Environmental Law in Denmark

Environmental Law in Denmark

Third Edition

Ellen Margrethe Basse

This book was originally published as a monograph in the International Encyclopaedia of Laws/Environmental Law.

Founding Editor: Roger Blanpain
General Editor: Frank Hendrickx
Volume Editor: Kurt Deketelaere

DJØF Publishing

Wolters Kluwer

Published by:
Kluwer Law International B.V.
PO Box 316
2400 AH Alphen aan den Rijn
The Netherlands
E-mail: international-sales@wolterskluwer.com
Website: lrus.wolterskluwer.com

Sold and distributed in North, Central and South America by:
Wolters Kluwer Legal & Regulatory U.S.
7201 McKinney Circle
Frederick, MD 21704
United States of America
Email: customer.service@wolterskluwer.com

Sold and distributed in all other countries by:
Air Business Subscriptions
Rockwood House
Haywards Heath
West Sussex
RH16 3DH
United Kingdom
Email: international-customerservice@wolterskluwer.com

Sold and distributed in Denmark by:
Djøf Publishing
Gothersgade 137
DK 1123 Copenhagen
Denmark
Website: www.djoef-forlag.dk

ISBN 978-94-035-1940-1 (Kluwer)
ISBN 978-87-574-4707-1 (DJØF Publishing)

e-Book: ISBN 978-94-035-1965-4
web-PDF: ISBN 978-94-035-1954-8

The Author

Ellen Margrethe Basse is a Doctor Habilitation of Law (Doctor Juris), Professor in Environmental Law, Aarhus Business and Social Sciences (Aarhus BSS), Aarhus University, Denmark. She is also an honorary doctor, Juris Doctor (H.C.), in Environmental Law at Uppsala University, Sweden. She is a former Professor in Procedural Law, and an Associated Professor in Administrative Law. In 1993, 1996 and 1998, she worked as Visiting Professor at the University of Florida, US. In 2005, 2008, 2010, 2013, 2015 and 2019, she served as visiting Professor at Georgia State University, US.

She is a member of the Royal Danish Academy of Sciences and Letters, a member of the Centre on International and Transnational Tendencies in Law (INTRALaw) and a member of the Centre for Legal Informatics (CREDI) at the Department of Law, Aarhus BSS, Aarhus University.

During 1992–2001, she was the Director of the interdisciplinary social science environmental research center (CeSaM), and during 2008–2010, she was the Chairman of AU's Climate Panel and Secretary. She is a former member of the Danish Research Council and a member of the Board of the National Transport Research Institute, Chairperson of the Board of National Environmental Research Institute, member of the Research Advisory Board for the Minister for Environment and Energy, member of the Parliamentary Board of Technology, the Common Committee on Environment of the Danish Research Councils, and the Danish Social Science Research Council. In 2003, she finalised the trial period as a lawyer by working full-time in law firms (1990–1991 and 2002–2003). In 2004, she was awarded the Order of Dannebrog by HM, The Queen of Denmark.

She has published many books and articles on international, EU, Arctic and national environmental law, energy and climate law, as well as judicial theory. Her focus is now on the emerging new legal thinking within environmental laws with a special focus on the vertical harmonisation of international, EU and Danish environmental laws, as well as the digitalisation-ready Danish environmental legislation and automation of the decision-making processes.

The Author

Table of Contents

Table of Contents

List of Abbreviations

AA	Appropriate assessments under the Habitats Directive
AAQD	Ambient Air Quality Directive (2008/50/EC)
Aarhus Convention	UNECE Convention on Access to Information, Public Participation in Decision-making and Access to Justice in Environmental Matters
ACCC	Aarhus Convention Compliance Committee
Air Quality Directive	Directive on Ambient Air Quality and Clean Air for Europe (2008/50/EC)
ApS	Private limited company
APAE II	Action Plan for the Aquatic Environment (covering the period 1998–2004)
APAE III	Action Plan for the Aquatic Environment (covering the period 2005–2015)
A/S	Public limited company
BAT	Best Available Techniques
BAT-AELs	BAT Associated Emission Limit Values (under the IED)
BBP	Benzyl butyl phthalate
BEP	Best Environmental Practice
BPS Scheme	Basic Payment Scheme
BREF	BAT notes
BSAP	HELCOM Balkan Sea Action Plan
BSPA	Baltic Sea Protected Areas
CAP	Common Agricultural Policy
CAPE	Clean Air Programme for Europe
CARS 21	Comprehensive Regulatory System for the 21st Century
CBD	Convention on Biological Diversity
CBDR	Common But Differentiated Responsibility
CCA	Copper chromium arsenate
CCS	Carbon capture and storage (CCS Directive – 2009/31/EC),
CDM	Clean Development Mechanisms

List of Abbreviations

CEN	Comité Européen de Normalisation (European Committee for Standardisations)
CENELEC	European Committee for Electro Technical Standardisation
CER	A certified emission reduction unit generated by a CDM project
CFC	Chlorofluorocarbon
CFP	Common Fisheries Policy
CFP Regulation	Regulation on the Common Fisheries Policy (1380/2013)
CH_4	Methane
CHP	Combined Heat and Power Plant
CITES	Convention on International Trade in Endangered Species
CJEU	Court of Justice of the European Union
CLC Convention	International Convention on Civil Liability for Oil Pollution Damage
CLRTAP	Convention on Long-Range Transboundary Air Pollution
CMR	Carcinogenic, Mutagenic or toxic to Reproduction
CO	Carbon monoxide
CO_2	Carbon dioxide
CO_2 equivalent	Carbon dioxide equivalent
COM	EU Commission Communication
Commission	European Commission
COP	Conference of the Parties
CQM	Catch Quota Management
Cr	Chromium
CSA	Chemical Safety Assessment
CSR	Chemical Safety Report
Cu	Copper
DANVA	Danish Water and Waste Association
dB	Decibels
DBP	Dibutyl phthalate
DEHP	Diastyl phthalate
DK ETR	Danish Allowance Registry under the EU ETS
DKK	Danish kroner
Drinking Water Directive	Directive on the Quality of Water intended for Human Consumption (98/83/EC, as amended by Regulation 1882/2003/EC, Regulation 596/2009/EC and Commission Directive 2015/1787/EU))
DUC	Danish Subsoil Consortium
EAFRD	Rural Development by the European Agricultural Fund for Rural Development (Regulation 1305/2013/EU)

EAP	Environmental Action Programme (1EAP (1972–1976); 2EPA (1977–1981); 3EPA (1982–1986); 4EAP (1987–1992); 5EAP (1992–1999); 6EAP (2001–2012) of the EU; and 7EAP (2013–2020)
ECE Water Convention	UNECE Convention on the Protection and Use of Transboundary Watercourses and International Lakes
ECHA	European Chemical Agency
EEA	European Environmental Agency
EEB	European Bureau (active in the co-decision process of the IED)
EEC	European Economic Community
EECS	European Energy Certificate System
EED	Energy Efficiency Directive (2012/27/EU, as amended by 2018/844/EU)
EEZ	Exclusive Economic Zone
EFSA	European Food Safety Authority
EIA	Environmental Impact Assessment
EIA Directive	Environmental Impact Assessment Directive (2011/92/EU as amended by Directive 2014/52/EU)
EINECS	European Inventory of Existing Commercial Chemical Substances
ELD	Environmental Liability Directive (2004/35/EC as amended by Directive 2006/21/EC on the Management of Waste from Extractive Industries; through Directive 2009/31/EC on the Geological Storage of Carbon Dioxide and through Directive 2013/30/EU on Safety of Offshore Oil and Gas Operations)
ELVs	End-of-life Vehicles
ELVs Directive	End-of-life Vehicles (Directive 2000/53/EC, as amended by Directive 2018/849/EU)
EMAS	Environmental Management and Audit Scheme
EMAS III Regulation	Regulation on the Voluntary Participation by Organisations in a Community Eco-management and Audit Scheme (1221/2009/EU), as amended by Commission Regulation 2017/1505/EU amending Annexes I, II and III
EMFF	European Maritime and Fishing Fund (Regulation No. 508/2014/EU)
EMSA	European Marine Safety Agency
END	Environmental Noise Directive (2002/49/EC)
EPA	Environmental Protection Agency (the Danish)
EPBD	Directive on the Energy Performance of Buildings (2010/31/EU as amended by Directive 2018/844/EU)
EPI	Environmental Performance Index

List of Abbreviations

E-PER	European Pollutant Emission Register
EPR	Extended Polluter Responsibility
E-PRTR	European Pollution Release and Transfer Register
E-PRTR Regulation	Regulation concerning the Establishment of a European Pollutant Release and Transfer Register (166/2006/EC)
ERDF	European Regional Development Fund
EQS	Environmental Quality Standards
EQS Directive	Environmental Quality Standards Directive (2008/105/EC)
ERU	An emission reduction unit generated by a Joint Implementation Project
ESI Funds	European Structural and Investment (ESI) Funds
ESM	Environmentally Sound Management
ETSI	European Telecommunication Standard Institute
ETS sector	Industries covered by the EU ETS
EU	European Union
EUAs	EU ETS Allowances
EUAAs	Allowances for aircraft operators
EU ETS	EU Emissions Trading Scheme
EU ETS Directive	Directive establishing a Scheme for Greenhouse Gas Emission Allowance Trading within the Community (2003/98/EC, as amended by Directive 2004/101/EC, Directive 2008/101/EC, Directive 2009/29/EC – now in a consolidated version of 30 April 2014)
EU SDS	EU Sustainability Strategy
EWC	European Waste Catalogue
FAO	Food and Agriculture Organisation
ff.	Following pages
FLEGT	Forest Law Enforcement, Governance and Trade
FLEGT Regulation	Regulation on establishing FLEGT licensing Scheme for Imports of Timber into the European Community (2173/2005/EC)
Floods Directive	Directive on the Assessment and Management of Flood Risks (2007/60/EC)
FMSP	Framework for Maritime Spatial Planning
FMSP Directive	Directive on Framework for Maritime Spatial Planning (2014/89/EU)
F_{msy}	The maximum rate of fishing mortality (the proportion of a fish stock caught and removed by fishing)
GAEC	Good Agricultural and Environmental Conditions
GDP	Gross Domestic Product
GES	Good environmental status

GHGs	Greenhouse Gases
GHS	Globally Harmonised System
GMM	Genetically Modified Microorganism
GMM Directive	Directive on the Contained Use of Genetically Modified Micro-organisms (2009/41/EC)
GMO	Genetically Modified Organism
GMO Directive	Directive on the Deliberate Release into the Environment of Genetically Modified Organisms (2001/18/EC)
GNP	Gross National Product
Green Growth Agreement	It is a political agreement between the majority of the political parties signed 2009 to ensure a higher level of environmental, nature and climate protection
GRI	Global Reporting Initiative
Groundwater Directive	Directive on the Protection of Groundwater against Pollution and Deterioration (2006/118/EC)
GSD	Geological Survey of Denmark
GWP	Global warming potential
ha	Hectare
HCB	Hexachlorobenzene
HCFC	Fully halogenated CFCs
HCl	Hydrogen chloride
HDVs	Heavy-duty vehicles
HELCOM	Helsinki Commission
HF	Hydrofluoric acid
HFCs	Hydrofluorocarbons
Hg	Mercury
HM	Heavy Metals
HNS	Hazardous and Noxious Substances
HNS Convention	Convention on Liability and Compensation for Damage in Connection with the Carriage of Hazardous and Noxious Substances by Sea
ICCM	International Conference on Chemicals Management
ICES	International Council for the Exploration of the Seas
ICZM	Integrated Coastal Zone Management
IEA	International Energy Agency
IED	Industrial Emission Directive (2010/75/EU)
IETS	International Emissions Trading Scheme
IIR	Information Inventory Report
ILO	International Labour Organization
IMCAM	Integrated Marine and Coastal Management

List of Abbreviations

IMO	International Maritime Organisation
IMP	Integrated Maritime Policy
IOMC	Inter-Organisation Programme for the Sound Management of Chemicals
IPCC	Intergovernmental Panel on Climate Change
IPPC Directive	Integrated Pollution Prevention and Control Directive (2008/1/EC) – now replaced by the IE Directive
ISO	International Standardisation Organisation
ISWM	Integrated Solid Waste Management
ITQ	Individual Transferable Quota
IUCN	International Union for Conservation of Nature
IUU Regulation	Illegal, Unreported and Unregulated (IUU Regulation 1005/2008/EC)
IWC	International Whaling Commission
JI	Joint Implementation
JRC	European Commission's Joint Research Centre
JREC	Johannesburg Renewable Energy Coalition
km	Kilometre
km^2	Square kilometre
km^3	Cubic kilometre
kW	Kilowatt
kWh	Kilowatt hour
Landfill of Waste Directive	Directive on the Landfill of Waste (1999/31/EC as amended by Directive 2011/97/EU and Directive 2018/850/EU)
LLMC 76	International Convention on Limitation of Liability for Maritime Claims
LMO	Living modified organism
LULUCF	Land Use, Land-Use Change and Forestry
m	Metre
MAPP	Major Accident Prevention Policy
MARPOL	Convention on Prevention of Pollution from Ships
MARS	Major Accident Reporting System
MCP Directive	Directive on Limitation of Emissions of Certain Pollutants into the Air from Medium Combustion Plants (Directive 2015/2193/EU)
MCPFE	Ministerial Conferences on the Protection of Forests in Europe
Mining Waste Directive	Directive on Management of Waste from Extractive Industries (2006/21/EC)

MPA	Marine Protected Area
MRL	Maximum residual levels
MSFD	Marine Strategy Framework Directive (2008/56/EC)
MSY	Maximum Sustainable Yield (catch) that can be taken from a specific fish stock over an indefinite period under constant environmental conditions measured in tonnes
MW	Megawatt
N	Nitrogen
NAFO	Convention on Future Multilateral Cooperation in the Northwest Atlantic Fisheries
NaMMCO	North Atlantic Marine Mammal Convention Organisation
NAPs	National action plans
NASCO	North Atlantic Salmon Conservation Organisation
NEAFC	Northeast Atlantic Fisheries Commission
NEC	National Emission Ceilings for Certain Pollutants
NEC Directive	Directive on National Emission Ceilings for Atmospheric Pollution (2001/81/EF)
NECD	Directive on National Emission Ceilings for Certain Atmospheric Pollutants (2016/2284/EU)
NEEAP	National Energy Efficiency Action Plan
NECP	National climate and energy plan
NERI	National Environmental Research Institute (Danish research that was closed in 2011 and replaced by DCE)
NGOs	Non-governmental organisations
NH_3	Ammonia
Nitrates Directive	Council Directive 91/676/EC of 12 December 1991 concerning the Protection of Water against Pollution caused by Nitrates from Agricultural Sector
NMPA	Network of Marine Protected Areas
NMVOCs	Non-Methane Volatile Organic Compounds
N_2O	Nitrous oxide – commonly known as laughing gas
NO	Nitrogen monoxide
NO_2	Nitrogen dioxide
NO_x	Nitrogen oxides (refers to NO and NO_2)
NOVA	National Programme for Monitoring of Aquatic Environment
NOVANA	National Programme for Monitoring of Aquatic and Terrestrial Environment
NSA	Nitrate-Sensitive Areas
O_3	Ozone
ODS	Ozone-Depleting Substances

List of Abbreviations

OECD	Organisation for Economic Co-operation and Development
OIEF	Oil Industry's Environmental Fund
OSPAR	Convention on the Protection of the Marine Environment of the North-East Atlantic
P	Phosphorus
Packaging and Packaging Waste Directive	Directive on Packaging and Packaging Waste (94/62/EC as amended by Directive 2004/12/EC, Directive 2005/20/EC, Regulation 219/2009/EC, Commission Directive 2013/2/EU, Directive 2015/720/EU (consolidated version 2015) and Directive 2018/852/EU)
PAH	Polycyclic Aromatic Hydrocarbon
Pb	Lead
PBT	Persistent, Bio accumulative and Toxic
PCB	Polychlorinated biphenyl
PFCs	Perfluorocarbons
PIC	Prior informed consent
PJ	Gross energy consumption transformed to fossil fuel equivalents
PM	Particulate matter
$PM_{2.5}$	Particulate Matter which passes through a size-selected inlet as defined in the reference method for the sampling and measurement of $PM_{2.5}$, EN 14907, with a 50% efficient cut-off at 2.5 μm aerodynamic diameter
PM_{10}	Particulate Matter which passes through a size-selected inlet as defined in the reference method for the sampling and measurement of PM_{10}, EN 12341, with a 50% efficient cut-off at 10 μm aerodynamic diameter
POPRC	Persistent Organic Pollutants Review Committee
POPs Convention	Stockholm Convention on Persistent Organic Pollutants
POPs Protocol	Aarhus Protocol on Persistent Organic Pollutants
PPPs	Plant Protection Products
PRTR	Pollution Release and Transfer Register
PRTR Protocol	Kiev Protocol on the PRTR (established under the Aarhus Convention)
PRTR Regulation	Regulation concerning the Establishment of a European Pollution Release and Transfer Register (166/2006/EC)
PSO	Public Service Obligations
PWRH	Waste Reception and Handling Plan
RAC	Committee for Risk Assessment
RDP	Rural Development Programme

REACH	Registration, Evaluation, Authorisation and Restriction of Chemicals (Regulation 1907/2006/EC)
REDD	Reduced Emission from Deforestation and Degradation
REDD+	Reduced Emission from Deforestation and Degradation, but it goes beyond those initiatives and includes the role of conservation, sustainable management of forests and enhancement of forest carbon stocks
RECS	Certificate system under EECS
RES	Renewable energy sources
2009 RES Directive	Directive on the Promotion of the Use of Energy from Renewable Sources (2009/28/EC, as amended by Directive 2015/1513/EU)
2018 RES Directive	Directive on the Promotion of the Use of Energy from Renewable Sources (2018/201/EU)
RMU	Removal Unit Generated by an LULUCF Project
RoHS Recast Directive (RoHS 2)	Directive on the Restriction of the Use of Certain Hazardous Substances in the Electrical and Electronic Equipment (2011/65/EU as amended by Directive 2017/2102/EU)
SAC	Special Areas of Conservation (Internationally important habitat areas for wild birds as designated under the Habitats Directive – 92/43/EEC)
Safety of Offshore Oil and Gas Operations Directive	Directive on Safety of Oil and Gas Operations (2013/30/EU)
SAICM	Strategic Approach to International Chemicals Management
SCI	Sites of Community Importance
SDS	Safety Data Sheet
SDG	Sustainable Development Goal
SEA	Strategic Environmental Assessment
SEA Directive	Strategic Environmental Assessment Directive (2001/42/EC)
SEA Protocol	Strategic Environmental Assessment Protocol (under the Espoo Convention)
SEAC	ECHAs Committee for Socio-Economic Analysis
Seveso I Directive	Directive on the Control of Major-Accident Hazardous involving Dangerous Substances (82/501/EEC)
Seveso II Directive	Directive on the Control of Major-Accident Hazardous involving Dangerous Substances (96/82/EC)
Seveso III Directive	Directive on the Control of Major-Accident Hazards involving Dangerous Substances (2012/18/EU)

List of Abbreviations

Sewage Sludge Directive	Directive on the Protection of the Environment, and in particular of the Soil, when Sewage Sludge is used in Agriculture (86/278/EEC as amended by Directive 91/692/EEC and some regulations)
SF_6	Sulfur hexafluoride
SMC	Sound Management of Chemicals
SO_2	Sulphur dioxide
SPA	Special Protection Areas (internationally important habitats, as designated under the Wild Birds Directive – 2009/147/EC
SPS Agreement	WTO Agreement on the Application of Sanitary and Phytosanitary Measures
SPS Scheme	Single Payment Scheme (under the CAP)
SVHCs	Substances of Very High Concerns
T	Tonne
TAC	Total Allowable Catch (TAC is a catch limit set for a particular fishery, generally for a year or a fishing season. TACs are usually expressed in tonnes of live-weight equivalent, but they are sometimes set in terms of number of fish)
TBT	Tributyltin
TEU	Treaty on the European Union
TFC	Transferable Fishing Catch
TFEU	Treaty on the Functioning of the European Union
TOC	Total Organic Carbon
TSP	Total Suspended Particulate matter
TVQ	Transferable Vessel Quota
UN	United Nations
UNCED	United Nations Conference on Environment and Development
UNCLOS	United Nations Convention on the Law of the Sea
UNDP	United Nations Development Programme
UNECE	United Nations Economic Commission for Europe
UNEP	United Nations Environmental Programme
UNESCO	United Nations Educational, Scientific and Cultural Organisation
UNFCCC	UN's Framework Convention on Climate Change
UNIDO	United Nations Industrial Development Organization
UNWC	United Nations Watercourses Convention
Urban Waste Water Directive	Directive concerning Urban Waste Water Treatment (91/271/EEC)
VAT	Value Added Tax
VOC	Volatile Organic Compound

vPvB	very Persistent and very Bio accumulative
Waste Framework Directive	Directive on Waste (2008/98/EC), as amended by Directive 2018/851/EC (consolidated version of 5 July 2018)
WEEE	Waste Electrical and Electronic Equipment
WEEE II Directive	Directive on the Waste Electrical and Electronic Equipment (2012/19/EU, as amended by Directive 2018/849/EU)
WFD	Water Framework Directive (2000/60/EC)
WHO	World Health Organization
WMO	World Metrological Organisation
WoG	Whole-of-Government
WSR	Waste Shipment Regulation (1013/2006/EC)
WTO	World Trade Organization
Zn	Zinc

Preface

Modern Danish environmental law has a strong international dimension due to Denmark's membership of the EU, and participation by the EU and Denmark in global and regional agreements. Most of the various EU directives and regulations implement such international environmental obligations. Based on the Lisbon Treaty, the regulations are part of Danish law with direct legal effect for the Danish citizens and companies, and the Danish authorities must transform the directives into national law in harmony with the legal principles on application of EU law that have been developed by the Court of Justice of the European Union (CJEU).

As just indicated, EU environmental legislation is very important in the description of Danish environmental law. Therefore, the focal point is on EU environmental law, including case law. The clear relation between EU law and international conventions is described in the book to make it clear that the Danish environmental law is part of a vertical harmonised legal system. The Danish implementation of EU law – as it is made by acts of the Danish Parliament, by statutory orders passed by different governments, and by the application of the provisions by Danish courts, – is assessed, both in the light of the obligations of the Danish authorities and the rights of citizens arising from EU rules and CJEU case law. The information provided by the EU Commission, the European Environment Agency and the Danish authorities and research institutions on emission data and the status of the environment is included in the evaluation of the effect that the legislation has on the quality of the environment. The political agreements concluded between a changing political majority and the government are included in the explanation of the complicated Danish legislation.

The legal provisions have been updated according to the current law and practice followed at international, EU and national levels as the law in force in Denmark took effect on 1 July 2019.

The new election to the Danish Parliament held on 5 June 2019 resulted in a change of government. On 27 June 2019, a new Social Democrat Government took over power. Its power is based on a deal with three other political parties on the left – the Social-Liberal Party, the Socialist People's Party and the Red Green Alliance. This deal includes an ambition to achieve a 70% reduction of the GHGs in 2030 compared with the level in 1990, just as it includes high ambitions for environmental issues in general. This monograph includes information on the change made in June 2019 with respect to the competences of the Danish ministries.

Aarhus, August 2019
Ellen Margrethe Basse

General Introduction

Chapter 1. General Background

§1. Geography and Population

1. The Kingdom of Denmark covers an area of 43,092.85 km^2 (16,632 square miles), spread over Jutland and about 400 islands, of which only about 100 are inhabited. In the south, Jutland borders on Germany. Besides, Denmark consists of two larger islands, Zealand and Funen, eight smaller islands and around seventy small, inhabited islands. The largest island is Zealand, where the capital Copenhagen is situated. The population of Zealand is as large as that of Jutland, which is geographically three times its size. Zealand is only separated from the southern part of Sweden by a narrow strait (Oresund). Besides the mentioned areas of Denmark, two other special regions, namely Greenland and the Faroe Islands are part of the Kingdom of Denmark with special status as self-governing communities.[1]

In 1814, Greenland and the Faroe Islands became Danish territory. Greenland is the largest island in the world and covers an area of 2.2 million km^2. However, 85% of the area is covered with ice. The icecap reaches a height of more than 3,000 m above sea level. The northern part, Nordpynten, lies only 700 km from the North Pole – the southern part Cap Farwell lies 2,600 km further south. The number of inhabitants amounts to 56,000. The Faroe Islands consist of eighteen small, mountainous islands situated in the North Atlantic at about 62° north and 7° west. The highest point is on the northern islands. It is almost 890 m above the sea. The islands extend over 113 km from north to south and 75 km from east to west. The total area amounts to 1,399 km^2. The islands have 47,000 inhabitants – only seventeen of the islands are inhabited. Their environment and cultures are different from each other and from the rest of the Danish Realm. They are both located in the Arctic region far from each other and far from Denmark. Neither the state of the environment nor the population or the environmental law for these special Arctic regions of Denmark is included in this monograph.

1. Concerning the special status of Danish regions Greenland and Fareos Islands, *see infra* para. 4.

2. Denmark (exclusive of Greenland and the Faroe Islands) has a population of 5.7 million.[2] The population growth has been relatively small during the last forty years. In January 2017, immigrants and descendants comprised 12.9% of the total Danish population – about 9.9% were immigrants and 3.0% were descendants. About 52% of all immigrants and descendants originate from a European country. On 1 January 2014, Denmark had a population density of 131.1 per km^2. The population is expected to reach 6 million before the year 2040.

More than 66% of the land area is used for agricultural purposes, while 14.3% is forested.[3] Around 10% of Denmark has towns, roads and other infrastructures. Cities, roads, bridges and other types of man-made surfaces cover a total of 10%. Urban centres, such as residential and industrial districts, dominate and account for three-fourths of the man-made surfaces.[4] The urban population has increased over the last years as a result of population growth.

Around 85% of the Danes live in towns. Approximately one-third lives in the capital, Copenhagen, around one-third in towns of more than 10,000 residents and around one-third in small towns and rural areas. About 51% is rural areas. Of the rural area, 66% is agricultural land while forest cover 14%. Thirty per cent of the population lives in rural areas.[5] Dykes or other coastal protections constitute a total of about 1,800 km of the coastline protection.[6]

Most enterprises, institutions, etc. are situated in towns. Since the 1970s, the combination of spatial planning systems and the zoning on land as binding regulatory instruments has ensured a development in Denmark without sprawl problems.[7] The law has been so strong and so well coordinated with other environmental decision-making that it has been nearly impossible to locate industry and housing in rural areas. Since 2001, the legal design of the Planning Act has, however, been made more flexible and focused more on economic growth. A former Danish liberal-conservative coalition Government[8] – with support from the Danish People's Party – started this trend.[9]

3. Denmark is a typical low-lying country characterised by a long coastline and several hundred islands. The marine area for which Denmark has environmental responsibility covers a total of 100,000 km^2 (this figure is exclusive of the marine area surrounding Greenland and the Faroe Islands). It covers an area of 2.5 times

2. Statistics Denmark, *Statistical Yearbook, 2017*. Danish Ministry of Climate, Energy and Building, *Denmark's Seventh National Communication and Third Biennial Report, Under the United Nationals Framework Convention and Climate Change, December 2018* (hereinafter *Denmark's Seventh National Communication and Third Biennial Report*), at 252.
3. Danish Ministry of Climate, Energy and Building, *Denmark's Seventh National Communication and Third Biennial Report*, at 14.
4. Statistics Denmark, *Statistical Yearbook 2011*.
5. European Commission, *Fact sheet: 2014-2020 Rural Development Programme for Denmark*, 12 December 2014.
6. *Denmark's Fifth National Communication on Climate Change*, at 49ff.
7. The urbanisation as such is, however, a problem for the sparsely populated areas that lose their schools and shopping facilities.
8. It was a minority coalition government that consisted of the Liberal Party and the Conservative Party.
9. Concerning the Danish Planning Act, *see infra* in Part III, Chapter 2.

that of the landmass. Spatial planning of the maritime activities is now part of the management system at the sea area of Danish jurisdiction as Denmark had to implement the EU Directive on Maritime Spatial Planning no later than 18 September 2016.[10]

The Danish Continental Shelf was originally only determined in accordance with the Convention of 29 April 1958 on the Continental Shelf as interpreted for the North Sea in the decision made on 20 February 1969 by the International Court of Justice.[11] The maritime areas consist of a 3 nautical miles territorial sea, a 4 nautical miles custom zone, a 24 nautical miles nature conservation zone, a 200 nautical miles exclusive economic zone (EEZ), a 200 nautical miles continental shelf and various special zones.[12] The Danish territorial sea was expanded on the basis of the UN Convention on the Law of the Sea (UNCLOS) – before Denmark ratified the Convention in 2004 – by the Act on the Territorial Sea[13] and the Act on the Exclusive Economic Zones.[14]

Perched on the northern flank of continental Europe, Denmark protrudes between the Kattegat and the North Sea. It forms the threshold between the Baltic freshwater basin and the salty marine areas of the North Sea and the Atlantic Ocean. Of the marine waters, approximately half of it constitutes the Danish part of the North Sea, while the Kattegat and the Belt Sea (including Oresund) each account for 15%, and the Skagerak and the Baltic Sea each account for 10%. This borderline location creates major natural variations across a relatively small area. In an international perspective, Denmark is important to biodiversity due to its geographical location between the north and the south, and between the saltwater of the North Sea and the brackish water of the Baltic Sea. The coastlines are in some places (in the east) rocky outcrops and in other places (in the west) deserted unspoiled beaches. To protect low-lying land against flooding and storm surge, it has been necessary to build dykes or other permanent installations along the about 1,800 km long coastline. Today, sandbags, breakwaters, etc. protect some parts of the coastline, which would otherwise erode because they consist of soft materials deposited during the last Ice Age.

The inland area is 669.68 km^2, and the coastline is 7,313.9 km^2. It corresponds to almost 1.5 m coast per inhabitant. With more than 1 km watercourse per km^2, the watercourses and the coastal areas are an important element in the landscape and an important home for many species and types of habitats of European and international significance. This includes the shallow-water marine areas, and the plant and animal life in the coastline, as well as the dunes heaths along the west coast of Jutland. There are approximately 35,000 km natural watercourses. During the winter season, the Wadden Sea, the shallow areas of Danish waters and the wetlands are home for waterfowl from Scandinavia and large parts of Russia. In the springtime, millions of migrating birds arrive in Denmark to breed or forage on their way north.

10. European Parliament and Council Directive 2014/89/EU, *see infra* para. 130.
11. Promulgation Order No. 1189 of 21 September 2018 on the Danish Continental Shelf.
12. European Parliament, Directorate-General for International Policies, Policy Department, Structural and Cohesion Policies B, *Fisheries in Denmark*, 2013, at 17.
13. Act No. 200 of 7 April 1999 on the Territorial Sea.
14. Act No. 411 of 22 May 1996 on the Exclusive Economic Zones.

Surface water in Denmark is constituted partly by freshwater in the form of watercourses and lakes, and partly by salt water in the form of coastal marine areas. The physical conditions range from small coves, to closed estuarine fjords with poor water exchange, to open estuarine fjords, to straits as the Oresundand the Belt Sea, to open marine waters such as the Baltic Sea. A large number of watercourses have been straightened, canalised or subjected to rigorous maintenance. Today, only about 2% of the remaining watercourses, according to the seventh national communication, follows a naturally meandering course, and this 2% is the result of watercourse restoration projects.[15]

By European standards, all Danish watercourses are small. The two largest watercourses, the rivers Skjern Aa and Gudenaa, are each about 2,500 km^2. Together, they cover 11% of the area of Denmark. There are more than 100,000 standing water bodies greater than 100 km^2. By far the majority are ponds and small lakes. There are only 2,762 true lakes, i.e., with an area greater than 1 ha (10,000 m^2). Denmark is home to many species and types of nature of European and international significance. This includes the shallow-water marine areas and the plant and animal life near the coastline, as well as the dunes heaths along the west coast of Jutland. In the international and regional regimes, several conventions have been signed and ratified by Denmark. 'Natura 2000 in Denmark' consists of the 'Sites of Community Importance' (SCI) designated under EU's Wild Birds Directive as SCAs, as Special Protection Areas (SPAs) under the Habitats Directive or Ramsar sites in the Danish territory.

Compared to other countries, Denmark has a unique groundwater resource of very high quality and in large quantities. It is so clean that it provides the direct source of the drinking water. Thus, groundwater accounts for 98–99% of the consumption of water. Often, the treatment is limited to removal of iron and manganese by oxidation and filtration. The majority of the groundwater will flow into the bottom of lakes and watercourses and will flow out to the sea with the watercourses. There are considerable variations from year to year and from region to region. Denmark's available groundwater resources (about 1 billion m^3 per year) are generally sufficient to meet national water supply requirements (between 600 and 700 million m^3 per year in recent years).[16]

Denmark lies in the Temperate Zone and has a distinctly coastal climate. It has mild winters without large amounts of snow, but with much rain. A natural feature of everyday life in Denmark is overcast days and many clouds in the sky. There is an average of four hours sunshine a day; in summer from May to August, there are more than six hours of sunshine a day. In a year, the average temperature varies from 0°C in January to 16°C in August. Great variations occur in relation to the average. The coldest day in more than 100 years was a day in January 1982 with a temperature of -31°C, and the warmest day was a day in August 1975 with a temperature of 36°C.[17] Since 1873, the temperature has been rising by about 1.5°C, and precipitation has increased to 15%. Long-term winter temperature is expected to rise

15. OECD, *Environmental Performance Reviews. Denmark. 2007*, at 96–98.
16. OECD, *Environmental Performance Reviews. Denmark. 2007*, at 77.
17. Statistics Denmark, *Statistical Yearbook, 2011* and Statistics Denmark, *Statistical Yearbook, 2014*, at 456.

by 2°C–3°C, and plant growing seasons will be extended by one to two months on an average as a consequence of climate change. In the long term, summer temperatures are expected to rise a further 1°C–3°C, leading to greater evaporation. The sea level in Danish marine waters has generally risen in the past 100 years and especially in the past thirty years as a consequence of global warming. A general rise in sea level of 0.15–0.75 m is anticipated on the west coast and in Danish waters as a consequence of climate change. There is also a tendency towards more powerful storms and more extreme weather.[18]

The country is largely flat with gently sloping hills; the highest point in Jutland is approximately 170 m above sea level. The landscape is moraine from the two latest glacial periods in the area. Of the once richly wooded land, only a few forest areas remain. About 6% of the country consists of dunes and moorland. Forest and other wooded land take up to 13% of land, while permanent grasslands take up to 8%, arable and permanent cropland take up to 54%, and 25% of the areas for other purposes. Most of the country is cultivated. Around 66% of the total area (i.e., 28,900 km^2) is used for agriculture.[19] To a great extent, Danish landscape is a cultivated landscape. Farms manage 2.6 million ha. Over 90% of this utilised agricultural area is arable land characterised by intensive and specialised production putting pressure on certain ecosystems and high nature value areas.[20] Over the past 100–200 years, the landscape has been transformed by intensive land use, primarily attributable to the expansion of farmland, the intensification of agriculture and the development of built-up areas. Another characteristic of Denmark's geography is the many islands, a total of 407.

Transport infrastructure takes up space and impinges upon the natural ecosystem by using land and fragmenting the landscape. The total land area used for transport purposes in Denmark is estimated to be approximately 3% of the landscape. Of this, the majority is used for the road network.

§2. Legal and Political Structure

4. Denmark is one of the European Union (EU) Member States. In 1973, Denmark became a member along with the United Kingdom and Ireland. The Act on Denmark's accession to the European Economic Community (EEC)[21] contains the necessary provisions for the transfer of constitutional authority to the EU institutions on the basis of section 20 of the Danish Constitution. As outlined in the 1992 Edinburgh Agreement, Denmark maintains four opt-outs from the EU policies – concerning the European Monetary Union, the Common Security and Defense Policy, the Justice and the Home Affairs. The Lisbon Treaty that entered into force on 1 December 2009 is the constitutional basis for the EU institutions and its

18. *Denmark's Fifth National Communication on Climate Change*, at 49ff.
19. OECD, *Environmental Performance Reviews. Denmark. 2007*, at 13 and 104; *Statistical Yearbook 2014*, at 465. Over the last forty years, the agricultural area in Denmark has fallen from 72% (30,900 km^2) of the total land area in 1960 to 66%.
20. European Commission, *Fact Sheet: 2014-2020 Rural Development Programme for Denmark*, 12 December 2014.
21. Act No. 447 of 11 October 1972 on Denmark's Accession has been changed several times.

twenty-seven Member States.[22] It was signed on 13 December 2007 and entered into force on 1 December 2009. It consists of the Treaty on the European Union (TEU), the Treaty on the Functioning of the European Union (TFEU) and some protocols. Denmark can use the new opt-in mechanism of legislation and legislative initiatives which are allowed by a protocol to the Lisbon Treaty.

The Danish monarchy is based on a written Constitution, the history of which dates back to 1849. The Constitution has been amended only rarely since then.[23] The basic constitutional philosophy followed is one of careful change, respecting precedents but taking account of changes in the values of society. The latest amendment was made in 1953.[24] Since this amendment, the parliamentary system has been a one-chamber system. The Parliament (Folketinget) does not have the power to amend the Constitution unless it can gain the assent of two-thirds of the members of Parliament.

The Constitution has, as basic principles, the integrated monarchy and the division of powers, as well as certain fundamental rights: personal liberty, property rights, freedom of opinion, freedom of organisation and freedom of assembly. Section 3 of the Constitution lies down that the legislative power shall be jointly vested in the King (the Government) and the Parliament, while the executive power shall be vested in the King. The ministers, and not the King, bear the responsibility for government actions.

The Danish environmental democracy is among the most advanced in the Organisation for Economic Co-operation and Development (OECD).[25] It is a representative democracy. The citizens influence the political power by voting in elections for the members of the municipalities and regional councils,[26] the Danish Parliament and the European Parliament. The Parliament has 179 members of whom two are elected in Greenland and two in the Faroe Islands. The proportional method is used in elections of the members. A minimum of 2% of votes is required for a party to be represented in the Parliament. As of July 2019, fourteen parties are represented in the Parliament. Four of these parties represent the citizens of Greenland and Faroe Islands. The Prime Minister has the power to decide on a new election. The political system is known as 'negative parliamentary' which means that the Government may never have a majority against it in the Parliament, but it is not required to have the support of an actual majority. No single political party has had the majority in the Parliament since the beginning of the twentieth century. The last election took place on 5 June 2019. The minority Government that came into power on 27 June 2019 consist of the Social Democratic Party.[27] It can stay in power for

22. Croatia joint the Union from 1 Jul. 2013 as Member State number 28.
23. It has only been amended in 1855, 1866, 1915, 1920, and in 1953, *see* now Act No. 169 of 5 June 1953 on the Danish Constitution.
24. Act No. 169 of 5 June 1953 on the Constitution of the Danish Kingdom
25. OECD, *Environmental Performance Reviews. Denmark. 2007*, at 181.
26. Concerning the municipalities and regional councils, *see infra* para. 5.
27. On 27 Jun. 2019, a new Social Democrat Government took over the power. This power is based on a deal with three other political parties on the left – the Danish Social-Liberal Party, Socialist People's Party and Red Green Alliance. This deal is based on a higher ambition on environmental issues and the ambitions on a 70% reduction of the GHGs in 2030 compared with the level in 1990.

four years (2019–2023). According to the Constitution, there must be a general election at least once every four years. Before that, all governments since 1980 have been coalition governments and almost all of them were minority governments.[28] Any member of the Parliament as well as members of the Government is authorised to put forward legislation (sections 21 and 41 of the Constitution). No legislation may be passed until it has been read three times in the Parliament and has received Royal Assent. A minority of Parliament (at least one-third of the 179 members) may ask that a bill passed by the Parliament shall be subject to a referendum before Royal Assent is given. If a referendum is requested, Royal Assent will be refused if the majority votes against the bill and that majority constitutes not less than 30% of the electorate. Some bills, however, are exempt from this provision, particularly bills regarding taxation or any other financial legislation. With regard to expropriation bills, it is possible to ask for a postponement of the third reading.

The Parliament as the legislative power may delegate its authority to the Government, except where the Constitution specifically demands that the legislative assembly shall give the rules in question. The Government is subordinate to Parliament both with respect to its legislative powers and its executive powers. Any Member of Parliament may put questions to the ministers during a weekly questioning time. A number of members of Parliament may collectively request discussion of a particular matter. The fact that ministers are politically answerable to the Parliament implies a measure of cohesion between the legislature and the ministries. Because of this, the Danish administration is relatively centralised.

The Constitution includes the legal basis for the Government's competence to act in international affairs on behalf of the Danish Realm. The Government cannot act without the consent of the Parliament in any way that increases or restricts the competence of the Parliament and Government in international cooperation.

The Danish regions Greenland and the Faroe Islands are not members of the EU. Greenland became a member of the EEC when Denmark joined in 1973, but after the Home Rule Governmental system was established by a 1978 Act,[29] Greenland held a consultative referendum on membership of the EEC in 1982. A transfer of legislative and administrative powers from the Danish Parliament to Greenland came into force in July 2005.[30] On 21 June 2009, the Act on Greenland Self-Government[31] came into force. It replaces the Greenland Home Rule Arrangement.

28. The coalition government that was in power from 2015 to 2019 – a minority liberal-conservative government – consisted of the Liberal Party, the Conservative Party and the Liberal Alliance. They were in power with support from the Danish People's Party. From 2011 to 2015, the coalition government consisted of the Social Democratic Party and the Danish Social-Liberal Party. The Socialistic People's Party was also involved in the first two years. From 2001 to 2011, a liberal-conservative coalition Government – supported by the Danish People's Party – had a very important impact on a change in the environmental policy focusing more on economic growth and reduction of taxes than the former Government. The coalition government that was in power from 1993 to 2001 consisted of the Social Democratic Party and the Social-Liberal Party – in some periods with other small political parties involved in the government. This coalition government had a very high environmental profile.
29. Act No. 29 of 29 November 1978 on Home Rule for Greenland.
30. Act No. 577 of 24 June 2005 on the conclusion of agreement under international law by the Government of Greenland.
31. Act No. 473 of 12 June 2009 on a Self-Governmental System in Greenland.

The Self-Government Act gives full powers to Greenland to negotiate and to conclude under international law where such agreements relate solely to Greenland – for example, mineral resource activities in Greenland. It does not apply to international agreement, which shall also apply to Denmark or agreements to be negotiated within an international organisation of which the Kingdom of Denmark is a member. Greenland's authorities consist of a directly elected Greenland Parliament, Inatsisartut, comprising thirty-one members and the Government, Naalakkersuisut, which is responsible for the central administration under the Prime Minister. Greenland is divided into four administrative regions. The Self-Government Act provides for a system of information and cooperation with the High Commissioner of Greenland to ensure that the full powers are used within the limits of the statutes and that they are not used contrary to the general interests of the Kingdom. As Greenland is not covered by the EU membership, Denmark has the power to act in the event of conflict of interests which cannot be resolved, i.e., to safeguard the interests of Greenland without harming the interests of the EU.

The Faroese Parliament, Lagting, governs the Faroe Islands' internal affairs.[32] This 2005 Act on Self-Government provides that the Faroese authorities may decide unilaterally to exercise legislative and administrative powers with respect to the Faroe Islands in all matters not already under Faroese authority, with the exception of the Constitution, citizenship, the Supreme Court, foreign, security and defence policy, and monetary and currency matters. As the Faroe Islands are not covered by the EU membership, Denmark has the power to act in the event of conflict of interests, which cannot be resolved, i.e., to safeguard the interests of the overseas territory, without harming the interests of the EU. The island's relations with the EU are governed by a 1991 Free Trade Agreement, which was followed by a new agreement in 2014.

5. The structural framework of the Danish State administration is that of a hierarchy in which each minister is the top executive within his or her field. Where traditional State authorities are concerned, the hierarchical relationship implies that the superior authorities have the right to interfere ex officio.[33] Part of the responsibility of the ministries has been left to agencies.

Normally, the decisions of lower instances must be appealed to an appeals board, which has been formed on a collegiate basis and which primarily has the function of settling disputes.[34] The Danish preconditions concerning the interpretation of Article 9(1) of the Aarhus Convention related to the access to an appeal to a court of law or other independent and impartial body established by law are problematic. In reality the two administrative appeal bodies with competences in environmental

32. The ordinary status of the Faroe Islands was laid down in Act No. 137 of 23 March 1948. Act No. 579 of 24 June 2005 on the Self-Government of the Faroe Islands, and Act No. 578 of 24 June 2005 has widened the scope and procedures for the transfer of legislative and administrative powers to the Faroe Islands' authorities.
33. Concerning the hierarchical relationship between the ministries and their agencies, *see infra* paras 40–44.
34. Concerning the appeal system, *see infra* para. 47.

cases – the Environmental Protection and Food Appeals Board and the Spatial Planning Appeals Board – are both part of the Ministry of Industry, Business and Financial Affairs with their secretariats located directly under the minister in the 'Appeals Boards' House' in Viborg, Jutland. The same is the case with the Danish Energy Appeals Board. The traditional guaranties on impartiality are not ensured in the relation between the Ministry of Industry, Business and Financial Affairs and these three appeals boards.[35]

As declared by section 82 of the Constitution, the municipalities and the regional councils are in a relatively independent position. The Constitution does not regulate how the system of local government is to be organised. From the beginning of the nineteenth century until 1972, Denmark consisted of more than 1,300 urban and rural municipalities. A reform changed the institutions. All the municipalities were then amalgamated into 275 municipalities and 14 county councils. In March 2005, a broad political agreement on the future structure and mapping of ninety-eight municipalities and five new regions was reached in the Parliament. A minimum size for the new municipalities was set at 20,000 inhabitants and the suggested target was 30,000. Municipalities with less than 20,000 inhabitants had to merge into new municipalities. A new structural reform of municipalities and regions came into force on 1 January 2007 and gave rise to major changes in the public sector. The reform consisted of a new distribution of power and new institutions. Popularly elected councils govern both municipalities and regions. The elections of new political members to the municipality and regional councils are fixed to take place every fourth year on the third Tuesday in November. The governing of the local democracy falls under the parameters of the Parliament (Folketinget). The Parliament empowers the Government as responsible for the control of the municipalities' implementation of the legislation.[36] The municipalities are handling several environmental issues at the local level. The regional councils have only very few competences.

6. There are three stages in the judicial system. The lowest courts of first instance are the twenty-four city courts. The superior Courts of First Instance are the Higher Courts – one for the eastern circuit (Eastern High Court) and one for the western circuit (Western High Court). They are courts of appeal from the lowest courts. The Supreme Court is at the highest level. All the courts are ordinary courts.

The courts' independence is based on section 64 of the Constitution, which provides that in the performance of their duties, judges shall be directed solely by 'the law'. Today, the law includes not only acts passed by the Parliament and given the Royal Assent but also the EU regulations and directives as well as national administrative rules (statutory orders), which the ministers may have issued under an

---

35. It is a problem based on CJEU case law, *see* Case 222/13 *The Danish Telecommunication Complaints Board*. It its judgment the CJEU stated: 'Those guaranties and impartiality require rules, particularly as regards the composition of the body and the appointment, length of service and the grounds for abstention, rejection and dismissal of its members, in order to dismiss any reasonable doubt in the minds of individuals as to the imperviousness of the body to external factors and its neutrality with respect to the interest before it … .'
36. Since the Constitution was passed in 1849, there has been a special ministry with responsibility for the steering and control of the local government.

authority given by the legislative power. The courts also include customary law, general legal principles and judicial practice as legal sources. There is no constitutional court in Denmark.

The Constitution lays down the right for the court of law to review administrative decisions as well as conflicts between private persons. Section 63 of the Constitution contains a special provision on the competence of the courts to decide on any question bearing upon the extent of the powers of the administration.[37] When taking a stand on the role of the courts as a controlling body of environmental practice of the authorities, it is necessary to distinguish between the part of the acts within civil law (including administrative law as well as private law) and the part within criminal law. The Danish procedural law is based on the Administration of Justice Act which was rooted in the first Danish Constitution of 1849. The Act was completed in April 1916. It came into force in October 1919.[38]

7. In addition to the courts, there is a special instance called the Parliamentary Ombudsman, appointed by the Parliament under section 55 of the Constitution and the Act on the Parliamentary Ombudsman.[39] The Ombudsman has no competence in relation to the courts. If cases concerning administrative decisions – including cases on environmental issues – are brought to the courts, the assessment by the courts has priority, and the Ombudsman will consequently stop his investigation. The same is expected to be the case in relation to the interpretation of EU law.[40]

A citizen who feels unjustly treated by the public administration or other public bodies making decisions on environmental issues in any respect may turn to the Ombudsman. One of the great advantages of this institution is that, unlike review by appeal authorities and courts, the claimant does not have to prove specific interests, and the methods of handling appeals against administrative decisions are direct, informal, speedy and cheap. All that a claimant has to do is to write a letter addressed to the Ombudsman asking him to investigate, inspect, recommend, reprimand and give advice concerning an administrative action or inaction. There is a time limit of one year. The Ombudsman may also implement investigations on his own initiative, *see* section 17 of the Act. The competence and power of the Ombudsman is described in the Constitution and in Chapter 2 of the Act. He has the power to control all parts of the public administration and those parts of semi-private or private organisations that are covered by the administrative management acts. When the Ombudsman assesses the municipalities' or the regional counties' administration, he has to take into consideration 'the special conditions, under which the local governments function', *see* section 8 of the Act. The recourse is primarily a legal protection remedy for the citizens, which they have to use before the Ombudsman

37. Concerning the Danish Constitution's provisions on the competences of the courts, *see infra* para. 363.
38. Concerning the Administration of Justice Act, *see infra* paras 365–366.
39. Promulgation Order No. 349 of 22 March 2013 on the Parliamentary Ombudsman.
40. It was stressed in the 'Report No. 1272/1994 concerning the content of the Ombudsman Act' that the Ombudsman had to stop his investigation if a case was brought to a Court of First Instance or to the European Court of Justice – now replaced by the Court of Justice of the European Union (CJEU).

will accept a complaint. As the public administration in Denmark is quite large, there are a lot of cases coming into the Ombudsman Institution.

The main task of the Ombudsman's activities is to ensure that the administration complies with the statutory legislation and administrative principles, and that the public bodies behave in a proper manner in their relations with citizens.[41] The Ombudsman has the right to concentrate on those problems in the public administration which, on the basis of considerations for the protection of the public and the intentions laid down in the acts, are the most important at any time to secure the efficiency of the Ombudsman Institution. He is, in other words, an individual who personally decides his jurisdiction on each claim made to him and is personally responsible for the consequences of his decision in each case. The words of the acts as well as preparatory work published in reports from committees and especially the comments of the Parliaments attached to the bills are important parts of the legal sources used by him in his decision-making. The Ombudsman regards himself particularly obliged to attach great importance to the assumptions on which the Parliament has based its passing of an act – as he is, in spite of everything, the *Parliamentary* Ombudsman.

The Ombudsman may request an explanation from the authority concerned and may request and study relevant public files. In accordance with the inquisitorial principle, he has the duty of securing the necessary information. No formal court-like hearings are held. If the Ombudsman finds it necessary, he has, however, the right to arrange for civil servants and other people to be interrogated by the courts. It is not possible for the Ombudsman to use Article 267 TFEU as the basis for references for preliminary rulings in cases concerning the proper implementation of EU law.

The Ombudsman has no power to reverse or quash administrative decisions – he has to control the administration on behalf of the Parliament only. Therefore, the Ombudsman's power does not interfere directly with administrative actions, but he has had considerable influence on the behaviour of the administration. Generally, the head of the authorities decides to follow the advice given by the Ombudsman. So, even though his 'decisions' are not legally binding, they commonly have a very great effect. The Ombudsman prepares an annual printed report with recommendations to the legislature (the Parliament). The report may include criticism of the decisions made by the public authorities. Continuously since 1955, he has, as a very important part of the control system, been urging for the promotion of requirements relating to administrative procedures embodied in what he has called 'code of good administrative practice'. Some of these recommendations have been transformed to statutes in the Administrative Procedure Act.

8. The Nordic countries consist of Denmark, Sweden, Norway, Finland and Iceland. The 'North' is the term for the five Nordic countries collectively. The Nordic Council of Ministers, established in 1952, operates as the formal organ in the cooperation between the Nordic countries. A treaty did not establish this Council. It was rather established by national legislation in each of the Nordic countries, as is customary practice in the Nordic cooperation. However, Nordic treaties do exist. The

41. Concerning the administrative law principles, *see infra* para. 30.

Treaty of Cooperation between Denmark, Finland, Iceland, Norway and Sweden (the Helsinki Agreement), entered into force on 1 July 1962. While neither as a Parliament nor as a supranational body with authority to make binding decisions on Member States, the Nordic Council serves as a forum for discussion and cooperation in attempting to resolve the problems and issues facing the Nordic region. The chairmanship of the Council is rotated between the Nordic countries on an annual basis. The annual budget in 2018 for the Nordic Council was Danish kroner (DKK) 996,679,000. The total expenditure for 2019 is unchanged in real terms. The resources for environmental projects in 2019 are DKK 47,100,000.[42]

Although, the Nordic cooperation and uniform Nordic legislation took place prior to the establishment of this Council, and much of the cross-national cooperation in the North takes place outside the framework of it, the Council nevertheless serves a significant function by the sponsorship of regular meetings and formal establishment of responsibilities. Contacts between officials and civil servants in the Nordic countries can take place directly without the necessity of going through the ministries of foreign affairs as if the North was one unified political jurisdiction. This is partly due to historical practice and the attitude that it is acceptable to contact an official or one's counterpart in another Nordic country along with the formal recognition of this practice by Article 38 of the Helsinki Agreement. It is especially within the international organisations that the Nordic countries' delegates and staff work together by sharing information and agreeing upon joint positions for the Nordic region as a whole.

In 1973, an Official Committee for Environmental Affairs was established to take care of environmental matters. The Nordic Environmental Protection Convention (1973) is a result of an initiative taken by the Nordic Council. It covers all kinds of activities dangerous to the environment. The purpose of the Convention is to secure the Nordic citizens in matters relating to environmental protection. It seeks to accomplish this goal by giving administrative authorities and individuals the right of access to courts and puts administrative authorities in other Nordic Member States in a position as if they were parties within the same jurisdiction. In other words, the primary principle of the Convention is that pollution of a neighbouring country is to be equated with pollution of one's own country. The consultation principle regarding notification and information of States potentially affected by activities that may have significant adverse transboundary effects has been codified by the Convention. Therefore, entering this Convention was a significant step in 1973 in relation to state cooperation on the issue of environmental democracy. The Convention is, however, not very important any longer, as the ratification of the Aarhus Convention by all Nordic countries in 1998 has ensured common procedural rights.

Although the Nordic countries do not have uniform environmental protection legislation, each nation's legislation and administration are quite similar and is based upon the same basic principles. The Nordic ministers have established common environmental strategies titled 'Programme for the Nordic Cooperation on the Environment and Climate 2019-2024'. The plan prioritises: (1) circular economy; (2) climate changes and air pollution; (3) chemicals – environment and health; (4)

42. Nordic Council, *Plans and Budget 2019. Summary.*

biodiversity; (5) oceans and coastal areas; and (6) implementation. It is a framework for the Nordic countries' environmental cooperation both within the Nordic area and in relation to its neighbouring areas.

In 1990, the Nordic Environmental Finance Corporation (NEFCO) was established by Denmark, Norway, Sweden and Finland. Its activities are focused on projects that achieve cost-effective environmental benefits across the region. Until 1995, Denmark was the only Nordic country being a full member of the European Community. Sweden and Finland became members in 1995 while Norway and Iceland are not members of the EU. They are members of the European Economic Area and the Schengen system. In July 2014, Iceland delivered its application for membership of the EU.

§3. Economic Characteristics

I. General

9. The Danish economy is one of the strongest in Europe having a diversified economic structure with high-tech industry and advanced business services. It is a very open – and thus sensitive – economy, in which export accounts for a substantial part of the total demand. The trust between different actors and societal groups – often referred to as 'social capital' – has also been an important factor for Danish economy.[43]

The public expenditure accounts for a large part of the Gross Domestic Product (GDP). The extensive public services and facilities are funded through taxes.[44] In the period 1993–2007, Denmark benefited from considerable economic growth, with a Gross National Product (GNP) rising on an average of 2.7% per year. In 2007, after a long consumption-driven upswing, Denmark's economy began slowing. From 1997 to 2007, it dropped from number 6 to number 12 among the richest OECD nations. In 2010, Denmark was the eighteenth richest country in the world.[45] After the economy contracted in 2008–2009, positive growth rates have returned to an average of 1.6% annually in 2014–2016, and at an average of 2% in 2016–2018.[46] In 2016, the GDP amounted to 2,065 billion, corresponding to DKK 360,000 per capita.[47] The Danish Government's debt has the highest possible rating (AAA/Aaa) from the largest international credit rating agencies due to, *inter alia*, the low debt level and its composition of long-term liabilities.[48]

In 2009, Denmark was violating the 3% budget norm outlined in the Stability and Growth Pact,[49] and it accordingly entered the excessive deficit procedure.[50] The

43. BertelsmanStiftung, *Sustainable Governance Indicators, 2014 Denmark Report*, at 3.
44. Concerning the Danish taxes, *see infra* paras 11–12.
45. *Statistical Yearbook 2011* & The European Commission, *Taxation trends in the European Union. Data for the EU Member States, Iceland and Norway*, 2011, at 175ff.
46. The Danish Government, *Denmark's Convergence Programme 2018*, at 7.
47. *Denmark's Seventh National Communication and Third Biennial Report,* at 18.
48. The Central Bank of Denmark, *Danish Government Borrowing and Debt*, 2014.
49. The Pact entered into force in 1999 as part of the assessment bases for countries entering the common currency – the Euro.

Commission recommended that Denmark in the period 2010–2013 should bring the deficit below the 3% norm and improve the structural budget by 1.5% relative to the GDP.[51] With the Budget Act which took effect from 2014, the framework for the fiscal policy management has been strengthened. Denmark is holding the number 38 position by nominal position at an international level. In the Government's Convergence Programme 2018, it is stated that the economic expansion means that in 2018 the GDP is expected to increase in coming years.[52]

In accordance with the TFEU and the EU directives on the financial markets, Denmark enjoys free movement of capital. Denmark participates fully in the economic cooperation but has not yet adopted the Euro. In 2000, the 2001–2011 Liberal-Conservative Government and a large majority of the Parliament recommended the opt-out from the Economic and Monetary Union, but the proposal was rejected by a referendum. Denmark participates in the second Exchange Rate Mechanism (ERM II) Agreement which links currencies of Member States outside the Euro area to the Euro. In contrast with the United Kingdom and Sweden, Denmark has a long-standing firm policy of a fixed exchange rate vis-à-vis the Euro (previously the Deutschmark). One Euro equals approximately DKK 7.46766.[53] The fixed exchange rate policy was introduced in 1982 and has been a crucial element in making Denmark a low-inflation economy.

Since 1987, Denmark's total export of goods and services have exceeded the total import. The surplus on the balance of goods and service rose from DKK 77.4 billion in 2009 to DKK 150.0 billion in 2015. In 2016, the surplus amounted to DDK 141.7 billion.[54]

In recent decades, the business structure has experienced comprehensive changes. Denmark has changed from an agricultural and industrial society to a society where services are the dominant activity. In 2014, there were 299,800 active enterprises in Denmark.[55] Trade and transport account for most of these enterprises (22%) as well as business services (17%), with 10% of the enterprises having their activity within agriculture, forestry and fishing, and 7% having their main activity in manufacturing, mining, and quarrying. It is first and foremost the small- and medium-sized firms that dominate the manufacturing and service sectors. Trade and transport accounted for the largest share of enterprises and for the largest share of turnover (46%).[56]

Denmark is one of the world's leading maritime nations[57] and is among the world's four largest tonnage operators. On 1 January 2016, there were 1,735 Danish ships of at least 20 gross tonnage (GT), which is a decrease of 7 ships compared to

50. BertelsmanStiftung, *Sustainable Governance Indicators, 2014 Denmark Report*, at 7.
51. BertelsmanStiftung, *Sustainable Governance Indicators, 2014 Denmark Report*, at 7.
52. The Danish Government, *Denmark's Convergence Programme 2018*, at 8.
53. This exchange rate as of 16 May 2019.
54. *Statistical Yearbook 2017*, in the section that is titled 'External economy'.
55. *Statistical Yearbook 2017,* in the section titled 'Business sectors in general'.
56. *Statistical Yearbook 2017,* in the section titled 'Business sectors in general'.
57. Danish Ministry for Foreign Affairs. *Focus on the Maritime Sector*, 2014.

2015, of which 29% of the ships were dissing vessels and 31% were cargo vessels. The Danish merchant fleet is made up by cargo and passenger ships of at least 100 GT.[58]

In the fishing sector, fewer than 10,000 individuals are employed in catching, selling, processing and transporting fish. Employment was almost halved in the past decade.[59] During the period 2003–2013, the total catch by Danish fishermen as to salt-water fishing has fallen from 1.0 million tonnes to 670,000 tonnes.[60] In 2016, the total catch by Danish fishermen from salt-water fishing amounted to 672,000 tonnes.[61] Fishing is an important industry in Denmark, considering that Denmark is the fifth largest exporter of fish and fish products in the world, and it represented about DKK 3.7 billion in 2016.[62] The poor condition of fish populations, especially cod, has implied that the EU has imposed fishing quotas on Danish waters, which are considered some of the best fishing grounds in the world.[63] The fishing industry is made up of owner-captains rather than commercial fleets.[64]

Over the years, the agricultural sector's importance for the national economy has declined. In 1975, this sector had a share of 4.9% of the total Danish GDP at factor costs. In 2015 this share had decreased to 1.3%.[65] Over many years, structural trends within agriculture have been marked by a steady annual decline in the number of farms. In 1985, Denmark had around 92,000 farms. In 2012, there were 39,900 farms with at least 5 ha of farm area. Over a period of twenty years, the number of farms has drop of about 50%.[66] In 1985, the average farm cultivates were 71.9 ha against 30.7 hectares only, and 78% of all farms had livestock.[67] In the same period the livestock farms have increased in size to 117 animals in cattle farms compared to 58 in 1985. The pig farms increased from 200 pigs to 3,300 in the mentioned period.[68] Nevertheless, there are still many small farms – 54% of the farms are less than 30 ha. A total of 7% of all farms are organic.[69] The processing of agricultural products is carried out through a network of cooperative enterprises with quality control staff and sales companies. Historically, the legal approach to ownership in the agricultural sector has been very strict, but the Agricultural Act[70] in force also accepts companies as owners. In 2016, the meat and meat manufacture represented 4% of the external trade in goods.[71] The agricultural sector is facing economic problems with continuing low profit margins, significant capital gains and a continuing increase in agricultural property prices. In recent years, productivity growth, which

58. *Statistical Yearbook 2017,* in the section titled 'Business sectors'.
59. European Parliament, Directorate-General for Internal Policies, Policy Department, Structural and Cohesion Policies B, *Fisheries in Denmark,* 2013, at 11.
60. *Statistical Yearbook 2014*, at 405. Concerning fishing in Denmark, *see also infra* paras 281–286.
61. *Statistical Yearbook 2017,* in the section titled 'Business sectors'.
62. *Statistical Yearbook 2017,* in the section titled 'Business sectors'.
63. OECD, *Environmental* Performance Reviews. Denmark, 2007, at 94.
64. Concerning the Catch-Share Programme, *see infra* para. 284.
65. *Statistical Yearbook 2017,* in the section titled 'Business sectors'.
66. *Statistical Yearbook 2014,* at 398.
67. In 2015, it was reduced to 60%.
68. *Statistical Yearbook 2017,* in the section titled 'Business sectors'.
69. *Statistical Yearbook 2017,* in the section titled 'Business sectors'.
70. Promulgation Order No. 27 of 4 January 2017 on Agricultural Properties.
71. *Statistical Yearbook 2017,* in the section titled 'External economy'.

historically has been high, has been falling dramatically. The real prices of agricultural products fell by nearly 90% from 1966 to 2007.[72] Although agriculture's role in the Danish economy has steadily declined with the rise of industrialisation and economic development, it remains an important sector in the political decisions on how to design environmental law. This priority is a result of the sectors foreign currency earning capacity, its effect on employment, and its importance in supplying everyday foodstuffs. A number of important industrial branches such as slaughterhouses, dairies, canneries, breweries, skin and fur production, and pharmaceutical and biochemical firms are related to agriculture. The Danish forests cover 12.4% of the total land area. It contributes 0.24% to the Danish GDP. The combined forest, paper and furniture industries contribute 3.67% to the GDP.

The largest industries in Denmark are the food, drink and tobacco, engineering, electronics and the chemicals. The main branches of industry (in terms of GDP) are the chemicals, iron and metal works, food, drink and tobacco, paper and printing, and wood and furniture. Since 2000, the manufacturing industry's total turnover for enterprises with ten employees or more has increased from DKK 476 billion to DKK 763.9 billion in 2016. Manufacturing of food, drink and tobacco accounted for 22% of the turnover and had the largest turnover of all industries. This was followed by manufacturing of machinery with 21.5%, pharmaceuticals with 11.8%, and manufacturing of chemicals and oil refineries, etc., with 8.9%.[73]

Production in the building and construction sector has increased. In recent years, house building activities have accounted for slightly more than half of all investment in building activities. The economic growth of the mid-2000s led to an increase in the number of dwellings completed from 2003 to 2007 when it peaked with 31,000 dwellings completed. The economic crisis resulted in a strong slowing-down in the construction of dwellings.[74] The development have changed, starting with 18,000 completed dwellings in 2016. The sector is responsible for some of the largest and most important material streams in Denmark as the sector consumes most of the mineral resources produced, the majority of which consists of sand, gravel and stone.

In the 1970s, exploitation of the deposits of oil and natural gas in the Danish part of the North Sea began, and since then it has been of great importance. Since 1990, Denmark's total production of energy has almost tripled. Primarily due to the production of oil and gas in the North Sea, Denmark has been more than self-sufficient in oil since 1993, resulting in an annual net export. In 2010, the degree of self-sufficiency in oil was 168%.[75] Since 2004, oil production from Danish fields has declined by about 20%, and in 2007 natural gas sales also ended at a lower level. In the period 1963–2013, the State revenue from hydrocarbon production in the North Sea aggregated DKK 383 billion in 2013 prices. In 2013, the State generated a revenue of DKK 22.1 billion from North Sea oil and gas production.[76] The five-year

72. Danish Economic Councils, *Economy and Environment 2010*, at 457ff.
73. *Statistical Yearbook 2017*, in the section titled 'Business sectors'.
74. *Statistical Yearbook 2017*, in the section titled 'Business sectors'.
75. Danish Energy Agency, *Energy Statistics 2010*, at 5.
76. Danish Energy Agency, *Oil and Gas Production in Denmark 2013 and Subsoil Use*, 2014 at 24.

forecast of the Danish Energy Agency for the period 2015–2019 included information on the declining production of oil and gas. The total estimated value of Danish oil and gas production in 2014 was DKK 40.7 billion, a decline of 18% compared to the production value in 2013.[77] Renewable energy is also increasingly contributing to the country's energy supply. It accounts for about 35% of the actual energy consumption.[78]

The two main types of company used in most of the Danish business sectors are the private type of limited companies and the public limited companies (A/S). Both are limited liability companies. An A/S must have a board of directors consisting of at least three members. The board of directors must appoint and supervise a manager or board of managers who are responsible for the day-to-day operation of the company. None of the members are personally liable for the debts of the company. The board of directors is responsible for the general policy and decisions concerning unusual transactions. State-owned corporate firms are based on the same company structure. There are several public-owned stock companies, for example, in the electricity, heating and waste treatment sectors. The Water Sector Reform[79] – that came into force on 1 January 2010 – promoted liberalisation of the water supply and sewerage supply sectors. The municipalities are the owners of most of the water utilities.[80] The rules regulating the municipality's economic management can be found in the Local Government Act.[81] The municipality's investments and the investments of the municipality-owned water utilities are regulated by a 'pay-as-you-go' financial system, under which each year's expenditure must be financed out of the tax revenue. Investment in water utilities by taking on debt is also restricted. As regards loans for projects, the municipality is obligated to deposit funds equal to the full project investment costs in unusual water services activities – such as energy-related activities – upfront under the Statutory Order on Municipality Loans.[82] All economic benefits from the establishment of ownership of the water companies by the 2010 Act have to be paid back to the State.[83] None of these rules are results of EU legislation. In 2013–2014, the Water Section Act was evaluated. On 29 April 2014, the political parties reached an agreement on more flexible rules for the cooperation between public and private parties in the sector.[84]

---

77. *See* Danish Energy Agency, *Oil and Gas Production in Denmark 2014*, at 30. According to the estimate, oil production accounts for about DKK 33.6 billion and gas production for DKK 7.1 billion of the total production value. The production value is determined by supply and demand in oil and gas, the dollar exchange rate, and the volume of production.
78. The Economic Councils, *Economy and Environment 2014*, at 325.
79. Act No. 469 of 12 June 2009 on the Organisation of and the Economic Conditions for the Water Sector.
80. Concerning the Danish water supply system and the municipality owned utilities, *see infra* paras 113 and 123.
81. Promulgation Order No. 47 of 15 January 2019 on Local Government.
82. Statutory Order No. 1580 of 17 December 2013 on the Municipality Loans, as amended by Statutory Order No. 830 of 21 June 2018.
83. Promulgation Act No. 634 of 7 June 2010 on Municipalities Transforming of Water Utilities in to Public Owned Companies, as this Act was amended by Act No. 132 of 16 February 2016 and by Act No. 690 of 8 June 2018.
84. Act No. 132 of 16 February 2016 on the Follow up on the Political Agreement on a New and Better Regulation of the Water Sector.

The Danish model for the labour market is known as a 'flexicurity' model, meaning that it is not costly to fire employees, and that the social welfare state will step in with motivation and training when necessary.[85] The official full working time in most of the labour market is thirty-seven hours a week with six weeks of vacation per year. The share of the workforce employed in goods-producing industries (agriculture, manufacturing, energy and construction) has been continuously declining for several years. The number of hours worked by women is lower than the number of hours worked by men. In 2015, 39.6% of women were working part time, while only 26.6% of men were working part time.[86] More than 1.3 million full-time employers – or 62% of all full-time employers – work in the largest enterprises with 100 or more full-time employers.[87]

The service sector accounts for the highest number of persons employed in 2015. The largest groups are the public administration, education and health employment (31.3%), the second largest group is trade and transports, etc. (24.5%), and the smallest group is agriculture and fishing, etc. (2.7%).[88] Denmark has the highest employment rate for women in the EU as 76.7% of the women were in employment in 2012.[89] It was also the women that had the highest unemployment increase from 2008 as a consequence of the economic crises. [90]

The overall level of job inflows and outflows remained high during the economic crisis, showing that the Danish 'flexicurity' model is intact.[91] Prior to the global economic crisis, the level of unemployment was close to 2%.[92] In 2012, the average number of persons employed was approximately 2,795,801,[93] and the unemployment rate was 6.1. In 2014, employment was back at the 2006 level – before the overheating of the Danish economy. Since the beginning of 2013, in the labour market, employment has increased by almost 20,000 persons, and it is expected to increase further.[94] From 2012, there has been a slightly falling tendency in unemployment from around 6.0% to 4.2% of the labour force in 2016.[95]

10. Command-and-control regulation in the form of legal rules and principles are supplemented by different economic instruments. With the focus on genuine saving and circular economy, the interest in the use of economic instruments is getting still more important. First and foremost, it is a national competence to make decisions on the use of economic instruments as the competence of the EU is limited by Article 192(2) litter a. Only if the Council is acting unanimously the legislation on provisions of a fiscal nature can be adopted at EU level. In its Circular

85. BertelsmanStiftung, *Sustainable Governance Indicators. 2014 Denmark Report*, at 7; and BertelsmanStiftung, *Sustainable Governance Indicators. 2017 Denmark Report*, at 7.
86. *Statistical Yearbook 2017,* in the section titled 'Labour, earning and income'.
87. *Statistical Yearbook 2017,* in the section titled 'Business sectors in general'.
88. *Statistical Yearbook 2017,* in the section titled 'Labour, earning and income'.
89. *Statistical Yearbook 2014,* at 481.
90. *Statistical Yearbook 2017,* in the section titled 'Labour, earning and income'.
91. BertelsmanStiftung, *Sustainable Governance Indicators. 2017 Denmark Report*, at 6.
92. BertelsmanStiftung, *Sustainable Governance Indicators. 2014 Denmark Report*, at 8.
93. *Statistical Yearbook 2014,* at 481.
94. Danish Ministry for Economic Affairs and the Interior, '*Economic Survey – August 2014*', at 14–15.
95. *Statistical Yearbook 2017,* in the section titled 'Labour, earning and income'.

Economy Action Plan *Closing the Loop – EU Action Plan for Circular Economy*,[96] on the transition to a more circular economy, the EU encourages the Member States to use financial incentives and economic instruments to ensure that the 'polluter pays principle' and the 'user pays principle' are respected.

Consequently, focus in this part of the monograph is on the national use of economic instruments.

There are legal barriers in relation to the use of economic instruments at national level. The use of the economic instruments is limited by the ban on state aids laid down in Article 107 TFEU. This Article provides that any aid granted by a Member State or through State resources in any form whatsoever, which distorts or threatens to distort competition by favouring certain undertakings or production of certain goods, will, insofar as it affects trade between Member States, not be accepted. In certain cases, however, the Commission may consider it compatible with the internal market if the state aid facilitates the development of environmental protection at a level above the mandatory environmental standards, or if it promotes the use of renewable energy.[97] Furthermore, Article 110 TFEU aims at guaranteeing the neutrality of internal taxation by prohibiting discrimination against products of other Member States and the protection of domestic products. The Member States are free to decide which environmental taxes they consider most appropriate and, in particular, to spread, e.g., the tax burden as they see it fit across the various factors of production as long as the taxes are in accordance with EU law. Case law of the CJEU settle that, in the absence of EU rules governing the matter, it falls within the competence of the Member States or of infra-state bodies having fiscal autonomy to designate bases of assessment and to spread the tax burden across the various factors of production and the economy sectors.[98] In the Court's judgments about taxation of large retail establishments in Spain, the CJEU accepted that the purpose of the relevant tax was to contribute to environmental protection and town and country planning, and that it did not constitute state aid.[99] However, the Court has also established that it is not necessary to prove that the aid has real effect on trade between Member States and that competition is distorted, but only necessary to examine whether aid is liable to affect such trade and distort competition.[100]

II. Environmentally Market-Based and Economic Instruments

11. Over the last twenty to twenty-five years, Denmark's tax-to-GDP ratio has been relatively constant, fluctuating from 47.9% to 50.8%. OECD data shows that Denmark had the highest tax-to-GDP ratio compared to other OECD members in

96. COM(2015) 614 final. The Action Plan for Circular Economy was published on 2 Dec. 2015.
97. *See* the Commissions Guidelines (2014/C 200/1) on State Aid for Environmental Protection and Energy 2014–2020.
98. CJEU joined Cases C-106/09 P and C-107/09 P, *Commission and Spain v. Government of Gibraltar and United Kingdom.*
99. C-233/16 *ANGED*; the joined cases C-234/16 and C-235/16 *ANGED*; and C-236/16 and C-237/16 *ANGED.*
100. C-74/16 *Congregación de Escuelas Pias Provincia.*

2013 (48.6%).[101] Personal income tax is the tax that ensures approximately half the state income from taxes. Other taxes are value added tax (VAT), duties, corporate taxes, and labour-market contributions.

Denmark's Statistics divided the total taxes into four main types: Income (including taxes on enterprises) and property taxes, production and import taxes (including VAT and green taxes), capital taxes and compulsory contribution to social security schemes. The conclusion is that income and property taxes account for the largest share. Tax on capital and compulsory contribution to social schemes are not significant in terms of revenue.[102] The extensive welfare state is funded through a tax burden above 50% of the GDP.[103] The tax structure differs from most countries in that direct income and indirect (VAT) taxation serve as the predominant taxes, while social security contribution plays a modest role.[104] The Danish income tax system is progressive. The percentage paid in tax increases as income increases. The top tax bracket is only paid on the highest income levels ('the top tax threshold'). The 2001–2011 Liberal-Conservative Government introduced a tax freeze as a means of controlling public expenditure and bringing about a gradual reduction of the tax burden. The tax freeze applies to both direct and indirect taxes. A tax reform was agreed between this former government and the Danish People's Party in 2004 (the 'Spring Package'). It ensured a special deduction of taxes to everyone engaged in active employment. In 2009, a new major tax reform was agreed between the same parties (Spring Package 2.0). The tax reform increased the threshold for the top income tax,[105] and the Act implementing the reform between 2010 and 2019 reduced the overall marginal tax rate by 7.5%. The top tax rate was unchanged, but the income level at which it began was raised. The tax reform was designed to be neutral as a whole, but it was underfinanced in the short run in order to stimulate the economy. In May 2010, to consolidate the budget, a Fiscal Consolidation Agreement was reached between the former Liberal-Conservative Government and some of the other political parties, somewhat modifying the scope of the reform. In 2011, personal income tax constituted about 50.7% of total tax revenues.[106] In 2012, the following coalition Government[107] presented a new reform titled 'Denmark at work' with the goal of reducing the taxes on earned income that was implemented by an Act in September 2012.[108] From 2013, the reform raised the top tax threshold,[109] and it changed the taxation of persons who are not domiciled in, but who were

101. The GDP per capita amounted to EUR 43,700 in March 2013.
102. *Statistical Yearbook 2017,* in the section titled 'National accounts and government finances'.
103. BertelsmanStiftung, *Sustainable Governance Indicators. 2017 Denmark Report*, at 8.
104. BertelsmanStiftung, *Sustainable Governance Indicators. 2017 Denmark Report*, at 9.
105. In 2010, the threshold was increased from DKK 377,400 in 2009 to DKK 423,800. It also ensured a reduction in the top marginal tax rate from 63% to 56%.
106. *Denmark's Sixth National Communication and First Biennial Report to the UNFCCC*, December 2013, at 139.
107. This Government consisted in 2012 of the coalition between the Social Democratic Party, the Social-Liberal Party and the Socialistic People's Party.
108. Act No. 921 of 18 September 2012 on Reduction of Ceiling on Travel Allowance, increased Taxation of Free Cars, Taxation of the full Taxpayer's foreign Salary Income, Taxation on Labour Hire and extended Taxation of Wage Labour in Denmark. In 2014, the top tax threshold decreased to DKK 449,100.
109. In 2019, the threshold is DKK 498,900 – compared to DKK 389,900 in 2012.

working in Denmark. Both in the 2009 reform and in the 2012 reform, decreasing income tax rates have to a large extent been financed by broadening the tax basis by the use of environmental taxes.[110] The corporate tax rate has been gradually reduced from 50% in 1986 to 30% in 2005, to 25% in 2007, and to 22% in 2017.[111] In 2013, the Government in power[112] presented a reform titled 'Growth Plan DK' starting in 2014 with a 1% reduction of the rate for company tax from 2014 to 2016 when it will be restated at 22%.

The ninety-eight Danish municipalities receive revenues from income and profit taxes, property taxation, the central government grants and fees paid by the citizens for specific services (water and waste services). Local tax rates are flat and vary from one municipality to the next (on average 24.91%, which include church tax). There are no local taxes on corporations, but municipalities receive a share of corporate income tax revenue. Municipal councils themselves decide the tax rates within certain limitations set by law and the annual agreements established between the Ministry of Finance and the Local Government Denmark.[113] The agreements are normally concluded in June the year before the year in question. As a consequence of the size of the local authorities, for a number of years, the Government has endeavoured to influence spending through the above-mentioned negotiations. The agreements have to be approved by the Parliament. Most welfare tasks in Denmark are devolved to the municipalities.

The municipal annual budget can be divided into the following categories: roads and environment (clearly the smallest percentage of all the categories), care for the elderly, day-care institutions, other social services, primarily education, around-the-clock services, and administration.[114] The citizens pay green taxes to the State and fees to the municipalities for management of the water supply, wastewater treatment, waste management and heating. For some municipal services (mainly day-care services and institutions for the elderly), the municipality pays approximately 70% of the costs, while the users pay the remaining part in monthly fees.

The five regions are financed directly by a grant from the government and by a small contribution directly paid by the municipalities when citizens are hospitalised.[115] In 2009, the five regions' expenditure on environmental tasks amounted to 4.4% of the total budget for the regions.

For municipalities and regions, there is no special framework for the annual environmental investments. The level of spending and investment depends on the legislative acts and the agreements entered into between the State and the municipalities/regions.

The total national expenditure in million DKK on protection of the environment in 1992 was DKK 30.2 million, in 1994 DKK 32.4 million, in 1996 DKK 37,300

110. BertelsmanStiftung, *Sustainable Governance Indicators. 2014 Denmark Report*, at 9.
111. BertelsmanStiftung, *Sustainable Governance Indicators. 2017 Denmark Report*, at 9.
112. The Government consisted until January 2014 of the coalition between the Social Democratic Party, the Social-Liberal Party and the Socialistic People's Party.
113. Local Government Denmark is the interest group and member authority of the Danish municipalities.
114. Local Government Denmark, *The Danish Local Government System*, at 13.
115. Local Government Denmark, *The Danish Local Government System*, at 15–16.

million, in 1998 DKK 42.3 million and in 2000 DKK 42.8 million.[116] The liberal-conservative coalition Government that was in power from 2001 to 2011 changed the budget for the environment and reduced it dramatically, and the different coalition governments that were in power until 27 June 2019 did not change the now priority to environmental public spending. The Ministry of Environment of Food's overall budget has decreased.[117] In 2016, it was only 0.8% of the GDP that was related to environmental protection.[118]

12. The use of green taxes is common in Denmark – both as a way of reducing the negative effects of production processes and parts of consumption and as an important part of the state revenue. The revenue from the green taxes is high in Denmark compared to our neighbouring countries and the average in the OECD countries.[119] In 2017, the revenue from green taxes was 4% of the GDP – the average was 1.6% in the other OECD countries.[120] In an assessment by the EU Commission in 2017, it is stated that the environmental tax revenues relative to GDP are high compared to the EU although there is room to align the design of the environmental taxes in Denmark with their environmental objectives.[121] An environmental tax is tax based on a physical unit – or a proxy of it – of something that has a proven, specific negative impact on the environment. It is used as an incentive to ensure internationalisation of external costs in harmony with three environmental principles: the 'polluter pays principle', the 'resource user pays principle' and the 'precautionary principle'.[122]

For more than two decades, Denmark has applied a broad spectrum of environmental taxes.[123] The history of the use of such taxes started in the 1970s with taxation of certain oil products. The balance of taxation among the various economic sectors is uneven: thus, household energy taxes and the taxes on the service sector are considerably higher than those levied on industry. Industry is often granted exemptions or given opportunities for rebates to protect international competitiveness.[124] The general tax reform which was phased in over the period 1994–1998 should gradually shift the balance in the tax system away from income taxation towards environmental taxation. The green tax burden peaked in 1999 with 5.3% of the GDP. The taxes were at a stable level from 2000 to 2007. The financial crisis in 2008 affected the environmental tax revenue downwards. The Eurostat tax statistics

---

116. The Ministry of Finance, *The economic benefits and costs of the environmental policy*, 2001, at 17.
117. OECD, *Environmental Performance Review. Denmark 2007*, at 108 and 143. In the period from 1999 to 2017, it decreased by one-third. The decrease started in 2001, *see* concerning the different coalition government, *supra* in para. 4.
118. *Statistical Yearbook 2017,* in the section titled 'National accounts and government finances'.
119. The Danish Economic Council, *Economy and Environment 2017*, at 335.
120. The Danish Economic Council, *Economy and Environment 2017*, at 102.
121. European Commission staff working document of 3 February 2017, *The EU Environmental Implementation Review Country Report – Denmark*, SWD(2017) 39 final, at 20.
122. European Environmental Agency, *Environmental Taxes: Recent Developments in Tools for Integration*, November 2000, at 14.
123. European Environmental Agency, *Environmental Taxes: Recent Developments in Tools for Integration*, Report No. 18/2000, at 33.
124. OECD, *Environmental Performance Reviews Denmark*, at 127, and the Danish Economic Council, Economy and Environment 2017, at 337.

show that Denmark in February and March 2014 headed the ranking among the twenty-eight Member States with environmental taxes equivalent to 3.9%. In 2015, the Government's total revenue from environmental taxes developed to DKK 81.1 billion, which corresponds to 8.5% of the total taxes. Measured as a percentage of the GDP, green taxes amounted to 4.0%.[125] Although the Danish environmental taxes, energy taxes and transport-related taxes are meant to influence the behaviour of enterprises and individuals, they are a source of finance for public environmental activities. The financial motives behind the taxes have been a convenient way in which to cover deficits on the State budget. A European study based on the levels of the Danish environmental taxes that already exist in similar countries show that there might be a considerable potential for shifting taxes from labour to environmental taxes.[126] However, in 2017–2018 developments in Denmark show a gradual reduction in both the green taxes and the labour taxes.

There are many different environmental-related taxes – some of the most important are described in the following. In 1987, an amendment to the Environmental Protection Act was included as a new Chapter 12a, which laid down some common rules on *waste taxes*. In the remarks connected to these rules, it was stressed, that it was the intention of the Government to base its tax policy on the 'polluter pays principle', and that it was anticipated that the use of economic instruments would lead to the development of cleaner technologies, to more initiatives by the industry itself, and to a more conscious use of mineral resources, etc. In 1989, the tax levels were laid down in the Act on Taxes on Waste and Mineral Resources. The levels have been increased – e.g., as part of the 1993, 1997 and 1999 tax reforms. Based on the Act on Taxes on the Mineral Resources and Waste, from 1 January 2001, the tax on waste amounted to DKK 375 per ton for the delivery of waste to deposits. For waste treated at an incineration plant, the price amount to DKK 330 per tonne, and for waste used as energy resources, heating houses, the price was DKK 280 per tonne. In 2009, a new tax reform was agreed to, changing the taxes on waste incineration, including the utilisation of waste as an energy source. It came into force on 1 January 2010. The landfill tax is still regulated by the Act on Taxes on Mineral Resources and Waste – in 2018, it amounted to DKK 475 per tonne.[127] Enterprises that exclusively receive waste for recycling are exempted from these taxes in order to encourage recycling. To ensure that hazardous waste is handled by the public system, the authorities have decided not to collect taxes on such waste until 2014. The rules imposing taxes on certain types of packaging and plastic waste are laid down in the Act on Packaging Taxes.[128] The tax comprises five separate systems: (1) a volume-based tax on beverage packaging; (2) a mass- and environmental impact-based tax on the packaging of certain commodities (e.g., food, animal food, cosmetic); (3) a mass-based tax on paper bags and plastic bags; (4) a mass-based tax on disposable plastics dishes; and (5) a mass-based tax on PVC foil. In 1997, a

125. *Statistical Yearbook 2017*, at 411.
126. The Commission's staff working document, *The EU Environmental Implementation Review. Country report – Denmark*, SWD(2017)39 final at 20 with reference to Eunomia Research and Consulting, IEEP, Aarhus University, ENT, 2016.
127. Section 9 of the Promulgation Order No. 412 of 21 April 2017 on Taxes on Mineral Resources and Waste.
128. Promulgation Order No. 1236 of 4 October 2016 on Packaging Taxes.

wastewater tax on households and industry was imposed. There are also taxes on the use of drinking water in Denmark. The tax on water consumption in 2018–2020 amounts to DKK 6.37/m^3.[129] The parties to the 'Action Plan for the Aquatic Environmental II' of February 1998 (APAE II) introduced a general nitrogen tax. The third 'Action Plan for the Aquatic Environment III' (2005–2015) introduced a tax that amounted to DKK 4 per kg of mineral phosphorous in feed. Revenues from this tax are returned to agriculture through a reduction in land taxes. Within the agricultural sector (horticulture and forestry), only farmers that are subject to fertilisation planning control have the possibility to purchase tax-free fertilisers. Since 2012, a special act has ensured the legal basis for taxes on pesticides. The act is based on the environmental and health impacts of these chemicals, implying a higher tax the more environmentally hazardous they are.[130] A higher tax on pesticides has been passed since.[131]

In 2000, a tax on PVC was introduced, following the failure of an environmental agreement. It was set to a rate amounting to DKK 2 per kg of hard PVC for phthalate-softened PVC. The precise tax rates on the softened PVC depend on how much phthalates they contain.[132]

There are two types of energy and climate taxes: the taxes on heating, which are levied on all fossil fuels as well as on waste used for energy production, and the energy tax on electricity, which is an output tax. This last-mentioned *electricity tax* is payable only for households, non-commercial uses and industrial space heating. The electricity tax system was introduced in 1998 along with the implementation of the first Electricity Directive. The current system is a result of many amendments to the Act Electricity Taxes.[133] Energinet.dk[134] collects the data on electricity consumption in a hub as the basis for the tax authorities' collection of taxes. The energy tax rates levied on the energy sources *used for heating* are different across the different energy products according to the energy content of each fuel type. With effect from 1 January 2008, the tax rates set out in the four acts (the Mineral-Oil-Tax Act, the Gas-Tax Act, the Coal-Tax Act and the Electricity-Tax Act) were subject to an annual regulation of 1.8% in the period 2008–2015.[135] Taxes on nitrogen oxides (NO_x) emission (particles) were introduced in 2008. A new NO_x tax was introduced as part of the 'Energy Agreement 2008'. The tax rate amounted to DKK 5 per kg NO_x effective from 1 January 2010. New political initiatives on higher energy taxes were discussed in the Danish Parliament as part of the energy policy for the period 2012–2020.[136] As part of the follow-up on the 'Energy Agreement 2012', several

129. Act No. 924 of 18 September 2012 on Different Taxes on Consumption.
130. It was implemented with the legal basis in Act No. 594 of 18 June 2012 on Taxes on Pesticides.
131. Danish Government, *The National Reform Programme Denmark* 2015, at 62. The rules are now found in the Promulgation Order No. 232 of 26 February 2015.
132. Promulgation Order No. 1110 of 19 September 2017 on PVC Tax.
133. Promulgation Order No. 308 of 24 March 2017 on Electricity Taxes.
134. Energynet.dk is a combination of an enterprise and an authority owned by the Ministry for Climate, Energy and Utilities.
135. The taxes to be plaid in are stated in Act No. 1385 of 28 December 2011. The taxes amount to between DKK 2 and 4 per litre.
136. *Statistical Yearbook 2011*, and European Commission, *Taxation trends in the European Union. Data for the EU Member States, Iceland and Norway*, at 175ff.

amendments to the legislation were passed with effect from 1 January 2013.[137] The NO_x tax increased to DKK 26.4 per kg from 1 January 2015 as a result of an Act on Taxes on Air Pollution from NO_x etc.[138] The rate was reduced in 2016 to DKK 5 per kg NO_x.[139] From 2016, the tax rates set in the four tax acts has been following an annual regulation based on the consumer price index of the last two years.[140] A political agreement on 'Business and Entrepreneurial Initiatives' from 2017 reduced the tax on electric heating for the industry. The tax on electricity for heating purposes will be reduced from 4.1 EUR cent/kWh to 2.1 EUR cent/kWh from 2021. The general electricity tax will be reduced from 12.3 EUR cent/kWh to 10.4 EUR cent/kWh in 2025. For certain types of business, the electricity tax will be reduced to the EU minimum level.[141]

Denmark was one of the first countries in Europe to introduce a carbon dioxide (CO_2) tax on top of already existing energy taxes levied on oil products, coal and electricity consumption. The CO_2 tax rate on energy sources (such as CO_2 taxes on gas oil, fuel oil, electricity, natural gas and town gas, heating tar, crude oil, coke, crude oil, lignite briquettes and lignite, LPG and other gases) is used as an incitement to change the use of energy resources.[142] The CO_2 tax was introduced in May 1992 as a tax for households. In June 1993, the Parliament accepted a comprehensive tax reform which came into force on 1 January 1994 and which included a substantial package of new energy taxes as well as green taxes. This tax reform, named the 'CO_2 Package', increased the energy taxes on coal and coal-based electricity. During the period 1993–1995, industry was granted a 50% reduction in CO_2 taxes.[143] In May 1995, the social democratic and liberal coalition Government presented 'The Danish Energy Reform – Green Taxes' based on the results of the European Council meeting in Essen in December 1994, the conclusion of which called for a report on the linkage between economic growth and the environment and the consequences of this for the economic policy. As a result, the energy tax on trade and industry was revised. Under this reform, a green tax on energy consumption by trade and industry was phased in during the period 1996–2000. The package introduced higher CO_2 taxes, energy taxes on space heating, a gas tax on natural and town gas, and SO_2 taxes on emissions for trades and industries. The energy tax was also raised between 1996 and 2002, and the tax on sulphur in fuels was phased in until 2000 with a rate amounting to DKK 20 per kg sulphur in fuels and a rate amounting to DKK 10 for SO_2 emitted to the air.[144] As part of the implementation

---

137. *See* Act No. 1353 of 20 December 2012 and Statutory Order No. 1403 of 21 December 2012
138. Promulgation Order No. 1144 of 13 October 2017 on NOx Tax.
139. *Denmark's 7th National Communication on Climate Change*, at 152.
140. *Denmark's 7th National Communication on Climate Change*, at 152.
141. *Denmark's Draft Integrated National Energy and Climate Plan under the Governance Regulation*, December 2018, at 50.
142. Promulgation Order No. 321 of 4 April 2011 as amended many times – the last amendment was made by Act No. 331 of 30 March 2019.
143. NERI (Denmark), Cambridge Econometrics (UK), ESRI (Ireland), EEIP (Czech Republik), PSI (UK) and WiiW (Austria), *Competitiveness Effects of Environmental Tax Reforms*, 2007, at 34.
144. *Denmark's 7th National Communication on Climate Change*, at 152.

of the EU ETS in 2005, a decision taken by the Danish Parliament decided to pay back the CO_2 taxes paid for fuels and heating used in the industries covered by the EU Emissions Trading Scheme (ETS sectors). In the non-ETS industries (i.e., services and industries not covered by the ETS quota system), a scheme was set up in order to ensure equality of treatment of similar industries in the ETS and non-ETS sectors after the Commission did not accept the Danish exemption of the ETS sector from the CO_2 taxes, and the ETS sectors were taxed at the minimum level established by the Energy Taxation Directive.[145] The deduction scheme was removed simultaneously with the introduction of auctioned quotas, starting from 2013. In June 2013, a Danish Act on reduction of the energy and CO_2 taxes of energy used for business processes to the EU's minimum tax rate was passed with effect from 1 January 2014.[146] Businesses continue to pay energy and CO_2 taxes on energy used for space heating and cooling, and these taxes will increase over the next years for both the businesses and households. There are no energy-related taxes on bioenergy. In contrast to this, bioenergy is included in the objectives that are covered by CO_2 taxes, NO_x taxes and methane (CH_4) taxes.

Since 1 March 2001, imports of industrial F-gases – hydrofluorocarbons (HFCs), perfluorocarbons (PFCs) and sulphur hexafluoride (SF_6) – in the industry/business sector have been subject to climate change-related taxation.[147] The taxes correspond to the global warming potential (GWP) of these greenhouse gases (GHGs). In 2009, the tax system was reformed to equate to a CO_2 tax rate amounting to DKK 150 per ton. As it was estimated that without further initiatives there would be a shortfall in the needed reduction in the total Danish emission of GHGs – primarily CH_4 and N_2O from agricultural activities – approximately 12.25 million tonnes of CO_2 equivalents each year during the period 2008–2012, a tax on CH_4 were introduced in 2008, and the taxes rate on CO_2 taxes was increased from DKK 3 to DKK 90 per tonne. As these taxes on industrial gases are based on the CO_2 tax, there was an increase in 2011 from DKK 0.10 per kg of CO_2 equivalents to DKK 0.15.[148]

In 2012, taxes on energy constituted 59% of the total environmental tax revenue compared to 70% on average in the thirty-nine OECD countries.[149] The energy-related taxes – taxes on electricity, gasoline and certain petroleum tax – are the most dominant among energy taxes. In 2015, they constituted up to 56% of the total environmental-related taxes.[150] In 2015, the revenues from energy taxes amounted to DKK 37.8 billion, which was a 3.3% decline compared to 2014. Compared with 1990, prices increased by 172% in 2015.[151] In its report from 2017, the Danish Economic Council is stating that the tax on electricity has only doubtful or indirect

145. Council Directive 2003/96/EC restructuring the Community Framework for the Taxation of Energy Product and Electricity.
146. Act No. 903 of 4 July 2013 amending several acts on taxation. It was the result of a political agreement of 24 April 2013 between the Government and several political parties initiated by the Government's 'Reform Programme 2013'.
147. Promulgation Order No. 69 of 17 January 2017 on CFC Taxes and Taxes on some other Industrial Greenhouse Gases.
148. *Denmark's 7th National Communication on Climate Change*, at 157.
149. OECD, *Environmental-related taxes. Taxes on Energy use.*
150. *Statistical Yearbook 2017*, at 412.
151. *Denmark's 7th National Communication on Climate Change*, at 56.

effects on the environment. It is also the opinion of the Danish Economic Council that the high tax on electricity might even contribute to increasing the total emission of CO_2 as it could counteract the transition away from fossil fuels in non-ETS sectors.[152] The Public Service Obligation (PSO) tariff, which has been a supplement to the price of electricity paid by all consumers until 2017, was based on a model used to calculate expected future expenditure on subsidies for renewable electricity production (calculating the expenses for offshore wind, onshore wind, biogas and photovoltaics, combined heat and electricity production, etc.). The calculation of the PSOs has been based on gross electricity consumption before grid losses. The PSO tariff will be phased out at the end of 2021 as a consequence of the Commission's criticising of the subsidies that the Danish companies receive.[153]

Transport-related taxes cover CO_2 taxes, SO_2 taxes, registration tax (taxes paid to the State when a person buys a car) and an annual tax for owning a vehicle. The transport taxes are relatively important in Denmark.[154] Since 1 July 1997, this annual tax has been based on energy consumption (the green owner tax) that is calculated in accordance with the Energy Taxation Directive adapting to the technical progress that has impact on the fuel consumption of the motor vehicles. The tax rates on transport fuel are higher than on fuels used for heating and process purposes or electricity generation.[155] In 1999, a tax difference between light diesel and diesel low in sulphur was introduced to encourage the use of the latter, which is less polluting than light diesel. The tax rate fell from 2002 onwards as a consequence of rising fuel taxes. A further differentiation from 1 January 2005 favouring sulphur-free diesel was likewise introduced to phase out lead in diesel. The rules on taxation of different types of petrol are also based on a differentiation promoting the phasing out of lead.[156] By 2013, the minimum rates for motor fuels were completely harmonised in all Member States. The car registration tax was established already in 1925. It is calculated on the basis of the value of the vehicle. A registration tax reduction for highly energy-efficient cars was introduced in 1999 and modified in 2007. A reduction of the registration tax applies to new diesel fuelled vehicles if they meet the emission requirements for particulate matter. Electricity vehicles are granted deduction until 2021.[157] Car owners have to pay half-year taxes, which are differentiated in accordance with the fuel efficiency of the cars.[158] The structure of car taxation is based on low annual taxes, and high registration taxes are criticised by the Commission as the taxes do not meet its environmental objectives.[159] Public transport is exempt from fuel taxes. The CO_2 tax rate on gasoline and diesel was increased in 2007. Biofuels are exempt from CO_2 taxes. Income

---

152. The Danish Economic Council, *Economy and Environment 2017*, at 335–337.
153. Concerning the replacement of PSO funding by financing over the Danish Budget Bill, *see infra* para. 15.
154. Based on data from Eurostat Statistics, February–March 2014.
155. David Brandbury and Kurt Van Dender, *Environmentally Related Taxes. Taxes on Energy Use*, OECD.
156. Danish Government, *Denmark's 5th National Communication on Climate Change*, at 145f.
157. *Denmark's 7th National Communication on Climate Change*, at 156.
158. *Denmark's 7th National Communication on Climate Change*, at 156.
159. The Commission's staff working document, *The EU Environmental Implementation Review. Country report – Denmark*, SWD(2017)39 final at 20 with reference to Eunomia Research and Consulting, IEEP, Aarhus University, ENT, 2016.

tax breaks are granted to commuters. In 2013, the Danish Economic Councils stated that there are a number of problems with the design of the current car taxation as most of the taxes are not directly targeting the external costs of driving. In addition, the overall tax level is higher than what can be motivated by the level of the marginal costs of driving.[160] In a staff working document of the Commission, it is stated that there is a large potential in getting both a reduction of the emission from the car transport sector and a high revenue by a future amendment of the Danish transport fuel taxes.[161] However, it is not on the Danish agenda. Currently, there is no road pricing system in Denmark.

13. For some services, the municipalities are by law allowed to collect special user charges (fees). As regards user charges, the full-cost recovery principle applies to all of the following areas: public waste treatment, water supply, and sewage and wastewater treatment. The Danish Competition and Consumer Authority[162] – which is an agency under the Ministry for Business – is responsible for ensuring that water services respect the 'full-cost recovery principle', centralised pricing levels, and the performance benchmarking mentioned below. It has also the competence to calculate an annual 'price cap' for the individual water utilities, partly on an individual result-oriented benchmarking basis and partly on a calculation of the traditional costs of water services.[163] The ambition with these rules is to ensure a modernisation process in the water sector, increasing the efficiency of operations and transparency. The users of water have to pay charges, which also cover compensation for the economic loss inflicted on farmers by conversion of land use from normal agricultural production to more extensive methods to ensure protection of areas of special interest in the drinking water supply.[164]

Based on Chapter 4 of the Heat Supply Act, the price for receiving the services from the municipality-owned district heating supply system has to be equivalent to the long-term marginal costs of producing the heat. The price-calculation principle ensures that the charge each individual consumer has to pay is a genuine reflection of the long-term marginal costs of producing heat. The municipality-owned waste handling enterprises also have to use the revenue from user fees as the basis for covering the costs connected with the infrastructure facilities and services, etc. In section 48 of the Environmental Protection Act, it is stated that the municipal council must fix user fees at such a rate as to cover expenses relating to planning, establishment, operation and administration of waste schemes. This principle means that income and expenditures must balance over a sequence of years. The fees may

160. Economic Councils, *Economy and Environment 2013*, at 375ff.
161. The Commission's staff working document, *The EU Environmental Implementation Review. Country report – Denmark*, SWD(2017)39 final, at 20, with reference to Eunomia Research and Consulting, IEEP, Aarhus University, ENT, 2016. The road transport emissions in Denmark are among the highest in the EU.
162. This Authority is part of the Ministry of Industry, Business and Financial Affairs.
163. *See* ss 6–8 in the Water Sector Act. Concerning the regulation of the water utilities E.M. Basse, *The Existing Regulatory Conditions for 'Energy Smart Water Utilities': Promotion of Sustainable Energy Transition,* at 111–136.
164. This is specified in section 52a–52c of the Water Supply Act, *see infra* para. 121 concerning the Danish price on water supply.

include payment for assignment schemes, separation and collection of waste, etc. The party having a registered right to the property must pay the fees relating to waste. The fees enjoy the same privileges in the property as public direct and indirect taxes. Because of the need for consistency in the amount of delivered and treated waste, the above-mentioned 'full-cost recovery principle' may cause problems and may lack ecological justification in relation to waste-recycling treatments. The Act on Taxation of Real Estate provides that where household waste is disposed of by order of the municipal council, the fee may wholly or in part be calculated on the basis of the public land value assessment. Furthermore, a judgment of the Eastern High Court in 1977 stated that the municipal councils were entitled to collect the revenue to cover the costs of general local waste treatment from the general income taxes.

There are also other fees to be paid. By way of example can be mentioned the fee on tires imposed on the user. The fee depends on the size of the tires. The money received as a result of the collection of the used motorcar tires is spent on ensuring reuse of the raw materials.[165]

14. In its 2017 report, the Danish Economic Council is assessing how to regulate the agriculture nitrogen emissions to coastal waters, and the outcome is the recommendation of 'targeted crop taxes'. Included in the assessment are two other economic instruments: (1) 'allowance-based leaching rights' and (2) 'tradeable leaching rights' that are assessed as less costly both for the farmers and for Danish society. Based on the recommendation, the 'targeted crop taxes' are to be paid by the individual farmer, and the obligation depends on the size of the cultivated areas and the farmer's choice of crops. It is recommended that the taxes should differ between farmers due to geographical differences in soil types and how much of the leached nitrogen that never reach the surface and ground water. The Government[166] did not follow the recommendation.

Allowance-based leaching rights and tradeable leaching rights are only used in Denmark in the area covered by the EU Emissions Trading Directive (EU ETS Directive). On 2 June 1999, the Parliament adopted an Act on CO_2 Quotas for Electricity Production.[167] This Act was replaced by the Carbon Dioxide Allowance Act[168] that implemented the EU ETS Directive. Until 1 January 2013, the European operators of ETS stationary installations that were obligated to acquire CO_2 quotas received free CO_2 allowances. One CO_2 quota equals the right to emit 1 ton of CO_2 within a year. Today, the operators must pay for the CO_2 allowances (also named 'tradable emission permits') or (until the end of 2020) by credits from JI or Clean Development Mechanism (CDM) projects.

165. *See infra* para. 158. The rules are laid down in the Statutory Order No. 1347 of 21 November 2016 concerning Fees and Subsidies for Recycling and Recovery of Used Tires.
166. It was the liberal-conservative Government that was in power from June 2015 to June 2919.
167. Act No. 376 of 2 June 1999 on CO2 Quotas for Electricity Production.
168. Act No. 493 of 9 June 2004 on Carbon Dioxide Allowance. Concerning the EU ETS Directive and the Danish legislation on the EU ETS scheme in force, *see infra* paras 82 and 84.

15. The European Structural and Investment Fund (ESI Fund) regulations are very important for the promotion of environment-friendly developments.[169] They provide the funding strategies and programmes of the Member States for economic, social and territorial cohesion, rural development and maritime policy. They also reinforce the capacity of implementing bodies to deliver cost-effective and sustainable investments in these areas. The regulations cover eligibility of expenditure on financial management and the management and control system. In the preamble of the regulations, it is underlined that the objectives of the ESI Fund should be pursued in the framework of sustainable development and the Union's promotion of the aim of preserving, protecting and improving the quality of the environment as set out in the Lisbon Treaty.[170] The partnership agreements under the ESI Funds that aim to play a significant role in the achievement of the objectives of the 'Europe 2020' strategy[171] create a common and coherent overall framework for all EU's funds that aim to improve coordination between them.

Denmark was the first Member State to sign a 'Partnership Agreement' with the Commission on 28 February 2014 covering the period 2014–2020. The regional development funding for Denmark amounting to EUR 206.6 million is to be used on investment in energy efficiency measures. The economic support from the Agricultural Fund for Rural Development amounted to EUR 919 million.[172] The budget for agri-environmental-climate measures represents 22.5%. The Danish Rural Development Programme (RDP) – titled 'Green Conversion and Green Jobs' – was adopted by the Commission on 12 December 2014 – and outlines Denmark's priorities for using EUR 860 million of the money that is available during the period 2014–2020.[173] About 75% of the amount will be used on better management of natural resources and to encourage climate-friendly farming practices. The aim is to double the organic area. Other schemes have focus on the environmental performance of farms, as the RDP aims to support the restructuring of roughly 8% of the farms in the pig and cattle sectors. Finally, it can be mentioned that other schemes aim to boost innovation, provide training opportunities and create jobs in the rural areas. The Danish biodiversity financing based on this funding is criticised in the Commission's staff working document. It is stated that Denmark do not in its rural development plan activate as a means to implement the protection of Natura 2000 sites the measures on compensation for restrictions that are laid down on the agricultural activities. Denmark takes an 'island approach' that do not consider the protection of areas outside Natura 2000 sites although the protection of these areas directly contributes to the objectives of Natura 2000, as well as to the realisation of

---

169. The current ESIFs are the following: the European Regional Development Funds (ERDF), the European Agricultural Fund for Rural Development (EAFRD – explained *infra* in para. 258), the European Maritime and Fishing Fund (EMFF – explained *infra* in para. 280), and the European Social Fund (ESF).
170. *See* Art. 11 TEU on the principle of integration, and Art. 191(1) TFEU on environmental principles, etc., taking into account the 'polluter pays principle'. Concerning these articles in the Treaty, *see infra* paras 27–28.
171. Regulation No. 1303/2013 laying down the Provisions on the European Funds in the period 2014–2020.
172. *See* the Commission's staff working document, *The EU Environmental Implementation Review. Country Report – Denmark*, SWD(2017) 39 final, at 21.
173. The EUR 629 million is from the EU budget, while the EUR 230 million is national funding.

the EU Biodiversity Strategy 2020.[174] In its 2017 assessment of the Danish implementation of the ESI Funds, the Commission states that this 'island' approach that do not consider areas outside Nature 2000 sites is a problematic biodiversity financing.[175]

The development of environmental friendly and renewable energy has been promoted in Denmark since the late 1970s by paying the owners of the facilities a supplement to the electricity production price. It was used in the very first action plan on waste and reuse in the energy conservation acts in the 1980s. As part of the energy policy, a pool of special funds for small enterprises was established in the late 1990s. As part of the former 2001–2011 Liberal-Conservative Government's policy, the public and development funds for environmental non-energy-related research were gradually reduced, and the share of public energy research and development expenditure in this area increased. The overall focus was on private sector research with a more immediate commercial potential than before.[176] The same priority characterised the former coalition Government that were in power until 27 June 2019.[177] There is still a direct support for energy producers in the form of investment subsidies in research and demonstration, tax credits, premium systems and feed-in tariffs. Feed-in tariffs on wind energy have been used since the first electricity liberalisation reform (1999).

The environmental investments from national sources include money from the Budget Bill as well as from the PSO funding.[178] The Budget Bill 2015 that was based on a political agreement of 13 December 2014 between the Government and the Socialist People's Party and the Red-Green Alliance allocated DKK 400 million to an enhanced environmental and ecological effort, development of sustainable construction, and development of green national accounts in 2015–2017.[179] The priority of investment in such green issues by the Budget Bill under the Government that was in power in 2015–2016, as well at the priority under the former Government in the period 2017–2019[180] has been criticised as not high enough compared to the need for such investment. From 2017, PSO funding was partly replaced by financing over the Danish Budget Bill and will be discontinued at the end of 2021. Until 2021, the feed-in tariffs are only used on established wind mills that have an established right based on the rules that were in force when they were established. The political agreement of 17 November 2016 on the abolition of the PSO between the majority of the political parties in the Danish Parliament was the consequence of the Commission's critiques. The Commission was of the opinion that the economic support of Danish business by the PSO funding was illegal state aid. In connection with this agreement, a new green climate fund was established. This fund is

174. *See* the Commission's staff working document, *The EU Environmental Implementation Review. Country Report – Denmark*, SWD(2017) 39 final, at 22.
175. European Commission staff working document of 3 February 2017, *The EU Environmental Implementation Review Country Report – Denmark*, SWD(2017) 39 final, at 22.
176. Danish Economic Councils, *Economy and Environment 2010*, at 355.
177. Concerning the different Danish coalition governments, *see supra* in para. 4.
178. The PSO funding will be stopped in 2021, *see supra* para. 12.
179. Danish Government, *The National Reform Programme Denmark 2015*, at 58.
180. It was a coalition Government consisting of the Liberal Party, the Conservative People Party and Liberal Alliance.

used to support initiatives across all sectors that promote the green transition. The total budget for the fund is DKK 375 million for the period 2017–2020 – disturbed on DKK 50 billion in 2017, DKK 50 billion in 2018, DKK 100 million in 2019 and DKK 175 million in 2020.[181] The 'Energy Agreement 2018'[182] increased funding for energy and climate research to DKK 1 billion in 2024. It also includes a reserve of 400 million DKK in 2025 and 500 million annually for further efforts from 2026 to promote renewable energy. On 1 September 2018, the former coalition government presented its Circular Economy Strategy with a focus on economic support to technology innovation.[183]

§4. Social and Cultural Characteristics

16. The social and cultural characteristics are part of Scandinavian traditions. Each Nordic country has its own language, but the Swedish, Norwegian, and Danish languages sound more or less alike. The language spoken in Denmark is Danish, a Germanic language[184] closely related to the old Norse language. The Finnish and Icelandic languages are quite different, but Finns and Icelanders normally speak Swedish or Danish. Therefore, the languages do not prevent Nordic cooperation in areas of mutual interest whether informally or formally because various people normally understand one another.

The main religion is Protestantism, and 89.7% of the Danish population are members of the National Church. This is the state-financed church, which is regulated and protected by the Constitution. The population in the main country is relatively homogenous, and the number of foreigners living in the country is relatively small.[185]

17. Denmark is a liberal-minded and social democratic nation with a market economy. Like the other Nordic countries, Denmark is a welfare society with a relatively even distribution of income. To a large extent, wage and employment conditions are traditionally determined by collective agreements between the labour market parties.

The Danish income distribution is among the most even ones of all OECD countries, which in particular reflects that a large part of income is redistributed through the tax burden and speeded on the public sector. The size of the public sector is influenced by the fact that many services (such as education, care of the elderly and health) are almost entirely supplied by the public sector – most of it at regional and local levels. Health and welfare are cornerstones of the Danish State. The highly

181. *Denmark's 7th National Communication on Climate Change*, at 28.
182. The political 'Energy Agreement' of 29 Jun. 2018 that all the political parties are part of. It is not yet implemented.
183. *See supra* the notes in para. 4 concerning the different Danish coalition governments that have been in power since 1993.
184. However, the official language in Greenland is 'kalaallisut' being part of the eskimo-aleut, closely related to the languages spoken by the Inuit in Canada, USA, and Siberia. In the Faroe Islands, the language is faroese.
185. Concerning the Danish population, *see supra* para. 2.

developed health sector is largely covered by tax revenues. Visiting a doctor or being hospitalised is free of charge. At school, children have medical and dental check-ups. The eligibility age for retirement is 65 years in 2019, but it is changed in 2020 to 66, in 2021 to 66.5, in 2022 to 67 and in 2030 to 68 years. Around 800,000 people aged 18–64 years are receiving public benefits. Today, average life expectancy is 82.8 years for women and 78.8 years for men.[186] The literacy rate is near 100% as it might be expected in a developed country with high educational standards. Compulsory school attendance is nine years, and many children stay in school longer. The education level has increased since 1969. In 2010, 69% of the 30–69 year olds had completed education providing them with professional qualifications, defined as vocational or higher education aimed at specific types of jobs. In 2016, 71% of the 30–69 years olds were at this education level.[187]

18. In general, Danish homes are comfortable with very good sanitation, waste and heating facilities, as well as many electrical appliances. Apartment buildings are common in most cities, but the large majority of Danes live in their own houses with gardens. The housing situation was as follows in 2010: 58% one-family houses and 38% multi-dwelling houses, while the remaining dwellings were other types of dwellings. As of 1 January 2017, 43% of all the dwellings were detached houses/farmhouses, 15% were terraced, linked or semi-detached houses and 39% were dwellings in multi-family buildings, while the remainder were other types of dwellings. Dwellings occupied by the owners make up just over half of all the dwellings.[188]

Over the last 100 years, the marital relations have seen considerable changes. Many people are financially independent, and unlike previously it is no longer necessary to marry to achieve a reasonable living standard. Consequently, the number of households in Denmark has increased. More than one-third of all adults live without a partner. In 2011, the total number of households was 2,584,479. Among these were many single men (493,599) and women (660,508) living with or without children. The total number of other households was 175,724. In 2017, 75% of all couples living together were married.[189]

The Danish consumers are among the most critical in Europe. Today, the household sector accounts for more than half of the total consumption of goods and services. Over the past ten years, the average private consumption has increased by 19%. Today, most households have a refrigerator, microwave oven, automatic dishwasher, freezer, washing machine, one or more TVs, video, CD players, computers and several mobile phones. The growth of the number of households with PC and an internet connection means that Denmark is ranking amongst the top five in the world. In 2017, household energy consumption accounts for approximately 31% of

186. *Statistical Yearbook 2017,* in the section 'Living conditions'.
187. *Statistical Yearbook 2017,* in the section 'Education and knowledge'.
188. *Statistical Yearbook 2017,* in the section 'Living conditions'.
189. *Statistical Yearbook 2017,* in the section 'Population and elections'.

the total energy consumption. It is expected to fall to 27% by 2030. The share of energy consumption used for heating is expected to be around 82% throughout the period.[190]

19. Denmark is one of the countries in Europe with the greatest land area under cultivation. Ninety-four per cent of Denmark's land is private owned. Over the period 2000–2006, the annual land taken for urban and other artificial land development in Denmark was 0.44%, representing 1,495 ha per year. It was mainly driven by diffuse residential developments.[191] State authorities own and manage a number of terrestrial natural areas. It is primarily the Ministry of Environment and Food (1,880 km^2). The Ministry of Defence, the Ministry of Ecclesiastical Affairs and the Ministry of Transport are also owners of some land. A total of approximately 2,570 km^2 or 6% of Denmark's area are owned by the State.[192] The Ministry of Defence manages approximately 33,000 ha of land, most of which is owned by the Danish Defence. This makes the Ministry of Defence Denmark's second largest landowner after the Ministry of Environment. The Ministry of Defence has – as a large land owner – prepared a 'Environmental and Nature Strategy' for the period 2012–2015 in which it is explained that working out long-term nature management plans is one of the tools that is used to secure future training possibilities in these areas, while taking the required measures for nature protection and access by the public.[193]

Since the mid-1940s, there has been a clear trend towards locating manufacturing industries away from the centre of the large towns. This development has led to a large increase in the extent of urban area and caused a spread of houses, industrial workplaces and cultural facilities, which has disrupted a number of the functional relationships in towns. Social development over the last forty years has helped to draw stronger attention to the rational use of infrastructure and the protection of the cultural environment in a broader sense. This development has been brought about by the major conversion of the Danish landscape and urban structure in the form of industrial districts, a fine-meshed network of railways and motorways, large infrastructure installations, electricity pylons, tourist facilities along the coast, and intensive large-scale agricultural production, etc. The agricultural landscape in Denmark is changing, mainly driven by structural changes such as changes in the ownership structure of farm properties. The changes are related to developments in agricultural policies and legislation, as well as to change in intensive farming practices. Former production functions with small biotopes and many semi-natural landscapes, such as heath lands, wet meadows and salt marshes, are no longer an integrated part of the agricultural production system. The changes in the agricultural landscape are also part of new multifunctional developments in agriculture relating

190. Danish Energy Agency, *Denmark's Energy and Climate Outlook 2018. Baseline Scenario Projection Towards 2030*, at 33.
191. European Commission staff working document of 3 February 2017, *The EU Environmental Implementation Review Country Report – Denmark*, SWD(2017) 39 final, at 12.
192. Danish Government, *Action Plan for Biodiversity and Nature Conservation in Denmark 2004-2009*, at 35.
193. *Environment and Nature Strategy of the Ministry of Defence 2012-2015*, at 6.

to new urban-rural relationships, where a growing proportion of people living in the agricultural landscapes are urban employees.

The mobility is high in Denmark. In 2011, there were 389 passenger cars per 1,000 inhabitants. Nowhere in Denmark is more than fifteen minutes away from the network of main roads and railways. On 1 January 2016, there were 74,405 km of public roads in Denmark. The public road network has increased by nearly 2,135 km over the past ten years, mainly because of municipal roads.[194] Denmark has spent five to six times more money on road network infrastructure (for a total road network length of some 72,000 km) than on the rail network infrastructure (for a total rail network length of some 2,600 km).[195] Since the 1990s, Denmark has experienced an average annual increase of 2% in road traffic (in number of kilometres driven) due to a growing number of passenger cars, the extension of the motorways and the increased distance between home and work or school. Since 2006, the motorway network has been extended by 20% to 1,237 km in 2016, and in 2016, the length of the dual carriageways has increased by 4% to 377 km. The volume of public transport – especially travel by coach and by train – has grown over the last ten to twelve years. The growth in passenger kilometres is mainly attributed to the fact that journey distances have increased markedly due to changes in settlement patterns. One of the possible explanations for Denmark's high transport volume is that fuel prices in Denmark are relatively low compared to the other EU Member States measured in terms of purchasing power parity.[196]

The railway network has existed since 1920, and it would benefit from being totally modernised. On 1 January 2016, the length of the rail network was 2,573 km. The main part of the rail network is operated by the state-owned Rail Net Denmark 'Banedanmark'. In relation to the total land area of Denmark, there is 62 km of railway per 1,000 km^2. At the beginning of 2016, a quarter of the rail network was electrified.

Since 1995, domestic air traffic and ferry transport has been declining which is largely due to the opening of the fixed link over the Great Belt and the Oresund Street. In 2009, more than 30,000 cars crossed the Great Belt every day; this is an increase of 61% compared to the year when the bridge was opened, while ferries between Eastern and Western Denmark carried 2,200 cars every day, compared to 12,700 in the year before the bridge was opened to road traffic. Rail traffic between the Eastern and Western Denmark also increased considerably after the opening of the bridge. In February 2012, the Government had to redraw a proposal on introducing a congestion charge on all cars coming into Copenhagen. Local politicians and the mass media blocked the proposal.

Planning for bicycle transport is an integrated part of traffic planning. Since 2000, traffic by bicycles has decreased further by 6%.

Denmark is number seven on a global ranking of ship operators. It is number 13 flag state on a global scale, and number 4 in the EU. The Danish merchant fleet is made up of cargo and passenger ships of at least 100 GT. The fleet is growing. In

194. *Statistical Yearbook 2017,* in the section 'Geography, environment and energy'.
195. OECD, *Environmental Performance Reviews. Denmark. 2007*, at 137.
196. NERI, *The State of the Environment in Denmark 2001*, at 52, and *Statistical Yearbook 2011*.

2017, there were 683 ships, of which the container ships represented the largest segment. Shipping remains Denmark's largest export industry.[197] In 2015, there were 111 Danish ports handling freight. The 28 largest ports each handled more than 1 million tonnes of goods annually and accounted for 83% of the total goods transported by sea.[198] Seventy-three ports were engaged in transport of passengers, of which 32 had more than 2,000 passengers arriving and departing every year.

§5. Main Environmental Problems

20. Nature habitat types such as heaths, dry grasslands, meadows and salt marshes have, however, declined considerably in Denmark during the twentieth and early twenty-first centuries as a consequence of converting land to farmland. Over the last 100–170 years, the Danish landscape has become drier and drier. Only a few wetlands are left compared to previously. In the 2017 assessment made by the Commission on the Danish implementation of EU environmental policy and legislation it is stated that one of the main challenges with regard to implementation is the pressures on nature from intensive agriculture, inclusive the use of pesticides and nutrients.[199]

The main pollution pressure of Danish marine waters results from land-based sources of nitrogen (N) and phosphorus (P). About 25% of the Danish land mass drains into the North Sea, 72% into inner marine waters (the Kattegat, the Great Belt, the Little Belt and the Belt Seas), and 3% into the Baltic Sea. The inner marine waters and almost enclosed marine waters are particularly vulnerable to environmental pressures. The geographical conditions with a long coastline, a large share of coastal waters in relation to its land area, and the intensive agricultural production makes it complicated for Denmark to reach the common goals of the Water Framework Directive (WFD).[200] The largest surface and sea water pollution problem at present is the emission of N as well as P from the agricultural sector. The shallow marine waters are especially vulnerable to eutrophication because water exchange with the stratification of the water masses often limits the input of oxygen to the bottom water. Over the last ten years, the concentration of nutrients has decreased in coastal waters. There are, however, still problems with the aquatic vegetation and benthic invertebrates. Only 2% of coastal waters have achieved the goal of good ecological status.[201] The oxygen depletion, algae growth and pesticides pollution that has taken place over the last few decades, as well as the discharges of nutrient salts into surface waters and the sea, have all been sources of problems in relation to ensuring a good environmental quality of the water. The quality of the nature as well as the water has also been affected by extensive physical regulation in connection with agricultural and urban development. This includes lowering of the groundwater table, drainage, cultivation, channelling, obstructions and weed

---

197. Danish Shipping, *Danish Shipping Industry. Facts and Figures,* December 2017.
198. *Statistical Yearbook 2017*, in the section 'Geography, environment and energy'.
199. *See* the Commission's staff working document, *The EU Environmental Implementation Review. Country Report – Denmark*, SWD(2017) 39 final, at 4 and 9–14.
200. Danish Economic Councils, *Economy and Environment 2015*, at 362.
201. Danish Economic Councils, *Economy and Environment 2015*, at 362.

cutting. The dominant role of agriculture in the Danish landscape also means that the use of chemical pesticides is a great danger to nature. Pesticides are used to combat weeds, pests and fungal infections.

The political interest on reduction of wastewater emission started in the 1980s, and it has resulted in an improvement of the water quality. In 1986, the first Danish scientific report established oxygen deficits occurred in large parts of the Kattegat. It called for intensification and dephosphorisation and denitrification treatment efforts throughout the country. Accordingly, in January 1987, the Danish Parliament reached the agreement on the first 'Action Plan for the Aquatic Environment I' (APAE I). The environmental authorities launched a very extensive national monitoring programme in 1988, focusing on N in all parts of the aquatic environment. It derived from the APAE I. Denmark was the first EU Member State to establish N emission targets for the surface water. The target groups were municipal and industrial sewage water treatment plants which had to ensure a reduction of discharges from large cities. The APAE I achieved a reduction in the impact of urban wastewater. However, it did not reach the desired quality targets, with the phosphorus concentration remaining high. This was partly due to a previously discharged P concentration that had accumulated in the sediment. In addition to this were discharges from sparsely populated areas and from agricultural activities. The Danish legislation was an inspiration for the Urban Waste Water Directive.[202] In the late 1990s, the Commission asked the Danish authorities to ensure that Denmark respected the Nitrate Directive's quality norms.[203] To achieve this, some new rules in the Water Supply Act, the Environmental Protection Act and the Nature Protection Act concerning the protection of areas with drinking water resources were brought into force in 1998. In February 1998, the political parties in the Parliament agreed on 'The Agreement Relating to Action Plan for the Aquatic Environment II' (APAE II). This second plan was more precise and ambitious. It aimed to increase the land cultivated using organic farming practices by a total of 170,000 ha by 2003 – a significant increase compared to the situation in 1998. It also called for a reduction in N emissions by 10% compared to the 1998/1999 levels. The plan introduced a number of additional measures, including re-establishment of wetlands, afforestation, agreements on environment-friendly agricultural measures, organic farming on an additional 170,000 ha, improved use of fodder, reduced animal density, use of catch crops, reduced fertilisation norms and stricter requirements concerning the use of nitrogen in manure. The aim, which had been reached, was to reduce N leaching by 100,000 tonne per year by 2003. In 2002, an 'Action Plan for Reduction of Ammonia Volatilisation in Agriculture' was introduced. This Action Plan, covering the period 2002–2007 introduced a ban on surface spreading. The plan aimed to ensure a reduction of about 9,500 tonnes of N per year. The 'Manure Action Plan' involving tightened distance requirements came into effect on 20 March 2004. The objective was to protect neighbours by establishing zones where new farming facilities

202. OECD, *Environmental Performance Reviews. Denmark, 2007*, at 53. Concerning the Urban Waste Water Directive (91/271/EC), *see infra* para. 106.

203. The Nitrates Directive (91/676/EEC) includes zoning issues protecting the groundwater against pollution. Under this Directive, Member States have to identify eutrophic waters or waters at risk of becoming eutrophic, including estuaries, coastal and marine waters. The whole area of Denmark is considered a 'vulnerable zone' under the Nitrates Directive, *see infra* para. 106.

were not allowed. The distances depend on the number of neighbours and the size of the livestock herd. The APAE III covered the period 2005–2015. The political agreement of the plan was conducted in April 2004 by the 2001–2011 Liberal-Conservative coalition government, the Danish People's Party and the Christian Democrats. It was closely related to the implementation of the WFD and the Habitats Directive. Organic farming was one of the several elements in this Action Plan. It included a target on the reduction of P by 50%. The means to ensure this reduction of the P was the establishment of a crop-free buffer zone of 10 m along rivers and lakes before 2009 (covering close to 30,000 ha of agricultural areas) and a further 20,000 ha of agricultural areas before 2015. The buffer zones were to be established by voluntary transfer of set-aside land along lakes and rivers. The leaching of N from agricultural activities was to be reduced to a minimum of 13% by 2015 compared with 2003. The rules on late crops and the rules on utilisation of nitrogen in livestock manure were also tightened under this action plan. On 22 December 2015, a political agreement on the 'Food and Agricultural Package' changed the political agenda. The package made it possible for the agricultural and the aqua farming sectors to have a higher level of emission of N as well as P into surface water and coastal waters. The EU Commission is questioning if this political agreement is in harmony with the WFD, the Nitrate Directive and the Habitats Directive. [204] In 2012, pesticides have been identified in more than 40% of the monitoring points in Danish groundwater, and the drinking water requirement was exceeded in 12% of the monitoring points.[205]

The impact on the marine water areas of discharges from other countries is also very significant. Such pollution can come from both east and west. In the west, pollution of the North Sea by the great European rivers is carried along the west coast of Jutland and from there to some extent into the Kattegat and the Danish inlets. In the east, the polluted rivers of Eastern Europe, Sweden and Germany flow into the Baltic Sea and later spill into Danish sea areas. However, the latter source of pollution, as far as nutrient salts are concerned is relatively modest. This is due to the fact that the residence time of waters in the east is very long (e.g., in the Bay of Bothnia it is thirty to forty years). In Danish marine waters, the biological quality objective set under the Environmental Marine Protection Act is achieved in the Skagerrak and the open part of the North Sea and is close to being met in the open northern and central Kattegat. In the remaining marine waters, the objective has not been met primarily due to a nutrient loading, and also in some fjords and coastal waters, due to the high concentration of Tributyltin (TBT), organ chlorines, Polycyclic Aromatic Hydrocarbons (PAHs) and/or heavy metals (HM) in sediment. There is no sign of general improvement in the oxygen content of the bottom water neither for coastal waters nor for open marine waters. Denitrification and the sedimentary deposit of phosphates have largely been accomplished by the time the polluted waters reach Danish areas.[206]

204. The EU Commission's letter 8540/16/ENVI on 'Implementation in Denmark of Directives 91/676/EC, 2000/60/EC, 92/43/EEC, in relation to the recently adopted agriculture package', May 2016.
205. Danish Economic Councils, *Economy and Environment 2015*, at 367.
206. OECD, *Environmental Performance Reviews. Denmark, 2007*, at 59, 94.

21. In their 2012 report, the Danish Economic Councils have stated that about one-fifth of all the 32,000 known Danish species are likely to be threatened. The most serious threats are explained as the loss and deteriorations of habitats, which, to a high degree, can be traced back to forestry and agriculture activities.[207] In the OECD, *Environmental Performance Reviews. Denmark. 2007*, it was also stressed that botanists estimate that one-third of Denmark's wild plant species are on the verge of disappearing.[208] Over the past 150 years, the marked decrease in the quality of open nature habitats and the decline in the quality of the habitat that remains as a result of intensive agriculture, urbanisation, land reclamation and infrastructure development have led to the extinction of 340 species. Approximately 30% of those species included in the Danish Red List as internationally protected (International Union for Conservation of Nature's (IUCN's) categories) are threatened and vulnerable. The quality of Denmark's nature and biodiversity has never been as poor as it is today. In its 2017 assessment of the Danish implementation of EU's environmental policy and legislation, the Commission stated that the red list species associated with forest habitats are facing treats caused by fragmentation of populations, deteriorating habitats, disturbances and climate change. Intensive agriculture continues to impact habitats.[209] The various natural and semi-natural areas are spread out as large or small areas, divided by cultivated land, roads, railroads, and built-up areas. The area of original forest, which is especially valuable to biodiversity, has also been steadily reduced over the last 200 years. The woodland makes up only a fraction of the total area.

All the farming activities have affected the ecological conditions for a number of animals and plants associated with the wetlands, watercourses and lakes. For a number of the natural habitat types covered by section 3 of the Nature Protection Act,[210] ammonia (NH_3) deposits comprise a major threat. A large number of rare and threatened plants in these natural habitats become outcompeted by more nitrogen-demanding and nitrogen-tolerant (and often common) plants to the detriment of biodiversity. The whole spectrum of species narrows, and variation within the individual natural habitat types and landscapes is thereby reduced. In the 2016 pilot letter of the Commission, it is stated that the political agreement on 'Food and Agricultural Package' of 22 December 2015 is very likely to exert an increasing pressure on certain habitat types, such as coastal habitats and grassland habitats, which are already in a bad conservation status due to agricultural intensification, fertilisation, nitrogen input and diffuse pollution to surface water due to agricultural and forestry activities, as reported by the Danish authorities themselves to the EU.[211] According to the Danish report sent to the Commission under the Article 17

207. Danish Economic Councils, *Economy and Environment 2012*, at 445.
208. *See* p. 89 and also *infra* para. 261.
209. European Commission staff working document of 3 February 2017, *The EU Environmental Implementation Review Country Report – Denmark*, SWD(2017) 39 final, at 10.
210. Promulgation Order No. 240 of 13 March 2019 on Nature Protection. Concerning the protection under s. 3 of the Nature Protection Act, *see infra* para. 244.
211. EU Pilot 8540/16/ENVi.

Habitats Directive, almost 70% of the habitats assessments are in an unfavourable-bad status. Only 5% of the assessments show favourable status.[212]

According to the Danish reporting to the Commission, marine habitats are under the influence of N supplied from surface water and from atmospheric deposition, but in recent years, there are some signs of a better situation. The Commission 2017 assessment report stated that 34% are at a favourable status, 13% at an unfavourable-inadequate status and 28% have unfavourable-bad status.[213] At sea, fishing (especially bottom trawling), dumping of materials and mineral exploitation has altered the aquatic ecosystem. The release of micro pollutants, such as organ chlorines, hexachlorobenzenes (HCBs) and toxins, from the marine waters are spread throughout the environment through shipping channels. Furthermore, the return of oxygen depletion to large areas of the sea has a negative impact on the survival and distribution of many marine species.[214]

22. The use of ever-larger agricultural machinery throughout the period of mechanisation of agricultural practice causes *soil compaction* in Denmark. Compaction of the soil's structural elements and particles reduces its pore volume, which among other things is important for aeration of soil. Compaction also reduces the capacity in relation to the transport of water. Moreover, compacted soil provides poorer living conditions for plants and soil animals. Wind erosion also comprises a considerable problem in certain Danish wind-blown areas that have sandy soil with a loose, dry and fine particular composition (e.g., the sandy soils of western and northern Jutland). In these areas, erosion can be a significant factor in relation to plant growth conditions. The Common Agricultural Policy (CAP) reform is expected to reduce such negative effects as a consequence of the agri-environmental criteria and the cross-compliance conditions.[215]

Groundwater is threatened due to leakage of organic compounds from point sources, in particular sites contaminated by chemicals and oil.[216] Many of these substances are emitted with wastewater into aquatic areas, as general sewage treatment does not normally target these substances. In certain places, the detrimental impact is so heavy that abating measures, e.g., pumping up water round the source, have proven insufficient. In these cases, it has been necessary to close drinking water boreholes. A nation-wide survey of the heavy metal content of soil outside urban areas revealed generally low concentrations. However, high concentrations can be found locally in the vicinity of waste deposits, polluted sites from old enterprises, busy roads, etc. In 2003, the Environmental Protection Agency (EPA) estimated that there were 14,000 contaminated sites in areas of priority, 31,000 actually polluted

212. European Commission staff working document of 3 February 2017, *The EU Environmental Implementation Review Country Report – Denmark*, SWD(2017) 39 final, at 10. It is mentioned in the report that this situation is below the other EU Member States.
213. European Commission staff working document of 3 February 2017, *The EU Environmental Implementation Review Country Report – Denmark*, SWD(2017) 39 final, at 12.
214. OECD, *Environmental Performance Reviews. Denmark, 2007*, at 94.
215. The CAP reform is described *infra* in paras 258–259.
216. Concerning the mapping of the sensitive drinking water resources areas under the Water Supply Act and the protection under the Contaminated Soil Act, *see infra* paras 176–177.

sites and 55,000 possibly polluted sites. A total of 10,000 of the 14,000 sites in priority areas needed to be removed because of risk for human health. Also, 4,000 of the sites that had a high priority were a risk to drinking water and other parts of the protected groundwater. The preliminary status in 2010 was 6,000 sites in areas of priority, 13,000 definitely polluted sites and 26,000 sites mapped as potentially polluted.[217]

23. The production and use of chemical substances since the 1950s have resulted in the dispersal of chemical substances in the environment. Attention regarding undesirable substances has traditionally focused on heavy metals and the persistent organ chlorines such as dioxins, polychlorinated biphenyls (PCBs) and compounds that were previously widely used as pesticides, e.g., DDT. Even though emissions of chemicals from industries and other point sources of pollution have declined considerably over the past decade, their release into the environment is still significant. Pesticides, particularly herbicides, are widely detected in watercourses and in groundwater used for drinking water.

In 2004, three of the five most commonly used herbicides were detected in concentrations exceeding the detection limit in the five large watercourses: the herbicides were glyphosate (found in 77% of the samples), 2-methyl-4-chlorophenoxyacetic (found in 37% of the samples) and terbuthylazine (found in 25% of the samples). Such pesticides have environmental consequences in terms of poorer living conditions for wildlife (flora and fauna) on cultivated land. Several reservoirs of drinking water have been closed in recent years due to contamination or the risk of contamination by pesticides. In 2004–2005, ten of the 2,400 wells used for drinking water abstraction had to be permanently abandoned to maintain the Danish political decided principle that drinking water should not need purification. In 2008, pesticides were found in four of ten of the wells monitored by the Geological Survey of Denmark[218] (GSD) – it was a 9% increase compared with the results from the year before, and a 63% increase compared with the results in 2000. The amount of pesticides was also 400% higher in 2008 compared with the level in 1990,[219] and the problems caused by pesticides to the Danish drinking water is still growing in 2019. From 30 April 2019, the use of some pesticides are consequently prohibited.[220]

The use of pesticides makes poorer living conditions for wildlife (flora and fauna) on cultivated land. The harm is caused partly as a consequence of their direct toxic effects, and because the use of pesticides leads to a shortage of food for species that live off the plants and insects targeted by pesticides. In addition to this, pesticides can alter the substance cycle of fields, thus causing the workings of soil ecosystems to deteriorate. Such pesticides through driftage also affect areas adjoining cultivated

217. EPA, *Current trends within the administration of contaminated sites in Denmark.*
218. The Geological Survey of Denmark (GSD) – in Danish: 'Danmarks og Grønlands Geologiske Undersøgelser' (GEUS) – is a research institution with laboratories that can perform routine and some more advanced analyses under the Ministry of Climate, Energy and Buildings.
219. GSD's information on the monitoring results of 18 October 2010, and OECD, *Environmental Performance Reviews. Denmark. 2007*, at 173 and 176.
220. Statutory Order No. 354 of 2 April 2019.

land that has been sprayed with pesticides, including forests and small biotopes. The amount of pesticides in the Danish groundwater has increased over time.

Denmark has some of the OECD's highest rates of mortality from certain forms of cancer, and allergy, and respiratory diseases affect about 20% of the population.[221] Some of these problems may relate to environmental factors including chemical substances. There are a number of different heavy metals in the atmosphere that cause respiratory diseases, such as coal dust, solvent harmful to the nervous system, substances that indicate asthma and dermatitis or carcinogens that constitute a great concern for human health.[222]

24. On 15 March 2018, Denmark sent its latest Annual Information Inventory Report (IIR) to the UNECE Convention on Long-Range Transboundary Air Pollution (CLRTAP) and to the Commission under the NEC Directive with information on the status of the air quality.[223] In June 2015, as its key findings on the air pollution in Denmark, the EEA published its opinion and stated that the national authorities face various challenges in terms of air quality, mainly caused by the important acidification factors that are non-methane volatile organic compounds (NMVOCs) and NH_3.[224] Denmark has lowered some of its targets, and it has allocated NMVOC, SO_2 and NERCs under the NEC Directive.[225]

The Danish problems are related to the emission of NH_3, NO_2 and PAH beyond the emission ceilings established by the NEC Directive.[226] There have been some breaches of the annual average of NO_2 in Denmark, especially in the big cities. Denmark submitted to the Commission (in a letter of March 2011) a notification of a postponement of the deadline for an extension regarding the annual NO_2 limit values from 2010 to 2015 in three air quality zones (Copenhagen, Aarhus and Aalborg). In its decision of 2 February 2011, the Commission raised objections to the postponement of the deadline because Denmark had failed to demonstrate that compliance would be achieved by the extended deadline. Based on the 2015 findings, there is not a general problem with the NO_2 emission limit level. The air in the capital (Copenhagen) did not meet the new NO_2 limit value in one of the big streets of Copenhagen.[227]

PM concentrations in the air are generally a major health concern in all EU countries.[228] The size of PM is expressed in micrometres, where the largest is PM_{10}. Based on the EEA report from 2013, the daily mean concentration of PM_{10} as well

221. OECD, *Environmental Performance Reviews. Denmark. 2007*, at 25, 169.
222. ILO, *Background Information for Developing an ILO Policy Framework for Hazardous Substances*, at 10.
223. DCE, *Annual Danish Informative Inventory Report to UNECE. Emission Inventories from the Base Year of the Protocol to Year 2016*, report no. 267, 2018.
224. Concerning this air quality issue, *see also infra* paras 76 and 98.
225. AirClim, ClientEarth and European Environmental Bureau, *Clearing the Air. A Critical Guide to the New National Emission Ceilings Directive*, 2017, at 15 and 17.
226. Concerning the EU air quality legislation, *see infra* para. 75.
227. It is the air quality in the H.C. Andersens Boulevard (Copenhagen) that is not respecting the EU NO2 limit target.
228. Concerning the protection of the air quality in the EU, *see infra* paras 75–77, and concerning the Danish implementation *infra* paras 78–79.

as the concentration of $PM_{2.5}$ in Denmark was below, but close to the EU maximum level.[229] The people most sensitive to this are those with heart problems, or respiratory diseases like emphysema, bronchitis and asthma. The elderly and children are also very sensitive. The main sources for PM_{10} are resuspended dust and combustion. PM_{10} particles are also created in the atmosphere by NO_2 and SO_2. Submicron particles, which are formed by combustion and chemical reactions in the atmosphere, are suspected to be the most harmful for health.[230] Overall, wood combustion represent 49% of Denmark's total PM emission.[231] The largest sources are the agricultural sector and the residential sector. The largest $PM_{2.5}$ emission sources are the residential sector (55%), followed by road traffic (18%) and other mobile polluters (85%). Total suspended particulate (TSP) matter from transport is also important and includes both exhaust emissions and the non-exhaust emissions from brake and motorcar tire wear (26%) and road abrasion. The PM emission inventory has only been produced for 2000–2004 – covering TSP, PM_{10} and $PM_{2.5}$ – and the emission levels did not change over that period. The EU air quality limit values for $PM_{2.5}$ have been legally binding since 1 January 2010.[232] Emissions of PAHs have increased in the last ten years as a result of increased wood combustion for residential heating. The most important source is combustion of wood in the residential sector making up 68% of the total emission in 2013.[233]

Acidification, caused by atmospheric SO_2 pollution, was a problem for biological life in a number of Denmark's freshwater lakes thirty years ago. This is not the case today. SO_2 emission per unit of GDP, or SO_2 intensity, is now the lowest in the OECD.[234] The main part of the sulphur dioxide (SO_2) emission originates from combustion of fossil fuels. From 1990 to 2013, the total emission decreased by 92%.[235]

The heavy metal emissions – especially lead (Pb) and zinc (Zn) – have decreased substantially in recent years as a result of the use of gas devices at power and district heating plants. The reduction of Pb is due to a gradual shift towards unleaded gasoline. The emission of copper (Cu) is, however, not decreasing. The major source of Cu is automobile tire and break wear (93% in 2013).[236] Lead pollution in Danish towns has also decreased markedly in line with the introduction of unleaded petrol.

CH_4 and nitrous oxide (N_2O) emissions as GHGs mainly come from the agricultural sector, which contributes with 67% of the total CH_4 emission and 92% of N_2O emissions in 2007. The biggest contribution comes from dairy cows.[237] NH_3 volatilisation contributes to the GHG effect because some of the ammonia nitrate ends up as N_2O in the atmosphere. This emission particularly occurs during handling of manure in animal housing, storage of manure, the transport of manure and from

229. EEA, *Air Quality in Europe – 2013 Report*, at 33.
230. NERI, *The Danish Air Quality Monitoring Programme. Annual Summary for 2005,* at 40.
231. Danish Government, *The National Reform Programme Denmark 2015*, at 62.
232. Concerning EU's air quality standards, *see infra* paras 75–76.
233. DCE, *Annual Danish Informative Inventory Report to UNECE*, 2015, at 42.
234. OECD, *Environmental Performance Reviews. Denmark. 2007*, at 35.
235. DCE, *Annual Danish Informative Inventory Report to UNECE*, 2015, at 35.
236. DCE, *Annual Danish Informative Inventory Report to UNECE*, 2015, at 40.
237. Danish Government, *Denmark's Fifth National Communication on Climate Change* at 174f.

grazing animals. Model calculations show that NH_3 sources comprise to a high percentage of the atmospheric input of nitrogen to Danish marine waters and land. NH_3 is also the dominant alkaline gas in the atmosphere. It neutralises a large amount of oxidised sulphur and nitrogen compounds in ambient air, and consequently pays a very central role in the chemical reactions occurring in the atmosphere. Between 1985 and 2013, emissions of NH_3 from the agricultural sector decreased by 42% resulting in a reduction in related acid deposition. The reduction is particularly the result of the different political action plans, which led to legislation and other measures to prevent the loss of nitrogen (N) in agricultural production.[238] In its 2014 report to the United Nations Economic Commission for Europe (UNECE), the EPA stated that the reduction achieved by Danish agriculture (20% reduction in the period 1999–2010) is among the highest reductions among the parties to the Gothenburg Protocol.[239]

The emission of NMVOC originates from many different sources. The total emission has decreased in Denmark by 44% from 1990 to 2013, largely due to the increased use of catalyst cars and reduced emissions from use of solvents.[240] Denmark exceeded the NMVOC ceilings in 2013 and the NH_3 ceilings in 2010, 2011, 2012 and 2013.[241] Denmark applied the EU for adjustment from the national emission reduction commitments both in 2017 and in 2018.[242]

The quantity of ozone in the stratosphere varies greatly, being highest in the spring and lowest in the autumn. The ozone column over Denmark is declining by an average of 0.4% per year, slightly more in the spring and slightly less in the autumn. Ozone is formed in photochemical reactions between volatile organic compounds (VOCs) and NO_x in the presence of sunlight. A total of 70% of the NO_x comes from the transport sector.[243] The ground-level ozone concentration in cities is generally lower than that in rural areas because ozone reacts with NO and forms NO_2. The ground-level ozone is the air pollutant found in the highest concentrations in forests and rural area – it is the gaseous air pollutant that harms vegetation the most. Annual ozone concentration in Denmark is well below the EU target value laid down in the Ambient Air Quality Directive (AAQD).

In 2011, the CO_2 emission was the most important GHG contributing to the Danish national emission in CO_2 equivalent with 78.0% followed by N_2O with 10.7%,

238. DCE, *Annual Danish Informative Inventory Report to the UNECE 2015*, at 9. Concerning the development in Denmark from 1985 to 2004 with a decrease of 32%, *see* OECD, *Environmental Performance Reviews. Denmark. 2007*, at 35ff, and the Danish Government *Denmark's Fifth National Communication on Climate Change*, at 175.
239. Danish EPA Environmental Technology Letter of 19 March 2014, j.nr. MST-5269-00007.
240. DCE, *Annual Danish Informative Inventory Report to UNECE*, 2015, at 37.
241. EEA, *NEC Directive Status Report 2014*, at 6, 8, 10, 17–18 and 23–24.
242. EEA, *NEC Directive Reporting Status 2018*, at 3.
243. Danish Government, *The National Reform Programme Denmark* 2015, at 62.

CH_4 with 9.8% and F gases (HFCs, PFCs and SF_6) with 1.5%.[244] The transport sector is responsible for 23% of the emission.[245] From 1990 to 2011, it increased by 19.7%, mainly due to increasing road traffic.

25. Denmark is facing environmental challenges resulting from unsustainable consumption patterns. The latest material flow analysis, performed in 1997, showed that 185 million tonnes of materials is directly used by Danish economy (35 tonnes per inhabitant). Denmark has one of the world's highest levels of resource consumption: it is almost double the EU average. The generation of household waste is growing nearly twice as fast as the economy and has reached one of the highest generation rates in the OECD. Denmark has the highest amount of municipal waste generated in EU.

In 2014, the generation of waste per inhabitant was 758 kg per year compared to the EU average of 475 kg per year,[246] and Denmark had the second highest proportion of incineration waste (54%). The recycling accounted for 44%. Most incineration plants treat municipal waste as an energy source. Those plants are engaged in combined heat and power production. From 1990 to 2010, the combined heat and power (CHP) production that was based on waste increased by 146%. Today 48% of the waste used in energy production is renewable energy.[247] In November 2013, the Government launched a resource strategy titled 'Denmark Without Waste. Recycling More – Incinerate Less' for public waste management with the object of increasing waste recycling. In February 2015, it was followed by the strategy 'Denmark Without Waste II – A Draft on Strategy for Waste Prevention'.[248] In 2017, the Commission recommended that Denmark must reinforce policies to promote waste prevention and make reuse and recycling more economically attractive, especially by shifting away from incineration in order to improve resource effectiveness.[249]

244. DCE, *Denmark's National Inventory Report 2013. Emission Inventories 1990-2011 – submitted under the United Nations Framework Convention on Climate Change and the Kyoto Protocol*, at 18.
245. DCE, *Denmark's National Inventory Report 2013. Emission Inventories 1990-2011 – submitted under the United Nations Framework Convention on Climate Change and the Kyoto Protocol*, at 18.
246. European Commission staff working document of 3 February 2017, *The EU Environmental Implementation Review Country Report – Denmark*, SWD(2017) 39 final, at 17.
247. OECD, *Environmental Performance Reviews. Denmark. 2007*, at 156 and Energy Agency, *Energy Statistics 2010*.
248. Danish Government, *The National Reform Programme Denmark 2015*, at 60.
249. European Commission staff working document, *The EU Environmental Implementation Review Country Report – Denmark*, SWD(2017) 39 final of 3 February 2017, at 14.

Chapter 2. Basic Principles of Environmental Law

26. Environmental law is the area of law at international, regional, EU (subnational) and national levels that seek to manage human impacts on the environment with respect to the use of resources, pollution and climate change. The word 'law' refers broadly to those that lay out behavioural prescriptions issued by an authoritative source in a written form, whether or not mandatory or backed by a dispute settlement or other enforcement systems. Whereas mainstream legal disciplines (e.g., constitutional law, contract law, commercial law, tort law and administrative law) deal only with state-state interaction and human-human interactions (e.g., government-citizen interactions), environmental law also deals with the interactions among humans and the other several million species on the planet, in complex interconnected systems, transboundary interactions and over long-term horizons. In other words, environmental law is concerned with the inextricable connection between humanity and the common exterior world. Most of today's environmental problems are global and complex, and development of principles and norms are often developed at global and regional levels. Multilateral and unilateral institutions are taking part in the development of such principles as well as in the codification of the environmental principles in conventions, protocols, declarations and guidelines.

Environmental law refers to all aspects of the natural environment, including land, air, water, flora and fauna/ecosystems (including biodiversity), the climate, the landscape, cultural heritage, renewable energy, the operation of socio-economic systems, human health and quality of life, neighbour-to-neighbour situations (e.g., noise and vibrations) and any interaction between these factors. The area of law seeks to manage human impacts on the environment with respect to the use of resources, water and ecosystem services, reduction of pollution and reduction of emission of GHG caused by human activities. Since natural resources underpin the economy and the localisation of enterprises is depending on spatial planning, environmental approvals, product type approvals, etc., modern environmental law has become a very important part of business law. The consequences that the utilisation of natural resources and land has are important aspects of environmental law. The recognition of resources as a common concern of humankind provide for a change in the legal approach. Also, the transboundary pollution of dangerous or polluting materials, emissions, etc. as well as the increasing international trade in chemical and other dangerous goods has impact on environmental law. The negative environmental effects mean that there is a need for a common and effective effort to minimise the damages to environment and health on a global level.

Environmental themes have recurred through different generations of regulatory designs. It started at international level in 1972 at the UN's Stockholm Conference on the Human Environment with a presentation of ideas for the simplification of rules for national states in order to implement general principles of human rights and obligations towards nature, environment and future generations. The 'Founex Report on Development and Environment' was prepared as part of the basis for the discussion at the Conference ensuring a focus on the combination of strategies on environmental protection and the need for economic development in developing countries.

It resulted in the Stockholm Declaration that set the stage for the future development of environmental principles[250] as well as the establishment of the first international intergovernmental organisations focused on environmental protection. Twenty years after the Stockholm Conference, the UN's Conference on the Environment and Development was held in Rio (the Rio Conference or the UNCED). The World Commission on Environment and Development (the Brundtland Commission) prepared the report – titled 'Our Common Future' – for this Conference in 1987. The report recognises the consideration of ecological/resource dimension alongside economic and social dimensions stating that the interdependency of the new challenges and issues today contrast sharply with the nature of the institutions that exist.[251] The parties taking part in the UNCED agreed on environmental priorities that were essentially divided into two categories that are still very important in the understanding of the regulatory approach used by the legislators at all regulatory levels: those related to the protection of various environmental media and those related to the regulation of particular activities or products.[252] The Conference resulted in the very important Rio Declaration,[253] the Agenda 21, the United Nation's Framework Convention on Climate Change (UNFCCC), the Biodiversity Convention and the Global Consensus on the Management, Conservation and Sustainable Development of all types of Forests. In 2012, the UN's Conference on Sustainable Development ('Rio+20') was held. The ambitions behind this conference was to make it possible to transform the global economy into an inclusive and green economy in the context of sustainable development and poverty reduction.[254]

27. One of the most important aspects in environmental policy and law is *the concept of sustainability* – a concept that has been developed over the last forty years. As stated in the Brundtland Report, the sustainability concept implicates not only the limits on economic activities in the interests of preserving or protecting the environment, but it was also an approach to development, which emphasises the fundamental importance of equity within economic systems.[255] Sustainable development contains both substantive and procedural elements. The substantive elements include the environmental principles on the equitable allocation of resources both within the present generation and between generations (intra- and intergenerational equity), the sustainable utilisation of resources and the right of development, including the least developed countries. It modifies the purposes of conventional development by adding a wide range of environmental protection goals, by incorporating the environment into social goals and by insisting that economic goals should be compatible with environmental protection. The concept also

250. Stockholm Declaration of the United Nations Conference on the Human Environment.

251. WCED, 1987 at 310.

252. Philippe Sands and Jacqueline Peel, with Adriana Fabra and Ruth MacKenzie, *Principles of International Environmental Law*, Cambridge, 2018, at 4.

253. United Nations Rio Declaration on Environment and Development.

254. The outcome document from the Rio+20 Summit was titled *The Future that We Want*. The conference was not as successful as the former one.

255. *See* Jonas Ebbesson, *A Modest Contribution to Environmental Democracy and Justice in Transboundary Contexts: The Combined Impact of the Espoo Convention and the Aarhus Convention*, RECIEL, 20(3), 2011, at 248–257. Concerning the two Conventions, *see infra* para. 32.

modifies the purpose of development by recognising the present generation's responsibility to future generations. The principal procedural elements of the concept are related to the human rights to environmental information, public participation and access to justice.[256] The concept of sustainability emphasises a far-sighted approach to decision-making at all levels, and the need for environmental impact assessment (EIA). It rests on an integration of environmental concern and a balanced consideration of social, economic and environmental goals and objectives in both public and private decision-making as well as cross-sectorial coordination.

The ambition to ensure a sustainable development by the laws and other regulatory instruments was especially highlighted by the Report 'Our Common Future' (1987). The concept means a shift away from the traditional thinking based on state sovereignty in international law towards cooperative and inclusive governance structures founded upon a sense of responsibility for humanity's common future. Based on this concept, the protection of the global atmosphere, temperature and biodiversity from hazardous products and waste, etc. is a common responsibility for all states. Most fundamentally, sustainable development would have governments – including international regimes (e.g., the UN), the EU institutions, the national as well as the local governments – to protect the entire range of natural resources and ecosystems as well as the atmosphere from every significant threat, including the threat from GHGs. The importance of this international concept is, e.g., illustrated by the UN's '2030 Agenda for Sustainable Development' (adopted in 2015) with its 17 'sustainability development goals' and 169 targets.

Based on the Agenda 21 that was agreed at the Rio Conference in 1992, the parties (the national states as well as the EU) are called to delegate sustainable development responsibilities to the lowest level of public authority consistent with effective action. In other words, subsidiarity is an important aspect of sustainability. The local and regional governments have central roles within their jurisdiction, although it is obvious that they need a supportive institutional, regulatory and financial framework from international bodies and from higher levels of government. In its broadest context, sustainability is a concept of economic change – from a brown to a green economy[257] – and a change in which the population and intended functions of a community can be maintained into the indefinite future without degrading community institutions, the means of production, systems of infrastructure, the resource base, and natural and man-made environments. *Self-determination and accountability* are other important aspects in sustainable development, and the respect for the procedural principles that are embedded in third generation human

256. These procedural principles are laid down in the Rio Declaration's Art. 10 and the UNECE's Aarhus Convention, *see infra* para. 31.

257. United Nations Environmental Programme (UNEP) 'Green Economy Report', 2011, in the Introduction (at 02), outlines its definition and approach to the green economy. 'In a green economy, growth in income and employment should be driven by public and private investments that reduce carbon emissions and pollution, enhance energy and resource efficiency, and prevent the loss of biodiversity and ecosystem services. These investments need to be catalyzed and supported by targeted public expenditure, policy reforms and regulation changes'. http://wedocs.unep.org/bitstream/handle/20.500.11822/18966/Green_EconomyReport_Final_Dec2011_UNEP.pdf?sequence=1&isAllowed=y.

rights can assist to foster more legitimate decision-making in the balancing of economic and environmental interests. Principle 10 of the Rio Declaration stressed:

> Environmental issues are best handled with the participation of all concerned citizens, at the relevant level. At the national level, each individual shall have appropriate access to information concerning the environment that is held by public authorities, including information on hazardous materials and activities in their communities, and the opportunity to participate in decision-making processes. States shall facilitate and encourage public awareness and participation by making information widely available. Effective access to judicial and administrative proceedings, including redress and remedy, shall be provided.

As it is clearly stated in this principle, access to environmental information, public participation and access to justice are closely connected parts of the participatory regime. The UNECE Convention on Access to Information, Public Participation and Access to Justice in Environmental Matters (the Aarhus Convention)[258] establishes such procedural rights, and it is open for all countries that want to be a party. The parties to the Convention recognise that sustainable and environmentally sound development depends on effective governmental decision-making that contains both environmental considerations and external inputs. In order to protect the rights of present and future generations to live in a healthy environment, Article 1 of the Convention requires the parties to guarantee these procedural rights as the three 'pillars' that primarily concern relations between members of the public and governing institutions.

Sustainability as part of the EU Constitution can be understood in the light of development of the concept under international environmental law. The Treaty of Amsterdam (1997) clarified as the first Treaty the legal regime of sustainability as an integrated part of the European Community's constitution.[259] The Maastricht Treaty (1992) ensured the environmental policy integration as a relatively prominent substantive basis in Article 11 TFEU. In June 2001, at the Gothenburg Summit, EU leaders launched the first EU Sustainability Strategy (EU SDS), and the next version of the strategy was adopted by the European Council in June 2006. In 2009, a Commission communication reviewed the EU SDS to respond to the most recent economic and financial crisis from the perspective of a long-term sustainable development with the objective of furthering the mainstream EU SDS into the EU policy fields.[260] In December 2009, the European Council confirmed that sustainable development remains a fundamental objective of the EU under the Lisbon Treaty. Article 3(3) TEU of the Lisbon Treaty states that the EU must work for a

258. The Convention was adapted in 1991 in the second largest city in Denmark (Aarhus), and it came into force in 2001. Currently, there are now forty-seven parties to this Convention – including the EU and Denmark.
259. European Commission, *The Law of Sustainable Development. General Principles*, 2000, at 5.
260. *See* COM(2009) 400 final.

sustainable development of Europe and globally with a focus on the uneasy relationship between environmental protection and economic development.[261] According to Article 21 TEU, the external actions of the EU shall foster the sustainable economic, social and environmental development of developing countries with the primary aim of eradication of poverty. EU and all of its Member States have signed and ratified the Aarhus Convention as a 'mixed agreement'.[262] With a focus on the need to have the accurate data collected, the Protocol on Pollution Release and Transfer Registers (the PRTR Protocol)[263] was adopted during the Fifth 'Environment for Europe' Ministerial Conference under this Convention in May 2003. Thirty-three parties to the Aarhus Convention have ratified the PRTR Protocol – EU and Denmark are both parties to the Protocol.[264] As a party, Denmark has direct reporting obligations to the Protocol. Both the Aarhus Convention and the PRTR Protocol prohibit discrimination on the basis of citizenship, nationality or domicile against persons that seek to exercise their rights. The obligation to respect the Aarhus Convention has been implemented in EU law by the 'Aarhus Regulation' with effect on its own institutions, bodies, offices or agencies established by, or on the basis of, the Treaty of Lisbon.[265]

The European ambition is to help develop international measures to prevent and improve the quality of the environment and the sustainable management of global natural resources in order to ensure sustainable development. Horizontal policy integration and sustainable development is commonly understood as balancing economy, social and environmental interests and policies in a way that trade-offs (or negative effects) between them are minimised, and synergies are maximised. Sustainability thinking is now a central part of the EU's general political strategy 'European 2020. Smart, Sustainable and Inclusive Growth' that was adopted in 2010.[266] The EU's 7th Environmental Action Programme (7EAP) 'Living Well, Within the Limits of Our Planet' (2013) refers to this general strategy as well as to the UN's Conference on Sustainable Development ('Rio + 20'), which aims to transform the Union into an inclusive and green economy in the context of sustainable development and poverty reduction.[267]

There are no rules on sustainability and no rules on the citizen's rights to a safe, healthy and ecologically balanced environment in the Danish Constitution that is

261. Susanne Kingston, Veerle Heyvaert and Aleksandra Cavoski, *European Environmental Law*, 2017, at 12–13.
262. Denmark ratified the Convention in 2000 with reservation for Greenland, and the EU ratified it in 2005. The Convention was implemented in Danish legislation by Act No. 447 of 31 May 2000 on the Amendments to Certain Environmental Acts.
263. The Protocol is also titled the Kiev Protocol.
264. *See infra* paras 60 and 71. The EU and Denmark have ratified the PRTR Protocol. The Protocol came into force on 9 Oct. 2009. It has thirty-five parties – including the EU and Denmark.
265. Article 2(1) letter (c) of the European Parliament and Council Regulation No. 1367/2006/EC on the Application of the Aarhus Convention on Access to Information, Public Participation and Access to Justice in Environmental Matters to Community Institutions and Bodies. The Regulation entered into force on 28 Sept. 2006.
266. *See* the Commission's proposal in COM(2010) 2020 final and the Council's conclusion of 17 June 2010.
267. Decision No. 1386/2013/EU of the European Parliament and of the Council of 20 November 2013 on a General Union Environment Action Programme to 2020 'Living well, within the limits of our

very old.[268] The constitutional rights laid down in the Constitution are 'negative' in character rights to be free from government intrusion, rather than rights to affirmative governmental assistance. The Danish political strategy on sustainable development is from 2014.[269]

28. The concept of sustainability is codified in principles of environmental action laid down as soft law in the Stockholm Declaration, the Rio Declaration and several other international declarations and treaties as well as in the Lisbon Treaty. The objectives for the EU's participation in international environmental governance are also among the overall objectives stated in Article 3(5) TEU and Article 21(1) letters d) and f) TEU. Based on these treaty rules, the EU pursues the object of playing a global leadership role. In Article 191(1) TFEU, it is stated that the objectives of the EU environmental policy are to contribute to preserving, protecting and improving the quality of the environment, protecting human health, prudent and rational utilisation of natural resources and promoting measures at an international level to deal with regional or worldwide environmental problems, and in particular combating climate change.[270]

In its relations with the wider world, the EU is supposed to contribute to the sustainable development of the Earth, cf. Article 3(5) TEU. In order to ensure sustainable development, the EU must also help foster the sustainable economic, social and environmental development of the developing countries, cf. Article 21(1) letter d) TEU. Furthermore, the EU must help to develop international measures to preserve and improve the quality of the environment and the sustainable management of global natural resources, cf. Article 21(1) letter f) TEU.[271] Both the principles of environmental actions codified in the TFEU and other environmental principles are often mentioned in secondary EU legislation. They are also very important legal sources in the CJEU case law. When the principles are mentioned in directives and regulations, they will have binding effect on the national authorities in their implementation of the relevant legislation.[272]

The 'principle on common but differentiated responsibilities and respective capabilities' (the CBDR principle) is a leading principle of international law that is based on an equity approach.[273] The principle is a guiding future action with respect to biodiversity, climate change and several other environmental problems. Principle 7 of the Rio Declaration declares:

---

planet', and concerning the EU EAPs, *see infra* para. 39. Concerning the environmental governance as a stronger conceptual for the awareness of environment, economy and society, *see* Susanne Kingston, Veerle Heyvaert and Aleksandra Cavoski, *European Environmental Law*, 2017, at 36–43.

268. The Danish Constitution is from 1849, *see supra* para. 4.
269. The strategy was passed by a former coalition Government that consisted of the Social Democratic Party and the Social-Liberal Party. Concerning the different coalition governments, *see supra* para. 4.
270. Ludwig Krämer, *EU Environmental Law*, 2016, at 8–14.
271. When the EU is exercising its shared competences in the area of environmental issues, it is bound by the principles of subsidiarity and proportionality, *see infra* para. 56.
272. The binding effect is stated in Art. 288 TFEU.
273. Philippe Sands et al., *Principles of International Environmental Law*, 4th edition, at 244–251.

> States shall cooperate in a spirit of global partnership to conserve, protect and restore the health and integrity for the Earth's ecosystem. In view of the different contribution to the global environmental degradation, States have common but differentiated responsibilities. The developed countries acknowledge the responsibility that they bear in the international pursuit to sustainable development in the view of the pressure their societies place on the global environment and of the technologies and financial resources they command.

The CBDR principle is recognising the obligation of all states to work in a spirit of global partnership in protecting and restoring the Earth's ecosystems. But, the responsibility is differentiated between developed, developing countries and least developed countries. The developed countries have a special responsibility in two respects: an implicit legal responsibility to others because of past and current acts, and an equitable responsibility to use their technical and financial capacity to alleviate the world's environmental and developmental problems. One of the important examples of the codification of the principle is Article 3(1) UNFCCC. The consequences of the CBDR principle emerge in Articles 4(2) and (8) UNFCCC, where the developed countries commit themselves to take all practicable steps to promote, facilitate and finance, as appropriate, the transfer of, or access to, environmentally sound technologies and know-how to other parties, particularly developing countries, to enable them to implement the provisions of the Convention. The use of the CBDR principle has been under a lot of pressure in the Conference of the Parties (COP), and the outcome of the discussion is a reduced importance of the principle in the framing of the Paris Agreement. It is not dividing the parties in such strict categories, but employs the bottom-up approach to CBDR where each party must formulate and promote the most ambitious emission reduction goals that its economic, social and other sources and capacities allow (NDS), cf. Article 4(3) of the Paris Agreement. Article 2(2) of the Agreement states that the obligations:

> will be implemented to reflect equity and the principle of common but differentiated responsibilities and respective capabilities, in the light of different national circumstances.

A regulatory design with an integrated and holistic approach is based on the concept of sustainability, and such a design is a very important part of environmental law today. The 'principle of integration' is an important environmental principle laid down in several international conventions and declarations, including principle 13 of the Stockholm Declaration, principle 4 of the Rio Declaration and the UN's 2030 Agenda for Sustainable Development'.[274] The content and importance of this principle as an international principle is explained in the 'New Delhi Declaration of Principles of International Law Relating to Sustainable Development'. It:

274. *See* target 17.14 of the UN's '2030 Agenda for Sustainable Development', 2015.

> reflects the interdependence of social, economic, financial, environmental and human rights aspects of principle and rules of international law related to sustainable development as well as the interdependence of the needs of current and future generations of humankind.

The principle of integration of environmental protection requirements is also stated as an important principle in Part II 'Provisions having general application' of the TFEU. Article 11 declares that environmental protection must be integrated into the definition and implementation of all the Union's policies and activities by its institutions, in particular with a view to promote sustainable development. The principle is, e.g., codified in the legislation on EU financing of environmental protection.[275] The ambition behind the principle is to achieve greater coherence of policies and actions at all regulatory levels and to avoid contradicting policies at different levels. Integration of environmental concerns into other policy areas should be ensured both horizontally and vertically between all levels of governments and all actors in the private sector. Institutionally and procedurally, the regulatory design should ensure good opportunities for cooperation across competencies and regulatory systems and levels. The use of integrated policies and Whole-of-Government (WoG) approaches is also presented by the UN's Economic & Social Affairs as important aspects of sustainable development.[276] It states that high-quality, disaggregated data for policymaking, as well as for monitoring progress, strengthen government's capacity to formulate and carry out integrated policies and increase the potential for policy integration among government agencies.[277] The need to deal with the integrative challenges of sustainable development is important when dealing with closely interlinked policy domains, such as climate change, food and water security, sustainable agriculture, biodiversity and nature protection at international, regional and national levels.[278] Transparency and accountability of the institutions can be enhanced by assess to environmental information and by rules on public participation in the decision-making. Such procedural environmental rights are also important aspects of the principle of integration.[279]

The 'precautionary principle' is another important environmental principle. It is stated as a guiding principle in several conventions, declarations and other international instruments. Principle 15 of the Rio Declaration notes that the precautionary approach shall be widely applied by states according to their capabilities:

---

275. The 'polluter pays principle' is, e.g., an important part of the objectives of the Waste Framework Directive (2008/98/EC, as amended), the End-of-Life Vehicles Directive (2002/96/EC, as amended), the Environmental Liability Directive (2004/35/EC as amended), the Directive on Promotion of Renewable Energy (the RES Directive – 2009/28/EC, as amended) and the Directive on Industrial Emissions (IED – 2010/75/EU).
276. United Nations Economic & Social Affairs, *The United Nations E-government Survey 2016. E-government in Support of Sustainable Development.* The WoG systems are presented as governmental systems in which the digital features enabling different systems to seamlessly exchange information, and the citizens are ensured access to the status of such online transactions, at 7–8.
277. United Nations Economic & Social Affairs, *The United Nations E-government Survey 2016. E-government in Support of Sustainable Development*, at 15–18.
278. United Nations Economic & Social Affairs, *The United Nations E-government Survey 2016. E-government in Support of Sustainable Development*, at 11.
279. The procedural principles are described *infra* paras 31–33 and 347–348.

> Where there are threats of serious or irreversible damage, lack of full scientific certainty shall not be used as a reason for postponing cost-effective measures to prevent environmental degradation.

This principle of precaution has its basis in the more traditional environmental agreements dating back to, e.g., the 1974 Paris Convention on the Prevention of Marine Pollution from Land-Based Sources.[280] Central to the principle is the element of anticipation, reflecting a requirement for basing effective environmental measures upon actions which take a long-term approach, and which might anticipate changes on the basis of scientific knowledge. The principle asks political and administrative decision-makers to remain mindful of their responsibility also for the life of future generations, the nature and animal health. It states that if an action or policy has a suspected risk of causing serious harm to the environment, to human health or to animal health, the burden of proof that such products/activities are not harmful falls on those taking the action (applying for an approval, etc.). The 'precautionary principle' is one of the guiding principles in the UNECE Convention on the Protection and Use of Transboundary Watercourses and the International Lakes,[281] the Cartagena Protocol on Biosafety under the Convention on Biological Diversity (CBD),[282] the Vienna Convention on the Protection of the Ozone Layer with its Montreal Protocol,[283] the UNFCCC with its Kyoto Protocol and Paris Agreement,[284] the UN Fish Stocks Agreement,[285] Article 191(2) TFEU and several EU regulations and directives. The principle establishes obligations on the authorities in situations of scientific uncertainties. It has, e.g., been used by the CJEU to ensure a strong protection of Nature 2000 sites and Annex IV species under the Habitats Directive.[286]

A high level of environmental protection[287] – considering the diversity of situations in the various regions of the Union – is one of the important aims and principles of the EU, cf. Articles 3(3) and 21(2) letter f) TEU as well as Articles 6 and 191(2) TFEU.

The 'polluter pays principle' is another example of how the concept of sustainability is steering the policy through principles, cf. Article 16 of the Rio Declaration. It declares that:

> National authorities should endeavour to promote the internalization of environmental costs and the use of economic instruments, taking into account the

280. Philippe Sands et al., *Principles of International Environmental Law*, Cambridge, 2018, at 4.
281. Article 2(5). Concerning this Convention, *see infra* para. 102.
282. Concerning the Cartagena Protocol on Biosafety, *see infra* paras 298 and 334.
283. Concerning the Vienna Convention on the Protection of the Ozone Layer with its Montreal Protocol, *see infra* para. 74.
284. Concerning the UNFCCC, the Kyoto Protocol and the Paris Agreement, *see infra* paras 80–81.
285. Agreement for the implementation of the UNCLOS related to the conservation and management of straddling fish stocks and highly migratory fish stocks. Concerning the international regimes for the conservation of marine living resources, *see infra* para. 279.
286. *See, e.g.,* C-127/02 *Waddenzee*, C-441/17 *Bialowieza Forest*, and the joined cases C-293/17 and C-294/17 *Coöperatie Mobilisation for the Environment et al.*
287. The 'principle of a high level of environmental protection' is, e.g., stated in the Air Quality Framework Directive and in the Eco-design Framework Directive.

approach that the polluter should, in principle, bear the cost of pollution, with due regard to the public interest and without distorting international trade and investment.

Based on this principle, it appears that the principle is aimed at striking a balance between the market forces and the power of the authorities to use taxes and other economic instruments in the internalization of the economic valuable consequences into the prices of the products/services, etc. The basic reasoning behind this principle is that the operator should be responsible for the cost of preventing harm to the environment necessitated by his use of resources and other environmental harming activities. The principle was presented already in 1972 as a guiding principle concerning international economic aspects by the OECD as a new approach to economic growth.[288] It prescribes a quasi-regulatory regime of environmental taxation for the application of this principle arguing that the companies have to be taxed according to the level of pollution they produce. The principle is mentioned in international treaties, protocols, etc. as well as in the Lisbon Treaty, cf. Article 191(2) TFEU. It serves as an economic rule according to which a portion of the profits accruing to polluters as the result of their activities must be returned to the public authorities responsible for protecting, inspecting, monitoring and controlling the quality of the environment. It is also used as a principle in liability regimes as the basis for an ex ante allocation of the costs of pollution prevention and control measures designed to encourage rational use of scarce environmental resources. In the context of the overall concept of sustainable development and modern view of common and shared resources, the content of the principle is that there is an obligation for the EU institutions to ensure economic efficiency, equitable distribution of costs and to put requirements on the Member States to make a regulatory system, for example, demanding the operators to include the cost of the emissions from conventional energy production in the prices of energy production. The use of energy taxes is an example of instruments used to ensure that it becomes more expensive to buy conventional energy compared to the price of energy based on renewable energy.[289]

There are other important principles such as the principles that have been developed in international law. The 'principle of prevention' has been introduced by declarations, conventions, Article 191(1) TFEU as well as international tribunals[290] and courts.[291] The principle is also important in the guiding of the interpretation and

288. OECD's recommendation of 26 May 1972 – C(72)128 – of the Council on Guiding Principles concerning International Economic Aspects of Environmental Policies.

289. Council Directive 2003/96/EC restructuring the Community's Framework for Taxation of Energy Products and Electricity.

290. In 2005, the arbitral tribunal stated in the *Iron Rine case* Belgium/Netherlands (PCA 2003-02), Final Award 24 May 2005, that the 'duty of prevention' is a principle of general international law that applies not only in the case of autonomous activities but also activities undertaken in implementation of specific treaties between state parties. *See* Philippe Sands et al., *Principles of International Environmental Law*, 4th edition, at 211.

291. The International Court of Justice used the 'principle of prevention' as a customary rule in its judgment of 13 July 2006. It solved the conflict between Argentina and Uruguay in the Pulp Mills case. *See* Philippe Sands et al., *Principles of International Environmental Law*, 4th edition, at 211.

application of several EU directives and regulations.[292] The principle that 'environmental damage should, as a priority be rectified at source' (the 'source principle') that is also mentioned in Article 191(2) TFEU is close to the just-mentioned 'principle of prevention'. It is of special interest in the regulation of waste and polluting activities. The principle of 'prudent and rational utilisation of natural resources' is a central part of the concept of sustainability, and it is also mentioned in Article 191(2) TFEU as well as in EU directives.[293]

The 'combined approach' used since 2000 by the EU is an example of a regulatory approach used in accordance with the environmental principles. The principles of the water policy guiding the design and the implementation of the WFD[294] on the basis of the combined river basin approach are: (a) high level of protection; (b) the 'precautionary principle'; (c) the 'prevention principle'; (d) the 'source principle'; (e) the 'polluter pays principle'; and (f) the 'principle of integration'.[295] The environmental objectives and principles mentioned in the Treaty of Lisbon – including Article 191 – are all binding on the EU institutions when they are framing secondary legislation, and when they are making any decisions in the environmental area. When the environmental objectives and principles are codified in EU secondary legislation, they are binding on the national authorities – and it is very often the case.[296] The CJEU has also included the 'precautionary principle' in its interpretation of the Habitats Directive that does not mention this principle in its preamble.[297]

The *Danish notion* of the mentioned environmental principles is that they are only political signals to the administrative authorities, and the interest in these principles is not very strong in terms of legal decision-making. The environmental principles need to be formalised and specified in the wording of Danish legislation in order to become applicable by national courts and administrative bodies. The 'polluter pays principle' is the only environmental principle that is described as a legally binding principle in the acts. A binding effect of the polluter pays principle is (partly) ensured only in the Contaminated Soil Act, the Act on Strict Liability for Pollution Cost by Heavily Polluting Activities,[298] and in the rules implementing the Directive on Environmental Liability.[299] The OECD has stated in an assessment of Danish legislation that the problem with implementation of the principles in Denmark is that the practice 'polluter pays principle' applies primarily to households

292. The EIA Directive and the IE Directive are important examples on such instruments.

293. The principle of prudent and rational utilisation of natural resources can, e.g., be found in some secondary rules, for example the Nitrates Directive (91/676/EEC) and the SEA Directive (2001/42/EC). *See* Philippe Sands et al., *Principles of International Environmental Law*, 4th Edition, at 219–227.

294. European Parliament and Council Directive 2000/60/EC Establishing a Framework for Community Actions in the Field of Water Policy.

295. Concerning the WFD, *see infra* paras 103–104.

296. Concerning the principle of integration that is relevant in the national authorities' use of the ESI-funding, *see supra* para. 15.

297. *See, e.g.*, C-127/02 *Waddenzee*, C-441/17 *Bialowieza Forest*, and the Joined Cases C-293/17 and C-294/17 *Coöperatie Mobilisation for the Environment et al.*

298. Concerning the Danish Act on Strict Liability for Pollution Cost by Heavily Polluting Activities, *see infra* para. 343.

299. Concerning the implementing the Directive on Environmental Liability, *see infra* paras 337–341.

and, to a lesser extent, to industry.[300] The 'precautionary principle' is not codified in Danish legislation as a legal principle, and it is not always accepted as a relevant guiding principle by the Danish authorities in the application of conventions,[301] EU directives and regulations. The principle of integration has no role to play for the reduction of the problems connected to fragmentised environmental law, but the WoG approach – highlighted by the UN as mentioned *supra* – is important in the design of environmental legislation.[302] It is mandatory for the Ministry of Environment and Food of Denmark (and for all other Danish ministries) to use a digitalisation-ready design in the drafting of legal acts that – as far as possible – will contribute to ensure digital management and decision-making at the administrative level. When formulating new rules, they must be able to ensure that all options for adjusting the rules for automatised decision-making have been sought, and that the regulation of business is 'agile', adaptable and foreseeable in relation to meet a society in rapid change.

29. The role of modern environmental law is both an issue relating to ensuring the competitive position of the private sector actors in global trade, the protection of developing countries against discrimination and an issue relating to environmental regulation and reduction of the negative impacts of production and global trading and transport of goods. Article 3(3) TEU states that the Union shall establish an internal market, and it shall work for the sustainable development of Europe based on balanced growth. The internal market shall comprise an area without internal frontiers in which the free movement of goods, persons, services and capital is ensured in accordance with the provisions of the Treaties, cf. Article 26(2) TFEU. The intent behind the Union's environmental policy is to facilitate sustainable development by use of ways, that respect trade as well as environmental policy, accepting some exceptions from the principles of the four freedoms. Therefore, EU environmental law has to be understood in the light of the balance between the principle of the internal market and the environmental principles, especially the 'principle of a high level of environmental protection'. As a consequence, there is also a difference between the traditional legal state-based approach in international and national law compared with the approach in the legal order of the EU: The traditional legal separation between public and private law is not part of EU law. The Treaty uses the terminology 'public' versus 'private'. It is not containing an express

300. OECD, *Environmental Performance Reviews. Denmark. 2007*, at 17.

301. By way of example it may be mentioned, that Denmark in 2017 – as the only party to the Helsinki Convention – made reservations for the application of the precautionary principle, which the other parties presume to apply in connection with the transfer of quotas by a party from an additional reduction of nutrient emissions from one sea-area to another sea-area. Concerning the Helsinki Convention, *see infra* para. 130.

302. The most important political documents the joint-public digitization strategy, *A Stronger and More Secure Digital Society. The Common Public Digitization Strategy 2016-2020* (2017), the Government's Action Plan '*Simple Rules, Less Bureaucracy – Digital Actuality*' (2017), and the Political Agreement between all the political parties represented in the Danish Parliament on 'Digitization Clearance Agreement' (2018).

distinction between public versus private institutions or a distinction between private versus public law. It is not the public power of the authorities versus the private actors that is the focal point in the EU legal order – rather it is the access to the internal market without the states disturbing the market forces more than necessary with an environmental legislation that conflicts with the treaty rules.

The interaction between economic and environmental issues is part of the concept of sustainable development, and it has been central both at international and EU levels in the development of modern environmental law. At the Rio Conference in 1992, the ambition was to make trade and environment mutually supportive.[303] Principle 12 of the Rio Declaration states that:

> States should cooperate to promote a supportive and open international economic system that would lead to economic growth and sustainable development in all countries, to better address the problems of environmental degradation. Trade policy measures for environmental purposes should not constitute a means of arbitrary or unjustifiable discrimination or a disguised restriction on international trade. Unilateral actions to deal with environmental challenges outside the jurisdiction of the importing country should be avoided. Environmental measures addressing transboundary or global environmental problems should, as far as possible, be based on an international consensus.

This regulatory approach is part of one of those conventions that were adopted at the Rio Conference – the UNFCCC.[304] It was also stated at the Declaration from the Rio+10 meeting in Johannesburg (2002) and the Rio+20 meeting (2012) in Rio that the economic and trade agenda and the work on environmental efficiency and protection, are mutually reinforcing efforts. The General Agreement on Tariffs and Trade (GATT)[305] regulates the market access of World Trade Organization (WTO) Member States. It is a condition under this regime that environmental legislation and decision-making by the authorities at regional and national levels must not result in quantitative restrictions or measures having equivalent effect on trade.[306] The WTO rules mandate equal treatment of like products. GATT Article I sets out provisions in respect to the most favoured nations (MFN) principle, according to which Members must extend any advantage granted to a product from one WTO Member to 'like' products from all other WTO Members; and Article III set out provisions on the national treatment principle, according to which internal taxes and

303. *See* Philippe Sands et al., *Principles of International Environmental Law*, 4th edition, at 841–843.
304. The United Nations Framework Convention on Climate Change was adopted on 9 May 1992. Article 3(5) UNFCCC states that measures taken to combat climate change should not constitute a means of arbitrary or unjustifiable discrimination or a disguised restriction of international trade. *See* Edith Broun Weiss, *The Evolution of International Environmental Law*, 54 Japanese Y.B International Law (2011), at 12–15.
305. GATT is an international agreement signed on 30 Oct. 1947 and changed by the Marrakesh Agreement establishing the World Trade Organization with annexes, final Act and Protocols from 15 Apr. 1994.
306. The GATT 1994 has in its Preamble a reference to the aim of sustainable development. A Committee on Trade and Environment was established to study, e.g., the relationship between environmental conferences/regimes and the WTO.

legal regulations must treat imported products not less favourable than 'like' domestic products. However, Article XX provides exceptions which may justify environment-related criteria, if the criteria can be justified as necessary to protect human, animal or plant life or health (Article XX(b)), or they can be justified as necessary because of the need for conservation of exhaustible natural resources, and the measures are made effective in conjunction with restrictions on domestic production or consumptions (Article XX(g)). The general condition for accepting such exceptions is that the relevant national legislation is not causing 'arbitrary or unjustified discrimination between countries' or 'a disguised restriction on international trade', cf. the 'chapeau' of Article XX. The legality of economic incentives, standards, technical requirements and mandatory environmental criteria under WTO rules can be decided by ruling under dispute settlement. The Agreement on Technical Barriers to Trade under the GATT aims to ensure that technical regulations and standards, and uniform assessment procedures related to the environmental regulations, do not create unnecessary obstacles to international trade. It lays down obligations, which apply to technical standards and conformity assessment procedures issued either on a national or a regional basis.

The trade rules as '"barriers" for the national EU legislators' use of their environmental competence by use of stronger standards or economic instruments are also importance parts of the Lisbon Treaty. National taxation and charges, which form part of a general system of national taxation, are regarded as a 'charge having equivalent effect'. State aid is prohibited. Article 107(1) TFEU provides that any aid granted by a Member State, which distorts competition by favouring certain undertakings or products, is, insofar as it affects trade between Member States, prohibited as incompatible with the internal market. Article 107(2) and (3) provides for an exhaustive list of grounds on which aid may be considered compatible with the Internal Market. The Community Guidelines on State Aid for Environmental Protection established the relevant criteria.[307] It is stressed that the 'polluter pays principle' is applicable as one of the important criteria that sets limits to economic support, including the use of environmental taxes.[308] According to Article 110, Member States are prohibited from imposing any internal taxation of any kind on the products of other Member States in excess of that imposed on similar domestic products. They are also prohibited from imposing on the products of other Member States any internal taxation of such a nature as to afford indirect protection to other domestic products. Tax on an imported product must be compared with tax on an equivalent domestic product. It is a consequence of EU law that the Danish authorities have to treat nationals and non-nationals from other EU Member States, taking the different EU obligations into account. According to settled CJEU case law, the rules regarding equality of treatment between nationals and non-nationals forbid not

307. Commission Guidelines 2014/C 200/01 on State Aid for Environmental Protection.

308. *See, e.g.*, C-233/16 *ANGED*, C-234/16 and C-235/16 *Anged*, and C-236/16 and C-237/16 *Anged* concerning taxes on large establishments in Spain that were accepted by the CJEU as non-State aid as the large retail establishments have a significant and adverse effect on the environment and on town and country planning compared with others.

only open discrimination by reason of nationality but also all direct forms of discrimination which by application of other criteria have the same consequences.[309]

Article 30 TFEU prohibits customs duties and all charges having equivalent effect on trade between Member States. There are also rules on free movements that are of importance for the environmental competences as it is prohibited to have national environmental standards and obligation that can be described as barriers that are incompatible with Articles 34–36. Technical rules are subject to the provisions of Article 34 TFEU, which prohibit quantitative restrictions on imports and all measures having equivalent effect, and Article 35 TFEU, which prohibits restrictions on exports, and all measures having equivalent effects. Article 36 declares that:

> provisions of Articles 34 and 35 shall not preclude prohibitions or restrictions on import and exports of goods in transit justified on grounds of public morality, public policy or public security, the protection of health and life of humans, animals or plants; the protection of national treasures processing artistic, historical or archaeological value; or the protection of industrial and commercial property. Such prohibition or restrictions shall not, however, constitute a means of arbitrary discrimination or a disguised restriction on trade between Member States.

It is up to the national authorities to prove that the conditions in national legislation allowing exceptions from the prohibition of quantitative restrictions have been met. One of the first cases in which the CJEU accepted documentation of environmental benefits is the *Danish Bottle* case, C-3012/86 *Commission v. Denmark*. However, Article 36 TFEU must be interpreted in the light of the 'precautionary principle', cf. Article 191(2).[310] Stringent environmental standards laid down in EU secondary legislation can impose potential problems for some Member States. To reduce the risk of unreasonable negative consequences, Article 191(2) TFEU requires that EU harmonisation measures answering environmental protection requirements shall include, where appropriate, a safeguard clause allowing Member States to take provisional measures, for non-economic environmental reasons, subject to a procedure of inspection by the Union.

While it follows from Article 345 TFEU that the Treaty is not affecting Member States' right to decide whether a given asset should be in public or private ownership, CJEU case law shows that this do not have the effect of exempting expropriation measures from the fundamental rules on the Treaty. Accordingly, expropriation measures used by a Member State should be non-discriminatory and proportionate to attain their legitimate objective, e.g., by providing for adequate compensation.

The prior informed consent (PIC) procedure is an important part of EU legislation, and it is therefore also described in the regulations and directives. It is a principle for the regulation of hazardous trade between states. It is done by means of procedural rules preventing and controlling transboundary environmental harm and

309. The CJEU considers Art. 18 TFEU to be a specific expression of the general 'principle of equity' which applies across the boarders in EU law.

310. Concerning the Art. 36 TFEU, *see supra* at para. 29.

respecting the rights of the transit and the recipient state to make informed decisions.[311] The procedural rules are related to import, export and transboundary transport of hazardous substances, such as hazardous wastes, chemicals and genetically modified organisms (GMOs). A State of export is obliged to notify, in writing, the competent authority of the State(s) concerned of any proposed transboundary movement of hazardous wastes, chemicals and GMOs. Standards and guidelines are vitally important in creating a harmonised system in several of the EU environmental policy areas. The reason for this is the fact that directives and regulations cannot contain all the detailed technical information without being too inflexible.[312] In the Council Resolution of 3 December 1992 on the relationship between the industries' competitiveness and environmental protection, the Council and the Member States were asked to encourage standardisation.[313] The International Standardisation Organisation (ISO) has developed a new global approach to environmental protection. The ISO has, for example, published the ISO 14000 series on environmental management standards and ISO 9001 on quality management. Implementation of the ISO 14000 series in the EU is ensured by agreements on standardisation. International and European standards are as harmonised standards incorporated directly into the directives and regulations. Standards are not legally binding by themselves.

30. The Danish legislator's competence is not only framed by international and EU obligations. The provisions of the Danish Constitution have also to be respected by the legislator as well as by the administrative authorities. Section 73 of the Constitution protects the private property rights and other economic rights against expropriations and also against restrictions on the use of property laid down in Danish Acts, administrative rules and decisions, if such restrictions are not respecting the criteria developed by case law on the balancing of individual economic interests against the public interests.

The current Danish implementation policy is based on a 'minimum implementation strategy' under which the Implementation Council is an advisory body that was established in December 2015 to ensure that EU secondary legislation is implemented into Danish law in such a manner that Danish companies are not subject to stricter requirements than companies in other EU countries.

It has been stated by the Danish Supreme Court that legal interference by public authorities with property rights by legal acts has to be based on a documentation for weighing of the need to protect important and strong public interests (e.g., environmental protection) against the relevant private interests. The rules that ensure the legal basis for expropriation have to be designed as general regulation of future activities, and the interference has to be necessary. If the expropriation is to be accepted it is also a condition that the interference is compensated economically.

311. All States of export or import and transit States are considered as 'States concerned'.

312. *See supra* para. 39 concerning the 'New Approach' established in 1987 as part of the Internal Market.

313. The European Committee on Standardisation (CEN) is one of the standardisation bodies that have to adopt the requirements. The European Committee for Electro Technical Standardisation (CENELEC) and the European Telecommunication Standard Institute (ETSI) are other standardisation bodies with competences. The Commission presumes that products that follow the CEN, CENELEC or ETSI standards also fulfil the essential requirements laid down in the relevant directives.

Therefore, the Danish legal provisions on protection of water and restrictions on land use, etc. make widespread use of full compensation and other guarantees for the property owners (typically owners in the agricultural sector), and the actors in business sectors are in most cases protected against individual costlier regulation of their current use of their properties. Claims for compensation raised by companies and farmers related to loss caused by administrative law intervention on proprietary rights (expropriation) are also presented to the courts. Ownership normally follows landownership according to the 'proximity principle', e.g., those with a proprietary interest in the banks of the lakes or watercourses, are those who have the right to compensation. However, ownership of land is including ownership of the water as such, neither the groundwater nor the surface water. Therefore, the right to decide on the use of water is normally based on the rules and approval systems established in the Watercourse Act[314] and the Water Supply Act.[315]

There are no rules in the Constitution prohibiting acts with retroactive effect. There are, however, many Danish Supreme Court cases, as well as introductory provisions in Danish Acts and legal opinions from the Ministry of Justice, in which the question of retroactivity has been analysed, and the outcome of all these analyses is clearly that there is a common understanding of an existing constitutional tradition in Denmark based on which retroactive regulation by environmental legislation or by administrative decision-making is not acceptable.

Danish environmental law is strongly rooted in administrative acts and the principles of administrative law mentioned below. Except for the Act on Strict Liability for Pollution Cost by Heavily Polluting Activities,[316] part of the Act on Soil Contamination,[317] part of the environmental liability rules[318] and neighbour law,[319] all the environmental statutory acts are based on the administrative law approach. The provisions in the acts are often framework rules delegating the power to make more precise rules to the relevant minister. The principle of loyalty – and the duty on sincere cooperation – in the implementation and interpretation of EU legislation is one of the most important limits.[320] Under the Scandinavian legal tradition, the preparatory works of the legislator are an important legal source used in the interpretation of the rules. The political agreements used by the political parties in the Parliament are also very important sources used to understand the intentions behind the legal text. As mentioned *supra* the obligations to use a digitalisation-ready design in general regulation also serves limits to the discretionary power of the minister when he/she use the discretionary power to pass statutory order. Command-and-control regulation has been the traditional way of dealing with pollution control

314. Concerning the provisions of the Watercourse Act, *see infra* paras 109–110.
315. Concerning the provisions of the Water Supply Act, *see infra* paras 114–117.
316. Concerning the provisions of the Act on Strict Liability for Pollution Cost by Heavily Polluting Activities, *see infra* para. 343.
317. Concerning the provisions of the Contamination Soil Act, *see infra* paras 173–175, and paras 177–180.
318. Concerning the unwritten culpa rules developed by the courts and the Act on Strict Liability for Pollution Cost by Heavily Polluting Activities, *see infra* paras 170, and 343–344.
319. Concerning neighbour law, *see infra* paras 30, 35 and 193.
320. Concerning the duty of sincere cooperation, *see* Art. 4(3) TEU. Concerning this duty as one of the elements in the general supranational construction of the EU, *see infra* para. 56.

and nature conservation/protection. Decisions concerning the approval of new activities, as well as bans, orders and annulment of previous operating licences and product type approvals are very important means under environmental law. Bans, orders and annulments are relevant in cases where the addressee does not comply with the legal rules or the terms included in a permit (operating licences, authorisation, dispensation, etc.). The traditional principles of administrative law are important both in the EU and in Danish law as basis for protecting individual rights against the public authorities exercising their discretionary powers.[321] These principles are:

- *legality*: all administrative rules designed by administrative authorities as well as their decisions need to have clear legal basis in acts decided by the Parliament;
- *specialisation*: the administrative authorities have only the power to include the interests mentioned in the act, that they are referring to as the relevant legal basis for their action in the concrete case;
- *proportionality*: the administrative authorities must demonstrate that their intervention/use of instruments is not going beyond what is necessary to ensure goal effectiveness in the relevant area of competence;
- *fairness and non-discrimination*: the authorities have to treat seminar cases equally;
- *principle of good decision-making*: the public authorities must provide all the information required to ensure a correct decision-making process.

These administrative law principles are not mentioned in the Danish Constitution, but they have a very strong position in case law.

When the Danish acts are delegating discretionary power to the authorities, these public law principles play an important role in the decision-making – also compared with an application of the environmental principles that might be in opposition to the application of the public law principles. The principles are also part of the obligations that the Danish authorities have under the general principles of EU law when they are applying EU law, cf. Article 41 of the Charter of Fundamental Rights of the European Union.[322] Some limitations on the property rights to carry out property development are based on 'neighbour law', which determines the limits to the trespassing that a neighbour must tolerate from the use of the adjoining properties. It is part of Danish private law. The employment of sanctions depends on whether a neighbour will bring the case to court and submit relevant claims. Such claims generally seek prohibition of the emissions in question if they are not in compliance with legal requirements or the ordinary level of pollution in that nearby surrounding area, and/or pollution reduction or remedial measures to bring one's own property back to its original condition. The sanctions used by the courts in such cases can be divided into the following categories: (a) prohibition of the enterprise or other activities whether fully or partly; (b) an order for remedial action; and/or

321. The principles derive from the 'rule of law'. These principles are also part of the EU law, *see* Suzanne Kingston, Veerle Heyvaert and Alexandra Cavoski, *European Environmental Law*, 2017, at 90.
322. C-141/12 *YA*, paras 67 and 68.

(c) economic compensation. The general rule is that the owner of 'damaged' property may only demand compensation for restoration, if the cost of restoration is not disproportionate to the value of the damaged property.[323]

To be able to understand Danish legal and political structures and culture, it is important to be aware of the use of political agreements in the Danish legislative process as well as the importance of Danish tradition of close cooperation between the representatives of the regulated sector, the ministerial civil servants, and to a certain extent, the political parties. Both the political agreements and the agreements with the business sectors affect the legal design. Political agreements between (some of) the political parties represented in the Danish Parliament and the Government are used to ensure that the priority in the environmental legislation is not (always) changing by change of government. The use of such agreements was started in the 1970s to ensure more long-term energy political priorities. The political agreements are now also used to ensure a high priority to economic interest of the business – especially as a support to the agricultural sector and other parts of the food sector – with consequences for environmental protection. The use of environmental agreements between the Danish government and the business sectors was instituted directly by the Environmental Protection Act in 1992. It calls for the encouragement of voluntary commitments or agreements to achieve clear environmental objectives, including establishing procedures in the event of non-compliance. The agreements encourage polluters to accept certain standards on a voluntary basis in order to avoid a situation where other instruments may put a larger financial burden on them. The authorities also make use of voluntary agreements to reduce emissions and to ensure the recycling of waste materials, e.g., establishing take-back obligations (producer responsibility). Agreements with farmers – instituted in some acts in 1998 – are other examples of the compromise culture. By way of example can be mentioned, the voluntary agreements on full compensation to the farmers are used as far as possible to protect the drinking water against pollution from agricultural production.[324] Taking back the obligations ensured by voluntary agreements with the industry in combination with mandatory obligations are used in the implementation of several EU waste directives.

31. Access for the public to all environmental information collected by private as well as public actors and access to the environmental documents are one of the three important procedural rights. It is an important prerequisite to the exercise of the right to full participation in the political process as well as to the access to justice rights.[325] The PRTR Protocol provides more concrete obligations on how to ensure information about industrial pollution. The PRTR Regulation requires those EU institutions and bodies to assist and provide guidance to the public – including the public living in Denmark – with regard to access to environmental information.

323. Concerning the negligence approach in Danish case law, *see infra* para. 344.
324. Concerning the use of agreements as means to protect the drinking water against pollution from agricultural production, *see infra* paras 116.
325. United Nations Economic & Social Affairs, *United Nations E-Government Survey 2016*, at 22, with reference to this condition for achieving inclusive and participatory decision-making as called for in UN's 2030 Agenda.

The access to environmental information includes not only data on the status of environmental media but also information about the factors that affect human health and elements of the environment – such as relevant substances, activities, administrative measures, policies, legislation, plans and programmes. The parties to the Aarhus Convention are required to process and update environmental information that is relevant to their functions. It is mandatory for the parties, within their legislation, to make such information available to the 'public' in a transparent manner, cf. Article 5(1)–(2). The 'public concerned' must also be informed about decisions concerning the permission of specific projects and activities that may have a significant effect on the environment to make participation in the authorities' decision-making possible.

The Convention's 'first pillar' on public access to environmental information is implemented by two main secondary legislations. The Aarhus Regulation[326] establishes such rights for the European citizens and other parts of the 'public' if they want to receive information from the EU institutions and bodies,[327] and the Directive on Public Access to Environmental Information[328] establishes the obligation for the Member States to ensure such rights for their citizens and other parts of the 'public'. The Directive and the Aarhus Regulation are both following the Aarhus Convention in their description of scope, objectives and terms.[329] Therefore, the national parliaments – including the Danish Parliament – must adopt national legislation that establishes clear legal rights on access to environmental information in harmony with the objects and provisions of the Directive and the Convention. The provisions of this Directive and the Convention have 'direct effect' in the national systems, if the national provisions do not ensure such rights for the citizens to environmental information held by public authorities.[330] The definition of such authorities and bodies is laid down in Article 2(1) letter c) of the Aarhus Regulation and in Article 2(2) of the Directive on Access to Environmental Information. The definition includes both traditional authorities with and without a specific environmental public function or objective at all levels of government as well as private entities having public functions or responsibilities. It includes all aspects of the entities which have public functions, responsibilities and/or provide public services,[331] and it covers as a minimum utilities that are publicly owned, and it may furthermore

326. European Parliament and Council Regulation No. 1367/2006/EC on the Application of the Aarhus Convention on Access to Information, Public Participation and Access to Justice in Environmental Matters to Community Institutions and Bodies.

327. The Aarhus Regulation is supplemented by the general Regulation No. 1049/2001/EC regarding Public Access to European Parliament. As another regulation that ensures the public access to information at EU level, *see* the REACH Regulation (1907/2006/EC) that includes some rules on public access to environmental information held by the European Chemical Agency (ECHA). Concerning the REACH Regulation, *see infra* para. 210.

328. European Parliament and Council Directive 2003/4/EC on Public Access to Environmental Information.

329. There are several other directives containing similar information requirements that the Member States have to ensure. The Directive on European Emissions Trading Scheme, the Seveso III Directive, and the Directive on the Deliberate Release of GMO are examples.

330. Concerning CJEU case law on the direct effect of Directives, *see supra* para. 58.

331. Jonas Ebbesson, *Public Participation and Privatisation in Environmental Matters: An Assessment of the Aarhus Convention*, Erasmus Law Review, 4(2), 2011, at 71–89.

cover utilities performing environmental-related public services that are subject to regulatory control. In CJEU Case C-279/12 *Fish Legal v. Information Commissioner etc.* it was stated that for the purpose of interpreting the Directive, account is to be taken of the wording and aim of the Aarhus Convention. In the use of the phrase 'natural or legal persons performing public administration under national law', it should be examined, whether the relevant entities (in the relevant case: the water companies) are vested under the relevant national law with special powers beyond those which results from the normal rules applicable in relations between persons governed by private law. So, if anyone is asking for environmental information from a Danish municipally owned water utility (or any other utility covered by the just-mentioned criteria), this utility is required to disclose environmental information, which it holds in the context of supply of public water services.

The term 'environmental information' means any available information in written, visual, aural or database form on the state of water, air, soil, fauna, flora, land and natural sites, and on activities or measures adversely affecting or likely so to affect these, and on activities or measures designed to protect these (including administrative measures and environmental management programmes).[332] Access to such information is established by Article 3 of the Aarhus Regulation and Article 3 of the Directive. The EU institutions as well as the Member States have to respect the obligation established by the Directive to make such information available at national level upon request without the applicant has to state an interest. Article 4 of the Regulation and Article 3(5) of the Directive oblige EU institutions and the Member States to ensure that public authorities will provide information, guidance and advice on the right of access to environmental information. If a request is formulated in a very general manner, the public authority shall as soon as possible, and at the latest within the time-frame laid down in Article 3(2) letter a), ask the applicant to specify the request and shall assist the applicant in doing so, cf. Article 3(3) of the Directive. The accepted exceptions are listed in Article 4(1) of the Directive as:[333]

(a) the information is not held by the authority itself;
(b) the request is manifestly unreasonable;
(c) the request is formulated in too general manner, taking into account Article 3(3) of the Directive;[334]
(d) the request concerns material in the course of competition or unfinished documents or materials;
(e) the request concerns internal communication, taking into account the public interest served by disclosure;

332. *See* the definition of 'environmental information' in Arts 2(1) letter d) of the Aarhus Regulation and Art. 2(1) of the Directive on Environmental Information that are both in harmony with the definition laid down in the Aarhus Convention.

333. Concerning application and exception requests for access to the 'Community institutions and body's environmental information', *see* Art. 6 of the Aarhus Regulation.

334. Article 3(3) is stating that the authorities must as soon as possible ask the applicant to specify the request, and they shall assist the applicant in doing so.

(f) the confidentiality of personal data and/or files related to a natural person where that person has not consented to the disclosure of the information to the public, where such confidentiality is provided for by national or EU law;
(g) the interests or protection of any person who supplied the information requested on a voluntary basis without being under, or capable of being put under, a legal obligation to do so, unless that person has consented to the release of the information required; and
(h) the protection of the environment to which such information relates, such as the location of rare species.

The grounds for refusal shall be interpreted in a restrictive way, considering for the particular case the public interest served by disclosure. In every particular case, the public interest served by disclosure shall be weighed against the interest served by the refusal, *see* 'the public interest test' in Article 4(4) of the Directive.[335] The 'public interests test' laid down in the Directive and the Regulation is in harmony with Article 4(4) of the Convention that establishes a presumption of access, as the 'public authority' can only deny access on certain listed grounds and after having ensured a priority to the interest in access to information. The national authorities may not refuse requests that relate to information on emissions into the environment, if the reason for such a decision is the interest mentioned *supra,* if they are stated in Article 4(4) letters a), d), f), g) or h) of the Directive. The Member States also have to set up registers and lists of environmental information in order to facilitate access to this information, and they have to provide general information to the public on the state of the environment by such means as periodical descriptive reports, cf. Article 7 of the Directive.[336] It is an implementation of Article 5(9) of the Aarhus Convention that requires the parties and their public authorities progressively to establish a coherent, national wide system of pollution inventories or registers.

The Danish implementation of the provisions of the Convention and the Directive is complicated and problematic. The Danish Act on Access to Environmental Information[337] is a minimum implementation. It provides access to information from all administrative authorities and organisations and enterprises, which are partially or fully owned by the public, and in some instances information from the courts, cf. section 1 of the Act. There are no formal requirements regarding the form in which requests for information must be made. Where the information relates to emissions into the environment, the national authorities are obligated to accept the request under the same conditions that are stated in the Directive, cf. section 2(5) of the Act. The problems connected to the design of the Danish Act are related to the fact that the exceptions to access to environmental information are based on references to the rules laid down in the Act on Administrative Procedure (in the 2013

335. The public interest test is also part of the obligations placed on the EU institutions' and bodies' by Art. 6(1) of the Aarhus Regulation.
336. The obligations on the collection and dissemination of environmental information by the EU institutions and bodies are laid down in Arts 4–5 of the Aarhus Regulation.
337. Promulgation Order No. 980 of 16 September 2017 on Access to Environmental Information.

version of the Act)[338] and the rules laid down in the 1985 Act on Public Files.[339] The consequence of this design is that the content of the Danish rules are not exactly the same as those listed in the Directive.[340] Of these two old general acts, the Act on Administrative Procedure is establishing access to information and the rights of the individual person or company with a direct, personal and legitimate interest in an individual case in which they are parties (individual significant interest). This 'right of contradiction' is related to the traditional human rights to be protected against the public authorities' misuse of public power.[341] Neighbours and other third parties (e.g., environmental organisations), who require information from public authorities, have only access to such documents under the old 1985 Act on Access to Public Files.[342] Under this old Act, everybody has a right to inspect documents in administrative cases, if they can indicate the identity of the case in question. There are no formal requirements regarding the form in which requests may be made under this Act. It is a general modification to the use of these old acts that the authorities that are required to give access to environmental information have to respect the 'public interest test' when they assess the interest in the information and weigh the interest served by the refusal, cf. section 3(2) of Act on Access to Environmental Information. The time limits for the authorities' response established by the Act on Access to Environmental Information is following the Directive on Access to Environmental Information Article 3(2) letter a) – as soon as possible and

338. In s. 14 of Act No. 639 of 12 June 2013 on the Amendment of Several Acts as a Consequence of Act No. 606 of 12 June 2013 on Access to Public Information, it is stated that the new s. 6(2) in the Act on Freedom of Access to Environmental Information has to be used together with a version of the Act on Administrative Procedure from 2012 (Promulgation Order No. 988 of 9 October 2012). The newer versions of the Act (currently Promulgation Order No. 1284 of 14 November 2018) must not be used. This regulatory solution makes the use of the rules on access to environmental information very complicated and the application of the rules very inconsistent.

339. In s. 14 of Act No. 639 of 12 June 2013 on the Amendment of Several Acts as a Consequence of Act No. 606 of 12 June 2013 on Access to Public Information, it is stated that a new s. 6(2) in Act on Freedom of Access to Environmental Information still has to be used together with the old version of these acts. *See* s. 42(3) of Act No. 606 of 12 June 2013 (as amended) stating that its scope is not including environmental information.

340. The Danish rules are laid down in ss 2 and 4 of the Act on Access to Environmental Information.

341. Promulgation Order No. 433 of 22 April 2014 on Administrative Procedure, as amended by Act No. 503 of 23 May 2018. The amendment was passed to ensure respect for EU Regulation No. 2016/679/EU of 26 April 2016 on Protection of Natural Persons with regard to the Processing of Personal Data and the Free Movement of Such Data (General Data Protection Regulation). The 'right of contradiction' presumes that the public authorities are obliged to ensure that the addressee of a decision is aware of the existence of a case that affects him or her, and that the addressees have access to factual data in particular documents available to the authorities. Furthermore, he or she must be entitled to express an opinion prior to the decision of the authorities, or to apply for a suspension of the decision until he or she has had an opportunity to make a statement.

342. Act No. 572 of 19 December 1985 on Access to Public Files. In all other cases than cases related to environmental information, this Act is no longer in force. It has been replaced by Act No. 606 of 12 June 2013 on Access to Public Files, as amended by Act No. 503 of 23 May 2018 (passed to ensure respect for the General Data Protection Regulation).

normally within one month and in special situations within a two-month limit.[343] The payment obligations are those established by the Directive and the Aarhus Convention.[344]

32. The 'second pillar' of the Aarhus Convention ensures the public concerned their rights to public participation in decision making on projects (Article 6) and the Convention on Environmental Impact Assessment in a Transboundary Context (the Espoo Convention)[345] is another important international instrument that contributes to environmental direct democracy and transparency in decision making on projects.[346] The obligations on the parties (and their public authorities) to ensure environmental awareness by use of EIA procedures are part of EU and Danish legislations. The Aarhus Convention and the Espoo Convention prohibit discrimination on the basis of citizenship, nationality or domicile against persons that seek to exercise their rights.

The Espoo Convention introduces specific rules for an EIA of activities located on the territory of one contracting party (defined as the party of origin), and likely to cause significant transboundary impact in another contracting party, defined as the affected party. The term 'impact' that is very important in its broad scope means:

> any effect caused by the proposed activity on the environment including human health and safety, flora, fauna, soil, air, water, climate, landscape and historical monuments or other physical structures or the interaction among these factors; it also includes effects on cultural heritage or socio-economic conditions resulting from alterations to those factors.

The parties to the Conventions – e.g., the EU and Denmark – shall take the necessary legal, administrative or other measures to ensure that the specific rules for conducting an EIA procedure of proposed activities follow six key steps:

(1) notification and transmittal of information, cf. Article 3 of the Convention;
(2) preparation of the EIA information/report by the developer, cf. Article 4 and Appendix II of the Convention;
(3) public participation, dissemination of information and consultation, cf. Article 2(2) and (6), Articles 3(8) and 4(2) of the Convention;

343. In the 1985 Act on Access to Public Files the time scale for the authorities' response is ten days. Within this timeframe, the authorities have to state whether access will be permitted or not, or whether the case is uncertain.

344. There are two statutory orders on payments. Statutory Order No. 939 of 10 October 2015 on Payments for Access to Environmental Information in other forms than on Paper under the Ministry for Transport and the Ministry for Energy, and Statutory Order No. 1431 of 13 December 2006 on Payments for Access to Environmental Information in other Forms than on Paper under the Ministry of Environment and Food of Denmark.

345. The Espoo Convention was adopted in 1991 in Espoo/Finland. It came into force in 1997. There are forty-five parties to the Convention – including the EU and Denmark.

346. *See* Jonas Ebbesson, *A Modest Contribution to Environmental Democracy and Justice in Transboundary Contexts: The Combined Impact of the Espoo Convention and Aarhus Convention*, Review of European Community & International Environmental Law (RECIEL), 20(3), 2011, at 248–257.

(4) consultations between parties, cf. Article 5 of the Convention;
(5) examination of the information gathered and final decision, cf. Article 6(1) of the Convention; and
(6) dissemination of information on the final decision, cf. Article 6(2) of the Convention.

To improve the efficiency and transparency of the Espoo Convention's application and to increase synergies with other multilevel environmental agreements and other relevant legislations the 'Meeting of the Parties to the Convention' decided to amend some of the provisions of the Convention in 2004. These amendments came into force on 23 October 2017, ninety days after the date of deposit by Denmark of the last missing (thirteenth) instrument of acceptance by parties to the Convention.[347] The list of activities subject to the Convention was aligned with the EIA Directive that is described *infra*.

In the Preamble of the Aarhus Convention it is explained that public participation enhances the quality and implementation of decisions, contributes to public awareness of environmental issues, gives the public an opportunity to express its concerns and enables the authorities to take due account of such concerns. The 'second pillar' of this Convention involves rules on a right for the public concerned to take part in decision-making on projects, cf. Article 6 of this Convention. Each party (involving both the EU and Denmark) shall strive to promote effective public participation at an appropriate stage in decision-making on specific activities/projects (the 'second pillar' of the Convention).[348] Article 6(2) of the Convention states the obligations for the parties in respect to ensuring that the public concerned can take part in decision-making on projects. It says that:

> the public concerned shall be informed, either by public notice or individually as appropriate, early in an environmental decision–making procedure, and in an adequate, timely and effective manner, inter alia, of: (a) the proposed activity and the application on which a decision will be taken; (b) the nature of possible decisions or the draft decision; (c) the public authority responsible for making the decision; (d) the envisage procedure … and (e) the fact that the activity is subject to a national or transboundary impact assessment procedure.

The term 'public concerned' means the public affected or likely to be affected, or having an interest in, the environmental decision-making. For the purposes of this definition, non-governmental organisations (NGOs) promoting environmental protection and meeting any requirements under national law are deemed to have an interest, cf. Article 2(5) of the Aarhus Convention.

The Espoo Convention and the 'second pillar' of the Aarhus Convention have been implemented into EU law by the following secondary legislative acts:

347. Information on this issue is available at the homepage of the UNECE.
348. The general rules on public participation rights are in a Danish context, especially relevant as part of the planning process, cf. ss 23a–28 of the Planning Act. The rules on spatial planning are described *infra* in Part III.

- The decision-making at EU level is regulated by the Aarhus Regulation.
- The decision-making at national level has to be based on the minimum requirements laid down in the Directive on Public Participation,[349] the EIA Directive[350] and the IED.[351] The public concerned has rights at national level based on the direct effect of the provisions laid down in these directives.[352]

The scope of the general public participation procedure is defined primarily in Annex I of the Directive on Public Participation.[353] The obligations on use of the procedural steps included in an EIA are more complicated. In line with the drive for smarter regulation, the 2014 amendment of the EIA Directive aims to simplify and update the rules on EIA. The Directive includes a definition of EIA in Article 1(2) letter g). It means a process consisting of:

- preparation of an EIA report by the developer;
- carrying out consultations;
- examination by the competent authority of the information presented in the EIA report and any supplementary information provided, where necessary, by the developer and any other relevant information received through the consultations;
- reasoned conclusion by the competent authority on the significant effects that the project has on the environment; and
- integration of the competent authority's reasoned conclusion into any decisions full or partly made on the basis of the reasoned conclusion.

The EIA Directive is based on the 'polluter pays principle' and the 'prevention principle'. The duty to carry out an EIA therefore lies with the developer of the project. The EIA obligations always apply to public and private project types included in Annex I, cf. Article 4(1). The projects listed in Annex I are, e.g., crude oil, thermal power stations and other combustion installations, installations for the intensive rearing of poultry pigs, wastewater treatment plans, extraction of petroleum and natural gas for commercial purposes, pipelines for transport of gas, oil or

349. European Parliament and Council Directive 2003/35/EC of 26 May 2003 provides for Public Participation in Respect of drawing up Certain Plans and Programs related to the Environment – as amended by Directive 2016/2284/EU on the Reduction of National Emissions of Certain Atmospheric Pollutants.
350. European Parliament and Council Directive 2011/92/EC of 13 December 2011 on the Assessment of the Effects on certain Public and Private Projects on the Environment, as amended by European Parliament and Council Directive 2014/52/EU of 16 April 2014. An unofficial document with the amendments is available at: http://ec.europa.eu/environment/eia/pdf/EIA_Directive_informal.pdf. The present content of the EIA Directive (as amended in 2014) came into force on 15 May 2014, and it had to be implemented by the Member States in national law no later than 17 May 2017.The first EIA Directive was Council Directive 85/337/EEC of 27 June 1985 on the Assessment of the Effects on certain Public and Private Projects on the Environment.
351. European Parliament and Council Directive 2010/75/EU of 24 November 2010 on the industrial emissions (integrated pollution prevention and control). *See infra* para. 61 the description of the IE Directive.
352. Concerning CJEU case law on the 'direct effect' of clear directive rules, *see infra* para. 58.
353. European Parliament and Council Directive 2003/35/EC on the Public Participation in respect of drawing up certain Plans and Programmes relating to the Environment, as amended by Directive 2016/2284/EU on the reduction of national Emissions of certain Atmospheric Pollutants.

chemicals, offshore wind farms, and installations for storage of petroleum, petrochemical, or chemical production. This Annex on mandatory EIA – with the rights for the public concerned to public participation in the decision-making – is not covering all the projects that are included in Article 6(1) and Annex 1 of the Aarhus Convention. The projects that are not covered by the EIA Directive are covered by the Directive on Public Participation, and some are covered by Annex II of the EIA Directive. The developers of Annex II-projects have only to respect the EIA obligations, if the responsible national authorities are of the opinion that the consequences of the proposed projects are expected to be significant. The detailed information that needs to be provided as part of the assessment by the developer when determining whether a project listed in Annex II requires an EIA are listed in Annex II.a. The current rules are providing the Member States the choice to establish a system under which the authorities on a case-by-case examination (a scoping) assess the necessity of EIA of Annex II projects or to set general thresholds and/or other criteria in a clear and transparent legal framework. The case-by-case assessment and the general thresholds/criteria have to be determined by the criteria listed in Annex III, cf. Article 4(3) of the Directive. The characteristics of projects that are listed in Annex III under point 1 are: (a) their size and the design of the whole project; (b) accumulation with other existing and/or approved projects; (c) the use of natural resources, in particular land, soil, water and biodiversity; (d) the production of waste; (e) pollution and nuisances; (f) the risk of major accidents and/or disasters, which are relevant to the project concerned, including those caused by climate change, in accordance with scientific knowledge; (g) the risks to human health (e.g., due to water contamination or air pollution). The location of the projects is another aspect that the authorities have to include in the scooping, cf. Annex III under section 2. Among these location-related aspects are areas classified or protected under national legislation and Natura 2000 sites designated by Member States pursuant to the Wild Birds Directive or the Habitats Directive.

The information that is required from the developer that applies for the approval of a project listed in Annex I and the approval of a project listed in Annex II in situations in which EIA is required is stated in Article 5(1) and Annex IV:

- *Project description*: A description of the location and the physical characteristics of the whole project, including, where relevant, requisite demolition works, and the land-use requirement during the construction and operational phases; the main characteristics of the operational phase of the project, for instance, energy demand and energy used, natural resources used; expected emissions and waste produced.
- *Project alternatives*: Any aspects of the project that could be achieved in a number of ways should be explained. The description has to include an outline of the main alternatives studied by the developer and an indication of the main reasoning for the developer's choice, taking into account the environmental effects.
- *Baseline scenario*: A description of the relevant aspects of the current state of the environment and an outline of the likely evolution thereof.
- *Environment description and the significant environmental effects*: The factors that have to be described include the factors specified in Article 3(1) likely to be

significantly affected by the project: population, human health, biodiversity, land, soil, water, air, climate, material assets, cultural heritage and landscape.
- *Mitigation*: A description of the measures envisaged to avoid, prevent, reduce or, if possible, offset any identified adverse effects that the project has on the environment.
- *Non-technical Summary*: The EIA has to include a summary that makes it possible for the public to understand the project and the assessment.
- *A reference list*: If the authority needs further information, it has the power to require the developer to provide such information. When the competent authority has received the project proposal including the EIA, the authority shall circulate it to relevant authorities and make it available to the public concerned (incl. NGOs) for comments. The consultation on the basis of the Directive can be transboundary, if the proposed project will have effects in other states.[354] The comments received from the public concerning any EIA shall be taken into account by the responsible authority in its EIA examination, and the authority is under a duty to consider whether the EIA report is up to date at the point of decision. The final decision must include a reasonable conclusion on the significant effects that the project has on the environment. The EIA shall be completed before a decision on approval of projects likely to have significant effects on the environment is made, and the decision-maker shall consider it.

Denmark has implemented the obligations under the Espoo Convention and the EIA Directive by the following legislative acts and statutory orders:

(1) Part III of Act on Strategic Environmental Assessment and EIA (hereinafter the Danish SEA and EIA Act)[355] and the Statutory Order on the Coordination of Environmental Impact Assessment and Digital Self-Service[356] that covers the situations in which EIA problems have to be solved.
(2) Statutory Order on the Monitoring, Coordination and Publication of the Environmental Impact Assessment (EIA) of State-Owned Road and Railway projects.[357]

The municipalities are responsible for the EIA procedure in most cases, cf. section 17(1) of the Danish SEA and EIA Act. The regional councils have the EIA competences in cases on the extraction of mineral resources, cf. section 17(2) of this Act. The Ministry of Environment and Food of Denmark and its agencies have the EIA competences in connection with most of the projects that are located on the sea area. If such a project is regulated by the Coast Protection Act, it is the municipality that

354. Cf. Art. 7 of the EIA Directive.
355. Promulgation Order No. 1225 of 25 October 2018 on the Strategic Environmental Assessment of Plans and Programmes and the Environmental Impact Assessment of Individual Projects – the SEA and EIA Acts.
356. Statutory Order No. 1470 of 13 December 2017 on the Coordination of Environmental Assessment and Digital Self-service etc. of Plans, Programs and Individual Projects covered by the Act on SEA and EIA.
357. Statutory Order No. 451 of 8 May 2017 on the Monitoring, Coordination and Publication of the Environmental Impact Assessment (EIA) of State-Owned Road and Railway Projects.

has the competence, cf. section 17(2) of the Danish SEA and EIA Act. If the sea-based project is related to extraction of hydrocarbons, the location of pipelines or of energy production utilities, the Ministry for Climate, Energy and Utilities and has the competence, cf. section 17(3) of the Danish SEA and EIA Act. The establishment of offshore wind turbines can follow two different procedures: a government tender procedure run by the Energy Agency and an open-door procedure. The right to exploit wind energy within the Danish waters is in both situations depending on a permission to carry out preliminary investigations (including as a minimum an EIA as well as geophysical and geotechnical surveys of the seabed to clarify what type of foundation should be used) and later a final approval of the project granted by the Energy Agency. Public participation is ensured in both these decision-making processes.

The 'public concerned' concept has *not* been implemented into Danish legislation that implements the Convention – the rules use only the term 'the public'. The involvement of the public is today ensured by publications on homepages without a special focus on the interests of the 'public concerned'. As the CJEU has clarified the doctrine of direct effect of clear provisions in directives that ensure rights for the citizens and the principle of judicial protection in relation to the EIA directive before the national courts and other national authorities, any Danish rules that are incompatible with the clear rights established under the Directive have to be set aside by the Danish authorities.[358]

The number of EIA screenings in Denmark has increased dramatically since 2000. This is first and foremost a consequence of increased pig production as well as the concentration of large farms. In the same period, EIA rules have been developed primarily due to an increased focus on the protection of groundwater and Natura 2000 sites. As an alternative to the case-by-case decision-making (scoping) on Annex II projects, Denmark is using its competence under the Article 4(3) of the EIA Directive to establish general thresholds and criteria laid down in its digitalisation-ready legislation. This regulatory design is used with the ambition to make it possible for the State to automatise the decision-making process without giving the authorities a discretionary power.[359] Large-scale transboundary projects – including projects presented by operators outside Denmark – have to be assessed in accordance with the Espoo Convention, the EIA Directive and the Danish EIA legislation, if the projects are located inside the Danish jurisdiction. This is currently relevant with the Russian Nord Stream 2 AG's application and EIA report handed in April 2017 to the Danish Energy Agency on a pipeline system passing through Danish territorial waters as well at the application and an EIA report of 10 August 2018 to the Danish Energy Agency for an alternative route passing through the Danish EEZ to the north-west of Bornholm. Germany, Sweden, Finland and

358. *See, e.g.*, the judgment in C-201/02 *Delena Weels* and the description of the CJEU case law *infra* in para. 57.

359. By way of example it may be mentioned, Act No. 204 of 28 February 2017 on the New Regulatory Design of Agriculture.

Denmark consider themselves as 'parties of origin' under the Espoo Convention. The Russian Federation is acting as a 'party of origin' in so far as it is possible according to its legislation.[360]

33. The 'second pillar' of the Aarhus Convention involves also rules on a right for the public concerned to take part in decision-making on plans, programmes and politics related to the environment (Article 7), and to take part in the decision-making on the preparation of executive regulation and/or generally applicable legally binding normative instruments (Article 8). The same applies to the aims behind the passing of the Protocol on Strategic Environmental Assessment (hereinafter 'SEA Protocol') under the Espoo Convention.[361] The Aarhus Convention and the Protocol prohibit discrimination on the basis of citizenship, nationality or domicile against persons that seek to exercise their rights. These obligations are part of EU and Danish legislation.

The implementation of the obligations under Articles 6 and 7 of the Aarhus Convention into EU law has been made by different secondary legislative acts, where the obligations for the EU institutions again have to be found in the Aarhus Regulation. The obligations for national authorities are laid down, e.g., in:

- The Waste Framework Directive that established the obligation to ensure public participation in the waste management planning and the decision-making on waste prevention programmes.[362]
- The Packaging and Packaging Waste Directive that established the obligation to ensure public participation in the decision making on waste management plans.[363]
- The Air Quality Directive that established the obligation to ensure public participation in the decision-making on the design of the air quality plans for zones in which the air emission exceeds the limit values.[364]

---

360. Russia is a signatory, but not a party, to the Convention. The project on 'Nord Stream II' is a planned twin pipeline system through the Baltic Sea that can transport natural gas from the world's largest reserve in Northern Russia to the EU. *See* the EIA of the alternative pipeline route presented by the operator on 10 Aug. 2018, https://ens.dk/sites/ens.dk/files/OlieGas/11_-_environmental_impact_assessment_denmark._nord_stream_2_-_north-western_route._august_2018.pdf (visited December 2018). The permit is being evaluated by the Minister of Foreign Affairs as the construction can only be granted, if the project is compatible with national foreign, security and defence policy interests, cf. s. 3a(2) of the Act on the Continental Shelf and Certain Pipeline Installations in the Territorial Waters.
361. The SEA Protocol was passed in 2003, and it entered into force on 11 Jul. 2010. The EU signed it on 12 Nov. 2008. Denmark signed it on 4 Jun. 2012.
362. Concerning European Parliament and Council Directive 2008/98/EC on Waste, as amended, *see infra* para. 145.
363. Concerning European Parliament and Council Directive 94/62/EC on Packaging and Packaging Waste, as amended, *see infra* para. 156.
364. Concerning European Parliament and Council Directive 2008/50/EC on Ambient Air Quality, *see infra* para. 75.

– Nitrates Directive that established the obligation to ensure public participation in the decision-making on the programmes for the protection of vulnerable zones.[365]

It is not always enough to ensure public participation – in some cases the obligations under the SEA Protocol to make a strategic environmental assessment (SEA) have to be respected by the authorities. The Strategic Environmental Assessment Directive (SEA Directive)[366] is the EU's implementation of the obligations with effect on the Member States. The content of a SEA is explained by the OECD as analytical and participatory approaches to strategic decision-making that aims to integrate environmental considerations into policies, plans and programmes, and evaluate the interlinkages with economic and social considerations.[367] The SEA procedure and demand on making environmental reports under the SEA Protocol and the SEA Directive is comparable to the EIA procedure under the Espoo Convention and the EIA Directive. SEA is mandatory for plans and programmes which are prepared for agricultural, forestry, fisheries, energy, industry, transport, waste management, water management, telecommunications, tourisms, town and country planning or land use and which set the framework for future development consent of projects listed in Annex I and II of the EIA Directive.[368] It is also mandatory to make an SEA as part of the preparation of plans and programmes, in view of the likely effect on Natura 2000 sites. For all other plans and programmes, which set the framework for future development content of projects, the SEA is optional. The authorities must ensure that the public is given early and effective opportunities to participate in the preparation and modification or review of projects, plans or programmes required to be drawn up under the provisions listed in the Directives. The environmental report and the result of the consultation, including transboundary consultations, have to be taken into account in the preparation of the plans/programmes, and the final plans/programmes have to be communicated to the authorities, the 'public concerned' and other parties involved in the consultation. The SEA Directive was implemented in Denmark in July 2004 by the Act on Strategic Environmental Assessment of Plans and Programmes. This Act is now replaced by the Danish 'SEA and EIA Act'.[369] Part II of this Act describes the SEA process and the competences of the authorities. Part IV of the Act explains how the authorities have to decide on who has the status as the affected authorities, who has the right to take part in the hearing process and how to ensure a publication of the SEA making it possible for the public to participate in the decision-making. The

365. Council Directive 91/676/EC of 12 December 1991 concerning the Protection of Water against Pollution caused by Nitrates from Agricultural Sector, *see infra* para. 121.

366. European Parliament and Council Directive 2001/42/EC on the Assessment of Certain Plans and Programmes on the Environment.

367. OECD, *Applying Strategic Environmental Assessment. Good Practice Guidance for Development Cooperation,* 2006.

368. Article 4 of the Protocol established the obligations for the State Parties to ensure, that the plans and programmes listed in Art. 4(2)–(3), which are likely to have significant environmental, including health, effects, are not passed without an SEA.

369. Promulgation Order No. 1225 of 25 October 2018 on the Strategic Environmental Assessment of Plans and Programmes and the Environmental Impact Assessment of Individual Projects (the SEA and EIA) – Part II consists of ss 8–14.

Danish authorities shall ensure that both the affected authorities and the public are given early and effective opportunities to participate in the preparation and modification or review of the plans or programmes. The procedural rights established by the Act have to be applied in harmony with the SEA Directive and the Directive has direct effect based on CJEU case law if it is not respected by the Danish authorities.[370] The Danish act is not using the 'public concerned' concept to ensure a special position for the NGOs. It is a right for 'the public' that is stated in section 35 of the Act, but the discretionary power of the Danish authorities in their interpretation of this term is limited by the principles of equivalence and effectiveness developed by CJEU case law that means that the national procedures cannot render implementation of EU law ineffective.[371]

34. Monitoring and reporting of emissions and the environmental status of the external environment are necessary parts of an effective environmental regulation. The rapid development of data-management technologies and WoG systems demands and enables more accurate responses, both from the authorities and those impacted, either directly or indirectly by the emissions and the environmental policy. High-quality environmental information has to be routinely provided by the authorities as the basis for their design of environmental policy and legislation, and such information has to be dismissed to the public in a user-friendly manner to ensure openness and transparency.

The INSPIRE Directive[372] lays down the rules for the establishment and operation of an infrastructure for the collection and dissemination of environmental information within the EU of relevance for the implementation of Article 5(1) of the Aarhus Convention. It sets the minimum conditions for interoperative sharing and exchange of spatial data across the EU as part of a larger European Interoperability Framework and the E-Government Action Plan that contributes to the Digital Single Market. The Directive requires Member States to establish and operate a set of network services to discover, view, transform and download spatial digitalised data set and invoke other spatial data services by the EU. It facilitates coordination between users and suppliers of information in order to combine and disseminate information originating from different sectors. Among the data included are land cover data, hydrography and ecological data on hazardous waste disposal sites, spatial planning and management, species migration and biodiversity assessment, water supply and assessment and monitoring in estimation of watercourses. The Danish Spatial Information Act[373] was passed to ensure the implementation of the INSPIRE Directive. According to Article 19(1) of the Directive, each Member State must designate a Contact Point to be responsible for the contacts with the Commission. It is the Danish Geodata Agency (CENIA) under the Ministry of Environment and Food of Denmark that is the Danish Contract Point. A wide range of environmental information

370. Case law on the direct effects of directives is described *infra* in para. 58.
371. Concerning case law on these principles, *see infra* para. 57.
372. European Parliament and Council Directive 2007/2/EC establishing an Infrastructure for Spatial Information in the Community.
373. It is now Promulgation Order No. 746 of 15 June 2017 on Spatial Information.

is publicly available and frequently updated on the Danish Environmental Portal.[374] The Portal makes it possible for any interested person to find data on emissions from the three levels of national authorities – the State, the five counties and the ninety-eight municipalities. The Portal allows the authorities to access data across administrative units, sectors and geographical areas, and consequently used as a basis for cooperation between the authorities with regard to data and E-Government. In the Commission's 2017 assessment, the status in Denmark on effective coordination of data, sharing arrangements and identification of spatial datasets, as well as the documentation of datasets and services (metadata) on the trend of the implementation is described as positive.[375] However, the provision of services for identified spatial datasets (discovery, view, download) and the provision of interoperable spatial datasets are only assessed as neutral.[376]

374. Statutory Order No. 415 of 13 May 2005 established an Obligation for the Public Authorities to Communicate Environmental Information on their own Initiative.

375. JRC Technical Reports, *Summary Report on Status of Implementation of the INSPIRE Directive in EU*, 2017, at 8, 10, 13 and 17.

376. JRC Technical Reports, *Summary Report on Status of Implementation of the INSPIRE Directive in EU*, 2017, at 20 and at 22.

Chapter 3. Historical Background

35. The Danish legal system is generally considered to be a civil law system, although in common with other Scandinavian legal systems not as influenced by Roman law as other European civil law systems. In part, the legal traditions are characterised by the traditions of continental European law in which the administrative law is central.

The description of the history of Danish environmental law starts in this paragraph with information on the first generation dating back more than 200 years.[377] The vertical harmonisation of international law, EU and national environmental law has a strong impact on the third generation of Danish environmental law.[378] The protection and conservation of the landscape were initially (as the first generation of environmental law) based on neighbour law, tort law and some public regulation of building activities. The protection of coastal areas by zoning dates back to 1792. Protection of forests has been part of Danish policy since 1805, the year of the Royal Decree concerning the improvement, maintenance and conservation of forests. Already in this decree, it was decided that all forest areas have to be kept forested in perpetuity, and the owners would be responsible for the maintenance and improvement of those forests. The Watercourse Act dates back to 1880. The most important element of this Act was to ensure the right to drain water away from farmland. However, in the eighteenth and the nineteenth centuries, the landscape in Denmark was also radically changed by projects to prevent sand drifts and other projects accepted by the legislator. The Danish waste handling system was based on landfills until 1900. The first municipal waste incineration plant was built in 1903 in Copenhagen using the energy generated for production of both heat and electricity. Two other municipalities followed the example in the 1930s. As part of the first generation of environmental law, general regulations on the protection of health were laid down in the by-laws on Health already in the 1850s. The Public Health Statutes of 1852 was the first – and very weak – legislation providing regulation for sanitation, water supply and water protection. The burying of toxic waste in containers made out of a perishable material was covered by the local by-laws, which were made by special communities in accordance with the Act. Most of the sewerage network in the capital (Copenhagen) was laid down between 1860 and 1910. Until 1892, the contents of latrines were still collected and driven to the countryside for fertilisation. The rest of the sewage was let into the sea, causing extreme odour and sedimentation of sludge. The first overall plan for the public services in relation to water, sewerage and gas was approved in 1851 and implemented from 1860 to 1885 in order to improve the conditions of the city. Water closets were not used before 1897. Intercepting sewers were installed along the harbours from 1893 to 1903 to pump most of the wastewater into the sea. The sewerage system of the western part

377. General pollution control and the protection of health as part of the second generations of environmental law are described *infra* in para. 36. The special aspects relating to the protection of drinking water and health against soil contamination and the handling of liability issues in case law are described *infra* in para. 37. Concerning the third generation of environmental and planning law – introduced by the 1992 reform – *see infra* para. 38.

378. Concerning the vertical harmonisation of environmental law, *see infra* paras 39 and 54–59.

of Copenhagen was established as a biological treatment system from 1904 to 1920 to reduce the water pollution. Before 1950, wastewater from homes and enterprises was mostly sent directly into the watercourses, lakes and sea without having been treated. It was a fundamental assumption under Danish law that the environment could and should be used as a medium for disposal of every kind of fluid and solid waste. And, as assumed, the aquatic, atmospheric and terrestrial environment were capable of performing tremendous scavenging, assimilating and dispersing functions. In the 1930s, new rules on the general planning of cities, etc. came into force – based on the Act on City Planning. The Danish protection and conservation of the landscape and the cultural heritage in Denmark were recognised to be of utmost importance by a Royal Decree of 1805 on the conservation of communal forest and by the Parliament's adoption of the Nature Conservation Act in 1917. In 1937, some protection lines were introduced as part of the Nature Conservation Act. Such protection lines limited (and they are still limiting) the landowners' building rights in a zone around forests and the coast. Until 1937, protection of ancient monuments was based on voluntary preservation. From 1969, the Nature Protection Act replaced the 1917 Nature Conservation Act. Adoption of the first Building Conservation Act in 1918 created the foundation for the preservation of the finest old buildings. The basic principles laid down in this Act have been maintained up to the present time. The provisions have been expanded and made more stringent on several occasions.

Before the 1973 environmental protection reform, the protection of fresh water against pollution had been regulated in the Water Supply Act of 1926, the later version thereof dating from 1969. The first Watercourse Act was passed by the Parliament in 1949. By an amendment to this Act in 1963, the former regional counties and the municipal councils took over the bank owners' obligation to maintain public watercourses under the Watercourse Act.

The Forest Act of 1935 replaced the Royal Decree of 1805, ensuring that a large proportion of the country remained forested by imposing a special maintenance obligation on the owners.

36. Historically, the legal status of real estate and land ownership has been very similar in the Scandinavian countries, but recent administrative and environmental developments have led to different national legislative measures and procedures. One reason for this difference has been the ongoing change in the functions of the main institutions such as land use, planning, pollution control (with its permit systems), and the protection of nature resources. At the same time, the impact from EU environmental law on the horizontal harmonisation of the national legislation is of importance in all these countries as three of them (Sweden, Finland and Denmark) are Member States, and the other States (Norway and Island) are members of the Agreement on the European Economic Area.[379]

Two acts on spatial planning were passed in the 1970s: The National and Regional Planning Act of 1973 and the Municipal Planning Act of 1975. They were all part of the second generation of environmental and planning law. The Urban and

379. As mentioned *supra* in para. 30, Danish environmental law is strongly rooted in the traditions of administrative law.

Rural Zones Act was as indicated introduced as the first stage of a planning act reform. The Act was no ordinary Planning Act, which confers powers to make plans, but it worked on the basis of plans and the planning system. In conformity with this, the principal purpose of the Act was to reduce urban sprawl and to ensure a planned and expedient development in terms of the national economy, in accordance with the national, regional and municipal planning. Another of the important goals of the Act was to contribute to the safeguarding of the population's recreation interests and the maintenance of rural amenities. Finally, the Act aimed to help to secure an expedient use of raw material resources and agricultural area resources. By means of two other Acts, the Act on National and Regional Planning and the Municipal Planning Act, a system was instituted whereby sector authorities could veto a coordinated plan if the plan conflicted with the special interests which those sector authorities were designed to safeguard. In Denmark most sector planning has, at least for the last sixteen years, been included in the physical planning. The Nature Protection Act was amended in 1978 in order to incorporate conservation planning into overall physical planning. Under the Act, an elaborate planning system was provided for including prior mapping, analysis and assessment of the conservation interests within each region. Since the amendment of the Conservation of Nature Act in 1978, there have only been a very few concrete cases on conservation. With the passing of an Act on the Changing of Different Environmental and Planning Acts in 1987, sector plans are no longer binding.

The first act on recycling and reduction of waste was the 'Can Act' from 1971, relating to containers for beer and soft drinks. It provided the framework for economic instruments and recycling activities.[380] The most important part of the second generation of environmental policy was institutionalised by the first Environmental Protection Act, which came into force on 1 October 1974. It required the operators of new landfills to apply for an environmental approval before starting up new polluting industrial activities. The primary objectives of this Act were to establish environmental regulations based on considerations of hygiene and ecological balance, to prevent and combat the pollution of air, water and soil through the use of end-of-line technologies, to stress protection of nature and the environment as a factor in its own right and to prevent and combat noise nuisance, as well as to provide the necessary administrative basis for the planning and implementation of pollution control. In accordance with this Act, which was in force until 1 January 1992, enterprises did not have to apply for approval, as long as there were no construction-related or operational changes. According to the first Environmental Protection Act, the Minister could pass administrative provisions making it mandatory for specific enterprises and plants to apply for an environmental approval within a specified time if further testing of the pollution factors was deemed especially necessary. In October 1974, the wastewater regulations of the Watercourse Act were transferred to the Environmental Protection Act. In 1982, the Watercourse Act was replaced by a new act. The idea behind the 1982 Act is expressed in its object clause. It states that the watercourse maintenance must be undertaken in a

380. Act No. 297 of 8 June 1978 on Recycling of Paper and Beverage Containers and Reduction of Waste amended the Can Act. After 1 Jan. 1992, the rules are incorporated in the new Environmental Protection Act as Chapter 7; *see infra* para. 38.

manner that takes into consideration the environmental conditions that should pertain to the water in order to ensure that the water quality norms laid down in the regional (now municipal) plans can be met. The aim of the Act was also to resolve conflicts between landowners regarding watercourse utilisation and maintenance. The first Act to regulate the marine environment exclusively was adopted in 1980 by the Environmental Marine Protection. The Enforcement Act from 1984 made the rules on enforcement in the environmental and planning acts more stringent. The first Environment and Genetic Engineering Act was adopted in 1986. It was an attempt to establish an adequate regulatory response to developments in the area of genetic engineering. In response to acidification problems, the Danish Parliament in 1989 adopted the Act on Reduction of Emission of Sulphur Dioxide and Nitrogen Oxides from Power Plants.

37. Only in the last five decades or so it has become a recognised fact that waste deposits are a threat to the environment and a health hazard for people. Since the early 1970s, Danish legislation on environmental protection has been made progressively stringent with a view to limiting such pollution. Many old urban areas are contaminated by diffuse sources.

Based on the Act on the Disposal of Oil and Chemical Waste, the Minister for Environment had the competence to make binding statutory orders concerning the duties of any person or industrial enterprise on whose premises oil or chemical waste was found. In accordance with this Act, the Statutory Order on the Disposal of Oil Waste and the Statutory Order on the Disposal of Chemical Waste were adopted. They entered into force on 1 November 1972 and 1 April 1976 respectively. These statutory orders provided that anyone storing, transporting or disposing of oil and chemical waste was responsible for ensuring that such activities did not cause any pollution of air, soil or water. According to the same statutory orders, oil and chemical waste were to be delivered to municipal receiving plants, and the municipal authorities were responsible for ensuring that disposal of the waste was made in an environmentally sound manner. The first act on investigations and remedial action on old sites was the 1983 Act on Chemical Waste Sites. The Act covered sites on which oil waste had been spilled before 1 November 1972 and/or chemical waste had been spilled or deposited before 1 April 1976. It contained requirements for the preparation of surveys of polluted sites, registration of the same sites and public financing of remedial action. On 1 September 1990, this Act was replaced by the Act on Waste Deposits. The Act governed investigations and remedial action in relation to previous waste deposits. The scope of the Act was laid down in section 1, according to which it applies only to waste deposits that may cause harmful effects to people or the environment. The waste deposits included in the scope of this historical Act were only those established before the entry into force of the legislation on environmental protection against oil and chemical waste from the beginning of the 1970s with its requirements for the public as well as internal enterprise supervision and control. The purpose of the Act was to limit environmental as well as health-related effects of pollution caused by activities in the past in all parts of Denmark. One of the characteristics of the Act was that the public authorities (the

Ministry of Environment and the former county councils) were to pay for investigations and remedial action in relation to removal of waste and reduction of environmental damage caused by the previous waste deposits. However, it was left to the same environmental authorities to determine the circumstances in which such measures needed to be taken.

In June 1991, the Supreme Court handed down a judgment stating that the liability of a property owner for polluting activities harming the environment should be based on an evaluation of negligence (culpability), if the statutory rules do not provide sufficient evidence to show that the legislator had the intention to deviate from basic principles of tort law (*culpa*) in the Rockwool Case.[381] In a judgment of 3 February 1998, the Supreme Court ruled that a landowner that had been the user of an oil tank could not be ordered to pay the cost of prevention and cleaning-up the polluted soil, if he or she had not acted in breach of the tort rules on negligence. Demonstrating liability involves certain difficulties for the environmental authorities. In practice, the result of these court judgments was that no public authority wanted to use its power to demand that polluters clean up polluted sites.[382]

38. In December 1988, the government presented its action plan on sustainability to follow-up on the recommendations in the 1987 Report 'Our Common Future' by the World Commission on the Environment (the so-called Brundtland Report). A theme of the government's action was to work towards initiatives for sustainable development in the context of international cooperation. This was regarded as the first phase of integration of environmental interests into other policy areas.

In 1991, the Parliament passed the third generation of Danish environmental law partly as a compilation and updating of the above-mentioned acts: a new Environmental Protection Act, a Planning Act and a new Mineral Resources Act. At the same time, the Parliament agreed on a new Environment and Genetic Engineering Act. Furthermore, on 1 July 1992, a new Act on Nature Protection came into force, repealing the Nature Conservation Act, the Nature Management Act and the Act on Sand Drifts. The reform was not very revolutionary, but it ensured a reduction in the number of acts, and to some degree, it ensured a more integrated approach based on the environmental principles.[383] The development of environmental and planning laws under 'the third generation of environmental law' is not only a result of national traditions and policy, but also to some extent the result of EU law, and international conventions and declarations.[384] In 1995, the Parliament amended the Watercourse Act with the aim of accelerating the recreation of an ecologically well-functioning watercourse system. In watercourses where sluices are highly detrimental to watercourse quality, the water authority may decide pursuant to the provision

381. The judgment is published in the Danish Weekly Law Reports 1991, at 674.
382. Concerning negligence as the most important legal basis, *see infra* para. 344.
383. Concerning the general reform of the Danish environmental acts in 1992, *see supra* at para. 38.
384. This coalition Government that was in power until 27 Jun. 2019 has not passed an action plan on sustainability and its policy has been focused primarily on a strong position in international competition – especially for the agriculture and food industry. On 27 Jun. 2019, a new Government took over power with the ambition to ensure a higher level of environmental protection. *See supra* para. 4 concerning the different Danish coalition governments.

of the Act to implement whatever measures are necessary to restore satisfactory environmental quality, including regulating the watercourse.

The Act on Strict Liability for Pollution Cost by Heavily Polluting Activities came into force in July 1994.[385] It was based on a Report of the Committee constituted by the Danish Ministry of Justice No. 1237/1992 on 'Liability for Environmental Damage'. The Act introduces a regime of strict liability with respect to the economic cost of restoring damage caused by the plants, i.e., only plants listed in the Environmental Protection Act of 1995 and only for damage cost incurred after the Act entered into force. In 2000, the Contaminated Soil Act came into force. The purpose of the Act is to clarify the responsibility of the polluter on an administrative law basis and to base such responsibility on the 'polluter pays principle'.[386] A Committee on the Modernisation of the Danish Environmental Law in 2017–2018 was working on a proposal on a modernisation of the law, but this report has not been part of any new proposal on a modernisation of the law.[387] Denmark has four derogations or 'opt-outs' from the cooperation in the EU, but it is not of big importance for the environmental law.[388] Many amendments of the Danish environmental legislation have been necessary to ensure implementation of the EU's more modern legislation. Other amendments are results of national compromises.

39. EU environmental action programmes (EAPs) and the modernisation of the design of environmental law have nearly a fifty-year history. Modern environmental legislation is increasingly interrelated, reflecting the overriding objective of promoting sustainable development. The obligations are more than just a matter of more or less total protection. It is also a matter of specific environmental thresholds and limits that must not be exceeded as well as the protection of ecosystems and the amount of resources.

The EU has as a 'regional economic integrated organisation' a strong power of influence on the development of international environmental law as well as the design of national environmental law – the consequences on Danish environmental law is that this national law is both increasingly interrelated and vertically harmonised with international and EU environmental law.[389] The European environmental history can be explained with focus on the EAPs, as these plans have stated the overall ambitions and guidelines for the development of legislation. For a period of some years, they set out the priority objectives, the principles and the measures to be taken as part of the EU's actions in the environmental area. The EAPs have been developed since the early 1970s before the Treaty included provisions on the legislative power of the EU institutions in the area of the environment. The EU's first

385. Concerning the Act on Strict Liability for Pollution Cost by Heavily Polluting Activities, *see infra* para. 343. This Act has, however, not been used before the Supreme Court used it in 2018 in two cases.
386. Concerning the Contaminated Soil Act, *see infra* paras 173–180.
387. The report was titled *The Legal Compass* ('Lovkompasset'). The report is in Danish, it is published at https://mfvm.dk/fileadmin/user_upload/MFVM/Lovkompas_rapport.pdf.
388. With respect to environmental law, it is first and foremost the reservations for justice and home affairs that can have impact on the Danish approach to the EU's initiatives.
389. Concerning the characteristic of the Danish environmental law as part of the vertical harmonised international, EU and national provisions, *see infra* para. 54.

five-year EAP (1EAP) was adopted in November 1973 after the first United Nations Environmental Programme (UNEP) conference (the Stockholm Conference) was held in 1972. It established the general principles: (a) the 'prevention principle'; (b) the 'polluter pays principle'; (c) the 'source principle'; and (d) the 'subsidiarity principle'. The second EAP (2EAP) covered 1977–1981. It was a follow-up in terms of approach and objective with a greater range of problems to be dealt with. Nature protection received special attention. The third EAP (3EAP – 1982–1986) reflects a considerable change in political approach, being much more closely related to the completion of the Internal Market than its predecessors. Issues linkage between the Internal Market and environmental policies became a key driver for EU policy. In 1985, the European Council adopted a Resolution on a 'New Approach' to technical harmonisation and standards that are of importance for the environmental sources of today. It was introduced as a general approach in EU legislation to ensure that environmental standards were harmonised to avoid distortion to industry competition. Product standards had to be harmonised to avoid non-tariff barriers emanating from different national products. With the decision concerning this approach, the use of voluntary means as part of the strategies concerning implementation of the 'essential requirements' applied to various products as a result of different framework directives. The harmonised standards put – as part of the 'New Approach'– a presumption of conformity with the corresponding essential requirements laid down in directives and regulations. Accurate information on existing air, water, nature, soil, etc. quality is the starting point for effective management and planning of environmental improvements.[390] Reference measurement methods for each pollutant and other relevant aspects are often developed as standards by the standardisation bodies.[391] Technical standards related to product characteristics or procedures can be either legally defined or set in voluntary standards developed by national, European or international standardisation bodies. The legislation can also include reference to standards already developed by standardisation bodies, thus making them legally binding. The technical standards applied in the EU noise directives constitute a mix of such situations. The environmental policy approach was also changed under the 3EAP, as it had more focus on waste avoidance, efficient resource use, integrated environmental technologies, emission (more than environmental quality) and a global focus (e.g., with reference to IUCN's first global strategy for 'World Conservation Strategy Living Resource Conservation for Sustainable Development', 1980). The approach in the fourth EAP (4EAP – 1987–1992) was based on an ambition to ensure a more 'integrated approach' in the regulation of the whole production process. Focus was on a sectorial approach, analysing the impact of strategic economic sectors on the environment. The evaluation of new economic and other incentive instruments was announced. The fifth EAP (5EAP – 1992–1999) was produced as the Community's main response to the 1992 Rio Earth Summit, which called the international community to develop new policies as outlined in Agenda 21. The 5EAP was divided into five target sectors (industry, energy, transport, agriculture and tourism) and seven themes (climate change, acidification/air quality, urban environment, coastal zones, waste management,

390. Concerning the PRTR provisions on data collection and reporting, *see infra* in para. 60.

391. *See*, for example, EN 12341 for the measurement of PM10 of relevance for the air quality rules.

water resources and biodiversity). It sets out objectives for each of these areas divided into EU and global levels and describes the targets and general actions needed to meet each objective. It was focused on: (a) the principal aim of sustainable development according of the definition in the Brundtland Report from 1987 and the need for an integration of environmental dimensions into all major policy areas. In the 5EAP, it was stated that in order to maintain sustainable development, environmental obligations must also be indispensable for agriculture.[392] The strategic reorientation of the policy took place as a consequence of a global approach, partly inspired by the UNECE Conference in 1992 (the Rio Conference) and the EU's participation in the environmental regimes. As a response to Member States' reaction and interest in a renationalised environmental policy, a new regulatory approach emerged that focused on procedural requirements, framework directives, voluntary agreements and self-regulatory information and management tools. In the last years of the 1990s, a revival of the sustainability approach was ensured, partly by the Amsterdam Treaty (1987) and the Cardiff Process. Directives with focus on the 'combined approach' (as the important approach in the WFD), new environmental instruments (e.g., 'extended producer responsibility' (EPR) in the Waste Framework Directive) and 'minimum environmental quality standards' (in the Air Quality Directives) were passed. Since 1987, such policy action programmes are being decided as part of EU policy instruments.[393] The 'Lisbon Strategy' (2000) agreed by the Heads of State and Government in the same period aimed at making the EU the most competitive economy in the world and achieving full employment in 2010. It rested on three pillars: (a) an economy pillar preparing the ground for the transition to a dynamic, competitive and knowledge-based economy; (b) a social pillar designed to modernise the European social model; and (c) an environmental pillar drawing attention to the fact that economy must be decoupled from the use of natural resources. The sixth EAP (6EAP – 2001–2012) was less ambitious than its predecessors. It was the ambition to address the shortcomings in the implementation of the 5EAP, as well as new issues which have emerged. The starting point was the so-called persistent environmental problems, such as climate change; the loss of biodiversity and the over-consumption of resources which require a broader approach beyond environmental legislation. It was a formulation of a framework of general principles and objectives, which were to be more specified by thematic strategies on key issues.[394] In 2010, the EU adopted the 'Communication on Trade, Growth, and World Affairs'[395] that stressed that the EU trade policy should support and promote green growth around the globe in relation to its activities in the areas of climate change, energy, resource efficiency and protection of biodiversity. In comparing the development of environmental law in different regions, it can be stated that it has been the EU that has pioneered new refinements in environmental law, especially in the use of a holistic regulatory approach in the legal design. The

392. The programme included specific objectives on conservation of water, soil and genetic processes, the reduction of chemical inputs, the achievement of a balance between nutrient input and the absorption capacity of the soil and plants, to promote rural environment management practices, to conserve biodiversity and the natural habitats and to minimise natural risks.

393. *See* now Art. 192(3) TFEU.

394. Christian Hey, *EU Environmental Policies: A Short History of the Political Strategies.*

395. COM(2010) 612 final on the 'Communication on Trade, Growth, and World Affairs'.

WFD was the first example of this new regulatory design.[396] The Marine Strategy Framework Directive (MSFD) is another important example of this. It created the basis for a merged approach enabling a harmonised, seamless transition from catchment through transnational waters and coasts to an open marine system in which the regional conventions also covering sea areas outside the jurisdictions of the Member States are included in EU law.[397]

The 7EAP (2013–2020) with the title 'Living Well, Within the Limits of Our Planet' is the policy programme that is behind the current initiatives of the EU institutions. It is based on the ambition to make the environment more resilient to systematic risks and change, and to ensure a more harmonised environmental policy in the Member States by enforcement of the EU environmental rules. In executing the programme, the EU institutions have the following objectives: (a) to protect, conserve and enhance the Union's natural capital; (b) to turn the Union into a resource-efficient, green and competitive low-carbon economy; (c) to safeguard the Union's citizens from environment-related pressures and risks to health and well-being; (d) to maximise the benefits of the Union's legislation; (e) to improve environmental integration and policy coherence; (f) to enhance the sustainability of the Union's cities; and (g) to increase the Union's effectiveness in confronting regional and global environmental challenges. The programme is also guiding the new EU initiatives in the direction of smart regulation, subject to comprehensive impact assessment where appropriate. This programme identifies as the three thematic priorities: (a) the protection, conservation and enhancement of the EU's natural capital; (b) the transformation of the EU waste management into a resource-efficient, green and competitive low-carbon economy; and (c) the protection of the citizens against environmental-related pressures and risks. It is also an important goal in this strategy – mentioned as the first enabling condition in the programme – to ensure a better control and implementation of EU legislation in the Member States. Scientific research, monitoring and reporting of environmental developments will be used as the second enabling condition to improve the knowledge base. As the third enabling condition, it is a priority to ensure adequate investments and innovation in products, services and public policies such as regional policy, agriculture, fisheries, energy and transport. The fourth enabling condition in the programme is full integration of environmental requirements and considerations into other policies (as this principle of integration is stated in Article 11 TFEU). The two additional horizontal priority objectives are mentioned to complete the program: (1) to make the EU's cities more sustainable; and (2) to help the EU address international environmental and climate challenges more effectively.[398]

---

396. *See supra* at para. 28 concerning the 'combined approach' and its relation to the environmental principles. *See* a more detailed description of the WFD, *infra* at paras 103–104.
397. The Directive is described *infra* para. 130. Concerning the Directive *see also* Long, R., *The Marine Strategy Framework Directive: A New European Approach to the Regulation of the Marine Environment, Marine Natural Resources and Marine Ecological Services*, 29(1), 2011, at 1–44; and Borja. A., Elliott M., Carstensen J., Heiskanen A.S. and van de Bund, W., *Marine Management – Towards an Integrated Implementation of the European Marine Strategy Framework and the Water Framework Directives*.
398. Concerning the history of the political programmes, *see supra* para. 39.

Environmental action plans are also used at national level. The plans – which are normally sector-based – interact with the various regulatory systems that apply in the relevant sector. The plans include an expression of the Government's political intentions and ambitions. Such plans are not very important for the long-term political strategies in Denmark if they are not supplemented by political agreements between the Government and some of the political parties that are in opposition to the Government. Is it not a tradition in Denmark to make such political programmes on the general development of environmental policy and legislation? Only very few programmes have been made on how to ensure a policy and legislation based on the concept of sustainability. In August 2002, the Danish national sustainable development strategy entitled 'A Shared Future – Balanced Development' was adopted by a liberal-conservative coalition Government.[399] It involves the following themes: a developed welfare society and economic growth decoupled from the environmental impact; a safe and healthy environment with a high level of protection; a high degree of biodiversity and protection of ecosystems; an effective use of resources; coordinated action at international level; accounting for environmental concerns at all levels; market support for sustainable development; shared responsibility and measuring of progress.[400] In 2007 the OECD stressed that there is a need for Denmark to develop a long-term, comprehensive environmental plan or framework with specific objectives, including targets and deadlines. The environmental efforts were characterised as scattered across a large number of unrelated programs, policies and ministries.[401] In 2009, the strategy was replaced by a new strategy – made by the same Government – titled 'Precautionary Growth – The Governmental Strategy for Sustainable Growth'. Both strategies had a focus on economic growth. In October 2014, the replacing coalition Government that consisted of the Social Democratic Party and the Social-Liberal Party published a strategy titled 'A Sustainable Denmark' with targets on mitigation of GHGs, recycling of waste, reduction of the effects from pesticides, clean air and diverse nature and protection of waters. This strategy has not been replaced by any of the liberal-conservative coalition governments that were in power in the period 2015–2019.

399. The different Danish coalition governments that have been in power since 1993 are mentioned (in the notes) *supra* in para. 4.

400. *A Shared Future – Balanced Development,* at 2.

401. OECD, *Environmental Performance Reviews. Denmark. 2007,* at 122f, 137.

Chapter 4. Role of Government Institutions in the Shaping and Administration of Environmental Law and Policy

§1. The Governmental Institutions and Their Competences

40. All power and duties vested in the Parliament, the Government and the courts originate from the basic structure of the Danish Constitution. The Parliament has three primary functions in terms of environmental matters: it lays down the rules for environmental policy in Denmark respecting the obligations laid down in EU law and the international conventions ratified by the Danish Government; it appropriates money to fulfil the purposes of the legislation; and it oversees the administrative implementation of the legislation based on an interest in achieving the goals.

The Parliament has a special Committee for Physical Planning and another Committee for Environmental Protection and Agriculture, which consists of members of Parliament and represents the political parties proportionally.

The Constitution establishes a Government of separated, divided and limited powers. An important power of the ministries – e.g., the Ministry of Environment and Food of Denmark – is the right to implement existing environmental laws through statutory orders, circulars, guidelines and national plans, and not so much through ex officio interference. The guidelines are generally issued after due negotiations with the affected business organisations. Environmental programmes and regulatory power are scattered throughout the Government. This is partially because the location of an environmental programme in a particular ministry results from the influence of lobbyists, and the parliamentary committee that created it on the basis of input from such lobbyists, opponents of the proposed programme and the draft from one or more ministers. The Minister for Climate, Energy and Utilities has the power in relation to water utilities, energy resources, renewable energy, energy efficiency and mitigation of GHG issues. In relation to traffic policy and regulation, it is the Minister for Transport who has the power, and in relation to agriculture and fisheries, it is the Ministry of Environment and Food. The Ministry of Industry, Business and Financial Affairs has the competence to regulate spatial planning and competition issues. Some ministries implement and administer the environmental statutes; some have an effect on the environment while pursuing other objectives; and some have the right to negotiate with the environmental authorities on specific issues. The Minister for Environment is normally Denmark's representative in national and international environmental cooperation on environmental issues, e.g., with Danish business organisations, EU authorities and the authorities of other Nordic countries.

41. The Ministry of Environment of Denmark was founded in 1972, and since then many other environmental authorities with environmental competences have come into existence.[402] In 1993, the Ministry of Environment and the Ministry of Energy were merged. In 2001, the Ministries were separated again, as the energy

402. Concerning the info on the other Danish authorities with environmental competences, *see infra* paras 46–49.

issues were transferred to the Ministry of Economy and Business. Since 2015, the Ministry of Environment and the Ministry of Agriculture have been merged (the Ministry of Environment and Food). From 2011 to 2015 energy and climate issues were under the Ministry of Energy, Utilities and Climate, but from 27 June 2019 these issues fell under the Ministry of Climate, Energy and Utilities. Since 2015, all issues related to spatial planning at land and at the sea are under the competence of the Ministry Industry, Business and Financial Affairs.

There are two ministers that share the responsibility for the competences in the Ministry of Environment and Food. These two ministers are the Minister for the Environment and the Minister for Food, Fisheries and Equal Opportunities and Nordic Cooperation.

The Ministry consists of the department and four agencies, each of which is headed by a Director-General. The Permanent Under-Secretary serves as the secretariat of the minister, advising her and assisting her in the preparation of resolutions and the setting of priorities, as well as in the management of the Ministry's overall activities. At present, the main areas of responsibility of the Ministry includes pollution control, reuse, recycling, promotion of cleaner technologies, protection and management of nature, environmentally acceptable forestry, wildlife administration, physical planning, preservation and protection of buildings, and the building-up of knowledge regarding the environment, geology and cleaner technology. The Environmental Protection and Food Appeals Board with its civil servants is not included in this Ministry.

42. The basic expert and administrative work of the Ministry of Environment and Food of Denmark is carried out by five agencies: the National EPA; the National Nature Agency (with the Coastal Authority); the Agriculture Agency; the Fisheries Agency; and the Veterinary and Food Administration.

The agencies have a staff of administratively and technically trained personnel: law graduates, economists, engineers specialised in different branches, chemists, doctors, biologists, etc. Within their particular fields, they advise the minister, lay down rules in a number of situations, advise municipalities and provide guidance and information services to the public, the business community, etc. on environmental problems and ways to solve them. The agencies, furthermore, collect and process data, e.g., on the condition of the environment, issue draft acts and orders and prepare circulars and general guidelines.

Unlike in many other countries, civil servants in Denmark are not replaced when the Government changes hands, and the civil servants are expected to be loyal towards successive ministers regardless of their personal political beliefs.

43. The EPA[403] is responsible for the daily administration of environmental protection and nature protection at national level and deals exclusively with environmental protection. Its tasks include the administration of many of the environmental acts, primarily the Environmental Protection Act,[404] the Environmental Approval for

403. The EPA's homepage: https://eng.mst.dk (visited on 14 Jul. 2019).
404. Promulgation Order No. 681 of 2 July 2019 on Environmental Protection.

Livestock Holdings Act,[405] the Watercourse Act,[406] the Water Supply Act,[407] the Environmental Marine Protection Act,[408] the Chemical Substance and Products Act,[409] and the Act on Contaminated Soil.[410]

The EPA is responsible for some competences under the just-mentioned acts. Based on these acts, the EPA has the power to permit and control many enterprises and local waste handling facilities. It is responsible for the preparation of the statutory rules as well as the drafting of the guidelines. The Agency is also the approval authority as well as the supervision authority for the (s)-marked installations regulated by the Statutory Order on Environmental Approval of Listed Enterprises.[411] Decisions made by the Agency may be brought before the Environmental Protection and Food Appeals Board, if the relevant legislation so prescribes.[412]

In conjunction with the research institutes, the Agency must be up-to-date with the national and international state of knowledge in the field of environmental protection.

44. The Danish Nature Agency[413] is involved in the management of the nature, forest and wildlife, as well as some special nature schools. Under this Agency, there is a Coastal Authority that manages the function and protection of the coast, ensures dunes conservation and represents the Danish State in respect to its sovereignty over the territorial waters.

Wildlife administration,[414] as well as the running of the National Forest Service,[415] which manages one-third of Denmark's forested area, is a very important aspect of the Agency's work. It functions in accordance with the sustainable development objective, with the purpose of combining utilisation with the protection of the land. It carries out the conservation planning at national level and endeavours to remedy any damage already done to nature and the environment. Protection of nature and the environment can take place through preservation, building lines and other bans on some types of land, restrictions on hunting activities and the establishment of nature and wildlife reserves. The Agency is the supervising authority for national forest systems, which consists of local forestry districts. It manages approximately 2,000,000 ha of forests and natural areas; it registers the development of natural areas and improvement of the agricultural environment. The monitoring activities concern the condition of the forests, the living conditions of fauna and flora, and of raw material resources on land and on the seabed.[416] The Agency can buy natural areas and thus ensure environmentally appropriate management of the areas or grant loans and subsidies for projects aiming at nature conservation and

405. Promulgation Order No. 520 of 1 May 2019 on Environmental Approval for Livestock Holdings.
406. Promulgation Order No. 127 of 26 January 2017 on Watercourses.
407. Promulgation Order No. 118 of 22 February 2018 on Water Supply.
408. Promulgation Order No. 1033 of 4 September 2017 on Environmental Marine Protection.
409. Promulgation Order No. 115 of 26 January 2017 on Chemical Substances and Products.
410. Promulgation Order No. 115 of 26 January 2017 on Contaminated Soil.
411. Statutory Order No. 1317 of 20 November 2018 on Environmental Approval of Listed Activities.
412. Concerning the Environmental Protection and Food Appeals Board, *see infra* paras 47 and 355.
413. The Nature Agency's homepage: https://eng.naturstyrelsen.dk (visited on 14 July 2019).
414. Concerning the wildlife administration, *see infra* paras 241–247 and 251–256.
415. Concerning the Danish management of forests, *see infra* paras 274–278.
416. Concerning the monitoring activities of the Nature Agency, *see supra* para. 34 and *infra* para. 273.

restoration. Furthermore, the Agency is responsible for the protection and administration of national parks and the administration of the Hunting and Wildlife Management Act. The Danish Coastal Authority is a department within this Agency. This part of the Agency is the authority for 7,300 km coastline and 103,000 km^2 of Danish territorial waters.

45. The Agricultural Agency[417] is responsible for the administration of the agricultural funding under the European CAP funding systems. The Agency takes care of the administration of the money under the 'Basic Payment Scheme' and the 'Uniform Payment Scheme'. It is also responsible for the administration of the Danish acts on the use of fertiliser and vegetation cover, etc. The Fisheries Agency[418] is responsible for the Danish administration of the fishing quotas and other parts of the fishing legislation. The inspection of the fulfilment of EU legislation on fisheries in the Danish territorium is also part of the Agency's competences. The Veterinary and Food Administration has, e.g., the competence to take care of the authorisation of people that work as a veterinarian, protection of animals as well as food control.[419]

46. There are thirteen independent nature conservation boards in Denmark. They are composed, in accordance with the rules of the Nature Conservation Act, of a chairperson, who must be a judge – and whom the Minister of Environment and Food appoints. The local municipal authorities appoint one of the members, and the Minister of Environment and Food appoints two members of the boards. Their decision-making process is regulated by a statutory order.

The nature protection boards have the competence to preserve areas as sanctuaries (conservation orders) and to grant exemption from the protection of forests, beaches and seashores as well as of ancient monuments and churchyards. They have no right to interfere ex officio: someone with the right to raise a case has to ask for a decision. It is important to note that the preservation authorities are the primarily decision-makers in the evaluation of whether to allow or reject any activity adversely affecting a protected area. These decisions must be made in conformity with special procedural rules. The procedural rules and the composition of the preservation boards, both at first instance and at the appellate level, ensure that legal experts hear the matters, and that they will be balanced against the environmental protection interests. The decisions made by the boards may be appealed before the Environmental Protection and Food Appeals Board.

47. The administrative appeal system is the most common means of appeal used in environmental matters.[420] The Environmental Protection and Food Appeals

417. The Agricultural Agency's English homepage: https://eng.lbst.dk (visited on 14 Jul. 2019).
418. The Fisheries Agency's English homepage: https://fiskeristyrelsen.dk/english/ (visited on 14 Jul. 2019).
419. The Veterinary and Food Administration's English homepage: https://www.foedevarestyrelsen.dk/english/Pages/default.aspx (visited on 14 Jul. 2019).
420. Concerning the Danish administrative appeal system, *infra* paras 349–353.

Board[421] is the appeal body in sixty-four legal acts concerning environmental legislation, agriculture, fishery and food. This Appeals Board has authority, e.g., in relation to environmental protection, water supply, chemical product, nature protection and the marine environment. The Spatial Planning Appeals Board[422] has the competences under the Planning Act, the Maritime Spatial Act and two more acts. The Energy Appeals Board[423] is the third administrative appeals board. These three appeals boards are the final instance of administrative appeal, and they have in some cases the authority to carry out a complete re-examination, in other cases their competences are limited to the review of the application of the legal criteria. If the total compensation and indemnification that has to be paid to the owners covered by the restrictions put on their land use as results of the adoption of a conservation order based on the Nature Protection Act and other decisions concerning expropriation, the Environmental Protection and Food Appeals Board has to review the entire decision of the conservation boards.

The chairpersons of these appeals boards are professors of law who are working full-time as professors. The composition of the appeals boards depends on the planning, environmental, nature protection, energy etc. acts. In most cases it is the civil servants located in the 'House of the Appeals Boards' – an agency under the Minister for Industry, Business and Financial Affairs – that make the decisions without any independent judges or expert members.[424]

48. The ninety-eight municipalities discharge numerous powers. The field of competence is in general as follows: to assist sustainable local development, to take into account local environmental protection considerations, spatial planning, nature and water protection, waste administration and waste collection/disposal, wastewater treatment and water supply, administration of permit systems in many areas, e.g., under the Environmental Protection Act and the Water Supply Act. It is normally municipal councils, which give permission in rural zones to parcel land, to construct new buildings and take existing buildings and areas that have not already been built on into use. In accordance with the Building Act, they issue building licences. Under this Act, new buildings may not be constructed, and old restorable buildings may not be demolished without permission. Before deciding, the council has to make an examination of whether the project respects all the environmental acts. The municipalities carry out the majority of inspections as the main environmental inspection authority under all the environmental acts.

49. The environmental competences of the five regional councils are very limited. The regions are responsible for parts of the administration of Contaminated

421. The composition and competences of this Appeals Board is laid down in Act No. 1715 of 27 December 2016 on Environmental Protection and Food Appeals Board.
422. The composition and competences of this Appeals Board is laid down in Act No. 1658 of 20 December 2016 on Spatial Planning Appeals Board.
423. The Energy Appeals Board is established by the energy legislation, and its competence is laid down in the different energy-related acts.
424. The Danish preconditions concerning the interpretation of the wording of Art. 9(1) of the Aarhus Convention related to 'a court of law or other independent and impartial body established by law' by these appeal bodies are problematic.

Soil Act and part of the Mineral Resources Act.[425] The activities under the Contaminated Soil Act include mapping and investigation, monitoring, prioritisation of cleaning-up activities covered by public money and some processing cases within an insurance scheme. The public traffic service by buses is also a competence of the regional councils.

§2. The Current Role of the Governmental Institutions

50. The powers of ministries have, in certain respects, become broader than in the past. The Ministry of Environment and Food of Denmark is an important authority in the area of environmental and nature protection. The Ministry of Industry, Business and Financial Affairs is responsible for spatial planning on the sea as well as on land. The Ministry of Climate, Energy and Utilities has competences in respect to the climate change policy and legislation, as well as all energy issues, including the renewable energy legislation, and this Ministry also has the competence in relation to the operation of and the regulation of the prices for the supply of waste and water services. The Ministry of Transport, the Minister of Taxation, the Ministry of Justice, the Ministry of Finance and the Ministry of Economic Affairs and Interior also have some competences of importance for the management of the environment and the resource efficiency. It is normal practice within rather wide limits of the ministries to delegate administrative functions to agencies. This competence has been used to make statutory orders on delegation of power.

51. As many duties as possible that are not performed centrally are delegated by the legislature to the municipalities. Under the Environmental Protection Act and several other environmental acts, the main responsibility for administration of environmental protection, the nature protection, the waste management, etc. rests with the municipal councils. This is based on the principle of subsidiarity, which implies that decisions are made at the lowest possible level.

Where the deciding authority is a municipal council or a regional council, the governmental authorities or other authorities will normally not have the competence to interfere ex officio unless expressly empowered to do so by law. There are, however, some rules that ensure the power for the ministries/agencies to take over the competences, and there are rules on general powers to give instructions on general guidance to the municipalities.

Where the right of complaint rests on a superiority/subordination relationship, the superior authority, in addition to its powers as a recourse authority, has the other normal powers of superiority in relation to the body whose decision is being considered. This means the right to give official orders, to amend on its own initiative decisions made by the subordinate authority and the right to superintend the subordinate authority. These additional powers have the effect that in such cases the usual procedural prerequisites – including the right of complaint – do not have to be satisfied for the recourse body to consider a complaint as to the issues of fact.

425. Concerning the Contaminated Soil Act, *see infra* paras 173–180, and concerning the Mineral Resources Act, *see infra* paras 291–293.

52. Many municipalities are undergoing substantial restructuring today, and this leads to radical changes in the ways in which municipal environmental tasks are carried out. In recent years, more and more municipalities have tried to find new forms for their environmental tasks. Some of them have begun to label themselves 'green municipalities' to indicate their involvement. The 2007 structural reform has changed the geography of public administration and the functional responsibility for environmental administration. As an important consequence of this, the municipalities took over several competences from the former regional councils.[426]

It is normal to establish municipal-owned enterprises as well as joint municipal companies in the waste, water and water supply sectors. The joint municipal companies play an important role in the waste areas and the water supply areas. There are also joint municipality companies that carry out the supervision and preparation of enforcement of environmental obligations. In the energy sector, one finds several consumer-owned electricity supply companies. The Danish Competition Council has several times approached the Minister of Environment and Food as well as the National Association of the Local Authorities to try to ensure free competition in the 'market' for waste. As an important example, the Council has pointed out that the rules laid down by the Municipal Council of Copenhagen regarding waste treatment may have potentially harmful effects on competition. Also, a Danish Eastern High Court judgment of 1997 stated that the practice of the Municipal Council of Copenhagen was without basis in the Environmental Protection Act. A judgment from the CJEU (Case C-209/98, *Sydhavnen Sten & Grus v. Copenhagen Municipality*) stated that the requirement in the local by-law that certain goods should only be delivered to domestic companies in fact means that the export of those goods was prohibited. The regulation was thus subject to the prohibition on quantitative restrictions under the Treaty. The Court also decided that the treatment of waste could, under certain conditions, be regarded as a service of general economic interest within the meaning of the Treaty. The Court further confirmed that environmental reasons can justify the grant of exclusive rights for the public-owned waste handling utilities, but those exclusive rights must have direct relation to the environmental objectives pursued.[427] A 2010 reform of the waste sector has ensured that the waste now is handled in accordance with the EU waste rules, including the Internal Market.[428]

53. Self-regulation or voluntary compliance programmes have some impact on the role of all the environmental authorities. The revised version of the Danish Environmental Protection Act of 1992, as a tool to change the administrative law tradition, contained a rule in section 10, providing for the use of environmental agreements – and, consequently, accepting public-private cooperation as part of the regulatory approach.

According to section 10(1) of the Act, the Minister for the Environment has the authority to establish a binding set of objectives with respect to the environment.

426. *See*, e.g., concerning the municipal spatial planning of the municipalities that replaced the former regional spatial planning, *infra* paras 313–317.

427. Concerning Arts 34–36 TFEU, *see supra* para. 29.

428. Concerning the Danish implementation of EU waste law, *see infra* para. 148.

According to section 10(2), the Minister can make environmental contract with companies or organisations representing different branches. The Minister can set the rules to determine the basis of agreements, as well as rules regarding the subject having the right to enter into agreements. In the examples of environmental contract currently in force, organisations normally have appeared as the parties to the agreements. To ensure equality and that agreements are fair to all parties involved, including for companies behaving as 'free-riders', i.e., non-signatories to the agreement, the agreements are supplemented by statutory rules, and also by regulatory rules and sanctions. According to section 10(4), the Minister has the power to compel administratively relevant parties that have not agreed to an ongoing agreement to meet the same environmental obligations as laid down in the agreement. The Minister can, according to this subsection, by means of a statutory order, applying to non-signatories:

> lay down similar requirements to limit the use, discharge or disposal of such products, substances or materials for enterprises not covered by the agreement.

The use of environmental agreements was emphasised as an appropriate instrument in the 'Danish Action Plan for Waste and Recycling 1993-1997', which was maybe the reason why the majority number of environmental agreements are on waste treatment.[429] Agreements combined with integrated management and production programmes are used as comprehensive, flexible instruments for reduction of emission of VOCs and CFCs. Normally, the public authorities' interest in voluntary instruments is either to reach higher quality levels than the standards stipulated in the statutory quality norms or to reduce the public resources used in the particular case. In relation to the regulation of goods, including the utilisation of waste products, a voluntary, market-based approach is easier to implement. Other rules imposing agreement on the farmers' land use as means to protect drinking water resources are based on the principle of least intervention necessary.[430] The agreements with the farmers provide for flexible regulation of land use matters, safeguard individual properties and disposal rights, and provide an incentive to farmers to cooperate with the local authorities in making environmental improvements while at the same time focusing on possible benefits for the farmers. Moreover, the formal integration of agreement options into the statutory rules of drinking water protection clearly helps to improve the legitimacy of this instrument. As can be seen from the examples of agreements within the agricultural and waste sectors, there are positive experiences in relation to the negotiated decision-making. There are, however, limits to the extent to which regulation of environmental areas can be managed by way of negotiated decision-making. The regulated business sectors have to be interested in taking part in agreements. The general administrative law principles of non-discrimination, impartiality, proportionality and fairness also have to be respected.

429. Concerning the Danish agreements with the Danish Retursystem A/S on the on the management of special waste categories, *see infra* paras 155–159.

430. Concerning the obligation for the authorities to use agreements before they use public power, *see infra* para. 267.

Furthermore, there are also some procedural and administrative law problems relating to the use of the voluntary approach in relation to recipient quality, as the interest involved are so different and complex.[431]

431. Ellen Margrethe Basse and Martin Enevoldsen, *Negotiated Decision Making in Denmark: Public-Private Agreements in Land Use and Waste Management Policy*, in Doudewijn de Ward (ed.) 'Negotiated Decision-Making', Schoordijk Institute, Center for Legislative Studies, Boom Juridische Uitgevers, Den Haag, 2000, at 125–159.

Chapter 5. Sources of Environmental Law and Instruments

54. It is a characteristic of environmental legislation in Denmark that there is a lack of a true multimedia approach. A complicated system of many acts has been created whereby many decision-makers should, but do not necessarily, collaborate. Environmental law is fragmented horizontally as various problems are regulated by various pieces of legislation, some of which are the result of implementation of international and EU legislation, whereas others are the result of national traditions and political compromises. The number of acts and statutory orders are enormous.

Environmental themes have recurred through different generations of regulatory designs, and national traditions are still very important. Several of the different regulatory styles and means used in Danish legislation are in reality still in force as part of national traditions.[432] Modern Danish environmental law has at the same time some elements of a strong international dimension due to membership of the EU and the participation in global and regional agreements.[433] Under Danish law, the dualistic principle applies to the relation between international law and national law. International conventions have to be formally internalised into national law. Normally, the Danish authorities will interpret the legislation in such a way that a violation of international obligations under the Convention of Treaties is avoided. The dualistic approach is modified by Denmark's membership of the EU.[434]

The EU has ratified and signed most of the international environmental conventions, protocols and declarations. Parts of various EU directives and regulations therefore consist of an implementation of international environmental law. The regulations passed by the EU institutions are part of national legislation, and the implementation of the directives has to be in harmony with the aims and the minimum harmonisation obligations established by the provisions that the Council has ratified and signed. The Danish authorities are therefore obliged to apply EU law – including EU law that transform international obligations into the EU legal order, with the modification that a number of provisions ensure some room for manoeuvre within national law. As a member of the EU, Denmark is bound by EU legislation, and the approach taken by the CJEU with respect to the status of international agreements concluded by the EU.

55. The EU is a special supranational legal construction. It can act as a party to regional and international environmental agreements, and it has competences in nearly all environmental areas. The EU has increasingly placed itself in between international and national legal actors as a lawmaker – and as a powerful market. The EU also applies its environmental requirements extra-territorially, effectively imposing its standards on others.[435] The relationship between international law and

---

432. Concerning the historical development of Danish environmental legislation, *see supra* in paras 35–38.
433. Concerning the legal sources, *see infra* para. 56.
434. The EU has shared competence with its Member States in areas for the conclusion of an international environmental agreement, cf. Art. 4(2) TEU and Art. 191(4) TFEU. The international and regional agreements that are ratified by the Council are binding on its institutions and its Member States, cf. Art. 288 TFEU. Concerning these issues, *see infra* para. 56.
435. Concerning Art. 3(2) TEU and Arts 216(2) and 288 TFEU, *see infra* para. 56.

national law that generally was a dualistic system in Denmark is – as a consequence of the development of EU environmental law – gradually replaced by a new triangular relationship: international environmental law/EU environmental law/national environmental law.

The legal order of the EU is different from this traditional approach to law. The EU, which is not viewed as an international regime (confederation of sovereign states), is neither a federation, which shares its sovereignty with its Member States, nor a nation state. The constitutional basis for the EU is the Treaty of Lisbon that includes the TEU, the TFEU, the Charter of Human Rights of the European Union (Charter) and several protocols. EU legislation takes the form of the Treaties' rules – including the Charter and the protocols – the regulations, directives and decisions. The EU legal order differs from traditional international law due also to its body of autonomous law-making institutions and its courts.[436] The legal authority of the CJEU – that consists of one judge from each Member State – is like that of a supreme court enforcing federal constitution.[437] It was stated by the Court in Case 26/62 *Van Gend en Loos* that the EU constitutes a new legal order in international law, for whose benefit the states have limited their sovereign rights, albeit within limited fields. By this judgment – and several latter judgments – the CJEU has developed a special legal order that has consequences for the competences of the Member States and for the traditional legal theory.

The competences of the EU have two dimensions: the relation between the EU and its Member States ('internal dimension') and the EU's external relations ('external dimension').

Since the early 1990s, the EU has established itself as an international leader in environmental governance pushing especially for stringent global commitments on sustainable environmental policy under the UNEP and outside this regime. As a 'regional economic integrated organisation', the EU is exercising a strong power of influence especially in the cooperation on global commitment, e.g., under the United Nations (UN) – directly as a party to multilateral agreements, and indirectly through its Member States in the regimes, where the EU has not been accepted as a party. The Treaty of Lisbon formulates the principles and objectives of the EU's internal and external actions, and it confirms the legal personality of the Union, cf. Article 47 TEU. EU institutions are in their relations with the wider world obliged to do all that lie in their power to enhance the international legal order and to do this under the guidance of the principles, which have inspired the creation of the Union, its development and its enlargement, cf. Articles 3(5) and 21(1) TEU. In Article 3(5) TEU, it is stated that one of the aims of the EU is to promote its values globally supporting the role of it as a normative global power. Among the general provisions on its external actions is the obligation to respect the principles, which have inspired its own creation, including the principle of sustainability, *see* Article 21 TEU. According to Article 21(2), the EU institutions shall define and pursue

436. Concerning the process to be followed in the decision-making on secondary legislation, *see infra* para. 57.

437. The General Court and the national courts are also integral to the system of the interpreting, application and enforcement of EU environmental law, *see* Susanne Kingston, Veerle Heyvaert and Alexandra Cavoski, *European Environmental Law*, 2017, at 67–68.

common policies and sustainable actions. It shall work for a high degree of cooperation in all fields of international relations, e.g., in order to improve the quality of the environment and the sustainable management of global natural resources. The EU has competence to act externally, alone or together with its Member States. In the areas of environmental law, negotiation and conclusion of international and regional agreements are 'mixed agreements' in which both the Member States and the EU have to take part and to sign the agreement, cf. Article 191(4).[438] The Commission negotiates, and the Council makes the final decision on international commitments with binding effect on the Member States, unless secondary legislation accepts that the Commission has the competence to make the final decision. Once the Council has concluded a bilateral or multilateral agreement, its legal effects are twofold: the EU as well as its Member States are bound, as the ratification by the Council of bilateral and multilateral agreements has binding effect, cf. Articles 216(2) and 288 TFEU. Based on case law of the CJEU, the conventions concluded by the Commission and approved by the Council form an integral part of the EU legal order.[439] Both the EU institutions and the Member States are bound by such international agreements and, consequently, those agreements signed by the Council have authority over secondary EU legislation transposing the obligations into EU law.[440] The CJEU has explained that the reasoning behind this hierarchy of the legal sources is made to show third parties to the international agreements that the EU is a reliable international partner. The *principle of sincere cooperation* regulates the general obligations of the Member States and the EU to support each other also in their relations with third parties, cf. Article 4(3) TEU.[441] This Principle is important to remember in the understanding of Danish environmental law as it has impact on how the Danish authorities have to ensure a correct interpretation also of international conventions and protocols, etc. that Denmark and the EU are parties to.

Based on Article 191(4), the EU institutions and the Member States shall cooperate with third countries and with the competent international organisation in the area of environmental law. The EU has exclusive competence in all areas as to the conclusion of an international or regional agreement when its conclusion is provided for in an environmental legislative act of the EU or is necessary to enable the

438. Article 191(4) TFEU declares that Member States and the Union shall cooperate with third countries within their respective spheres of competences.

439. As a rule, upon becoming binding, the international norms automatically start to form 'an integrated part' of EU law, cf. the Case C-181/73 *Haegeman v. Belgian State*.

440. Once the Council has concluded a multilateral agreement, its legal effects are twofold: the EU and its Member States are bound, as the ratification by the Council has binding effect under Arts 216(6) and 288 TFEU. *See* Case C-61/94 *Commission v. Germany*, para. 52.

441. In C-404/13 *Client Earth* (para. 52) the CJEU states with reference to the Treaty:

> As regards Article 4 TEU, it should be recalled that according to settled case law, under the principle of sincere cooperation laid down in para. 3 of that Article, it is the Member States to ensure judicial protection of an individual's right under EU law ... In addition. Article 19(1) TEU requires Member States to provide remedies sufficient to ensure effective protection in the fields covered by EU law.

EU to exercise its internal competence, or in so far as its conclusion may affect common rules or alter their scope, *see* Article 3(2) TFEU.[442] This means that the EU shall only act insofar as the objective of the initiatives cannot be sufficiently achieved by the Member States at national level and will better be achieved at EU level. The international and regional environmental agreements for the EU cooperation may be subject to arrangement between the Union and third parties concerned (as 'mixed agreements'). The Member States have no right to enter into international or other commitments, which might affect or alter the scope of 'internal' EU rules and the external negotiations by the EU. [443] The CJEU has held[444] that the international agreements signed by the Council are an integrated part of the EU's legal order and that international agreements concluded by the Council may under certain circumstances be directly applicable in the Member States. The international obligations and/or criteria are higher-ranking then EU secondary legislation transforming these obligations/criteria into obligations for the Member States. According to the CJEU case law, a provision in a convention or protocol signed by the Council is also directly applicable in some situations:[445]

> when, regard being had to its wording and the purpose and nature of the agreement, the provision contains a clear and precise obligation, which is not subject, in its implementation or effects, to the adoption of any subsequent measure.

To decide upon whether certain provisions have those attributes lies within the jurisdiction of the CJEU. The correct interpretation may not be decided solely by the national courts of the Member States.[446] Thus, the provision of an international agreement can become part of national legislation – directly or indirectly. Based on CJEU's case law, the Member States are under an obligation to ensure, if necessary, by a separate provision, that in case of conflict between domestic law and the EU rules transforming international obligations into EU requirements, the EU requirements have supremacy. Some conventions – e.g., conventions under the International Maritime Organisation (IMO) – are not ratified by the EU as a consequence of the IMO's non-acceptance of economic integrated organisations with the EU as a party. However, by means of several directives and regulations, the EU is also supporting the transformation of such international agreements into the national legislation of its Member States.[447] According to the principle of external competence

442. Concerning the exclusive versus the shared competences, *see infra* para. 56. When the EU has passed secondary environmental law, which is the case in relation to the use of the regulatory initiatives, all subject matters of such secondary law fall within the scope of the exclusive external EU power, cf. Art. 3(2).
443. In the judgment C-246/07 *Commission v. Sweden*, the CJEU stated that a proposal to list PFOS in Annex A to the Stockholm Convention presented by the Swedish Government to the body set up under the Convention was against the exclusive competence of the Commission.
444. *See* Case C-213/03, *Syndicates professional coordination des pêcheurs de l'étang de Berre et de la region v. Electricité de France* and Case C-239/03, *Commission of the European Commission v. Franche Republic*.
445. *See* the judgment in C-240/09 *Slovak Brown Bear*, para. 44.
446. *See* the judgment in C-240/09 *Slovak Brown Bear*, para. 43.
447. Concerning the implementation of IMO conventions into EU law, *see infra* para. 129.

developed by the CJEU,[448] the EU acquires external competence, also in situations where it adopts internal EU rules on the same subject matter that is discussed in connection with transport issues in the IMO that is not accepting the EU as a party. As a rule, upon becoming binding, the international norms automatically become 'an integrated part' of EU law.[449] The governance by such an incorporation of international norms into the EU legal order is legally based on Article 216(2) TFEU. The consequences that European integration has on the position of international requirements in Denmark, after the rules have entered the national legal order via the EU legal order, illustrate the emergence of a complicated triangular relationship between international law, EU law and national law. The principle of loyalty and the duty to sincere cooperation have the consequence that the Danish authorities, as far as possible, must accept the multilevel regulatory system as an integrated part of Danish environmental law. In other words, the provision of a multilateral agreement can become part of Danish legislation without national transformation of it into legislation.[450] In this aspect, it is also important to mention that the interpretation of the procedural rights of the public and the public concerned established by the Aarhus Convention is applied both by the CJEU and by the Aarhus Convention Compliance Committee (ACCC) to ensure control of the national implementation of multilevel environmental law.[451]

56. Within the EU, the highest legal ranking is obviously enjoyed by the TEU and TFEU articles, the Charter and the protocols included in the Treaty of Lisbon. All these articles bind the EU institutions. The treaty rules clarified the EU competences by articulating the exclusive EU competences, shared competences, complementary competences and the principle of conferral.

The principle of conferral is a fundamental principle of EU law, cf. Article 5(2) TEU and Article 4(1) TFEU. Under this principle, the EU is a union of Member States, and those Member States voluntarily confer all its competences on it. The areas of the environment, energy, the Internal Market, economic issues, agriculture and fisheries (excluding the conservation of marine biological resources) and transport are covered by shared competences, cf. Article 4(2) TFEU. It is modified by Article 3(2) TFEU under which the EU has exclusive competence in:

- areas of importance for establishing the competition rules necessary for the functioning of the Internal Market;
- the conservation of marine biological resources under the Common Fisheries Policy (CFP);

448. *See, e.g.*, Case C-22/70 *Commission v. Council (the AETR-case).*
449. Cf. the judgment Case C-181/73 *Haegeman v. Belgian State.*
450. International law is considered a body of law distinct from national law. Such legal systems that require the intervention of the national democratically elected legislator before an international multilateral agreement, which can be applied by national authorities as national law, are based on the dualistic approach. The impact of the dualistic approach on the interpretation of the environmental rules is reduced by the role of the EU as an environmental legislator.
451. Concerning the procedural rights, *see supra* paras 32–33, *infra* paras at 347–348 and *infra* para. 373.

– in all areas for the conclusion of an international or regional agreement when its conclusion is provided for in an environmental legislative act of the EU or is necessary to enable the EU to exercise its internal competence, or insofar as its conclusion may affect common rules or alter their scope. The exclusive EU competence includes areas, where internal market harmonisation and measures related to international trade are required: prohibition and restrictions of production, export, import or export, placing on the market and use of products.

When competences are shared with the Member States, both the Union and the Member States may legislate and adopt legally binding acts. Member States are in the areas of shared competences only permitted to exercise their competence to the extent that the Union has not exercised its competence, cf. Article 2(2) TFEU. The treaty provisions that are primarily employed as the frame for development of environmental law at EU level are laid down in Article 11 (the 'principle of integration') and Articles 191–194. The power of the EU institutions in this policy area are shared among the Member States, cf. Article 4(2) TFEU.

In cases in the areas of shared competences (e.g., most of environmental policies) where agreement on a measure cannot be attained within a reasonable period by the EU as a whole, the Member States, which are willing to go further, have the option to adopt such measures via the EU institutions and exercise those competences by applying the relevant provisions of the Lisbon Treaty.[452] EU policy must take into account the diversity of situations in the various regions of the EU, cf. Article 3(3) TEU. On the other hand, according to settled case law, the need for a uniform application of EU law and the principle of equality require that the terminology, etc. used in secondary EU law must normally be given an autonomous and uniform interpretation throughout the Member States. Based on the principle of loyalty and the duty of sincere cooperation,[453] the Member States must ensure the correct implementation of EU legislation. Interpretation at national level must take into account the context of the provision and the purpose of the legislation in question.[454]

In relation to land use, it is important to remember that the system of property ownership is not a competence of the EU institutions, cf. Article 345 TFEU. Some initiatives by the Commission on regulation of land use by directives have therefore failed.[455] While it follows from Article 345 TFEU that the Treaty is not affecting Member States' right to decide whether a given asset should be in public or private ownership, the CJEU case law shows that this do not have the effect of exempting expropriation measures from the fundamental rules on the Treaties. Accordingly, expropriation measures used by a Member State should be non-discriminatory and proportionate to attain their legitimate objective, e.g., by providing for adequate

452. Such a decision has to be based on the procedures laid down in Art. 20 TEU and Arts 326–434 TFEU.

453. The duty for both the EU institutions and the Member States to take part in a sincere cooperation is laid down in Art. 4(3) TEU.

454. *See*, *inter alia*, the CJEU C-204/09 *Flachglas Torgau*, para. 37.

455. Concerning the proposed Soil Framework Directive that has not been accepted by the Member States, *see infra* para. 168.

compensation. EU legislation is not stipulating how the division of powers and responsibilities has to be designed between national, regional and local administration in national law.

When implementing EU legislation, Denmark has to respect the harmonisation obligations established by the Treaty of Lisbon, including the general principles on sincere cooperation and non-discrimination.[456]

As in other Member States, the choice of means to be used to ensure correct implementation of EU law into Danish law often depends on the national traditions. The onus for the correct application of EU law is primarily on the Member States' legislator, administration and judiciary. They must ensure an effective implementation of EU law at national level and, if necessary, establish effective, dissuasive and proportionate sanctions in order to implement and enforce EU law. In its case law, the CJEU has established that the procedural rules of each Member State generally apply to cases where national law implements EU law, but with two modifications. The 'principle of equivalence' means that the procedure, which the Member States use in the implementation of EU directives, must be equivalent to the procedures used in domestic cases. The other principle, the 'principle of effectiveness', means that the national procedures cannot render implementation of EU law ineffective.

Under Article 17(1) TEU, legal responsibility for ensuring compliance with regulations and directives in the EU system lies with the Commission.[457] The Commission monitors the implementation of EU law by individual Member States. In cases of suspected non-implementation, it initiates Article 258 TFEU infringement proceedings. Invariably, these proceedings begin informally, with a series of bilateral negotiations between the Commission and the Member State. Typically, this is sufficient to settle legal disputes. Where the dialogue fails to produce a satisfactory conclusion, proceedings may move to a formal stage, where the Commission sends a 'formal letter of notice', detailing the grounds of the suspected infringement, and inviting feedback from the Member State. If a satisfactory response is not forthcoming, the Commission may deliver a 'reasoned opinion', laying out its view of how Member State action remains inadequate, and establish a deadline to rectify the infringement. Failure to comply with the reasoned opinion may result in the case being referred to the CJEU. Article 260 TFEU makes it possible to launch infringement proceeding against Member States with financial sanctions decided by the CJEU. Another of those novelties was the possibility for the Commission to request, at an earlier stage of the procedure, financial sanctions against Member States for failure to notify measures transposing a directive adopted under the legislative procedure, cf. Article 260(3) TFEU. In its monthly package of infringement decisions, the Commission pursues the actions taken against Member States.[458] The Member

456. Concerning the Lisbon Treaty and CJEU case law of importance for the obligations of the Member States, *see infra* paras 54–58.

457. The entry into force of the Treaty of Lisbon brought important changes in infringement management at EU level.

458. *See* concerning the praxis the homepage of the Commission with information on such cases: http://ec.europa.eu/environment/legal/law/press_en.htm.

States also have power to control the Commission's exercise of implementing power.[459] The control is applied through the comitology procedures.

Enforcement at national level has to be based on national law or EU regulations, if it is the citizens that are enforced to respect the rules, as international conventions, and EU directives are not binding on the citizens. If it is the enforcement of provisions laid down in the conventions and/or the directives that are unconditional and sufficiently precise ensuring some rights in the interests of the public concerned and/or individual citizens, such provisions are also enforceable at national level. If it is not possible to interpret the national provisions in line with the provisions laid down in the convention or the directive, the national courts are obliged to set the national provisions aside and other national authorities are obliged to undertake all measures necessary to secure the correct implementation of the EU provisions.[460] With respect to the Aarhus Convention, the CJEU stated that a provision is directly applicable:[461]

> when, regard being had to its wording and the purpose and nature of the agreement, the provision contains a clear and precise obligation which is not subject, in its implementation or effects, to the adoption of any subsequent measure.

The European Union Network for the Implementation and Enforcement of Environmental Law (IMPEL) at national level is an information network organisation established by the Member States. It was set up in 1992 to create the necessary inputs in the EU to make progress in ensuring more effective application of environmental legislation.[462] The core of the activities concerns awareness raising, capacity-building, peer-review, exchange of information and experience on implementation, international enforcement collaboration as well as supporting the practicability and enforcement of environmental legislation. In many EU directives and regulations, there are rules on the national monitoring and reporting obligations that ensure the basis for effective control of national implementation in practice. By way of example can be mentioned, the Industrial Emission Directive (IED) sets out minimum criteria for organising, performing, follow-up and publishing environmental inspections.

57. The process to be followed by the EU institutions when they are making new secondary legislation is laid down in Articles 289 and 294–297 TFEU. Article 192(1) on environmental issues, Article 194(2) on energy issues and the first paragraph of Article 42 and Article 43(2) on agricultural issues recognise co-decision as

459. European Parliament and Council Regulation No. 182/2011/EU laying down the Rules and general Principles concerning Mechanisms for Control by Member States of the Commission's exercise of Implementation Power.

460. *See* as examples C-361/88 and C-59/89 *TA Luft* concerning health aspect.

461. C-240/09 *Slovak Brown Bear*, para. 43.

462. IMPEL is now an international non-profit association of the environmental authorities of the EU Member States that is working together with the Commission on the basis of a Memorandum of Understanding (signed in 2009) and the 7EAP.

the ordinary legislative procedure,[463] where both the European Parliament and the Council by majority voting can bring new rules into force, cf. Article 289.

The Commission takes the initiatives. The Parliament and the Council, acting in accordance with the just-mentioned treaty rules – after consulting the Economic and Social Committee and the Committee of the Regions – together decide on the final wording of secondary legislation. The EU institutions must pass two tests when they are regulating in policy areas that they share with the Member States: The 'principle of subsidiarity'[464] and the 'principle of proportionality' govern how the EU institutions can use their power, cf. Article 5 TEU. The 'principle of subsidiarity' permits action at the Union level only and insofar as the objectives of the proposed action cannot be sufficiently achieved by the Member States and can therefore, by reason of the scale or effects of the proposed action be better achieved by the Community. Article 6(1) TEU states that the Charter shall have the same legal value as the TEU and the TFEU, but it shall not extent in any way the competences of the Union as defied in the Treaties. It applies only to the institutions, bodies, offices and agencies of the EU with due regard to the 'principle of subsidiarity'. The provisions of the Charter are only addressed to the Member States when they are implementing Union law, cf. Article 51(1) of the Charter. Any action taken by the EU institutions in areas which do not fall within the EU's exclusive competence has to respect the subsidiarity and proportionality principles, cf. Article 5(3)–(4) TEU.[465] *First*, they have to demonstrate that the objectives of the initiatives cannot be sufficiently achieved at national level, and *second*, they should demonstrate that the actual initiative by reason of its scale or its effects can be better achieved at EU level than at national level – e.g., by being more effective, more democratic, more consistent with the internal market, more consistent with international obligations, more environment-friendly, etc. On the other hand, the Member States shall only exercise their competence to the extent that the EU has not exercised, or has decided not to exercise its competence. Under the proportionality principle, the EU institutions' involvement must be limited to what is necessary to achieve the objectives of the Treaties, *see* Article 5(4) TEU and Article 296 TFEU. This means that when various forms of intervention are available to the Union, it must, where the effect is the same, opt for the approach that leaves the greatest freedom to the Member States and individuals. National parliaments of the Member States are obliged to contribute to the good functioning of the Union by receiving draft EU legislation, ensuring

463. The Lisbon Treaty places more policy areas under the co-decision procedure than the former Treaty establishing the European Community (TEC). It makes the co-decision procedure the ordinary legislative procedure, and thus, ensures the Parliament more decision-making power.

464. The subsidiarity principle was introduced together with the environmental rules in the Single Market in 1987, cf. Art. 130r(4) EEC. The history of this principle in the EU is described by Ludwig Krämer in *EU Environmental Law*, 2016, at 1718. Concerning the special approach to the subsidiarity principle in the EU compared with the approach in US, *see* Richard L. Revesz, Philippe Sands and Richard B. Stewart, *Environmental Law, the Economy and Sustainable Development*, 2000, at 69–73.

465. Protocol No. 2 of the Lisbon Treaty sets out the requirements on the application of these principles, and Protocol No. 1 sets out the role of national Parliaments in the Union and empowers them to check that these principles are respected.

that the principle of subsidiarity is respected, taking part in the evolution mechanisms for the implementation of the EU policies and taking part in the inter-parliamentary cooperation between national parliaments and with the European Parliament, cf. Article 12 TFEU.[466]

Under Article 192(2) the unanimity of the Council, acting after consultation of the Parliament and the Economic and Social Committee is needed in special situations. According to Article 192(2) TFEU, the following EU regulatory initiatives have to be decided by the Council acting unanimously: (1) provisions primarily of a fiscal nature; (2) measures affecting; (a) town and country planning; (b) quantitative management of water resources or affecting, directly or indirectly, and the availability of those resources; (c) land use, with the exception of waste management; and (d) measures that significantly affect Member States' choice between different energy sources; and the general structure of its energy supply. According to Article 113, provision for taxes also has to be decided by the council acting unanimously. On this basis, there is no derogation from qualified majority voting in the Council.

58. The harmonisation levels ensured by the legislative basis of EU's secondary legislation as well as the instruments used by the EU institutions (directives or regulations) are of importance for the competences – including the discretionary power – of the Member States.

The EU institutions have to base their legislative initiates on the right primarily law substantive basis, cf. Article 296 TFEU. According to settled case law of the CJEU, the choice of substantive basis for an act of the Union must rest on objective factors amenable to judicial review, which include the aim and content of the measure. The substantive basis for environmental legislation is normally Article 192 TFEU. When this substantive basis is used, the rules consist of minimum harmonisation rules/standards, where Member States are expressly permitted to take more stringent environmental measures than provided for in the EU rules in question, cf. Article 193 TFEU. In contrast to this, measures based on Article 114 TFEU (the Internal Market), Article 194(2) TFEU (energy policy), Articles 38–44 TFEU (agriculture and fishery) and Article 91(1) TFEU (transport) are all intended to provide a uniform European standard by total harmonisation of the legislation (including procedural rules) in all Member States. The choice of harmonisation level made by the EU institutions must be based on objective factors, which are amenable to judicial review and in particular include the aim and content of the measure. When using Article 114, it must be shown that without the harmonisation measures the functioning of the Internal Market would be endangered and competition distorted. Member States may invoke the procedure under Article 114(4) and (5) TFEU to maintain or introduce stringent measures. The main rule is that the EU institutions may only use a single substantive basis when taking decisions in relation to new measures. However, the CJEU does accept exceptional situations, where an act

466. The Protocol on the Role of National Parliaments in the European Union and the Protocol on the Principles of Subsidiarity and Proportionality included in the Lisbon Treaty provide greater detail. The Danish Parliament has to organise its scrutiny process in a manner that makes it possible for it to take part in this decision-making process. It is not always easy.

simultaneously pursues a number of objectives or has several components that are involved, without one being secondary and indirect in relation to the other. The use of both legal bases is, for example, relevant with respect to the Directive on Promotion of the Use of Energy from Renewable Resources (the 2009 RES Directive).[467] The Directive establishing a Framework for Maritime Spatial Planning (FMSP) is another example of a secondary act relying on several treaty rules,[468] as it is based on the following rules: Article 43(2) TFEU (provisions for the agriculture and fisheries politics), Article 100(2) TFEU (provisions for sea and air transport politics), Article 192(1) (provisions for environmental politics) and Article 194(2) TFEU (provisions for energy politics). The last-mentioned Article provides the EU institutions with competence to adopt energy measures. However, it does not provide competence to regulate in a manner that would affect the Member States' right to determine the conditions for exploiting their energy resources, their choice between different energy sources or the general structure of their energy supply.

Directives and regulations are both used as measures to establish environmental obligations on the Member States and their citizens, cf. Article 288 TFEU. Such measures are also used to implement the international obligations that the EU has accepted by ratification in order to transpose the content into EU and national laws. By virtue of the nature of regulations and their function in the system of sources of EU law, the provisions of a regulation, as a general rule, have immediate effect in the national legal systems without it being necessary for the national authorities to adopt measures of application, cf. Article 288(2) TFEU:

A regulation shall have general application. It shall be binding in its entirety and directly applicable in all Member States.

Parallel or conflicting national rules in areas covered by a regulation have to be repealed. Generally, the regulations covering environmental issues are adopted in the field of environmental protection, cf. Article 192(1) when the subject concerns EU's external trade. The Waste Shipment Regulation (WSR)[469] is the implementation of the obligations under the UN Basel Convention on the Control of Transboundary Movement of Hazardous Waste and their Disposal (the Basel Convention).[470] The Rotterdam Regulation[471] and the Regulation concerning the Registration, Evaluation, Authorisation and Restriction of Chemicals (REACH)[472] are both parts of the implementation of the Rotterdam Convention. Both the

467. European Parliament and Council Directive 2009/28/EC on Promotion of the Use of Energy from Renewable Resources, as amended, *see infra* para. 229. From 2021, this Directive will be replaced by European Parliament and Council Directive 2018/201/EU on the Promotion of Energy Renewable Sources. This new 2018 RES Directive has its legal basis in Art. 194 TFEU.

468. European Parliament and Council Directive 2014/89/EU establishing a Framework for Maritime Spatial Planning. The Directive is described *infra* in paras. 130–131.

469. European Parliament and Council Regulation No. 1013/2006/EC on Shipment of Waste, as amended by Regulation No. 660/2014/EU. The Regulation is described *infra* in para. 141.

470. Concerning the vertical harmonisation, *see infra* paras 140–142.

471. European Parliament and Council Regulation No. 649/2012/EU concerning the Export and Import of Hazardous Chemicals is described *infra* in para. 209.

472. European Parliament and Council Regulation No. 1907/2006/EC concerning the Registration, Evaluation, Authorisation and Restrictions in Chemicals is described *infra* in para. 210.

WSR[473] and the Rotterdam Regulation contain certain measures that are more stringent than those of the conventions. Regulations are also used as the basis for voluntary EMAS and eco-labelling schemes. The EMAS Regulation[474] and the Ecolabel Regulation are relevant examples.[475] The just-mentioned Regulations transform the obligation under the Aarhus Convention Article 5(7)–(8) into national legislation ensuring, in a voluntary manner, that producers make available to the public information concerning the environmental performance of the production process and their products. Regulations, in principle, take effect on adaptation and publication in the EU's Official Journal. About 10% of EU environmental legislation takes the form of regulations. The Danish agri-environmental legislation in force is based on national as well as EU law, including several directly applicable EU regulations. At national level, the immediate direct effect of regulations may be given in the first instance by a measure of constitutional status providing for the supremacy of EU law. Regulations do often require national measures for their implementation as regards certain matters. The types of measures that Member States have to adopt in order to make regulations apply in practice in their jurisdiction include the appointment of competent national authorities to inspect and control the implementations and respect for the regulation. For example, the national authorities have to inspect and control that trade is not restricted in a manner that is in conflict with the REACH Regulation.

Most EU environmental legislative texts are, however, adopted in the form of *directives*. The legal characteristics of such secondary legislations are explained in Article 288 TFEU, third paragraph:

> A directive shall be binding, as to the result to be achieved, upon each Member State to which it is addressed, but shall leave to the national authorities the choice of the methods.

The directives oblige each Member State to achieve a given result when they transpose the rules into national law, but very often leave the means and methods to the decision of the Member States. EU law requires Member States to implement directives in such a way that the national implementing law is accessible to those affected by the rules, and that it is clear as to the legal effects of the rules. Some directives are framework directives used as the 'lead directives' to provide the outline for the relevant daughter directives. The important definitions and requirements of relevance for competent authorities and administrative infrastructure for the whole sector (water, waste, air, etc.) are set up in such framework directives. They set the framework for identifying and prioritising the quality planning needs, whilst other directives are dealing with the quality standards (legally binding limit values

---

473. The Waste Shipment Regulation do not apply only to EU-flagged ships, but to all waste exports from EU Member States, and thus end-of-life ships that leave EU ports, so ship-owners are not able to escape controls by reflagging to non-European flags.

474. European Parliament and Council Regulation No. 1221/2009/EC on the Voluntary Participation by Organisations in a Community Eco-Management and Audit Scheme (EMAS), as amended by Commission Regulation No. 2017/1505/EU, amending Annexes I, II and III.

475. European Parliament and Council Regulation No. 66/2010/EC on the EU Ecolabel.

and guide values), the technologically and economically feasible standards, communication and information as well as regulatory controls (such as prohibition on the use of certain types of chemicals, fuels etc.). A key consideration behind the framework directives is phasing the implementation of daughter directives in a cost-effective way, so that industries have a time period to respond to the new requirements. Existing 'daughter' directives are scheduled by the framework directives to be replaced by more stringent directives or by the framework directive itself in a defined time period.[476] The Directive on Ambient Air Quality and Cleaner Air for Europe[477] merged most of the existing legislation into a single directive.

Most directives have only vertical direct effect, as the third paragraph of Article 288 TFEU states that directives are addressed to Member States and not to individuals. Undertakings and individuals can invoke the objectives of directives vis-à-vis: (a) all national authorities; and (b) public bodies, whatever its legal form is.[478] It was stated by the Court in this judgment, that a body, which has been made responsible pursuant to a measure adopted by the State for providing a public service under the control of the State, falls within the broad definition of the 'emanation of the State', if that body has received – for the purpose of ensuring public services – special power beyond those traditional marked powers, which result from normal rules applicable in relations between individuals. In the individual directives, the Member States must be given time to bring their legislation in line with the requirements. It follows from the principle of loyal cooperation, cf. Article 4(3) TEU that during the implementation period, the Member States must refrain from taking any measures liable seriously to compromise the result prescribed by the directive under preparation. In the absence of concrete and specific provisions and requirements, it is primarily for the Member States to determine the concrete design of transformations into national legislation. Normally, the Member States will enjoy considerable discretion, at least in respect of how the environmental minimum quality standards are transposed into national legislation and enforced within the limits of the principle of loyal cooperation – effective, preventive, non-discriminatory and proportional. National law must provide the instruments, which public authorities can use to attain the appropriate level of environmental protection, nature management, etc. One modification of the need for implementation before the directive has effect is based on the 'principle of the direct effect of directives' developed by CJEU case law. In deciding whether a particular provision in a directive is directly effective, the following criteria are applied: (a) the provision must establish protection and/or rights to the private party; (b) the description of the protection and/or rights must be sufficiently clear, precise and unconditional, leaving no room for the exercise of discretion in implementation by the Member States; and (c) it is only after the time limit for national implementation that direct effect is relevant. Directives laying down precise and detailed conditions to which products harmful to the environment must conform before being placed on the market will normally be directly

476. By way of example it may be mentioned, the WFD described *infra* in para. 103. Concerning the Waste Framework Directive, *see infra* para. 145.

477. Concerning the European Parliament and Council Directive 2008/50/EC on Ambient Air Quality and Cleaner Air for Europe, *see infra* para. 75.

478. Cf. CJEU Case C-188/89 *Foster v. British Gas.*

effective. A 'direct effect' of directives cannot be invoked to establish a breach of provisions in relations between individuals, as directives do not directly impose obligations upon persons or undertakings. The horizontal direct effect of directives has however been accepted by the CJEU in very special situations.[479] EU law, in furtherance of the 'principle of legal certainty', requires also implementation of the directives to be carried out at national level by way of legally binding provisions.

The objectives of *secondary EU environmental legislation* may usefully be grouped into:

- designation of competent authorities at both national and regional/local levels;
- procedural rules and the establishment of systems for notification of the public and stakeholders;
- obligations on operating licences, including environmental approvals;
- emissions limit values that are legally binding thresholds on concentration that must not be exceeded;
- environmental quality standards (EQS) (i.e., limit on levels of specified pollutants, chemical and ecological potential);
- development of quality management strategies and plans for improving environmental quality;
- quality assessment and management;
- prevention of hazardous risks, risk management and safety reporting obligations;
- technical standards, product type approvals, and material handling;
- free movements of goods and services;
- monitoring and information exchange.

As mentioned above, the type approval is an instrument used in environmental law. It is based on rules making it mandatory to follow a procedure whereby a manufacturer can obtain certification – from a competent accredited body – documenting that the product meets the requirements of the relevant regulation or directive. Type approvals need to be handled by accredited testing laboratory and implemented as part of the national registration process. The CE marking symbolises the conformity of a product with the applicable EU requirements imposed on the manufacturer.[480] The principle of the type approval rules is that the competent body that grants a type approval for a component or technical unit is responsible for ensuring the conformity of production during the whole period of validity of the approval in question. Each Member State shall register and permit the sale and entry into service of new products on grounds relating to their construction and functioning, if they are accompanied by a valid certification of conformity. The ISO standard on environmental management standards is one of the many ISO standards that are part of EU secondary legislation. It is integrated in the EMAS III Regulation.[481] The key stakeholders involved in this voluntary management system are: (a) the

479. *See* C-201/02 *Delena Weels*.

480. The 'CE Mark' is used by the manufactures as a mark on the compliance of the labelled product with the essential requirements laid down in EU product directives.

481. European Parliament and Council Regulation No. 1221/2009/EC on the Voluntary Participation by Organisations in a Community Eco-Management and Audit Scheme (EMAS), as amended by Commission Regulation No. 2017/1505/EU amending Annexes I, II and III.

national accreditation body; (b) the verification bodies; (c) industries and public institutions; (d) environmental regulators; (e) the public; and (f) company stakeholders. Under the Accreditation and Certification Scheme connected to the EMAS regulation, the National Accreditation Body (in Denmark – DANAK) accredits the Environmentally Sound Management (ESM) certification body. These accredited ESM certification bodies are competent to assess and certify companies/institutions, which have properly designed and implemented EMSs in compliance with the ISO 14000 series.[482] Under the Lisbon Treaty, the national environmental authorities must, if necessary, take effective, dissuasive and proportionate sanctions in order to implement and enforce EU law. Most secondary EU legislation requires environmental quality monitoring to be undertaken, and the Member States have to report the results and the degree of compliance to the Commission, the European Environmental Agency (located in Copenhagen, Denmark) and the public. The design of reporting is specified by the Directive on Standardizing and Rationalizing Reports on the Implementation of Certain Directives relating to the Environment.[483] On a sectoral basis, the Directive aims at rationalising and improving the provisions on the transmission of information and the publication of reports concerning certain environmental directives. In relation to some directives, the Commission has established the questionnaires for the Member States' reports on the implementation.

59. Danish environmental legislation consists of framework rules empowering the Minister for Environment (or other ministers) to implement EU directives as well as Danish acts through statutory orders, circulars, plans, guidelines and decisions. The statutory orders are binding administrative rules. They set best available techniques (BATs)-based effluent emission limit values typically established by the EU, which are then incorporated in the environmental approval system and its operating licences.[484] More generally, the rules provide substantial discretion to decision-makers and institute procedural procedures. The decisions on environmental protection and nature conservation, etc. are usually made on the basis of planning: either in the form of spatial plans or sector plans. The Danish rules on supervision and control generally leave it to the authorities to determine the extent of the supervision and the measures to be taken (provided they respect the proportionality principle). The implementation of the IED in 2013 has made the supervision obligation clearer.[485] The supervisory authority must take the necessary steps in accordance with the 'official principle'[486] in every case of established or possible adverse effect on the environment, so that the authority has the correct basis on which to make its decision.

Decisions concerning approval of new activities, as well as decisions of an encumbered nature (bans, orders and annulment of previous environmental approvals/permits/operating licences) are all very important means under environmental law. Bans, orders and annulments are relevant in cases where the addressee

482. The accreditation is based on the ISO Guide.
483. European Parliament and Council Directive 91/692/EEC, as amended by Regulation No. 1882/2003/EC of the European Parliament and of the Council of 29 September 2003.
484. Concerning the environmental approval systems, *see infra* paras 61–66.
485. Concerning the mandatory inspection system, *see infra* paras 67–66.
486. The 'official principle' is established as an important, binding principle by traditional public law.

does not comply with the conditions attached to a permit (approval, operating licences, authorisation or dispensation), the rules of a statutory order or an act. A series of environmental acts requires the authorities to impose injunctions/prohibitions, which are registered in the real estate register. The registration will impose a burden on the property, and also on the creditors and potential buyers. The authority in question will then cancel the injunction from the registry as soon as the necessary adjustments have been made. The authorities often impose conditions on permission to mitigate harm to neighbours of real estate, to the sensitive nature, or to the public generally.

Another type of means is notification. Such instruments make it mandatory for the private actors to inform the authorities about a certain type of activity (e.g., small building activities, change in the permitted production, transport of contaminated soil, etc.) before starting the activities. The authorities will normally have a short time period to respond on the notification. If the authority is not responding, it is then legal to start as the passivity is regarded as acceptance of the activity. Product type approval systems are other examples of instruments used by the Danish Parliament and very often as a consequence of EU legislation.[487] Most of the mentioned Danish environmental acts are the result of implementation of EU directives. If there is a need for inspection, the authorities must respect the special rules based on the 'law and order principle' protecting private person against the authorities' use of their public power.[488] This Act is reflecting the fundamental human right of privacy that is also protected by the Danish Constitution.

The following Danish acts are important sources of relevant public, private and environmental statutory legislation.

Agriculture

- *Agricultural Holdings Act* (Promulgation Order No. 27 of 4 January 2017, as amended by Act No. 1518 of 18 December 2018).
- *Agricultural Aid Act* (Promulgation Order No. 231 of 22 March 2018 on the Administration of the EU Regulations under the CAP).
- *Environmental Approval for Livestock Holdings Act* (Promulgation Order No. 520 of 1 May 2019.
- *Hedgerow and Subsidies for Planting of Hedgerows Act* (Promulgation Order No. 15 of 14 January 2017).
- *Land Allocation Act* (Promulgation Order No. 31 of 4 January 2017).
- *Management of Agricultural Land Act* (Promulgation Order No. 958 of 10 July 2017).
- *Organic Farming Act* (Promulgation Order No. 21 of 4 January 2017).
- Use of Fertilisers by Agriculture and on Nutrient-reducing Measures Act (Promulgation Order No. 338 of 2 April 2019).

487. Concerning type approvals as part of Danish legislation, *see supra* para. 59.
488. *See, e.g.*, the Act No. 442 of 9 June 2004 on the Supervisory Authority's Use of Enforcement Powers and the Obligation on Information. This Act is also titled 'the Rule of Law Act'. The Act has been amended several times.

Chemicals and GMOs

- *Chemical Substances and Products Act* (Promulgation Order No. 115 of 26 January 2017).
- *Environment and Genetic Engineering Act* (Promulgation Order No. 9 of 4 January 2017).

Energy

- *Atomic Plant Act* (Act No. 170 of 16 May 1962, as amended by Act No. 332 of 19 June 1974, Act No. 244 of 12 May 1976 and Act No. 69 of 4 February 2004).
- *Electricity Supply Act* (Promulgation Order No. 52 of 17 January 2019).
- *Energy Efficiency Act* (Promulgation Order No. 1065 of 12 November 2012, as amended by Act No. 345 of 8 April 2014, Act No. 1498 of 23 December 2014, Act No. 1876 of 29 December 2015 and Act No. 7690 of 8 June 2018).
- *Energy Labelling of Energy Related Products* (Promulgation Order No. 1026 of 4 November 2011).
- *Heating Supply Act* (Promulgation Order No. 64 of 21 January 2019).
- *Natural Gas Supply Act* (Promulgation Act No. 1127 of 5 September 2018).
- *Nuclear Safety Measures and Environmental Issues relating to Nuclear Plants Act* (Act No. 244 of 5 December 1976).
- *Promotion of Renewable Energy Act* (RES Act – Promulgation Order No. 356 of 4 April 2019).
- *Sustainable Biofuels Act* (Promulgation Order No. 62 of 17 January 2019).
- *Use of Nuclear Substances Act* (Act No. 94 of 31 March 1953 on the Use of Nuclear Substances, as amended by Act No. 99 of 10 February 2009, and by Act No. 23 of 15 January 2018).

Fishery

- *Fisheries Act* (Promulgation Order No. 261 of 21 March 2019, as amended by Act No. 558 of 7 May 2019 and Act No. 559 of 7 May 2019).

General environmental and climate legislation

- *Carbon Dioxide Allowances Act* (Act No. 1095 of 28 November 2012, as amended by Promulgation Order No. 1070 of 9 September 2014, Promulgation Order No. 1307 of 24 November 2014, Act No. 1497 of 23 December 2014 and Promulgation Order No. 1605 of 14 December 2016).
- *Climate Policy Act* (Act No. 716 of 25 June 2014).
- *Contaminated Soil Act* (Promulgation Order No. 282 of 27 March 2017, as amended by Act No. 278 of 17 April 2018).
- *Environmental Protection Act* (Promulgation Order No. 681 of 2 July 2019).

General administrative rules on environmental procedural rights and rules on trade

- *Access to Public Files Act* (Act No. 572 of 19 December 1985 – only in force in respect to environmental issues – in other cases it is replaced by Act No. 606 of 12 June 2013 as amended).
- *Administration of Justice Act* (Promulgation Order No. 1284 of 14 November 2018 as amended many times in 2018 and 2019).
- *Administrative Procedures Act* (Promulgation Order No. 1365 of 7 December 2007 with amendments in respect to access to environmental information – in relation to other rules of this general Act it is now replaced by Act No. 433 of 22 April 2014 as amended).
- *Decision-Making Concerning Expropriation of Real Estate Act* (Promulgation Order No. 1161 of 20 November 2008, as amended by Act No. 1520 of 27 December 2014 and Act No. 1895 of 29 December 2015).
- *Freedom of Access to Environment Information Act* (Promulgation Order No. 980 of 16 August 2017).[489]
- *Strategic Environmental Assessment of Plans and Programmes and the Environmental Impact Assessment of Individual Projects* (SEA and EIA Act) (Promulgation Order No. 1225 of 25 October 2018).
- *Parliamentary Ombudsman Act* (Promulgation Order No. 349 of 22 March 2013).
- *Spatial Information Act* (Act No. 746 of 15 June 2017).
- *Statute of the Municipalities Act* (Promulgation Order No. 47 of 15 January 2019).
- *Competition Act* (Promulgation Order No. 155 of 1 March 2018).

Jurisdiction, subsoil and rules on self-government, etc.

- *Agreement under International Law with the Government of the Faroe Islands on Self-Government* (Act No. 579 of 24 June 2005).
- *Agreement under International Law with the Government of the Greenland on Self-Government* (Act No. 473 of 12 June 2009).
- *Constitution of the Danish Kingdom Act* (Act No. 169 of 5 June 1953).
- *Continental Shelf Act* (Promulgation Order No. 1101 of 18 November 2005).
- *Delegation of Power to Government of the Faroe Islands Act* (Act No. 578 of 24 June 2005).
- *Danish Territorial Sea Act* (Act No. 200 of 7 April 1999).
- *Denmark's accession to the European Community Act* (Act No. 447 of 11 October 1972, as amended by Act No. 259 of 28 May 1984, Act No. 352 of 4 June

489. In s. 14 of Act No. 639 of 12 June 2013 on the Amendment of Several Acts as a Consequence of Act No. 606 of 12 June 2013 on Access to Public Information, it is stated that the new s. 6(2) in the Act on Freedom of Access to Environmental Information has to be used together with a version of the Act on Administrative Procedure from 2012 (Promulgation Order No. 988 of 9 October 2012) and not newer versions (currently Promulgation Order No. 433 of 22 April 2014, as amended by Act No. 503 of 23 May 2018). This legal solution makes the use of the rules on access to environmental information very complicated and inconsistent.

1986, Act No. 281 of 28 April 1993, Act No. 322 of 6 June 1998, Act No. 499 of 7 June 2001, and Act No. 321 of 30 April 2008).
- *Exclusive Economic Zones Act* (Act No. 411 of 22 May 1996).
- *Subsoil Act* (Promulgation Order No. 1190 of 21 September 2018, as amended by Act No. 500 of 1 May 2019).

Nature, coast, wildlife and landscape, culture protection and management

- *Coastal Protection Act* (Promulgation Order No. 57 of 21 January 2019).
- *Environmental Objectives Act* (Promulgation Order No. 119 of 26 January 2017).
- *Forest Act* (Promulgation Order No. 315 of 28 March 2019).
- *Hunting and Wildlife Management Act* (Promulgation Order No. 265 of 21 March 2019).
- *National Parks Act* (Promulgation Order No. 120 of 26 January 2017).
- *Nature Protection Act* (Promulgation Order No. 240 of 13 March 2019).
- *Museum Act* (Promulgation Order No. 358 of 8 April 2014, as amended by Act No. 1715 of 27 December 2016).
- *Conservation of Buildings and the Culture in the Cities Act* (Promulgation Order No. 219 of 6 March 2018).

Maritime water, watercourses and water supply activities/management

- *Environmental Marine Protection Act* (Promulgation Order No. 1033 of 4 September 2017, as amended by Act No. 463 of 15 May 2017, Act No. 1534 of 19 December 2017 and Act No. 1552 of 18 December 2018).
- *Marine Strategic Management Act* (Promulgation Order No. 117 of 26 January 2017, as amended by Act No. 1554 of 19 December 2017).
- *Ochre Act* (Promulgation Order No. 1581 of 10 December 2015).
- *Sewage Works Payment Obligation Act* (Promulgation Order No. 663 of 7 June 2010, as amended several times – the last amendments are made by Act No. 132 of 16 February 2016).
- *Water Basin Management Planning Act* (Promulgation Order No. 126 of 26 January 2017).
- *Watercourse Act* (Promulgation Order No. 127 of 26 January 2017).
- *Water Sector Act* (Act No. 469 of 12 June 2009, as amended several times the last amendments are made by Act No. 662 of 8 June 2017).
- *Water Supply, etc. Act* (Promulgation Order No. 118 of 22 February 2018).

Liability

- *Environmental Damage Act* (Act No. 277 of 27 March 2017).
  Act on Strict Liability for Pollution Cost by Heavily Polluting Activities (Promulgation Order No. 994 of 9 September 2014).

- *Claims for Damages by Nuclear Installations Act* (Promulgation Order No. 993 of 9 September 2014, as amended by 492 of 17 June 2008).
- *Product Liability Act* (Promulgation Order No. 261 of 20 March 2007, as amended by Act No. 261 of 20 March 2007).
- *Statute of Limitations Act* (Promulgation Order No. 1238 of 9 September 2015, as amended by Act No. 140 of 28 February 2018).

Physical planning, zoning, construction, registration and mineral resources

- *Building Act* (Promulgation Order No. 1178 of 23 September 2016, as amended by Act No. 734 of 8 June 2018, Act No. 1711 of 27 December 2018, and Act No. 368 of 9 April 2019).
- *Land Registration Act* (Promulgation Order No. 1075 of 30 September 2014, as amended by several acts, the last amendments were made by Act No. 1722 of 27 December 2018).
- *Parcelling-Out Act* (Promulgation Order No. 769 of 7 June 2018, as amended by Act No. 80 of 24 January 2017 and Act No. 1711 of 27 December 2018).
- *Planning Act* (Promulgation Order No. 287 of 16 April 2018, as amended by Act No. 1712 of 27 December 2018, Act No. 1714 of 27 December 2018, Act No. 1715 of 27 December 2018).
- *Summer Cottage and Camping Act* (Promulgation Order No. 949 of 3 July 2013, as amended by Act No. 86 of 28 January 2014, Act No. 1658 of 20 December 2016 and Act No. 368 of 9 April 2019).
- *Mineral Resources Act* (Promulgation Order No. 124 of 26 January 2017, as amended by Act No. 427 of 18 May 2016 and Act No. 720 of 8 June 2018).

Tax Law and Law on State Aid

- *Coal-Tax Act* (Promulgation Order No. 1080 of 3 September 2015, as amended several times – the last amendments were made by Act No. 331 of 30 March 2019).
- *CO_2 Tax Act* (Promulgation Order No. 321 of 4 April 2011, as amended several times – the last amendments were made by Act No. 331 of 30 March 2019).
- *CFC-Tax Act* (Promulgation Order No. 69 of 17 January 2017, as amended by Act No. 1431 of 5 December 2018 and by Act No. 1728 of 27 December 2018).
- *Electricity-Tax Act* (Promulgation Act No. 308 of 24 March 2017, as amended several times – the last amendments were made by Act No. 331 of 30 March 2019).
- *Income Taxes on Hydrocarbon Extraction Act* (Promulgation Order No. 1153 of 18 September 2018).
- *Natural Gas-Tax Act* (Promulgation Order No. 312 of 1 April 2011, as amended several times – the last amendments were made by Act No. 331 of 30 March 2019).

- *NO_x Tax Act* (Promulgation Order No. 1144 of 13 October 2017, as amended by Act 1385 of 28 December 2011, Act No. 104 of 13 February 2018 and Act No. 1728 of 27 December 2018).
- *Mineral-Oil-Tax Act* (Promulgation Order No. 1118 of 26 September 2014, as amended several times – the last amendments were made by Act No. 331 of 30 March 2019).
- *Pesticides Taxes Act* (Promulgation Order No. 232 of 26 February 2015, as amended by Act No. 1728 of 27 December 2018).
- *SO_2 Tax Act* (Promulgation Order No. 335 of 18 March 2015).
- *Taxes on Lead-Batteries and Hermetically Sealed Nickel-Cadmium Accumulators Act* (Promulgation Order No. 244 of 10 March 2017, as amended by Act No. 1431 of 5 December 2018 and by Act No. 1728 of 27 December 2018).
- *Mineral Resources and Waste Taxes Act* (Promulgation Order No. 412 of 21 April 2017, as amended by Act No. 1728 of 27 December 2018).

Transport and infrastructure

- *Aviation Act* (Promulgation Order No. 1149 of 13 October 2017, as amended in 2018 by Act No. 731 of 8 June 2018 and Act No. 1706 of 27 December 2018).
- *Harbours Act* (Promulgation Order No. 457 of 23 May 2012, as amended by Act No. 658 of 8 June 2016 and Act No. 144 of 28 February 2018).
- *Public Roads Act* (Act No. 1520 of 27 December 2014 as amended several times – the last amendments were made by Act No. 523 of 22 May 2017).
- *Shipping Act* (Promulgation Order No. 1505 of 17 December 2018).

Part I. Pollution Control

Chapter 1. General Law

60. Pollution is one of the most serious threats to life on Earth. Many of the problems related to direct and indirect harm and damages are caused by pollution from point sources (such as industrial installations) as well as diffuse sources. The enforcement of environmental obligations is depending on the monitoring and reporting obligations that are established both by international agreements, especially the PRTR Protocol, by EU secondary environmental legislation and by national legislation. The access for the public to such information is also very often a precondition for the fulfilment of environmental obligations.[490]

The PRTR Protocol was adopted on 21 May 2003 by the 'Extraordinary Meeting of the Parties to the Aarhus Convention'. In accordance with Article 4 of the Protocol, each party shall establish and maintain a publicly accessible national pollutant release and transfer register that:

(a) is facility-specific with respect to reporting on point sources;
(b) accommodates reporting on diffuse sources;
(c) is pollutant-specific or waste-specific, as appropriate;
(d) is multimedia, distinguishing among releases to air, land and water;
(e) includes information on transfers;
(f) is based on mandatory reporting on a periodic basis;
(g) includes standardised and timely data, a limited number of standardised reporting thresholds and limited provisions, if any, for confidentiality;
(h) is coherent and designed to be user-friendly and publicly accessible, including in electronic form;
(i) allows for public participation in its development and modification; and
(j) is a structured, computerised database or several linked databases maintained by the competent authority.

The Protocol was the first legally binding international instrument on registration of pollution release and on the establishment of an electronic database with environmental information received on pollutants emitted from and reported by the largest industrial facilities. The term 'release' is defined in Article 2(7) as:

490. *See supra* para. 28 on the PRTR rules, *supra* para. 29 on access to environmental information, and *supra* para. 34 on the importance of monitoring and reporting of general information on the status of the environment.

> any introduction of pollutants into the environment as a result of any human activity, whether deliberate or accidental or not routine, including spilling, emitting, discharging, injecting, disposing or dumping, or through sewer systems without final waste-water treatment.

It was an ambition behind the design of the provisions to balance the reporting burden against the relevance of the information provided as well as to create pressure on the companies to avoid being identified as major polluters and provide incentives for facilities to invest to reduce emission that have to be registered.[491] Reporting on diffuse sources is also included as a core element of the Protocol, cf. Article 4(b). The concept of 'transfer' that is included in the scope of the Protocol applies to the movement of pollutants within and between facilities. It is using the term 'off-site-transfer' as:

> the movement beyond the boundaries of the facility of either pollutants or waste destined for disposal or recovery and of pollutants in wastewater destined for wastewater treatment', cf. Article 2(8).

The database – that consists of data on sixty-four categories of activities with capacity thresholds (Annex I) and eighty-six substances and categories of substances with pollutant thresholds (Annex II) – is now linking to other relevant environmental and ancillary information that may be spread over different databases.[492]

The Protocol is signed both by Denmark[493] and the EU.[494] The EU signed and ratified the Protocol with a declaration on its great satisfaction with it as an essential step forward in further encouraging and supporting public awareness in the field of environment and better implementation of environmental legislation in the UNECE region, in accordance with the principle of sustainability. EU has implemented the obligations that are laid down in the Protocol by means of the Regulation concerning the Establishment of the European Pollutant Release and Transfer Register (E-PRTR Regulation).[495] Based on the requirement in Article 14(1) of the Regulation, the Commission published a guidance document in May 2006. The guidance document is available in twenty-two EU languages on the webpage of the Commission and the EEA. The E-PRTR builds upon and expands the former European Pollutant Emission Register (E-PER) that was established in 2000.[496] Reporting obligations are linked to specific types of industrial activities (listed in Annex I

491. UNECE, Guidance on Implementation of the Protocol on Pollutant Release and Transfer Registers to the Convention on Access to Information, Public Participation in Decision-making and Access to Justice in Environmental Matters, at 2.
492. The portal is open for the pubic, *see* https://prtr.unece.org.
493. Denmark signed the Protocol on 21 May 2003 with reservation for Greenland and the Faroe Islands.
494. The Council signed the Protocol on 21 May 2003 and ratified it on 21 Feb. 2006.
495. European Parliament and Council Regulation No. 166/2006/EC of 18 January 2006 concerning the establishment of a European Pollutant Release and Transfer Register. The PRTR Regulation replaced the Decision 2000/479/EC on the implementation of a European Pollutant Emission Register (E-PER). The E-PRTR is hosted by the Environmental Agency in Copenhagen.
496. Commissions Report on Progress in implementing Regulation 166/2006/EC concerning the Establishment of a European Pollutant Release and Transfer Register (E-PRTR), at 3.

to the Regulation)[497] and pollutant thresholds (listed in Annex II)[498] with a view to address the major sources of industrial pollution, notably activities covered by the Industrial Emission Directive (IED). According to Article 10(1) of the Regulation, the Commission shall make the E-PRTR publicly accessible. It has been ensured by a portal that can be visit at the internet.[499] The E-PRTR has now key environmental data from 33,000 industrial facilities, covering sixty-five economic activities across the Europe (not only from the Member States).[500] The data covers mass releases to air, water and soil as well as the types of waste transferred from facilities to waste handlers – both inside and outside each European country. In an assessment of the coherence between this data collection and the reporting under EU's directives, it was concluded that there is not only a high level of coherence but also some incoherence between E-PRTR and EU legislation on air, water and waste.[501] The Regulation is directly applicable as part of the national law in the Member States and it imposes duties on the Danish companies covered by the scope of it, cf. Article 288(2) TFEU.[502] The information on these obligations is published as a statutory order by the Ministry of Environment and Food of Denmark.[503] The facility operators have to report specific data annually to the competent national authority with an indication of whether the information is based on measurement, calculation or estimation as well as information on the analytical methods and/or the method of calculation that the operator has used, cf. Article 5(1). The competent national authorities have to check the quality of the reported data and transmit them to the Commission and the European Environmental Agency (EEA). It is the Danish Agency on Environmental Protection that is the Danish competent authority in respect to the general administration and the municipalities have to receive the reports and to check the quality of the data received.[504] The Member States must

497. The list largely reflects the pollutants lists in Annex I of the former IPPC Directive as well as the Annex I of the IE Directive. It also reflects the 2006 scientific understanding of the main environmental issues associated with Annex I Activities, cf. the Commission's *Service Request – Annex 'Specific Terms of References'. Review of E-PRTR implementation and related guidance*.
498. The list largely reflects the pollutants lists in Annex II of the IE Directive.
499. *See* https://prtr.eea.europa.eu/#/home.
500. The 2013 data on the industrial installations in thirty-two European countries – the EU-28, except Croatia, Iceland, Lichtenstein, Norway, Switzerland and Serbia – are now available in the EEA's data service.
501. Commission Staff Working Document, REFIT evaluation of Regulation (EC) No. 166/2006 concerning the Establishment of a European Pollutant Release and Transfer Register (E-PRTR), SWD(2017) 710 final, at 18–20. It is, e.g., mentioned that the E-PRTR has added five substances to the list in order to streamline it with the Water Framework Directive, but the new Directive on the Environmental Quality Standards in the Field of Water (EQSD) is evolving more quality to take account of new treats, e.g., endocrine disrupter. Concerning the Water Framework Directive and the EQSD, *see infra* para. 105. The reporting under the Urban Waste Water Treatment Directive has a number of different and much lower thresholds.
502. Concerning regulations as part of national law, *see supra* para. 58.
503. Statutory Order No. 1172 of 13 October 2013 on a Pollution Release and Transfer Register (PRTR).
504. Sections 4 and 5 of the Statutory Order on a Pollution Release and Transfer Register (PRTR).

put rules for penalties in case of infringements of their national legislation, cf. Article 20. The Danish rules establish the legal basis for periodic penalty payments.[505]

61. The regulation of polluting activities within the EU is covered by several regulations and directives. Some of the most important secondary acts are the following: (a) the Industrial Emission Directive (IED),[506] Directive of Landfill of Waste (hereinafter Landfill of Waste Directive),[507] the Seveso III Directive,[508] the Directive on the Safety of Offshore Oil and Gas Operations[509] and the EMAS Regulation III.[510] In accordance with Article 193 TFEU, as these directives are built on Article 192(1) TFEU as the legal basis, the provisions do not prevent Member States from maintaining or introducing more stringent protective measures.

The IED had to be transposed into national legislation by Member States by 7 January 2013. It replaced several directives.[511] It establishes a mandatory environmental approval system to prevent and control pollution by a case-by-case assessment of installations listed in the Annex I of the Directive, cf. Article 10. The terminology ‘installation’ is defined in Article 3(3) as:

> a stationary technical unit in which one or more activities listed in Annex I or in Part 1 of Annex VII are carried out, and any other directly associated activities on the same site, which have a technical connection with the activities listed in those Annexes; and which could have an effect on emission and pollution.

The threshold values for activities covered by the IED provisions are included in its Annex I in which the categories of activities are listed with reference to Article 10. Most of these thresholds are the same as those used in the former Integrated Pollution Prevention and Control Directive (IPPC Directive). New activities have been included in the IED as covered by the environmental approval obligation. It is for example the case with the waste disposal and recovery activities of non-hazardous waste. The Directive applies to the industrial activities – including pigs and poultry

505. Section 7 of the Statutory Order on a Pollution Release and Transfer Register (PRTR).
506. European Parliament and Council Directive 2010/75/EU on Industrial Emissions (integrated pollution prevention and control); *see infra* at para. 164 concerning the Arts 42–55 of the IED that deal with special provisions for waste incineration and waste co-incineration plants.
507. Council Directive 1999/31/EC on the Landfill of Waste, as amended – *see infra* para. 162.
508. European Parliament and Council Directive 2012/18/EU on the Control of Major Accident. Concerning this Seveso III Directive, *see infra* para. 203.
509. European Parliament and Council Directive 2013/30/EU on Safety of Offshore Oil and Gas Operations.
510. European Parliament and Council Regulation No. 1221/2009/EC on the Voluntary Participation by Organisations in a Community Eco-Management and Audit Scheme, as amended. Concerning the EMAS Regulation, *see supra* at para. 57.
511. European Parliament and Council Directive on Industrial Emissions (IED) integrates and codifies the IPPC Directive (2008/1/EC), the Directive on Waste Incineration (2000/76/EC), the VOC Directive (1999/13/EC), the LCP Directive (2001/80/EC), and three directives on Titanium Dioxide (78/176/EEC, 82/883/EEC and 92/112/EEC).

farms – giving rise to pollution referred to in Chapters II–VI. The IED has tightened up requirements for industrial operators as well as competent authorities. It is based on the 'integrated approach' ensuring a holistic assessment of all environmental aspects of the polluting activities. It lays down the principles governing the procedures and conditions for the grant of environmental approvals to construct and operate large industrial installations. The polluting substances that are of relevance in the approval system established by the Directive are listed in its Annex II. There are thirteen air polluting substances, and thirteen water pollutant substances on the list.[512] The IED do not in all respect set uniform EU targets. Applicable emission limits, quality criteria and other environmental conditions that have to be respected in the approval of installations are provided through the EU environmental directives as implemented by national rules, spatial plans, management plans, etc. on:

- the air quality obligations established in accordance with the Directive on Ambient Air Quality and the Fourth Daughter Directive and controlled under the NEC Directive;[513]
- the status of 'good ecological status' and 'good chemical status' in the relevant water recipient established on the basis of the WFD[514] and the Strategic Marine Framework Directive;
- the waste reduction and reuse of waste established in accordance with Waste Framework Directive and the daughter directives;[515]
- the noise quality established in accordance with the Environmental Noise Directive (END);[516]
- the Nature 2000 sites established in accordance with the Habitats Directive and the Wild Birds Directive.[517]

The IED sets out performance criteria as BAT for each IE activity which operators need to meet fixed through the term included in the individual operating licence delivered by the national authorities. Under the IED, the existing emission limits must be used in combination with the use of BAT and BAT conclusions as BAT Associated Emission Limit Levels (BAT-AELs). BAT is defined in Article 3(10):

> '*best available techniques*' means the most effective and advanced stage in the development of activities and their methods of operation which indicates the

512. The term substance is defined in Art. 3(1) of the IED as any chemical element and its compounds with the exception of radioactive substances and some GMMs. The term 'pollution' is defined in Art. 3(2) identical with the use of the term, e.g., in the Water Framework Directive.
513. Concerning the directives on the protection of the air quality, *see infra* paras 75–76.
514. European Parliament and Council Directive 2000/60/EC establishing a Framework for Community Action in the Field of Water Policy. The Water Framework Directive and its daughter directives are described *infra* in paras 103–107.
515. The Waste Framework Directive and the many daughter directives are described *infra* in paras 145–146, 149–152, and 154.
516. European Parliament and Council Directive 2002/49/EC relating to the Assessment and Management Environmental Noise. The Directive is described *infra* in para. 188.
517. Concerning the Habitats Directive and the Wild Birds Directive, *see infra* paras 241 and 252–253.

practical suitability of particular techniques for providing the basis for emission limit values and other permit conditions designed to prevent and, where that is not practicable, to reduce emissions and the impact on the environment as a whole:

1) '*techniques*' include both the technology used and the way in which the installation is designed, built, maintained, operated and decommissioned;
2) '*available techniques*' mean those developed on a scale which allows implementation in the relevant industrial sector, under economically and technically viable conditions, taking into consideration the costs and advantages, whether or not the techniques are used or produced inside the Member State in question, as long as they are reasonably accessible to the operator;
3) '*best*' means most effective in achieving a high general level of protection of the environment as a whole.

The BATs are defined per sector in reference documents, BREFs (also called BAT notes) that serve as benchmarks for environmental performance. The BREFs deal with resource use, energy efficiency, air pollution, soil and groundwater pollution, waste, as well as odour, noise and accident prevention, cf. Annex III of the IED. The Commission produces BREFs for each IE sector. The roles of the BREFs for environmental performance have been strengthened by the BAT conclusions that are defined in Article 3(12) as:

> a document containing the parts of the BAT reference document laying down the conclusions on the best available techniques, their description, information to assess their applicability, the emission limit levels (ELVs) associated with the best available techniques, associated monitoring, associated consumption levels and, where appropriate, relevant site remediation measures.

Article 13(5) provides that decisions on BAT conclusions to be made by the Commission shall be based on the criteria mentioned in Annex III and adopted with the regulatory committee procedure with publication of comitology decisions, cf. Article 75(2). The Member States are involved in the review of existing BREFs[518] and the BAT conclusions of these. The Commission publishes the BREFs and the BAT conclusions without delay in all official languages of the EU, cf. Article 13(6).

The Directive is based on the 'polluter pays principle'. The definition of the operator is established by Article 3(15):

> any natural or legal person who operates or controls in whole or in part the installation or combustion plant, waste incineration plant or waste co-incineration plant or, where this is provided for in national law, to whom decisive economic power over the technical function of the installation or plant has been delegated.

518. The CEUJ has stated in Case 235/02 *Saetti and Frediani* that BREFs are relevant in the decision-making on the categorisation/definition of waste.

In respect to the subsidiarity principle, Recital 16 of the IED states that it is for the Member States to determine the approach for assigning responsibilities to operators of installations provided that compliance with this Directive is ensured. The Member States have to establish national legislation that ensures that the operator is the primarily responsible for the protection of the environment through:

- Applying for a permit before starting up any activities or changing the permitted installations with negative consequences for the environment, cf. Recital 11 and Articles 4 and 20.
- Notifying the competent authorities of any planned change, which might affect the environment, cf. Recital 18.
- Ensuring adequate information in the decision-making process in the application for an approval and in situations where the competent authority requests necessary information, cf. Recital 11 and Articles 12 and 21(2).
- Respecting the general governing principles that are stated in Article 11 as basic obligations as well as the terms laid down in the permit, cf. Article 14.
- Describing the level of significance of pollution of soil and groundwater caused by the activities and paying the cost of bringing the environmental quality back to the baseline quality level when the activities are stopped or the installations as such are closed, cf. Recital 25 and Article 22.

The operator applying for an environmental approval must demonstrate to the satisfaction of the authority, in his/her application and during the licensing process, that the installation/facility will be operated in such a way that all the appropriate preventative measures are taken against pollution through: (a) following the guidelines of the BAT notes (BREFs), and if any BAT conclusion is established ensuring respect for this; (b) the environmental limit values (based on BAT); (c) not breaching the quality standards for the recipient; (d) preventing waste, and where that is not possible respecting the waste hierarchy established by the Waste Framework Directive; (e) using energy efficiently; (f) preventing accidents and limiting their negative effects; (g) returning the site to a satisfactory state when the installation closes; and (h) seeing to that monitoring and reporting is carried out within a quality-assurance regime by an accredited actor. The identification of BAT emphasis is placed on pollution prevention techniques rather than end-of-pipe treatment. Operators of the IE activities that typically cause soil and groundwater pollution will have to provide a 'baseline report' on the environmental impact with information about the state of soil and groundwater by relevant 'hazardous substances' classified under the CLP Regulation,[519] cf. Article 3(19) the definition of 'baseline report' and the provisions laid down in Article 22 on when and how the approval authority has to ask the operator to provide such a report as a condition for getting a permit. Where activities involve the use, production or release of relevant hazardous substances, baseline reports are to be drawn up by the operator before starting or changing activities. This obligation to send a report aims to prevent and tackle

519. European Parliament and Council Regulation No. 1272/2008/EC on the Classification, Labelling and Packaging of Substances and Mixes. *See infra* paras 216–217 concerning this CLP Regulation.

potential soil and groundwater contamination, cf. Article 22(2). In 2014, the Commission published a guidance on how to understand this provision.[520] The report formed the basis for a comparison with the state on contamination upon definitive cessation of activities. As an important part of the application, the operator also has to prepare an EIA following the conditions established by the EIA Directive. The EIA report has to be assessed by the relevant authority before it is possible to make a decision on an approval under the IED, cf. Article 5(3). It is accepted by Recital 11 and Article 12(2) of the IED that the operator should be able to use information resulting from the application of the EIA Directive and the Seveso III Directive when submitting permit application.

The assessment of applications for approvals by the competent national authority must involve all media (air, land, soil, nature and water) as well as the use of resources (waste, energy and water). If there are any Natura 2000 sites close to the location of the IE activities, the approval process also has to include an assessment under Article 6(3)–(4) of the Habitats Directive. On the basis of the obligation under the Article 6(3)–(4), the CJEU has judged that if the appropriate assessment (AA) under the Directive concludes that adverse effects cannot be ruled out, then there are strong restrictions on the national authority.[521]

The approval process is therefore complex. In granting operating licences, the authorities have to take into consideration any relevant information obtained through the mandatory EIA procedure, including data on transboundary effects. At the installation/facility level, the most appropriate BATs will depend both on the content of the BAT notes and on local factors. A local assessment of the costs and benefits of the options available may be needed to establish the best option. The choice may be justified on the basis of the technical characteristics of the installation/facility, its geographical location, the local environmental considerations and the economic and technical viability of upgrading existing installations. The overall objective of ensuring a high level of protection of the environment as a whole will often involve making a judgment of different types of environmental impact, and these judgments will often be influenced by local considerations. In accordance with Article 17, it is mandatory for the Member States to ensure the use of an integrated approach and a high level of environmental protection equivalent to that achievable with individual permit conditions when they pass general rules as part of their environmental permit system. They also have to ensure that the environmental approval include measures necessary for compliance with Articles 11–18, cf. Article 14(1) that lays down the mandatory permit conditions. The BAT obligations for the operators and the obligations related to prevention of pollution and waste in accordance with waste hierarchy are also mentioned as general principles in Article 11(a)–(e). According to Article 11(e), the generation of waste is to be prevented. If waste is generated, the waste hierarchy has to be applied. It is also mandatory to ensure that energy is used efficiently, and the necessary measures are taken to prevent accidents and limit their consequences, cf. Article 11, letters f)–g). The

520. Commission Guidance 2014/C 136/3 concerning Baseline Reports under Art. 22(2) of the Directive 2010/75/EU on Industrial Emissions.

521. Illustrated by the judgment in Case C-127/02 *Waddenzee* and the Joint Cases C-293/17 and C-294/17 *Coöperatie Mobilisation for the Environment et al.*

environmental approvals have to contain several terms (conditions) to ensure that the installation can be operated in compliance with the Directive. It is stating in the IED that the Member States must take the necessary measures to ensure: (a) that the emission limit values (ELVs) for polluting substances to the air, the water or the soil are respected;[522] (b) the protection of the soil and groundwater and the management of waste generated by the installation; (c) the operator in monitoring frequently in accordance with the measurement methodology follows the evaluation procedure established by EU law specifying an obligation to submit to the competent authority the results of the emission monitoring and other required data that enable the authority to verify compliance with the permit conditions. The authorities also have to include requirements for the regular maintenance and surveillance of measures taken to prevent emissions causing soil and groundwater pollution as an important part of the terms included in the approvals. The BAT conclusions shall be the reference for setting the permit conditions by the national authorities, cf. Article 14(3). If there is no BAT conclusion, the authorities making decisions on BAT conditions have to follow the criteria laid down in Annex III of the Directive, cf. Article 14(5). According to the articles mentioned, the competent national authority must ensure in the designing of concrete operating licences that, under normal operating conditions, emissions do not exceed the emission limit levels associated with the BAT-AELs, as laid down in the BAT conclusions. The authority may set individual terms in a permit that differs from those associated with BAT notes in terms of values, periods of time, and reference conditions applied, if it can be shown through monitoring that the emissions from the installations do not exceed the levels associated with the BAT. In specific cases, where the BAT-AELs would lead to 'disproportionately higher costs compared to the environmental benefits', it is accepted to set less strict limit emission levels, if the high costs are consequences of the geographical location or the environmental conditions of the installations concerned or the technical characteristics of the installations, cf. Article 15(4). The reasons for the derogations have to be explained in the approvals, and the procedures on such derogations are subject to public participation. Operating licences must include a requirement for the operators of polluting plants to carry out, or to have carried out on their behalf, monitoring of emission rates. Such monitoring must be carried out within a quality-assurance regime (accredited actors) to ensure that the data obtained are valid.

Article 19 of the IED requires a regular reconsideration and update of the permit conditions to ensure that they truly reflect the current BREFs and ensure incentives to continuous improvement of environmental performance of each IE activity. The permit received by the operators may therefore in principle be granted only for a limited period of time. According to IED, it is mandatory for the Member States to pass legislation that ensures that the competent authority periodically reconsiders, in accordance with Article 21(2)–(5), all permit conditions and, when necessary, to ensure compliance with the Directive, update those conditions, cf. Article 21(1). Recital 21 of the IED states that in order to take account of developments in BAT

522. Limit values are legally binding concentration thresholds on different substances that must not be exceeded.

or other changes to an installation, permit conditions should be reconsidered regularly and, where necessary, updated, in particular where new or updated BAT conclusions are adopted. Within four years of the publication of the comitology of a BAT conclusions, the competent national authorities shall, when it is assessing the permitted IED-activities: (a) reconsider, and if necessary, update the operating licences conditions so as to ensure that the emission limit level values (ELVs) are in line with the emission limit levels associated with the BAT (BAT-AELs); (b) reconsider/update all existing derogations granted; (c) ensure that the installation actually operates according to the new BAT conclusions within that deadline, cf. Article 21(3). The general binding national rules regulating the activities covered by the IED also need to be up to date with BAT and the BAT conclusions, in order to ensure compliance with the permit conditions, cf. Articles 14–15. The general approach behind the mentioned BAT rules is to ensure a continuous incentive to improve environmental performance and harmonisation in the industrial sector without adding uncertainties to the business conditions. According to Article 22(1) and (3)–(4), it is the task of the competent authorities to set permit conditions in the operating licences for special hazardous installations on the obligation for the operator to take the necessary measures to address the soil and groundwater pollution caused by the activities so as to return the site to the state it had at the time of the design of the 'baseline report' in order to ensure compliance with the site remediation provisions. Member States shall take the necessary measures to ensure that the applicants on special hazardous installations include such 'baseline reports' in their applications in situations where relevant hazardous substances are included in the IE activities, cf. Article 12. Once the activities stop, the operator needs to assess the state of soil and the groundwater contamination caused by hazardous substances against the content of the 'baseline report', and the authorities have to demand a cleaning-up to the level described as the status in the 'baseline report' prepared by the operator as part of the application for the licence of the activities, cf. Article 22(3). There are also rules on public access to environmental information, public participation and access to justice in the Directive, cf. Articles 24–25.

62. The obligation to limit the pollution caused by private and public industrial activities in Denmark is covered by the Environmental Protection Act, which is more traditional in its design compared to the holistic design used by the EU in the IED.[523] The Act aims to:

- abate and combat pollution of the air, water and soil, and nuisances caused by vibration, odour and noise;
- provide for administrative regulations based on considerations of hygiene which are important for both humans and environment;
- promote the use of cleaner technology and BAT;
- reduce the use and wastage of mineral resources and other resources;

523. The Environmental Protection Act has been used to ensure the legal basis for the implementation of EU directives – including the Industrial Emission Directive, the Ambient Air Quality Directive, the Waste Framework Directive and all its daughter directives, and part of the Water Framework Directive.

– promote recycling and reduce problems in connection with waste disposal.

The Act has been revised many times since. Many of the changes have been made to deal with specific national policy priorities and special problems although most of the changes have been made to ensure the implementation of EU directives – including the implementation of the mandatory environmental approval systems established by the former IPPC Directive in 1999 and the Industrial Emission Directive (IED) in 2012.[524]

63. Section 35 of the Environmental Protection Act and the Statutory Order on Environmental Approval of Listed Enterprises[525] establish the environmental approval system under which the enterprises can receive a licence to operate. Since 1 January 1992, when the second Environmental Protection Act came into force, all enterprises included in the Annexes to the Statutory Order on the Approvals of Listed Enterprises have to obtain an overall environmental approval.[526] Enterprises that are covered by the scope of the environmental approval obligation of this Act are called 'Chapter 5 Enterprises' or 'Listed Enterprises'. The obligation for the operator to have an environmental approval applies both to new activities and to process operational changes which will result in increased pollution, cf. section 33(1) of the Act.

There are two annexes to the Statutory Order – these to annexes content of a list of categories of installations and activities with (information on thresholds, etc.) that must have an approval as the basis for their operation. Annex I is a copy of the Annex I to the IED. The installations that Denmark need to regulate in accordance with EU rules are based on the definition laid down in Article 3(3) of the IED. The definition has been used in the Danish implementation of the Directive to reduce the impact of the stronger EU rules on the environmental approval system. The obligation to follow the provisions of the IED are based on a distinction between the most important issues (or characteristics) for the listening of an enterprise at Annex I – described as the 'main listed activities' versus other activities (secondary activities). Based on section 3(3)–(5) of the Statutory Order, the activities that are carried out as secondary 'not-main listed activities' as part of listed installations are *only* included in the mandatory assessment under the environmental approval system if: they a directly technical connection with the activities listed in the Annex, and if these 'non-main listed activities' have an effect on the level of emission and pollution.[527]

---

524. Act No. 446 of 23 May 2012 on the implementation of the IED. This implementation amended four Danish acts: the Environmental Protection Act, the Act on Environmental Approval for Livestock Holdings, the Contaminated Soil Act and the Environmental Marine Protection Act. These amending rules came into force on 1 Jan. 2013.
525. Statutory Order No. 1317 of 20 November 2018 on Environmental Approval of Listed Activities.
526. Concerning the history of the Danish environmental approval system, *see supra* para. 38.
527. This criteria is related to the obligation under the IED to include in the approval process all secondary activities that are directly associated activities on the same site which have technical connections with the activities listed in Annex I to the IED, and which could have an effect on emission and pollution, *see* Annex I to the IED.

Annex II includes installations and activities that are not covered by the scope of the IED. The provisions regulating such installations and activities are less restrictive than the provisions laid down in the IED. The rules on the obligation to have an environmental approval were changed in 2015 to reduce the number of enterprises covered by the national approval system. The case-by-case decision-making on approvals is replaced by general sector-specific statutory orders.[528] Five thousand enterprises are expected to be included in these new rules on notifications to the authorities as a simple decision-making condition compared to the case-by-case approval system. The statutory rules relating to such installations and activities involve provisions covering both the standard of information used by the authorities and the conditions for emission and environmental quality targets (emission targets), technologies, etc., and this regulatory system reduces the operator's information obligations as well as the public authorities' obligations to assess the projected activities.

64. A special environmental approval system for large livestock farms (approximately 30,000 head of cattle) is laid down in the Act on Environmental Approval for Livestock Holdings.[529] In February 2017, the Act was amended as part of the implementation of the political agreement on the 'Food and Agricultural Package'.[530] After this amendment, the environmental approval system applies only to pig and poultry installations, whereas land spreading of manure and other organic fertilisers are subject to another regulatory system.[531] As the IED is covering intensive rearing of poultry and poultry installation above clear thresholds stated in Annex I, Subsection 6.6[532] of the IED there is also in this Act a distinction between livestock holdings above the IED thresholds and other livestock holdings.

65. The competences of the Danish environmental approval authorities under the Environmental Protection Act and the Environmental Approval for Livestock Installations Act are laid down in these acts and in the supplementary statutory orders.[533]

528. The change of the Environmental Protection Act was made by Act No. 537 of 29 April 2015 on the Authorisation to lay down Rules on Notification, Terms of Establishment, Operation and Case Management.

529. Promulgation Order No. 520 of 1 May 2019 on Environmental Approval for Livestock Installations. *See also* Jussi Kauppita and Helle Tegner Anker, *The Role of Permits in Regulating Livestock Installations and Manure Spreading: Experience from Denmark and Finland*, European Energy and Environmental Law Review, 27(3), June 2018, at 88–100.

530. Concerning the political agreement on the 'Food and Agricultural Package' (of 22 December 2015), *see supra* paras 20–21, and *infra* paras 242, 262 and 265. Concerning the Act on Environmental Approval of Livestock Holdings as part of this agreement, *see infra* para. 262.

531. The Danish regulation of nutrients in agriculture is laid down in revised regulation of the spreading of livestock manure and individual requirements for establishing catch crops designed for each holding based on information from the fertiliser accounting system, *see infra* paras 262–263.

532. The correct interpretation of subs. 6.6(a), which applies to installations for rearing of poultry with more than 40,000 places was presented by the Danish courts for a preliminary ruling by the CJEU in the Case C-585/10 *Niels Møller v. Haderselv Municipality*.

533. Statutory Order No. 1317 of 20 November 2018 on Approval of Enterprises establishes the rules under the Environmental Protection Act, and Statutory Order No. 718 of 4 July 2019 on the Environmental Approval and Permits, etc. of Livestock Holdings establishes the rules under the Act on Environmental Approval of Livestock Holdings, respectively.

In most cases the municipalities are the competent approval authority. The EPA has the competence only in relation to the most complicated industrial installations and activities (including marine aquaculture) under the Environmental Protection Act. Such installations and activities are marked with an 's' in the lists of activities in Annexes I and II to the Statutory Order on Approval of Enterprises.

Applications for approval under Chapter 5 of the Environmental Protection Act must be submitted by use of the digital self-service system 'Byg & Miljø',[534] and the applications for approval under the Act on Environmental Approval for Livestock Holdings must be submitted by use of the digital self-service system 'Husgodkendelse.dk'.[535] The applications must be communicated to the municipalities[536] in a digitalised form and accompanied by the plans, drawings and descriptions required to evaluate the project, and by an indication of the nature and scope of the actual or anticipated pollution. The applications must contain detailed information about the production process, the identity of the applicant, the capacity of the plants/livestock holdings, a description of the site and the surroundings, the proposed methods for the monitoring, control plan, etc. The proposed projects must be based on the concept of BAT and detailed information about the proposed installation and technical facilities to be used to reduce the environmental impact of the installation. The obligation on BAT is covering more issues if the application is related to an IED installations/livestock holdings compared with the applications related to non-IED installations. It is always mandatory to ensure public participation in the decision-making on an approval related to the IE installation/livestock holdings, as the provisions in Article 24 of the Directive are clear and directly applicable based on CJEU's case law. If the proposed project involves an IED installation or activity that is also covered by the EIA Directive,[537] the operator must send an EIA report to the approval authority.[538] The approval authority must make a draft approval and publish it together with the draft on the EIA permit. The environmental approvals must not be given before the mandatory EIA process has been completed. If the proposed IE project is not covered by the EIA obligations, the approval authority must ensure public hearing allowing the neighbours, the NGOs and others likely to be concerned with the projects opportunities to express their opinion on: (a) the information supplied by the operator; and (b) the draft on an approval prepared by the approval authority. The authorities have the possibility to include information received from other authorities, neighbours and the public concerned in their

534. The English translation of the title of the digitalisation platform is 'Build & Environment'. Concerning this self-service system, *see supra* paras 48–49 and 50.

535. The English translation of the title of the digitalisation platform is 'Livestock holdings.dk'.

536. Only applications on environmental approval of combustion installations located on offshore oil and gas platforms – where an item of combustion plant on its own, or together with any other combustion plant installed on a platform have a rated thermal input exceeding 50 MW – have to be sent directly to the EPA.

537. *See* Art. 12(2) of the IED. Concerning the EIA rules, *see supra* para. 32. Concerning the direct effect of provisions of directives that ensures the citizens procedural rights, *see supra* para. 58.

538. Concerning the obligations to prepare an EIA of proposed projects, *see supra* para. 32.

assessment,[539] and they can also inform the applicants that they need more information. They must involve other authorities in the decision-making process in situations where an application includes special problems – e.g., in decision-making on approval of major accident hazardous activities covered by the Seveso III Directive.[540] Section 4(3) of the Act determines that an operator, who continues or initiates a polluting project, must take the necessary steps to prevent and combat the pollution. However, this is only a general policy guideline, which is not legally enforceable. The general control of the location of polluting enterprises and other plants takes place within the framework of the municipal and local spatial planning and the environmental approval system.[541]

The assessment to be made by the approval authorities must be based on the use of the half-automatised decision-making systems established by the digital systems 'Byg & Miljø' and 'Husdyrgodkendelse.dk'. It is mandatory for the authorities to protect the Natura 2000 sites,[542] to ensure that the emission targets on air pollutants,[543] and the obligation on a good environmental status (GES) of the water basins[544] are respected. The operating licence that the operator receive must include emission limit values for pollutants that are likely to be emitted from the plant, environmental quality levels of the recipient (i.e., ambient air quality standards and water quality goals) and BAT requirements. The terms included in the operating licence will, normally, include appropriate requirements ensuring the protection of the neighbours against noise, light, vibrations and odours. The operating licence must include terms aiming to ensure protection of the Natura 2000 sites, soil, groundwater and, especially, the drinking water resources at the site. Some terms regarding the management of waste generated at the plant can also be found in the licences, but only in relation to the handling of the waste at the plant itself.[545] If the relevant activity to be approved under the Environmental Protection Act is included

539. The obligations on access to environmental information and public participation – described *supra* in para. 31 – make it possible for the public concerned to send critical comments and other materials to the authority.

540. Concerning the Seveso III Directive and the implementation of this Directive into Danish law, *see infra* paras 203–204.

541. Concerning the Danish provisions on spatial planning, *see infra* paras 306–328. On the basis of a survey of the sources of pollution, the municipal councils draw up spatial plans for the future localisation of enterprises that may cause pollution problems.

542. Cf. Art. 6(3)–(4) of the Habitats Directive s implemented by Statutory Order No. 1595 of 6 December 2018 on Designation and Management of International Nature Conservation Areas and Protection of Certain Species. The mandatory protection on Natura 2000 sites is described *infra* paras 241–242.

543. The EU provisions on air quality have been implemented by the Statutory Order No. 1472 of 12 December 2017 on the Assessment and Regulation of the Air Quality. These provisions are described *infra* in para. 78.

544. It is an obligation stated by the CJEU in the landmark judgment C-461/13 *Weser*. There are several Danish statutory orders implementing the EU rules on water quality protection. The most important is the Statutory Order No. 1433 of 21 November 2017 laying down Requirements for the Discharge of certain Pollutants into Watercourses, Lakes, Transitional Waters, Coastal Waters and Marine Areas. Concerning the Danish provisions, *see infra* para. 108.

545. The municipal councils normally regulate the transportation of waste, reuse of waste and deposit of waste outside the plant by means of general local regulation on waste treatment.

in the Statutory Order on Standardised Information and Terms for the Listed Activities,[546] the authorities have to use the relevant standardised terms, unless there are special conditions that make it necessary to have special terms included in the licence.

66. The Danish environmental approvals were ordinarily regarded as time-unlimited based on the traditions that were established by the first Environmental Protection Act (from 1973). The design of the Environmental Protection Act was inspired by Swedish legislation, which is also characterised by a strong protection of the interests of the operators.[547] It is possible for the operators of existing enterprises belonging to a category of installations listed in the annexes to the Statutory Order to apply for approval even when they are not so obliged, cf. section 38 of the Act. It can be to the operator's advantage to have such an approval, since the approval provides some protection against subsequent intervention by the supervisory authority, cf. section 41a(2) of the Act.[548]

The general rules are now that only after a period of eight years from when the approval was granted, the supervising authorities may, on the basis of section 41b of the Environmental Protection Act, or section 40(1) of the Environmental Approval for Livestock Holdings Act, respectively, change the conditions under which the installations/livestock holdings are functioning.[549] However, it is a consequence of the IED that the approval authorities periodically must reconsider all conditions under which the IE installations/livestock holdings.[550] Consequently, the Danish competent supervision authorities must reconsider and update the terms stated in the operation licences received by the operators of IE installations/ livestock holdings, cf. sections 40–48 of the Order on Approval of Enterprises,[551] and section 40(2) of the Environmental Approval for Livestock Holdings Act, respectively. The competent authorities must also update the relevant terms included in such operating licences no later than four years after the publication of BAT conclusions, cf. section 44 of the Statutory Order on Approval of Enterprises, and section 40(4) of the Statutory Order on the Environmental Approval and Permits, etc. of Livestock Holdings, respectively.[552] Public hearing is a mandatory part of the

546. Statutory Order No. 1474 of 12 December 2017 on Standardised Information and Terms for the Listed Activities.
547. The provisions of the Environmental Approval Act for Livestock Holdings are passed on the same regulatory approach. *See* concerning Swedish traditions the article of Maria Pettersson and Patrik Söderholm, *Industrial Pollution Control and Efficient Licensing Processes: The Case of Swedish Regulatory Design*, in the Open Access Journal 'Sustainability', ISSN 2071-1050, www.mdpi.com /journal/sustainability.
548. Concerning the supervision system, *see infra* paras 67–70.
549. Review of the approval conditions may be ordered in conjunction with the limitations stated in ss 41a, 41b and 42 of the Act.
550. This is an obligation stated in Art. 21 of the IE Directive.
551. The distinction between 'main listed activity' and other activities in s. 3 of the Statutory Order on Approval of Enterprises is important in this respect.
552. These statutory rules are the implementation of the provisions laid down in Art. 21(4) of the IED.

supervision authorities' re-evaluation of the permits in existing environmental approvals of IED installations/livestock holdings.[553]

67. It is mandatory for the Member States under the IED to set up a system of environmental inspections addressing the examination of the full range of relevant environmental effects from the installations concerned, cf. Article 23. These inspections and obligations are defined in Article 3(22) as covering:

> all actions, including site visits, monitoring of emissions and check of internal reports and follow-up documents, verification of self-monitoring, checking of the techniques used and adequacy of the environmental management of the installation, undertaken by or behalf of the competent authority to check and promote compliance of installations with their permit conditions and, where necessary, to monitor their environmental impact.

Article 23(1) requirements on inspections are more strict than those laid down in the older recommendation on the minimum criteria for environmental inspection.[554] The Member States must under the IED ensure that operators afford the competent authorities all necessary assistance to enable those authorities to carry out any site visit, to take samples and to gather any information necessary for the performance of their duties for the purpose of this Directive. Article 23(2) makes it mandatory for the national authorities to establish an inspection plan, which must be regularly reviewed and, where appropriate, updated. Such a plan provides for routine and non-routine inspections depending on the environmental risk involved in the activities and the performance by the operators. In accordance with Article 23(4), non-routine inspections shall be carried out to investigate serious environmental complaints, serious environmental accidents, incidents and occurrences of non-compliance as soon as possible and, where appropriate, before the granting, reconsideration or update of a permit.

68. The Danish supervisory authority is the same as the approval authority. Consequently, the primary responsibility for the supervision of polluting enterprises rests with the municipal councils, cf. section 65(1) of the Environmental Protection Act and Chapter 4 of the Environmental Approval for Livestock Holdings Act, respectively. The supervision obligations established by the IED have been implemented into Danish law by the Statutory Order on Supervision of Environmental Polluting Activities.[555] It is covering all activities under these two acts.

When enterprises, plants or activities of the installations cause pollution that is considered to be significant, the supervisory authorities may order the adoption of

553. Cf. s. 17 of the Statutory Order on Approval of Enterprises and s. 42 of the Statutory Order No. 718 of 4 July 2019 on the Environmental Approval and Permits, etc. of Livestock Holdings. This mandatory involvement of the public is a consequence of the obligations established by IE Directives Art. 24.

554. Commission Recommendation 2001/331/EC provided for minimum Criteria for Environmental Inspection in the Member States.

555. Statutory Order No. 117 of 28 January 2019 on Supervision of Environmental Polluting Activities. The provisions are the result of the implementation of Art. 23 of the IED.

anti-pollution measures and other relevant means. Furthermore, in relation to approved installations, if the operator fails to respect the conditions under which the licence was given, the supervisory authority may issue an injunction against continuing the activities, in pursuance to section 41a of the Environmental Protection Act and section 40 of the Environmental Approval for Livestock Holdings Act, respectively. These two sections ensure the operators of the approved enterprises some legal protection against new environmental requirements. In eight years following the issuance of a licence, an order changing the conditions that are stated in the terms connected to the licence or – in very special situations to prohibit the activities (partly or totally) – may only be issued if the authorities are able to fulfil one or more of the requirements stated in subsection 2 of the mentioned two sections. The conditions are: (a) new information has come to light regarding the harmful effects of the pollution in question; (b) the pollution is causing environmental damage which could not have been foreseen when the licence was issued; (c) the pollution significantly exceeds considerably the clear conditions stipulated in the terms stated in the licence; (d) essential chances in the BATs make it possible to expect a radical reduction of the emissions from the utility and an operative order on a change to ensure that the new BREFs is not causing disproportionately higher costs compared to the environmental benefits; (e) the dependability of the process and/or the activity makes it necessary to change the conditions; or/and (f) new information about the risk of hazardous activities means that it is necessary to change the conditions. These conditions incorporated in the Environmental Protection Act as a consequence of the implementation of the IPPC Directive to ensure an administration based on the BAT principle.[556] The IED rules on BAT conclusions, which make it mandatory to change the term if they are not in harmony with the conclusion, have not been implemented as a change to the criteria just mentioned.

Enterprises *not* covered by the environmental approval systems do not enjoy the same protection under the 'law and order principles', as the protection of the addressee described *supra*. Orders may be issued to industrial enterprises, which do not need environmental approval if their activities cause unhealthy conditions or significant pollution including waste generation that is not handled in a proper manner, cf. section 42 of these two acts. The use of the requirements in relation to the removal of polluted soil, water etc., depends on the risk of pollution, the time span and the activeness or passivity of the authority after the risk of pollution has become known. The time limit specified in the individual decision by an order has to be decided partly on the actual danger and partly on the basis of the cost of immediate action. An administrative order on cleaning-up, etc. issued pursuant to these acts presupposes that the activities are still ongoing. Moreover, an intervention presupposes that the responsible operator owns the contaminated site.

69. If an operative order or a prohibition given by the supervisory authority to an installation/livestock holding is not complied within the specified time period decided by the supervisory authority, the authority might take measures to ensure protection of the environment.

556. The Environmental Approval of Livestock Holdings Act was not existing at that time. When it was designed, the provisions were based on a copy of the Environmental Protection Act.

The supervisory authority must first demand that the illegal activities be rectified, unless the matter is relatively insignificant, cf. section 68 of the Environmental Protection Act and section 48 of the Environmental Approval for Livestock Holdings Act, respectively. According to section 69 of the Environmental Protection Act and section 49 of the Environmental Approval for Livestock Holdings Act, the authority in charge of the supervising of a polluting enterprise/livestock holding may itself initiate investigations and remedial action at the expense of the responsible operator, if – and only if – the operator does not comply with an operative order or prohibition. According to settled case law, the following conditions must be met before the authorities are allowed to take the measures required: (a) an operative order must have been issued to the operator and, the law must vest the environmental authority with the power to issue such orders; (b) the operative order must be formulated in exact terms to ensure that the operator understands its content; (c) the operative order must be addressed to the right operator (i.e., the responsible operator); (d) the time limit specified in the operative order must be respected by the supervisory authority to make it possible for the operator to take action before the deadline; (e) there must be some proof of the risk or danger; and (f) the costs incurred must be within reasonable limits. Under these conditions, the supervisory authority may prohibit continued operation and, where required, order removal of the activity and/or order the responsible party to restore the original situation. It can also decide to start self-help actions to ensure a legal situation.

In the event of imminent danger to health and where immediate action is required in order to avoid pollution or the spread of pollution, the supervisory authority may in accordance with section 70 of the Environmental Protection Act and sections 48–49 of the Environmental Approval for Livestock Holdings Act, respectively, take any measures required as self-help action without giving prior notice and at the expense of the responsible party. Section 75 of the Environmental Protection Act and section 58 of the Environmental Approval for Livestock Holdings Act contain a clause on the 'right of the contradiction'.[557] This means that the administrative authority must, prior to deciding on an order or restriction, give written notice to the addressee of the decision and inform it of the right to be heard. Such obligation concerning communication may be waived if a prompt decision is required or if notification can be regarded as obviously unnecessary.

70. Both the responsible authorities and the private parties in an environmental case need to have sufficient information at their disposal to make the right decision. Under section 72 of the Environmental Protection Act and section 53 of the Environmental Approval for Livestock Holdings Act, respectively, any operator responsible for the activities that are likely to cause pollution must, at the request of the supervisory authority, provide all information relevant to the evaluation of the pollution risk and the possible remedial action. The authorities may order the operator to submit samples of material, etc. that are being used or processed, and of waste products. All the expenses are borne by the operator – but the demand for information must be based on the proportionality principle, i.e., not more intensive and

557. Concerning the 'right of contradiction', *see supra* para. 31 and *infra* paras 69, 178, 350 and 365.

expensive than necessary to be goal-effective.[558] The parties responsible for activities likely to cause pollution must – under sections 21 and 71 of the Environmental Protection Act and section 52 of the Environmental Approval for Livestock Holdings Act – immediately inform the competent authority when either the interruption of operations or an accident result in (or run the risk of causing) substantial pollution. This obligation is only relevant if a significant quantity of pollutants escapes from a plant into the external environment.

71. Chapter 9a of the Environmental Protection Act and Chapter 5a of the Environmental Approval for Livestock Holdings Act are implementing the Environmental Liability Directive (ELD).[559] These two Chapters establish the standards and criteria for the supervisory authorities' decision-making on whether there is environmental damage or an imminent threat thereof that make it mandatory for the municipalities to follow the special provisions on environmental liability described. These Chapters include rules about who is the right addressee for an administrative order as the 'operator' individually responsible for the environmental damage (or risks of an environmental damage) and how to order the 'operator' to take preventive and restorative initiatives. There are rules on the sharing of the responsibility between the farmer as the 'operator' using damaging products (modified organisms, pesticides, and/or fertiliser), the producer of such products and the importer of such product used by the farmer.[560] The rules include most possible exemptions stated in the ELD.[561]

72. Under the Environmental Protection Act and the Environmental Approval for Livestock Holdings Act, most decisions made by the municipal councils and the EPA may be brought before the Environmental Protection and Food Appeals Board.[562] Moreover, section 82 of the Environmental Protection Act and section 65 of the Environmental Approval for Livestock Holdings Act, *inter alia,* include provisions which empower the Minister for Environment in matters of more far-reaching importance to decide on concrete cases, where the decisions based on statutory rules would otherwise have been made by municipal councils. These provisions concerning ex officio interaction have not been used very extensively in practice.

73. With the legal basis in section 35a of the Environmental Protection Act, the Minister for Environment has passed the PRTR-Statutory Order[563] as a supplement

558. Concerning the application of s. 72 of the Environmental Protection Act, *see infra* para. 171.
559. Concerning the Environmental Liability Directive and implementation of the Directive into Danish law, *see infra* paras 336–341.
560. Concerning the environmental approval system, *see supra* paras 63–64.
561. Concerning the Danish implementation of the Environmental Liability Directive, *see infra* paras 337–341.
562. Concerning the Environmental Protection and Food Appeals Board, *see supra* para. 47, and *infra* para. 355.
563. Statutory Order No. 1172 of 13 October 2015 on a Pollutant Discharge and Transmission Register (PRTR).

to the PRTR Regulation establishing the obligation for enterprises/activities covered by the Danish rules on environmental approval obligation to collect their emission data to be registered under the E-PRTR. The E-PRTR provides an overview of the major ninety-one pollutants (e.g., heavy metals, pesticides, GHGs and dioxins) emitted to air, water and soil as well as on waste.[564] There are obligations on the operators to provide the E-PRTR with data regarding the quantity of hazardous chemicals and pollutants released to the air, water and soil and transferred off-site as waste for treatment or disposal.

564. The Protocol is related to the Aarhus Convention, *see supra* para. 60.

Chapter 2. Air Pollution

§1. Industrial Pollution

74. Air pollutants cause substantial harm to human health, the vegetation and ecosystem, the build environment as well as the climate.[565] It is both an international and a local problem. Air pollution is first among the environmental causes for premature death. Some air pollutants persist in the environment for long periods of time, and they may accumulate in the environment and in the food chain, affecting humans and animals not only via air intake but also via water and food intake.[566]

Every year 7 million people die prematurely globally because of exposure to air pollution.[567] Owing to its ability to spread over long distances, and the absence of aggressive intervention, air pollutants affect a larger area. The number of premature death resulting from ambient air pollution is estimated to increase by more than 50% by 2050.[568] Heart disease and stroke are the most common reasons for premature death attributable to air pollution and account for 80% of such deaths, followed by lung diseases and lung cancer.[569] Estimates of health impacts attributable to exposure to air pollution indicate that fine particulate matters ($PM_{2.5}$) were responsible for about 428,000 premature deaths originating from long-term exposure in Europe (over 41 countries), of which around 300,000 were in the EU Member States.[570] The estimated impacts on population in these 41 countries due to exposure to nitrogen dioxide (NO_2) and ozone (O_3) concentrations in 2014 were around 78,000 and 14,400 premature deaths per year, respectively, of which around 75,000 and 13,600 occurred in the EU Member States. The number of people that died in Denmark in 2012 as a consequence of air pollution are estimated as: 2,900 people caused by $PM_{2.5}$, 110 caused by O_3 and 50 caused by NO_2. Some air pollutants, such as black carbon (BC), CH_4 and ground-level O_3 are also short-lived climate pollutants. Industrial production, fuel-based and biomass-based energy production, transport, agricultural activities and domestic (household) solid fuel combustion facilities[571] contribute to air pollution. Atmospheric deposition of sulphur and nitrogen compounds mainly derived from emission of sulphur dioxide (SO_2), nitrogen oxides (NO_x) and ammonia (NH_3) causes air pollution. Air pollutants contribute to

565. EEA, *Air Quality in Europe 2015*, 2015, at 7.
566. EEA, *Air Quality in Europe 2015*, 2015, at 7.
567. *See* the homepage of UNEXE https://www.unece.org/environmental-policy/environment-for-europe/initiatives/baca.html (visited on 1 Feb. 2019).
568. *See* the World Health Organization, Ambient Air Pollution: A global assessment of exposure and burden of disease, 2016 and the Resolution 3/8 'Preventing and reducing air pollution to improve air quality globally' decided at the UN Environment Assembly of the UNEP, third session in Nairobi, 4–6 December 2017 (UNEP/ÆA.3/res.8).
569. EEA, *Air Quality in Europe 2015*, 2015, at 11 with reference to WTO, WHO, 2014a, and World Health Organization, *Burden of Disease from Ambient Air Pollution for 2012 — Summary of Results*.
570. EEA, *Air quality in Europe – 2017 Report*, Report No. 13/2017, at 9.
571. The domestic (household) solid fuel combustion facilities has historically been a major PM driver in many EU Member States, *see* the Commission's staff working document SWD(2013) 531, at 29.

eutrophication, atmospheric ozone and the acidification of water and soil. NH_3 contributes to eutrophication. Ammonia, which is deposited from the air onto vegetation and water surfaces, can be further converted into nitrate through biological processes in the soil. When this nitrate leaches, the upper soil layers become acidified. Agriculture accounts for nearly all atmospheric emission of NH_3. Transport accounts for only 2%. The proportion is increasing because the use of catalytic converters is increasing, whereas the proportion caused by agriculture is decreasing. NO_x, SO_2 and NH_3 contribute to the acidification of soil, lakes and rivers, causing the loss of animal and plant life and biodiversity.[572] It also impacts agricultural production and forests, causing yield losses.[573] Europe's sustained ground-level O_3 concentrations damage agricultural crops, forests and plants by reducing their growth rates. The largest sources of black carbon (BC)[574] are also problematic pollutants caused by fossil fuel, biomass and biofuel combustion. BCs have impact both on the health of people (causing respiratory diseases) and on the climate as it warms the atmosphere by absorbing sunlight.

The World Health Organization (WHO) Air Quality Guidelines: Global Update 2005 provides an assessment of health effects of air pollution and thresholds for healthy and harmful pollution levels. In 2016, 91% of the world population was living in places where these quality guidelines were not met. The WHO Regional Office for Europe held its Sixth Ministerial Conference on Environment and Health in Ostrava in 2017. The declaration of this conference resolved to protect and promote people's health and well-being by actively improve air quality to meet the WHO Air Quality Guidelines.

The first international convention on air pollution was the UNECE Convention on Long-Range Transboundary Air Pollution[575] (the Geneva Convention, the CLRTAP or the Air Convention). It was adopted in 1979 by the USA, Canada and several European countries (including Denmark) as well as the EU. The history of the Convention dates back to the 1960s, where scientists demonstrated the interrelation between sulphur emissions in continental Europe and the acidification of Scandinavian lakes. By 1980, the disappearance of forests in Eastern Europe and in Canada due to pollution was another alarming signal. It obligates its parties to endeavour to limit and, as far as possible, gradually reduce and prevent air pollution, including long-range transboundary pollution. It was initially focused on the effects of acid rain through the control of SO_2. Later, the scope was widened to cover the ground-level ozone (ground-level O_3 – smog) and later several other pollutants.

There are eight protocols adapted to complement the Convention. The obligation for the parties to use the BAT is one of the important regulatory instruments. Since 1999, the Centre for Integrated Assessment Modelling (CIAM) has been responsible for the monitoring and evaluation of the progress under the CLRTAP.

572. EEA, *Air quality in Europe 2015, 2015*, at 9.
573. EEA, *The European Environment. State and outlook 2015, Synthesis report*, 2015, at 69.
574. BC is a strong light absorbing carbonaceous material emitted as solid particulate matter created through incomplete combustion of carbon-based fuels.
575. It is ratified both by Denmark and by the EU – concerning EU's ratification, *see* Council Decision 81/462/EEC of 11 June 1981 on the conclusion of the Convention on Long-range Transboundary Air Pollution.

There are three Protocols on the reduction of sulphur emissions. It is first and foremost the 1985 Helsinki Protocol and the 1994 Oslo Protocol. The last-mentioned Protocol sets emission ceilings until 2010 and beyond, including measures on energy efficiency and renewable energy, measures on reduction of sulphur in the fuels, and obligations to use BAT. Under the Oslo Protocol, there is focus on the use of economic instruments for the adoption of cost-effective approaches and solutions. The 1987 Protocol on Reduction of Nitrogen Oxide or their Transboundary Fluxes (named the Sofia Protocol) is related to reduction of nitrogen dioxide (NO_2). The parties to this Protocol have to control and reduce their emission of NO_2 with the reference year 1987 in the counting of reductions. It is also mandatory for the parties to introduce pollution control for major existing stationary sources and to apply national emission standards both to new major stationary and to mobile sources. The management to be used has to be based on BAT. The Gothenburg Protocol mentioned *infra* also includes provisions on the reduction of emission of NO_2. The 1991 Protocol on Reduction of Volatile Organic Compounds (VOC) or their Transboundary Fluxes (also called the Geneva Protocol) also established obligations for the parties to use BAT to promote commercial exchange of available technologies, to secure monitoring and to exchange knowledge. The contracting parties may use voluntary cooperation such as environmental contracts as means to comply with these obligations. The 'Heavy Metals Protocol' (the Aarhus Protocol) from 1998 sets targets on three particularly harmful metals: cadmium, lead and mercury (Hg). It aims to cut emissions from industrial sources (iron and steel industry, non-ferrous metal industry), combustion processes (power generation, road transport) and waste incineration plants. It lays down stringent emission limit values (EVLs) for emissions from such stationary sources and the obligation to use BAT for the reduction of these sources. Examples of BAT are special filters or scrubbers for combustion sources or mercury-free processes. The parties have to reduce their emissions for these three metals below their levels in 1990 (or an alternative year between 1985 and 1995). The Protocol also requires a phase-out of leaded petrol. Furthermore, it introduces measures to reduce heavy metal emissions from other products, such as mercury in batteries. It proposes the introduction of management measures for other mercury-containing products (such as electrical components, measuring devices, fluorescent lamps, dental amalgam, pesticides and paint). Amendments on more stringent emission limits were agreed on in 2012 but they are not in force. The Aarhus Protocol on Persistent Organic Pollution (the 'POPs Protocol') – that was signed in 1998 under UNECE – focuses on a list of sixteen chemical substances that have been singled out according to the agreed risk criteria. The substances comprise eleven pesticides, two industrial chemicals and three by-products/contaminants. It obliges parties to reduce their emissions of dioxide, furans, PAHs[576] and HCB) below their levels in 1990 (or an alternative year 1985 or 1995). For the incineration of municipal, hazardous and medical waste, it lays down specific ELVs. On 18 December 2009, the Protocol was amended to

576. Based on the information on the homepage of UNECE, Denmark has – based on the reported emission data of 2 Nov. 2017 – not met the limits set for its emission of NH3, *see* www.unece.org/env/lrtap/status/lrtp_s.html (visited on 2 Feb. 2019).

include seven new substances. Furthermore, the parties revised obligations for dichlorodiphenyltrichloroethane (DDT), heptachlor, HCB and PCBs, as well as the emission from waste incineration.

The Gothenburg Protocol (the Multi-Pollutant Protocol) was signed in 1999. Under the ordinary version of the Protocol, it sets reduction obligations to be met by the parties before 2010 for the following pollutants: SO_2, NO_x, NMVOCs and NH_3.[577] The revised Protocol includes reduction obligations on $PM_{2.5}$. The revision thereby also promotes the reduction of BC as a component of $PM_{2.5}$. The provisions on BC are voluntary. The revised Protocol sets reduction commitments for each party on the emission of SO_2, NO_x, NMVOCs, NH_3 and $PM_{2.5}$ to be reached by them in 2020 (taking the year 2005 as the base year). It also sets reduction obligations for 2030 (taking the year 2010 as the base year).[578] Among the new initiatives used to reduce uncertainties inherent in setting national emission commitments, the revised Protocol includes both flexibilities and obligations on national air pollution control programmes. In 2015, the International Institute for Applied Systems Analysis (IIASA) and the European Commission have published a technical report on the BATs for mobile sources to be used under this Protocol.

The CLRTAP established a broad framework for cooperative actions on monitoring and exchange of information. The EMEP Protocol from 1984 is an instrument for international cost-sharing of the monitoring costs and other resources. The monitoring is related to the status of the emission of $SO_{2,}$ $NO_{x,}$ VOCs and other air pollutants in Europe. It includes measurement of air and precipitation quality and the modelling of atmospheric dispersion. At present, more than 200 monitoring stations in 40 UNECE countries participate in this programme.[579] At the Eighth Ministerial Conference in June 2016, the parties to the CLRTAP has agreed on the 'Batumine Action Cleaner Air (2016-2021)' with the objective to encourage and support governments and other actors in their work to improve air quality. The initiative includes:

- the establishment of systematic, comparable and transparent monitoring activities and emission inventories;
- the establishment of national programmes that reduce air pollution;
- the improvement of public awareness, capacity-building and technical support; and
- policy actions.

The parties are invited to submit voluntary commitments to the initiative, preferable by Monday, 9 May 2016.[580] Denmark has not yet submitted its commitment,

577. Based on the information on the homepage of UNECE, Denmark has – based on the reported emission data of 2 Nov. 2017 – not met the limits set for its emission of PAH, concerning the international obligations *see* www.unece.org/env/lrtap/status/lrtp_s.html (visited on 2 Feb. 2019).
578. Denmark was against the acceptance of the obligations that were placed on it under the revised Protocol with respect to the emission of ammonia, *see infra* on the Danish statement under the EU's ratification of the Protocol.
579. *See* https://www.unece.org/env/lrtap/emep_h1.html (visited on 2 Feb. 2019).
580. ECE/CEP/S/2016/2.

and there is currently no information on the reasoning behind this. On 1 February 2019, the question was presented to the Danish Minister for the Environment.

The BC darkens snow and ice thus reducing the albedo (ability to reflect sunlight) effect. Melting snow and ice expose dark ocean or land that has a much lower albedo and absorbs even more sunlight thus creating a positive feedback loop.[581] The Arctic Council has passed a new initiative to reduce the emission of BC in the sensitive Arctic nature and society.[582] The reduction of the emission of BC is covered by measures of a non-binding Framework on Black Carbon and Methane of this Council. The Framework allows the parties to send the Arctic Council the same submission that they sent to the CLRTAP (under the Gothenburg Protocol), or more simply, the information regarding where it can be collected on the CLRTAP public webpage.[583] In 2015, the IMO published a study on new international technological standards on the measures needed to reduce BC emission from international shipping.[584]

The UNEP Minamata Convention on Mercury was adopted on 10 October 2013 with the aim to protect human health and the environment from the adverse effects of mercury (Hg) including the air borne mercury emission.[585] Annex VI to the Convention on Prevention of Pollution from Ships (MARPOL 73/78) includes the Regulations for the Prevention of Air Pollution from Ships. The rules set limits on SO_x and NO_x emissions and prohibit deliberate emissions of ozone-depleting substances (ODS). It contains provisions allowing for special 'SO_x Emission Control Areas' (SECA) with stringent control of the content of SO_x. The EU has implemented Annex VI to the MARPOL 73/78 by an amendment to the Directive on Sulphur Content of Certain Liquid Fuels.[586] It established the maximum permitted sulphur content of heavy fuel oil, gas oil, marine gas oil and marine diesel oil used in the Union.

75. In order to limit air pollution responsible for acidification, eutrophication and ground-level pollution, the EU has become a party to the CLRTAP and its protocols. These international provisions have been implemented by the air quality directives described *infra* that contain several measures on reducing and controlling the diffuse emissions of harmful substances into the atmosphere,[587] the quality standards on fuels and the Eco-design Directive. Air pollution from stationary sources

581. *See* Darian Shapovalova, *The Effectiveness of the Regulatory Regime for Black Carbon Mitigation in the Arctic*, Arctic Review on Law and Polities, 7(2), 2016, at 137.

582. The Arctic Council, *The Fairbanks Declaration*, 2017. *See* Darian Shapovalova, *The Effectiveness of the Regulatory Regime for Black Carbon Mitigation in the Arctic, in Arctic Review on Law and Polities*, Vol. 7, No. 2, 2016, at 136–151.

583. Darian Shapovalova, *The Effectiveness of the Regulatory Regime for Black Carbon Mitigation in the Arctic*, Arctic Review on Law and Polities, 7(2), 2016, at 144.

584. IMO, *Investigating of Appropriate Control Measures (Abatment Technologies) to Reduce Black Carbon Emission from International Shipping*, 2015.

585. EU and Denmark are parties to the Convention.

586. European Parliament and Council Directive 2012/33/EU amending the Council Directive 1999/32/EC regarding the Reduction of Sulphur of certain Liquid Fuels.

587. The 2012 revised Protocol means that they shall jointly cut their emissions of SO2 by 59%, NOx by 42%, NH3 by 6%, VOCs by 28% and PM2.5 by 22% during the period 2005–2020. For comparison, the underlying scenario analysis showed that full implementation of existing legislation is

within the EU is regulated, e.g., by the Industrial Emission Directive's[588] requirement on the framing of the terms in the operating licences to ensure that ambient air quality standards are not breached by the number of individual sources. In 1996, the first Air Quality Framework Directive ('Directive on Ambient Air Quality Assessment and Management')[589] was adopted by the Council. Ambient air means outdoor air in the troposphere. The rules of this Directive define and establish objectives for ambient air pollution in the Member States, and they ensure the basis for the assessment of ambient air quality in Member States on the basis of common methods and criteria. The first Directive on National Emission Ceilings for Certain Pollutants (the 2001 NEC Directive) established the upper emission limits for each Member State for the total national emissions ceilings (NECs) for four pollutants. The aim was to protect public health and the ecosystems against the transboundary impact of air pollution.[590] The 2001 NEC Directive established binding NEC for four pollutants namely: SO_2, NO_x, NMVOCs and NH_3. EU's Sixth Environmental Action Programme (6EAP covering 2001–2012) called for the development of a thematic strategy on air pollution. One of the priority actions to achieve was to strengthen a coherent and integrated policy on air pollution to cover priorities for further actions, the review and updating, where appropriate, of air quality standards and NECs with a view to reach the long-term objective of respect for the critical loads and levels and the development of better systems for gathering information, modelling and forecasting.

The first important initiative made in the EU to ensure a higher level of air quality was made by the 'Thematic Strategy on Air Pollution' (TSAP) in 2005. In accordance with the former First Daughter Directive, the Council Decision of 22 April 1999 relating to emission limit values for SO_2, NO_x and NO, PM and lead in ambient air puts legally binding limits on the mentioned pollutants. The limits have been binding since 1 January 2005. The 7th EAP 'Living Well, Within the Limits of Our Planet' confirms the EU's long-term objective for air policy to achieve levels of air quality that do not give rise to significant negative impacts on and the risk to human health and environment. The 'Clean Air Policy Package' adoption on 18 December 2013 included the 'Clean Air Programme for Europe' (CAPE)[591] that aims to ensure full compliance with existing legislation by 2020 at the latest, and to further improve Europe's air quality, so that by 2030 the number of premature deaths is reduced by half when compared with the situation in 2005. The draft on a new Directive on Medium Combustion Plants,[592] the draft on the Council Decision on the ratification of the amendment of the 2012 Gothenburg Protocol[593] and the draft

expected to result in emission reductions in the EU of 66% for SO2, 50% for NOx, 4% for NH3, 36% for VOCs, and 34% for PM2.5 over the same time period.

588. European Parliament and Council Directive 2010/75/EU on industrial emissions (integrated pollution prevention and control).
589. Directive 1996/62/EC.
590. European Parliament and Council Directive 2001/81/EC on national emission ceilings for certain atmospheric pollutants.
591. *See* the Commission's proposal on the strategy; COM(2013) 918 final and COM(2013) 920 final.
592. Adopted as Directive 2015/2193 on Medium Combustion Plants.
593. Adopted as Council Decision 2017/1757/EU.

on second NEC Directive[594] on the reduction of emission of certain atmospheric pollutants were included in the package. The TSAP was implemented through the Directive on Ambient Air Quality and Clean Air for Europe (or just the AAQD)[595] which replaced the first Framework Directive, the Directive on Exchange of Information[596] and the following three of the four daughter directives:

(1) the *First Daughter Directive*: the Sulphur Dioxide, Nitrogen Dioxide and Oxides of Nitrogen, Particular Matter and Lead in Ambient Air Directive;[597]
(2) the *Second Daughter Directive*: The Directive relating to Limit Values for Benzene and Carbon Monoxide in Ambient Air;[598] and
(3) the Third Daughter Directive: the Directive relating to ozone in the Ambient Air.[599]

The Directive relating to Arsenic, Cadmium, Mercury, Nickel and Polycyclic Hydrocarbons in Ambient Air[600] (*Fourth Daughter Directive*) was not replaced by the new AAQD. The EU thresholds established by the air quality standards have to be implemented and prescribed in national legislation for each pollutant. The AAQD establishes emission limit values (ELVs) that are legally binding concentration thresholds that must not be exceeded, target values (TVs) that are to be attained where possible by taking all necessary measures not entailing disproportionate costs, and (3) expose reduction obligations in respect to $PM_{2.5}$ urban background concentration from 2008–2010 to 2018–2020.[601] The main purpose of the AAQD is to lay down measures aiming at defining and establishing objectives for ambient air quality to avoid, prevent and reduce harmful effects on human health and the environment as a whole, cf. Article 1(1), as well as assisting the ambient air quality in Member States on the basis of common methods and criteria, cf. Article 1(2). It is the aim of both Directives to maintain air quality, where it is good and improve it in other cases, cf. Article 1(5) of the AAQD and Article 1(b) of the Fourth Daughter Directive. It is also the aim of both the AAQD and the Fourth Daughter Directive to obtain information on ambient air quality in order to help combat air pollution and nuisance and to monitor long-term trends and improvements resulting from national and EU measures, cf. Article 1(3) of the AAQD and Article 1(d) of the Fourth Daughter Directive. It is also the subject matters of these Directives to ensure

594. The European Parliament and Council Directive 2016/2284/EU on national emission ceilings for certain atmospheric pollutants.
595. The European Parliament and Council Directive 2008/50/EC on the ambient air quality and cleaner air for Europe.
596. Council Directive 97/101/EC on Exchange of Information.
597. Council Directive 1999/30/EC Relating to Limit Values for Sulphur Dioxide, Nitrogen Dioxide and Oxides of Nitrogen, Particulate Matter and Lead in Ambient Air.
598. European Parliament and Council Directive 2000/69/EC relating to Limit Values for Benzene and Carbon Monoxide in Ambient Air.
599. European Parliament and Council Directive 2002/3/EC relating to Ozone in Ambient Air.
600. European Parliament and Council Directive 2004/107/EC relating to Arsenic, Cadmium, Mercury, Nickel and Polycyclic Aromatic Hydrocarbons in Ambient Air. The Directive was amended by Commission Directive 2015/1480/EU laying down Rules concerning Reference Methods, Data Validity and Location of Sampling Points for the Assessment of Ambient Air Quality.
601. EEA, *Air quality in Europe 2013 Report,* at 7.

that information on ambient air quality is made available to the public, cf. Article 1(4) and Article 26 of the AAQD and Article 7 of the Fourth Daughter Directive. Finally, it is the matter of the AAQD to promote increased cooperation between the Member States in reducing air pollution, cf. Article 1(6). The AAQD includes twenty-eight definitions. The definitions that are to be used are laid down in Article 2 of the AAQD and most of them are also used in the other air quality Directive. Such definitions are binding on the Member States and the correct interpretations are decided by the CJEU if it is requested for a preliminary ruling under Article 267 TFEU from one of the Member States' courts. Both the AAQD and the Fourth Daughter Directive require that Member States divide their territories into zones and agglomerations for the assessment and management of air quality, based on pollution levels and population. They require the Member States to measure the ambient air quality in specific areas, including the zones and the urban 'agglomeration'. The term 'zone' is defined in Article 2(16) as:

> part of the territory of Member State, as delimited by that Member State for the purpose of air quality assessment and management.

The term 'agglomeration' is defined in Article 2(17) as:

> a zone that is a conurbation with a population in excess of 250.000 inhabitants or, where the population is 250.000 inhabitants or less, with a given population density per km2 to be established by the Member States.

In setting ambient air quality standards at national, regional and local levels, any zones that require special environmental protection must be identified to avoid damage to sensitive ecosystems (as a protection of biodiversity) and to the health of human in urban and industrial areas, cf. Article 4. Air quality assessment and air quality management shall be carried out in all zones and agglomerations, cf. Article 4 AAQD. The AAQD's ELVs legally imply a duty to achieve a specific result at the deadline, as these limits must actually be attained by the Member States. Most of the standards used in the AAQD are ELVs. These values are the strictest regulations for the levels of air pollution by the EU legislation. The most important ELVs for health protection are those set for particulate matter (PM) and nitrogen dioxide (NO_2) concentrations. The $PM_{2.5}$ are regulated both by ELV and by TVs. The ozone emissions are not regulated by LVs, they are only regulated by TVs. When the limit values are exceeded, the authorities are obliged to define measures to reduce the levels of pollutant concentrations. The AAQD is more demanding on LVs compared to the former provisions. The most significant news are the provisions laid down in Articles 15–16 for the national $PM_{2.5}$ exposure reduction target, the TVs and the LVs of such pollutants. The term 'margin of tolerance' is defined by Article 2(7) AAQD as the percentage of the limit value by which that value may be exceeded subject to the conditions laid down in the Directive. The AAQD sets upper and lower assessment thresholds for SO_2, NO_x, NO, PM_{10} and $PM_{2.5}$, lead, benzene and carbon monoxide (CO). The content of the definition of the term 'target value' is different in the two directives. In the Fourth Daughter Directive, the definition has to be understood in the light of the very hazardous pollutants covered by this Directive that cause cancer. The term is explained in Article 2(a) as:

> a concentration in the ambient air fixed with the aim of avoiding, preventing or reducing harmful effects on human health and the environment as a whole, to be attained where possible over a given period.

The *Fourth Daughter Directive* is setting the target value for the concentration of the pollutants covered by this Directive for the total territory of each Member State. Based on this Directive, Member States shall draw up a list of zones and agglomerations in which the levels of arsenic, cadmium, nickel and benzo(a)pyre are below the respective target values, cf. Article 3(2). They shall maintain the levels of these pollutants in these areas below these values, and they shall endeavour to preserve the best ambient air quality, compatible with sustainable development. The Member States also have to draw up a list on the areas in which the target values are exceeded. For such areas they shall demonstrate the application of all necessary measures not entailing disproportionate costs, directed in particular at the predominant emission sources, in order to attain the target values, cf. Article 3(3). The AAQD is defining the same term target values in Article 2(9) as:

> a level fixed with the aim of avoiding, preventing or reducing harmful effects on human health and/or the environment as a whole, to be attained where possible over a given period.

Member States shall take all necessary measures not entailing disproportionate costs to ensure that concentration of $PM_{2.5}$ in ambient air does not exceed the target value laid down in section D of Annex XIV as from the date specified therein. There are also reduction targets on $PM_{2.5}$ exposure for the protection of human health in section B of that Annex that the Member States have to measure, cf. Article 15 AAQD. They shall ensure that the average exposure indicator for the year 2015 established in accordance with section A do not exceed for the exposure concentration obligation laid down in section C of that Annex. The average exposure indicator of these pollutants shall be assessed in accordance with section A. There are obligations on where to locate the sampling points. It is also mandatory for the Member States to take all necessary measures not entailing disproportionate costs to ensure that the target values and long-term objectives on ozone concentration in zones and agglomerations are attained. For zones and agglomerations in which a target value is exceeded, Member States shall ensure that the programme prepared pursuant to the NEC Directive and, if appropriate, an air quality plan is implemented in order to attain the target values.

The common methods and criteria to be used under the AAQD are laid down in Chapter II of the Directive. The Chapter is divided into sections 1–2. Section 1 lays down the assessment regimes for SO_2, nitrogen dioxide NO_2, oxides of nitrogen (NO_x) particulate matter (PM_{10} and $PM_{2.5}$), lead, benzene and CO in Article 5 with the description of the procedure to follow in respect to the review in Annex II, section B. The assessment criteria for these pollutants that are binding on the Member States in their zones or agglomerations are laid down in Article 6 and Annex IV. The conditions on the location of sampling points are laid down in Article 7 and Annex V, and the reference measurement methods are described in Article 8 and Annex VI. The assessment of ambient air quality in relation to *ozone* is described in section 2. The assessment criteria for ozone that are binding on the Member States in their zones or agglomerations are laid down in Article 9 and Annex VII, section C, the conditions on the location of sampling points are laid down in Article 10 and Annex IX, and the reference measurement methods are described in Article 11 and Annex VI, section A. The Member States have the obligation under the AAQD to ensure compliance with the critical levels specified in Annex XIII for the protection of vegetation. The term 'critical level' is defined by Article 2(6) as a level fixed on the basis of scientific knowledge, above which direct adverse effects may occur on some receptors, such as trees, other plants or natural ecosystems but not on humans. The relevant pollutants are listed in Annex III – included in the list are SO_2, NO_x, $PM_{2.5}$, lead, benzene and CO. 'Limit value' (LVs) is defined in the AAQD as a level fixed on the basis of scientific knowledge, with the aim of avoiding, preventing or reducing harmful effects on human health *and/or* the environment as a whole, to be attained within a given period and nor to be exceeded once attained, cf. Article 2(5). The Member States have the obligation to comply with the LVs for the different pollutants set by the AAQD for every zone and agglomeration no later than in 2010. Article 13 sets the LVs and alert thresholds for SO_2, NO_2, NO_x, PM_{10} and $PM_{2.5}$, lead, benzene and CO as a protection of human health. The air quality in each zone has to be classified, monitored and assessed with respect to upper and lower assessment thresholds based on the measurement over the previous five years. Member States shall transmit to the Commission, for a given year, list of zones and agglomerations where the established LVs are not respected, cf. Article 20. AAQD primarily sets long-term objectives, target values, an alert threshold as well as an information threshold for *ozone* to avoid, prevent or reduce harmful effects on human health and the environment. It provides for common methods and criteria for the assessment of the ozone concentrations in ambient air and on adequate information available to the public and promotes increased cooperation between the Member States in reducing ozone levels. Where, in given zones or agglomerations, the level of pollutants in ambient air exceed any LVs or TVs, plus any relevant margin of tolerance in each case, Member States shall ensure that air quality plans are established for those zones and agglomerations in order to achieve the related LVs or TVs specified in Annexes XI and XIV, cf. Article 23(1). The Member States have a general obligation under Article 23 to prepare plans to improve air quality in areas where it does not meet the ambient air quality standards. Such plans have to be implemented at national level through the use of legislation, economic instruments, voluntary agreements, etc. The plan must set out appropriate measures so that the period during which the limit values are exceeded can be kept as short as possible and may also include specific measures aimed at protecting sensitive population groups, including children. The first subparagraph of Article 13(1) AAQD provides that the Member States are to 'ensure' that the LVs on SO_2, PM_{10}, lead and CO are not exceeded. The second subparagraph of Article 13(1) states that, as regards NO_2 and benzene, the LVs 'may not be exceeded' after the specified deadline. The time limits are set by the AAQD, cf. Annex XI. By Article 22(1) it is allowing Member

States additional time (a maximum of five years) to meet limit values for NO_2 and for benzene in a given zone or agglomeration, provided that:[602]

- the Member States have passed air quality plans;
- the air quality plans are established in accordance with Article 23 for the relevant zone or agglomeration to which the postponement would apply;
- the air quality plans shall be supplemented by the information listed in section B of Annex XV related to the pollutants concerned;
- the air quality plans shall demonstrate how conformity will be achieved with the limit values before the new deadline in place;
- the Member States have to notify the Commission of the zones and the agglomerations to which it considers that Article 22(1) applies and to submit the air quality plan referred to Article 22(4).

The notification made by Member States to the Commission are assessed by the Commission in accordance with the guidance set out in the Commission's Communication on Notification of Postponements of Attainment Deadlines and Exemptions from the Obligation to Apply Certain Limit Values.[603] Article 22(2) of the Directive includes the possibility for derogation from limit values for PM_{10} as specified in Annex XI in specific areas until June 2011, if the limits cannot be achieved because of site-specific dispersion characteristics, adverse climate conditions or transboundary contributions, provided that the conditions laid down in Article 22(1) are fulfilled, and the Member State shows that all appropriate measures have been taken at national, regional and local level to meet the deadlines. This possibility is however no longer relevant.[604]

The Commission's Decision of 12 December 2011 is laying down rules for the Member States on reciprocal exchange of information and reporting on ambient air quality. Chapter III (Article 6) includes special provisions on zones and agglomerations, including provisions on the obligations for the Member States to ensure information on postponement of the quality of the air accepted pursuant to Article 22 AAQD. The reference methods, data validity and location sampling points to be used in the assessment of ambient air under these two Directives are regulated by the Commission Directive from 2015.[605] This Directive on the reduction of national

602. In Case C-404/13 *ClientEarth*, the correct interpretation of this provision was made clear by the CJEU.
603. COM(2008) 403 final.
604. The just-mentioned difference is highlighted by the CJEU in the judgment C-404/13 *Client Earth* by which the Court makes the interpretation that there is an obligation to achieve the LVs sets for the NO2 and benzene as a result. In para. 56 of its judgment, the Court stated that natural or legal persons directly concerned by the limit values being exceeded after 1 January 2010 must be in a position to require the competent national authorities, if necessary, by bringing action before the courts having jurisdiction, to establish an air quality plan, which complies with the second subparagraph of Art. 23(1) of AAQD, where a Member State has failed to secure compliance with the requirements of the just-mentioned Art. 13(1) subs. 2 on the LVs of NO2 and benzene, if the Member State has not applied to the Commission for a postponing of the deadline.
605. It was amended by the Commission Directive 2015/1480/EU laying down Rules concerning Reference Methods, Data Validity and Location of Sampling Points for the Assessment of Ambient Air Quality.

emissions of certain atmospheric pollutants that includes measures to control NH_3 emissions, and measures to control emissions of PM and BC,[606] is part of the Clean Air Policy Package. It makes it mandatory for the Member States to establish emission inventories, adjusted emission inventories, project and informative inventory report using the methodologies adopted by the parties to the CLRTAP (EMEP Guidelines).

The number of monitoring locations required under the AAQD depends on population size and whether ambient air quality concentration exceeds the upper assessment threshold, are between the upper and lower assessment thresholds or are below the lower assessment threshold.

76. The NEC Directive and the AAQD are complementary. They are covering the same pollutants. While the NEC Directive from 2001 addresses the overall amounts of emissions (in kilotons), the AAQD addresses the quality of the air. The 2016 NEC Directive (NECD) implements the amendments that were passed under the Gothenburg Protocol mentioned *supra.*

The NEC Directive remain applicable until the end of 2019, cf. Article 21(1)(a) and (2) NECD. In 2020, the NECD establishes new emission reduction commitments for 2020 onwards, and later for 2030 onwards for the Member States as agreed under the Protocol. Further, it requires the Member States draw up National Air Pollution Control Programmes that should contribute to the successful implementation of their air plans established under the AAQD. There is also an emission ceiling for PM_{10}, $PM_{2.5}$ and total suspended particular matters (TSP) as well as obligations on monitoring and reporting on BC laid down in this Directive. The NECD also involves amendments to the Directive on Public Participation in Respect to Drawing up of Certain Plans and Programs,[607] cf. Article 19 of the NECD.[608]

Member States must comply with the obligations arising from the Directive to adopt or envisage, within the framework of national programmes, appropriate and coherent policies and measures capable of reducing, as a whole, emissions of *inter alia* those pollutants to amounts not exceeding the ceilings in Annex I to that NEC Directive and the new NECD by the end of 2010, 2020 and 2030, *respectively* at the latest. The reason for this is that the Directive is based on a purely programmatic approach under which the Member States enjoy wide flexibility as regards the choice of the policies and measures to be adopted or envisaged, within the framework of national programmes concerning all sources of pollution, in order to progressively achieve a structural reduction of emissions not exceeding the emission ceilings laid down in Annex I of the Directives. The Directives makes it mandatory for the Member States to ensure the monitoring of negative impacts of air pollution upon ecosystems, cf. Article 9. They have to prepare an annually update national emission inventories for the pollutants set out in Table A of Annex 1, in accordance

606. COM(2013) 920 final.
607. European Parliament and of the Council Directive 2003/35/EC providing for Public Participation in Respect of the Drawing up of Certain Plans and Programmes relating to the Environment and amending with regard to Public Participation and Access to Justice the Council Directives 85/337/EEC and 96/61/EC.
608. Both the 2001 NEC Directive and the new NECD are closely connected to the CLRTAP, which in its Gothenburg Protocol establishes binding national emission ceiling for the EU and its Parties.

with the requirement set out therein, cf. Article 8. It is also mandatory for the Member States to provide a national air pollution control programme and to send the first programme to the Commission by 1 April 2019, cf. Article 10. These obligations are based on the implementation of the revised Gothenburg Protocol.

As of 2010, Member States should not under the NEC Directive have exceeded their emission ceilings, but many Member States breach the air pollution ceilings every year, mostly due to high emissions from agriculture and transport sources. The EEA report 'NEC Directive Status Report 2014', which include preliminary data for 2013 and summarises data for 2010–2012 conforms that Denmark and other Member States did not do so for these years. Denmark exceeded the NMVOCs in 2013 and NH_3 ceilings in 2010, 2011, 2012 and 2013.[609] Denmark applied for adjustment from the national emission reduction commitments both in 2017 and in 2018.[610] The Danish problems are related to the emission of NH_3, NO_2 and PAH beyond the emission ceilings. It is possible for the Member States that have problems meeting the national ceilings to apply the Commission for a dispensation. It is a condition for getting such a postponement of the deadline that the Member States have applied improved emission inventory methods in accordance with updated scientific knowledge available since 2010. The Member States shall be deemed to comply with the obligation for a maximum of three years, cf. Article 5(4) NEC Directive. Member States wishing to adjust their data in this way must first notify the Commission by 15 February each year and subsequently submit a range of documentation by 15 March for review by the Commission. The CJEU has granted Member States wide flexibility when developing programmes for the progressive reduction of emissions of pollutants under the NEC Directive. It was stated by the Court that the Member States must comply with the obligations arising from the NEC Directive to adopt or envisage, within the framework of national programs, appropriate and coherent policies and measures capable of reducing, as a whole, emissions of those pollutants covered by the Directive. But it was not a consequence of this obligation that the national authorities must include, among the conditions in the individual operating licences, the ELVs for pollutants laid down in the Directive before the deadline laid down on minimum quality of the air. [611]

77. The EU has also implemented the 2012 amendments to the Gothenburg Protocol by the new Directive on Limitation of Emissions of Certain Pollutants into the Air from Medium Combustion Plants (MCP Directive).[612] The Directive was passed as part of the 'Clean Air Policy Package' in 2013, and it regulates emissions from the combustion of fuels in plants with a rated terminal input equal to or greater than 1 MWth and less than 50 MWth.

The MCP Directive addresses the potential need for the Member States to apply stricter emission limits on SO_2, NO_x and PM to air in areas where this can improve

609. EEA, *NEC Directive Status Report 2014*, at 6, 8, 10, 17–18 and 23–24.

610. EEA, *NEC Directive Reporting Status 2018*, at 3.

611. The Joint Cases C-165/09 and C-167/09 *Stichting Natuur en Milieu and others v. College van Gedeputeerde Staten van Groningen and College van Gedeputeerde Staten van Zuid-Holland.*

612. It is now the European Parliament and the Councils Directive 2015/2193/EU on the limitation of emissions of certain pollutants into the air from medium combustion plants.

air quality. The medium combustion plants covered by the Directive are used for a wide variety of applicable generation, domestic heating and cooling, providing heat/stream for industrial processes, etc.

78. Article 14(2) of the Danish Environmental Protection Act provides the Minister for the Environment the competence to regulate the air quality with binding provisions if such rules are necessary to fulfil the international and EU obligations described *supra*. The Act applies to all activities that through emission of solid, liquid or gaseous substances may cause pollution with consequences for the quality of the air.

In relation to global air protection, the problems are handled partly by use of economic and fiscal instruments.[613] Nevertheless, most Danish regulations are based on end-of-pipe technology, emission and input norms laid down in the statutory orders as well as the obligations for the big industrial companies and agriculture farms to have operation licences under Chapter 5 of the Environmental Protection Act.[614] Based on section 14(2), the Minister for the Environment has the power to lay down binding rules on air quality if such rules are necessary for Danish fulfilment of international obligations. The Minister has published the Statutory Order on Assessment and Regulation of Air Quality.[615] It is an implementation of the above-mentioned EU AAQD, the 4th Daughter Directive and the MCP Directive. This Statutory Order provides the necessary administrative basis for the planning and implementation of environmental quality and pollution control. The 2016 NEC Directive is implemented by Statutory Order on the Reduction of Emission from SO_2, NO_x, VOCs, PM and NH_3.[616] It is the EPA that is the competent authority under these administrative rules. There are only local air quality management plans for the four largest cities (Copenhagen, Aarhus, Aalborg and Odense). According to Article 22(2) of the AAQD, in a letter dated 31 October 2008, the former liberal-conservative government[617] gave the Commission notification of a postponement of the deadline from 2005 to 2010 for an extension regarding the PM_{10} emission limit values in three air quality zones as well as the annual limit value in two of those zones. The notification indicates that several structural abatement measures have been introduced and implemented. Those measures address primarily traffic and include, *inter alia*, the possibility of establishing environmental zones in major cities. However, in the absence of a Danish air quality plan with a short-term action plan setting out measures effective for the controlling or, where necessary, suspending activities which contribute to the risk of the limit values being exceeded, the Commission could not assess whether the measures, which were already taken would ensure compliance with the daily limit value. The notification indicates that the Danish authorities intend to make use of the possibility in Articles 20 and 21 of the AAQD to deduct

613. Concerning the use of economic and fiscal instruments, *see supra* paras 11–14.

614. Concerning the environmental approval system, *see supra* paras 62–64 and *infra* in para. 77.

615. Statutory Order No. 1472 of 12 December 2017 on the Assessment and Regulation of the Air quality.

616. Statutory Order No. 491 of 16 May 2018 on the Reduction of Emission from SO2, NOx, VOC, PM and NH3.

617. This Government was in power from 2001 to 2011. Concerning the different coalition governments, *see supra* para. 4.

contributions from natural sources, such as sea-salt from concentration levels as well as to identify zones where winter sanding or salting of the roads is a contributing cause to the exceeding of the limits. The Commission raised objections against the notification of an exemption. The limit values for NO_2 have been legally binding since 1 January 2010 in accordance with the AAQD and the NEC Directive. In a letter of 1 March 2011, the 2001–2011 Liberal-Conservative Government gave the Commission notification of a postponement of the deadline for an extension regarding the NO_2 limit values in three cities until 2015 (in a letter of 30 May 2011, the notification of a postponement of the deadline in one of the three cities). The traffic and temporary local construction works were identified as the main source contributing to the high NO_2 concentration levels at the local and urban levels. The notification was this time accompanied by air quality plans that fulfil the requirements provided for in the Framework Directive. The Commission notes that the relevant sources have been addressed. However, the Commission raised objections against the notification of an exemption.[618] The concentrations for most pollutants have been decreasing during the last decades. There was no exceedance of the NO_2 limit values in 2017 in Danish cities covered by the assessment programme. The limit value was exceeded in 2016 at one street station (H.C. Andersens Boulevard). Annual averages of PM_{10} and $PM_{2.5}$ were below limit values at all stations and the average exposure indicator ($PM_{2.5}$ in urban background) has decreased by about 30% since 2010.[619]

The Danish EPA Guidelines No. 2 from 2001 on 'Limitation of Industrial Air Pollution' are based on the BAT principle.[620] These contain technical regulations on the monitoring technology and guideline targets for the authorities to include when making decisions on the establishment or enlargement of industrial plants. For those who manage or intend to establish enterprises that cause or may cause air pollution problems, these guidelines also indirectly indicate the conditions that the authorities have to follow when they design the operating licences under the environmental approval provisions.[621] The air pollution guidelines explain how regulations limit emissions and monitor industrial pollution. They also explain the use of B-values and the OML-model (air dispersion calculations) to assess the extent of pollution by harmful substances.

79. In relation to air problems for neighbours regarding odour, EPA has published Guidelines No. 9 from 2002 on 'Industrial Odour Control'. The purpose of the guidelines is to provide the basis for uniform consideration of complaint and approval cases relating to odour problems in the ambient air. The problems normally lie in measuring odour in an objective manner and to prove the economic cost of such pollution. The guidelines state that the enterprises must not cause significant odour problems. The 'monitoring' of such pollution is based on a six-person

---

618. Draft Decision of 2 December 2011 on the notification by the Kingdom of Denmark on a postponement of the deadline for attaining the limit values for NO2 in two air quality zones. Concerning the status, *see infra* para. 98.
619. *See* the scientific Report No. 281/2018, *The Danish Air Quality Monitoring Programme. Annual summary for 2017*, Danish Centre for Environment and Energy (DCE).
620. Concerning BAT, *see supra* para. 61.
621. Concerning the environmental approval system, *see supra* paras 62–73.

panel. In some situations, the courts will also protect the neighbours' interest on the basis of the unwritten 'neighbour law'.[622]

§2. Global Climatic Change

80. Climate change represents one of the most difficult challenges in global governance. The changes in the global atmosphere induced by the growing amount of GHGs affects the climate in every region, no matter where emissions are produced. The UNFCCC from 9 May 1992 established the international regime for climate actions. The Convention has 192 parties – nearby universal membership – and it sets out a framework for the tackling climate change by means of mitigation/reduction of GHGs; adaptation/protective measures against the negative effects of climate change; and financing of initiatives. The Convention has set up what is known as the COP as its supreme authority. In formal terms, the negotiations take place in the conference of parties that meet once a year in December, and each meeting is given a number. The Convention is the parent treaty of the 1997 Kyoto Protocol.

In the case of climate change, there may be a 'tipping point' at which the thermohaline circulation of the oceans is disrupted, with significant negative implications for all communities. The consequences of anthropogenic-influenced GHG emissions can be irreversible due to the long lifetime of many GHGs in the atmosphere. The major GHGs include CO_2, CH_4, N_2O and chlorofluorocarbons (CFCs). Anticipating the critical role that the scientific consensus would play in building the political will to respond to climate change, the UNEP and the World Meteorological Organization (WMO) created the Intergovernmental Panel on Climate Change (IPCC) in 1988. As it has been pointed out by the IPCC in its reports on climate change, it is a global problem of an unprecedented scale triggered by anthropogenic influence. The IPCC works with six main categories: CO_2, CH_4, N_2O and the so-called industrial gases, which include HFCs, PFCs and sulphur hexafluoride (SF_6). The industrial gases are covered by the Montreal Protocol, described *infra*. HFCs, which replaced ozone-depleting CFCs, are primarily used in the refrigeration industry. These gases are the largest contributors to industrial GHG emission.

The UNFCCC was adopted at the Rio Conference in 1992 with the objective to achieve stabilisation of GHG concentration in the atmosphere at a level that would prevent anthropogenic interference with the climate system.[623] The Convention lays down the CBDR principle as a guide to action on climate change. There is a basic division between the parties laid down in the Convention between the developed countries (Annex I Parties) and developing countries (non-Annex I Parties). Annex I Parties commit themselves under the Convention to take all practicable steps to promote, facilitate and finance, as appropriate, the transfer of, or access to, environmentally sound technologies and know-how to other parties, to enable them to implement the provisions of the Convention. The non-Annex I Parties is differentiated for the purpose of economic help into 'least developed countries and small

622. Concerning the unwritten 'neighbour law', *see supra* paras 30 and 35, and *infra* para. 193.
623. The Convention was supplemented by the Kyoto Protocol in 1997 and the Paris Agreement in 2015. Both the EU and Denmark are parties to these international instruments.

islands developing states' on the one hand and on the other hand to other non-Annex I Parties (China and other emerging economies). In addition to the polluting industrial practices of Annex I Parties, the Convention is related to the abusive exploitation of the tropical and temperate forests, which influence and degrade the life cycle of all living organisms and human beings by use of REDD+ mechanisms.[624] The Kyoto Protocol is the only instrument under the Convention that establishes binding GHG emission reductions obligations. The obligations covered the period from 2008 to 2012.[625] The Protocol allows parties that have emission units to spare (emission permits permitted to them but not used) to sell this excess capacity to countries that are over their targets. The other units which may be transferred under the International Emissions Trading Scheme (IETS), each equal to one ton CO_2, may be in the form of: (a) an emission reduction unit (ERU) generated by joint implementation projects (JI-projects) between developed countries; (b) a certified emission reduction (CER) generated from CDM-projects between a developed and a developing country; and (c) a removal unit (RMU) on the basis of Land Use, Land-Use Change and Forestry (LULUCF). The rules on JI- and CDM-projects are set up in the Kyoto Protocol as financial instruments that represent a tonne CO_2 removal or reduction from the atmosphere as a result of emission reduction projects. The JI-agreements are used between developed countries. A CDM-agreement is a contract between a developed and a developing country by which they agree on the covering of the cost of the CDM-project that is located in the developing country, but the cost is paid by the developed country. They also agree on certification of the emission reductions as well as on the trading of the CER credits earned by the CDM-project. The creation of ERUs as the result of a JI-agreement and the CERs can be sold to companies and developed countries to be used by them as means to meet their emission reduction targets. Pursuant to the wording of the Protocol, these flexible mechanisms are only accepted as a supplement to domestic actions. The main objectives of the JI- and the CDM-project agreements[626] is to support all parties' efforts to finance and implement energy-efficient renewable energy, and clean technology measures to reduce GHG emissions and to help Annex I Parties to reach their reduction targets.[627] At COP15, held in Copenhagen (Denmark) in December 2009, most parties accepted by 'the Copenhagen Accord' that GHG emissions should be reduced by 50% no later than 2050 (with 1990 as the base year)

624. Concerning the REDD+ mechanisms, *see infra* para. 272.
625. Under the Protocol, forty-one States, consisting of UNFCC Annex I Parties (industrialised countries), were in the commitment period 2008–2012 covered by legally binding emission limitation and reduction commitments. The reduction commitments of each Annex I party were shown in Annex B of the Protocol. The Protocol is now covering the period until 2020 for the Parties that have accepted this. Among these parties are EU and its Member States, cf. *infra*.
626. A CDM-project is used to ensure emission reduction or emission removal. The CDM-agreement is a contract between a developed and a developing country by which they agree on the covering of the cost of the CDM-project that is located in the developing country, but paid by the developed country. They also agree on certification of the emission reductions as well as on the trading of the credits CERs earned by the CDM-project. The CERs can be sold to companies and developed countries to be used by them as means to meet their emission reduction targets.
627. Article 6 of the Paris Agreement that replaces the Kyoto Protocol from 2021 has replaced the possibility of using the JI- and CDM-mechanisms with a new market mechanism with effect from 2020.

to ensure that the average global temperature increase can be kept below the 2°C above pre-industrial level. The mentioned level is based on IPCC's Fourth Assessment Report, AR4 from 2007.[628] The IPCC assumed in this report that the Annex I Parties must reduce by 25–40% no later than 2020 and that it must be reduced by 80% no later than 2050 than the 2006 level.[629] In 2011 at the COP17 meeting in Durban, South Africa, some of the parties, including the EU and its Member States, agreed on a second commitment period of the Kyoto Protocol from 1 January 2013 to December 2020.[630]

81. The 'Paris Agreement' on climate change was adopted at the COP21 (on 12 December 2015).[631] Nearly all States[632] are parties to the Agreement. On 4 October 2016, it was ratified by the Council,[633] and on 5 October 2016 the Council deposited its ratification instrument together with its Member States (incl. Denmark).[634]

It is the ambition behind this agreement to pursue efforts toward 1.5°C by the reduction of GHG emission by different means, including the means available to remove carbon from the atmosphere. The parties decide on a voluntary basis how much GHG emission they are able and willing to reduce. Their decisions have the form of National Determined Contributions (NDCs) that are reported by them to the UN. The NDCs are policy plans reflecting the parties' highest possible ambitions and representing progression over time – striving to formulate and communicate long-term low GHGs development strategies, mindful of the objectives of the Agreement.[635] Under the COP24 (December 2018), the parties were not capable of reaching an agreement on new binding mitigation obligations. They agreed only on new binding provisions on monitoring and reporting of their GHG emissions. One of the weaknesses of the UNFCCC, the Kyoto Protocol,[636] and the Paris Agreement

628. IPCC, 2007, Chapter 13, Box 13.7, at 776.
629. The reductions have to be 95% in relation to the 1990 levels.
630. To achieve rapid clarity, parties to this second period of the Kyoto Regime turned their economy-wide targets into quantified emission limitation or reduction objective and submitted them for review on 1 May 2012. In 2013, the COP19 that was held in Warsaw/Poland decided, in the context of its determination to adopt a protocol, another legal instrument or an agreed outcome with legal force under the Convention applicable to all Parties at its twenty-first session (December 2015) and for it to come into effect and be implemented from 2020. The COP19 adopted a decision establishing the 'Warsaw international mechanism on loss and damage', and the 'Warsaw REDD+ framework', a series of seven decisions on REDD+ finance, institutional arrangements and methodological issues. As part of the efforts by countries to accelerate pre-2020 climate action, it was decided at the COP20 held in Peru in December 2014 that the Secretariat should organise a showcase on how policy and action could be scaled up and how many countries and non-state actors could taking action across themes ranging from renewable energies to more sustainable land use.
631. The Paris Agreement entered into force on 4 November 2016.
632. Syria is not a party. Trump has after his election as the President of US decided that they will not continue as a party to the Paris Agreement.
633. Council decision (EU) 2016/1841 of 5 October 2016 on the conclusion, on behalf of the European Union, of the Paris Agreement adopted under the United Nations Framework Convention on Climate Change.
634. Denmark ratified the Paris Agreement with reservation for Greenland.
635. Denmark published a draft of its NDC under the EU's Governance Regulation on Governance of the Energy Union and Climate Change in December 2018.
636. Article 2(2) of the Kyoto Protocol declares that the Annex I Parties (developing countries) shall pursue limitation or reduction of emissions of GHGs – not controlled by the Montreal Protocol –

are the exclusion of sources outside the land-based territory (i.e., aerial and maritime sources are excluded). By 2050, global aviation and shipping are together expected to contribute almost 40% of global CO_2 emission unless further actions are initiated.[637] In 2018, the IMO adopted an initial emission strategy to reduce GHG emissions. The ICAO Assembly adopted a Resolution in 2017 for a Global Market-Based Measure to Address CO_2 Emissions from International Aviation (COSIA) that is decided to start in 2021, the same year as the Paris Agreement.

82. Together EU and its Member States (including Denmark) are the third biggest emitter in the World. Article 4 of the Kyoto Protocol – which became known as the 'EU Bubble'– allowed the EU Member States to meet their targets jointly through a differentiated commitment among Member States.[638] In the second commitment period under the Protocol (2012–2020), all 28 Member States jointly committed to limit their average annual GHG emissions in the years 2013 to 2020 to 80% of their base year emission (mostly 1990).

EU's current binding commitments covering the national obligations until December 2020 are divided into the EU ETS Directive[639] and the common emission bubble covering the emission from non-ETS sectors (e.g., transport, agriculture, buildings and waste) titled the 'Effort Sharing Decision'.[640] The reduction of GHG emissions under these two schemes is designed to ensure that the ordinary EU's goal of a 20% reduction of GHG emissions across the entire economy is met. The schemes are described *infra*, starting with the EU ETS scheme. This scheme is one of the most important common tools for fulfilling the EU's commitment under the international Kyoto Protocol. The EU ETS is based on the 'polluter pays principle' and it identifies certain types of industrial entity within the EU that are required to acquire CO_2 allowance[641] equals entitling them to emit specified quantities of CO_2. It addresses the GHG emissions from more than 12,000 installations in thirty-one countries.[642] The energy-intensive sectors – including electricity generation, cooking, mineral-oil refineries, ferrous-metal production, cement, lime, ceramics, bricks, glass, pulp and paper – are ETS sectors. The EU ETS allowances are called EUAs. Receipt of such a permit is a precondition for the production process. The permit may include a number of conditions. Once the permit is obtained, the industrial entity receives CO_2 quotas free of charge in accordance with the

from aviation and marine bunker fuels, working through the International Civil Aviation Organisation (ICAO) and the International Maritime Organisation (IMO).

637. The interviews with Anke Lükewille in the European Environmental Agency's Newsletter, Issue 2018/1 of 15 March 2018 with reference to EEAs Annual Transport and Environmental Reporting Mechanism (TERM).

638. The bubble target was to emit 8% less CO2 in December 2012.

639. European Parliament and Council Directive 2003/87/EC establishing a Scheme for Greenhouse Gas Emission Allowance Trading within the Community, as amended.

640. European Parliament and Council Decision 406/2009/EC on the efforts of EU Member States to reduces their Greenhouse Gas (GHG) Emissions to meet the EU's GHG Emission Reduction Commitments up to 2020.

641. One CO2 allowance equals the right to emit 1 ton of CO2 within a year.

642. EEA, *The European Environment State and Outlook 2015. Synthesis Report*, at 103 and EEA Technical report No. 3/2015 *Application of EU Emission Trading Directive. Analysis of national responses under Article 21 of the EU ETS Directive in 2014*, at 9.

national CO_2 allocation plans (the plan has to be accepted by the Commission). Operators of ETS installations must pay for supplementary GHG emissions by means of CO_2 allowances, or by credits from JI or CDM projects. If an industrial entity emits CO_2 in excess of the level of emissions covered by its CO_2 quotas, including any extra CO_2 quotas purchased and extra JI or CDM credits obtained, the entity must pay a fee for every excess ton of CO_2 emitted. In addition, the operator is obliged to make up for the shortfall in allowances during the following year. CO_2 allowances may be bought and sold in all EU Member States, irrespective of where in the EU they were issued. The prices for one CO_2 allowance and JI and CDM credits are determined by supply and demand. A permit to emit CO_2 issued by the national authorities allows the operator to emit CO_2. The EU ETS Directive provides that industrial entities are obliged to monitor their CO_2 emission levels, which must be verified annually by an independent body and reported to the national authorities. Each year the companies must calculate their GHG emissions, obtain verification for their emissions from an independent body and report the result to the responsible national authority. To ensure a coordination approach, Article 8 of the EU ETS Directive requires coordination of the procedure for EU ETS permits and the permits under the Industrial Emission Directive (IED) where installations are subject to both systems.

The implementation of 'the Climate and Energy Package' (2008) included an amendment of the EU ETS Directive[643] as well as the current 'Effort Sharing Decision' (also titled the 'GHG Reduction Decision',[644] a new Directive on the Promotion of the Use of Energy from Renewable Sources (the 2009 RES Directive),[645] the Community Guidelines on State aid for Environmental Protection,[646] the Directive on the Geological Storage of Carbon Dioxide[647] and the Regulation on Environmental Performance Standards relating to Private Cars.[648] The Package aims to achieve three targets by 2020 (titled the '20-20-20 targets'): (1) a 20% reduction of GHG emissions compared to the 1990 levels; (2) a 20% reduction in primarily energy use (based on projected levels) through improved energy efficiency; and (3) a 20% reduction of energy consumption originating from renewable energy sources (RES). The consequence of this is that EU law provides binding emission reduction targets for the Member States to be complied with in the next commitment period 2013–2020. The current conditions on auctions of GHG's allowances under the EU

643. European Parliament and Council Directive 2009/29/EC amending Directive 2003/87/EC so as to Improve and Extent the Greenhouse Gas Emission Allowance Trading Scheme of the Community.
644. European Parliament and Council Decision 406/2009/EC on Effort Sharing.
645. European Parliament and Council Directive 2009/28/EC on the Promotion of the Use of Energy from Renewable Sources.
646. EU Commission Communication 2008/C 82/01 on the Community Guidelines on State Aid for Environmental Protection. The guidelines are now replaced by Community Guidelines 2014/C 200/01 on the Community Guidelines on State Aid for Environmental Protection and Energy 2014–2020.
647. European Parliament and Council Directive 2009/31/EC on the Geological Storage of Carbon Dioxide.
648. European Parliament and Council Regulation No. 443/2009/EC on Environmental Performance Standards relating to Private Cars.

ETS are laid down in a Decision of the European Parliament and the Council.[649] On 16 October 2008, the EU ETS Directive was changed so that it included the IETS under the Kyoto Protocol (Article 17) after the successful connection to the International Transaction Log. The Directive, as it was amended in 2008, includes aviation activities in the scheme for GHG emission allowance trading within the territory of the EU Member States from 1 January 2012. Allowances for aircraft operators are called EUAAs. Surrender of such emission allowances and reporting for 2013 was not required until 2015.[650] As a consequence of protects from US, Russia, and other States as well as the promise on a new ICAO agreement, the Council decided to limit the scope of the EU ETS to intra-European Economic Area-flights from 2017 onwards.[651] The Directive was amended by a 2014 regulation,[652] and again by a 2017 regulation which kept the systems' coverage confined to flights within the European Economic Area.[653] In 2014 the auctioning of 900 million allowances was postponed from 2014–2016 to 2019–2020.[654] The amendment of the EU ETS Directive made the scheme more flexible and cost efficient in order to reach the reduction target of 20% set for 2013–2020 (Phase III with 2005 as the base year). The amendment included a broader list of enterprises covered by the scheme from 2013. The scope of the amended Directive covers:

---

649. European Parliament and Council Decision No. 1359/2013/EU amending Directive 2003/87/EC clarifying Provisions on the Timing of Auctions of Greenhouse Gas Allowances.
650. A number of American and Canadian airlines and airline associations contested the measures transposing this Directive in the United Kingdom. They contend that, in adopting the Directive, the EU infringed a number of principles of customary international law and various international agreements. The High Court of Justice of England and Wales asked the CJEU whether the Directive is valid in the light of international law. In its judgment of 21 December 2011 C-366/10 *Air Transport Association of America et al.*, the CJEU has stated that the amendment of the EU ETS Directive is not in conflict with international law. As regards the Kyoto Protocol, the Court observed that the State Parties might comply with their obligations in the manner and at the speed upon which they agree with that. The Court points out that EU policy on the environment aims at a high level of protection. Thus, the EU legislature may in principle choose to permit a commercial activity, in this instance air transport, to be carried out in its territory only on conditions that operators comply with the criteria that have been established by the EU. Furthermore, the fact that certain matters contributing to the pollution of air, sea or land territory of the Member States originate in an event which occurs partly outside that territory is not such as to call into question, in the light of the principles of customary international law capable of being relied upon, the full applicability of EU law in that territory. On 21–22 February 2012, a number of non-European countries met in Moscow to coordinate their opposition to aviation's inclusion in the EU ETS Directive. The meeting resulted in a joint declaration, and a series of suggested retaliatory measures to be used against European industry.
651. As stated *supra*, the ICAO adopted the Resolution for a Global Market-Based Measure to Address CO2 Emissions from International Aviation in October 2016.
652. Regulation No. 421/2014/EU amending EU ETS Directive in the View of the Implementation by 2020 of an International Agreement Applying a Single Global Market-based Measure to International Aviation Emissions.
653. European Parliament and Council Regulation No. 2017/2392/EU amending Directive 2003/87/EU to continue limitations of scope for aviation activities and to prepare to implement a global market-base measure from 2021.
654. EEA, *The European Environment State and Outlook 2015. Synthesis Report*, at 104.

- CO_2 emissions from the petrochemicals, NH_3 and aluminium sectors as well as CO_2 emissions from installations carrying out GHGs capture, transport and geological storage (carbon capture and storage (CCS) facilities);
- N_2O emissions from the production of nitric, adipic and glyocalic acid;
- PFCs emission from the aluminium sector.

The EU ETS Directive continued to primarily address CO_2 emissions in the large energy sector and energy-intensive sectors. It covers around 45% of the total EU GHG emission.[655] The trading of credits is in the EU ETS Registry[656] and the Union Transaction Log (EUTL) that tracks the ownership of allowances by recording the amounts owned in the accounts and the transactions between accounts. An agreement between the European Parliament and Council resulted in the Monitoring Mechanism Regulation. The Commission has published a Regulation in 2012 on the Monitoring and Reporting of Greenhouse Gas Emissions.[657] Denmark has taken advance of the provision offered by Article 13 to allow the use of simplified monitoring plans in low-risk cases for stationary installations.[658] The auctioning is progressively replacing the free allocation of allowances to the ETS sectors. Most of the operators of the ETS installations have under the current phase to buy allowances in accordance with the Commission Auctioning Regulation.[659] The Commission makes the exact allocation of allowances to the ETS installation under the Phase III period (2013–2020) on the basis of data from the Member States. Based on the data, preliminary freely allocation per installation is calculated for each year until 2020. Partial treatment is given to installations in sectors or subsectors that are deemed to be at risk of 'carbon leakage' because they face competition from industries in third countries that are not subject to comparable carbon restrictions. Article 10a of the EU ETS Directive ensures the right to free allocation on national level based on a fully harmonised benchmarking scheme established by the Commission. In addition to the free allocation, the Member States may grant State aid to compensate some electro-intensive industries for direct carbon costs. The use of aid must respect the EU State Aid Guidelines.[660] Allowances issued from 2013 onwards can be banked for use in the subsequent phase of the scheme. On 23–24 October 2014, the Council stated that the emission reduction target of at least 40% should

---

655. EEA, *Application of the EU Emissions Trading Directive. Analysis of national responses under Article 21 of the EU ETS Directive in 2014*, at 15f.
656. Commission Regulation No. 389/2013/EU establishing a Union Registry pursuant to Directive 2003/87/EC of the European Parliament and Council, as amended by Regulation No. 2018/208/EU.
657. Regulation No. 601/2012/EU on the Monitoring and Reporting of Greenhouse Gas Pursuant to Directive 2003/87/EC.
658. Commission, *Report on the Functioning of the European Carbon Market*, COM(2018) 842 final, at 13.
659. Commission Regulation No. 1031/2010/EU on the Timing, Administration and other Aspects of Auctioning of GHG Emission Allowances, as amended by Regulation No. 176/2014/EU in particular to determine the Volume of GHG Emissions Allowances to be auctioned in 2013–2020.
660. Guidelines 2014/C 200/02 State Aid for Environmental protection and Energy 2014–2020.

be delivered collectively by the Union in the most cost-effective manner possible.[661] The ETS sectors had to reduce their emission in the period 2020 to 2030 with at least 43%, and the non-ETS sectors had to reduce their emissions with 30%.

83. In 2018 the EU passed a new package on the '2030 Framework for Climate and Energy'. It includes EU-wide targets and policy objectives for the period 2020 to 2030 in 2014.[662] The EU targets for 2030 are a 40% reduction of GHG emissions, 32% renewable energy sources and at least 32.5% energy efficiency target for 2030.

A new Regulation on the Governance of the Energy Union and Climate Action[663] – that is part of the national law in the Member States (incl. Denmark) – is linked to sectoral law implementing the 2030 targets for energy and climate. It ensures a more ambitious linear reduction factor for the GHG emissions, new rules for free allocation and carbon leakage and provisions for funding innovation and modernisation. It aims to simplify the process of monitoring and to address weaknesses in implementing the goals of Energy Union, in particular EU targets on renewable energy, energy efficiency and GHGs. It envisages national and EU registries and inventories on GHGs for the post-2020 period as means to assess progress in meeting the goals of the Paris Agreement.[664] A '2018 Market Stability Reserve' was established as part of the Package to reduce the imbalance on the carbon market. The EU ETS Directive was revised in 2018[665] as art of the '2030 Framework for Climate and Energy' with the aim of facilitating a 43% GHG emissions reductions by 2030 in line with EU's commitments under the Paris Agreement. The amendment has effect for the fourth trading period (2021–2030). The revised Directive allows the Member States to continue providing indirect carbon cost compensation and to complement it with enhanced transparency and reporting provisions. International credits from CDM and JI projects will no longer be used. Across the entire EU, GHG emissions from non-ETS sectors must be reduced by an average of 10% compared to 2005 levels by 2020 regulated by the 'Effort Sharing Decision'.[666] Member States with a low GDP per capita and strong prospects for economic growth (primarily the new Member States) may increase their carbon emissions by up to 20%, whereas those with high national income per capita (e.g., Denmark) must cut the emission by up to 20% by 2020. In order to set a trajectory to meet the target reduction in emission by 2020, the burden sharing decision sets annual binding emission limits for each Member State. Denmark, Ireland and Luxembourg have

661. Council Conclusion of 24 October 2014, EUCO 169/14.
662. COM(2014) 15 final, *A Policy Framework for Climate and Energy in the Period from 2020 to 2030.*
663. European Parliament and Council Regulation No. 2018/1999/EU on the Governance of the Energy and Climate Action.
664. Concerning the obligations that each Member State have to produce an integrated national plan for energy and climate (NECP) every ten years covering the period until 2030, *see infra* para. 229.
665. European Parliament and Council Directive 2018/410/EU amending Directive 2003/87/EC to enhance cost-effective emission reductions and low-carbon investments, and Decision 2015/1814/EU.
666. European Parliament and Council Decision 406/2009/EC on the efforts of EU Member States to reduce their greenhouse gas (GHG) emissions to meet the EU's GHG emission reduction commitments up to 2020.

– as the most significant obligation – to reduce their emissions by 20%. On 6 March 2015, the Council decided a reduction of GHG emissions at EU level. The EU ETS sectors have to reduce their emissions by 43% and the other sectors (agriculture, small companies, buildings and transport) have to reduce their emissions by 30%. The Effort Sharing Decision is, with effect for the period 2021–2030, replaced by the Effort Sharing Regulation.[667] The non-EST sectors have to reduce their emission with 30%. One of the key measures for the Common Agriculture Policy of the EU for the period 2014–2020 is to increase the carbon sink by encouraging more grassland and protecting the forest etc.[668]

84. Denmark is bound by the UNFCCC, the Kyoto Protocol, the Paris Agreement, and the EU's climate legislation described *supra*. The Danish reduction obligation is one of the hardest reduction targets in the world. Denmark has chosen 1995 as the base year for industrial GHGs, and in the calculation under the Kyoto Protocol, it has included the removals of GHGs in forests occurring as a consequence of afforestation since 1990. Under the first burden-sharing-agreement, Denmark must, in accordance with this agreement, reduce its annual GHG emissions by 21% before the end of 2012 (compared with the 1990 levels). In accordance with the second burden-sharing-agreement, Denmark has undertaken to reduce its average GHG emissions between 2013 and 2020 by 20% (compared with 2005 levels). Under the Burden Sharing Regulation Denmark is committed to a 39% reduction in non-ETS emissions in the period 2021–2030 relative to 2005.

In 2014, the Climate Policy Act[669] came into force. It has not been changed since. The Act is only a framework for transitioning to a low-emission society in 2050. It is without precise legal obligations in respect to the reduction of GHG emission. In December 2017, the 'Seventh National Communication and the Second Biennial Report' was submitted by the Danish Government to the UNFCCC Secretariat covering the Kingdom of Denmark, inclusive Greenland and the Faroe Islands. In the summary of this report it is stated that most of the CO_2 emissions in Denmark come from combustion of coal, oil and natural gas in energy industries, residential properties and from the manufacturing industry (44% in 2015).[670] Road transport is also a major contributor (34% in 2015). The relatively large fluctuations in the emissions from year to year are due to trade in electricity with other countries (primarily the Nordic countries). In 2015, the total actual CO_2 emissions inventoried under the UNFCCC, excluding LULUCF, were about 34% lower than in 1990.[671] If LULUCF is included, net emissions were about 32% lower. In 2015, total CH_4 emissions that are made by agriculture, landfills and the energy sector (among which agriculture

667. European Parliament and Council Regulation No. 2018/842/EU on the Binding Annual Greenhouse Gas Emission Reductions.
668. Concerning the Common Agriculture Policy of the EU, *see infra* para. 258.
669. Act No. 716 of 25 June 2014 on Climate Policy.
670. *Denmark's 7th National Communication and the 2nd Biennial Report under the UNFCCC*, at 21.
671. CO2 made up 73.3% of the total Danish emission of GHGs in 2015. The total GHGs (excluding of the emissions from two Arctic regions) were estimated to 47.9 million tonnes of CO2 equivalents, cf. *Denmark's 7th National Communication and the 2nd Biennial Report under the UNFCCC*, at 22.

contributes the most by far) were 10% below the 1990 level.[672] The N_2O emissions – that first and foremost come from agriculture – were in 2015 reduced by 34% (compared with the level in 1990).[673] The total emissions of HFCs, PFCs and SF6 increased by 128% from 1995 to 2015.[674] In 2017, the Danish emissions from installations participating in the EU ETS scheme were estimated to have increased slightly by 0.18% compared to 2016 based on the information recovered in the EU Registry. This increase is explained in the 'Seventh National Communication and the Second Biennial Report' with the growth of 2.4% in real GDP which is higher than in any year since the beginning of the third trading period.[675] The number of allowances cancelled on a voluntary basis amounts to 84,827 allowances in 2017.

On 9 October 2018, the former liberal-conservative government published its climate plan 'Together for a Greener Future'. This plan was based on what the former government – that was in power until 27 June 2019 – titled 'a green realism'. The lack of a high ambition was criticised by the Danish Council on Climate Change[676] and by many other actors. Another new step of importance for the future climate policy in Denmark is the citizen initiative that was sent to the Danish Parliament in Spring 2019. It called for a new Climate Act and gained over 50,000 signatures. On 27 June 2019, the new Social Democrat Government came into power with very high ambitions on a 70% reduction of the Danish GHG emission by 2030 compared with the Danish GHG emission in 1990.[677]

Denmark has not ensured a formal integration of its implementation of the IED and the EU ETS permit systems as it is not the same competent body that oversees the application of the IED rules[678] and the EU ETS rules in Denmark.[679]

---

672. The methane counted for 14.3% of the total Danish emission of GHGs in 2015 (excluding the emissions from two Arctic regions).
673. The emission of N2O counted for 10.8% of the total Danish emission of GHGs in 2015 (excluding the emissions from two Arctic regions).
674. From 1995 to 2015, annual emissions of HFCs increased from 241 to 677 Gg of CO2 equivalents – 1.5% of the total Danish emission of GHGs in 2015 (excluding the emissions from two Arctic regions).
675. *Commission's Report on the Functioning of the European Carbon Market*, COM(2018) 842 final, at 28.
676. The Council is established as the most important institution under the Danish Climate Policy Act. The former liberal-conservative coalition government's plan is cruised in the Council's 2018 report. Concerning this government, *see supra* para. 4 note 28.
677. The history of the Danish policy is the following: The Parliament approved the *Cost Efficient Climate Strategy* in March 2003, setting out the overall guidelines for prioritising domestic versus international action to meet the Danish climate target. Initially, in 2003, funds were allocated for government procurement of JI credits, while CDM was included from 2004 onwards. In March 2005, a major ex-post analysis of Denmark's efforts in 1990–2001 to reduce emissions of CO2 and other GHGs, and associated costs was finalised and published in the Report, *Denmark's CO2 Emissions – The Effort in the Period of 1990-2001 and the Associated Costs*. In August 2013, the Liberal-Conservative coalition government's Climate Policy *Towards a Low Carbon Society* was published. It was the Government's ambition to put Denmark on track for the 2050 of an 80–95% GHG emission reduction by 2050 compared with 1990. The strategy included an interim target of a 40% reduction by 2020 in all Danish GHG emissions, and electricity and heating supply had to be completely based on renewable energy in 2035. The current Government has the ambition to reduce a 70% reduction of the GHG emissions by 2030.
678. It is the municipalities and the Ministry of Environment and Food of Denmark that have the competence.

85. The Energy Agreement of 29 June 2018 and the above-mentioned energy strategy of 9 October 2018, titled 'Together for a Greener Future', set the path towards making renewable energy's share of the total energy consumption 55% by 2030 and a net zero emissions situation by 2050. On 25 June 2019, the Social Democratic Party – as its political basis for getting the positions, as the new minority Government – made an agreement with three other political parties in order to be able to form the Government with effect from 27 June 2019.

The new Government has to present a bill in the autumn of 2019 on a new Climate Act with binding sub-goals and binding long-term goals. This new Act will include a target of a 70% reduction of GHG emissions by 2030 compared with the emission levels in 1990. A climate policy plan will include binding targets on reducing national emissions for each year and it will be mandatory for the Government to ensure an annual assessment of the fulfilment of the plan. This follow-up will be coordinated with the decision-making in the yearly finance bill process. It is also the ambition to change the transport sector by means of a new mobility plan. Sale of new petrol and diesel cars will be phased out in 2030, and the environmental zoning in the cities will be more demanding. The subsidies for the agricultural sector that Denmark receives from the EU will be used more proactively to ensure a sustainable production. It is also part of this political agreement to push the climate policy of the EU in a more ambitious direction.

86. Denmark implemented the EU ETS Directive by adopting the Carbon Dioxide Allowances Act in 2004.[680] The Act has been amended several times to ensure the implementation of new versions of the EU ETS. The Act regulates CO_2 emissions from a number of identified categories of industrial activities at land and on the sea as listed in sections 8–10. Denmark has 360 installations under the EU ETS rules under the administration of the Ministry for Energy, Utilities and Climate.[681] All aviation activities within Danish territory are also included by the scheme for GHG emission allowance trading from 1 January 2012, cf. section 11 of the Act.[682]

Under the second commitment period under the EU ETS Directive, Denmark submitted its National Allocation Plan (NAP2) for CO_2 certificates for the period of 2008–2012 on 17 January 2007 to the Commission. In the first version of this NAP2, Denmark had ordinarily imposed a ceiling for the use of quotas deriving from JI- and CDM-projects at a maximum of 19% from each operator. The Commission found that the ceiling was inconsistent with Denmark's supplementary obligations under the Kyoto Protocol and with the prohibition of State aid under the

679. It is the Ministry of Climate, Energy and Utilities that has the competence.
680. Act No. 493 of 9 June 2004 on Carbon Dioxide Allowances. It is now Promulgation Order No. 1605 of 14 December 2016.
681. EEA, *The European Environment State and Outlook 2015. Synthesis Report*, Appendix 4, at 76.
682. Amended by Act No. 1267 of 16 December 2009. The Act No. 1497 of 23 December 2014 ensured conformity with the European Parliament and Council Regulation No. 421/2014/EU amending Directive 2003/87/EC establishing a Scheme for Greenhouse Gas Emission Allowance Trading within the Community, in View of the Implementation by 2020 of an International Agreement applying a Single Global Market-based Measure to International Aviation Emission.

Treaty.[683] The plan was finally approved by the Commission in August 2007, subject to one amendment concerning the use of the JI- and CDM-projects. The approved NAP2 was then transformed into rules, changing Chapter 4 of the Act. Under the NAP2, an average annual allowance of 24.5 million tonnes CO_2 were allocated for the period of 2008–2012. Denmark allocated a total of 125 million CO_2 emission quotas during the second commitment period. Of these, 2.5 million have been allocated to new production units and major expansions of existing enterprises. The rest was allocated free of charge to those production units covered by the trading scheme in 2007.

Under the current EU ETS, it is the Commission that allocates the allowances.[684] The Minister for Climate, Energy and Buildings allocated the allowances that Denmark has received from the Commission. The allocation of free allowances to the sectors that are covered by the modification established by the EU ETS is based on the benchmarking criteria established by the Commission.[685] The revenue from the sale of credits is regarded as a State income, cf. section 18 of the Act. Under sections 15–16 of this Act, the Minister for Industry, Business and Financial Affairs is the administrator of the Danish approvals given to the enterprises covered by the EU ETS obligations.[686] The operators must have enough allowances to cover the CO_2 emissions that their activities are resulting in, and they are responsible for the monitoring and the reporting of the emission. The aircraft operators have the same obligation regarding enough allowances to surrender allowances calculated in the light of the whole of their national or international flight, cf. sections 27–28. If an operator emits CO_2 in excess as to the level of emissions covered by its CO_2 quotas, including any extra CO_2 quotas purchased and extra JI or CDM credits obtained, the operator must pay an excess emission penalty for each ton of CO_2 emitted without surrendering the allowances. The Minister for Climate, Energy and Utilities is responsible for the correct implementation of the EU ETS Directive, and he has to control that the operators are following the rules and to ensure that any operator who do not surrender sufficient allowances by 30 April each year to cover the emissions from its activities during the preceding year is held liable, cf. section 27. In addition to paying the excess emission penalty, the operator must surrender an amount of allowances equal to those excess emissions, cf. section 28. The supplementary Danish rules on monitoring, verification and reporting are adopted by the Minister for Climate, Energy and Utilities, cf. section 25.[687] It is the Danish supplement to the Commissions regulations.[688]

---

683. Concerning guidelines on state aid, *see supra* in para. 82.
684. The third commitment period is implemented by Act No. 1095 of 28 November 2012 to provide for CO2 allowances.
685. The allowances for the installations have been calculated for 2013–2020 in accordance with the EU benchmarking decision 2011/278/EU.
686. Statutory Order No. 1636 of 13 December 2917 on the EU ETS Registry and the Danish Kyoto Registry.
687. Statutory Order No. 1180 of 12 December 2012 on Monitoring, Verification and Reporting of CO2 emission and Tonne-kilometre.
688. Commission Regulation No. 600/2012/EU on Verification of Greenhouse gases reports and tonne-kilometre Reports and Accreditation of Verifiers pursuant to the EU ETS Directive and regulation No. 601/2012/EU on Monitoring and Reporting of CO2 emission.

§3. ACID RAIN

87. Acidification causes buildings to degenerate, threatens the aquatic environment and contributes to forest destruction. The most harmful air pollutants in terms of damage to ecosystems are ozone O_3, NH_3 and NO_x. Deposition of substances or chemically transformed compounds of sulphur, nitrate and ammonium compounds can acidify the soil as well as lakes and watercourses, and thereby indirectly affect many chalk-poor and nutrient-poor natural ecosystems, as well as forest productivity and the biological state of forests.

The effect of acidification depends on a combination of two factors: the amount of acid deposition and the natural capacity of the terrestrial or aquatic ecosystem in question to counteract the acidification, i.e., the ecosystem's buffering capacity. Transport accounts for only 2%. The proportion is increasing because the use of catalytic converters is increasing, whereas the proportion caused by agriculture is decreasing. Acidification causes buildings to degenerate, threatens the aquatic environment and contributes to forest destruction. The greatest acidifying factor in Denmark is nitrogen from the NH_3 emitted by agriculture.[689]

88. The Danish government admitted in the 1980s that because of the prevailing southwesterly wind, the SO_2 emission from Denmark made a significant contribution to Swedish problems, and consequently several regulatory as well as technical initiatives had to be taken especially in the energy sector. The first energy action plan 'Energy 2000' aimed at an increased use of natural gas instead of other more polluting fossil fuels and a halving of SO_2 emissions and a reduction by about one-third of NO_x emissions before the year 2000.[690]

Section 7 of the Environmental Protection Act empowers the Danish Minister for the Environment to issue statutory orders which may include emission limits targets for the content in fuels of sulphur and other substances that may cause air pollution, including rules on the purification of discharges from sources of air pollution.[691]

The cars and the fuels used in Denmark have to be designed in harmony with EU's standards to ensure the reduction of the emission of SO_2, NO_x and NH_3.[692] There is no car production in Denmark. The Directives on the quality of fuels used

689. The air quality legislation at the international, EU and national levels is described *supra* in paras 74–76.
690. This goal has been met, *see infra* para. 98. *See also infra* para. 87.
691. Of such statutory orders on pollution from plants, the first most important orders were: Statutory Order No. 885 of 18 December 1991 on Limitation of Emission of Sulphur Dioxide and Nitrogen Oxide from Power Plants (as amended by Statutory Order No. 321 of 4 June 1998). The former, already in 1991, established SO2 and NOx emission quotas. The power plants were able, to a large extent, to choose technology and location when new flue gas cleaning plants were to be built. The mentioned statutory orders are no longer in force.
692. Concerning the standards on cars, *see infra* para. 90.

in cars are implemented as statutory rules.[693] The emission from ships are also regulated at international and EU levels with binding effect in Denmark.[694] These EU obligations on the maximum sulphur content of heavy fuel oil and gas oil are implemented into Danish law by Statutory Order on the Content of Sulfur in Solid and Liquid Fuel.[695] There are Danish rules on the quality of the biomass used in the households of small combustion plants.[696] The MCP Directive[697] has been implemented by Statutory Order on Environmental Requirements for Medium-sized Combustion Plants.[698] There are also statutory rules on the emission from the large combustion plants,[699] on Emission of Nitrogen Dioxide, Un-burnt Hydrocarbons and Carbon Monoxide from Gas Engines and Gas Turbines,[700] and on the quality of the wood waste used in the energy sector.[701] Most agricultural NH_3 emissions in Denmark derive from manure (76%). Other important sources include commercial fertiliser (7%), crops (15%) and NH_3 treatment of straw (2%). Application of sewage sludge to fields also emits NH_3.

The current regulation of the emission of NH_3 and nitrogen from agriculture is based on the political agreement on the 'Food and Agricultural Package' from November 2015 that has been implemented by the Act on Approval of Livestock Installations,[702] Act on Farms with Animals[703] and the Act on the Use of Fertilisers by Agriculture and on Nutrient-reducing Measures.[704] Denmark has in relation to the EU accepted a limit of 69,000 tonnes of NH_3 in 2010 as part of the EU quality rules. As a signatory to the Geneva Convention on Long-range Transboundary Air Pollution, Denmark has accepted an emission limit that entails a 43% reduction in NH_3 volatilisation relative to the 1999 level, corresponding to an emission limit of 69,000 ton of NH_3. The predominant source of NH_3 is agricultural activities (96%) and the major part comes from livestock manure.[705] In a scientific report from 2009 covering the period of 2010–2030, it is stated that the emission is expected to

693. Statutory Order No. 1024 of 23 August 2017 that is implementing Directive No. 98/76/EC as amended.
694. European Parliament and Council Directive 2012/33/EU amending the Council Directive 1999/32 as regards the Sulphur Content of Marine Fuels. The amendment ensures vertical harmonisation with the MARPOL Annex VI – as means to reduce SO2 emission from shipping.
695. Statutory Order No. 640 of 12 June 2014 on the Content of Sulfur in Solid and Liquid Fuel.
696. Statutory Order No. 49 of 16 January 2018 on Reduction of Air Pollution from Small Combustion Plants for Solid Fuels below 1 MW.
697. It is now the European Parliament and the Council Directive 2015/2193/EU on the Limitation of Emissions of Certain Pollutants into the Air from Medium Combustion Plants.
698. Statutory Order No. 751 of 28 May 2018 on Environmental Requirements for Medium-sized Combustion Plants.
699. Statutory Order No. 513 of 22 May 2016 on Limitation of Emission of Certain Polluting Substances from Large Combustion Plants.
700. Statutory Order No. 1473 of 12 December 2017 on Emission of Nitrogen Dioxide, Un-burnt Hydrocarbons and Carbon Monoxide from Gas Engines and Gas Turbines.
701. Statutory Order No. 1471 of 12 December 2017.
702. Act on Approval of Livestock Installations is mentioned *supra* in paras 63–64.
703. Promulgation Order No. 1 of 2 January 2019 on Farms with Animals.
704. Act No. 338 of 2 April 2019 on the Use of Fertilisers by Agriculture and on Nutrient-reducing Measures.
705. DCE Report No. 81, *Projection of S02, NO x, NMVOC, NH3 and Particle Emission 2012-2035.*

decrease by 19% from 2009 to 2020 – and 23% before 2030.[706] An economic analysis made by the Organisation of Farmers from February 2015 – with references to the EEA emission 2012 data – states that Denmark now has the lowest NH_3 level per kg milk produced among the 10 largest milk producers in the EU.

89. When the 1991 Geneva Protocol on VOCs that specifies options for emission reduction came into force the 29 September 1997, Denmark was obliged (in accordance with Articles 1 and 2 of the Protocol) to control and reduce its emissions of VOCs by at least 30% by the year 1999, using either 1988 as a basis or any other annual level during the period of 1984–1990, which it had to specify upon signature of the Protocol.

In 1994, an environmental contract for reducing the emissions of VOCs was made between the Confederation of Danish Industries and the Minister for Environment. It was part of the agreement that the Minister made branch guidelines for those branches of industry. The EPA stated that the guidelines associated with this agreement was to be used by the supervisory authorities with respect to all firms within the relevant branches, even including those branches and companies that are not parties to the contract. The agreement of the contract is primarily that of an action plan for the involved branches. It is based on technical statements about the possibilities of reduction as well as statements about the possible technical and economic barriers to reduction. For the industry, the advantage of this agreement lies precisely in the agreement itself, as the Ministry promised, already in 1989, not to raise the threshold limits for VOCs in air quality guidelines, if the industry would prepare a plan for substantial reduction of VOC emissions by the year 2000. The possibilities of sanctions were not included in the agreement. The Competition Council examined the agreement in September 1994 as it wanted to ensure that differential treatment did not lead to monopoly relationships. After EPA had informed the Council that preferential treatment was not intended, and after it had been disclosed that the possibilities of being included in the agreement were open for everyone in the relevant branches, the Council declared that the agreement was not subject to the obligation to report under the Trade Act.

A traditional top-down regulation of the VOC issues is laid down in the Statutory Order on the Limitation of Emission of Volatile Organic Compound from the Utilisation of Organic Solvents in Certain Activities and Plants[707] and the environmental approval system in Chapter 5 of the Environmental Protection Act.[708] The VOCs decreased dramatically in 2004–2008 and has continued to do so.[709]

§4. Vehicles and Fuels

90. The transport sector emits a number of substances into the air that influence human health, ecosystems and the climate. The World Forum for Harmonisation of

706. DCE Report No. 7, *Projection of S02, NO x, NH3 and Particle Emission 2010-2030.*
707. Statutory Order No. 1491 of 7 December 2015.
708. The Danish system is described *supra* paras 62–66. Concerning the EU rules, *see supra* para. 61.
709. DCE Report No. 281, *The Danish Air Quality Monitoring Programme 2017.*

Vehicle Regulation agreed in March 2010 on the need to review and update the 1958 UNECE Agreement and its regulations, along with a view to introduce the concept of international whole vehicle type approval. EU regulations and directives refer to the international agreements as developed under the CLRTAP.[710]

In June 1992, an agreement was signed between the Commission, the European umbrella organisation on oil industry, the European Petroleum Industry Association – Europia, and the European Automobile Manufacturers Association (ACEA) to deal with the pollution from the cars by means of voluntary environmental performance standards. The European Auto-Oil Programmes from 1992 to 2000 resulted in proposals for vehicle emission limits and new fuel standards. These experiences were also the background for the Clean Air for Europe (CAFE) Programme, which was launched in May 2001.[711] The first directive on a common legal framework for the type approval of cars, vans, trucks, buses and coaches was passed in 2007.[712] EU's Climate and Energy Package from 2008 included three regulations setting the legally binding performance standards for CO_2 emissions from new cars and vans by vehicles type approval rules.[713] The Regulations are part of the national law and are setting the standards for an average reduction of emissions from new cars to 120 g CO_2 per km. This is to be achieved in two ways: a reduction to 130 g CO_2 per km through engine technology plus an additional cut of 10 g CO_2 per km through more efficient vehicle features, for instance, air conditioning systems or tires. The Regulation makes these objectives binding for the average fleet of a given car manufacturer in successive stages. From 2015, the whole fleet needed to comply with the CO_2 emissions objective. To give a signal to the industry for further production cycles, the Council and European Parliament introduced additional objective of 95 g CO_2 per km for 2020. Manufacturers may improve their fleet's emissions performance by including eco-innovations, i.e., new technology that is not measured through the standard EU CO_2 emissions test, or by producing ultra-low emissions cars, which emit less than 50 g CO_2 per km. If car manufacturers do not comply, they face penalties depending on the extent to which their fleet exceeds the targets and on the number of their new passenger cars. Other emission performance standards for vehicles have been passed to ensure better air quality. Following the Regulation for Euro 6 vehicles, the Commission performed a study on the real driving emissions (RDE) of Euro 5 vehicles in 2010. The study showed that RDE, in particular NO_x emissions of Euro 5 diesel vehicles significantly exceeded regulatory

---

710. *Cars 21 High Level Group on the Competitiveness and Sustainable Growth of the Automotive Industry in the European Union. Interim Report 2011* at 5, 8 and 30.
711. COM(2001) 245 final.
712. European Parliament and Council 2007/46/EC establishing a Framework for the Approval of Motor Vehicles and their Trailers, and of Systems, Components and Separate Technical Units intended for such Vehicles.
713. European Parliament and Council Regulation No. 692/2008/EC on Type Approval of Motor Vehicles with respect to Emissions from Light Passenger and Commercial Vehicles (Euro 5 and 6) and on Access to Vehicle Repair and Maintenance Information; European Parliament and Council Regulation No. 443/2009/EC setting the Emission Performance Standards for New Passenger Cars as Part of the Community's Integrated Approach to reduce CO2 Emissions from Light-Duty Vehicles; and European Parliament and Council Regulation No. 595/2009/EC on Type Approval of Motor Vehicles and Engines with Respect to Emission from Heavy Duty Vehicles (Euro VI) and on Access to vehicle Repair and Maintenance Information.

emission limits. In its 'CARS 2020 Communication', the Commission noted the shortcoming of the current procedures and committed a new test procedure in the type approval framework to assess NO_x emissions of light-duty vehicles (LDVs) under real world driving conditions.[714] The shortcoming has also been highlighted by the 2013 impact assessment of the general regulation of air pollution.[715] It was concluded in 2013 that while vehicles in general have delivered substantial emission reductions across the range of regulated pollutants, this is not true of NO_x emissions from diesel engines (especially the light passengers and commercial vessels –named the 'light-duty vechicles' or the LDVs). Type approval emissions requirements for motor vehicles have been tightened through the introduction of and subsequent revision of Euro standards.[716] The implementation of the Regulation on mandatory Euro 6 vehicles in 2014, together with the implementation in 2017 of the RDE procedure[717] that are applied for type approval of LDVs (Euro 5 and Euro 6) as well as the 'Euro IV' on heavy-duty vehicles (HDVs),[718] together with the robust not-to-exceed (NTE) emission limits ensure a reduction in the emissions of $NO_{x,}$ emissions from HDVs as well as from LDVs.[719] Other legislative instruments address emissions to the air from the use of fuels, supporting fuels with a lower content of sulphur and the use of alternative fuels, such as electricity, hydrogen, biofuels, CH_4 (natural gas and bio-methane), LPG and others. The Regulation on the Worldwide Harmonised Light Vehicle Test Procedure[720] and the RDE tests (Act 4)[721] are defining the new test procedures for vehicle type and enable real world testing, including testing by independent certified laboratories.

The Fuel Quality Directive[722] sets out environmental standards for fuel, with the objective of improving air quality and reducing GHG emissions. It aims to facilitate the more widespread blending of biofuels into petrol and diesel and, to avoid negative consequences. Suppliers must, each year by 31 December, gradually reduce life cycle GHG emissions by 10% per unit. 'Life cycle GHG emissions' means all net emissions of CO_2, CH_4 and N_2O that can be assigned to the fuel or energy supplied.

---

714. COM(2012) 636 final and COM(2013) 918 final, at 3.
715. The impact assessment is published as the Commission staff working document. Impact assessment SWD (2013) 531, at 21.
716. Concerning the performance standards, *see* Directive 2007/46/EC and Commission Regulation 692/2008/EC as amended by the Commission Regulation 136/2014/EU.
717. Commission Regulation No. 136/2014/EU of 11 February 2014 as regards the reduction of pollutant emission from road vehicles. The RDE are measured on the road by a Portable Emission Measurement System (PEMS). Exhaust control systems must perform under a broad range of different operating conditions, the logistics of type approval processes are forced to be restructured and new measurement technology has to be applied.
718. Commission Regulation No. 582/2011/EU as amended by the Commission Regulation No. 136/2014/EU.
719. COM(2013) 918 final, A Clean Air Programme for Europe, at 3.
720. Commission Regulation No. 2017/1151/EU.
721. This is a test procedure agreed by the Member States on 3 May 2018 ensuring a transparent and independent control of the emissions.
722. European Parliament and Council Directive 2009/30/EC amending Directive 98/70/EEC as regards the Specification of Petrol, Diesel and Gas-oil and introducing a Mechanism to monitor and reduce Greenhouse Gas Emissions and amending Council Directive 1999/32/EC as regards the Specification of Fuel Used by Inland Waterways Vessels and repealing Directive 93/12/EEC. Amended by European Parliament and Council Directive 2016/802/EU.

The Directive on the Sulfur Content of Liquid Fuels[723] lays down the maximum permitted sulphur content of heavy fuel oil, gas oil and marine gas oil used in the EU. The Directive was amended five times. The amendments in 2005[724] and in 2012[725] regarding the sulphur content of marine fuels ensures reduction of SO_x emission from the transport sector were the most important amendments. In 2012, an amendment of the Directive ensured the implementation of the new Annex VI of the MARPOL 73/78. The Directive with amendments was codified in 2016.[726] By 2030, the goal proposed by the Commission for the transport sector, currently discussed by the Council and European Parliament, will be to reduce GHG emissions from the transport sector to around 20% below their 2008 level. It represents 80% of the energy used by all transport modes in the EU. It is estimated that HDVs cause 26% of CO_2 emissions from road transport in EU, which is about 5% of total CO_2 emissions. The traffic also emits hydrocarbons – including CH_4 – covered by UNFCCC. Other substances emitted from traffic are nitrogen oxides (NO_x/NO_2) that are covered by the rules on acid rain.[727] Several particles, including lead and particulate matter (PM_{10} and $PM_{2.5}$) and ozone, are also emitted by vehicles.[728]

91. The 2009 RES Directive[729] as well as the Fuel Quality Directive aims to ensure production of biofuels to be used by vehicles in a sustainable way. Both Directives set ambitious sustainability criteria for biofuels, and they ensure total harmonisation of the sustainability criteria.[730] The 2009 RES Directive obliges all Member States to ensure, that their share of RESs in the transport sector has to reach 10% by 2020. They are obliged to require suppliers to ensure that diesel fuel used on their territories respect the specifications set out in the Directive. They must also ensure the provision of appropriate information to consumers concerning the biofuel content of petrol and, in particular, on the appropriate use of different blends of petrol.

The energy from biofuels may only be taken into account for the purposes of GHG emissions reduction, if they fulfil the subsidiarity criteria set out in the Directives. The 2009 RES Directive emphasises the obligations to demonstrate the protection of biodiversity (globally and locally) and the reduction of GHG emissions from cultivated soil through implementation of sustainability criteria. The criteria relate to GHG savings, land with high biodiversity value, land with high carbon

723. European Parliament and Council Directive 1999/32/EC relating to a Reduction in the Sulphur Content of Certain Liquid Fuels.
724. European Parliament and Council Directive 2005/33/EC amending Directive 1999/32/EC.
725. European Parliament and Council Directive 2012/33/EU amending Directive 1999/32/EC as regards the Content of Sulphur Content of Fuels.
726. European Parliament and Council Directive 2016/802/EU on the Reduction in the Sulphur Content of Certain Liquid Fuels (heavy fuel oil, gas oil, marine gas oil and marine diesel oil).
727. Concerning the rules on acid rain, *see supra* paras 85–89.
728. Concerning the Danish notification to the Commission in accordance with Art. 22(2) of the Framework Directive, *see supra* para. 76.
729. European Parliament and Council Directive 2009/28/EC on the Promotion of the Use of Energy from Renewable Sources. This Directive is from 2021 replaced by European Parliament and Council Directive 2018/201/EU on the Promotion of Energy Renewable Sources, *see infra* para. 227.
730. The rules on the sustainability criteria are based on the Treaty rule on the Internal Market – now Art. 114 TFEU.

stock and agri-environmental practices. The effect of the sustainability criteria is not limited to the production of biofuels inside EU.[731] The reasoning behind the sustainability criteria's exterritorial effect is the need to avoid an unjustified competitive advantage for the producers of biofuel in third countries over their EU competitors. Based on the sustainability criteria, mineral resources (biomass) for biofuels and bioliquids cannot be produced on land with high carbon stock or on wetlands, forests and areas with other wooded land of native species etc. if the Member States wish to use biofuels or bioliquids to fulfil their RES obligations or to use subsidies. Biofuels are not permitted to be made from materials obtained from land that was peat land in January 2008, unless evidence is provided that the cultivation and harvesting of the raw material do not involve the draining of previously undrained soil, cf. Article 17(5). With respect to imports, this Directive states that only third countries that supply biofuels and other bioliquids, which meet the total harmonised sustainability requirements (both relating to domestically produced and imported), should be able to benefit from the promotion of RES in the EU. Vertical harmonisation must be ensured by means of international conventions' concepts and criteria. The sustainability criteria are therefore related both to national, EU and international criteria.

Biofuels used for compliance with the GHGs reduction targets laid down in both Directives are required to fulfil sustainability criteria irrespective of whether the mineral resources were cultivated inside or outside the territory of the EU.[732] The reasoning behind the sustainability criteria's extra-territorial effect is the need to avoid an unjustified competitive advantage for the producers of biofuels in third countries over their EU competitors.[733] The Directive was amended in 2015 making it possible also to include exterritorial emission into the reporting.[734] The GHG emissions saving from the use of biofuels must be at least 35%. With effect from 1 January 2017, the GHG emissions saving must be at least 50%, and from 2018 at least 60%.

92. It was stated in OECD 2007 evaluation of the Danish environmental policy that little progress has been made at the strategic level in integrating environmental concerns into transport policy.[735] The Danish transport policy aims at facilitating accessibility and is mainly aimed at increasing or upgrading the supply of road infrastructure supply. Solutions to the negative consequences of transport are only focused on improving efficiency, cleaning the technological means of transportation and, to some extent, shifting the mode of transport from car transportation to collective transportation.[736] During the past decade, central part of the Danish road and

731. Article 7b of the current version of the Fuel Quality Directive lays down that, irrespective of whether the mineral resources were cultivated inside or outside the territory of the EU, energy from biofuels shall be taken into account for the purposes of GHG emission reduction only, if they fulfil the subsidiarity criteria set out in the Article.
732. Concerning energy and climate policy, *see infra* para. 229.
733. Concerning the transformation to Danish legislation, *see infra* para. 230.
734. European Parliament and Council Directive 2015/1513/EU on the Reduction of Indirect Land Use Change for Biofuels and Bioliquids amending the RES Directive.
735. OECD, *Environmental Performance Reviews. Denmark 2007*, at 24.
736. T.B. Christensen & T. Kjær, *Planning for Sustainable Transport: The Case of Copenhagen,* at 127.

rail network has been experiencing growing capacity and congestion problems, especially during gradually expanding peak hours.

The 'predict and provide approach' under the Danish policy is a significant barrier to solving air pollution caused by transport activities as it lessens the effect of policy measures that aims to reduce transport activities as such. The money spent on infrastructure in Denmark is first and foremost used on new roads. Traffic in Denmark has increased by more than 50% since 1990, and it is expected to increase at the same rate for the foreseeable future. Public transport increased about 25% over the period of 1990–2010, while car transport increased by about 14% over the same period. The increase in public transport can be attributed to the Great Belt Fixed Link, which has connected the western and eastern parts of Denmark since 1997, and the Øresund Link which has connected Denmark and Sweden since 2000. In the recent past, the freight transport infrastructure has been based on the 'Big H' covering the major road and railway networks that connect Denmark from east to west, and from north to south. In addition, it provides links to neighbouring countries. A forecast published by the Danish Infrastructure Commission shows that by 2030, traffic on the national road network is expected to increase by nearly 70%. This corresponds to an average annual growth rate of 2.2%. The growth will create critical congestion problems on major parts of the motorway network in Denmark and feeder routes as well. In 2014, the Economic Council stated that car transport accounts for about 75% of the total passenger transport in passenger kilometres, while public transport accounts for about 10%.[737]

The first action plan on traffic from the Danish Ministry of Transport was published in 1990 and laid down the CO_2 reduction targets in relation to the transport area. The next action plan was 'Traffic 2000' (1993), which encompassed a detailed survey of environmental problems in relation to this sector. It was followed by a clarifying paper entitled 'Transport, Environment and Carbon Dioxide Emissions' (1995) and the action plan 'The Danish Government's Action Plan for Reduction of CO_2 Emission of the Transport Sector' (1996). The 2001–2011 Liberal-Conservative Government presented a vision for 'Sustainable transport – better infrastructure' to ensure a higher mobility as an integral part of a strong society in terms of individual freedom, dynamic impetus and economic growth. The green investment plan ensures a state investment of DKK 150 billion in Danish infrastructure in the period up to 2020. In January 2009, the 2001–2011 Liberal-Conservative Government reached an agreement on 'Green Transport Vision Denmark' with the majority of the members of the Parliament. The focus of this political agreement is an environment-friendly renewal of vehicle tax, CO_2 tax and fuel consumption taxes, more and better public transport plus new sustainable technologies. In January 2008, the Danish Infrastructure published the strategy 'The Danish Transport Infrastructure 2030' based on the 'predict and provide approach' to transport planning. The 'Big H' remains the basis of the road and rail infrastructure, but the report recommended ensuring secondary links from the different regions.[738] The Finance Act of 2010 confirmed the agreement. Based on this, support may be given via a scheme for the testing of more energy-efficient transport

737. Economic Councils, *Economy and Environment 2014*, at 337.
738. Report from the Danish Infrastructure Commission, *The Danish Transport Infrastructure 2030*.

solutions for public and private companies. The aim of the scheme was to reduce CO_2 emissions from the road transport sector.[739] In 2012, the total subsidy to public transport was about DKK 8.5 billion.[740] Two large-scale projects (the Fehmarn Belt Fixed Link between Denmark and Germany and the Metro Circle Line in Copenhagen) are partly financed by this investment plan. A new Infrastructure Fund is financing the remaining amount of DKK 90 billion, which will cover the major investment in roads and railways in the coming years. The political Energy Agreement of 29 June 2018 ensured funding to ensured 100 million DKK in the period 2020–2024 to support green solutions in the transport sector. On 9 October 2018 the former liberal-conservative government published its proposal on a strategy for climate and air quality 'Together for a Greener Future' that included several initiatives related to the emissions from cars.[741] There is no Danish policy on the development of cycling as a mode of transportation. However, there are two relevant public campaigns that aim to promote environmentally sound behaviour. The 'We cycle to work' is a national strategy in which the Danish Cyclist's Federation has ensured a good cooperation with many cities and companies. The Danish capital, Copenhagen, has the highest rate of cycling of any major European city.

93. Taxes on motor vehicles and fuels, etc. are used as an instrument to reduce the negative effect on the air quality.[742] For the period of 2008–2012, the Finance Act reserved DKK 35 million, and for the period 2004 and 2005, the Finance Act reserved approximately DKK 24 million for a scheme to support installation of particulate filters on buses and HDVs. Financial support for a test scheme relating to electric vehicles provides finance for projects and has been established for the period of 2013–2015. DKK 70 million was earmarked for the project in the 'Energy Agreement' of 22 March 2012. It was agreed in the Energy Agreement of 29 June 2018 to increase funding for energy and climate research to DKK 1 billion in 2024 in support to the course towards a climate-neutral society by 2050.

94. Rules on reducing air pollution were established as part of the Traffic Act in 2002. Both the municipal council of Copenhagen and Aalborg wanted to create 'low-emission zones' in Copenhagen and Alborg City. These municipal councils presented their plans, but they were dismissed by the Ministry of Justice as expropriations (takings).[743] New rules on 'low-emission zones' are now part of the Environmental Protection Act (sections 15–15d), making it possible for the municipal councils in the four biggest cities to reduce the access by HDVs unless they are equipped with particulate filters approved by the Danish Road Safety and Transport

739. Danish Ministry of Climate and Energy, *National Action Plan for Renewable Energy in Denmark*, at 85ff.
740. Economic Councils, *Economy and Environment 2014*, at 338.
741. The Government was not re-elected on 5 May 2019. On 27 Jun. 2019, it had to entrust power to a new red-green Government that has higher climate ambitions. Based on the proposal of the former government, the last petrol and diesel cars will be sold in 2030. Concerning the different coalition governments in power since 1993, *see supra* para. 4.
742. Concerning the use of green taxes in Denmark, *see supra* para. 12.
743. Concerning s. 73 of the Constitution, *see supra* para. 30.

Agency. The filters reduce particulate emissions by 80%. The rules on how to pass local rules on such zones are laid down in a statutory order.[744]

The municipal council of Copenhagen passed its rules on such filters with effect from 1 September 2008. The normal requirement was that the HDVs complying with Euro 2 or older European standards had to have a particulate filter installed. In July 2010, the requirement was tightened to include HDVs in this obligation that comply with Euro 3. All duty HDVs that drive inside the 'law emission zone' must carry a certificate in the window of the truck. Before this initiative, the HDVs made up only 7% of Copenhagen's traffic, but were responsible for 50% of PM emissions. Aalborg municipality passed rules with effect from 1 September 2009, and Aarhus and Odense followed later. The filters have also been mandatory on Euro 0–2 HDVs from July 2008 and on Euro 3 HDVs from July 2010, except for vehicles that are more than thirty years old. Estimates show that the concentration of $PM_{2.5}$ can be reduced to 20% by installation of filters on all diesel-powered vehicles in Denmark.[745]

Copenhagen has also considered whether to introduce congestion charges as a means to reduce the traffic and the pollution without success. It was part of a political strategy of a former centre-left coalition government[746] to implement such a project by means of an act in 2011, but no bill was presented as the public opinion was against such an initiative.

§5. Enforcement and Control

95. In relation to air pollution from industries and agriculture, it is primarily the municipal councils that are the supervising authority as regards the observance of the enterprises activities, emission and immissions. The council must see to it that the Environmental Protection Act, the statutory orders and approvals issued under the Act are observed by the individual enterprises. They also have to ensure that the targets laid down in environmental approvals based on Chapter 5 of the Act are complied with. The authorities may give orders and prohibitions and see to it that conditions laid down in such orders are observed.[747] The councils and persons authorised by them have access to public and private property for the purpose of information retrieval. Furthermore, the supervisory authority may order persons responsible for enterprises which may be potential air polluters to present such data as is necessary to analyse and abate the pollution. They may also oblige them to supply samples of material and documentation concerning the emission to the surroundings, if any.[748]

744. Statutory Order No. 1323 of 21 December 2011 on Environmental Zoning.

745. OECD, *Environmental Performance Reviews. Denmark. 2007,* at 37ff.

746. This Government consisted of the Social Democrats, the Social-Liberal Party and the Socialist People's Party. Concerning the different coalition governments that have had impact on Danish environmental policy since 1993, *see supra* para. 4.

747. Concerning the competences of the supervisory authorities, *see supra* para. 68.

748. The obligations of the operator to ensure the necessary information is laid down in s. 72 of the Environmental Protection Act, *see supra* para. 70.

96. The control of air pollution from traffic is not directly a matter for the municipal councils. A report made by the Danish EPA in 1998[749] presents the experience gained from the first generation of traffic and environmental actions plans and puts forward proposals for new and different measures. It states that the authorities have concentrated on reducing traffic safety problems and on converting and building new roads and paths. It proposes that in the future local authorities should also support ideas, such as car sharing and company transport plans, and shows greater consideration for cyclists in their traffic planning. A link to local 'Agenda 21 work' is essential if the environmental impact of traffic is to diminish. There are plans on sustainable development that exists at the municipal level as part of the mandatory 'Local Agenda 21 Strategy'.[750]

97. Air quality is monitored regularly under the Nationwide Air Quality Monitoring Programme established in 1982. The state of selected air pollution has been monitored in Denmark since 1987. This monitoring was undertaken as part of a major EU programme that presently encompasses approximately 80% of EU forests. The modelling is normally based on the Danish OML (Open Modeling Language) urban background model. The aim has been to follow the concentration levels of toxic pollutants in the urban atmosphere and to provide the necessary knowledge to assess the trends, to perform source apportionment, and to evaluate the chemical reactions and the dispersion of the pollutants in the atmosphere. The assessment of the air is based on air modelling. The air pollution monitoring stations are located in different air zones.

The existing reporting obligations on ambient air quality require Member States to submit data at various designated periods. By way of example can be mentioned, Regulation on a Mechanism for Monitoring and Reporting of Greenhouse Gas Emissions, etc. is putting annual reporting obligations on the Member States.[751] These rules are replaced by the Regulation on the Governance of the Energy Union and Climate Action.[752] With effect from 2021, it ensures the registration of the use of land accounting categories of managed forest land and managed wetland under the LULUCF flexibility and in respect of the accounting of transactions under this Regulation, including the use of flexibilities, the application of compliance checks and the accurate function of the safety reserve, through the registry established pursuant to Article 10 in the 'Union Registry'. The Commission has also established the rules for the reciprocal exchange of information and reporting on ambient air quality by its Decision 2011/850/EU. The reporting and exchanging of air quality information are based on e-reporting.[753] The information is collated, analysed and

749. The Danish EPA, *Traffic and Environment in Municipalities – New Inspiration*.
750. Concerning the 'Local Agenda Strategy' of the municipalities, *see infra* para. 303.
751. Regulation No. 525/2013/EU on a Mechanism for Monitoring and Reporting of Greenhouse Gas Emissions and for Reporting other Information at National and Union Level relevant to Climate Change.
752. The obligations are replaced by Regulation No. 2018/842/EU on binding Annual Greenhouse Gas Emission Reductions by Member States from 2021 to 2030 contributing to Climate Action to meet Commitments under the Paris Agreement.
753. EEA, *Reporting and Exchanging Air Quality Information Using e-Reporting*, Technical Report No. 5/2012.

shared by the EEA. On behalf of the Ministry of Environment and Food of Denmark, the 'Danish Centre for Environment and Energy', Aarhus University (DCE) is responsible for the preparation and submission of the Annual Danish Emission Report and the inventories in the required format.

§6. Evaluation of the Effectiveness of Legal Provisions

98. The air quality in Danish cities has been monitored continuously since 1981. In 2017, the air quality was measured in four cities and at two background sites. In addition, model calculations were carried out. The concentration for most pollutants has been decreased. No exceedances of the emission limit values for the NO_2 were observed. Annual averages of PM_{10} and $PM_{2.5}$ were below emission limit values at all stations and the averages exposure indicator $PM_{2.5}$ in urban background has been decreased with about 30% since 2010.[754] Both the implementation of the EU requirements on cleaner fuel and imposition of fuel-related taxes have had a pronounced effect on air quality.[755] Danish emissions of SO_2 were peaked at 463,000 tonnes in 1977, hereafter decreasing to approximately 150,000 tonnes in 1995 – a fall of 67% during that period. SO_2 emissions declined by 27% from 1998 to 1999 due to first and foremost a decrease in the use of coal and more use of natural gas and renewable energy. From 1990 to 2013, the total emission decreased by 92%.[756] It is first and foremost due to installation of desulfurization equipment and use of fuel with lower sulphur content in public power and district heating plants. The introduction of a sulphur tax on fuels has also contributed to the reduction.[757] CO, benzene and lead concentration have been decreasing for more than two decades. They are far below the limit values set in the Fourth Daughter Directive.[758] In 1990, general ban on burning of agricultural crop residues on fields caused a significant reduction of emission. Non-industrial combustion plants are the main source to the total CO emission at the same level in 1990 and in 2013. Emissions of PAHs are increasing due to the increased combustion of wood in the residential sector.

99. Danish GHGs emissions have decreased by 30.7% from 1990 to 2015. The decrease is mainly caused by decreasing emission from the energy sector. It is estimated that the emission will be reduced by 40% by 2020 compared with the level in 1990. CO_2 is the most important GHG contributing in 2015 to the national total in CO_2 equivalents excluding LULUCF with 73.2% followed by N_2O with 11.0%, CH_4 with 14.3% and F-gases with 1.5%.[759] The emission of GHG emissions from stationary combustion plants, transport and agriculture represents the largest contribution followed by industrial processes and product use, waste and fugitive emissions. The decrease in the emission from the energy sector is mainly due to increasing production of renewable energy. The CO_2 emission from the transport

754. DCE, *The Danish Air Quality Monitoring Programme 2017*, Report No. 281/2018, at 2.
755. OECD, *Environmental Performance Reviews. Denmark 2007,* at 33.
756. DCE, *Annual Danish Informative Inventory Report to UNECE*, 2015, at 9.
757. OECD, *Environmental Performance Reviews. Denmark 2007,* at 33, 35ff.
758. Concerning the Fourth Daughter Directive (2004/197/EC), *see supra* para. 75.
759. *Denmark's Seventh National Communication and Third Biennial Report*, at 14.

sector has increased by 15.3% from 1990 to 2015, which is mainly a consequence of increasing road traffic.[760] Agriculture contributed with 21.5% of the total GHG in 2015, and it is the most important contributor to the emission of N_2O and CH_4.[761] The emission of N_2O from agriculture decreased with 28.5% from 1990 to 2015 as an effect of legislative rules on livestock farms and the use of fertiliser. The emission of CH_4 decreased as a consequence of a decreasing number of cattle. However, the emission from manure management has increased due to changes in stable management systems towards an increase in slurry-based systems. Altogether, the emission of CH_4 from the agricultural sector has increased by 1.1% from 1990 to 2015. The waste sector contributes with 2.4% to the total GHG emissions, 14.0% of the total CH_4 emission and 3.4% of the total N_2O emission in 2015. Emissions removal (sinks) from the forest sector is estimated to be 1.0% of the total emission incl. LULUCF.[762] On 18 June 2019, the Danish draft integrated national energy and climate plan (NECP)[763] was evaluated by the Commission.[764] The Commission estimates that Denmark would miss the target of a 39% reduction of the non-EST emission. It is stating that the draft NECP indicates that implementation of additional measures, use of ETS flexibility and potential credits from LULUCF may be used to reach the non-ETS target, as provided for in the Effort Sharing Regulation,[765] but it is the assessment of the Commission that it is uncertain whether the described measures will be sufficient.

100. Concerning acid rain caused by NH_3, the state of acidification of a number of vulnerable ecosystems in Denmark corresponds largely to that in Europe, as a whole, the overall effect being a decline. NH_3 emissions, which derive from agricultural activities, decreased slightly during the 1990s. Ammonia nitrogen and ammonium nitrogen are only transported over short distances and approximately 80% of the total disposition derives from sources in Denmark. Between 1985 and 2013, emissions of NH_3 from the agricultural sector decreased by 42% resulting in a reduction in related acid deposition.[766] Based on the NEC Directive, Denmark has to reduce its emission of NH_3 with 24% before 2020.

101. The most important instruments to reduce the emissions from the traffic are the EU legislations mentioned supra. Although all new petrol-fuelled cars in Denmark have been equipped with catalytic converters since 1990, road traffic is still the dominant source of CO and several other pollutants. The VOC emissions were estimated at 116,000 ton in 2004, a 28% decrease since 1995. Emissions have

760. *Denmark's Seventh National Communication and Third Biennial Report*, at 15.
761. *Denmark's Seventh National Communication and Third Biennial Report*, at 16.
762. *Denmark's Seventh National Communication and Third Biennial Report*, at 16.
763. *Denmark's Draft Integrated National Energy and Climate Plan*, 21 December 2018.
764. Commission Staff Working Document, *Assessment of the Draft National Energy and Climate Plan of Denmark*, SWD(2019) 275 final and *Demark. Summary of the Commissions assessment of the draft National Energy and Climate Plan 2021-2030*. Available at: https://ec.europa.eu/energy/en/topics/energy-strategy-and-energy-union/governance-energy-union/national-energy-climate-plans (visited on 30 Jun. 2019).
765. European Parliament and Council Regulation No. 2018/842/EU on the Binding Annual Greenhouse Gas Emission Reductions.
766. DCE, *Annual Danish Information Inventory Report to UNECE*, at 9.

declined since the introduction of catalytic converters in cars in 1990, and as a result of reduced emissions of solvents following the implementation of the VOC Solvent Emission Directive. Based on the 1991 Geneva Protocol on VOCs, the Danish obligation is to reduce VOC emissions by 30%. The effects of the agreement on VOC between the industry and the Ministry of Environment have contributed to the results.[767] Road traffic accounts for 18% of the $PM_{2.5}$. It is the second largest source of $PM_{2.5}$ emission.[768] Road transportation vehicles are also the main contributors to VOC emissions.

767. OECD, *Environmental Performance Reviews. Denmark 2007,* at 37.
768. Concerning the Danish problems with the limit established by EU legislation, *see supra* para. 78.

Chapter 3. Water Resources and Pollution

§1. The International Protection of water on Land

102. Surface water and groundwater resources are protected for all kinds of water uses, including water for drinking, production, recreation and the maintenance of adequate ecosystems. Chapter 18 of the UN Agenda 21[769] calls for protection of the quality and supply of freshwater resources by the application of the integrated approach to the development, management and use of water resources. The Agenda states that priority has to be given to the satisfaction of basic needs and the safeguarding of ecosystems. A number of the WHO Member States have expressed concern about the missing international protection of drinking water. As a response to this, the International Network of Drinking Water Regulators (RegNet) was established to share and discuss strategies to address challenges and experiences. The WHO has also published a publication in 1997 on 'Water Pollution Control: A guide to the use of water quality management principles' a report in 2006 on 'Protection of Groundwater for Health' and some guidelines for drinking water that are regularly updated.[770] In 2000, the United Nations Declaration on 'Millennium Development Goals' (MDGs) improved the focus on access to clean water as a world priority. The 'United Nations World Water Development' report from 2009 stated that the current patterns of water consumption have the consequence that two-thirds of the world will have big problems with their access to clean water. At the Rio+20 Conference in 2012, world leaders proclaimed that 'water is at the core of sustainable development as it is closely linked to a number of key global challenges'. In September 2015, the Agenda on Sustainable Development Goals (SDG) was adopted with a goal on 'water and sanitation'. Its Goal 6 states the need to 'achieve universal and equitable access to safe and affordable drinking water for all'.[771] In December 2016, the UN General Assembly unanimously adopted the resolution 'International Decade for Action – Water for sustainable Development' (2018–2028) in support of achieving the SDG goals and other water related targets.

The Biodiversity Conventions (1992) is the most important international convention that protects the ecosystems in the waters.[772] There are also two conventions on the protection of transboundary waters – including the groundwater – that are open for participation by all UN members. Both individually and in their relationship they established the most authoritative parameters of the general customary law process in the area of water protection.[773] They are both based on: the concept of sustainable development, the limited territorial sovereignty approach, the no-harm principle, the principle of the equality use and participation by water states in the

769. The 21 Agenda was agreed at the United Nations Conference on Environment AND Development in Rio De Janeiro, Brazil, 3–14 Jun. 1992.

770. The latest version of these guidelines is from 2017.

771. United Nations General Assembly Resolution of 25 September 2015, *Transforming Our World: The 2030 Agenda for Sustainable Development*, *see supra* para. 27.

772. The Biodiversity Convention is described *infra* in para. 234.

773. UNECE, *The Economic Commission for Europe Water Convention and the United Nations Watercourse Convention. An Analysis of Their Harmonized Contribution to International Water Law*, 2015, at 80.

allocation of water, and the implications of the interdependence between quality and quantity of the water running through the watercourses. They apply to uses of international[774] watercourses,[775] and for purposes other than navigation. On 17 March 1992, the UNECE Convention on the Protection and Use of Transboundary Watercourses and International Lakes (the ECE Water Convention) was adopted in Helsinki.[776] Both the EU[777] and Denmark[778] are parties to this Convention. It was originally designed as a regional convention for European and Central Asian countries, but in February 2013 it was open to all UN members.[779] The Convention is focusing on the ecosystem approach. This approach was explained in a common understanding adopted by the parties at the meeting in 1995 as a strategy for the integrated management of land, water and living resources that promote conservation and sustainable use in an equitable way.[780] In taking the measures, the parties shall be guided by the three principles:

(1) the 'precautionary principle', by virtue of which action to avoid the potential transboundary impact of the release of hazardous substances shall not be postponed on the ground that scientific research has not fully provided a causal link between those substances, on the one hand, and the potential transboundary impact, on the other hand;
(2) the 'polluter pays principle', by virtue of which costs of pollution prevention, control and reduction measures shall be borne by the polluter;
(3) water resources shall be managed so that the needs of the present generation are met without compromising the ability of future generations to meet their own needs.

The ECE Water Convention aims to strengthen national measures for the protection and ecologically sound management of transboundary surface waters and ground waters. Parties bordering the same transboundary waters shall cooperate by entering into specific agreements and establishing joint bodies. It includes provisions on monitoring (Articles 4 and 11), prevention and warning of pollution risks (Articles 3 and 14), mutual assistance (Article 15), exchange of information

774. The UN Water Convention states the definition of 'International watercourse' in Art. 2b as: 'means watercourse, parts of which are situated in different States'.
775. The definition of watercourses laid down in Art. 2a of the UN Water Convention explains that the term watercourse 'means a system of surface waters and ground waters constituting by virtue of their physical relationship a unitary and normally flowing into a common terminus'. This definition of watercourses is restrictive by comparison with the overly integrated and ecosystem approach taken by the ECE Water Convention, *see* UNECE, *The Economic Commission for Europe Water Convention and the United Nations Watercourse Convention. An Analysis of Their Harmonized Contribution to International Water Law*, 2015, at 22.
776. Entry into force on 6 Oct. 1996.
777. The EU signed it on 18 Mar. 1992 and ratified it on 14 Sept. 1995. Twenty-two European countries signed the Convention in 1992.
778. Denmark signed it on 18 March and ratified it on 28 May 1997 with reservation for the Faroe Islands and Greenland.
779. This was made possible by the amendments to Arts 25 and 26 of the ECE Water Convention. Denmark approved the amendments on 5 Jan. 2012, and the amendments were approved by the EU on 20 December 2013.
780. COP Decision v/6 Ecosystem Approach, Nairobi, 26 May 1995.

(Articles 6 and 13), responsibility and liability (Article 7) as well as access to information by the public (Article 16).[781] The parties to the Convention have agreed to prevent, control and reduce water pollution coming from all sources, especially dangerous substances. There are also two protocols connected to this Convention. It is the 1999 Protocol on Water and Health that neither the EU, nor Denmark have ratified,[782] and the 2003 Protocol on Civil Liability and Compensation for Damage Caused by the Transboundary Effects of Industrial Accidents on Transboundary Waters.[783] The last-mentioned Protocol is not in force. The 2006 'Model Provisions on Transboundary Flood Management', and the 2012 'Model Provisions on Transboundary Groundwaters' are soft law instruments connected to the Convention. The other – and closely related agreement on the protection of transborder watercourses – is the UN Convention on the Law of Non-Navigation Uses of International Watercourses (the UN Watercourses Convention – UNWC). It was adopted in May 1997. It came into force on 17 August 2014 with 36 States as parties. Denmark is a party to the Convention.[784] The EU promotes accession to and implementation of it as well as to other international agreements on water cooperation.[785] The parties have an obligation not to cause significant harm in their utilisation of international watercourses, cf. Article 7. They have to exchange data and information regularly and to cooperate on water management – including the protection and preservation of ecosystems, cf. Article 11. The information-rich countries, which are mostly the developed countries, shall share their wealth of information with less fortunate countries.[786] The Convention requires notification concerning planned measures which may have significant adverse effects upon other watercourse states. Such notification shall be accompanied by available technical data and information, including the result of any EIA, in order to enable the notified states to evaluate the possible effects of the planned measures, cf. Article 12.

§2. The WFD and Other Directives

103. Water is one of the most comprehensively regulated areas of EU environmental legislation. The WFD[787] is the overall regulatory framework of the fresh

781. Concerning the importance of access to environmental information, *see supra* para. 31.
782. Denmark signed the Protocol in 1999, but has not ratified it.
783. Denmark signed the Protocol on 21 May 2003, but has not ratified it.
784. Denmark ratified the Convention on 30 Apr. 2012. The EU ratified it on 19 Nov. 2018.
785. The Council of the European Union's Conclusions (13991/18) of 19 November 2018 on Water Diplomacy.
786. UNECE, *The Economic Commission for Europe Water Convention and the United Nations Watercourse Convention. An Analysis of Their Harmonized Contribution to International Water Law*, 2015, at 61.
787. European Parliament and Council Directive 2000/60/EC establishing a Framework for Community Action in the Field of Water as amended by the European Parliament and Council Decision No. 2455/2001/EC establishing the List of Priority Substances in the Field of Water Policy; the European Parliament and Council Directive 2008/32/EC establishing a Framework for Community Action in the Field of Water Policy as regards the Implementing Powers conferred on the Commission; the European Parliament and Council Directive 2008/105/EC on Environmental Quality Standards in the Field of Water Policy; the European Parliament and Council Directive 2009/31/

water. The WFD aims to protect all bodies of surface water (watercourses, lakes and coastal waters)[788] and groundwater, subdividing surface water into classes of ecological quality ('high', 'good', 'moderate' and 'bad'). It was adopted in Autumn 2000.

The WFD takes a holistic and 'combined approach' to water, with the river basins as the focal points. Its general objectives are:

- to protect ecosystems depending on water;
- to prevent any deterioration in the existing status of surface water and groundwater;
- to ensure that all bodies of surface water and that all bodies of groundwater achieve at least 'good status';
- to prevent any increase in direct and indirect pollution of water;
- to ensure a progressive reduction of pollution caused by hazardous substances in all water bodies, where the substances are prioritised for action at EU level;
- to ensure sufficient provision of drinking water and sufficient provisions of water for other (economic) requirements;
- to design the most cost-effective set of measures to achieve load reduction of prioritised substances, taking into account both products and process sources.

The holistic approach used as guideline in the Directive also includes the protection of Natura 2000 sites, cf. Article 1(a) that clearly mentions that the protection also includes the terrestrial ecosystems and wetlands directly dependent on them. Article 6 of the WFD stipulates the establishment of a register of protected areas 'which have been designated as requiring special protection' under EU legislation. Under the 'combined approach' that is stated in Article 10, the WFD requires that as part of the basic measures to be taken in the river basin, all existing technology-driven source controls must be implemented, the quality objectives established in the WFD and its daughter directives must be met. The 'precautionary principle' and the 'principle that environmental damage should as a priority be rectified at the source' (the 'source principle'), as well as the 'polluter pays principle' and the 'principle that environmental conditions in the various regions' must be taken into consideration as guiding principles in the interpretation of the WFD as well as in the implementation of the rules at national level.

The monitoring and the establishment of programs of measures etc. of the water quality – that are established as very important means by the WFD – must be implemented through coordination of administrative efforts rather than by the imposition of a single authority. The Member States are obliged to respect the WFD's key aims, namely to:

EC on the Geological Storage of Carbon Dioxide; the European Parliament and Council Directive 2013/39/EU amending the WFD as regards Priority Substances in the Field of Water Policy and European Parliament and Council Directive 2014/101/EU amending the WFD establishing a Framework for Community Action in the Field of Water Policy.

788. The scope of the WFD extends to 1 nautical mile from the coast of the Member States.

- Incorporate all requirements for management of water status into one single water basin management system, coordinate all the different objectives related to the protection of water and to fill any gaps in the current administration.[789] By 2003, all the Member States had to identify the individual river basins lying within their national territory and assign them to individual river basin districts, and identify competent authorities, cf. Articles 3 and 24.
- Make programmes of both basic and supplementary measures to be taken on the basis of individual problems and sectors to achieve the objectives defined in the water management plan, and to define the relationship between emission limit value measures and quality standards.
- Increase public participation in water policy to achieve greater transparency, with the advantages in enforceability that will result.[790]

The national authorities have to respect the criteria laid down in the WFD concerning two elements, one concerning general ecological protection ('good ecological status') and one relating to minimum chemical standards ('good chemical status'), both of which respect the ecological variability across the EU. '*Good ecological status*' is the ecological status that is required in order to meet the environmental objectives for a water basin established by Annex V of the WFD.[791] The concept must be interpreted as meaning that there is deterioration as soon as the status of at least one of the quality elements, within the meaning of Annex V, falls by one class, even if that fall do not result in a fall in classification of the body of surface water as a whole. If the quality element concerned, within the meaning of that Annex, is already in the lowest class, any deterioration of the element constitutes a 'deterioration of the status' of a body of surface water, within the meaning of Article 4(1)(i). The concept binds the national authorities to such an extent that decline of the quality of the surface water is no longer allowed unless the relevance of the criteria for derogation – granted in Article 4(7) – is proved by the national authorities.[792] The definition of good ecological status in respect to groundwater includes not only the protection of the proper groundwater, but also the directly dependent surface water and terrestrial ecosystems.

'*Good chemical status*' means the chemical status achieved by a body of water in which concentrations of the substances listed in the WFD do not exceed the EQS established by this Directive or by other relevant EU legislation setting EQS, cf. Article 4(1) and Annex X of the WFD. The first list of priority substances was adopted in 2001.[793] The Decision of the European Parliament and Council set a total

789. The WFD also requires Member States to include the effects of hydro morphological alteration in the management plan.
790. Concerning the right to public participation, *see supra* para. 32.
791. The ruling of the CJEU in the landmark Case C-461/13 *Weser* settled the legal status of environmental objectives laid down in Art. 4(1)(a)(i)–(iii) and Annex V. The Court ruled that the objectives on GES are legally binding. On the basis on this judgment, national authorities are obliged to refuse authorisation from individual projects estimated to compromise these objectives. They also have to respect the concept of 'deterioration of the status' of a body of surface water.
792. The CJEU took in its Case C-461/13 *Weser* a strong stance on this concept.
793. European Parliament and Council Decision 2455/2001/EC establishing the List of Priority Substances in the Field of Water Policy.

harmonised list of thirty-two priority hazardous substances. It is supplemented by the Directive on Priority Substances[794] that sets the EQS for these substances and for eight substances regulated by other directives. The chemical status of surface waters is considered good if they do not exceed these EQS.[795]

River Basin Districts are the fundamental and natural unit for the protection and use of water under the WFD. The term 'river basin' means the area of land from which all-surface run-off flows through a sequence of streams, rivers and, possibly, lakes into the sea at a single mouth, estuary or delta. The term 'river basin district' means the administrative area of land and sea, made up of one or more neighbouring river basins together with their associated groundwater and coastal waters. The national authorities must set out all the elements on standards in relation to the protection of groundwater and surface water quality in relation to chemical and quantitative status, and coordination of different measures in a water management plan for each river basin. The Danish Ministry of Environment and Food is responsible for the water management planning in Denmark. Based on the WFD, the national river management plans had to be published at the latest nine years after the directives entered into force, i.e., no later than 22 December 2009. Denmark did not published the final management plans by this deadline, and it did not send a copy thereof to the Commission by 22 March 2010. Therefore, the Commission sent an initial warning letter dated 3 June 2010 to Denmark concerning the absence of river basin management plans required by the WFD.[796] On 4 November 2014, the CJEU made the judgment in Case C-190/14 *Commission v. Denmark*. It concluded that Denmark has failed to fulfil its obligations under the WFD. Before 22 December 2012, all Member States had to carry out surveillance and notification pursuant to Articles 5, 8 and 15 of WFD. However, the Danish managements' plans were not final before October 2014.

The WFD's underlying philosophy is that the cost of wastewater treatment should be transparent, and that any failure to make water users responsible for the complete costs generated by their use is a source of water misallocation. It also states that cross-subsidization between sectors should be avoided where this would create misallocation. Based on the WFD, water users must pay 'full-cost recovery' prices for water supply, and wastewater collection and treatment.[797] Such services include all kinds of use of water and treatment of wastewater, not only the services of the water utilities. Member States are required to ensure that the price charged to polluters integrate the true costs. However, they are allowed to grant some exemptions from the full-cost recovery principle based on justified social and environmental

794. European Parliament and Council Directive 2008/105/EC on Environmental Quality Standards in the Field of Water Policy, as amended by Directive 2013/39/EU.
795. The definition of 'good surface chemical status' is defined in Art. 2(24) of the WFD. Concerning quality of water, *see supra* para. 104.
796. Concerning the Danish implementation of the WFD, *see infra* para. 108.
797. Concerning the Danish price on water supply, *see infra* para. 121, and concerning the Danish price on waste water treatment, *see infra* para. 128.

objectives, as well as for project development in regions entitled to the EU's Structural Funds. In its Guidance document, the Commission explains how to use economic analyses to support the development of river management plans.[798] In 2012, the Commission published 'A Blueprint to Safeguard Europe's Water Resources'[799] in which it stated that many Member States and water-using sectors were only partly applying the cost recovery principle. The Danish Ministry of Finance is responsible for the economic analysis of the water basin management plans, assessing the least costly way for the economy or for specific economic sectors achieving the environmental objectives defined by the Ministry of Environment and Food for the water resources.

104. The WFD replaces three daughter directives seven years after it came into force, cf. Article 22(1). It was the former Directive on the Quality required of Surface Water intended for the Abstraction of Drinking Water,[800] the Directive on Exchange of Information about Water Quality,[801] and the Directive on the Measurement and Analysis of Water for the Abstraction of Drinking Water.[802] From December 2013, the following directives were repealed by the WFD:

- Directive on the Quality of Fresh Waters needing Protection or Improvement in order to Support Fish Life;[803]
- Directive on the Quality or Shellfish Waters – the Shellfish Water Directive;[804]
- Directive on the Protection of Groundwater against Pollution caused by certain Dangerous Substances;[805]
- Directive on Pollution caused by certain Dangerous Discharges into the Aquatic Environment – the Aquatic Directive;[806]
- Directive concerning the Bathing Water – Bathing Water Directive;[807]
- Council Directive concerning the Methods of the Measurement and Frequencies of Sampling and Analysis of Surface Water intended for the Abstraction of Drinking Water in the Member States – Sampling Drinking Water Daughter Directive;[808]

798. Commission, *Economics and the Environment. The Implementation Challenges of the Water Framework Directive,* (the so-called WATECO), Guideline Document No. 1, 2003.
799. Communication of 14 November 2012, COM(2012) 673 final.
800. Council Directive 75/440/EEC on the Quality required of Surface Water intended for the Abstraction of Drinking Water.
801. Council Directive 77/795/EC on Exchange of Information about Water Quality.
802. Council Directive 79/869/EC on the Measurement and Analysis of Water for the Abstraction of Drinking Water.
803. Council Directive 78/659/EEC on the Quality of Fresh Waters needing Protection or Improvement in order to Support Fish Life.
804. European Parliament and Council Directive 2006/113/EC on the Quality or Shellfish Waters.
805. Council Directive 80/68/EEC on the Protection of Groundwater against Pollution caused by certain Dangerous Substances.
806. Council Directive 91/692/EEC on Pollution caused by certain Dangerous Discharges into the Aquatic Environment – the Aquatic Directive.
807. Council Directive 76/160/EEC concerning the Bathing Water.
808. Council Directive 79/869/EEC concerning the Methods of the Measurement and Frequencies of Sampling and Analysis of Surface Water intended for the Abstraction of Drinking Water in the Member States.

- Council Decision Establishing a Common Procedure for the Exchange of Information about the Quality of Surface Fresh Water in the Community.[809]

The quality standards and monitoring programs used to protect and improve the quality of water are now included in the WFD, but Articles 16–17 of the WFD foreseen that new rules on quality of groundwater and surface waters will replace these provisions. As a follow-up on this, the Parliament and the Council adopted the Directive on Environmental Quality Standards (EQS Directive) in the Field of Water establishes EQS. The EQS Directive provides in particular for an amendment of the list of priority substances and the corresponding EQS. It amends and repeals five Daughter Directives relating to the WFD:

- Directive on Limit Values and Quality Objectives for Mercury Discharges in the Aquatic;[810]
- Directive on Limit Values and Quality Objectives for Cadmium Discharges in the Aquatic;[811]
- Directive on Limit Values and Quality Objectives for Mercury Discharges in Sectors Other than by the Chlor-alkali Electrolysis Industry;[812]
- Directive on Limit Values and Quality Objectives for Discharges of Hexachlorocyclohexane in the Aquatic Environment;[813]
- Directive on Limit Values and Quality Objectives for Discharges of certain Dangerous Substances included in List I.[814]

The quality standards of the EQS Directive aims to combat surface water pollution by thirty-three priority chemical substances listed in Annex II. It sets transparent criteria for designated mixing zones, within which standards may be exceeded under certain conditions. It is the aim of the Directive to prepare an inventory of emissions, discharges and losses. This inventory was used in 2018 to prepare a report. In this report, the EEA checks the progress in reducing or eliminate ceasing emissions of pollutants.[815] Article 8b of the Directives states that the Commission shall establish a watch list of substances for which EU-wide monitoring data are to be gathered for the purpose of supporting future prioritisation exercises. The EQS Directive and Annex X of the WFD (that lists the chemicals) were amended in

809. Council Decision No. 77/795/EEC Establishing a Common Procedure for the Exchange of Information about the Quality of Surface Fresh Water in the Community.
810. Council Directive 82/176/EEC on Limit Values and Quality Objectives for Mercury Discharges in the Aquatic.
811. Council Directive 83/513/EEC on Limit Values and Quality Objectives for Cadmium Discharges in the Aquatic.
812. Council Directive 84/156/EEC on Limit Values and Quality Objectives for Mercury Discharges in Sectors Other than by the Chlor-alkali Electrolysis Industry.
813. Council Directive 84/41/EEC on Limit Values and Quality Objectives for Discharges of Hexachlorocyclohexane in the Aquatic Environment.
814. Council Directive 86/280/EEC on Limit Values and Quality Objectives for Discharges of certain Dangerous Substances included in List I.
815. EEA, *Chemicals in European Waters. Knowledge developments*, Report No. 18/2018.

2013[816] as regards twelve new priority substances in the field of water policy amongst those that pose a significant risk to the aquatic environment. It now lists 45 'priority' substances for surface waters. The new list is binding on the Member States from 14 September 2015. However, the deadline for 'good chemical status 'of surface water can be extended and less stringent environmental objectives set on grounds of technical impracticality, excessive cost and socio-economic requirements, provided there is no further deterioration in the water concerned. Chemical status of groundwaters is measured by reference to the concentration of specified pollutants. The electrical conductivity is also relevant, cf. Annex V of the WFD. The qualitative status of groundwater as such is expressed by the measures to which a body of groundwater and/or its dependent surface waters are affected by direct and indirect abstractions.

105. There are daughter directives that establish specific quality standards for drinking water and bathing water. Access to safe drinking water and sanitation is regarded as inextricably linked to the right to life and human dignity, as recognised by the Charter of Fundamental Rights of the EU, and to the need for an adequate standard of living.[817]

The Drinking Water Directive[818] sets quality standards for water quality at tap (microbiological, chemical and organoleptic quality parameters) as well as for hazardous substances (including total 'pesticides, benzo(a)pyrene, cadmium, lead, mercury nickel and PAHs, and it establishes the general obligations that drinking water quality must be wholesome and clean. It obliges the Member States to monitor the drinking water quality and to provide consumers with adequate and up-to-date information. Water suppliers serving fewer than fifty persons and supplies that provide less than 10 m^3 of drinking water per day as an average can be exempted from the standards by the national authorities. For a limited time, Member States may deviate from the chemical quality standards specified in Annex I of the Directive. They are also allowed to include additional requirements, e.g., regulating additional substances that are relevant within their territory, or to set higher standards, as the Directive is a minimum harmonisation directive.[819] On May 2011, the Commission adopted a decision establishing a series of symbols giving information to the public on bathing water classification and showing any bathing prohibition. In the EU, bathing is prohibited when pollution cannot be reduced to a level, which is acceptable for human health, and if bathing water does not comply with microbiological parameters for three successive bathing seasons. In 2017, 96% of the European bathing sites met the minimum quality requirements and 85% of the bathing water

816. European Parliament and Council Directive 2013/39/EU amending Directives 2000/60/EC and 2008/105/EC as regards to Priority Substances in the Field of Water Policy.
817. Concerning this approach, *see* the Commission's Communication on the European Citizens' initiative, 'Water and Sanitation are a Human Right! Water is a Public Good, not a Commodity', COM(2014) 177 final.
818. Council 98/83/EC on the Quality of Water intended for Human Consumption, as amended in 2003, 2009 and 2015.
819. Concerning minimum harmonisation, *see supra* para. 58.

sites met the Bathing Water Directive's most stringent 'excellent' quality standards.[820] A draft to a revision of the Directive was presented by the Commission on 1 February 2018.[821] The intention behind the proposal is to complement Articles 6, 7, 8 and 11 of the WFD that concern the requirements to identify and monitor the water bodies used for abstraction of drinking water and to design protected areas covering those water bodies. The proposal is also presented as part of the EU's fulfilment of Goal 6 of the UN's '2030 Agenda for Sustainable Development', the WHO's recommendations on the protection of people from the emergence of hazards to human health, the EU's 7EAP, and as part of the EU's transition to a circular economy. The European WHO report on the 'Drinking Water Parameter Cooperation Project' was published in 2018 with aims to provide policy relevant, science-based advice to inform the policymakers in the EU. It includes guidelines on selected parameters.[822]

The Bathing Water Directive[823] concerns the minimum quality criteria of bathing water, with the exception of water for therapeutic purposes and water used in swimming pools. The physical, chemical and microbiological parameters applicable to bathing water are laid down in the Annex to the Directive. The scope of the Directive is covering those waters in which bathing is authorised by the national authorities. Member States may fix more stringent values than the criteria. In addition, where the Directive does not give any values for certain substances, Member States are not obliged to fix any. The Directive requires monitoring of bathing areas according to specific rules for sampling frequencies and parameters. All appropriate measures have to be taken in order to comply with the mandatory minimum quality standards.

106. The Urban Waste Water Directive (UWWD)[824] aims to protect surface inland waters and coastal waters by regulating the collection and treatment of urban wastewater and the discharge of certain biodegradable industrial water.

More advanced treatment is required for so-called *sensitive areas*.[825] The sensitive areas are designated according to one or more of the following criteria: (a) water bodies which are found to be eutrophic or which may in the near future become eutrophic if protective action is not taken; (b) surface fresh water intended for the abstraction of drinking water and which could contain more than 50 mg/l of nitrates if action is not taken; and (c) areas where further treatment is necessary to fulfil other directives. The Directive requires for pre-authorisation of all discharges of urban wastewater, discharges from the food-processing industry and industrial

---

820. EEA Report No. 2/2018, *European Bathing Water Quality in 2017*, at 4–5. Concerning the Danish bathing waters quality, *see infra* para. 136.
821. COM(2017) 753 final of 1 February 2018, *Proposal for a Directive of the European Parliament and of the Council on the Quality of Water Intended for Human Consumption*, at 2.
822. WHO Europe, *Drinking Water Parameter Cooperation Project. Support to the Revision of Annex Council Directive 98/83/EC on the Quality of Water Intended for Human Consumption*, Recommendations, 2018.
823. European Parliament and Council Directive 2006/07/EC concerning the Management of Bathing Water Quality.
824. Council Directive 91/271/EEC concerning the Urban Waste-Water Treatment.
825. Concerning the Danish implementation, *see supra* para. 20.

discharges into urban wastewater collection. Member States must establish monitoring of the performance of treatment plants and receiving water as well as controls relating to sewage sludge disposal and reuse. The Annex to the Directive establishes that if the waters receiving the effluent of any waste treatment plant have to comply with the conditions laid down by other EU legislation, the functioning of the concerned plant will ensure the required quality of the effluents.

The Groundwater Directive[826] establishes a regime, which sets underground water quality standards and introduces measures to prevent or limit inputs of pollutants into the groundwater. It aims to protect groundwater against pollution from direct or indirect discharges of certain dangerous substances. For certain substances and groups of substances, any discharge to groundwater is prohibited (List I substances), whilst others (List II substances) are subject to an elaborate authorisation procedure. The Members States must monitor compliance with the authorisation – and the effect – of discharges. The Directive relates to assessment of the chemical status of groundwater and the identification and reversal of significant and sustained upwards trends in pollutant concentration. It states that Member States must ensure compliance with 'good chemical status'.[827] By using the measures set out in the Directive, the Member States must ensure that the environmental objectives are respected by December 2015.

The Nitrates Directive[828] aims to protect both groundwater and fresh water against pollution caused by nitrates from agricultural sources. It forms an integrated part of the WFD, and it complements the Urban Waste Water Treatment Directive in the protection of the water against nitrates. The Directive requires each Member State to draw up one or more 'codes of good agricultural practice', to be implemented by farmers on a voluntary basis. These codes must contain provisions covering at least the items mentioned in Annex IIA to the Directive. This Annex states that the following items are relevant: (a) periods when the land application of fertiliser is appropriate; (b and c) the land application of fertiliser to steeply sloping ground and to water-saturated, flooded, frozen or snow-covered ground; (d) the conditions for land application of fertiliser near watercourses; (e) the capacity and construction of storage vessels for livestock manures; and (f) procedures for the land application, including the rate and uniformity of spreading, both of chemical fertiliser and livestock manure, that will maintain nutrient losses to water at an acceptable level. Where necessary the Member State must set up a program, including the provision of training and informing farmers, promoting the application of the code(s) of good agricultural practice. Details on the 'codes' and praxis must be reported to the Commission. Member States must assess whether they should identify vulnerable zones or apply the more stringent system to the whole of their territory and designate accordingly. Denmark has decided to apply the last-mentioned and to set up an action plan.[829] An action programme may relate to all vulnerable zones in the territory of a Member State or, where the Member State considers it

826. European Parliament and Council Directive 2006/118/EEC on the Protection of Ground Water against Pollution and Deterioration. *See infra* in para. 104.
827. Concerning the criteria on good chemical status, *see supra* para. 103.
828. Council Directive 91/676/EEC concerning the Protection of Waters against Pollution caused by Nitrates from Agricultural Sources.
829. Concerning the Danish nitrate policy, *see supra* para. 110.

appropriate, different programmes may be established for different vulnerable zones or parts of zones. The criteria for such programmes are stated in Annex III of the Directive. It is possible to take additional measures into account. The Member States must, as part of their implementation of the Nitrate Directive, establish measuring and monitoring systems for the concentration of nitrate in fresh waters and groundwater. In a judgment by the CJEU, it was stated that the Member States must respect the 'polluter pays principle' as well as the 'proportionality principle' in their decision-making.[830]

107. The Directive on the Assessment and Management of Flood Risks (Floods Directive)[831] provides the Member States with a common framework for identifying, evaluating and addressing flood risks as well as management of flooding risks related to the adaptation to climate change. The Directive follows the holistic approach of the WFD and requires Member States to assess watercourses and coastlines that are at risk of flooding.

The identification by the Member States of those areas where there is a potential significant flood risk or where a flood might be expected to occur, makes it possible to reduce the adverse consequences of a flood for human health, the environment, nature, cultural heritage and economic activities by means of a proactive approach to the risks. The Directive requires that Member States draw up national flood hazard maps and flood risk maps, establish flood scenarios etc. and to follow up on these instruments with flood risk management plans. Such management plans must contain appropriate objectives and focus on the reduction of potential adverse effects of flooding in the designated risk areas. The Directive makes it possible for Member States to exclude sewage systems from their flood assessment and management systems.

§3. The Danish Water Legislation

I. Danish River Basin and Watercourses Management

108. Until 1 January 2016, the Environmental Objectives Act was the Act transposing the provisions of the WFD into Danish law. As a consequence of several problems – including a case against Denmark at the CJEU – this Act was replaced by the Water Basin Management Planning Act.[832] The new Act regulates the decision-making of water basin management planning in respect to the plans covering the second period of 2016–2021. It describes the work and planning process to be implemented in order to achieve the objective established by the WFD.[833] The Act stipulates the distribution of competences between the Ministry of Environment

830. C-293/97 *Stanley.*
831. European Parliament and Council Directive 2007/60/EC on the Assessment and Management of Flood Risks.
832. Act No. 1606 of 26 November 2013 on Water Basin Management Planning. This Act has been amended – it is now Promulgation Order No. 126 of 26 January 2017.
833. Concerning the objectives of the WFD, *see supra* in paras 103–104.

and Food (delegated to the EPA)[834] and the municipalities on the management of the water sources. The Act requires four river basin management plans to be drawn up in Denmark, one for each of the four river basin districts.[835]

The first preparation of the baseline characterisation of the river basins was performed in Denmark over the period of 2004–2006 by the decentralised units of the Ministry of Environment. The characterisation of the water basins included an assessment of the risk that the individual surface water bodies and groundwater bodies failed to achieve 'good status' by the year 2015 under the environmental measures already adopted. The next step was the preparation of a programme of measures and river basin management plan for each of the individual river basins. The first draft on the plans were presented in 2011 by the Minister for Environment, and the final versions were adopted as a Statutory Order two years after the deadline stated in the WFD Article 13(6).[836] The decision-making process used by the Ministry of Environment and Food of Denmark on the river basin management plans for the period of 2009–2015 was unsuccessful. On 20 June 2011, a case against Denmark (C-323/11) was brought by the Commission to the CJEU. It was lifted by the Commission in December 2011 as Denmark reported that the Ministry had adopted the water management plans. These plans were appealed to the former Nature and Environmental Protection Appeals Board.[837] In its judgment of 6 December 2012, the Board did not accept these plans as the hearing period of only eight days that had been followed by the Ministry was too short to ensure the involvement of the stakeholders. The consequence of this Appeals Board decision was that the Ministry had to start up a new planning process. The Commission started a new process against Denmark by a new reasoned opinion. In October 2014, the Ministry then passed new water management plans, and 150 stakeholders loaded a complaint against these next versions of the plans to the Appeals Board.[838] In its judgment of 6 November 2014 C-190/14 *Commission v. Kingdom of Denmark*, the CJEU declared that by failing to publish the final river basin management plans by 22 December 2009 at the latest and by failing to send a copy of those plans to the Commission by 22 March 2010 at the latest, Denmark has failed to fulfil its obligations under Article 13(1), (2) and (6) and Article 15(1) of the WFD. The decision-making process on the second generation of water plans (2016–2021) started in December 2013. The Ministry's guidelines for the municipalities' water management plans were published in April 2014 under the new Water Basin Management Planning Act. October 2014, the municipalities' proposals on the future water planning that had to be assessed by the Ministry were sent to the Nature Protection

834. Statutory Order No. 1577 of 14 December 2017 on the Delegation of Duties and Competences to the Environmental Protection Agency.
835. Section 26 of the Danish Water Basin Management Planning Act. The more detailed regulation is laid down in Statutory Order No. 119 of 7 February 2014 on the Geographical Scope of the River Basins and Sub-basin Districts.
836. Statutory Order No. 1208 of 15 December 2011 concerning the coming into force of the Environmental Goals, Programmes and Priorities of the Danish Water Basin Management Plans for 2012–2015.
837. This Board is now replaced by the Environmental Protection and Food Appeals Board.
838. This information was published by the Nature and Environmental Protection Appeals Board on 4 Mar. 2015.

Agency.[839] In December 2014, a draft on the State's water basin management planning for the next six years period (2016–2021) was made public.[840] The appealed water basin management plans mentioned *supra* were replaced on 1 January 2016 by the second generation water management plans that are not legally binding, as they are not (as the former plans) included in the spatial planning hierarchy. They are also without the former direct connection to the Natura 2000 plans. Most of these issues are now laid down in the following statutory orders that form a general implementation of the WFD:

- Statutory Order on the Content of Water Plans;[841]
- Statutory Order on Analyses of the Characteristics of a River Basins and the Impacts of Human Activities on the Water Quality;[842]
- Statutory Order on the Process for the Decision Making on the Environmental Goals established for Surface Waters and Groundwaters;[843]
- Statutory Order on the Environmental Goals established for Surface Waters and Groundwaters;[844]
- Statutory Order on the Programme of Measures that is an integrated part of the river basin management plans;[845]
- Statutory Order on the Cooperation Between Denmark and Germany;[846]
- Statutory Order laying down Requirements for the Discharge of certain Pollutants into Watercourses, Lakes, Transitional Waters, Coastal Waters and Marine Areas.[847]

The EPA has the overall responsibility for ensuring the correct implementation of these statutory orders by the municipalities as well as other authorities. The municipalities are under the Act required to ensure the implementation of these river basin management plans as part of an amendment of their municipality plans and by municipal water action plans. The relations between the action plan and other plans shall be described in the municipal plans.[848]

Public participation and consultation are important aspects of the water management planning. The participation of stakeholders in the decision-making process in

839. Concerning the competences of the Ministry of Environment and Food of Denmark and the municipalities, *see* ss 7–14, 22(2) and 25 of the Water Basin Management Planning Act.
840. The obligation to make the proposal available for the public is laid down in s. 15 of the Water Basin Management Planning Act.
841. Statutory Order No. 836 of 27 June 2016 on the Content of Water Plans.
842. Statutory Order No. 837 of 27 June 2016 on the Basic Analyses.
843. Statutory Order No. 1625 of 19 December 2017 on the Environmental Goals for Waters Streams, Lakes, River Mouth, Transitional Water and Ground Water.
844. Statutory Order No. 1522 of 19 December 2017 on the Environmental Goals for Surface Water and Ground Water.
845. Statutory Order No. 1521 of 15 December 2017 on the Programme of Measures.
846. Statutory Order No. 342 of 8 March 2016 on the Cooperation between Denmark and Germany on the Protection of Surface Water and Groundwater in the International Water Basin.
847. Statutory Order No. 1433 of 21 November 2017 laying down Requirements for the Discharge of certain Pollutants into Watercourses, Lakes, Transitional Waters, Coastal Waters and Marine Areas.
848. Concerning the spatial planning, *see infra* Part III and concerning the municipal plans, *see* paras 313–318.

the Danish water management plans has primarily been achieved through the establishment of Water Management Bodies as advisory boards at municipality level.[849] All the important elements in the preparation of the provisional river basin management plans, including the baseline characterisation of the river basin, the risk assessment, the development of a cost-effective programme of measures and the river basin management plan itself, have to be presented by the municipalities and discussed with the water management bodies. Based on the binding effects of the ruling of the CJEU in C-461/13 *Weser*[850] the Danish authorities may not permit activities that deteriorate the environmental quality of a water body or jeopardise its water quality standards.

As the implementation of the obligations under the Nitrate Directive, the Danish Nitrates Action Programme establishes that – to reduce the risk of leaching – the yearly amount of nitrogen applied is initially calculated as 10% below the economic optimum. Further, it was ensured until 2016 that the total amount of nitrogen that is applied do not exceed the total amount of the status in 2003/2004. As a consequence of the political Agreement on the 'Food and Agricultural Package' from 22 December 2015, the nitrogen standard was reduced by two-thirds for the period of 2015–2016, and it was completely removed in the period of 2016–2017 by new statutory orders.[851] The challenge related the protection of water was highlighted by the EU Commission in its pilot letter on the implementations problems connected to the just-mentioned political agreement.[852] On 16 May 2017, the EU Commission granted the cattle farms a two-year derogation from the maximum of 170 kg nitrates/ha – accepting 230 kg/ha on several conditions with reference to the need for an investigation of the consequences of the political agreement on the 'Food and Agricultural Package' (2015).[853]

109. There are approximately 30,000 km of watercourses of natural origin and an equivalent length of man-made watercourses in Denmark.[854] The majority of watercourses have been channelised to drain agricultural land and used to ensure fresh water to fish farms etc. Channelisation has often been accompanied by the construction of weirs and other facilities. Watercourses, lakes and ponds are under the Watercourse Act[855] classified as either private or public waters, cf. section 8 of the Act and Statutory Order on the Classification and Registration of Water

849. The rules are laid down in Statutory Order No. 217 of 2 March 2017 on Water Councils and Water Councils cooperation with the Municipalities.
850. This landmark case is explained, *see supra* in para. 101.
851. Statutory Order No. 280 of 16 March 2016 on Agricultural Use of Fertilisers during the 2015/2016 Planning Period, Statutory Order No. 1055 of 1 July 2016 on Agricultural Use of Fertilisers during the 2016/2017 Planning Period, Statutory Order No. 963 of 12 July 2017 on Agricultural Use of Fertilisers during the 2017/2018 Planning Period, Statutory Order No. 1008 of 2 July 2018 on Agricultural Use of Fertilisers during the 2018/2019 Planning Period and Statutory Order No. 762 of 29 July 2019 on Agricultural Use of Fertilisers during the 2019/2020 Planning Period.
852. EU Pilot 854040/16/ENVI, *Implementation of Directives 91/676/EC, 2000/60/EC, 92/43/EEC, in relation to the recently adopted agriculture package*, of May 2016.
853. Concerning the Danish implementation, *see supra* para. 20 and *infra* para. 262.
854. Ministry of Environment & NERI, *River Restoration – Danish Experience and Examples.*
855. The Water Course Act was amended by Act No. 720 of 8 June 2018 to ensure a better coordination of the municipalities' competences in coastal areas.

Courses.[856] This classification refers to the responsibilities of maintenance, monitoring and decision-making. By far the majority of Danish watercourses are private.

The management of watercourses is part of the fulfilment of the obligations under the WFD. The Watercourse Act contains provisions that can safeguard and restore good physical conditions in the watercourses. Such conditions are a prerequisite if the watercourses are to serve as habitats for a sound fish population and for natural flora and fauna.[857] Rules concerning maintenance of streams and watercourses are laid down in Chapter 7 (sections 27–36a) of the Act. There are some common rules for both public- and private-owned watercourses (sections 27–30) and special rules for the maintenance of the public-owned watercourses (sections 31–34) versus the private watercourses (sections 35–36a). Under section 10 of the Act, the municipality as the water authority has the competence to change the classification from public to private and vice versa as part of the water management planning and in other situations where it is necessary. The bank owners are obliged to restore private streams, streambeds and stream banks in accordance with the Local Stream Regulation drawn up by the Municipality, cf. section 27 of the Act. Part 8 of the Act is regulating the restoration obligations as supplemented by Statutory Order on the Criteria to be used in the Municipal Projects on Restoration of Water Courses.[858] The municipalities may order the private owners of watercourses to take initiatives on restoration, recreation, removal of physical barriers as well as cessation and reduction of watercourse maintenance to ensure the fulfilment of river management plans. A 1992 amendment of the Watercourse Act prohibited cultivation and physical changes in a 2 m wide border zone alongside rural lakes and watercourses of natural origin and those assigned the highest quality objectives (fish waters and areas of special scientific interest) in the former regional spatial plans.[859] In September 1998, the Supreme Court ruled that this general regulation and demand concerning extensification of the normal agricultural practices were neither very intensive nor were the financial consequences for farmers very large. Consequently, it was not to be categorised as an expropriation based on section 73 of the Constitution.[860] This general prohibition could apply without any compensation. Section 69 states that cultivation, soil treatment, planting, modification of the ground layout, the erection of fencing and the construction of buildings must not be carried out in a rural area within a 2 m border along natural or watercourses and lakes or those targeted as classified as good ecological status or maximal ecological status under section 7(1) of the Water Basin Management Planning Act. The provision does not apply to isolated lakes less than 100 m^2.

110. The Water Course Act permits the owners of adjacent properties to lower the groundwater level (drain) on adjacent land and to discharge both clean surface

856. Statutory Order No. 838 of 27 June 2016 on the Classification and Registration of Water Courses.
857. The list on Natura 2000 sites is laid down in Statutory Order No. 1595 of 6 December 2018 on the Demarcation and Management of International Nature Conservation Areas and Protection of Certain Species, *see infra* paras 240, 252 and 284.
858. Statutory Order No. 115 of 16 February 2018 on the Criteria to be used in the Municipal Projects on Restoration of Water Courses.
859. In 2007, the former regional spatial plans were replaced by the municipal spatial plans.
860. *See* the publication of the judgment in Danish Weekly Law Reports 1998, at 1669.

water and water from ordinary draining into the water body. Constructions that can hinder the free flow of water or in some other way harm the watercourse may not be built or modified without permit, cf. section 48 of the Watercourse Act.

Farmers have, as a starting point, the right to drain their land in such a way that the water level sinks sufficiently to allow the soil to be cultivated. section 3(1) gives any landowner the right to lower the groundwater level on his or her property to a depth necessary for cultivation, by means of ordinary ditching and draining with an outlet to existing watercourses. Section 3(2) permits the owners of nearby properties to discharge both surface water and water from ordinary drainage and ditching installations to the watercourses.

The right to draining was modified in 1998.[861] This amendment to the Watercourse Act and the other just-mentioned Acts was a consequence of the political agreement of February 1998 on the Aquatic Water Action Plan.[862] The new rules empowered the authorities to regulate access to drain low-level land, and to avoid potential wetlands being cultivated for agricultural use. They ensured that private and public land drainage pumping stations cannot be changed in low-level areas with a view to further lowering of the groundwater table. The right to drain was also restricted in some areas sensitive to ochre pollution. Alteration or regulation of watercourses require permission from the authorities under the Ochre Act[863] and sections 17, 18 and 21 of the Watercourses Act. Many watercourses, especially in the counties of Western Jutland, are affected by ochre. Ochre has a strong negative impact on the watercourse quality and on living conditions for fish. Watercourses affected by ochre have an impoverished macro invertebrate fauna with a highly reduced number of species and individuals. Ochre is dissolved in the water that flows to the watercourses. In the watercourses, the ochre is converted into fine particles when it becomes oxidised and comes into contact with weeds. The iron precipitates out of ochre, and it covers the bed and the plants. The Supreme Court's traditional interpretation of the general rules laid down in the Environmental Protection Act led to the view that draining water was not an activity that could be classified as 'pollution' under the Act. The reason for this judgment was that it took place as a result of normal farming practice.[864] So, the authorities cannot give a farmer an order to stop such ochre pollution, and the farmer will not be liable for the damage such draining activities may cause. Fish farming interests are only protected against activities that cause pollution from ochre discharges and other pollutants by a right to obtain prior information about the draining project not less than a week before the commencement of the draining procedures, cf. section 3(3) of the Watercourses Act. But the duty to take care of the consequences of the polluting activities in the water, where the fish live, is that of the owners of the fish farms – not the polluters. In the case of changes of watercourses whereby their natural state is affected, the conservation authorities must be consulted, since permission will

861. Act No. 478 of 1 July 1998 amending the Environmental Protection Act, the Nature Protection Act, the Watercourses Act and the Planning Act.
862. It is the Action Plan titled 'APAE II', *see supra* para. 135.
863. Promulgation Order No. 1581 of 10 December 2015 on Ochre.
864. *See* the publication of the judgment in the Danish Weekly Law Reports 1987, at 118.

often be required under sections 3 and 65(3) of the Nature Protection Act.[865] It is an important regulation with respect to surface water bodies and habitats. The power to take such decisions is vested in the municipal councils. Under section 3(1) of the Act, it is prohibited to alter the state of natural lakes of more than 100 m^2 and watercourses with a total length of 28,000 km. Such lakes and watercourses are protected habitats. However, this prohibition does not apply to any normal maintenance activity in watercourses. Section 3 allows the authorities to regulate these areas without granting the landowners any monetary compensation for losses caused as a result of the measures taken. As part of the 'Green Growth Agreement' (2009) the protection of such areas were reduced. An amendment to section 3 allows the planting of multiannual energy crops within the 150 m sea and protection line, where planting was not allowed before. In the event that a substantial majority of a draining association wishes to turn off the pumps in order to re-establish a lake in the area, and one or very few landowners refuse to surrender their land in the drained area to the nature restoration projects, the authorities may decide to expropriate the relevant land. The restrictions laid down in the Buffer Zones Act were reduced in 2014 as a consequence of a political agreement of 2 April 2014 on 'Policy on Growth in the Food Sector'.[866] The Buffer Zones Act was abolished by an Act in 2016 as a consequence of the political agreement on the 'Food and Agricultural Package'.[867] The EU Commission questioned this reduction of environmental protection by its pilot letter sent to Denmark in May 2016.[868]

111. As Denmark consists of many island and a long coastline that corresponds to almost 1.5 m coast per inhabitant, it is vulnerable to coastal flooding caused by climate change. In 2009, the Danish Act on Assessment and Management of the Flooding Risks was passed[869] and supplemented by the Statutory Order on Assessment and Management of the Flooding Risks from the Sea, Fjords and other Part of the Territorial Sea Area.[870]

The Danish Nature Agency and the Danish Coastal Agency appointed – due to potential flooding from storm surges and/or extreme river runoff – ten risk areas. The hazard, vulnerability and risk maps were incorporated into the risk reduction

865. Promulgation Order No. 240 of 13 March 2019 on Nature Protection, concerning this Act *see infra* paras 243–247.
866. The Agreement was implemented by Act No. 726 of 25 June 2014 on the Amendments of the Act on Buffer Zones and the Environmental Objectives Act.
867. Act No. 79 of 27 January 2016 on the Abolishment of the Buffer Zones Act.
868. EU Pilot letter 8540/16/ENVI, *Implementation in Denmark of Directives 91/676/EEC, 2000/60/EC, 92/EEC, in relation to the recently adopted agriculture package*, May 2016.
869. Act No. 1085 of 22 September 2017 on Assessment and Management of the Flooding Risks.
870. Statutory Order No. 121 of 2 February 2010 on Assessment and Management of the Flooding Risks from the Sea, Fjords and other Part of the Territorial Sea Area, now replaced by Statutory Order No. 78 of 19 January 2017 on Assessment and Management of the Flooding Risks from the Sea, Fjords and other Part of the Territorial Sea Area.

and risk management plans of the relevant municipalities – and the areas are including in spatial planning with binding effects.[871] It is the general principle as it is codified in the Coastal Protection Act[872] that it is the persons who profit on costal protecting projects who bear the economic coast of such protection, but it is the municipalities that have the power to decide on the establishment of such projects. The municipalities and their water utilities are cooperating on rainwater management.

II. Danish Water Supply Management

112. The Danish protection of the drinking water resources against overuse and pollution has been strong since the 1970s. In 1988, the Minister for Environment approved a statutory order on water quality and supervision of water supply plants that introduced quality monitoring of abstracted groundwater.[873] In 1994, the '10-Points Action Plan' on the protection of groundwater and drinking water, including classification of groundwater abstraction areas were decided by a majority of the political parties in the Parliament. The purpose of the Action Plan was to improve water protection, particularly the valuable areas for drinking water interests. It included the following initiatives:

- specific environmentally problematic pesticides were to be prohibited;
- the use of pesticides was to be halved and a pesticides tax was to be introduced;
- the nitrate pollution was to be halved before the year 2000;
- ecological farming was to be increased;
- areas with special sensitive drinking water interests were to be mapped and protected;
- restoration work on the waste deposits were to be increased, and a new act on contaminated land to be implemented;
- increases in afforestation and nature restoration were to be used as means to ensure the protection of groundwater;
- the Danish authorities were to promote stronger policies within the EU;
- the authorities were to ensure a better supervision of groundwater and drinking water; and
- the authorities were to ensure a better dialogue with the farmers.

The implementation of the Action Plan involved a zoning of the land into three categories: particularly valuable areas for drinking water interests; valuable areas for drinking water interests; and less valuable areas for drinking water interests. It was followed by a decision on a spatial dense hydro geological mapping of the groundwater resources within the 40% of the designated areas with particularly

871. Concerning the content of the spatial planning established by the municipal plans, *see infra* para. 313 and concerning the content of the local plans, *see infra* para. 321.
872. The Promulgation Order No. 78 of 19 January 2017 on the Assessment and Management of Fooling Risks from Lakes and Streams.
873. The water quality monitoring programme is now part of the NOVANA programme.

valuable drinking water interests. By the end of 1997, Denmark was classified according to the degree of drinking water interest. Several new political and legislative initiatives have been passed to ensure the protection of the drinking water against pesticides and nitrates. The planning of the protected drinking water areas is made under the Water Supply Acts section 11a that delegates the power to establish the general administrative rules to the Minister for the Environment. The Statutory Order on the GIS-Mapping of Protected Drinking Water Areas[874] ensures that the digitalised mapping is legally binding.

113. A 98–100% of the Danish water supply is based on the abstraction of high-quality groundwater, usually requiring very limited treatment with aeration, pH adjustment and filtration before it can be used as drinking water. Groundwater means water that can be extracted from the ground through wells, drilling and springs. A combination of low topography and widespread consolidation and unconsolidated aquifers ensures a plentiful and easily accessible groundwater resource. The utilisation of the groundwater is subject to a number of limitations, quantitative as well as qualitative criteria. All water supplied is of the same minimum quality regardless of whether it is used for drinking or other purposes.

In 2018, 87 municipalities owned, and 2,500 privately owned water supplies were registered. Most of the privately owned waterworks are consumer-owned and normally very small. The Water Sector Act,[875] which came into force on 1 January 2010, regulates the organisation of the large water suppliers. The municipality-owned water supply firms and privately owned with a capacity above 200,000 m^3 are covered by the scope of this Act. They must be organised as commercial companies on the basis of the rules for A/S or as private limited companies (ApS). The regulation of A/S and ApS is based on the Act on the Composition of Companies:[876] a situation in which none of the members are personally liable for the debts of the company but only to the extent of the capital contributed by the shareholders (the share capital) and the rest of the company's assets. The municipalities are the owners of the water utilities share capital. The aim of the Water Sector Act is to improve economic efficiency through a benchmarking system focusing on quality, the environment, security of supply and efficiency, based on user demand and to introduce centralised incentive-based price regulation. The Danish Competition and Consumer Authority is responsible for ensuring that water services respect the 'full-cost recovery principle', centralised pricing levels and the state driven performance benchmarking mentioned below. This Authority is part of the Ministry of Industry, Business and Financial Affairs. The Competition and Consumer Authority has the competence to calculate a yearly 'price cap' for the individual water utilities, partly on an individual result-oriented benchmarking basis and partly on a calculation of the traditional costs of water services.[877] The potential efficiency improvement

874. Statutory Order No. 209 of 12 March 2018 on GIS-Mapping of Drinking Water Areas.
875. Act No. 469 of 12 June 2009 on the Water Sector, as amended several times.
876. Promulgation order No. 1089 of 14 September 2015 on the Composition of Companies, as amended.
877. Sections 6–8 in the Water Sector Act.

assessed by this Authority is based on a comparison of the operating costs. The cost drivers that are included in the price calculation without figures relate to the cost of the energy supply.

114. The Water Supply Act[878] regulates the use of the groundwater and surface water. The objectives of this Act are to ensure:

- that the use of water resources takes place in accordance with integrated planning and through comprehensive evaluation of the considerations mentioned in section 2 of the Act;
- coordination of existing water supplies for an appropriate use of water resources;
- extension and operation of a water supply network that is adequate as regards volume and quality.

Section 1a states that the management of Act also has to be based on the 'polluter pays principle' and the 'principle of resource effectiveness'. Pursuant to section 59 of the Act, the Minister for the Environment has the competence to establish quality requirements on drinking water. The Minister may also lay down rules as to which substances may be added to the water used as drinking water or which may come into contact with food. These Danish quality standards must conform to the standards established by the EU as part of the Drinking Water Directive and the WFD.

115. The water supply plans must be drawn up by the municipality and incorporated into the municipality plans.[879] The municipal councils have the duty to undertake zoning between areas with specific drinking water interests, some drinking water interests and limited drinking water interests. The areas labelled 'areas with drinking water interests' are also designated as nitrate-sensitive areas (NSAs). The Ministry of Environment and Food of Denmark is responsible for the general mapping of groundwater and important drinking water areas. The drilling protection areas are included in Appendix 5 to the Statutory Order on the Mapping of Drinking Water Areas.[880] These attachments are also shown on the Danish Environmental Portal. The areas previously designated as recovery sites outside OSD are repealed by the Order.

Section 13 of the Water Supply Act and the Statutory Order on the Initiatives to be used to Ensure the Environmental Goals of the Water Basins Plans[881] establishes the procedural rules to be followed in the geographically planning of areas for future water supply activities. The Minister for the Environment has established supplementary area for the future water supply activities by Statutory Order on the Mapping of Drinking Water Resources Areas. This Order includes WEB-based GIS maps with constitutional effect. According to section 13a of Act, the municipalities must include stakeholders in the decision-making on the mapping of water supply

878. The Promulgation Order No. 118 of 22 February 2018 on Water Supply.
879. Concerning the municipal plans, *see infra* paras 313–318.
880. Statutory Order No. 209 of 12 March 2018 on GIS-Mapping of Drinking Water Areas.
881. Statutory Order No. 912 of 27 June 2016 on the Initiatives to be used to ensure the Environmental Goals of the Water Basin Management Plans.

areas. The municipal councils are obliged to carry out a survey of the location, size and quality of the water resources, and on the basis of the survey, it shall calculate the amount of water that will be available for extraction. The Minister may lay down rules for the execution of the surveys and the planning on the protection of drinking water, including time limits for their implementation of the surveys, cf. section 15 of the Act. Based on a survey and in view of the current and expected growth of the population and industry, the municipal councils must work out plans for the future extraction of water, cf. section 14. The coordination between the administrating authorities is primarily achieved by the municipal plans and the water basin plans, which provide the basis for decisions taken by the authorities, cf. section 14a.[882]

116. If there is a risk that a farmer (or another landowner) pollutes the soil as part of his or her normal lawful activities and by doing this causes serious risks to the water supply resources, the owner of the water supply plant in that area may ask the public authority to make an agreement with the landowner in accordance with the 'areas with drinking water interests' that are also designated as NSAs, cf. section 13d of the Water Supply Act. The farmer may order full compensation for reducing of the polluting activities on the basis of the expropriation rules. The use of 'water management agreements' of various forms are voluntary as part of a 'carrot-and-stick' approach to conservation and management of the water resources. The Commission has in April 2016 on its own initiative started an investigation questioning if the full compensation to the Danish farmers is in harmony with the 'polluter pays principle' laid down in the ELD.[883]

The municipal councils are also empowered to issue an administrative order with reference to the Environmental Protection Act, section 24 in cases where it is not possible to reach an agreement – and by ordering, restrict the right of use, including restriction of cultivation in nitrate-sensitive and pesticide-sensitive abstraction areas designed as NSA. Agreements and orders may only be used in cases where existing farming results in pressures on the drinking water resources, which require intervention to safeguard drinking water interests. The farmer that is restricted in the normal utilisation of the fields is entitled to receive full compensation.[884] The Land Tribunal settles the question of compensation. The Tribunal also decides whether compensation shall be paid as a result of a prohibition or order based on the Environmental Protection Act. The valuation authorities decide the size of the financial compensation; including the question of full or partial takeover.[885] The compensation may be reduced or dropped if the previous water supply and wastewater conditions of the property were unsatisfactory. The compensation may also be reduced by an amount corresponding to the increase in the value of the property caused by the connection to the common water supply plant.

882. Concerning water basin management plans, *see supra* para. 108, and concerning municipal planning, *see infra* paras 313–318.

883. *See* the Commission's answer of 11 October 2018 (P-004269/2018) related to some questions on the Danish politics – the questions were sent by Karmenu Vella to the Commission.

884. *See* concerning these rules also *infra* para. 267.

885. This approach is based on s. 73 of the Danish Constitution. Concerning s. 73, *see supra* para. 30.

117. Since the 1970s, one of the biggest challenges for water resource planning and administration has been to regulate the abstraction of surface water and groundwater to an acceptable level. The free water catchment right of landowners came to an end in 1978 when the Water Supply, etc. Act was revised.[886] Gradually, direct abstraction from surface water has been prohibited, and groundwater abstraction has been reduced to secure a certain minimum flow in all rivers, mainly through moving the abstraction away from riverbanks and wetlands. A landowner may still abstract groundwater for domestic use, but only on the basis of a permit received from the Municipality with reference to section 18 of the Water Supply etc. Act. Such an approval will only be granted if connection to a public water supply facility is not possible and only if water requirements are fulfilled. Riparian owners may abstract surface water only if the municipality with reference to section 20 of the Act approves the abstraction. Such permits can be given for watering cattle, not for irrigation or any other purpose.[887]

118. The administration of water-abstraction permits is regulated by the water management plan drawn up under the Water Basins Planning Act – in accordance with the WFD.[888] The quality standards that have to be respected in the decision-making on water supply activities are laid down in the Statutory Order on the Establishment of Environmental Targets for Streams, Lakes, Transition Waters, Coastal Waters and Groundwater.[889] When an application is being considered, it must be determined whether the water extraction will influence the watercourse quality, and the application may be refused on the basis of an expected deterioration.

The decision on whether or not to grant the licence is taken by the municipal council. It is easier for private households and agricultural applicants to obtain a licence than it is for the industrial applicants. Normally, a landowner only obtains permission if it is not possible for him to extract the water from the publicly owned waterworks in that area. Permission is based on an evaluation of the recipient quality plans, the water quality and volume of the watercourses in the area. Applications for water abstraction that are covering not more than the water for domestic and ordinary agricultural purposes of four households may only be refused if:

- it is possible for the water utility to provide the property or properties with another adequate water supply on reasonable financial terms; or
- there is an overwhelming probability that the water will not meet the requirements of drinking water quality or otherwise be injurious to health.

Normally the right to supply groundwater have a higher priority than the right to supply surface water. In the event of an application regarding the use of surface water, the authorities often refuse to grant licences because of conflict with water quality standards.

886. It was amended by means of Act No. 299 of 8 June 1978.
887. Concerning the conditions for water-abstraction permits, *see infra* para. 118.
888. Concerning the Water Framework Directive, *see supra* para. 103 and concerning the Danish implementation, *see supra* para. 108.
889. Statutory Order No. 1625 of 19 December 2017 on the Establishment of Environmental Targets for Streams, Lakes, Transition Waters, Coastal Waters and Groundwater.

The interests of a public water supply plant to obtain permission to use the water for the common good are normally of a higher priority than the interest of the private owners, as the public supply plant has a public duty to secure water for all the companies, farms and private households in relevant supply areas. In the event of conflict between the plant and the consumer, the plant may obtain an order from the local authority to make a connection to the consumer, so that he or she can obtain the necessary water. The possibilities of abstracting water are limited by the geological conditions and the groundwater chemistry, which – in a number of geographical areas – put an upper limit on the exploitation of fresh water reservoirs as a groundwater resource. Therefore, the publicly owned waterworks (as permit holders) sometimes brings a claim to the Environmental Protection and Food Appeals Board to stop utilisation of a licence granted by the municipality to landowners in the same area.[890]

Permits for water extraction are limited by terms relating both to the annual volume of water and the purpose of the licence (e.g., for household use only, for agricultural use, etc.). The validity of licences to extract water cannot exceed thirty years. Furthermore, licences to extract groundwater for the irrigation of agricultural crops and for fish farms may only be granted for a period not exceeding fifteen years and a period not exceeding ten years in the case of extraction of surface water. The right of the public authorities to withdraw permission is based on the words of the Act and limited by the traditional administrative law principles.[891] It is not easy to withdraw permission before the time limit has been met.

119. The Environmental Protection Act[892] constitutes a general very restricted encroachment on the rights of a property owner in relation to water supply issues as it contains rules on the designation of water supply plant protection areas within which activities cannot be carried out and substances, products and materials cannot be stored if they are likely to cause pollution of water. Section 11a of the Water Supply Act states that the Minister for the Environment shall issue regulations that designate the following protected groundwater areas with a constitutive effect:

1) Areas of drinking water interests.
2) Areas with special drinking water interests.
3) Recovery landings for general water supply outside the areas mentioned in No. 2.
4) Subdivisions within the areas mentioned in No. 2 and No. 3, which are particularly sensitive to one or more types of pollution (sensitive recovery areas), specifying which type of pollutants they are considered to be sensitive to transfer.
5) Sub-areas within the sensitive areas of recovery, cf. No. 4, based on an assessment of land use, pollution threats and natural protection of water resources, where special efforts to protect water resources are necessary to ensure the drinking water interests (areas of action).

890. Concerning the Environment and Food Appeals Board, *see infra* para. 355.
891. Concerning the importance of the traditional principle of administrative law, *see supra* para. 30.
892. Promulgation Order No. 681 of 2 July 2019 on Environmental Protection.

6) Drilling protection areas for drilling that collects groundwater for general water supplies.

The area designation is included as a GIS map with binding effect on other administrative decisions, plans, etc. Nitrogen-sensitive catchment areas are currently designated as sensitive catchment areas covered by the groundwater maps, and pesticide-sensitive collection areas have been designated on sand yards. On the other hand, no spray-sensitive clay soil has been designated as it was the opinion of the former government that was in power until 5 June 2019 that there was no sufficient academic basis for such a state designation. The protection against pesticides is therefore currently secured by different instruments. As a supplement to the protection areas designated, the municipal councils can issue enforcement or prohibition notices to prevent pollution risk of water supply plants, cf. sections 24 and 26a of the Environmental Protection Act.[893]As a supplement to the designation of protection areas, the municipal councils may issue enforcement or prohibition notices to prevent a pollution risk of water supply plants. Property owners may also be presented with orders to remove materials even if such waste was originally dug into the ground in accordance with the rules in force at the time. The councils must ensure that designation as a protected area is notified to the owner of the land in question, and it has to make this registration public in accordance with the Land Registration Act.[894] Non-offending property owners may claim compensation from the local authorities or the water supply company that have an interest in the remedial action being taken. This right to compensation is based on the reasoning behind section 73 of the Constitution concerning expropriations.

The municipalities also have the possibility of deciding to close down a water supply plant if the necessary remedial action is considered too costly, cf. the Act on Contaminated Soil.[895] According to this Act, the environmental authority itself can initiate investigations and remedial action at the expense of the responsible party, if – and only if – the responsible party do not comply with an administrative order laid down in accordance with the Act.

120. The municipal councils must ensure that orders are complied with, and that conditions laid down in licences are observed. Where orders are not complied with within the fixed time limit, the councils may initiate measures to be taken at the expense of the persons responsible, cf. section 65 of the Water Supply Act. Pursuant to the Act, some provisions have been laid down in the Statutory Order on Water Quality and Inspection of Water Supply Plants.[896] The municipal councils must inform the EPA of the results of the supervision and the measures they have ordered.

893. Concerning the protection of the drinking water, *see infra* para. 125.
894. Promulgation Order No. 1075 of 30 September 2014 on Land Registration, as amended.
895. Promulgation Order No. 282 of 27 March 2017 on Contaminated Soil, as amended. Concerning the protection of the soil against contamination under the Contaminated Soil Act, *see infra* para. 176. The conditions for the authorities that are using administrative orders under the Environmental Protection Act are described *infra* in para. 183.
896. Statutory Order No. 1068 of 23 August 2018 on Water Quality and Inspection of Water Supply Plants.

If the water from the plants is used in more than one municipal area, the municipal councils involved must reach an agreement on how public supervision is to be conducted. If an agreement cannot be reached, the EPA decides on the matter. The Agency may direct the municipal councils to consider and decide on questions concerning supervision of the water supply. It may also issue a prohibition or an administrative order to prevent the risk of pollution of existing or future plants for the extraction of groundwater.

121. The Danish price on water supply consists of fixed contributions, variable contributions, taxes and VAT. The municipality decides the payment fees (charge) for the use of water from the public water supply plant. The water price is not the same everywhere in Denmark. The consumers have to pay all the costs – and only the cost – connected with water supply management: costs incidental to drainage, treatment and discharge.[897] The prices are decided by the water utilities on the basis of their individual maximum price level as decided by the Danish Competition Authority on the basis of benchmarking. An average Danish family pays less than DKK 5,500 per year to have fresh, clean and inspected drinking water delivered to it, while at the same time getting rid of its wastewater.[898] Delivered water prices effectively represent at least three separate components: (a) a price for the protection of the water resources (e.g., by a ban on farmer activities and/or by establishment of forest in protected areas; (b) a price for the infrastructure services associated with its treatment, transmission and distribution; and (c) the cost of the resource itself. The water supply companies must also respect the Company Accounts Act,[899] including the common rules on accounts to ensure transparency and comparability. The utilities can finance their investments, renovation work, etc. either through borrowing or by increasing the price and saving up prior to making such investments. Differences in savings and debt commitments can result in considerable variations in price.

III. Wastewater and Other Pollutants at National Level

122. Since water pollution may have multiple causes, and clean or polluted water has numerous functions in modern society, water pollution and water quality touch upon a variety of other policy sectors. Water may be polluted as a result of approved or non-approved industrial, household or recreational water discharges. More diffuse water polluting sources are soil contamination (especially caused by industry and agriculture) and acid rain.[900] The protection of surface inland waters and coastal waters is covered by the Urban Waste Water Directive (UWWD) that must be implemented into national law.[901]

---

897. Concerning the use of fees in Denmark, *see supra* para. 13.
898. DANVA, *Water in Figures. DANVA's Statistics and Benchmarking 2017,* at 7.
899. Promulgation Order No. 1580 of 10 December 2015 on Company Accounts, as amended.
900. Concerning the Danish protection of the drinking water, *see infra* paras 170–187.
901. Concerning the UWWD, *see supra* in para. 106.

The Environmental Protection Act[902] controls land-based pollution by wastewater. It lays down general protection rules against pollution of groundwater and surface water. The Minister for the Environment may issue binding administrative regulations to prevent pollution and risks of pollution of the surface and/or groundwater by wastewater, including regulations concerning the installation and emptying of containers holding such liquids. In this connection, the Minister may issue regulations stipulating in which cases and under what conditions the licences will be issued, as well as regulations stipulating cases in which no licence is to be required. To fulfil international and EU obligations, the Minister must lay down binding statutory orders on the protection of the groundwater, cf. section 14(2) of the Act. The wastewater treatment plans are established at the municipality level in accordance with Chapter 4 of the Act. Section 32 of the Act makes it mandatory for the authorities to draw up plans for the sewage treatment. The plans for the sewage facilities, etc. must be prepared in such a way as not to affect the surface water quality plans (recipient quality plans) and/or the planning of the recovery of water – and all these guidelines are included in the municipality plans. The objective of the planning is to protect the groundwater (including drinking water), the surface water and the seawater.[903]

The Minister may also issue regulations concerning the matters to be taken into consideration to protect the groundwater and surface water by the municipal councils in the administration of the rules, cf. section 29 of the Act.[904]

123. The rules on the municipality-owned wastewater treatment plants were reformed by the Water Sector Act,[905] which includes rules on liberalisation of the sector. From 1 January 2010, it has been mandatory for the municipalities to establish A/S or ApS. In 2015, approximately 110 wastewater companies collectively processed more than 358 million m^3 water in their catchment areas.[906] There is no direct competition in the sector, as the connection of households and industries to the public-owned sewage system is mandatory, in most cases cf. section 28(4) of the Environmental Protection Act.

Bigger industrial companies have their own wastewater treatment facilities permitted as part of their operating licences under the environmental approval system established by sections 33–35 of the Act.[907] Some 94% of sewage discharges are subject to secondary treatment and 67% to tertiary treatment. Wastewaters are treated in several different stages at wastewater treatment plants: mechanical, biological and chemical purification and finishing treatment. Biological purification converts organically bound nitrogen into nitrate by mixing air with activated sludge and wastewater in tanks. Phosphorus is removed by using biological phosphorous

902. Promulgation Order No. 681 of 2 July 2019 on Environmental Protection.
903. The plans for the sewage facilities must be included in the water basin management plans described *supra* in para. 108. Concerning the municipal plans, *see infra* paras 313–318.
904. Statutory Order No. 1625 of 19 December 2017 on the Environmental Goals for Waters Streams, Lakes, River Mouth, Transitional Water and Ground Water is implementing the obligations on environmental targets laid down in the WFD, and the EQS Directive.
905. Act No. 469 of 12 June 2009 on the Water Sector, as amended.
906. DANVA, *Water in Figures. DANVA's Statistics and Benchmarking 2017*, at 7.
907. Concerning the Danish environmental approval system, *see supra* paras 63–73.

removal process under anaerobic conditions in which the phosphorous becomes incorporated into the activated sludge. Chemicals are sometimes added. Organic matter is removed with activated sludge, which is part of the wastewater. There are two kinds of sewerage systems today:

(1) *The combined system* leads both wastewater and storm water through a single pipeline to a wastewater treatment plant. Retention tanks are used to collect the water in situations of flooding, where the sewerage network and wastewater treatment plants are overloaded. Rainwater and wastewater from households, businesses, institutions, etc. are conducted to street sewers through service pipes, while rainwater from streets is supplied through service pipes.
(2) *The modern separate sewer system* which transports rainwater and sewage from homes and businesses through separate pipes to wastewater treatment plants, while storm water (rainwater) is led through another pipeline to streams, lakes and the sea. Climate change has already resulted in more rain and the water flows. These systems become overloaded in some extreme situations. Therefore, this system is combined with 'sewer overflows (known as 'combined sewer overflows' or CSOs) and small lakes that collect rainwater and allow it to gradually seep into rivers and the sea (it is titled 'storm water ponds'). It is the political ambition of several municipalities to phase such systems out in the next eighty to ninety years. Sewers have a lifetime of 50–100 years.

Discharge of wastewater from the sewers is regulated both by a sewage plan, cf. section 32 of the Act, and by permissions to discharge wastewater, cf. sections 27–28 and 34 of the Act.

124. There are about 100,000 households outside areas with wastewater treatments, which are regulated by sections 19 and 20 of the Environmental Protection Act. Discharges of wastewater from households outside areas with waste treatment facilities have been reduced since 2000 by two means which: (a) is local biological mini-treatment plants, often for single houses; and (b) is collection of wastewater by a transportable tank and transportation to centralised treatment plants. With respect to individual types of flows, pollution substances, products or materials may not be dug into or discharged on the ground unless a licence has been obtained, cf. section 19 of the Act. This rule is not referring to ordinary farming.

The general prohibition of waste disposal, oil tanks, etc. of such a polluting character being dug into – or disposed of – the ground applies irrespective of whether the water reservoir in question is used for water supply purposes or not. The decisive element of the prohibition is that the disposal takes place in a way likely to cause a risk of pollution of groundwater, soil and/or subsoil. Accidental discharge is also prohibited.[908] Section 19(1) and (2) of the Act contains a ban on the unauthorised installation underground of containers holding liquids and substances that may pollute the groundwater. This ban applies to both new and existing containers. Some

908. The judgment of the Danish Supreme Court is published in the Danish Weekly Law Reports 1987, at 256H.

modifications are established in section 19(3). It is the municipality that is the competent authority to permit an installation or a small deposit, *see* section 19(4). Pursuance to section 19(5) of the Act, the Minister for the Environment has laid down provisions in several statutory orders and circulars putting limitations on special activities and facilities. The most important provisions have been the Statutory Order on Oil Tanks[909] providing that the tanks must be of a type that has been approved by a central testing committee, and that the building authority must be informed at least eight days before the tank is covered. The criteria differ according to whether the tank located on the soil has a capacity of more than 200,000 litres, between 200,000 litres and 6,000 litres, and less than 6,000 litres. The users of tanks established underground before 1 April 1970 must ensure, at the latest twenty years after the installation that the tank conforms with the standards for tanks installed underground after 1 April 1970. If this is not the case, the user must take special protective measures and carry out subsequent regular checks. Should an oil tank be found to leak, the municipal council may require it to be emptied and dug up, and any contents that have leaked out and polluted the soil surrounding the tank must be removed by the tank user/owner. Orders to remove or clean the soil surrounding a tank may also be served on the oil supplier if substantial amounts of oil have escaped during filling.[910]

125. The Environmental Protection Act contains rules in sections 22 and 23 on the designation of protection areas within which activities cannot be carried out and substances, products and materials cannot be stored, if they are likely to cause pollution of drinking water to be extracted and used for water supply purposes.[911] When enforcement and prohibition notices are issued to non-offending property owners, compensation must be paid to the owners, cf. sections 63–64 of the Act. The owners can claim compensation in full for the expenses incurred from the water supply plant in whose interest the remedial action is taken or from the municipality in which the property is situated.

It is not permitted to discharge substances likely to pollute the watercourses, lakes or the sea, or to store the substances so close to such waters as to cause risk of pollution, cf. section 27 of the Act. However, pursuant to the Act, a licence may be issued to discharge wastewater into watercourses, lakes or the sea. The regulation is founded on a recipient principle, which means that the authorities assess the impact of the pollution on each single recipient, and on the basis thereof specify the acceptable emissions in each single licence. The principle originates from the principle that each recipient (e.g., a lake, watercourse or the sea) has a distinct capacity to absorb pollution. Licences to discharge wastewater into watercourses, lakes or the sea shall be issued by the municipal councils. Under section 28 of the Act, the municipal councils are the competent authorities regarding: (a) permission for linkage to or altering the emission to public sewage installations within the predetermined capacity of the latter; (b) connection to or alteration of domestic effluent to

909. Statutory Order No. 1611 of 10 December 2015 on Oil Tanks.
910. Concerning insurance obligations for the users of oil tanks in private homes, *see infra* para. 178.
911. Concerning the protection of drinking water under the Environmental Protection Act, *see supra* para. 119.

private sewage plants within the estimated capacity of the plant; and (c) in most cases of an installation of new or expansion of existing private sewage plants for domestic effluent. The municipal councils are not the relevant authorities in cases where the EPA has the competence to make the assessment on the basis of the IE Directive's rules, cf. sections 28(2) and 34(4) of the Act.[912]

126. It should also be mentioned that the prevention of water pollution is normally imposed as a specific condition for approval under Chapter 5 of the Environmental Protection Act for specially polluting enterprises.[913] The municipal council and the EPA are the first instance, e.g., regarding approval of the construction of large plants with alleged extensive pollution. It is only in special IED-cases marked with an 's' in the statutory rules, that the EPA is the competent authority – in most cases, the competence is at the municipal level. In taking decisions under section 33 of the Act, the municipal authorities and the EPA must take into account the limits laid down in subsections (4), (5) and (6) of section 41a of the Act.[914] They must also ensure that the environmental objectives in the water basin management plans are respected.[915]

127. The Environmental Protection Act and the Statutory Order on Mandatory Environmental Supervision[916] contains some broad general provisions concerning supervision by the municipal councils. Based on these rules the councils must frequently see that the Act and statutory orders issued under the Act are complied with. The municipal councils must control the water quality status of the watercourses, lakes and coastal sections of the territorial waters. This applies both to the state of pollution and the observance of the quality requirements set out in the Act, statutory orders and the water management plans. Supervisory activities must be carried out through sampling procedures, use of analysis methods and monitoring of analytical results in accordance with the requirements laid down in the Statutory Order on the Requirements on the Quality of Environmental Monitoring.[917]

When a wastewater treatment plant does not work properly from an environmental protection point of view, the municipal council may require that the necessary improvement or renewal of the plant will be executed, cf. section 30(1) of the Act. Where pollution cannot be remedied or where orders in pursuance of this provision are contravened, the council may issue a prohibition against the future operation of the plant and possibly require the removal of the plant. If the pollution gives rise to imminent and serious health risks, prohibition may be issued immediately. In respect to other plants not working properly, the competence to require the necessary improvement or renewal of the plant is found in sections 41, 42 and 72 of the Act.[918]

---

912. Concerning the environmental approval system established by the IE Directive, *see supra* para. 61.
913. Concerning the Danish environmental approval systems, *see supra* paras 62–73.
914. Concerning the supervision system, *see supra* paras 66–69.
915. Concerning the Danish water basin management plans, *see supra* para. 108.
916. Statutory Order No. 117 of 28 January 2019 on Mandatory Environmental Supervision.
917. Statutory Order No. 523 of 1 May 2019 on the Requirements on the Quality of Environmental Monitoring.
918. The competences of the supervision authorities are described *supra* in paras 66–68.

128. The users of common wastewater installations must pay contributions for their establishment and operation.[919] Costs in connection with the building, operation and maintenance of public and private water plants, including expenses in connection with common sewers, intercepting sewers, purification plants, acquisition of property and restrictive covenants must normally be borne and shared under the provisions of the Act on Sewage Works Payment Obligations.[920] The statutory rules are supplemented by local regulations laid down by the municipal councils. The exact charges and the use of the revenue vary depending on local conditions and the decision of the water utilities. The Danish Competition and Consumer Authority is responsible under the Water section Act for ensuring that the water utilities respect both the full-cost recovery principle and the price level for the individual utility.

Public sewer renovation costs about DKK 1 billion annually, and this is financed by user payment. As a consequence of adaptation to climate change, there is a need for reinvestments and fresh investments in sewers to ensure that they can accommodate increasing levels of rainfall. There are also major investments in increased basin capacity with a view to ensuring that unfiltered wastewater is not discharged into lakes or the sea during heavy downpours.

§4. Sea Water

129. With respect to environmental legislation, it is very important to take into account that the ocean is a planetary ecosystem, transient and balanced but vulnerable, threatened by degradation due to human activities.[921] Marine areas and coastal areas are among the most biologically productive systems on Earth. They also provide a wide range of services to mankind, including the storage and cycling of nutrients, a buffering capacity of land, protection against erosion, a filter system of pollutants and a regulation of water balances. Therefore, it is necessary to ensure global protection of the quality of the seawater, as it is a common good. A number of international and regional marine conventions and numbers of EU directives provide part of the frameworks of the efforts to improve the state of the marine environment.

The UNCLOS from 1982 serves as the constitution for the sea-related activities. It regulates the jurisdiction and obligations of coastal, port and flag States.[922] The

919. Concerning the use of fees, *see supra* para. 13.

920. Promulgation Order No. 633 of 7 June 2010 on Sewage Works Payment Obligations, as amended several times.

921. The ocean covers over 70% of the surface of the Earth, which for this reason is called the 'Blue Planet' by astronauts.

922. In Case C-15/17 *Bosphorus Quen Shipping Ltd Corp. v. Rajavartiolaitos,* the CJEU stated that the conventions signed and approved by the EU are an integral part of the European legal order and binding on it. Therefore, the Court has jurisdiction to interpret those provisions, and the Convention has primacy – a higher legal status in the EU's hierarchy of legal sources – over secondary EU legislation. It is also mentioned that the Baltic Sea is internationally recognised as being a special area characterised by geographical particularities and a particular sensitive ecosystem in need of special protection.

EU and its Member States (incl. Denmark) are parties to this Convention.[923] Coastal States have jurisdiction in their territorial waters (extending 12 nautical miles from the coast) with regard to the protection and preservation of the marine environment, cf. UNCLOS, Part II (Articles 3–16). Activities in such sea areas that affect resource deposits which lie across limits of natural jurisdictions must be conducted with due regard to the rights and legitimate interests of any coastal State across whose jurisdiction such deposits lie. However, third states enjoy freedom of navigation and other international 'innocent' (lawful) uses of the sea by foreign flagged vessels, cf. Articles 18–19. The EEZ is an area beyond and adjacent to the territorial waters, and this is subject to a special legal regime established by Part V (Articles 55–75). This zone can extend to a maximum of 200 nautical miles (approximately 370 km). In EEZ areas, coastal states have jurisdiction to explore and exploit natural resources of the sea (birds, fish, whales, etc.) as well as the seabed (minerals, oil, gas, etc.). The Convention addresses the continental shelf in Part VI. The coastal States have rights to the resources, and they can establish environmental protection legislation covering both the EEZ and the continental shelf. Part XI of the UNCLOS covers the obligation to respect the principles governing the common heritage of mankind, etc. in the resources of the high sea (the Area). That Convention also lays down a legal regime relating to the deep seabed and its resources as the common heritage of mankind. On the high seas, there is by definition no coastal State with jurisdiction. While all States are under a general obligation to cooperate for the protection and preservation of the marine environment, no State can impose its own legislation on the activities in such areas. Neither is it possible for the EU to regulate in relation to the high seas.

The IMO is – with a broad membership – the main rulemaking body in issues related to the maritime activities at the sea area. The EU is not a member of the IMO as such a membership is not accepted by the IMO.[924] Among the most important conventions of the IMO are: the MARPOL 73/78,[925] the Convention for Safety at Sea (SOLAS Convention), the Convention on the Prevention of Marine Pollution by Dumping of Wastes and Other Matter (London Convention), the Convention on Oil Pollution Preparedness, Response and Cooperation (OPRC Convention), the Convention Relating to Intervention on the High Seas in Cases of Oil Pollution Causalities (Oil Pollution Prevention Convention), the Convention for the Control and Management of Ship's Ballast Water and Sediments (the Ballast Convention) and the Convention on Carriage of Hazardous and Noxious Substances by Sea (2010 HNS Convention). The IMO rules are regarded as generally accepted rules and standards in the UNCLOS meaning. The IMO MARPOL Convention concerning vessel

923. It was approved by Council Decision No. 98/392/EC of 23 March 1998 concerning the conclusion by the EU of the UNCLOS and the Agreement of 28 July 1994 relating to the implementation of Part XI thereof.

924. Concerning the competences of the EU institutions, *see supra* para. 55, and concerning the marine protected areas *infra* paras 255–256.

925. The MARPOL 73/78 Convention covers any deliberate disposal of wastes or other matter from vessels, aircraft, platforms or other man-made structures into sea. Dumping do not include the disposal of waste or other matter arising from the normal operation of vessels, platforms or other man-made structures into sea or the placement of matter for a purpose other than disposal.

source pollution covers any deliberate disposal of wastes or other matter from vessels, aircraft, platforms or other man-made structures in or to seawater. In some of its conventions, the IMO is focusing on the 'flag state jurisdiction' with reference to UNCLOS Article 211(2). In accordance with this provision, States must adopt laws and regulations for the prevention, reduction and control of pollution of the marine environment from ships flying their flag or of their registry. Only flag States can adopt standards for ships. Such national standards must at least have the same effect as that of generally accepted international rules and standards. Article 217 UNCLOS exclusively addresses the enforcement of international rules and standards by flag States and provides that the enforcement must take place irrespective of where a violation occurs. The flag State is further free to uphold a higher standard on environmental rules for the ships registered in its registry than the standard required by the international conventions.[926]

Port State jurisdiction according to Article 218 UNCLOS relates to the enforcement of the applicable international rules and standards in respect to discharge from a ship outside the port States' internal waters, territorial sea or EEZ. Article 211(3) of the Convention implies that port States may put requirements on ships entering their ports. A port State is entitled to deny access according to Article 211(3) to a ship entering its port whenever the port entry requirements of such State concerning construction, equipment and manning of the ship are not complied with. The same Article further on expressly gives a right for cooperative arrangements concerning port entry requirements between two or more States in a region. The EU is developing its marine rules mainly based on 'port State jurisdiction' in accordance with the UNCLOS. After the Erika accident (1999) and the Prestige accident (2002), the EU has undertaken larger responsibilities on the protection of the marine area inside the jurisdiction of its Member States. From this follows that the EU has the right to implement the UNCLOS by the Port State Control Directive,[927] the Directive on Ship Inspection,[928] the COSS Regulation (Regulation on Establishing the Committee on Safe Seas and the Prevention of Pollution from Ships),[929] and the 'European Marine Safety System' established by Directive on Ship-source Pollution and on the Introduction of Penalties for Infringements.[930] The Preamble of the last-mentioned Directive states that it is part of the implementation of the MARPOL 73/78 to ensure

926. The Regional Action Plan on Marine Litter (RAP ML Recommendation 36/1) under the HELCOM II establishes common indications on marine litter and associated threshold values advancing the results on protection of the water. By 2018, the reporting on the implementation of this action plan is carried out under the EU chairmanship of HELCOM.

927. European Parliament and Council Directive 2009/16/EC on Port State Control. The purpose of this Directive is to reduce discharges of ship-generated waste and cargo residues into the sea, especially illegal discharges, from ships using ports in the Member States. The criteria for control of all ships in harbours are laid down in the Directive.

928. Council Directive 94/57/EC on Common Standards for Ship Inspection and Survey Organization and for the Relevant Activities of the Maritime Administrations.

929. European Parliament and Council Regulation No. 2099/2002/EC establishing a Committee on Safe Seas and the Prevention of Pollution from Ships (COSS).

930. European Parliament and Council Directive 2005/35/EC on Ship-Source Pollution and the Introduction of Penalties for Infringements. The CJEU made an interpretation of this Directive in Case C-15/17 *Bosphorus Quen Shipping Ltd Corp. v. Rajavartiolaitos* stating that it must be interpreted as meaning that it authorises the Member States to impose more stringent measures, in accordance with international law, than those set out in Art. 7(2) of the Directive where it is applicable.

incorporation of international standards for ship-source pollution into EU law, harmonisation of the safety policy and penalties for discharges. Based on this Directive, the European Marine Safety Agency (EMSA) is working together with the Member States in developing technical solutions and providing technical assistance in satellite monitoring, etc. The EMSA Clean Sea Net satellite service offers all Member States a near real-time marine oil spill and vessel detection service. The service is a recognised global monitoring for environment and security (GMES) service integrated within the national and regional oil pollution surveillance and response chains. Each coastal State has access to this service. The rules laid down in MARPOL 73/78 on Port Reception Facilities for Ship-related Wastes and Associated Issues have been implemented in the EU by means of the Directive on Port Reception Facilities for Ship-generated Waste and Cargo Residues (Port Waste Reception Facilities Directive).[931] The purpose of these rules is to reduce discharges of ship-generated waste and cargo residuals into the sea. The reason for these regulatory activities of the EU is to ensure that the Member States apply the international conventions that are passed by IMO efficiently.

Among important international and regional conventions covering the territorial waters of EU Member States (incl. Danish maritime territories) are: the Convention on Biodiversity,[932] the Basel Convention, the Convention on the Protection of the Marine Environment of the Baltic Sea Area (the Helsinki Convention), and the Convention for the Protection of the Marine Environment of the North-East Atlantic (the OSPAR Convention). The EU and its Member States are all parties to these conventions. The objectives of both OSPAR and the Helsinki Convention with regard to hazardous substances are to continuously reduce discharges, emissions and losses of such substances, with complete cessation by 2020. At their first joint Ministerial Meeting in June 2003, the OSPAR Commission and the HELCOM (the Baltic Marine Environment Protection Commission) made a common statement on the use of an ecosystem-based approach in their management of human activities under the OSPAR Convention and the Helsinki Convention. Their application of the ecosystem-based approach was explained to be part of – and a support to – the future development of the EU's marine strategy and its marine directives as well as measures adopted by other international organisations.[933] Denmark and the other

931. European Parliament and Council Directive 2000/59/EC on Port Reception Facilities for Ship Generated waste and Cargo Residues.

932. Concerning the Biodiversity Convention and the EU as well as the Danish implementation, *see infra* in para. 234. In 1995, the COP under this Convention encouraged the use of an IMCAM approach that today is integrated in EU legislation, *see infra* the description of the Marine Strategy Framework Directive and the coordination of these provisions with the provisions under the regional conventions (including the OSPAR Convention and the Helsinki Convention) in para. 130.

933. Statement at the First Joint Ministerial Meeting of the Helsinki and OSPAR Commission of 25–26 June 2003 on the Ecosystem Approach to the Management of Human Activities 'Towards an Ecosystem Approach to the Management of Human Activities', at 3.

North Sea countries as well as the EU[934] are committed under the so-called generation strategy, to achieve phase-out contamination in twenty-five years on the basis of these two regional Conventions. In implementing these provisions, the parties must apply the 'precautionary principle' and the 'polluter pays principle' and must adopt programmes and measures applying, *inter alia*, the BAT, the Best Environmental Practice (BEP) and, where appropriate, clean technology. Both Conventions established the concept of Marine Protected Areas (MPAs). Such areas can be defined as areas of seawaters that are given special protection through legal provisions because of their significance for a number of reasons.[935]

130. The 6EAP included the objective of conservation, appropriate restoration and sustainable use of marine environment, coasts and wetlands. On 24 October 2005, the Commission adopted the 'Thematic Strategy on the Protection and Conservation of the Marine Environment'.[936] The Marine Strategic Framework Directive (MSFD)[937] is a follow-up on its Strategy. It established a framework for the future regulation in the field of marine environmental policy to achieve a healthy marine environment and make ecosystems more resilient to climate change. MSFD is based on a more holistic and integrative (ecosystem) approach to the maritime resources than the approach used in the future regulatory instruments. It applies to marine waters of the Member States, without prejudice to the other EU legislative acts. The MSFD puts obligations on Member States to develop and implement marine strategies. It covers all marine waters from the baseline of territorial waters until the EEZ. The Member States must establish management measures that influence where and when an activity is to occur, and they must use coordination measures to ensure that different sectorial measures at different institutional levels are coordinated. Programs of measures must be based on an ecosystem approach, and they may include any of a number of instruments set out in the annex, including spatial and temporal distribution controls. Together with the FMSP Directive[938] and the general policy on an Integrated Maritime Policy (IMP),[939] it establishes an integrated approach to marine policy, in which maritime policy areas such as shipyards, shipping, ship safety, tourism, fisheries, ports, the marine environment, offshore

934. The Helsinki Convention was approved by the European Council by means of Decision 94/157/EC, and the OSPAR was approved by means of Decision 98/249/EC. The new Annex V on the Protection and Conservation of the Ecosystems and Biodiversity of the Maritime Area included in OSPAR was approved by Council Decision 2000/340/EC.

935. Concerning the biodiversity protection, *see infra* para. 234 and the protection of marine areas under the WCPA, *infra* para. 255.

936. COM(2005) 504 final. The EU has passed its IMP that sets the objective and guidelines for a coherent policy approach to the marine areas, with the aim of protecting the ecosystem, based in harmony with the Biodiversity Convention, and also taking the economic, environmental and social issues into account.

937. European Parliament and Council Directive 2008/56/EC establishing a Framework for Community Action in the Field of Marine Environmental Policy, as amended by Commission Directive 2017/845/EU as Regards the Indicative Lists of Elements to be Taken into Account for the Preparation of Marine Strategies.

938. European Parliament and Council Directive 2014/89/EU establishing a Framework for Maritime Spatial Planning is described in paras 130–131.

939. Laid down in Council Regulation No. 1255/2011/EU establishing a 'Programme to support the further Development of an Integrated Maritime Policy'.

energy production etc. are covered and their interdependence highlighted. It overlaps with the WFD and with the FMSP Directive in the coastal area.

The MSFD was adopted with the ambition to achieve GES across the EU by 2020 and to protect the resource basis for marine-related economic and social activities. Article 3 lays down the important definitions that the Member States have to respect in the implementation of the Directive. 'GES' is defined in Article 3(5), and it means that the overall status provides ecologically diverse and dynamic oceans and seas, which are healthy and productive within their intrinsic conditions. Environmental targets are qualitative or quantitative statements relating to the condition of the different components of, and pressures and impacts on, marine waters, cf. Article 3(7). MSFD's Annex I provide a set of eleven qualitative descriptors, which sets out in more detail the goals on 'good ecological status' to be achieved in the national and regional waters. Pursuant to Article 9(3), the Commission on 1 September 2010 adopted the decision on criteria and methodological standards on the GES of marine areas.[940] The MSFD is going further than the WFD in the use of an ecosystem-based perspective for maintaining healthy ecosystems in marine waters.[941] The MSFD also establishes an obligation to ensure that non-indigenous species introduced by human activities are at a level that do not adversely alter the ecosystem. According to Article 8, achievement of GES in a marine water body requires that concentrations of contaminants are at levels not giving rise to pollution effects. The definition of pollution in Article 3(8) is the following:

> inputs to the marine environment which result or are likely to result in deleterious effects such as harm to living resources and marine ecosystems, including loss of biodiversity, hazards to human health, the hindering of marine activities including fishing, tourism and recreation and other legitimate uses of the sea, impairment of the quality for use of the sea water and reduction of amenities or, in general, impairment of the sustainable use of marine goods and services.

The four European Marine Regions – the Baltic Sea (that is covered by Helsinki Convention),[942] the North-East Atlantic Ocean (that is covered by OSPAR Convention), the Mediterranean Sea and the Black Sea – that are the geographical and organisational frame for the national implementation and administration of the provisions is established on the basis of geographical and environmental criteria, cf. Article 4 of the MSFD. Denmark is a party to Helsinki Convention and OSPAR

940. Commission Decision 2010/477/EU. *See further*, the working paper, *Relationship Between the Initial Assessment of Marine Waters and Criteria for Good Environmental Status*, SEC(2011) 1255 final.

941. Concerning these issues, *see* Long, R., *The Marine Strategy Framework Directive: A New European Approach to the Regulation of the Marine Environment, Marine Natural Resources and Marine Ecological Services*, in Journal of Energy and Natural Resources Law 29(1), 2011, at 1–44; and Borja. A., Elliott M., Carstensen J., Heiskanen A.S. and van de Bund, W, *Marine Management – Towards an Integrated Implementation of the European Marine Strategy Framework and the Water Framework Directives*, U.S. National Library of Medicine, Elsevier full-text article (doi:10.1016/j.marpolbul.2010.09.026 Epub 2010 Oct 20).

942. Its name is also the Baltic Marine Environmental Protection Commission and the Helsinki Commission.

Convention.[943] The Member States are required to develop and implement marine strategies that include: (a) an initial assessment of their marine waters; the determination of GES of their marine waters; (b) the setting of environmental targets; (c) the establishment and implementation of coordinated monitoring programs; and (d) the identification of measures or actions that need to be taken in order to achieve or maintain GES. The national marine strategies must apply an ecosystem approach to the management of human activities, cf. Article 1(3) of the MSFD. As part of the preparation of their marine strategies, each Member State with a coast (twenty-three in all) under the MSFD had to provide a description of the current environmental status of their seas (initial assessment) by July 2012 and to establish environmental targets, drawing up its marine strategy together with other Member States in the relevant region, cf. Articles 5–6 of the Directive. In their initial assessment, the 'predominant' pressure and impacts must be addressed.[944] The development of targets and associated indicators must be carried out in the framework of the requirement for regional cooperation, keeping in mind the objective of coherence of frameworks within the different regions, cf. Article 5(2) and Article 6 of the MSFD, as well as the coherence across the EU, cf. Article 12. The monitoring programs of the Member States had to be coordinated with the monitoring under the regional conventions and the data resulting from the monitoring activities have to be sent to the Commission no later than July 2014.[945] The Commission decision on the qualitative criteria mentioned *supra* was replaced on 17 May 2017 by a new Decision[946] that ensures more flexibility, and the use of established thresholds values through regional cooperation, e.g., in the OSPAR Commission and in HELCOM. Based on this Decision, the threshold values are required to be set at appropriate geographic scales of assessment to reflect the different biotic and abiotic characteristics of the regions, subregions and sub-decisions. The scale of assessment depends on the individual Member States. Denmark has only one assessment area.[947] The national marine strategies must contain a detailed assessment of the state of the environment, a definition of GES at regional level, and clear environmental targets and monitoring programmes. Annex III – that was replaced by a Commission Directive of 17 May 2017[948] – contains an updated indicative list of characteristics, pressures and impacts, which the Member States are obliged to take

943. The EU, HELCOM and the OSPAR Commission are working together on monitoring of the environmental status, on reporting, and on enforcement.

944. In 2014, the Commission reported an assessment of these elements, concluding that Member States showed limited ambitions in setting environmental targets, *see* the COM(2014) 097 final, *The First Phase of Implementation of the Marine Strategy Framework Directive (2008/56/EC) – The European Commission's Assessment and Guidance*.

945. Denmark reported in time, *see* the Commission's *Commissioned Report of 16 January 2017 Assessing Member States' Monitoring Programmes under the Marine Strategy Framework Directive*, COM(2017) 3 final, at 3.

946. Commission Decision No. 2017/848/EU laying down Criteria and Methodological Standards on Good Environmental Status of Marine Waters and Specifications and Standardised Methods for Monitoring and Assessment.

947. David Langlet is highlighting the big differences between the Member States, *see* his article, *Scale, Space and Delamitation in Marine Legal Governance – Perspectives from the Baltic Sea*, Marine Policy, Marine Policy, 98, pp. 278–285, 2018.

948. Commission Directive 2017/845/EU amending the Directive 2008/56/EC as regards the Indicative Lists of Elements to be taken into Account for the Preparation of the Marine Strategies.

into consideration when assessing, monitoring, and establishing targets and programs. It is mandatory for Member States to draw up their programs of cost-effective measures and to make an EIA analysis of each measure. The methods required for assessment and monitoring under the MSFD of the marine environment must take into account and, where appropriate, be based on those applicable under existing EU legislation and, where relevant, knowledge and approaches developed in the framework of regional sea conventions. The Directive refines how the cooperation between EU Member States with other parties to the regional regimes inside the territory of the EU – including cooperation with the OSPAR Commission and HELCOM – should take place.[949] Where practical and appropriate, the OSPAR and HELCOM regimes should be used to ensure coordination among Member States and with third countries in the development of marine strategies.

131. Spatial planning is used in the EU with the ambition to consider the links between water management in the EU and territorial cohesion both on land and on the ocean.

The above-mentioned Framework Directive for Maritime Spatial Planning[950] – the FMSP Directive – lays down procedural rules on spatial planning.[951] It aims at promoting the sustainable growth of maritime economies, the sustainable development of maritime areas and the sustainable use of marine resources based on an eco-system approach, and it is based on the 'IMP' of the EU. The ambition behind the FMSP Directive is to foster coordinated and coherent decision-making, implementing the international Integrated Marine and Coastal Management (IMCAM) strategy adopted under the CBD in 2010. The Directive is also part of the codification of the Integrated Coastal Zone Management (ICZM) policy of the EU.[952] It is not affecting the sovereign rights and jurisdictions of Member States over marine waters, which derive from relevant international law, particularly UNCLOS. This includes the delimitation of maritime boundaries, cf. Article 2(4). Member States bordering marine waters shall cooperate with the aim of ensuring that the maritime spatial plans are coherent and coordinated across the marine region concerned, cf. Article 11. Where possible, the Member States shall also cooperate with third countries, cf. Article 12. The deadline for transposition of this Directive into national law was 18 September 2016. In their implementation of the FMSP Directive, each Member State shall take into account land-sea interactions. The Directive does not apply to coastal waters or parts thereof falling under a Member State's town or country planning, provided that this is communicated in its maritime spatial planning, cf. Article 2. The objectives of spatial planning are defined in Article 5, the minimum requirements are stated in Article 6 and the setting up of the plans are described in

949. Article 6 of the MSFD.
950. European Parliament and Council Directive 2014/89/EU establishing a Framework for Maritime Spatial Planning.
951. The FMSP Directive is based on Art. 43(2) TFEU (provisions for the agriculture and fisheries politics), Art. 100(2) TFEU (provisions for sea and air transport politics), Art. 192(1) (provisions for environmental politics) and Art. 194(2) TFEU (provisions for energy politics). Concerning the importance of the legal basis in the TFEU, *see supra* para. 58.
952. Concerning the Integrated Coastal Zone Management, *see infra* para. 248 and para. 302.

Article 8. Article 7 is stating that the land-sea interactions should not form part of the maritime spatial planning process as such. Member States may use other formal or informal processes, such as integrated coastal management. However, they shall reflect the outcome of the process in their maritime spatial planning. The FMSP Directive respects Member States' prerogatives to use national legal traditions in the design of plans and strategies, taking into account their economic, social environmental priorities as well as their sectorial policy objectives. It should help Member States to develop their plans and ensure the coordination of various marine activities and to avoid conflicts between diverse uses. It is relevant in several situations where a reservation for specific maritime activities is relevant, e.g., to ensure fishing areas.[953]

132. Denmark's marine waters are two and a half times as large as its land area and include fjords, the 'belts' and the open sea. Legislation on the protection of the environmental quality is the old Danish Marine Protection Act and the Marine Strategic Management Act implementing the MSFD.[954] The Directive on Safety of Offshore Oil and Gas Operations is implemented into Danish law partly as an amendment to the Danish Marine Protection Act.

The objectives of the Danish Environmental Marine Protection Act[955] are to prevent and reduce pollution and other negative impacts on marine nature and the environment caused by oil and other substances from ships, aircraft and mobile or fixed drilling platforms, and to maintain an emergency system for the sea, coasts and harbours. The Act protects the marine environment of the Danish territorial sea for all vessels, including foreign vessels, and prohibits any discharge of oil (section 11), chemical substances or waste in quantity (Chapter 9). The Act relates to the disposal of substances or materials by 'dumping', emptying or sinking them in the sea from ships, aircraft and platforms, whether fixed or floating. There is no definition of the word 'dumping', but it follows the MARPOL 73/78 approach. Such activities are however prohibited or restricted by Chapter 7 of the Act. The Act also includes rules on licensing and EIA procedures in relation to the use of fast ferries. The legal, financial and practical responsibilities of the different operators involved in delivery of ship-generated waste and cargo residues have been implemented by Denmark by means of sections 24(2) and 55(2) of the Act[956] and Statutory Order on Disposal of Waste from Ships and Obligation on Waste Planning.[957] The obligations concerning the need for adequate port reception facilities are the responsibility of the harbours. A waste reception and handling plan (PWRH-plans) must be drawn up in each port, and significant changes to PWRH-plans must include structural changes, changes to the physical area or boundaries of the port/port facility areas covered by the plan,

953. Concerning EU's fishery policy and legislation, *see infra* para. 280.
954. Act No. 522 of 26 May 2010 on Marine Strategy. It is now Promulgation Order No. 117 of 26 January 2017, as amended by Act No. 1554 of 19 December 2017.
955. Promulgation Order No. 1033 of 4 September 2017 on Marine Environmental Marine Protection, as amended several times.
956. Act No. 1275 of 21 December 2011 on the Implementation of parts of the Port State Control Directive amending the Environmental Marine Protection Act.
957. Statutory Order No. 1396 of 25 November 2016 on Disposal of Waste from Ships and Obligation on Waste Planning.

changes to the categories of traffic handling by the port/port facility, etc. The Minister for the Environment has the power to make the local county responsible for deciding on applications for the disposal of dredge material from harbour authorities, a competence that he or she has exercised in adopting the above-mentioned Statutory Order. Only the disposal of fresh fish or parts thereof is generally allowed. The details concerning the prohibitions and restrictions are laid down in the Statutory Order on Disposal of Refuse at Sea,[958] the Statutory Order on the Disposal of Oil at Sea from Vessels[959] and the Statutory Order on the Refuse of Waste Water from Pleasure Crafts.[960]

The implementation of the Directive on Safety of Offshore Oil and Gas Operations[961] was made by amendments to several acts, including the Environmental Marine Protection Act.[962] The amendment included section 34b of the Environmental Marine Protection Act that rules on the prevention of major accidents by a public risk management planning in which the responsible operators are only involved 'if it is relevant'. The obligations of the operator to have an internal risk management strategy are laid down in section 18a of the Act on Safety of Offshore Oil and Gas Operations.[963] The competence to decide on the operator's obligations is by section 4a delegated to the Minister for Employment. The 'operator' is defined in section 3, no. 17 as:

> the company designated by the rightsholder or by the Minister for Employment, on behalf of the rightsholder, performs the activities authorised by the rightsholder pursuant to the Act on the Use of Denmark's Subsoil, including planning and implementation of well activities, or the management of a production facility's functions.

The obligation for the Member States laid down in the Directive to require the operator to ensure that internal and external security plans are implemented by provisions in the just-mentioned Act that ensure competences for the Minister for Employment to pass statutory orders as general provisions in cooperation with the Minister for the Environment. The liability rules, included in this Act, are based on the Directive on Environmental Liability.[964]

The MSFD was implemented into Danish legislation in 2010 by means of the Marine Strategic Management Act. In July 2011, the Commission started a process against Denmark for its failing to implement Articles 5(3), 14(2) and 14(3) of the

958. Statutory Order No. 537 of 22 May 2017 on Disposal of Refuse at Sea.
959. Statutory Order No. 539 of 22 May 2017 on the Disposal of Oil at Sea from Vessels.
960. Statutory Order No. 360 of 22 March 2010 on the Refuse of Waste Water from Pleasure Crafts.
961. European Parliament and Council Directive 2013/30/EU on Safety of Offshore Oil and Gas Operations.
962. Amended by Act No. 1499 of 23 December 2014 on the Implementation of the Directive on Safety of Offshore Oil and Gas Operations.
963. Promulgation Order No. 125 of 6 February 2018 on Safety of Offshore Oil and Gas Operations.
964. European Parliament and Council Directive 2004/35/EC on Environmental Liability with regard to the Prevention and remedying of Environmental Damage and the Danish implementation of the Directive, *see infra* paras 336–341.

MSFD.[965] Denmark accepted that it had failed to implement the mandatory obligations on coordination with other Member States under Article 5(3), but it was the opinion of the Danish Government that Article 14(2)–(3) was correctly implemented. It accepted to make a more explicit implementation and an amending act was passed by the Parliament in February 2015.[966] The obligation to cooperate with other States is described in section 14, and the provisions on good ecological status etc. are laid down in section 11 of the Act. An amendment of the Act was passed the 19 December 2017 to implement the Commission 2017 Directive as regards the Indicative Lists of Elements to be taken into account for the Preparation of the Marine Strategies as a new Annex to the Act. In October 2014 Denmark reported under Article 11 on 54 monitoring sub-programs for the Baltic Sea marine region, and 62 monitoring sub-programs for the Greater North Sea subregion. The report identified monitoring gaps and plans to address them.[967] The 'Danish Marine Strategy I' was passed in 2012 comprising three reports:

(1) 'Initial Analysis' that provided an overview of the status of the Danish marine areas including info on the factors that are contributing to the situation that not all Danish maritime areas have GES. The most important challenges are identified as nutrient loads and contaminants dangerous to the marine environment.
(2) 'Environmental Targets' that identified targets for the environmental status of Danish marine areas – describing the threshold to be crossed in order to go from 'not good' to 'good', sub-targets to lead progress towards GES, as well as what would be considered as GES.
(3) 'Socio-Economic Analysis' with the general assessment that the measures to be used can result in considerable improvement in the marine environment, but that it is still too early to assess the final impacts of the measures at socio-economic level.

On 29 November 2018, a draft for the 'Danish Marine Strategy II' was sent out in a public hearing by the Ministry of Environment and Food of Denmark. It will ensure an updated monitoring programme by 2020 that takes into account new knowledge and new monitoring methods.

133. The Nordic countries made a common strategy on 'Maritime Spatial Planning in the Nordic Region – Principles, Perspectives and Opportunities' in 2009. In July 2010, the Danish liberal-conservative coalition Government published its strategy as 'An Integrated Maritime Strategy'. In 2012, the next coalition Government presented its 'Plan for Growth in the Blue Denmark'.[968] The implementation of the

965. The process was started by Commission letter No. 2014/2144.
966. Act No. 178 of 24 February 2015 on the Amendment of the Raw Materials Act, the Coast Protection Act and the Marine Strategic Planning Act ensured the implementation of the mentioned articles of the MSFD.
967. Report of the EU Commission of 16 January 2017, COM(2017) 3 final, on the *Assessment of Member States' Monitoring Programmes under the Marine Strategy Framework Directive*, at 15.
968. It was published by the former liberal-conservative coalition government that consisted of the Social Democratic Party, the Social-Liberal Party and the Socialistic People's Party. Concerning the different coalition governments that have been in power, *see supra* para. 4.

FMSP Directive into Danish legislation was made by an Act on Maritime Spatial Planning.[969] In relation to the protection of coastlines, the rules are to be found in the Planning Act,[970] the Nature Protection Acts[971] and the Act on Coastal Protection.[972] The Planning Act and the Nature Protection Act provide supplementary zoning and building lines as means to protect the coast.[973]

Denmark is part of the North Seas Energy Cooperation (NSEC) that was established in 2016 on a voluntary basis. One of the support groups under this cooperation focuses on maritime spatial planning. The Danish Act on Maritime Spatial Planning is not regarded by the Danish authorities as an important part of the environmental protection measures.[974] The ecosystem approach is not a part of the Act. The aim of the Act is to establish the geographical scope of the sea areas that can be used for, inter alia, offshore energy extraction, shipping, fishing, aquaculture and seabed mining – respecting that some areas have to be protected. The competent authority is the Agency on Maritime Fairs that is part of the Ministry of Industry, Business and Financial Affairs. The first maritime spatial plan was initiated in 2017 by the working group on maritime spatial planning – representing 12 maritime authorities. The Ministry for the Environment and Food is one of the authorities involved without any power to decide on the content of the maritime spatial plan. The design of the plan will be based on a need-oriented approach. When the Danish Maritime Plan is past – hopefully in 2020 with effect from 31 March 2021 – it will cover the period from 2021 to 2030, and it will be binding as a State spatial plan, cf. section 11(4), no. 8 of the Planning Act. Establishment of facilities, construction activities, etc. in the coastal area have to be in accordance with the Act on Coastal Protection and the maritime spatial planning established under the Maritime Spatial Planning Act. With an Act on the 'New Division of Competences and Simplification of Case Processing in connection with Coastal Protection, etc.'[975] the protection of coastal protection projects under several acts are now managed by the municipalities. They must include such considerations in their overall assessment under the Coastal Protection Act, cf. the new section 3a of this Act. The Renewable Energy Act[976] established the procedure for the approval of electricity production from water and wind at the sea. According to the Act, permission for preliminary studies and for exploitation of wind energy at sea may only be given either after applications have been requested in connection with a call for tenders or after an application has been made public, and other interested parties have been given the opportunity to apply, cf. section 25. The latter is known as an open-door procedure.

969. Act No. 615 of 8 June 2016 on Maritime Spatial Planning, as amended by Act No. 1714 of 27 December 2018.
970. Promulgation Order No. 287 of 16 April 2018 on Spatial Planning.
971. Promulgation Order No. 240 of 13 March 2019 on Nature Protection.
972. Promulgation No. 57 of 21 January 2019 on Coastal Protection.
973. *See infra* paras 243 and 311.
974. Economic growth is a strong focus for the maritime spatial planning of Danish marine waters, *see* European MSP 2017 platform at http://msp.ioc-unesco.org/world-applications/europe/denmark/ (visited 15 Jul. 2019).
975. Act No. 720 of 8 June 2018 on a new Division of Competences and Simplification of Case Processing in connection with Coastal Protection, etc.
976. Promulgation Order No. 356 of 4 April 2019 on the Promotion of Renewable Energy (the RES Act).

It is the Energy Agency that is the relevant authority. Any party applying to establish an offshore wind farm must prepare an EIA in order to ensure that the environmental conditions are the expected impact are described. If there are Natura 2000 sites in the neighbouring area, it is also mandatory to make an assessment based on Article 6(3) and (4) of the Habitats Directive.[977]

The Danish marine aquaculture production is located in shallow waters with low salinity and water flow. The farms are located in the Baltic Sea along and close to the southern cost of Jutland and a few farms along the coast of Zealand.[978] Such activities are causing eutrophication with nitrogen and to a lesser extent phosphorus from feed residues and faeces that are the most problematic environmental impact from these farms.[979] The aquaculture production of fish in floating grid cages, wire boxes, or the like that are anchored on the seabed where the plant is located in marine waters requires a permit under the Environmental Protection Act.[980] There are two categories of marine aquatic enterprises under the approval system:

(1) The marine aquaculture productions that are located partly or fully in the sea outside 1 nautical mile: It is the EPA that has the power to approve and supervise such activities.
(2) The marine aquaculture productions that are located in marine waters closer than 1 nautical mile from the coast and where operation requires the use of feed: The municipalities have the power to approve such activities and they also have the supervision power.

The owners of the aquatic farms have difficulties in obtaining environmental approval, as they cannot limit the emission of nitrates, phosphor and organic material (BI_5) adequately to the current environmental quality objectives and the protection of the integrity of Natura 2000 areas.[981] On 1 June 2017 the Danish Parliament passed an amendment to the Environmental Protection Act.[982] The amendment was a consequence of the political agreement on the 'Food and Agricultural Package' of 22 December 2015 that made it possible to use what the parties to the agreement

977. Statutory Order No. 1595 of 6 December 2018 on the Demarcation and Management of International Nature Conservation Areas and Protection of Certain Species, *see infra* para. 253. Concerning the EIA obligations, *see supra* para. 32, and concerning zoning and national planning, *see infra* Part III.
978. Concerning the marine aquaculture in Denmark, *see infra* para. 289.
979. The Ministry of Environment and Food of Denmark stated in a Consultation Note of 28 February 2018 – related to the Bill L 169 on the Supplementary Nitrogen Quota to the Marine Aquaculture Sector – that Denmark does not expect to reach the objective 'good ecological status' within the deadline specified in the MSFD.
980. Concerning the Danish environmental approval system, *see supra* paras 63–66.
981. The emission from this sector was in 2012 in total 330.6 tonnes nitrates, 36.4 tonnes phosphor and 1,057 tonnes organic materials (BI5). Concerning those numbers *see* the Ministry for Food, Agriculture and Fishery, *Strategy for a sustainable development of the aquaculture sector in Denmark 2014-2020* (in Danish), at 9.
982. Act No. 680 of 8 June 2017 on Compensatory Marine Instruments for the Establishment or Expansion of Marine Aquaculture.

titled 'the environmental space' of 800 tonnes of nitrogen for aquaculture production.[983] In addition, 43 tonnes of nitrogen were earmarked under this agreement to ensure that existing aquaculture within the water basins can utilise their already received discharge permit. It was also part of the agreement to postpone the handling of 6,200 tonnes of nitrogen for the third water planning period under the WFD (2021–2027) in favour of the food and agricultural sector. The marine instruments accepted by the new rules are planned to be mussel farming or/and cultivation of seaweed that are expected to remove some of the nutrients and phosphorus that are discharged into the neighbour marine environment. The intention behind the new rules is to make it possible for the authorities to approve new production activities also in situations where the principle that cleaning action should be taken at the source is not respected. The new rules in the Act are only establishing the legal power for the minister to publish the necessary administrative rules in a statutory order regulating the decision-making process on the approval of applications under the Environmental Protection Act.[984] Approvals cannot be granted before a new statutory order has been passed, and such an order can only be passed if the content of it is accepted by the political parties taking part in the agreement on passing the new rules. Such an order has not been passed yet (April 2019). Only very few farms have received an environmental approval, and after appeals to the Environment and Food Appeals Board the approvals of new activities have been rejected. The reasoning of the Appeals Board is that those farms have a negative impact on Nature 2000 sites. The 'Danish Aquaculture' has on behalf of its members – the owners of the fish farms – brought an action on this issue against the Appeals Board, because they disagree with the Board's interpretation of Article 6 of the Habitats Directive. An approval received from the Agency on Maritime Administration is also needed, before the operator of a fish farm can establish mussel farms in harmony with the Fishery Act.[985] An approval from the Agency for Coastal Protection is also needed, before the operator can establishes seaweed culture, if it is located close to the coast.[986] A political Agreement on Growth in the Aquaculture Sector was made on 30 June 2016 ensuring a mapping of possible location of the aquatic marine farms in the sea areas. The protection of Nature 2000 sites makes it very complicated to get an environmental approval to marine based fish farms that use open net pens. In 2018 and 2019 the Environment and Food Appeals Board has refused to accept marine based fish farms located close to Nature 2000 sites.

983. The Danish argumentation is based on an assumption that Denmark under the HELCOM has a space between the maximum permissible and the actual emission of nitrogen and phosphorus. The support for this argumentation is found, e.g., in DCE reports concerning flexibility (2014–2016). These natural scientific reports are based on the fact that reductions in nutrient supplies have wide-ranging effects. The argumentation is made with reference to HELCOM *Copenhagen Ministerial Declaration*, at 7.

984. The acceptance by the political parties to the voting-agreement behind the passing of the new Act has to be ensured on the design of these administrative rules.

985. Statutory Order No. 1387 of 3 December 2017 on Production of Mussels and Oysters in the Water Column.

986. Promulgation Order No. 57 of 21 January 2019 on Coastal Protection.

134. The Danish EPA shall as the supervisory authority be responsible for ensuring that the Environmental Protection Act's provisions on the Fish Farms.[987] It has the supervision competences. It must ensure water quality management and the assessment of biological conditions, regulation of marine fish farms, regulation of dredging, regulation of ship-based pollution, etc. The owners, users and captains of ships, and owners and users of platforms, and the persons responsible for the platforms must inform the authorities about disposals into the sea. Insofar as pollution from ships and platforms, etc. is concerned, the control is exercised by the Agency together with university researchers. They monitor the condition of the sea and carry out the inspection. Research is also carried on with respect to the impact of heavy metals and other toxic substances in the sea and its fauna and flora.

Oil spills from shipping, oil extraction and spillage from industrial processes in the sea are the main sources of PAHs, although about a quarter of the PAHs in the sea originate from land-based combustion processes. Many PAHs are toxic to marine organisms, and others may be both carcinogenic and mutagenic to man and animals. The Agency has requested offshore enterprises to regularly analyse the content of aromatic compounds in production water, and it has investigated possible techniques to remove PAH and other kinds of aromatic hydrocarbons from production water in offshore installations. The Directive on Ship-source Pollution and on the Introduction of Penalties for Infringements[988] is implemented as part of this Act.

§5. Evaluation of the Efficiency of the Legal Provisions

135. The EU commission has assessed the Danish water bodies' qualities, as they have been reported under the first generation of river basin management plans. Only 30% of natural surface water bodies achieved a good or high ecological status, and 17% of heavily modified[989] or ratified water bodies achieve a good or high ecological potential (61% unknown). Only 0.5% surface water bodies (99.5% unknown), 0.1% of heavily modified and artificial water bodies (99.6% unknown) and 57% of groundwater bodies achieved 'good chemical status'. About 65% of groundwater bodies are in 'good quantitative status'.[990] The Danish water legislation has not been changed as a consequence of the CJEU judgment in the *Weser* case. This is illustrated by the passing of the legislative amendments made as a consequence of the political agreement on 'Food and Agricultural Package', e.g., in

987. Concerning this supervision competence, *see supra* paras 67–70.

988. European Parliament and Council Directive 2005/35/EC on Ship-Source Pollution and the Introduction of Penalties for Infringements. The Commission was not satisfied with the Danish implementation and sent an open letter No. 2011/0081, but the answer from the Danish Ministry of Justice was that the implementation was in conformity with the EU Directive, *see* the Note of 29 March 2011 from the Danish Parliament's European Committee. However, the Parliament decided to make an explicit implementation of the Directive by its Act No. 423 of 10 May 2011.

989. Heavily modified water bodies are defined in Art. 4(3) of the Water Framework Directive.

990. The Commission's staff working document, *The EU Environmental Implementation Review. Country Report Denmark*, Brussels, 3 February 2017, SWD(2017) 39 final, at 17.

respect to the marine aquaculture in June 2017 – the effectiveness of this court judgment in Denmark is consequently not strong.[991] The Ministry of Environment and Food's Administration has stated that Denmark does not expect to reach the objective 'good ecological status' within the specified deadline.[992]

136. Today Denmark has 5,000 km of beaches suitable for bathing, and the quality of water is generally of high international standard. The Danish bathing water is regulated by Statutory Order on Bathing Water and Bathing Areas.[993] The assessment of bathing water results that was managed by the European Environment Agency in 2017 – based on the reported information under the Bathing Water Directive[994] – showed that 86.7% of the Danish coastal bathing waters met the excellent water quality, and 8.5% were of good quality, 2.7% were of sufficient quality, and 1.0% were of poor quality. [995]

However, the current environmental quality of the general water body is not a 'good ecological status'. Nitrogen from the agricultural sector is the most important source of pollution. In the most recent river basin management plans (decided in October 2014 and currently subject to appeal), a large number of reduction goals are postponed until after 2021 on the basis of disproportional costs. It is expected by the Danish Economic Council that just over 40% of the coastal waters and rivers, and 25% of lakes will meet the goals by 2021 under the policies already in place.[996]

In the EU's approval of the 2014–2020 RDP for Denmark December 2014, it is stated that although the water quality and the status of Danish water is generally quite good and improving, it is necessary to reduce emissions from nitrogen, phosphorus and pesticides in order to maintain and further improve the situation.[997] The three supporting key priorities for Denmark's Rural Development are: (a) better management of natural resources and encouraging climate-friendly farming practices and to double organic farmer's areas; (b) investment to improve the environmental performance of farms, restructuring farms and cattle sector; and (c) boosting innovation and creating jobs in rural areas.[998]

137. It is concluded in the draft of 29 November 2018 for the 'Danish Marine Strategy II' on the basis of the assessments made under the 'Danish Marine Strategy I' that for several parameters, GES has not yet been achieved. The cumulative analysis indicates that the most important pressures overall in Denmark are caused

---

991. Act No. 680 of 8 June 2017 on Compensatory Marine Instruments in the establishment or extension of Aquaculture. This Act amended the Environmental Protection Act.
992. It was stated in a Consultation Note of 28 February 2018 related to the Bill L 169/2017 on the Amendment to the Environmental Protection Act concerning the Phasing in of Nitrogen to the Aquaculture Sector.
993. Statutory Order No. 917 of 27 June 2016 on Bathing Water Quality and Bathing Areas.
994. European Parliament and Council Directive 2006/7/EC concerning the Management of Bathing Water Quality.
995. EEA Report No. 2/2018, *European Bathing Water Quality in 2017*, at 4–5 and at 21.
996. The Danish Economic Councils, *Economy and Environment 2015*, at 362–363.
997. European Commission, *Fact Sheet: 2014-2020 Rural Development Programme for Denmark*, 12 December 2014.
998. Concerning the CAP 2013 Reform of importance for the Danish Policy, *see infra* paras 258–260.

by three different categories of pressures. It is first and foremost nutrients that cause the problems, and the second and third most problematic pressures are caused by non-indigenous species and contaminants.[999] In the North Sea and the Skagerrak fisheries activities are the third most important parameter, and the same applies for noise in the Kattegat. The results concerning potential cumulative impacts – pressures combined with natural elements – indicate that such impact is generally high in certain inlets, fjords and coastal areas. The Wadden Sea is included in this problematic situation.[1000] Persistent organic pollutants (POPs) and heavy metals pose particular problems in the Baltic Sea because of the physical conditions in this marine area.[1001] The primarily means of achieving the quality objectives in relation to surface waters in Denmark is a reduction in nutrient discharges and emissions by the means of the general rules on good farming practice, the obligation to be connected to the municipal wastewater purification facilities and the obligations to have a licence to discharge polluted water into the lakes, rivers and coastal waters.

In 2000, the EU quality criteria were met in only a few estuaries, coastal areas and open water areas. The few coastal areas that met the criteria were generally non-stratified shallow-water areas with a relatively restricted load from land-based sources. The failure to meet the criteria was due to nutrient loading and oxygen depletion. The share of total N discharge from municipal waste treatment plants, industry and fish farms was 76%, 12% and 12%, respectively, in 2000. Land-based P discharges into estuaries and coastal areas have been significantly reduced due to the extension of sewage treatment. In 2000, the share of total P from such plants, industries and fish farms was 86%, 5.5% and 8.8%, respectively.[1002] The measures taken under the APAE III are insufficient to reach the desired reduction in nitrogen emissions from agricultural activities by a minimum of 13% by 2015 compared to 2003, as indicated in the Action Plan (covering the period of 2005–2015). In 2016, 62,400 tonnes of nitrogen were discharged to the seas around Denmark, which is a decrease compared with the previous year. In the last five years, normalised nitrogen emissions have been between 54,000 and 61,000 tonnes per year.[1003]

138. As an initiative to fulfil the SDG 12[1004] and SDG 14[1005] under the UN Sustainability Goals, the EU published its 'Plastic Strategy' in 2018[1006] and on 28 May

999. Ministry of Environment and Food, *Denmark's Marine Strategy II. Good Environmental Status. Basis Analyse. Environmental Goal*' (in Danish with an English summary), 2019, at 11.
1000. The Wadden Sea is an UNESCO World Heritage Area.
1001. The Helsinki Declaration adopted a target of 50% reduction in heavy metals and other persistent environmental hazardous substances from 1989 to 1995. It is estimated by the authorities that Denmark has achieved this reduction mainly as a result of important capacity in the municipal and industrial wastewater treatment plants.
1002. OECD, *Environmental Performance Reviews Denmark. 2007,* at 203ff.
1003. *See* the EPA's homepage, https://mst.dk/service/nyheder/nyhedsarkiv/2018/apr/udledning-af-kvaelstof-og-fosfor-i-2016/ (visited on 15 Nov. 2018).
1004. SDG 12 is related to responsible consumption and production.
1005. SDG 14 is stating the obligation to conserve and sustainability use of the Oceans, seas and marine resources for sustainable development.
1006. COM(2018) 28 final.

2018 the Commission presented its proposal for a single-use plastic directive.[1007] The proposal is stating that plastic makes up 80–85% of the total number of marine litter items. The Strategy addresses gaps in existing legislation with focus on microplastics, restrictions through REACH for deliberately added microplastics in products and oxo-plastic as well as measures for microplastics from tyres, textiles and plastic pellets etc. The main objective of the Draft Directive is the prevention and reduction of plastic marine litter from single plastic items and fishing gear containing plastic. The Danish Government published its 'Plastic Strategy' in December 2018.[1008]

1007. COM(2018) 340 final – Proposal for a Directive on the Reduction of the Impact of certain Plastic Products on the Environment.

1008. The Social Democratic Minority Government that took power on 27 Jun. 2019 wants to ensure a high priority of this strategy.

Chapter 4. Waste

§1. Sound Waste Management, Shipment of Waste and Resource Efficiency

139. Increasing globalisation and changes to the economy have led to greater imports and exports of mineral resources, semi-manufactured materials and waste. Therefore, the global context for sound waste management, resource efficiency and vertical harmonisation of the law on such management has become increasingly important. Wastes contain organic material, such as sludge sewage, food, paper, wood, plastic and garden trimmings, as well as hazardous materials. The waste management strategies for such waste categories are different. The strategies are also different in different countries, as the waste generation and waste composition vary between countries. Some of the important waste categories that show the difference between developing countries and developed countries are waste from households (municipality waste). Europe and USA are the main producers of municipal waste, and they are also frontrunners in respect of utilisation of such waste, for example, in energy production. Every waste management practice generates GHG emission, both directly and indirectly. The GHG emissions of particular relevance to waste management are emissions of CO_2, CH_4 and N_2O. The Governing Council of the UNEP has directed its International Environmental Technology Centre (IETC) branch to take climate-related actions in the area of waste management, as there are substantial co-benefits of waste management in the context of climate change.[1009] At international level, the UNEP has introduced its 'Resource Efficiency Program' (2012). It is also part of the United Nations 'Transforming Our World: the 2030 Agenda for Sustainable Development' (hereinafter UN's '2030 Agenda for Sustainable Development') in which Goal 12 is covering the sustainable consumption and production patterns.

Waste is defined under international law, EU law and national law as objects that are: (a) disposed of or recovered; (b) intended to be disposed of or recovered; or (c) required, by the provisions of national law, to be disposed of or recovered. Waste that contains environmentally dangerous substances and products are classified as hazardous in accordance with the European Waste Catalogue (EWC),[1010] and the OECD Waste Catalogue.[1011] Included in the definitions of hazardous waste are also wastes defined as, or considered to be, hazardous by the national legislation of the party of export, import or transit. The UNEP and the OECD introduced with respect to the transport of hazardous waste the two concepts of the quality of disposal facilities at the final location and the seeking of consent from the receiving country.

1009. UNEP *Waste and Climate Change. Global Trends and Strategy Framework*, (2010 and UNEP, *Emissions Gap Report*, 2015.

1010. Commission Decision 2000/532/EC establishing a List of Waste pursuant to Art. 1 of the Waste Framework Directive. In April 2018, the Commission published Notice No. 2018/C 124/01 on Technical Guidance on the Classification of Waste. Concerning the Waste Framework Directive, *see infra* para. 145.

1011. Concerning the OECD Waste Catalogue, *see infra* para. 140.

140. The most important international agreement on waste is the UNEP Convention on the Control of Transboundary Movements of Hazardous Wastes and its Disposal (the Basel Convention). The Convention was adopted on 22 March 1989 and entered into force on 5 May 1992. Denmark and the EU have ratified it in 1994. By December 2012 there were 180 parties to the Convention. In 1995, an amendment to the Convention called the Ban Amendment was adopted by Decision III/1 that provided for measures to be taken by the parties concerning prohibition of exporting of waste to countries listed in Annex VII. The amendment is not in force. The ultimate objective of the Convention is to protect human health and environment against the adverse effects that result from exposure to contaminants in waste or the mismanagement of waste. The Convention defines hazardous waste as any category contained in Appendix I (entitled 'Categories of wastes to be controlled') to the OECD Council Decision.[1012] Among the hazardous wastes are electric wastes, used lead-acid batteries, used oils, obsolete stocks of pesticides, PCBs, dioxins and furans, by-products from the dismantling of ships, biomedical and healthcare wastes. The codes and characteristics are identical to those in Annex III that includes the list of hazardous characteristics. It refers to those wastes which are characterised as hazardous under Article 1(1) letter a under the Convention. The provisions for hazardous waste prevention, minimisation and end-of-life destruction and long-term storage are applicable to POPs and therefore directly applicable to the POPs listed in the POPs Convention as well as to other POPs. The hazardous characteristics of the Convention and OECD are mainly defined by the UN classification criteria for the transport of hazardous goods. The EU hazardous characteristics are not totally the same as the international characteristics. The characteristics used by the EU are based on the classification under the REACH Regulation[1013] and CLP Regulation.[1014]

The Basel Convention offers a comprehensive and integrated approach for realising the entire range of waste management objectives. It recognises: (a) the PIC procedure; (b) the principle of the minimisation of the transboundary movement of hazardous waste; (c) the 'proximity principle'; (d) environmentally sound management (ESM) as an essential export condition; and (e) international cooperation to achieve these objectives. There is an administrative cooperation between this Convention and the two conventions on chemicals: the Rotterdam Convention and the Stockholm Convention. There are two types of activities required of the parties to the Basel Convention: capacity-building activities (including on chemical management) and activities undertaken as part of the programmes as directed by the parties to address specific issues in support of ESM. The provisions on ESM of waste infrastructure laid down in the 'Basel Declaration on Environmentally Sound Management' (1999) focused on strengthening capacity for domestic waste management. The Convention has established a network of fourteen regional and coordinating

---

1012. OECD Decision C(2001)107/Final, as amended by Decision C(2004)20.

1013. European Parliament and Council Regulation No. 1907/2006/EC concerning the Registration, Evaluation, Authorisation and Restrictions on Chemicals (REACH), establishing a European Chemical Agency.

1014. European Parliament and Council Regulation No. 1272/2008/EC on Classification, Labelling and Packaging of Substances and Mixtures. Concerning hazardous waste, *see infra* para. 149 and concerning the Rotterdam Regulation *see infra* para. 209.

centres for capacity-building and technology transfers. The ESM approach has linkage to the UNFCCC in that engineered landfills designed to recapture CH_4 as one of the important GHGs. Prior to commencement of each transboundary movement of waste, the exporter must provide written notification to the competent authority. The PIC procedure laid down in the Convention and the provisions relating to hazard communication run in parallel with the procedures established under the Rotterdam Convention on the Prior Informed Consent Procedure for Certain Hazardous Chemicals and Pesticides in International Trade (as revised in 2013).[1015] Since March 1992, transboundary movement of wastes destined for recovery operations between OECD Member Countries has been supervised and controlled under the terms of an OECD Council Decision. The procedure was harmonised with the Basel-procedure in 2001.[1016] The OECD Decision on the control of transboundary movements of wastes applies only to wastes, which are destined for recovery operations within the OECD area.

The UNEP is undertaking various programs and projects to assist its Member States to achieve improved waste management. These programs and projects include Integrated Solid Waste Management (ISWM) based on the 3 R (Reduce, Recycle and Reuse) approach, Sustainable Consumption and Production, E-waste management, converting waste agriculture biomass and waste plastics into useful energy and/or material resources, and management of hazardous waste. The UNEP is also proposing a 'Global Platform for Waste Management' to facilitate coherent delivery of international support for waste management.

The IMO has established a Protocol to the Convention for the Prevention of Pollution from Ships (MARPOL 73/78) that regulates the discharge of waste from ships. It requires the provision of adequate reception facilities in harbours. Denmark has ratified the Convention and the Protocol. The EU has not been accepted as a party of any of the IMO conventions, but it is implementing the obligations that its Member States have ratified under the IMO. The IMO rules on operations in ports are implemented into EU's legal order by the Directive on Port Reception Facilities for Ship Generated Waste and Cargo Residues.[1017] The provisions of this Directive make it mandatory for the Member States to ensure port receptor facilities and the delivery of waste to those facilities. The availability of port reception facilities for sewage is monitored, and facilities are maintained and upgraded in the cooperation under the HELCOM by using the cooperation platform on special area according to the Annex IV of MARPOL. The Baltic Sea control for sewage from passage ships under MARPOL Annex IV will take effect on 1 June 2021 for existing ships and on 1 June 2019 for new ships. The EU provisions are however not

1015. Concerning the international obligations on PIC, *see infra* para. 208.

1016. Decision C (2001) 107/FINAL on 14 June 2001.

1017. European Parliament and Council Directive on Port Reception Facilities for Ship Generated Waste and Cargo Residues was amended by Directive 2002/84/EC and Directive 2015/2087/EU. This Directive with the mentioned amendments is implemented by Statutory Order No. 1396 of 25 November 2016 on Harbour Reception Facilities for Ship Waste and Cargo Residues.

totally in line with the update of the subsequent amendments made to the MARPOL. This is why the EU is now preparing a new directive to replace it.[1018]

141. The EEC took the first step to its environmental regulation by passing the first general waste directive in 1975[1019] and with a waste directive on hazardous waste in 1978.[1020] The definition of waste was introduced in 1975 by the Waste Directive. The CJEU has through its case law supplemented these very unclear definitions by various criteria on how to understand the term 'to discard', and how to determine when and how an object or subject falls within the scope of the Directive. The Court has emphasised that the application of the concept of discarding waste implies that all the circumstances that are indicating whether the holder has the intention or obligation to discard have to be taken into consideration in the authorities' assessment of a product as waste or non-waste. This case law – that is still used in EU waste law – is binding on the national waste authorities in all Member States.[1021] The EEC Transfrontier Shipment of Hazardous Waste Directive was passed in 1984.[1022] A specific waste policy principle concerning the transport and disposal of waste was introduced by the first EC Strategy Paper on Waste (1989), which stated that disposal should take place at the nearest suitable waste treatment plant (the 'proximity principle'). It introduced high standards on waste disposal and the 'proximity principle' with the aim of reducing the movement of waste for disposal. Waste has to be disposed of at waste treatment plants, in which they are using the most appropriate technology to guarantee a high level of protection of the environment and public health.

The Basel Convention was originally transformed to EU law by means of Council Regulation on the Supervision and Control of Shipment of Waste,[1023] which was obviously directly applicable. It has since been replaced by the WSR,[1024] which is also directly applicable in Member States, and therefore forms part of Danish legislation. Provisions relating to inspections and enforcement laid down in Article 50 of the Regulation were strengthened from 1 January 2016.[1025] It transfers into EU law the provisions of the Basel Convention as well as the revision of the OECD

1018. *See* the Commission's proposal of 16 January 2018, and the European Parliament's Legal Resolution of 13 March 2019 on Port Reception Facilities for the Delivery of Waste from Ships, repealing Directive 2000/59/EU and amending Directive 2009/16/EC and Directive 2010/65, COM(2018) 33 final.

1019. Council Directive 75/442/EEC on Waste. It was a framework directive setting out the general principles and concepts.

1020. Council Directive 78/319/EEC of 20 March 1978 on Toxic and Dangerous Waste. The Directive was replaced by Council Directive 91/689/EEC of 12 December 1991 on Hazardous Waste.

1021. *See, e.g.,* C-242/94 and C-224/95 *Tombesi*, and *infra* para. 145.

1022. *See* EEA Report No. 35/2016, *Prevention of Hazardous Waste in Europe – The Status in 2015*, at 11.

1023. Council Regulation 259/93/EEC on the Supervision and Control of Shipment of Waste.

1024. European Parliament and Council Regulation No. 1013/2006/EC on the Shipments of Waste.

1025. It was strengthened by European Parliament and Council Regulation No. 660/2014/EU ensuring Provisions on Regular Inspection Planning and Stronger Rules on Enforcement. In 2012, every fourth inspected waste shipment revealed a violation of the WSR, *see* the EEA Report No. 35/2016, *Prevention of Hazardous Waste in Europe – The Status in 2015*, at 30.

Decision on the control of transboundary movements of wastes.[1026] The WSR concerns nearly all types of waste shipped. Only radioactive waste and a few other types are controlled by other separated control regimes. The requirements laid down in the Regulation aims to strengthen, simplify and further specify the previous procedures for controlling waste shipments to improve the level of environmental protection. It applies to shipments of waste: (a) between Member States within the EU or with transit through third countries; (b) imported into the EU from third countries; (c) exported from the EU to third countries; and (d) in transit through the EU, on the way to and from third countries. The Member States have to establish risk assessment-based inspection plans that include objectives, priorities, the geographical area covered, information about planned inspections, the tasks assigned to authorities involved in inspections, arrangements for cooperation between the authorities involved etc.

Waste shipments must be the subject of a contract between the person responsible for shipping the waste, or having it shipped, and the consignee of such waste. Shipping of waste intended for disposal and hazardous waste intended for recovery cannot legally be made without prior notification and the contract between the parties must include financial guarantees, cf. the prior informed consent principle. If a shipment cannot be completed, the person who made the notification of the shipment must take back the waste, normally at his or her own expense. The Commission Regulation[1027] concerning the export for recovery of certain waste listed in Annex III or IIIA to the Regulation includes supplementary rules. The WSR establishes a ban on exports of hazardous waste into non-OECD countries.

According to the WSR, non-hazardous waste destined for recovery or recycling can be exported relatively freely, if accompanied by a basic identification form. All hazardous waste movements must be notified in advance, and the Member State must report on waste that is shipped across its State borders. In spring 2016, Eurostat launched an interactive web-based map of transboundary waste shipments.

142. Statutory Order on the Transboundary Movement of Waste and Used Electrical and Electronic Equipment[1028] ensures the transformation of the WSR into Danish legislation. Based on the Order, the notification document must include all of the information listed in the WSR. Therefore, enterprises wishing to import oil or

1026. Decision No. C(2001) 107/FINAL on 14 June 2001 as amended by the Decisions C(2005)41 and C(2008)156.

1027. Commission Regulation No. 1418/2007/EC contains Procedures for Shipments of Waste of Annex III and IIIA to non-OECD Countries which have replied to the Requests of the Commission in accordance with the WSR. The Regulation has been amended by Commission Regulation No. 740/2008/EC amending Regulation No. 1418/2007/EC as regards the Procedures to be followed for Export of Waste to certain Countries, Commission Regulation 967/2009/EC amending Regulation No. 1418/2007/EC concerning the Export for Recovery of certain Waste to certain non-OECD Countries, Commission Regulation No. 837/2010/EU amending Regulation No. 1418/2007/EC concerning the Export for Recovery of certain Waste to certain non-OECD Countries, and the Commission Regulation 733/2014/EU amending Regulation No. 1418/2007/EC concerning the Export for Recovery of certain Waste to certain non-OECD Countries.

1028. Statutory Order No. 132 of 6 February 2014 on the Transboundary Movement of Waste and Used Electrical and Electronic Equipment.

chemical waste from abroad must notify the Danish authorities thereof in accordance with these rules. In March 2004, the Danish EPA published a guidance note titled 'Financial Resource Mobilisation for Implementation of the Strategic Plan for the Basel Convention'. On March 2017, a 'Danish Plan for Inspection of Import/ Export of Waste' was published as a follow-up on the amended Regulation.[1029]

143. Waste is not only an environmental problem. The EU's '1989 Waste Strategy' introduced the approach that waste has to be handled in harmony with the Common Market. In 1997 the second 'Community Waste Strategy' marked a shift in the main focus of waste policy away from a pure waste management to the recovery of resources, including energy from waste. The Strategy reaffirmed the 'proximity principle' and the self-sufficiency concept for waste disposal facilities as well as the three-step waste hierarchy: prevention, recovery and safe disposal.[1030] The EU principle regarding the right of free movement of goods, Articles 34–36 TFEU,[1031] and principle of free competition, Articles 101–102 TFEU, have now to be used to secure recycling and reuse of waste and the transportation of recycled materials – and to secure the Internal Market.[1032] The 'mandatory requirements' laid down in Article 36 TFEU, which override the free movement of goods, refer to legal advantages deemed worthy of special protection in the general interest of the EU. Interests of economic profitability or other economic interests do not number among the mandatory requirements. The national authorities are obliged to ensure proper competition between the public and the private sector: they must not unduly favour the public sector. In other words, the Danish municipal councils are restricted by the law in dealing with the business sector concerning the disposition of such materials.

The authorities can prohibit the export of waste for disposal to another Member State if a waste treatment plant which is located closer to the producer of waste, is prepared to accept the wastes (the 'proximity principle'). The policy behind this principle is waste-flow control and the support of BATs in order also to achieve the 'principle of regional or local self-sufficiency' in terms of waste disposal. These two principles – which are both part of the Basel Convention and the Waste Framework Directive – require every disposal region to ensure that sufficient disposal capacity is available for the disposal of all wastes generated within the territory of the region. In the *Walloon Waste* Case (Case C-2/90), the CJEU implemented the principle of self-sufficiency as part of EU waste legislation. The Court also held that only the local or regional bodies responsible for waste disposal might restrict the import of foreign waste. Member States are not authorised to make general restrictions. Furthermore, the use of the principles may not lead to a monopolisation of business conditions. The Court noted that wastes are goods of specific nature which may constitute a risk to the environment.

1029. Danish EPA's Memo No. 18/2017, *The Danish Plan for Inspection of Import/Export of Waste*.
1030. EEA Report No. 35/2016, *Prevention of Hazardous Waste in Europe – The Status in 2015*, at 11.
1031. Concerning the right of free movement of goods principle as part of EU law, *see* Suzanne Kingston, Veerle Heyvaert and Aleksandra Covoski, *European Environmental Law*, Cambridge, 2017, at 110–119, and Ludwig Krämer, *EU Environmental Law*, Sweet & Maxwell, 2016, at 224–226.
1032. Concerning the interaction between economic and environmental issues, *see supra* para. 29.

The waste management operators as well as other industrial operators (including public and private establishments and undertakings) carrying out activities listed in Annex I of the E-PRTR have to comply with the reporting and information requirements.[1033] The rules are implemented in the Danish Environmental Protection Act and the Statutory Order concerning the PRTR register.[1034]

144. The sustainable use and management of natural resources priority area of the 6EAP sets out a series of objectives to waste. It was followed by the 'Waste Thematic Strategy' on 21 December 2005.[1035] The long-term goal of the Strategy for the EU was to become a recycling society that seeks to avoid waste and uses waste as a resource. It placed the life cycle approach to waste management as the most important approach and included other key principles, including a shift towards a materials-based approach, a shift towards more flexible mechanisms of policy and standard setting at EU level. Under the 7EAP the objective to turn the Union into a resource-efficient, green, and competitive low-carbon economy has the positions as the second priority.[1036] The climate effects of waste practices result from avoiding landfill emissions, reduced raw material extraction and manufacturing, recovered materials and energy replacing virgin materials and fossil fuel energy sources, carbon bound in soil through compost application, and carbon storage due to recalcitrant materials in landfills. There are other environmental benefits related to the compost applied to land. The compost replaces synthetic fertilisers as soil improvers, and it reduces the need for pesticides, tillage and irrigation.

The strategy 'Closing the loop – EU Action Plan for Circular Economy' on the transition to a more circular economy was published 2 December 2015.[1037] A circular economy is defined in the strategy as:

> an economy where the value of products, materials and resources is maintained in the economy for as long as possible, and the generation of waste minimised.

The Action Plan contains the twofold objective to be achieved:[1038]

(1) enabling recycling and improving the uptake of secondary mineral resources, by limiting unnecessary burdens, and facilitating the cross-border circulation of secondary mineral resources to ensure that they can be traded easily across the EU;

1033. Concerning the European Pollution Release and Transfer Register, *see supra* paras 60 and 71.
1034. Statutory Order No. 1172 of 13 October 2015 on the E-PRTR Register.
1035. COM(2005) 666 final.
1036. Decision No. 1386/2013/EU of the European Parliament and the Council of 20 November 2013 on a General Union Environmental Action Programme to 2020, *Living Well, Within the Limits of Our Planet.*
1037. COM(2015) 614 final.
1038. Commission, *Communication on the Implementation of the Circular Economy Package: Options to address the Interface between Chemical, Product and Waste Legislation*, COM(2018) 32 final, at 2.

(2) substituting substances of concern and, where this is not possible reducing their presence and improving their tracking.

The Action Plan is stating that the Commission must emphasise circular economic aspects in future product design requirements under the Eco-design Framework Directive,[1039] the objective of which is to improve the efficiency and environmental performance of energy-related products taking also criteria related to reparability, durability, upgradability, recyclability, or the identification of certain materials or substances into systematically examination.[1040] On 22 May 2018, the 'Circular Economy Package' was published as an amendment of several waste directives with effect from 3 July 2018. The interplay in the 2009 RES Directive[1041] between instruments that support the utilisation of waste resources and ensure savings in the use of fossil fuels with a focus on the life cycle-wide environmental impact (LCA), avoiding unnecessary resource use, is an important aspect in a regulation based on the concept of resource efficiency and an important part of the circular economy concept. The Directive promotes energy from waste, landfill gas, sewage plants, biofuels and biogas. The Communication on Bio-waste Management[1042] proposes further action and notably the production of a guideline on bio-waste prevention and on applying life cycle thinking to bio-waste management. The 'Bio-economic Strategy' presented is also focusing on resource efficiency.[1043]

§2. Waste Framework Rules and Rules on Specific Waste Types

145. The Waste Thematic Strategy from December 2005 was accompanied by a proposal to revise the first Waste Framework Directive.[1044] The second Waste Framework Directive[1045] – that replaced the first version of the Directive – provides a common definition of waste and calls on the national authorities to take the necessary measures to ensure that waste is prevented, reused, recycled, utilised or disposed of without environmental or health risks and many other general provisions.

The Waste Framework Directive modernises the concept of 'waste' to encourage a life cycle approach, for example by clarifying the distinction between waste and 'by-products', introducing 'end-of-waste criteria' and improving the resource efficiency. On 12 December 2010, it was adapted. It establishes a framework for the

1039. European Parliament and Council Directive 2009/125/EC establishing a Framework for the Setting of Eco-design Requirements for Energy-related Products.
1040. COM(2015) 614 final, p. 4.
1041. *See infra* para. 228 for the description of European Parliament and Council Directive 2009/28/EC on the Promotion of Energy from Renewable Sources, as amended and replaced with effect from 2018 by the 2018 RES Directive.
1042. COM(2010) 235 final.
1043. COM(2012) 60 final.
1044. Council Directive 75/442/EEC on Waste, as this first version of the Directive was amended and codified by European Parliament and Council Directive 2006/12/EC on Waste. The second Waste Framework Directive repealed the first Framework Waste Directive (2006/12/EC), the Hazardous Waste Directive (91/689/EC) and the Waste Oil Directive (75/439/EC).
1045. European Parliament and Council Directive 2008/98/EC on Waste.

management of waste across the EU. The subject matter, the scope of, and the definitions and concepts used in the Directive were changed in 2018 as part of the 'Circular Economy Package'.[1046] The new wording of Article 1 on the objective of the Directive is:

> lays down measures to protect the environment and human health by preventing or reducing the generation of waste, the adverse impacts of the generation and management of waste and by reducing overall impacts of resource use and improve efficiency of such use, which are crucial for the transition to a circular economy and for guaranteeing the Union's long-term competitiveness.

In Article 3, no. 1, the definition of 'waste' is given as:

> any substance or object, which the holder discards or intends or is required to discard.

This is the same unclear definition of waste that was used in the first framework directive. The different categories of waste are listed and defined in the 2018 revised content of Article 3 – covering: 'hazardous waste' (no. 2); 'non-hazardous waste (no. 2a); 'municipal waste' (no. 2b); 'construction waste' (no. 2c); 'waste oils' (no. 3); 'bio-waste (no. 4), and 'food waste' (no. 4a). The Directive also sets other basic concepts and definitions relating to waste management, such as reuse, recycling, recovery and disposal. It explains when waste ceases to be waste and becomes a secondary raw material based on the 'end-of-waste' criteria, and how to distinguish between waste and by-products. The waste hierarchy under the Directive is as follows: it favours the prevention of waste, followed by reuse and then recycling, with disposal being the last resort. More detailed measures concerning waste are, in descending priority: (a) reduction in the volume of waste based on the use of cleaner technology; (b) waste sorting; (c) preparing reuse; (d) recycling; (e) other recovery, e.g., energy recovery; and (f), as the last resort, disposal. Thus, preventive measures have a higher priority than curative measures. Member States shall as a minimum take the measures mentioned in Articles 9–11 – as these articles were amended in 2018 – to prevent waste generation and to ensure that waste undergoes preparation for reuse, recycling and other recovery operations. These new rules add three new targets that increase the national obligation. The targets for the municipal waste by weight of preparation for reuse and the recycling are: 55% by 2025; 60% by 2030; and 65% by 2035, cf. Article 11(2) letter ii), sections c)–e). Article 11b of the revised Directive introduces a system of early warning reports to access Member States' progress towards these targets three years ahead of the respective deadlines. Member States shall ensure that bio-waste is either separated and recycled at source or is collected separately and is not mixed with other types of waste by December

1046. European Parliament and Council Directive 2018/851/EU amending Directive 2008/98/EC on Waste. The amending rules came into force 3 Jul. 2018.

2023, cf. Article 22. By January 2025, Member States shall set up separate collection for hazardous waste fractions produced by households to ensure that they are treated in accordance with the Directive and do not contaminate other municipal waste streams, cf. Article 20.

To limit the scope of the concept of waste the CJEU has by its case law introduced the criteria for the acceptance of by-products already under the first framework directive.[1047] Based on settled EU law as it has been developed by the Court, the by-products have to be an integral part of the production process, [1048] and the reasoning applicable to by-products should be confined to situations in which the reuse of the goods, materials or mineral resources is not a mere possibility but a certainty, within any further processing prior to reuse.[1049] In the revised Article 5(1) of the Directive, it is now stated that the Member States must take appropriate measures to ensure that 'by-products' are considered not to be waste, if the materials are in harmony with the criteria described by the Commission using the delegated power stated in Article 5(2). The revised Article 6 recognises the increasing importance of waste recovery by the obligations for the Member States to take appropriate measures to ensure that waste which has undergone a recycling or other recovery operations is considered to have ceased to be waste if it complies with the conditions stated in the Article ('end-of-waste'). Based on Article 6(2), the Commission shall monitor the development of national end-of-waste criteria and access the need to develop Union-based criteria on this basis.

The full costs of providing waste management services are substantial. The operators directly responsible for the provision of waste management facilities and services are obliged to move towards a position where their services recover the full costs of the services provided as the Directive is based on the 'polluter pays principle'. There are two broad ways of recovering the costs: (a) general fees paid directly or indirectly by the users of a specific service; and (b) earmarked fees on specific products (product charges) or activities, and where the revenues are earmarked for expenditure on waste management-related purposes such as to finance the take-back services and the waste-recycling facilities.[1050] Article 8 sets some principles regarding the implementation of the 'EPR' by the Member States. This principle is stating that preventive waste policy must begin with the economic agent who can play a decisive role in avoiding waste pollution, e.g., through design efforts. The operator has the responsibility to the post-consumer stage of the product life cycle.[1051] Compared to the traditional solid waste management approach, EPR involves a shift in responsibility from the public authorities to the entities that make and market the products that are destined to become waste. To this extent, the EPR constitutes the implementation of the 'polluter pays principle', but it induces

1047. *See, e.g.,* C-9/00 *Palin Granit Oy* in which the CJEU stated that there is no reason to hold that the provisions of the Directive, which are intended to regulate the disposal or recovery of waste, apply to goods, materials, or mineral resources, which have an economic value as products regardless of any form of processing and which, as such, are subject to the legislation applicable to those products (para. 35).

1048. C-9/00 *Palin Granit Oy*, paras 34 and 37.

1049. C-9/00 *Palin Granit Oy*, para. 36.

1050. Concerning the Danish use of economic and fiscal instruments, *see supra* paras 12–13.

1051. OECD, *Extended Producer Responsibility: A Guidance Manual for Governments*, 2001, at 164.

a change in the definition of the polluter. The economic agent who can play a decisive role in avoiding pollution through eco-design efforts is in this concept the polluter. The EPR aims at internalising environmental externalities providing an incentive to take into account environmental considerations in the design of the products. It is also a major instrument in support of the implementation of the waste hierarchy. In practice, EPR implies that producers take over the responsibility for collection of waste or taking back used goods. The producers also take over the responsibility for sorting, treating and eventual recycling. A study made for the EU shows that EPR policies have been designed and implemented in a very heterogeneous manner across the Member States.[1052] As a consequence of this problem with the inconsistent implementation of the minimum requirements for EPR, schemes are now included in the Directive, cf. Article 8a.

146. The Sewage Sludge Directive[1053] is one of the daughter priorities. The Packaging and Packaging Waste Directive[1054] and the Directive on Management of Waste from Extractive Industries[1055] (hereinafter 'the Mining Waste Directive') are other daughter directives covering waste categories that are not hazardous waste. These directives supplement the general waste management provisions laid down in the Waste Framework Directive.[1056]

The main aims of the Sewage Sludge Directive are to regulate the use of sewage sludge in agriculture in order to prevent harmful effects on soil, vegetation, animals and humans, and to encourage the correct use of sewage sludge. The Directive requires Member States to apply maximum emission limit values for certain metals, both in the sewage sludge and in the soil to which it is applied, to pre-treated sludge and to restrict its use on certain soils.[1057] The Packaging and Packaging Waste Directive[1058] includes requirements that are supplemented by harmonised standards based on the 'New Approach'. Thus, Annex II of the Directive lays down the 'essential requirements', which all packaging placed on the market within the EU must comply with. Waste from extraction, treatment and storage of mineral resources and the working of quarries are covered by the Mining Waste Directive.[1059] Such extractive waste must be managed in specialised facilities in compliance with specific rules on the location of the facility, the physical stability in respect of protection of soil, air and water against pollution, monitoring and inspection activities and

1052. Commission, *Development of Guidance on Extended Producer Responsibility (EPR)*, 2014.
1053. Council Directive 86/278/EC on the Protection of the Environment, especially of the Soil, when Sewage Sludge is used in Agriculture.
1054. European Parliament and Council Directive 94/62/EC on Packaging and Packaging Waste, as amended as part of the Circular Economy Strategy by the European Parliament and Council Directive 2018/852/EU.
1055. European Parliament and Council Directive 2006/21/EC on the Management of Waste from Extractive Industries (also titled the Mining Waste Directive).
1056. Concerning the use of such rules on special categories of waste, *see infra* paras 150–152, 154 and 156–.
1057. Concerning the Danish implementation of the Directive on Sewage Sludge, *see infra* para. 172.
1058. European Parliament and Council Directive 94/62/EC on Packaging and Packaging Waste, as amended.
1059. European Parliament and Council Directive 2006/21/EC on the Management of Waste from Extraction Industries.

arrangements for the closure of the facility, the rehabilitee of the land and the after-closure phase. According to the Directive, no management installation of extractive industries can operate without a permit from the competent authority. Operators of facilities presenting a potential risk for public health or for the environment must draw up a policy for prevention of a major accident, safety management systems and an internal safety plan. Strict environmental liability is applied in situations in which damages are caused by extractive waste activities.[1060]

147. In relation to the Danish waste policy, the first action plan was the 'Action Plan for Recycling 1987-89', which gave the highest priority in the 'waste hierarchy' to reuse and recycling. This plan was in 1992 followed by the 'Action Plan for Waste and Recycling for 1993-1997'. The next action plan called 'Waste 21' was accepted by the Parliament on 28 January 1999. It was presented to the Danish Parliament by the Government and accepted in 1999. In the plan, a description was given of the steps to be taken in order to reduce waste quantities considerably and to ensure the utilisation of the resources in the waste. The strategy indicated a large number of measures, including increased source separation, more focus on the products, focus on commercial and industrial waste, increased quality of waste treatment, etc. It named ways for a more consistent waste practice of enterprises and households. In 2004, the 'Danish Waste Strategy' for the period of 2005–2008 followed. The aim of the mentioned strategies was to prevent and control pollution, e.g., by banning certain types of non-returnable packaging and the use of particular substances and materials which may pose special waste disposal problems. The last-mentioned strategy was based on three fundamental elements: (1) the prevention of loss of resources and harm to the environment caused by waste; (2) the disconnection of waste generation from economic growth; (3) the ambition to achieve cost-effective solutions in its environmental activities through better waste treatment and an efficient waste sector. The next 'Danish Waste Strategy 2009-2012' aimed to ensure at least 65% recycling of the total waste and to reduce the total waste to landfill to 6% in 2012. The first part of the Danish waste strategy was published in November 2013 with the 'Denmark Without Waste. Recycle more – Incinerate Less', and it was followed in November 2015 by 'Denmark Without Waste. A Waste Prevention Strategy'. The ambition behind the Danish strategy is to increase the recycling of household waste from 22% to 50% in 2022. It outlines six initiatives on:

(1) more recycling of materials from households and the service sector;
(2) more recycling of materials from waste electric equipment and shedder waste;
(3) better exploitation of important nutrients such as phosphorus;
(4) improved quality in recycling construction and demolition waste;
(5) priority to bio-gasification and recycling of waste as alternatives to incineration of waste;
(6) promotion of green conversion ensuring new commercial opportunities.

1060. Concerning the Environmental Liability Directive, as amended, e.g., by the Mining Waste Directive, *see infra* para. 336.

The just-mentioned two strategies are still describing the Danish policy. A new Danish waste strategy will not be published until 2020. The Ministry of Environment and Food of Denmark wants to know the content of the new amendments to the EU's waste directives better before making the next updated waste strategy.[1061] In a report from the European Environmental Agency on prevention of hazardous waste, it is mentioned that Denmark aims to make it easier for consumers to have products and services that require fewer resources, contain fewer substances and generate less waste.[1062] On 11 October 2018, a political agreement on 'Circular Economy' was signed by the former liberal-conservative coalition government, the Danish People Party and the Social-Liberal Party.[1063]

148. The implementation of EU's waste rules into Danish legislation is part of the Environmental Protection Act.[1064] The transformation of the EU waste legislation has been a very long process, as the acceptance of waste as a 'commodity' in the internal market first became the relevant approach in the Danish rules from 2010. The liberal-conservative government that was in power in the period 2001–2011 stated that it wanted to let market-based principles be stronger in the waste management sector.[1065] A Waste Committee presented a proposal for a new organisation structure in the waste sector in 2004 to ensure a more efficient and cost-effective waste management sector, with a high environmental profile. In July 2009, it resulted in a change of the sector by means of the Act on a 'New Organisation of the Waste Sector'.[1066] The Mineral Resources Act,[1067] the Environmental Protection Act and the Marine Environmental Protection Act implemented the Mining Waste Directive[1068] by rules on planning and public hearing (section 6a) and by rules on application and after-treatment, cf. sections 6 and 7 of the Mineral Resources Act.[1069] In September 2011, the Commission started a process against Denmark for its failing to implement the mentioned Directive.[1070] The Danish Government in power would not accept that soil resulting from the extraction of mineral resources has to be handled as waste. On 9 March 2015, Denmark received the next letter from the Commission in this case. The correct implementation was not ensured until the Parliament in 2016 passed some amendments to the Environmental Protection Act.[1071]

The provisions on waste treatment are laid down in Chapter 6 of the Environmental Protection Act. Pursuant to section 45 of the Act, the municipal councils

1061. In July 2018, the amendments to the waste directives were pasted.
1062. EEA, *Prevention of Hazardous Waste in Europe – The Status in 2015*, Report No. 35/2016, at 33.
1063. Concerning the coalition government that was in power in 2018, *see supra* para. 4.
1064. Promulgation Order No. 681 of 2 July 2019 on Environmental Protection.
1065. Danish Government, *Making Markets Work for Environmental Policies. Achieving Cost-effective Solutions,* at 8.
1066. Act No. 513 of 12 June 2009 on a New Organisation of the Waste Sector (amending the Environmental Protection Act).
1067. Promulgation Order No. 124 of 21 January 2017 on Mineral Resources, as amended.
1068. European Parliament and Council Directive 2006/21/EC on the Management of Waste from Extraction Industries.
1069. Concerning the Mineral Resources Act, *see infra* paras 291–293.
1070. The process was started by Commission letter No. 2011/2056.
1071. The amending Act is No. 457 of 25 May 2016 on Rural Considerations and Public Participation.

have, with regard to household waste, industrial waste and construction waste, laid down some local rules (local council waste by-laws) governing the local waste schemes, including schemes for collection of different waste categories that are disposed of in different ways. The more detailed rules are laid down in the Statutory Order on Waste.[1072] The Order includes general provisions requiring households to use the public-owned waste plants, rules on waste treatment, waste planning (including public participation), waste storage and disposal of all waste, and leaves the management to the municipalities. The municipal councils must establish local by-laws on the management of household waste. They are also responsible for the collection and delivery schemes for polluted soil and other sorts of household waste, cf. section 44 of the Act. The schemes must include industrial enterprises as well as private households. The local rules and the decisions made by the authorities are not subjected to administrative appeal. The municipal council, by itself or through a contractor, is responsible for the collection of waste, cf. section 45(1) of the Act. As regards the collection of waste, the municipal councils, which are responsible for the setting up of schemes for the collection of waste, have to a large degree left it to private undertakings to operate the collection of waste on the basis of tenders. These enterprises may be of any kind: public companies, mixed companies or entirely private companies. The competences of the municipality remain an important part of the responsibility for the collection of waste. It is also possible for private companies to take part in the collection of waste. Such actors have to respect the rules laid down in the Statutory Order on the Waste Register and on Approval as a Collecting Company.[1073] Foreign waste conveyors, brokers and dealers must be registered in the Danish National Waste Register, before they work with waste in Denmark. The Order lays down rules on the reporting duties and also on the notification of the municipal council and of the EPA. Waste treatment enterprises are also obliged to provide information at the request of the authorities. The primarily responsibility for the supervision of waste rests with the municipal councils, cf. section 46(1) of the Act. The municipal councils are required to prepare a special plan for the disposal of waste within the local area. The plan must contain information about: existing and planned schemes for collection, transport, different forms of treatment and final disposal of the waste; delimitation of the areas from which the waste is carried to the individual treatment and deposit plants; the objectives of the distribution of the waste by means of various treatment and disposal methods; time limits for the introduction of the various schemes that are planned; and costs and financing in connection with implementation of the plan, cf. section 47(2) of the Act. Waste planning must not conflict with municipal spatial planning.[1074] The planning process is based on public participation, and it can be divided into three main phases: mapping, index of ideas, final waste plan and implementation of the plan.

1072. Statutory Order No. 224 of 8 March 2019 on Waste.
1073. Statutory Order No. 896 of 29 June 2017 on the Waste Register and on Approval as a Collecting Company.
1074. Concerning the municipal plans, *see infra* paras 313–318.

§3. Hazardous Waste

149. The EU hazardous waste rules were originally laid down in the Directive on Hazardous Waste[1075] covering chemical waste, oil waste, hazardous waste from hospitals, sludge from industrial undertakings and other toxic wastes listed as such. Also, the Directives on Waste from the Titanium Dioxide Industry[1076] aimed to prevent and progressively reduce pollution caused by waste from the titanium dioxide industry. The rules are now included in the Waste Framework Directive.

The Waste Framework Directive states that the classification of waste as hazardous should be based, *inter alia*, on the EU legislation on chemicals, in particular concerning the classification of preparations as hazardous, including concentration limit values used for that purpose.[1077] Hazardous waste means waste that displays one or more of the hazardous properties listed in Annex III, cf. Article 3, no. 2. Annex III includes a list of properties of waste, which render it hazardous. With a Decision of 18 December 2014, the Commission replaced it with a new Annex III. Hazardous waste is a small waste stream (less that 4% of total waste) covered by the rules of the Waste Framework Directive. The hazardous waste that poses a greater risk to human health and environment compared with other waste categories is covered by special rules on labelling, record keeping, monitoring, and control laid down in the Waste Framework Directive.[1078]

150. There are some special priority substances that are covered by daughter directives, e.g., the End-of-life Vehicles Directive (ELVs Directive),[1079] the Waste Battery Directive,[1080] the Directive on Waste Electrical and Electronic Equipment (the WEEE II Directive)[1081] and the RoHS Recast Directive (RoHS 2).[1082] The

1075. The first Directive was Council Directive 78/319/EEC on Toxic and Dangerous Waste. The next was Council Directive 91/689/EEC on Hazardous Waste.
1076. Council Directive 78/176/EEC on Waste from the Titanium Dioxide Industry, Council Directive 82/883/EEC on the Procedures for the Surveillance and Monitoring of Environments concerned by Waste from the Titanium Dioxide Industry, and Council Directive 92/112/EEC on the Procedures for Harmonizing the Programmes for the Reduction and eventual Elimination of Pollution caused by waste from the Titanium Industry.
1077. The EU approach to hazardous waste is based on a horizontal harmonisation with the legislation on chemicals. Therefore, hazardous waste in the EU and its Member States is not defined by the Basel Convention. Concerning this Convention, *see supra* para. 140.
1078. Article 17 (concerning control), Art. 18 (ban on mixing of hazardous waste), Art. 19 (labelling of hazardous waste) and Art. 20 (concerning hazardous waste produced by households). Concerning the special hazardous waste categories, *see infra* para. 149–153.
1079. European Parliament and Council Directive 2000/53/EC on End-life Vehicles, as amended as part of the Circular Economy Strategy by European Parliament and Council Directive 2018/849/EU.
1080. European Parliament and Council Directive 2006/66/EC on Batteries and Accumulators and Waste Batteries and Accumulators, as amended as part of the Circular Economy Strategy by European Parliament and Council Directive 2018/849/EU.
1081. European Parliament and Council Directive 2012/19/EU on Waste from Electronic and Electronic Equipment, as amended as part of the Circular Economy Strategy by European Parliament and Council Directive 2018/849/EU.
1082. European Parliament and Council Directive 2011/65/EU on the Restriction of the Use of certain Hazardous Substances in Electrical and Electronic Equipment, as amended by the Commission Delegating Directive 2015/65/EU as regards the List of Restricted Substances.

Directive on the Disposal of PCBs and PCTs[1083] is also one of these daughter directives of the WFD regulating hazardous waste.

The Directive on the Disposal of PCBs and PCTs aims to harmonise laws on the controlled disposal of PCBs and on the decontamination or disposal of equipment containing PCBs with the ambition to eliminate them completely. Equipment containing PCBs must be labelled and reported to the Commission, and the disposal of PCBs must be permitted and carried out in accordance with the conditions and plans made by the national authorities in accordance with the requirements of the Directive. The REACH Regulation and the CLP Regulation supplement this protection with a qualitative prevention of harmful substances.

The first version of the Electrical and Electronic Equipment Directive (WEEE Directive) has contributed to reducing hazardous substances contained in new EEE, hazardous substances such as mercury, cadmium, lead, hexavalent chromium and PCBs and ODS. It requires separate collection and reuse of WEEE. The Member States have to take measures to encourage the design of electrical/electronic products in such a way to consider and facilitate dismantling, recovery and recycling of WEEE. They have to ensure the set-up of a collection scheme. In addition, the producers are covered by the EPR principle. The current WEEE Directive[1084] replaced it on 15 February 2014. This environmental directive is based on Article 192(2) TFEU, and it covers all EEE used by consumers and EEE intended for professional use. The purpose of the Directive is to contribute to sustainable production and consumption by, as a first priority, the prevention of WEEE and, in addition, by the reuse, recycling and other forms of recovery of such waste so as to reduce the disposal and to contribute to the efficient use of resources and the retrieval of valuable secondary mineral resources. It also seeks to improve the environmental performance of all operators involved in the life cycle of EEE, e.g., producers, distributors, consumers and, in particular, those operators directly involved in the collection and treatment of WEEE. The term 'producer' means:

> any natural or legal person who, irrespective of the selling technique, including distance communication, established in a Member State, manufactures EEE under his or her name or trademark or has EEE designed or manufactured and markets it under his or her own name or trademark.

The person selling EEE by means of distance communication is also a producer. The best available treatment, recovery and recycling technologies should be used, provided that they ensure human health and a high level of environmental protection. Since 2016, each Member State has been required to meet a collection target of 45% of electric and electronic equipment sold. From 2019 that target is 65% of equipment sold or as an alternative 85% of electric waste generated annually. The WEEE Directive was amended 30 May 2018[1085] to ensure, with effect from 5 July

1083. Council Directive 96/59/EC on the Disposal of PCB and PCT.
1084. European Parliament and Council Directive 2012/19/EU.
1085. Amended by European Parliament and Council Directive 2018/849/EU.

2020, reporting obligations on Member States as well as their use of economic instruments and other measures to provide incentives for the application of a waste hierarchy.

The Recast Directive on Restriction of the Use of Certain Hazardous Substances in Electrical and Electronic Equipment (RoSH 2)[1086] is a quality waste prevention directive regulating hazardous waste as the second version that became effective on 3 January 2013.[1087] It is based on the Treaty's rule on the Internal Market, cf. Article 114 TFEU and it aims to contribute to the protection of human health and environment, sound recovery and disposal of waste by means of restrictions on the use of hazardous substances in new electrical and electronic equipment put on the market. The products must not contain lead, mercury, cadmium, hexavalent chromium, polybrominated biphenyls (PBB) or polybrominated diphenyl ethers (PBDE). It applies to the EEE falling within the categories mentioned in its Annex I. On 12 June 2019 the Member States shall bring into force national law that complies with the above-mentioned amendments.

151. The Waste Battery Directive[1088] prohibits the placing on the market of certain batteries and accumulators with a proportional mercury or cadmium content above a fixed threshold. The Directive seeks to improve the environmental performance of batteries and accumulators as well as the environmental performance of the activities of economic actors involved in the life cycle of batteries and accumulators. The Member States have to ensure efficient organisation of separate systems and, where appropriate, consider the use of economic instruments to encourage recycling. This system must ensure the maximisation of separate waste collection and the minimisation of disposal.[1089]

Member States shall monitor collection rates on a yearly basis according to the scheme set out in Annex I of this Directive. There is also an obligation to report on the levels of recycling achieved in each calendar year and whether the recycling efficiencies referred to in Annex III, Part B have been met.[1090] The Danish rules on the obligations to ensure recycling and reuse of waste from batteries and accumulators are laid down in section 9u, 9v, 9w, 9z and 9ø of the Environmental protection Act and the Statutory Order on Batteries and Accumulators and Waste from Batteries and Accumulators.[1091]

152. The ELV Directive[1092] restricts the use of heavy metals and sets recovery/ recycling targets. The ELV Directive aims to reduce the random disposal of such

1086. European Parliament and Council Directive 2011/65/EC, as amended by Directive 2017/2102/ EU.
1087. It was replacing European Parliament and Council Directive 2002/95/EC on the Restriction of the Use of certain hazardous Substances in Electric and Electronic Equipment.
1088. European Parliament and Council Directive 2006/66/EC on Batteries and Accumulators and Waste Batteries and Accumulators, as amended by Directive 2018/849/EU.
1089. Concerning the Danish use of economic instruments, *see supra* paras 11–13.
1090. Concerning examples on recycling, *see infra* paras 154–160.
1091. Statutory Order No. 1453 of 7 December 2015 on Batteries and Accumulators and Waste from Batteries and Accumulators.
1092. European Parliament and Council Directive 2000/53/EC on End-of Life Vehicles, as amended by Directive 2018/849/EU.

waste resources and to promote the Internal Market for such materials by demanding Member States to ensure that the end-of-life vehicles (ELVs) are traded by specifically authorised undertakings, and that certificates issued by such undertakings are mutually recognised throughout the Internal Market.

The Member States have to establish rules on the obligations for the operators to set up collection and treatment systems at no expense to the consumers. The storage and treatment of the ELVs are subject to strict control in accordance with the requirements of the Directive. The Directive on Motor Vehicle Type Approval regarding the reusability, recyclability and the recovery of motor vehicles is dealing with a type approval system supplementing the system established by the ELV Directive.[1093] The ELV Directive is implemented by the Danish Act on Environmental Subsidies on Re-use of Parts of Vehicles[1094] and the supplementary administrative provisions laid down in the Statutory Order on Treatment of Waste from Vehicles, etc.[1095] and Statutory Order on Fees and Subsidies in connection with Re-use of Parts of Vehicles.[1096]

153. The Danish rules on hazardous waste are following the international and EU rules. The conditions are laid down in the Environmental Protection Act and the general Statutory Order on Waste covering rules on notification, labelling, classification, registration, the duty to use the public-owned plants, etc.[1097]

The former Statutory Order on Waste was amended in 2015 to ensure a classification of the hazardous waste in harmony with the EWC.[1098] Companies have to inform the municipal councils when they produce oil or chemical waste or when such waste appears. The municipal councils direct the refuse collection or discharge systems that are not covered by special take-back schemes. The most important recipient company is Fortum Denmark. Companies must deliver their oil and chemical waste to the places designated by the municipal councils. The councils may lay down more detailed guidelines in the form of municipal by-laws to ensure that oil and chemical waste is stored and transported. The delivery obligation in relation to oil and chemical waste is not subject to a minimum quantity. The councils may allow a company not to deliver oil and chemical waste to the publicly appointed waste treatment plant if it is able to dispose of its waste by means of another acceptable method. Such permission may be granted, for instance, if the enterprise delivers its waste directly to a recycling plant. Furthermore, the local councils have powers of intervention. If pollution is caused during the storage, transport or disposal of oil or chemical waste, the municipal councils may, finally, issue orders concerning the elimination of the pollution at the expense of the responsible operator, cf. section 43 of the Environmental Protection Act. National Association of Local

---

1093. Concerning recycling of waste, *see infra* para. 154.
1094. Promulgation Order No. 224 of 6 March 2017 on Environmental Subsidies on Re-use of Parts of Vehicles.
1095. Statutory Order No. 1312 of 19 December 2012 on Treatment of Waste from Vehicles, etc.
1096. Statutory Order No. 618 of 28 May 2018 on Fees and Subsidies in connection with Re-use of Parts of Vehicles.
1097. Those instruments are established by Chapter 10 (ss 52–57) of the Statutory Order No. 224 of 8 March 2019 on Waste. Concerning the Danish implementation, *see supra* para. 148.
1098. This 2015 version of the rules was Statutory Order No. 715 of 13 May 2015 on Waste.

Authorities, the Fortum Denmark, and the EPA have set up a computerised register of enterprises generating oil and other hazardous waste.

§4. Recycling and Waste-to-Energy Utilisation

154. In the 'Handbook of National Counting: Integrated Environmental and Economic Accounting' published by the UN, EU, IMF, OECD and the World Bank, the definition of 'recycling' is the following:[1099]

> the re-introduction of residual materials into production processes so that they may be reformulated into new products.

The preparation for reuse, recovery and recycling of waste equipment and the substances, mixture or components thereof should be in accordance with the relevant legislation. Special EU secondary legislation that is part of the climate change law and relevant to mention is the Regulation on Substances that Deplete the Ozone Layer (ODS Regulation)[1100] that is an implementation of obligations under the Vienna Convention for the Protection of the Ozone Layer and the Montreal Protocol on Substances that Deplete the Ozone Layer as well as the Regulation on Certain Fluorinated Greenhouse Gases that is part of the EU's fulfilment of its obligations under the UNFCCC.[1101] Article 9 of the last-mentioned Regulation makes it mandatory for the Member States to establish producer responsibility schemes for the reuse of equipment that contains F-gases.

The general rules are laid down in the Waste Framework Directive. Recycling is explained in Article 3(17) as any recovery operation by which waste materials are reprocessed into products, materials or substances whether for the original or other purposes. It includes the reprocessing of organic material but do not include energy recovery and the reprocessing into materials that are to be used as fuels or for backfilling operations. Recycling is the third highest management tool in the waste hierarchy, cf. Article 4(1). The 2018 amendment of the Directive sets the following targets for the national preparation for reuse/recycling:[1102]

- 50% target for municipal waste;
- 70% target for construction and demolition waste.

1099. United Nations, European Commission, International monetary Fund, OECD, World Bank, *Handbook of National Accounting: integrated Environmental and Economic Accounting 2003, Studies in Methods*, Series F, No. 61, Rev. 1, Glossary, United Nations, New York, para. 3.51.
1100. European Parliament and Council Regulation No. 1005/2009/EC on Substances that Deplete the Ozone Layer.
1101. European Parliament and Council Regulation No. 517/2014/EU on Certain Fluorinated Greenhouse Gases.
1102. Commission, *Report on the Implementation of EU Waste Legislation*, COM(2018) 656 final, at 2–4.

Innovation in product design to avoid hazardous waste and other categories of waste is an important part of resource-efficient economy. There are minimum standards for recycling activities and recycled materials set across the EU in order to ensure the proper functioning of the internal market for recycling. Examples in EU waste law on daughter directives with a focus on recycling are to be seen in the Packaging and Packaging Waste Directive, the ELV Directive[1103] and the Directive on Motor Vehicle Type Approval regarding the reusability, recyclability and the recovery of motor vehicles[1104] facilitating the processing and reduction of waste from motor vehicles. Member States cannot grant EU type approval and national type approval to vehicles that do not comply with the requirements of the last-mentioned Directive. The minimum thresholds for recycling and recovery of components and materials for new vehicles are set out in Article 7(4) of the Directive. The essential requirements laid down in the Packaging and Packaging Waste Directive[1105] state e.g., that packaging must be manufactured in such a way that the packaging volume and weight are limited to the minimum adequate amount to maintain the necessary level of safety, hygiene and acceptance for the packed product and for its consumer. The essential requirements in the Packaging and Packaging Waste Directive have been translated into standards. The Commission mandated the European Committee for Standardisation (CEN) to draw up a set of CEN-standards and reports that are 'useful for the application of the Directive'. The current CEN standards are:

- CEN EN 13427:2004 Requirements for the use of European standards in the field of packaging and packaging waste.
- CEN EN 13428:2004 Requirements specific to manufacturing and composition – prevention by source reduction.
- CEN EN 13429:2004 Reuse.
- CEN EN 13430:2004 Requirements for packaging recoverable by material recycling.
- CEN EN 13431:2004 Requirements for packaging recoverable in the form of energy recovery.
- CEN EN 13432:2004 Requirements for packaging recoverable through composting and bio gradable – test scheme and evaluation criteria for the final acceptance of packaging.

Product design requirements laid down in the above-mentioned packaging and packaging waste rules have an impact not only on the composition of products in the use phase, but also in the waste phase and end-of-waste phase.[1106]

1103. Concerning the ELV Directive, *see supra* para. 152.

1104. European Parliament and Council Directive 2007/46/EC on Motor Vehicle Type Approval regarding the Reusability, Recyclability and the Recovery of Motor Vehicles, as amended several times – the consolidated version was published on 31 Mar. 2018.

1105. European Parliament and Council Directive 94/62/EC on Packaging and Packaging Waste, as amended.

1106. Some of these waste categories are hazardous waste, *see infra* paras 149–152.

155. In Chapter 7 of the Danish Environmental Protection Act, the term 'recycling of waste' is used – not the term 're-utilisation of waste'. The rules supplement the general waste rules in Chapter 6 and the specific product-related rules on collection, deposits, take-back obligations and deposits-return systems in section 9a–9å. The former Statutory Order on Waste was amended in 2014 to ensure the rights of the producers to establish a take-back scheme,[1107] and again in 2016 to ensure the adaptive climate-correction factor in the categorisation of the recovery of waste under Annex I, R1 concerning waste used principally as a fuel or other means to generate energy.[1108]

The first part of the 'Danish Waste Strategy 2009-2012' included the overall prioritisation, targets set for the recycling and disposal of waste, a strategy towards littering and a capacity plan for waste incineration. The second part of the strategy – 'Waste Strategy 10' – was issued in June 2010 and introduced a five-point waste hierarchy. The current Danish Waste Strategy 'Denmark without waste'[1109] includes measures to improve the recycling of phosphate in sewage sludge, and critical mineral resources found in e-waste. The strategy includes a target for the recycling rates of different materials from municipality waste – including paper, cardboard, glass, metal, plastic, bio-waste and wood. Deposit refund schemes entail the application of a surcharge or deposit on certain products, where a partial or total refund may be made when specific conditions are present. The municipalities are required to set up collection schemes for paper and other waste fractions not covered by private deposit-return systems. Collection systems for some types of waste, such as batteries, bottles, paper, electrical and electronic equipment etc., are based on sorting at source, and both households and enterprises use and support these systems. This involves end-users and consumers in the waste management chain and makes them more aware of the necessity and the ways to decrease the generation of waste. The by-laws must include rules on where to bring waste products for reuse. Agreements with the stakeholders have been used in Denmark to achieve objectives in relation to take-back schemes related to some waste categories.[1110] Under the terms of the agreements, retailers are obliged to accept the take-back products that they had processed. The agreements are supplemented by statutory orders. Some agreements have been replaced by statutory orders to ensure a correct implementation of the EU directives.

156. With respect to implementation of the Packaging Waste Directive, the most important Danish rules are to be found in an amendment to the Environmental Protection Act, the Statutory Order on Waste[1111] and the Statutory Order on Certain

1107. Statutory Order No. 422 of 10 April 2014 amending the Statutory Order on Waste to establish the Basis for Private Tack Back Systems, and Statutory Order No. 1331 of 4 December 2014 amending the Statutory Order on Waste to establish the Basis for Private Tack Back Systems covering Packaging Waste.

1108. Statutory Order No. 600 of 30 May 2016 amending the Statutory Order on Waste Climate with a correction Factor for Calculating the R1 Factor on Waste-to-Energy Utilisation.

1109. *See* concerning 'Denmark without waste' strategy, *see supra* para. 147.

1110. Concerning the use of agreements and statutory orders, *see infra* paras 155–159.

1111. Concerning the Statutory Order on Waste, *see supra* para. 148.

Packaging Requirements.[1112] The costs for the management of packaging waste are included in the revenue from the municipality charges treatment that are paid by the users of the packaging.

In relation to the recycling of soft drinks and beer packaging, specific rules were earlier laid down in the Statutory Order on the Labelling of Reusable Packaging[1113] and the Statutory Order on Packaging for Beer and Refreshing Drinks.[1114] These rules were assessed by the CJEU in the Danish Bottle Case.[1115] The liberal-conservative Government that came into power in 2001 repealed these two statutory orders.[1116] The system, requiring manufactures and importers to market beer and soft drinks only in reusable containers, was in conflict with the rule in the EC Treaty on quantitative restrictions, cf. now Article 34 TFEU. Dansk Retursystem A/S has been given the exclusive right to operate the Danish deposit and return system on bottles and cans containing beer, carbonated soft drinks, energy drinks, mineral water, iced tea, ready-to-drink beverages and cider products, as approved by Statutory Order on Mortgage and Collection, etc., of Packages for Certain Beverages.[1117] It is a requirement that any packaging assigned or transferred must have an International Article Number (EAN) barcode and Global Trade Item Number. Importers and producers wishing to sell drink products covered by the Danish deposit and return system must register their packaging with the 'Dansk Retursystem A/S'. One precondition for selling a product in Denmark is that the seller is either a Danish producer or importer, or the seller has an agreement with a Danish importer about the product. Importers and producers registered with the Danish deposit and return system must charge a deposit on the package that they sell on the Danish market. The companies must also pay fees to the 'Dansk Retursystem A/S'. Every year, the 'Dansk Retursystem A/S' sets the fee level, which is approved by the EPA. The fees charged and the actual overheads covered by the fee payments received are required to be in equilibrium over a six-year period. Before selling a product on the Danish market, importers and producers have a duty to label all one-way packaging with a deposit label. Deposit labels can only be purchased from the 'Dansk Retursystem A/S'. The correct deposit labels must be used on the packaging of beers and soft drinks to indicate that the full amount of taxes and customs, VAT payable for labelled containers, have been paid. The rules on enforcement of disposable packaging for beer and soft drinks were strengthened in 2005 by targeting restaurants and kiosks that were not complying with the rules on deposits needing to be paid for beverage containers. The rules are now included in the Statutory Order on Certain Packaging Requirements.[1118] This Order enables the Danish Custom and Tax Administration to confiscate cans and other non-returnable packaging for beer and soft drinks that do not have a label showing that a deposit has been

1112. Statutory Order No. 1455 of 7 December 2015 on Certain Packaging Requirements.
1113. Statutory Order No. 600 of 18 September 1987 on the Labelling of Reusable Packaging.
1114. Statutory Order No. 124 of 27 February 1989 on Packaging for Beer and Refreshing Drinks.
1115. C-302/86 *Commission v. Denmark*.
1116. Statutory Order No. 14 of 14 January 2002 on the Repeal of the Orders on Packaging for Beer and Soft Drinks.
1117. Statutory Order No. 357 of 29 March 2019 on Mortgage and Collection, etc., of Packages for Certain Beverages.
1118. Statutory Order No. 1455 of 10 December 2015 on Certain Packaging Requirements.

paid. In addition to seizure, dealers who break the deposit rules can be fined in criminal cases. Denmark is meeting the recycling targets set by the Packaging Directive.[1119]

157. In 1993, section 9a was added to the Environmental Protection Act to permit schemes whereby producers could recover used products and establish flexible collection and processing systems. Dansk Retursystem A/S handles the administration of the take-back schemes etc. It is a private non-profit organisation that has been given the exclusive right to operate the Danish deposit and return system. The more detailed rules are laid down in the Statutory Order on Waste.[1120]

The actual rules on Transport Packaging Waste Agreement, the Agreement on Plastic Soft Drink Bottles and the Agreement on Used Tires are based on the mentioned section of the Act. Importers and producers wishing to sell such products that are covered by the Danish deposit and return system must register their packaging with the 'Dansk Retursystem A/S'.

158. The Minister for the Environment signed the Agreement on Used Tires in February 1995. It concerns tires from motorcycles, private cars, commercial lorries and vans. The purpose of it was to increase the percentage of tires recycled within a five-year period, from the current 35% to 80%, to avoid the deposition of tires to landfills as well as to secure a resourceful utilisation of the materials, making recycling a priority over energy utilisation.

According to the agreement, the companies entering the scheme (as those responsible for the collection) took on their responsibility of collecting all used tires – including tires which the consumers delivered to the municipalities – as well as of making sure that there was sufficient capacity for re-gumming, material reuse and incineration. The firms selling tires are obliged to take a corresponding number of discharged tires back from the consumers without extra charge. A fee scheme became effective on 15 March 1995 established by Statutory Order. A fee of DKK 8 was paid for new tires and DKK 4 for used tires, upon purchase of such tires. An economic incentive to buy used tires was thereby established. The fee has been changed. The fee levels are now laid down in section 3 of the Statutory Order on the Use of Fees and Subsidies promoting the Re-use of Tires.[1121] The amount to be paid is now between DKK 10 and DKK 225. The fees are not imposed on tires that are exported, as the disposal of such tires does not contribute to the Danish environmental problems.

159. The implementation of WEEE I Directive[1122] was ensured by an amendment of the Environmental Protection Act[1123] by a new section 51(1), and by the supplementation of rules in the Statutory Order on the Management of Waste from

1119. Commission, *Report on the Implementation of EU Waste Legislation*, COM(2018) 656 final, at 7.
1120. Statutory Order No. 224 of 8 March 2019 on Waste.
1121. Statutory Order No. 1347 of 21 November 2016 on Fees and Subsidies to re-use of Tires.
1122. European Parliament and Council Directive 2002/96/EC on Waste from Electrical and Electrical Equipment (WEEE).
1123. Amended by Act No. 385 of 17 May 2005 on the Manufactures' Responsibility for Electric Scrap, etc.

Electronical and Electronic Equipment.[1124] The supplementing rules are now – as the implementation of the WEEE II Directive[1125] – laid down in the Statutory Order on Decree to place Electrical and Electronic Equipment on the Market and the Treatment of Waste from Electrical and Electronic Equipment.[1126]

Denmark has used the flexible agreements that were permitted already by Article 17(3) of the first WEEE Directive. 'Dansk Retursystem A/S' is the private actor who has the competence to ensure the implementation of the rules on producer responsibility.[1127] The collection of WEEE from households takes place largely through municipal collection schemes, i.e., either collection from people's homes or deliveries to municipal collection points. Producers have also established return arrangements, mainly in the form of voluntary collective take-back schemes. In 2015, Denmark collected 12 kg of household WEEE per person.[1128] WEEE from sources other than private homes is collected and processed pursuant to section 9j of the Environmental Protection Act. The rules are based on the principle that the producers are obliged to cover the costs of collecting, treating and disposing the WEEE. The basic principle is individual responsibility. When placing new products on the market, the producer must provide a financial guarantee to meet the future cost of managing waste from products. This can be achieved through a collective compliance scheme, insurance or a protected bank account. Producers may opt to fulfil their collection and return obligations partly via collective schemes and partly through individual programs. The financing arrangements for collective schemes involve a member's quota per producer and an environmental contribution depending on the type and quality of the electronic product placed on the market and registered in the collective scheme. The producer registration requires a financial security in the form of a guarantee on demand (i.e., a bank guarantee).

160. A waste-to-energy facility consists of the following main components: a reception and waste feeding system, one or more incineration units complete with bottom ash handling system boiler, flue gas treatment system and stack. If the facility is a combined heat and power plant (CHP plant) with a capacity above 25 MW, it has to be approved both in accordance with the Danish Electricity Supply Act[1129] and the Environmental Protection Act.[1130]

If the new plant's capacity is 25 MW or less, it has to be approved in accordance with the Heating Supply Act[1131] and the Environmental Protection Act. These waste-to-energy facilities have entered into binding agreements with the municipalities for treatment of the waste suitable for incineration generated in these

1124. Statutory Order No. 664 of 27 June 2005 on the Management of Waste from Electronical and Electronic Equipment.
1125. European Parliament and Council Directive 2012/19/EU, as amended by Directive 2018/849/EU.
1126. Statutory Order No. 148 of 8 February 2018 on Decree to place Electrical and Electronic Equipment on the Market and the Treatment of Waste from Electrical and Electronic Equipment.
1127. Concerning the implementation of the Packaging Waste Directive, *see supra* para. 156. The rules for these schemes are published on the internet, *see* https://www.dpa-system.dk/da/DPA (visited on 15 Jul. 2019).
1128. Commission, *Report on the Implementation of EU Waste Legislation*, COM(2018) 656 final, at 5.
1129. Promulgation Order No. 1009 of 27 June 2018 on Electricity Supply.
1130. Promulgation Order No. 1121 of 3 September 2018 on Environmental Protection.
1131. Promulgation Order No. 1211 of 9 October 2018 on Heating Supply.

municipalities acting as contractors for them.[1132] In 2014, more than 20% of all district heating and 5% of the electricity production in Denmark were based on waste as the energy resource. The slag from the incineration plants is sorted, and in this process iron and other metals are recovered. The sorted slag is recycled for construction works in accordance with the Statutory Order on the Utilisation of Soil and Sorted Waste from Building and Construction Activities[1133] that established the quality requirements for reuse of slag. There are also some incineration facilities where sewage sludge is used as alternative energy sources.

Biogas is an energy source that is normally generated on the basis of waste from agricultural activities (manure and organic wastes). It is the mix of CO_2 and the inflammable gas CH_4 that is produced by bacterial conversion of organic matter under anaerobic (oxygen-free) conditions. In the 1970s, biogas production plants were introduced in Denmark. There are both centralised biogas plants and farm scale biogas plants. The digestion of farmyard manure and organic waste is a well-established technological practice in Denmark. In 1987, a special action programme on biogas was established for the period of 1998–2001. Biogas has also been supported after this period as part of the general energy action plans and as part of the 2001–2011 Liberal-Conservative Governments 'Green Growth Agreement' with other political parties in July 2009. This Agreement had a target of at least 50% of all farm manure produced in the country being used to make biogas within the ten years timeframe. Enticements to encourage this development include 20% capital grants and high electricity prices where the farmers supply the current to the power network. Aid was paid to investments in biogas plants in 2010 and in 2012 as part of the Danish RDP 2007–2013. In 2012, support was awarded to both new and existing biogas plants to the amount of DKK 262 million.[1134] Biogas production is also seen as an important tool in the reduction of GHG emission from Danish agriculture. The Energy Agreement of March 2012 'Accelerating Green Energy towards 2020' includes the following initiatives on biogas:

- funding on biogas for CHP to continue;
- introduction of subsidy equality so that biogas sold to the natural gas grid receives the same subsidy as biogas used at CHP plants;
- introduction of a new subsidy for biogas used in industrial processes or as a fuel for transport;
- the start-up aid for new biogas projects was increased from 20% to 30%;
- a task force was established with a view to studying and supporting specific biogas projects.[1135]

On 29 June 2018, a new Energy Agreement was signed by all the political parties covering the period of 2018–2030. Based on this agreement, the subsidies for biogas production from existing biogas plants can be maintained until 2032 and at least

1132. RenoSam & Ramböll, *Waste-to-Energy in Denmark.*
1133. Statutory Order No. 1672 of 15 December 2016 on the Utilisation of Soil and Sorted Waste from Building and Construction Activities.
1134. *Denmark's 6th National Communication and First Biennial Report under the UNFCCC*, at 30.
1135. *Denmark's 6th National Communication and First Biennial Report under the UNFCCC*, at 123.

20 years for the individual plants. No new plants based on the current subsidies will be permitted as from 2020, at which time a ceiling will be established on production subsidies, and assessment will be conducted regularly to identify potential overcompensation. The parties agreed to earmark DDK 240 million annually over a twenty-year period to expand the use of biogas and other green gases. These funds will be used for upgrades, transport and industrial processes. The funding will be implemented during the period of 2021–2023 and allocated through tenders with price ceiling. It is the ambition to help the continued expansion and improvement of this technology. The Danish Energy Agency expects a five- to six-fold increase in the volume of manure used for biogas generation before 2020.[1136]

§5. Landfill Waste Treatment and Incineration Plants

161. According to the Waste Framework Directive, Member States are required to take appropriate measures to establish an integrated and adequate network of waste disposal installations, which will allow the EU and Member States to become self-sufficient as regards the disposal of waste. Member States are also obliged to ensure that existing plants operate in accordance with the provisions of the Framework Directive and its daughter directives.

162. The aim of the Landfill of Waste Directive[1137] is – with a view to support the Union's transition to a circular economy and meeting the requirements of the Waste Framework Directive – to prevent or reduce as far as possible negative effects on the environment from the landfilling of waste, by introducing stringent technical requirements for waste and landfills. The Directive applies to all landfills, defined as waste disposal sites for the deposit of waste onto or into land. It requires Member States to take a number of measures to achieve this aim. It sets up a system of operating licences (environmental approvals) for landfill sites following both the specific rules laid down in this Directive and the general rules laid down in the IED.[1138] The different categories of waste (municipal waste, hazardous waste, non-hazardous waste and inert waste) are defined in the Directive.

The 2018 amendment is part of EU 'Circular Economy Package'. A standard waste acceptance procedure is laid down in the Landfill Directive so as to avoid any risks: (a) waste must be treated before disposal; (b) hazardous waste must be assigned to hazardous waste landfills; (c) tipping sites for non-hazardous waste must be used for municipal waste and for non-hazardous waste; (d) tipping sites for inert waste must be used only for inert waste; and (e) criteria for the acceptance of waste in each landfill class must be adopted by the approval authority. The following types of waste may not be accepted in a landfill: liquid waste; flammable waste; explosive or oxidising waste; hospital and other clinical waste which is infectious; used

1136. *Denmark's 7th National Communication on Climate Change and Second Biennial Report under the UNFCCC*, at 188–189.

1137. Council Directive 1999/31/EC on the Landfill of Waste, as amended by European Parliament and Council Directive 2018/850/EU.

1138. Concerning the IE Directive, *see supra* para. 61.

tires, with certain exceptions; any other type of waste which do not meet the acceptance criteria laid down in Annex II of the Directive. The Directive has helped promoting the recovery of resources from waste by progressively diverting certain wastes from landfills: by 2006, the amount of biodegradable waste ending up in landfills had to be reduced to 75% of 1995 levels and by 2009 to 50%. The revised Directive (2018) puts more restriction on the Member States, requiring them to reduce the landfilling of municipal waste to a maximum of 10% by 2035, and it introduces a ban on the landfilling of separately collected waste, including biodegradable waste. Under Article 10 of the Directive, a duty is imposed on Member States to ensure that the operator site charges full costs for the waste producers setting up, running, closing and after caring related to the landfill site. In order to contribute to the objectives, the Member states are obliged under Article 15a to make use of economic instruments and other measures to promote incentives for the application of the waste hierarchy.

163. The conditions governing the establishment of final disposal at landfills have gradually been tightened in Denmark. Dumping of waste that can be incinerated – and consequently used for heating houses – has been prohibited since 1 January 1997.

The establishment of landfills is regulated both by the general rules on spatial planning in the Planning Act,[1139] by the rules on the environmental approval system established by the Environmental Protection Act,[1140] and by the Statutory Order on Landfills.[1141] According to the Statutory Order, CH_4 in landfills for mixed waste must be monitored. From landfills where significant amounts of biodegradable waste are disposed of, CH_4 gas must be managed in an environmentally sound way (e.g., as an energy source in the CHP plants).[1142]

The Environmental Protection Act stipulates that installations for the storage and treatment of some precisely defined forms of waste are subject to prior approval by the environmental protection authorities. New landfills have to be established as near to the coast as possible, but without coming into conflict with other land-use interests. They must also be approved in accordance with section 33 of the Environmental Protection Act, which implement the Landfill Waste Directive and the IED.[1143] Approval of discharge in accordance with section 33 must be obtained, e.g., in connection with the localisation of new municipal receiving stations and treatment plants causing soil pollution.[1144] Applications for approval must contain the following information: (a) the identity of the applicant and the operator; (b) a description of the types and total quantity of waste to be deposited; (c) the capacity of the disposal site; (d) a description of the site; (e) the proposed methods for pollution prevention and abatement; (f) the proposed operation, monitoring and control plan; (g) the plan for closure and aftercare procedures; (h) the applicant's financial

1139. Concerning the content of the municipal plans, *see infra* para. 314, and concerning the content of the local plans, *see infra* para. 321.
1140. Concerning the Danish environmental approval system, *see supra* paras 62–65.
1141. Statutory Order No. 1049 of 28 August 2013 on Landfills.
1142. *Denmark's 7th National Communication on Climate Change*, at 211.
1143. Concerning the IE Directive, *see supra* para. 61.
1144. Concerning the general issues related to soil pollution, *see infra* paras 170–171.

security; and (i) an EIA study where required. The authorities consider such applications on the basis of the applications and the information that the authorities themselves possess. The authority must know the composition; leach ability, long-term behaviour and general properties of the waste to be landfilled. Waste acceptability at the landfill is based on lists of accepted or refused waste types, defined by nature and origin, and on waste analyses methods and limit values for the properties of the waste to be accepted. The operating licence issued contains specific requirements aiming at minimising the harmful impact on the environment in connection with the activities to be undertaken. If this is not possible, measures shall be taken to protect the groundwater against pollution, for instance through a natural, sufficiently thick and impermeable layer of clay. Technical protection measures must be considered after a suitable site has been found. The aspects to be taken into consideration in connection with issuing a permit are the sensitivity of the area in which the plant is located. In the event of a breach of the conditions under which approval was given, the authority, which issued the operating licence (the municipal council or the EPA), may prohibit the continued operation at the disposal site. In the eight-year period after environmental approval has been granted, the competence of the authorities to issue prohibition notices or to make the terms more rigorous is limited by virtue of section 41a(2).[1145] It is a prerequisite for issuing orders under section 41a that the activity is ongoing, and that the responsible party is still in charge of the property. The operator of the landfills of waste has a duty to provide the authorities with a financial security covering the estimated costs of operation aftercare of the landfill.[1146] This obligation is part of the terms for receiving an environmental approval under Chapter 5 of this Act. The rules in Chapter 4 (sections 8–14) of the Statutory Order on Landfills[1147] are stating the criteria for the individual calculation of the financial security.

164. Where incineration takes place, the emission of pollutants must be minimised, in particular as regards metals, dioxin and furan. Strict monitoring of the installations is required to comply with the IED[1148] that replaced the Waste Incineration Directive[1149] in January 2014. Article 3(40) of the IED explains the definition of incineration plants. It:

> means any stationary or mobile technical unit whose main purpose is the generation of energy or production of material products and which uses waste as a regular or additional fuel or in which waste is thermally treated for the purpose of disposal through the incineration by oxidation of waste as well as other thermal treatment processes, such as pyrolysis, gasification or plasma process, if the substances resulting from the treatment are subsequently incinerated.

1145. Concerning the supervision authorities' competences, *see supra* paras 67–70.
1146. These Danish rules are the result of implementation of the Council Directive 1999/31/EC on the Landfills of Waste, as amended.
1147. Statutory Order No. 1049 of 28 August 2013 on Landfills.
1148. Concerning the IE Directive, *see supra* para. 61.
1149. European Parliament and Council Directive 2000/76/EC on the Incineration of Waste.

The definition of waste co-incineration plants is laid down in Article 3(41) of the IED. Chapter IV (Articles 42–55) of the Directive deals with special provisions for waste incineration and waste co-incineration plants and primarily recasts the Waste Incineration Directive. The various articles in this Chapter relate to scope, permit applications and conditions, control and monitoring of emissions, compliance, operating conditions, delivery and reception of waste, residues, substantial change and reporting and public information. The rules cover virtually all sorts of waste incineration and co-incineration plants. They aim at preventing or limiting as far as possible negative effects on the environment by way of establishing stringent operational conditions and emission limit values. It establishes a mandatory obligation to apply for an operating licence under Chapter I and lays down rules pertaining to operating conditions and emission from incineration plants to air and water. It applies to solid and liquid waste incineration plants as well as to co-incineration plants. Annex VI outlines the technical provisions relating to waste incineration and co-incineration plants and recasts Annexes I to VI of the Waste Incineration Directive. Today's energy-generating waste incinerators have little in common with the smoke belching models of the past. Air pollution from waste incineration has been reduced through improved terms on incineration conditions and effective abatement. The flue gas generated is cleaned of dust, heavy metals, acid gases (hydrogen chloride (HCl), HF and SO_2), NO_x and dioxins. At present, landfill is often the disposal method for residential products from flue gas abatement, and the material is difficult to deposit due to its water solubility. This is achieved in up to five subsequent treatment steps.

165. The environmental conditions required of Danish incineration plants are laid down in operating licence issued in accordance with the environmental approval system established by Chapter 5 of the Environmental Protection Act,[1150] the Statutory Order on Environmental Approval of Enterprises and the Statutory Order on Incineration of Waste.[1151]

The rules establish emissions limit values, e.g., on CO, dust, total organic carbon (TOC), HCl, hydrogen fluoride (HF), SO_2, NO_x, dioxins and several heavy metals. Specific limit values are stated in the operating licence and so is the mandatory requirement to use the BATs – following the criteria established under the IED. New plants must be approved in accordance with section 33 of the Environmental Protection Act. Applications for an operating licence must contain the following information: (a) the identity of the applicant and the operator; (b) a description of the types and total quantity of waste to be incinerated; (c) the capacity of the plant; (d) a description of the plant; (e) the proposed methods for pollution prevention and abatement; (f) the proposed operation, monitoring and control plan; and (g) an EIA study. The authorities consider such applications on the basis of the applications and the information that the authorities themselves possess. The operating licence issued

1150. Concerning the Danish environmental approval system, *see supra* paras 62–65.
1151. Statutory Order No. 1271 of 21 November 2017 on Incineration of Waste.

contains specific requirements aiming at minimising the harmful impact on the environment in connection with the activities to be undertaken. In connection with issuing an operating licence the aspects to be taken into consideration are the sensitivity of the area and water in which the plant is located.

166. All Danish landfills and incineration plants are owned or controlled by public authorities – the municipalities or companies owned by municipalities. Section 49 of the Act provides that the Minister for the Environment may lay down rules on the duty of municipalities to join inter-municipal waste facilities. This power has not yet been used, however. There are not any special provisions in the Act on the ownership of the waste incineration companies.

Based on section 45 of the Act the municipalities are responsible for handling the waste. The cost of waste services is decided by the municipalities, cf. section 48 of the Act. After the '2010 Waste Reform', the Danish waste system has, however, gradually become well organised into a number of inter-municipal waste companies and private recycling undertakings. The publicly owned companies, formed by an association of several municipal councils, have no power of their own, but act on behalf of the local councils. In 2016, there were twenty waste incineration utilities out of twenty-six municipality-owned waste incineration utilities. Two of these utilities were co-owned by the users and the municipalities. Seventy municipalities out of the ninety-eight municipalities were owner or co-owner of the 20 municipality owned waste incineration utilities. Two utilities were private owned, and four of the utilities were owned by the heat-consumers.[1152] It is only possible to establish new waste incineration utilities if it is accepted by the Energy Agency, cf. section 50b of the Act. The approval of such new facilities is based on a calculation of the amount of waste for incineration and the need for more capacity. The amount of waste that has been imported to Denmark for incineration – including waste used in the combined energy and heating sector – has increased. In 2015 Denmark imported 546,311 tons waste.[1153] The waste incineration utilities are responsible for 20–24% of the production of energy for the heating up of the houses.[1154]

§6. Evaluation of the Efficiency of the Legal Provisions

167. In all economic sectors, except industry and wastewater treatment plants, the generation of waste in Denmark has increased. The OECD 'Environmental Performance Review, Denmark 2007'[1155] is stating that Denmark faces numerous environmental challenges resulting from unsustainable consumption patterns, for

1152. The Danish Energy Agency, *Effektivisering af affaldsforbrændingsanlæg (in English: A More Effective Waste Incineration Sector)*, 2016.

1153. A Note of 23 November 2016 (MST-001-15354) from the Ministry of Environment and Food of Denmark sent to the Danish Parliament.

1154. Danish Waste Association, the Danish Industry, and the Danish Energy, *BEATE. Benchmarking af affaldssektoren 2016 (data fra 2015). Forbrænding (in English: BEATE. Benchmarking of the Waste Sector 2016 (data from 2015). Waste Incineration)*, at 21.

1155. OECD, *Environmental Performance Review, Denmark 2007*, at 115.

example waste generation. The generation of household waste increases nearly twice as fast as the economy. The amount of Danish waste has reached one of the highest generation rates in the OECD.

The total amount of waste arising (excl.) soil corresponding to waste generated in Denmark was in 2016 approximately 11.7 million tons.[1156] The volume of waste is increasing. The total amount of waste (excluding soil) in 2015 was 11.3 million tonnes of which 69% was recycled, 27% incinerated and 4% landfilled.[1157] Sixty-nine per cent of the Danish waste was recycled in 2016. As for commercial and industrial waste, 71% was recycled, while for household waste 50% was recycled in 2016. The assessment of the implementation of EU's waste directives published in September 2018 stated that the municipal waste represents around 10% of the total waste generated in the EU. Only 46% was recycled or composed, while 25% was landfilled.[1158] Some of the Member States have been identified as at risk of missing the 50% target for preparing such waste for reuse/recycling. Denmark is not one of these Member States.[1159] The Danish recycling rate for construction and demolition waste is above the 70%-target that has been set by the EU rules.[1160]

1156. Danish EPA, *The Danish Waste Statistics 2016*, at 6.

1157. *Denmark's 7th National Communication and Second Biennial Report under the UNFCCC*, at 208.

1158. Commission, *Report on the Implementation of EU Waste Legislation, including the Early Warning Report for Member States at Risk of Missing the 2020 Preparation for Re-use/Recycling target on Municipal Waste*, COM(2018) 656 final, at 1.

1159. COM(2018) 656 final, at 2.

1160. Deloitte et al., *Construction and Demolition Waste Management in Denmark V2*, September 2015, at 4.

Chapter 5. Soil Pollution

§1. Legislation

168. Soil pollution has an impact on the safety of the food as well as on the quality of the water and nature. There are four international instruments that have a significant impact on the protection of soil against pollution: the Basel Convention,[1161] the Rotterdam Convention,[1162] the Stockholm Convention[1163] and the Minamata Convention on Mercury.[1164] The outcome document of the UNs Conference on Sustainable Development 'The Future We Want' (2002) recognises the economic and social significance of good land management, including management and protection of the soil. Soil pollution is also one of the ten major threats identified in the FAO 2015 report 'Status of the World's Soil Resources'. The food safety issue is addressed by FAO's 'Revised World Soil Charter'[1165] and FAO's 'Voluntary Guidelines for Sustainable Soil Management'.[1166] Several of the UN SDGs have also focus on the problems.[1167]

Pollutants buried or spilt on the soil are seeping down to the groundwater from contaminated sites located in and around the old industrial towns. It is, consequently, necessary to reduce the seepage from waste deposits in order to secure future water quality. Such polluted sites are often defined as areas of land in which the soil or underlying groundwater contains either a special waste or listed substances in qualities or in concentrations in excess of criteria standards or conditions established by regulation. Soil formation is an extremely slow process, and soil of good environmental standard can be considered essentially as a non-renewable resource. Soil has a role as a habitat and a gene pool, and serves as a platform for human activities, landscape and heritage. Soil pollution is one of the environmental consequences of waste deposited and buried in the ground, accidents causing spills, and one of the consequences of diffuse sources from farming, industry and traffic as well. Some of the components' content of pesticides are, for example, found in the soil. Run-off of nitrates from the soil into groundwater and rivers following the application of fertilisers to the soil have resulted in nitrate levels in drinking water exceeding specified standards laid down in the EU quality norms. There is a long-term risk of seepage from polluted soil developing into more or less serious recipient pollution of the hydrogeological system, with corresponding ecological

1161. Concerning the 'Basel Convention – Controlling Transboundary Movement of Hazardous Waste and their Disposal', *see supra* para. 140.
1162. Concerning the Rotterdam Convention, *see infra* para. 208.
1163. Concerning the Stockholm Convention – Protecting Human Health and the Environment from Persistent Organic Pollutants', *infra* para. 208.
1164. Concerning the Minamata Convention on Mercury, *see supra* para. 74.
1165. The first World Soil Charter was adopted on the 39th session of the FAO Conference in November 1981. The second version was adopted in 2015.
1166. *Guidelines for Sustainable Soil Management (VGSSM)*, published in 2017. The parties developed the guidelines through an inclusive process within the framework of the Global Soil Partnership (GSP). The Guidelines aim to be a reference providing general technical and policy recommendations on sustainable soil management (SSM).
1167. FAO Concept Note, *Be the Solution to Soil Pollution. Global Symposium on Soil Pollution*, 2–4 May 2018.

consequences. The use of increasingly larger agricultural machinery causes soil compaction. Compaction of the soil's structural elements and particles reduces its pore volume, which among other things is important for the aeration of soil. Compaction also reduces capacity in relation to the transport of water. Moreover, compacted soil provides poorer living conditions for plants and soil animals. Wind erosion of soil can also comprise considerable problems in certain wind-blown areas with sandy soil that has a loose, dry and fine particular composition. Erosion in these areas can be a significant factor for plant growth conditions. In Denmark, restoration of contaminated sites is only required if there is a serious threat to water supply operation, human health or the environment. Consequently, in cases concerning soil pollution, a test of significant damage to human health, drinking water resources, flora and fauna and cost effectiveness of restoration is applied.

169. The EU's 6EAP requires the development of 'Thematic Strategy on Soil Protection' addressing the prevention of soil degradation. The scope of soil protection is not the same across the EU with the Danish policy being one of the most stringent. Also, the perspectives for dealing with soil protection are different.

In April 2002, the Commission adopted a communication on such a strategy, and the Thematic Strategy followed up the work for Soil Protection[1168] in September 2006. The objectives published in the Thematic Strategy for Soil Protection published are to protect the soil while using it sustainably, through the prevention of further degradation, the preservation of soil function and the restoration of degraded soils. A draft 'Soil Framework Directive' was presented in September 2006 by the Commission.[1169] It seeks to harmonise and raise the level of soil protection across the EU. In Article 1 it specifies that soil is the top layer of the Earth's crust situated between the bedrock and the surface, excluding groundwater as defined in the WFD. The current approach proposed in the draft Directive would require Member States to identify and remediate contaminated land, consider soil protection/functions in national policymaking and control loss of soil resources to development. In Article 9 of the draft it is stated that:

> For the purposes of preserving the soil functions referred to in Article (1), Member States shall take appropriate and proportionate measures to limit the intentional or intentional introduction of dangerous substances on or in the soil, excluding those due to air deposition and those due to a natural phenomenon of exceptional, inevitable and irresistible character, in order to avoid accumulation that would hamper soil functions or give rise to significant risks to human health or the environment.

The draft directive has not been accepted. One of the important aspects is the EQS concerning 'clean soil' and the possibility of including the costs of protection and restoration as being the expenses of the polluters, without harming the trade in the Internal Market. The 7EAP is still mentions the EU policy on soil contamination as one that has to be on the agenda. Soil as such has not to date been subject

1168. COM(2006) 231 final.
1169. COM(2006) 232 final.

to a specific protection policy at EU level, but soil contamination is included in the Landfill of Waste Directive,[1170] the ELD,[1171] the Sewage Sludge Directive,[1172] the IED[1173] and the 2013 CAP Reform.[1174] These instruments include not only requirements on quality standards, they also include supplementary economic means, e.g., public power to demand a cleaning-up and requirements in relation to fees (charges), insurance or other sorts of economic guarantees. Data on soil and subsoil characterised according to depth, texture, structure and content of particles and organic material, stoniness, erosion, anticipated water storage capacity, etc. have to be recorded in the INSPIRE systems.[1175] The general aim of soil mapping is to provide a spatial representation and description of the soils of countries, regions, farms and any other area of interest. Functional areas within urban and rural areas may be mapped through fieldwork, register information or through modelling using socio-economic data in a Geographical Information System (GIS). The recommended classification of land use is based on the UN International Standard Classification of All Economic Activities (ISIC Rev.3) fully compatible with the EU NACE Rev. 1. The data are relevant, for example in the administration of EIA rules, the ICZM,[1176] the water administration and the Seveso administration.

170. In Denmark, protection of soil is first and foremost to be seen in the light of the protection of the groundwater used by the water utilities for water supply (drinking water). About 98–100% of the water supply is based on the abstraction of groundwater of a high quality usually requiring very limited treatment.[1177]

The consequences of soil pollution in the payment of cleaning-up activities and restoration are laid down as follows:

– rules on prevention, protection and restoration are laid down in the main part of the Environmental Protection Act, the Environmental Approval for Livestock Holdings Act, and the Water Supply Act;[1178]

1170. Council Directive 1999/31/EC on the Landfill of Waste, as amended.
1171. European Parliament and Council Directive 2004/35/EC on Environmental Liability with Regard to Prevention and Remedying of Environmental Damage, as amended several times.
1172. Council Directive 86/278 on the Protection of the Environment, and in particular the Soil, when Sewage Sludge is used in Agriculture. Concerning this Directive, *see supra* in para. 146.
1173. European Parliament and Council Directive 2010/75/EU on Industrial Emissions. Concerning the obligations for the Member States to ensure national legislation demanding some of the operators under the IE Directive to make a 'baseline report' when they are applying for an approval and for the authorities to demand a cleaning-up once the activities on the plants stop, *see supra* in para. 61.
1174. Concerning the 2013 CAP reform, *see infra* para. 258.
1175. The INSPIRE Directive is described *supra* in para. 34.
1176. Concerning the ICZM, *see infra* para. 302.
1177. René Seerden & Kurt Deketelaere (eds.), *Legal Aspects of Soil Pollution and Decontamination in the EU Member States and the United States*, at 441–442.
1178. Concerning the competences of the supervisory authorities in the Environmental Protection Act and the Environmental Approval Act for Livestock Holdings, *see supra* paras 67–70.

- rules on investigations and remedial action are contained in the Contaminated Soil Act that includes special rules in Chapter 4b on the authorities' obligations to demand a cleaning-up to the level described in the 'baseline reports';[1179]
- environmental liability rules in the three just-mentioned acts implementing the ELD;[1180]
- culpa rules;[1181]
- liability law on damages in contractual relations (private law relations) that consists of the basic legal principles on claims against defect for sale of contaminated real estates.

Danish decision-makers must all apply these rules, but they must also take into account the difference in relation to the protection of drinking water that is required by different types of soil. Sand is not a good protector: clay secures the best protection.[1182]

171. The main considerations of the Environmental Protection Act concern the health of humans and interests related to the water supply as well as the sustainable use of natural resources. Under the Act, orders to remove pollution and restore the environment can be issued to the owner of the property, cf. section 24 of the Act. Compensation must, however, be paid to a non-offending property owner when an administrative order concerning soil pollution is issued to him or her, in relation to sections 63 and 64 of this Act.

Section 19 of the Act requires that a permit is obtained prior to the disposal of waste or substances likely to cause pollution of soil, subsoil or groundwater.[1183] Owners and users of land must notify the environmental authorities of any pollution of the soil or subsoil owned or used, cf. section 21 of the Act. Furthermore, anyone responsible for activities or installations likely to cause soil pollution must notify the authorities when interruption of operation or accidents result in substantial pollution or pollution risks, cf. section 71 of the Act. Even if an accident – such as for instance an oil spill – cannot be said to have been caused by the property owner, he or she must warn the owners of adjoining property and the authorities of the danger as soon as he or she becomes – or ought to have become – aware of it. Failure to give notification and warning is regarded as culpable negligence on the part of the owner who can be held liable for damages. According to section 72 of the Act, anyone responsible for activities likely to cause soil pollution must, at the request of the environmental authorities, must provide all information relevant for the evaluation of the pollution risk and possible remedial action.[1184]

1179. The IE Directive was implemented by Act No. 446 of 23 June 2012 amending the Environmental Protection Act, the Environmental Approval Act for Livestock Holdings, the Contaminated Soil Act and the Environmental Marine Protection Act.

1180. Concerning the Environmental Liability Directive and the Danish implementation of the Directive, *see infra* paras 336–341.

1181. Concerning the unwritten culpa rules, *see infra* para. 344.

1182. Concerning Danish land, *see supra* para. 2.

1183. Section 19 of the Act represents an extension of the protection: as the previous legislation – which was in force until 1 Jan. 1992 – only provided protection of groundwater.

1184. Concerning the competences of the supervisory authorities, *see supra* paras 69–70.

172. Additions of nutrients from agricultural activities constitute a significant negative impact on land (soil) as two-thirds of the open area in Denmark is managed by farms with a high pigment production totalling 25 million pigs per year. Pursuant to section 7 of the Environmental Protection Act standards on business farmyard manure and silage are laid down in statutory orders and guidelines.

The rules on the application of fertilisers on the fields are partly laid down in the Fertilisation Act[1185] and the Environmental Approval Act for Livestock Holdings[1186] and partly in the administrative filling of these two acts by Statutory Order on the Use of Fertiliser in the Individual Fertiliser Accounts,[1187] Statutory Order on Environmental Approval of Livestock Holdings[1188] and Statutory Order on Livestock Manure.[1189] The Statutory Order on Sewage Sludge[1190] protects the soil against the risk of pollution from the substances listed therein.[1191] Sludge originates from the process of treatment of wastewater. Due to the physical-chemical processes involved in the treatment, the sludge tends to concentrate heavy metals and poorly biodegradable trace organic compounds as well as potentially pathogenic organisms (viruses, bacteria, etc.) present in wastewater. Sludge is, however, rich in nutrients such as nitrogen and phosphorous and contains valuable organic matter that is useful when soils are depleted or subject to erosion. The organic matter and nutrients are the two main elements that make the spreading of this kind of waste on land as a fertiliser or an organic soil improver suitable. Slag from incineration plants can be used on farmyards (i.e., recycled), provided it complies with the limit values for certain heavy metals, but must otherwise be sent to a landfill. The Statutory Order establishing the Quality Requirements for Re-use of Slag supports the recycling of slag.[1192]

173. The most important rules on soil contamination are to be found in the Contaminated Soil Act.[1193] The Act is based on the recommendation from the Committee on Polluted Soil, which was set up by the Minister for the Environment in 1995. The Report 2/1996 contained a proposal that was meant to make it easier to secure re-establishment after soil pollution had occurred on the basis of the 'polluter pays principle'.[1194] The aim was to protect the soil and groundwater against future pollution from waste deposits and the removal of polluted soil from one property to

1185. Promulgation Order No. 996 of 25 June 2018 on Use of Fertilisers and Reduction of Emission from Fertilisers.
1186. Promulgation Order No. 520 of 1 May 2019 on the Environmental Approval Act for Livestock Holdings.
1187. Statutory Order No. 249 of 19 March 2019 on the Nitrogen Forecast for the Period from 2018 to 2019.
1188. Statutory Order No. 718 of 8 July 2019 on Environmental Approval of Livestock Holdings.
1189. Statutory Order No. 760 of 30 July 2019 on Commercial Animal Husbandry, Livestock Manure and Silage.
1190. Statutory Order No. 1001 of 27 April 2018 on Sewage Sludge.
1191. This statutory order is an implementation of Council Directive 86/278/EEC on the Protection of the Environment and in Particular of the Soil, when sludge is used in Agriculture (the Sewage Sludge Directive).
1192. Statutory Order No. 1672 of 15 December 2016 on the use of Residues, Soil and Sorted Waste and Construction Waste.
1193. Promulgation Order No. 282 of 27 March 2017 on Contaminated Soil.
1194. Concerning the 'polluter pays principle', *see supra* para. 28.

another. The competences to administer the rules on contaminated sites in the Contaminated Soil Act were changed by 1 January 2007 as a consequence of the 2007 structural reform, and new guidelines were published to support the authorities in their work.[1195] The five regions are now the responsible authorities. They are allocated DKK 3,000 million annually to investigate and clean up contaminated sites. Only 25% of the activities are privately financed.

174. The old gasworks, polluted industrial properties, polluted wood preservation sites, polluted oil tank stations, etc. constitute serious risk for the environment and people's health in the local surrounding area. As for the guidance of public authorities, the Minister for the Environment may lay down provisions as to the monitoring and quality values of soil differentiated on the basis of sensitivity. Several guidelines on these issues were published in 1998–2000.[1196] The major chemicals used in the wood-preserving industries are creosote (composed of phenol), copper chromium arsenate (CCA) and pentachlorophenol (PCP). Three different routes of exposure from such substances are typically considered: direct human exposure, leaching to groundwater and ecological risk. There are around 163 wood preservation sites in Denmark, some of them with a history going back to the 1860s.[1197]

175. As a central instrument, the Contaminated Soil Act established the use of pollution mapping and sensitivity mapping of larger areas. The regional councils are responsible for the mapping of contaminated sites. City areas, maps of spreading of solutes from polluted sites and risk management in relation to polluted sites is all drafted as a means to ensure better public awareness and public engagement in the protection of the groundwater.[1198]

Survey work is the basis for the mapping. There are two knowledge levels defined in sections 4 and 5 of the Contaminated Soil Act. The knowledge level of the pollution on a site is described as 'knowledge level 2' if the actual knowledge in relation to the pollution is based on documentation with a high degree of certainty. If the knowledge is based on a hypothesis and/or knowledge about the activities on the site or activities on the properties close to the site, it is classified as 'knowledge level 1'. The knowledge level is registered in the land register of the National Survey and Cadastre.[1199] The definition of lightly contaminated sites is according to section 50a of the Act established in the Statutory Order on the Definition of Lightly

1195. Concerning the reform of the municipal and regional council structure in 2007, *see supra* para. 52.

1196. *See* Guideline No. 8/1998 concerning Polluted Wood Preservation Sites, Guidelines No. 10/1998 on Soil Pollution from Tar Works and Asphalt Sites, Guideline No. 11/998 on Benzene and Oil Polluted Sites, and Guideline No. 13/998 on Sampling and Analyses of Soil.

1197. Lisbeth M. Ottosen, Alexandra B. Ribeiro & Eckhard Melcher, *Polluted Wood Preservation Sites*.

1198. In Denmark, 12,000 sites were mapped as polluted in 2012.

1199. On 1 Jan. 2007, several amendments to the Contaminated Soil Act entered into force as part of the 2007 structural reform. The survey criteria for contaminated sites were changed so that lightly polluted sites as found in most urban areas, no longer had to be surveyed, cf. Act No. 507 of 7 July 2006 on Modification of Surveying of Polluted Sites, etc.

Contaminated Soil.[1200] The Act states that the contaminated properties must be divided into two types of sites whereby the level of soil pollution and knowledge concerning the soil quality determine the concrete division into pollution areas. As for real estates within very polluted areas, the authorities must be able to lay down general directives for construction and for other land uses. As for such properties, it is furthermore ensured that according to law, a duty to notify applies, so that the owner or the user must submit a notification prior to any construction or any changed use of premises in the area. The regional councils make the division into above-mentioned two types of sites. The municipal councils help the regional councils to carry out the practical mapping of the areas that are currently used for housing, institutions and similar types of sensitive use. The mapping of areas is supplemented by guidelines of a more or less binding character.[1201]

176. As an important instrument, the Water Supply etc. Act requires that the municipal councils are mapping the sensitive drinking water resources areas.[1202] Hydrogeological mapping has provided a basis for establishing site-specific groundwater protection zones.

The combination of mapping of contaminated sites and mapping of sensitive areas ensures the authorities' knowledge at any time in terms of soil pollution and sensitivity – a knowledge that the mapping brings about. The interaction between sensitivity mapping and pollution mapping is decisive for concrete claims, which can be made against the owners and the users of real estates. According to the Contaminated Soil Act, sensitive areas are areas used for drinking water supply, and areas with homes, childcare centres or public playgrounds. The Act mentions the following as other sensitive areas: areas for recreation, areas accessible to the public, allotments, summer houses, and institutions. The authorities' knowledge at any time in terms of soil pollution and sensitivity, which the mapping brings about and which is used in connection with the mapping, has to be made public on the Danish Environment Portal as 'Areal Information'. Access to environmental information about the status of properties ensures that both the citizens and the authorities have the necessary insight to act adequately, i.e., as buyers of polluted sites and when assessing applications for building licences.

177. Soil quality criteria and cut-off criteria are set as the basis for the application of the rules on contaminated soil. These criteria are suitable for assessing the risk in an individual case. The Contaminated Soil Act distinguishes between: (a)

1200. Statutory Order No. 554 of 19 May 2010 on the Definition of Lighter Polluted Soil.

1201. Guideline No. 1/2007 was published to support more flexibility in the mapping of residential areas that are only contaminated by air borne pollution. It also included guidance to the people living in buildings located on contaminated sites. In most cases in residential areas, a leaking oil tank causes the contamination. Guidelines No. 3/2007 on Classification of Contaminated Sites and Guidelines No. 2/2009 on the Investigation and Cleaning Up of Contaminated Sites inform the authorities about the conditions for the administration of the supervision competences and the cleaning-up services of sites contaminated by oil resulting from oil tanks in residential areas. Concerning the different guidelines on polluted soil, cf. https://mst.dk/affald-jord/jordforurening/hvis-du-vil-vide-mere-vejledninger-mm/vejledninger/ (visited on 27 Aug. 2019).

1202. Concerning the protection under the Water Supply Act of the drinking water resources in the subsoil against pollution, *see supra* paras 112 and 114–117.

contamination that constitutes a risk for drinking water that means a public initiative is necessary; (b) contamination that constitutes such a human health risk that additional endeavours should be initiated; and (c) contamination that constitutes a health risk, that can be handled by public endeavours in the form of advices and careful use of the land.

The five regional councils are the competent authorities in relation to publicly financed investigation and cleaning-up activities on the basis of the abovementioned criteria, cf. sections 3–7 of the Act. As part of the administration of the Act, the regional councils and municipal councils make a survey of all sites on which activities are likely to cause serious soil pollution. Annual surveys are made of all registered property with specification of the measures to be taken and a timetable for their implementation. They give highest priority to supplementary investigations and cleaning-up measures in the special target areas mapped under the Act,[1203] i.e., areas with special drinking water interests, abstraction areas for common water supply plants, and areas which are used for sensitive purposes. Both the mapping of areas and the remedial action serve two essential purposes: partly to preserve the groundwater resources that form the basis of the drinking water supply, and to protect people against the health nuisances and hazards in connection with the use of polluted sites for environmentally sensitive activities.

178. The environmental authorities' approval is needed under the Contaminated Soil Act for any changes in the use of or construction on a property where soil pollution is found and mapped, and for any changed use of/construction on property that is mapped because it constitutes a risk of pollution, cf. section 8 of the Act. Mapping thus limits the rights of the owner as to the use of his or her property, which amongst other things can have significant financial consequences. The reason for this restriction of property rights is the need to limit public expenses in connection with any investigations and remedial action that may be initiated at a later point in time. The property owner of the polluted sites as well as independent contractors must submit an application to the municipal council before starting building activities. They may apply for voluntary removal and restoration of the polluted soil. If the application is approved, they must themselves pay all the costs of the examination and cleaning. Before accepting the planned project, the municipal council must ask the regional council for its opinion and include the answer from the regional council in its decision-making, as the answer is binding, cf. section 8a of the Act.

If a building is to be placed on top of polluted soil, threatening the groundwater or on a site with substantially increased concentrations of polluting matter, the regional council may determine the necessary conditions with regard to facilitating a public clean-up activity at a later stage. According to the proposal on a project, the council may instead choose to demand that the owner/user takes the necessary remedial measures before the construction can be started, on the grounds of precautionary and proportionality considerations. As can be seen, owners and users of real estate in very polluted areas incur a number of legal consequences. Therefore, the Contaminated Soil Act ensures that individuals are informed prior to the adoption

1203. Concerning the mapping of sensitive drinking water sites, *see infra* para. 176.

of mapping, just as – on the basis of 'law and order principles' – they are guaranteed a certain 'right of contradiction'. Mapping thus limits the rights of the owner as to the use of his or her property, which amongst other things has rather significant financial consequences, for instance if the owner wishes to obtain a mortgage loan from a mortgage-credit institute or a bank or if he wants to sell the property. The owners of such properties are therefore ensured some possibilities to involve the public authorities in investigation and cleaning-up of the pollution. The State has the duty to give a public guarantee that remedial actions will be taken within a specified period of time if the property owner pays part of the costs himself or herself, the amount of which is laid down in the public budget for such activities.

All private houses with oil tanks are covered by mandatory insurance, cf. section 49 of the Act. It is the private insurance firm 'Topdenmark' that covers the cost of investigation and cleaning-up. The municipalities can give an order to the owner of the polluted property with the consequences that the insurance firm has to act as the responsible party – also with the legal rights to appeal the decision to the Environmental Protection and Food Appeals Board. The Supreme Court has stated that the cleaning-up order must respect the 'principle of proportionality', and that it is not possible to give an order that goes beyond the necessary removal basis on an assessment of the sensitivity of the environment and human health.[1204]

179. The investigations and remedial measures in contaminated residential areas are in most cases to be initiated by the environmental authorities, cf. sections 6–7 of the Act. The investigations are to determine the nature and extent of the pollution problems relating to the indoor climate, infiltration of the pollution to the groundwater and the impact on nearby receiving waters. Public investigations and subsequent remedial action are undertaken in accordance with the time schedule drawn up by the authorities. If the authorities know exactly what kind of pollution exist in the soil, and they know that it can damage the environment and cause health problems, they will then map such properties as 'knowledge 2-level' properties, cf. section 5 of the Act. This mapping gives the owners of the properties the right to ask for more detailed investigations, and they can apply for public support to cleaning-up activities. The owners are not allowed to change the building or the use of such properties without a permit from the authorities.

180. The repeal of the restrictions established by the mapping of contaminated sites on a property by a licence – received on the basis of an application under section 8 of the Contaminated Soil Act – to build do not mean that all the restrictions as to its use are lifted. Typically, the property is cleaned to precisely such an extent that remaining pollution do not constitute any environmental or health-related problems in connection with the use that is specifically allowed. Such approvals for use must be entered into the register on the real estate at the expense of the addressee and into the municipal register relating to the property. The entry in the register of titles must comprise:

– specification of all buildings and installations on the mapped areas;

1204. *See* the judgment published in the Danish Weekly Law Reports 2005, at 2923.

- detailed description of the use of the mapped areas; and
- other conditions concerning remedial action, continued use, etc.

An entry in the register in accordance with the Act can only be cancelled, if the authorities consider it not to constitute any risk for the environment or human health. The environmental authorities do, however, have the possibility of cancelling the registration if evidence can be provided that the site is not or is no longer polluted. When the registration has been cancelled, which is entered in the register of titles, all restrictions relating to this ban as to the use of the property are abolished.

§2. Enforcement and Control

181. The Danish authorities have a general duty to exercise the powers conferred on them by the statutory rules in relation to soil pollution in such a manner that the groundwater quality objectives specified by the Drinking Water Directive are achieved and where the pollution cause a risk of damage to Natura 2000 sites protected by Article 6(1) of the Habitats Directive. Very high priority is given by the authorities to cleaning-up activities in vulnerable areas, where groundwater pollution already seems to have occurred, if the groundwater could be or is already being used for water supply purposes. In contrast to this, protection of the Nature 2000 Sites against damage caused by polluted soil is not a part of the public policy on cleaning up contaminated sites.

182. Pursuant to section 69 of the Environmental Protection Act, the environmental authority in charge of the supervision of an industrial enterprise may initiate investigations of polluted soil and remedial action at the expense of the responsible party.[1205] This public power must be used if – and only if – the responsible party do not comply with a prohibition order within the time limit specified in the order. Before giving an order to the responsible enterprise or private person, the authority must ensure, that:

- the administrative order has been issued, and it has been proved that the Contaminated Soil Act or the Environmental Protection Act vested the authority with the power used to issue such an order (the legality principle);
- the administrative order must be formulated in exact terms to ensure that the addressee understands its content (the law and order principles);
- the administrative order must be addressed to the right person (the public authority has to demonstrate that the addressee is the responsible polluter);
- the specified time limit laid down in the order has to be decided partly on the actual danger and partly on the possibility of the addressee to act before the deadline (the 'proportionality principle' and the 'principle of equity');
- there must be proof of the danger to health or the environment (the official maxim); and

1205. Concerning the competences of the supervisory authority, *see supra* paras 68–70.

- the costs incurred must be within reasonable limits (the proportionality principle), and the compensation demand must be based on economic interests.

It is also presumed that an order can only apply to the user of a property – who is responsible for the pollution provided – if the pollution is located on his or her own property and he or she has the right to use the property.[1206] So, in principle the Danish environmental authorities may demand that the responsible party pays the expenses in connection with the necessary investigations and remedial actions on the property. In practice, however, it is very complicated to ensure the enforcement by use of the supervisory power.[1207] If the damage is categorised as an environmental damage, the rules on environmental liability in Chapter 9a of the Environmental Protection Act has to be used.[1208] In the event of imminent danger to health and when immediate action is required to avoid pollution of drinking water, the supervisory authority will take the measures required without prior notice and at the expense of the responsible party, in accordance with section 70 of the Environmental Protection Act.

183. Chapter 5 of the Contaminated Soil Act contains rules on administrative orders relating to the operator of an 'occupational activity' (the 'polluter') that has received an environmental approval. The definition of the 'polluter' in this Act is:

> 1) a person who for commercial or public purposes has had a business or has used the plant from which the pollution comes. The pollution or a part of it has to be caused during the period in which the responsible person was the operator. 2) Other persons who have caused pollution if the pollution is due to culpability or a conduct which is subject to more strict liability rules according to other legislation.

So, it is not private owners of buildings that will be categorised as polluters under this Act. The competence to give an order is placed with the municipal councils unless, pursuant to the Environmental Protection Act, the EPA controls the enterprises in question.[1209]

An administrative order to the responsible polluter concerning the cleaning-up of soil pollution can be issued irrespective of how the pollution has happened (i.e., an assessment of negligence is not relevant). According to the Act, it is furthermore without importance whether the addressee of the order owns the polluted premises, cf. section 44 of the Act. If more than one polluter is involved in pollution, a compliance order must be given to all of them, cf. section 43 of the Act. The authority, which has conducted a cleaning-up, may sue the responsible persons and businesses for the cost of remedying environmental contamination, the damage to natural

1206. The judgment stating these conditions is published in the Danish Weekly Law Reports 1995, at 505ff.

1207. Concerning the Danish courts use of the culpa rules, *see infra* para. 344.

1208. Concerning the implementation of the environmental liability provisions into the Environmental Protection Act, *see infra* paras 336–341.

1209. Concerning the competences of the supervisory authority under the Environmental Protection Act, *see supra* paras 67–70.

resources (including the costs of assessing such damage); and the costs of studies necessary to determine the health effects of environmental contamination. However, an order is not to be given to one of the possible responsible polluters if the authorities assume that these polluters have only contributed to the pollution to a lesser extent. If the addressee of the administrative order does not freely dispose of the polluting premises, the authorities must, according to the Act, give an order to the person who can dispose of the real estate. That person can be ordered to tolerate that cleaning-up or other measures are taken at the cost of the polluter. Such orders on the owner of the neighbouring estate must be binding at any time on new owners and users of the premises.

According to the Act, the administrative order must be registered on the real estate at the expense of the addressee of the order. Orders concerning the operation of a business are pursuant to the Act, also binding on future entrepreneurs. In relation to oil pollution on premises from where commercial sales of oil products from tank plants take place or have taken place, the Act explicitly states that it is the responsibility of the oil company as well as the operator.

If the addressee of the administrative order do not have any legal rights to clean up the polluted soil, because someone else is the owner (or for some other reasons), the authorities must, according to the Contaminated Soil Act, give an order to the person who has the right to dispose of the real estate to tolerate that cleaning-up or other measures are made at the arrangement of the addressee of the order. Such orders are binding on the owner or user of the premises at any time. According to the Act, the administrative order given must be registered on the real property at the expense of the addressee of the order. The owners, tenants and other persons who have at their disposal polluted property can claim compensation for damage resulting from investigations or remedial measures. The compensation amount payable to the owner of the plant is agreed with the environmental authorities, and if agreement cannot be reached, a special expropriation authority fixes the amount of compensation. The amount is fixed without regard to the decrease in value caused by the pollution. However, full compensation cannot be paid, if the property owner was aware of the pollution at the time of purchase (i.e., the owner was in bad faith when buying the property).

In relation to buyers of real estates that are polluted, a legal basis for an administrative order on the cleaning-up or the needed information about the environmental status of the property, etc. is ensured in section 45 of the Act. The provisions are:

> Orders can be given to a future acquirer of a polluted property, if:
> the order on a polluter is based on a statutory obligation that had been given or notified before the acquisition but has not been carried out regardless of enjoinment or report;
> the acquirer at the time of acquisition already knew or should have known that an order was given or notified; and
> the acquisition comes from a person who himself was or could be committed to carry out the order. …

Compliance orders can only be given, if it appears from a given or notified order that this applies to future acquirers.

The authority, which has conducted a legal cleaning-up, may sue these persons and businesses for the cost of remedying environmental contamination, damage to natural resources (including the cost of assessing such damage) and the costs of studies necessary to determine the health effects of environmental contamination.

According to section 46 of the Act, the administrative order must be registered on the real estate at the expense of the addressee of the order. Orders concerning the operation of a business must, according to the Act, also be binding on future entrepreneurs.

An administrative order cannot be given, if thirty years or more have elapsed from the time of cessation of the activity/omission, which caused the pollution, cf. section 88(6) of the Act.

184. If the damage can be categorised as environmental damage covered by the rules on environmental liability in Chapter 4a of the Contaminated Soil Act, the special rules that implement the ELD must be respected.[1210] Section 38b(4) of the Act establishes strict liability for the manufacturer and importer of products (e.g., pesticides and GMOs) that cause environmental damage as a result of the direct or indirect introduction of substances, organisms or microorganisms in, on or under the surface of the land. Environmental liability is only relevant if the damage causes significant human health problems or damage to Natura 2000 sites/species or water. It entails that the manufacturer/importer is also liable for environmental damage.[1211]

Chapter 4b (sections 38k–38q) of the Contaminated Soil Act implements the rules laid down in the IED on the operator's obligation to assess the state of soil and groundwater contamination once their activities stop. The activities approved under the Environmental Protection Act as Annex 1 activities[1212] or the agricultural farms approved under the Environmental Approval for Livestock Holdings Act[1213] are covered by Chapter 4 b, if there are possibilities of soil and groundwater contamination at the site of the installation. Such operators shall prepare and submit to the competent authority an assessment of the soil and groundwater before closing down the approved plant. The pollution cost by the activities since the first baseline report was made has to be cleaned up by the operators.[1214]

§3. Evaluation of the Efficiency of the Legal Provisions

185. Over a quarter of Denmark's drinking water reserves could be contaminated by the fuel additive *methyl tert-butyl ether* (MTBE) despite a voluntary phase-out of substances in 2001, according to a report by the EPA. Its calculations were based on a survey in 2002 of forty-three polluted sites on the island of Funen (Fyn),

1210. These rules on environmental liability are described *infra* in paras 336–341.

1211. Ministry of Environment's Guidelines No. 9439 of 2 July 2008 on the *Definition of Environmental Damage in the Act on Environmental Damages*, at 57–58.

1212. Concerning the Annex I activities that are IE activities, *see supra* paras 63 and 65–66.

1213. Concerning the IE activities regulated by the special environmental approval rules in the Act on Environmental Approval of Livestock Holdings, *see supra* paras 64–65 and *infra* para. 264.

1214. Concerning the IE Directive, *see supra* para. 61.

where MTBE exceeding 30 ug/l had been found either in the secondary groundwater aquifers or the primarily groundwater aquifers or in nearby drinking water wells. From May 2001, the Danish oil industry voluntarily banned the use of MTBE entirely from 92- and 95-octane petrol, and cut supplies of 98-octane, essential to some older car models, by 90%. It was decided for the first time to focus on Denmark's next annual round of clean-up of former petrol stations on sites thought to be contaminated by MTBE.[1215]

186. One of the largest economic problems relating to the Danish waste deposit policy is the number of sites that have been registered or mapped under the Contaminated Soil Act as properties suspected to be polluted by old oil waste or chemical waste and the loss this represents for the landowners. Approximately half of all investigations and remedial action are undertaken on the initiative of property owners. A supervisory committee is formed in such cases with participation of representatives of the public authorities to ensure effective management of the voluntary investigation.

The amount of public money to be used for cleaning up polluted soil is insufficient, and consequently the organisations of oil importers as well as service stations have made an agreement with the environmental authorities concerning voluntary cleaning-up activities called the Oil Industry's Environmental Fund (OIEF). The goal of this fund is to finance efforts to clean up petrol station sites contaminated by petrol. It is clearly assumed that all companies, whether or not they had an interest in utilising the environmental fund – are covered by the contract. The assumption is justified by the relationships in the industry: that no company could tolerate unequal competition. The consumers pay for the soil clean-up through a price increase in the magnitude of DKK 0.03–0.05 per litre petrol. Normally such a cleaning-up project costs DKK 250,000, with the most expensive project expanded to DKK 11 million. At the same time, the oil industry has entered into a contract with the EPA, the National Association of Local Authorities in Denmark, the Association of County Councils in Denmark, and the Municipalities of Copenhagen and Frederiksberg on the industry's handling of the clean-up. If the contract between the authorities and the oil industry had not existed, then the reclamation initiative and the cost for old contaminated sites would have been the responsibility of the public, or the responsibility of the polluter, according to statutory rules and case law on fault-based liability, respectively. The contract has been subject to examination both by the Danish Competition Council and the Commission (DG Competition).

187. As a result of the agreement between the Government and the counties concerning the 1997 County Budget, DKK 270 million was set aside for public efforts to clean up contaminated sites. In addition, a DKK 75 million appropriation for cleaning up contaminated sites was included in the 1997 Finance Act. In 1999, the rules were strengthened in the Contaminated Soil Act. With the adoption of the Contaminated Soil Act in 1999, the regional authorities were given extended responsibilities. The total number of remediation in 2001 was estimated at a minimum of DKK 969 million. Of these, eighty-seven were financed by the public sector, 260

1215. Environment Daily No. 1432, 28 Apr. 2003.

were cleaned up under special programs, primarily the Danish Oil Industry's Association for Remediation of Retail Sites, 166 fell under the insurance scheme for oil tanks at houses, while the rest were voluntary remediation or compulsory (by means of an order), remediation financed by private funds.

In 2001, total expenditure for soil contamination was estimated at DKK 800 million. Interest in the programme was strong, and on 1 January 2002, 132 applications were pending, corresponding to an amount of DKK 95.3 million (EUR 12.7 million). The total cost of cleaning-up in 2008 was DKK 728 million (the private cleaning-up on the basis of administrative orders, as well as and the public spending) – the public expenditure at DKK 728 million. In December 2008, 24,000 contaminated sites were mapped. In 2009, the total expenditure for soil contamination was DKK 689 million of which DKK 437 million was paid by the public authorities. There were 36,430 mapped contaminated sites in 2017 and 434 DKK million was used by the five regions on cleaning-up, surveys, etc.

Chapter 6. Noise Pollution

§1. General Legislation

188. Noise causes a health risk for the neighbours to roads, railways, airports, wind turbines, leisure noise (e.g., nightclubs, pubs, live sporting events, concerts or live music venues), and industrial sites. Environmental noise is defined as noise emitted from all sources except industrial workplaces. Well-designed, powerful epidemiological studies have found cardiovascular diseases to be consistently associated with exposure to environmental noise. Environmental noise can consist of, for example construction noise, tonal noise, impulsive noise and low-frequency noise from various sources. The Regional Office for Europe of the WHO and the EU Commission have focused on the serious harms caused to human health by environmental noise.

In 1999, WHO summarised the scientific evidence on the harmful impacts of noise on health and made recommendations on guideline values to protect public health in its 'Guidelines for environmental noise'. Special night noise guidelines were published in 2009. In 2011 the WHO and the EU published an assessment of the burden for disease from environmental noise and quantified the healthy years of life lost in western European countries by environmental noise.[1216] It was estimated that the disability-adjusted life-years (DALYs) as the sum of the years of life lost from premature mortality and the years lived with disability for people living with the disease of health condition were 61,000 years for ischaemic heart disease, 45,000 years for cognitive impairment in children's, 903,000 years for sleep disturbance, 22,000 years for tinnitus and 654,000 years for annoyance (e.g., irritation).

Updated noise guidelines were published in 2018 with the title 'Environmental Noise Guidelines for the European Region'.[1217] These WHO Guidelines states that noise is one of the most important environmental risks to physical and mental health and well-being. Noise is measured in decibels (dB), and the intensity of the noise is measured using a method that mimics the ear's sensitivity and is represented by the unit decibel-A, dB(A).

The European Community has been working on the establishment and harmonisation of noise standards since 1992 with the Commission's proposal on the Fifth Environmental Action Programme (5EAP) stating that 'no person should be exposed to noise levels which endanger health and quality of life.[1218] The Commission's proposal for the 6EAP stated that noise was a growing problem that was estimated to affect the health and quality of life of at least 25% of the EU

1216. *See* the report published by the WHO Regional Office for Europe and the European Commission Joint Research Center, *Burden of Disease from Environmental Noise. Quantification of Healthy Life Years Lost in Europe*, 2011.

1217. The guidelines are published by the Regional Office for Europe of the WHO, and they are available at the internet, *see* http://www.euro.who.int/__data/assets/pdf_file/0008/383921/noise-guidelines-eng.pdf?ua=1 (visited 15 Jul. 2019).

1218. COM(92) 23 final, part 5.5.

population.[1219] One of the objectives was to address noise pollution in a wider context and to substantially reduce the number of people regularly affected by long-term above-average levels of noise, in particular from traffic and prepare the next steps in the work with EU legislation on noise. The priority of health protection is also part of 7EAP. This action plan is explaining that it is the ambition to move closer to the levels recommended by the WHO. The main focus of the EU noise policy is on noise-abatement through use of mandatory technical standards for products and type approvals laid down in a set of directives establishing emission limits for particular products. Existing EU source-specific environmental noise control legislation can be divided into the three following categories:

(1) *The noise emission from vehicles*, covered by the two directives introducing sound level limits: Directive on the approximation of the laws of the Member States relating to the permissible sound level and the exhaust system of motor vehicles[1220] lays down limits on the maximum levels of noise for road vehicle, and Directive on certain components and characteristics of two- and three-wheeled motor vehicles[1221] establishes limit values for the permissible level in relation to motorcycles. There is a Vehicle Type Approval system, which applies to all cars and motorcycles. In addition, the provisions of the Regulation Concerning Type Approval Requirements for the General Safety of Motor Vehicles, their Trailers and Systems, Components and Separate Technical Units Intended There[1222] are relating the tires from vehicles and their trailers, etc. by introducing limits on the noise generated where tires meet road.
(2) *The Framework Directive Relating to the Noise in the Environment by Equipment for Use Outdoors*[1223] has seven daughter directives on particular types of equipment that are placed on the market or put into service and aims to harmonise the standards on noise emission, etc.
(3) *The directives on noise emission limits from air plans*: Four directives are regulating the limit noise emissions from airplanes and their operation by reference to the Convention on International Aviation, e.g., the Directive on the Regulation of the Operation of Aero Plains[1224] that provides for the imposition of noise-related operating restrictions at airports.

1219. COM(2001) 31 final, at 48.
1220. Council Directive 70/157/EEC on the Approximation of the Laws of the Member States relating to the Permissible Sound Level and the Exhaust System of Motor Vehicles, with several amendments.
1221. European Parliament and Council Directive 97/24/EC on Contain Components and Characteristics of Two or Three-Wheel Motor Vehicles, with several amendments.
1222. European Parliament and Council Regulation No. 661/2009/EC concerning Type Approval Requirements for the general Safety of Motor Vehicles, their Trailers and Systems, Components and Separate Technical Units intended therefor.
1223. European Parliament and Council Directive 2000/14/EC on the Approximation of the Member States relating to the Noise Emission in the Environment by Equipment for Use Outdoors.
1224. European Parliament and Council Directive 2006/93/EC on the operation of aeroplanes covered by Part II, Chapter 3, Volume 1 of Annex 16 to the Convention on International Civil Aviation, second edition (1988).

Following a proposal by the Commission,[1225] the END[1226] was adopted in 2002. It defines 'environmental noise' as unwanted or harmful outdoor sound created by human activities including road, rail, air traffic and from sites of industrial activities such as those defined in Annex I of the Industrial Emission Directive, cf. Article 3(a). It does not set any source-specific limit values, but leaves the Member States the discretionary power to establish national limit values, if they wish to do so. The accepted noise levels depend on the surroundings. Pursuant to Article 2(1), the scope of the Directive covers environmental noise to which humans are exposed in particular in built-up areas, in public parks or other quiet areas in an agglomeration, in quiet areas in the open country, near schools, hospitals and other noise-sensitive buildings and areas. It is applying to noise that is caused by the exposed person himself or herself, noise from domestic activities, noise created by neighbours, noise at workplaces or noise inside means of transport or due to military activities in military areas, cf. Article 2(2). The main aim of the END is to define a common approach intended to avoid, prevent or reduce on a priority basis the harmful effects, including annoyance, due to exposure to environmental noise, cf. Article 1. To that end the Member States shall determine the exposure to environmental noise, through noise mapping, by harmonised methods of assessment. It is mandatory for the Member States to apply the noise indicators L*den* and L*night* as referred to in Annex I of the END, cf. Article 5. The values must be determined by means of the assessment methods as defined until the 1 January 2018 in Annex II of the Directive, cf. Article 6. From 31 December 2018 these standards were replaced by the standards laid down in the Commission Directive establishing common noise assessment methods according to END.[1227]

The Member States have to draw up their first strategic noise maps designed on the basis of the common assessment methods for the overall assessment of noise exposure in a given area due to different noise sources (major roads, railways, airports and agglomerations) or for the overall predictions for such areas (before 30 June 2012) as well as action plans (before 18 July 2013) to prevent and reduce noise where necessary, cf. Article 7. Member States are required to appoint competent authorities to draw up the strategic noise maps. The national authorities have to identify and report noise from major roads, railways, airports and agglomerations, using the harmonised noise indicators L*den* (day-evening-night equivalent level) and L*night* (night equivalent level), cf. Article 7. L*den* and L*night* are used in the making of strategic noise maps. The Member States must present strategic noise maps with the data on an existing or predicted noise situation in terms of a noise indicator, indicating breaches of any relevant limit value in force, and the number of dwelling exposed to certain values of a noise indicator in certain areas. The END provides for action plans to be made no later than 18 July 2008 designed to manage, within the territories, noise issues and effects, including noise reductions if necessary, cf. Article 8. The competent authorities are on the basis of the strategic

1225. COM(2000) 468 final.

1226. European Parliament and Council Directive 2002/49/EC relating to the Assessment and Management of Environmental Noise.

1227. Commission Directive 2015/49/EU Establishing Common Noise Assessment Methods according to Directive 2002/49/EC.

mapping to draw up action plans as means to reduce noise where necessary and to maintain environmental noise quality where it is good. There is neither a limit value, nor a prescription as to the measures to be used, which remain at the discretion of the competent authorities in the action plans. The END obliges the Member States to ensure that the public receives information about noise exposure, its effects and the measures considered to address noise, in line with the principles on public access to environmental information of the Aarhus Convention, cf. Article 9.[1228]

On 1 June 2011, the Commission submitted a report to the European Parliament and the Council on the implementation of the END.[1229] An evaluation of the Member States' implementation of the END relating to the assessment and management of environmental noise was published in 2016.[1230] In 2017, the Commission published a report on the implementation of Article 11 of the END.[1231] It is the conclusion that traffic noise remains the most dominant source affecting human exposure above the reporting levels defined by the Directive, with an estimated total of around 100 million people being exposed to road traffic noise above 55 DB L_{den}. Railways are the second most important noise sound with a total of more than 18 million people exposed above 55 DB L_{den}. Industrial noise within urban areas exposes around 1 million people to noise levels above 55 DB L_{den}.

189. The most important Danish rules on noise are laid down with legal basis in the Environmental Protection Act. In the provision on the objects it is stated, among other things, that it aims to prevent and abate the impact of noise on the public. There are a number of general instruments used for alleviating noise problems established by these acts.

The END is implemented by Statutory Order on the Mapping and the Environmental Noise Action Planning.[1232] The goal of the Statutory Order is to establish the rules for adoption of mapping of infrastructure plants in the biggest cities. The rules apply to environmental noise to which humans are exposed in particular in built-up areas, public parks, etc. following the scope of the END. The EPA is the competent authority to design the strategic noise maps, and guidelines have been adopted at national level for the mapping activities. The environmental authorities (either the EPA or the municipalities, depending on the case), are responsible for the monitoring of noise from airports and the action plans,[1233] and the larger IE industries and other noisy activities in cities.[1234] The mentioned authorities shall present noise

1228. Concerning the access to environmental information under the first pillar of the Aarhus Convention, *see supra* para. 31.
1229. COM(2011) 321 final.
1230. The Centre for Strategy & Evaluation Services of the European Commission, *Evaluation of Directive 2002/49/EC relating to the assessment and management of environmental noise, Final Report – Country Fiches, Second Implementation review of the Environmental Noise Directive*, July 2016.
1231. COM(2017) 151 final.
1232. Statutory Order No. 1596 of 13 December 2018 on the Mapping and the Environmental Noise Action Planning.
1233. Sections 7–8 of the Statutory Order on the Mapping and the Environmental Noise Action Planning.
1234. Sections 9–10 and 23–24 of the Statutory Order on the Mapping and the Environmental Noise Action Planning.

maps with the data on an existing or predicted noise situation in terms of a noise indicator, indicating breaches of any relevant limit value in force, the number of dwellings exposed to noise from the transport infrastructure, etc.[1235] The Ministry of Transport is responsible for mapping and strategic mapping of noise from the State roads and the main parts of the railways.[1236] The municipalities are responsible for the mapping of noise from the municipal major roads and for mapping of the noise from all roads in the major cities.[1237] In 2017, the noise levels in the neighbourhood to the roads were published by the four biggest cities: Copenhagen, Aarhus, Aalborg and Odense. It is available on the Danish Noise Mapp.[1238] The EPA carries out the coordination of mapping. The obligation to ensure public participation is stated in sections 29–30. The noise limit values in Denmark are depending on the sources causing the noise as well as the sensitivity in the recipient area.[1239]

190. To prevent noise pollution in cases of a significant impact on the environment, the Minister for the Environment may issue binding regulations concerning pollution by enterprises, plants, machinery, tools, furnaces and means of transport. Such rules are laid down in statutory orders on measuring methods covering noise emissions from production machines and activities as means used in the Danish implementation of the above-mentioned EU directives concerning noise limitation of vehicles, aircraft, etc. Other instruments are based on national traditions, such as statutory rules and guidelines for exposure levels covering daytime and night-time, physical plans, product types approvals, operating licences and economic instruments.

The authorities also use statutory orders and ministerial guidelines to determine the noise loads of different types of areas. Statutory Order on Noise from Wind Turbines[1240] is one of the most important examples. Other examples are the Statutory Order on Noise from the Training Grounds and Shooting Ranges of the Military Defence,[1241] and the Statutory Order on the Standard Conditions for Auto Repair Shops[1242] that regulates the specific activities of the mentioned enterprises.

The EPA has the competence to lay down guidelines for acceptable noise levels on different types of activities and different noise problems.[1243] Such noise emission guidelines are fundamentally important in the environmental decision-making system. Of special importance are the following:

1235. Sections 12–16 and 25 of the Statutory Order on the Mapping and the Environmental Noise Action Planning.
1236. Sections 5–6 and ss 17–20 of the Statutory Order on the Mapping and the Environmental Noise Action Planning.
1237. Section 11 of the Statutory Order on the Mapping and the Environmental Noise Action Planning.
1238. The Danish Noise Map is available at: http://miljoegis.mim.dk/spatialmap?&profile=noise (visited on 16 Jul. 2019).
1239. The Danish noise levels are published in the Centre for Strategy and Evaluation Service's report from 2016, at 68–72.
1240. Statutory Order No. 135 of 7 February 2019 on Noise from Wind Turbines.
1241. Statutory Order No. 1732 of 21 December 2015 on Noise from the Training Grounds and Shooting-ranges of the Military Defence.
1242. Statutory Order No. 1312 of 8 November 2016 on the Standard Conditions for Auto Repair Shops.
1243. Section 7 of the Environmental Protection Act.

- Guidelines No. 32/2019 on Quiet Delivery;
- Guidelines No. 16/2016 on the Noise Levels in Connection with the Establishment of Temporary Places for Refuges;
- Guidelines No. 9/1997 on Low Frequency Noise, Infrasound and Vibrations. These guidelines are based on the Directive on Approximation of the Laws of the Member States related to Common Provision for Construction Plant and Equipment[1244] establishing Harmonising Measures for Materials Utilised in Construction;
- Guidelines No. 5/1984 on Outdoors Noise from Enterprises with Supplements laid down in Guidelines No. 3/1996;
- Guidelines No. 6/1984 for the Monitoring of External Noise from Enterprises.

The EPA provides guidance for the work of the municipal councils and supports research and development of know-how on environmental noise issues. All the guidelines are first and foremost based on emission and input norms and in some ways on outdated technology-based thinking.

191. The Statutory Order on Emission by Outdoor Equipment[1245] is an implementation of the Outdoor Noise Directive ensures a harmonisation of the standards in the interest of the internal market.[1246] The Statutory Order has a number of objectives. It aims to protect the health and well-being of the neighbours and other citizens in the surroundings as well as protecting the environment. It is also a part of the harmonisation of trade in the EU. The rules apply to a wide range of product types from gardening equipment to construction and waste management equipment. All this machinery makes noise, such as, for example, equipment used in construction activities, cooling equipment for loading and unloading silos or tanks on trucks, and mortar mixers must be labelled with the EU harmonised marking (CE mark).[1247] All manufacturers of products subject to noise limits must follow conformity assessments under the supervision of notified bodies, which are appointed by the authorities. In 2017, the standards to be used were updated by the Commission.[1248]

192. Part of the Danish approach to noise control and abatement is to deal with noise in spatial planning. When planning new residential areas, the national guidelines for outside noise exposure are 58 dB (L_{DEN}). The activities have to respect the guiding noise level that are related to the accepted use of the area laid down in local

1244. Council Directive 84/532/EEC on the Approximation of the Laws of the Member States related to Common Provision for Construction Plant and Equipment.
1245. Statutory Order No. 29 of 11 January 2016 on Noise Emission in the Environment by Equipment for Use Outdoors.
1246. European Parliament and Council Directive 2000/14/EC on the Approximation of the Laws of the Member States relating to Noise Emission in the Environment by Equipment for Use Outdoors.
1247. *See* s. 3 of Statutory Order No. 29 of 11 January 2016 on Noise Emission in the Environment by Equipment for Use Outdoors.
1248. Commission, *Guidelines fort the Application of Directive 2000/14/EC of the European Parliament and Council Directive on the Approximation of the Laws of the Member States relating to the Noise Emission in the Environment by Equipment for Use Outdoors*, Update June 2017.

plans. Section 15a of the Act prohibits the municipalities (as the planning authorities) to establish local plans for residential, recreative or other noise-sensitive uses in the neighbourhood to industrial activities unless the local plan provides for the establishment of shielding measures etc., that can ensure the future for the industrial noise activities.

The Nordic noise prediction method was introduced in 2006 for the strategic mapping of road and railway noise on a 'pilot basis'. It has been used since 2007. Use of the method was a consequence of the implementation of the END by the first Statutory Order.[1249] The parameters used for the calculation, including the weather statistics and nine weather classes were specified in another Statutory Order.[1250] The Nordic prediction method, 'Nord 2000', is used for the monitoring of noise from road traffic. On the basis of the Planning Act, the municipal council must by means of the noise survey and other surveys, prepare plans for the location of enterprises, etc., for which special location requirements must be met to prevent pollution.[1251] In municipal planning, the focus must be on preserving sensitive areas from new facilities causing noise. As a result of the amendment of the Planning Act in 2003,[1252] it became possible to have a higher noise level in the existing enterprises compared to the normal noise levels in residential areas – but only for a short time period – if that area as an 'area of transformation' was to be transformed from a polluted business area into a residential area.

193. Environmental noise (e.g., from roads, railways and neighbours) is an integrated part of the building regulations to ensure low noise impact inside dwellings in connection with the construction of new buildings in noisy surroundings. Based on the Building Act,[1253] regulations on sound insulation between homes in the same building are required. There are also general rules on the required distance from one building to another. The neighbour law (law of nuisance) laid down by case law will also protect neighbours against very noisy activities.[1254]

§2. Noise from Fixed Sites

194. The Environmental Protection Act aims to prevent and combat noise nuisance from enterprises. The control over noise pollution from the most polluting enterprises is largely decided by the terms that are included in the environmental approvals that they receive under Chapter 5 of the Environmental Protection Act.[1255] There are some enterprises for which the licence requirement is based mostly on their noisiness. This is the case, for example in relation to shooting ranges

1249. Statutory Order No. 717 of 13 June 2006 and Guidelines No. 4/2006. The new Statutory Order No. 1596 of 13 December 2018.
1250. Statutory Order No. 647 of 18 June 2007. It is replaced by Statutory Order No. 1596 of 13 December 2018 on the Mapping of External Noise and on the Decision-Making on Noise Plans.
1251. Concerning the content of the municipal and the local plans, *see infra* paras 313 and 321.
1252. Act No. 440 of 10 June 2003 on the Amending of the Planning Act.
1253. Promulgation Order No. 1178 of 23 September 2016 on Construction of Buildings.
1254. Concerning the neighbour law, *see supra* para. 34.
1255. Concerning the environmental approval system, *see supra* paras 62–66.

and power bike sports clubs. There are some guidelines on how to design the terms on noise from such activities, cf. Guidelines No. 2/2005 on Noise from Power Bike Sports Clubs and Guidelines No. 2/1995 on Noise from Shooting-ranges.

An operating licence is not required for normal small enterprises, provided the enterprise is set up in accordance with approved local plans, i.e., in an area demarcated for industrial purposes.[1256] The accepted external noise level for enterprises is laid down in the Guidelines No. 5/1984 for enterprises.

195. Wind turbines emit a characteristic noise. Noise emanates from operation of the turbines' gear and generator as well as from the movement of the blades through the air. The wind turbines emit weak infrasound defined as sound that is lower in frequency than 20 Hz (fewer than twenty cycles per second). There is also some low-frequency noise, i.e., a deep sound with a low frequency from the compressor, a rumble from a boiler or a combustion plant, or the running of an idling engine. Such noise is technically defined as noise within a frequency range of 10–160 Hz (between 10 and 160 cycles per second). The Statutory Order on Noise from Wind Turbines[1257] includes rules on such noise for certain new types of series-produced wind turbines in specific situations. They apply to the values stated for correction for ground effects, which are based on the generally applicable method 'Nord 2000', as well as to the values stated for sound installations of dwellings, which are based on measurements of sound installation of low frequencies in fourteen representative Danish dwellings, cf. Annex I of the Statutory Order.

The noise in the open land may not exceed 44 dB(A) at a wind speed of 8 m/s and 42 dB(A) at a wind speed of 6 m/s in the neighbouring surroundings, cf. section 4 (1) of the Statutory order. In more densely built-up areas, such as residential areas, summer house areas and noise-sensitive recreational areas, the noise may not exceed 39 dB(A) at a wind speed of 8 m/s and 37 dB(A) at a wind speed of 6 m/s in the neighbouring surroundings, cf. section 4(2). The limit indoors is 20 dB for a wind speed of 6 and 8 m/s, cf. section 5 of the Statutory Order. Anyone who owns a wind turbine is responsible for installing, operating and maintaining it in such a way as to ensure compliance with the Statutory Order, cf. section 3. Before installation and modification of a wind turbine in a way that may lead to increased noise emission, the owner must submit a notification to the municipal council, cf. sections 8–9. Notification will be regarded as having been submitted when the municipal council has received all the information specified in section 8(3). Notification may take place when the required spatial planning, zoning permit, has been obtained – and if required, when an EIA permit for the wind turbine have been obtained. In areas which, according to municipal planning or local planning, have been reserved for the installation of several wind turbines or designated as wind farm areas, and where notification of individual wind turbines takes place consecutively, the municipal council may, to ensure that the total noise impact from all the wind turbines in the mentioned areas comply with the noise limits, set more restrictive requirements for the noise contributed by the individual wind turbine than the noise limit stated in section 4 and section 9(4). If a wind turbine is put into operation onshore after

1256. Concerning the spatial planning by local planning, *see infra* paras 319–328.
1257. Statutory Order No. 135 of 7 February 2019 on Noise from Wind Turbines.

installation, the municipal council must be informed of this. If the wind turbines are offshore, the information has to be sent to the EPA, cf. section 10.

The municipalities must inspect wind turbines to ensure that noise disturbance is not excessive, and they can require the owners to have the noise generated by their turbines measured to ensure that the requirements are meet, cf. sections 11 and 12. A survey of the noise must be carried out and the noise level calculated at the premises of immediate neighbours.

§3. TRAFFIC NOISE

196. The Road Safety and Transport Agency is responsible for development tasks concerning environment-friendly technologies for vehicles and public transport. Since 1995, the Agency has administrated part of the Ministry of Transport's Road Traffic Pool with the objectives to develop and test environment-friendly technologies. With support from the EPA's Pool and the Ministry of Transport's Traffic Pool, several research projects have been initiated, with the aim of reducing traffic-related environmental problems in towns.

197. Pursuant to section 10 of the Environmental Protection Act, the Minister for the Environment may, after discussion with the Minister for Transport, lays down regulations to the effect that projects for major road schemes and for the railways must be notified to him or her before work is commenced. The guidelines incorporate a compromise between a high quality of life and socio-economic considerations, accepting that a minor part of the public (typically the 10% most noise-sensitive people) might still feel highly disturbed. In Denmark, dwellings with road traffic noise of more than 58 dB (L_{DEN}) are considered exposed to noise, cf. the EPA's Guidelines No. 4/2007 for Road Noise. The Guidelines for railways have not been updated: it is still Guidelines No. 1/1997 on Noise and Vibrations from Railways that are used.

There are limitations concerning utilisation of areas near roads established by building lines. These are lines within which no buildings or extensions may be constructed, or important changes may be made to existing buildings without a licence. Such building lines are regulated partly by the Public Roads Act[1258] and partly by the Nature Protection Act.[1259] Although created for motives other than to prevent noise, the building lines do have a consequence for noise prevention, and they may be implemented while taking traffic noise problems into account.

198. The current 'Strategic Action Plan for the Noise from the State-owned Roads' was published in 2018, covering the period 2018–2023. Road traffic, especially on major urban roads in built-up areas is a very important contributing source to environmental noise. Roads and paths and other matters of importance to traffic, including the rights of access to traffic areas and the separation of the various kinds of traffic, must therefore be included in spatial planning. Under the Public Roads

1258. Promulgation Order No. 1520 of 27 December 2014 on Public Roads, as amended several times.
1259. Promulgation Order No. 240 of 13 March 2019 on Nature Protection.

Act, the public roads projects that are not decided by a specific road-related act may only be constructed in accordance with road preparation plans drawn up by the municipal councils in accordance with the overall spatial planning in the municipality and approved by the Minister for Transport.

Infrastructure projects are normally submitted in specific road acts by the Parliament. The special project-related acts evaluate the noise consequences of the new road and railway projects for the present or future use of the surrounding area.

199. Air transport is another important source of noise, particularly in and around airports and airfields. Therefore, airports and airfields must be considered in a spatial plan before their establishment.[1260] According to the Planning Act, the site for new airfields must normally be in open land that is not sensitive to noise and, if necessary, closely linked with other noisy transport installations and industrial areas.

Projects concerning airports are also covered by the environmental approval system laid down in Chapter 5 of the Environmental Protection Act.[1261] According to operating licences given on the basis of this Act, the owners of the airport must continuously monitor the noise level in the surroundings. There are also restrictions on the use of the airport in the evening and at night, terms concerning landing and take-off, etc. Based on Guidelines No. 5/1994 on Noise around Airports, it has to be ensured that new approved activities will not cause a higher noise level than the guideline values for day, evening and night laid down in the technical norm of these guidelines. The EPA's regional utilities handle approvals of airports. Copenhagen Airport (Kastrup Lufthavn) is a very special case under the authority of the Agency. As part of the approvals, noise mapping at various levels is carried out to ensure that the noise regulations are respected. The decisions on new airports are made by means of special development acts passed by the Parliament.

Aircraft used for aviation within Danish territory must have a certification of nationality and registration. It is an essential requirement for the registration of Danish aircraft that they meet the standards concerning noise pollution and other sorts of pollution laid down by the Minister for Transport, cf. section 82(1) of the Aviation Act.[1262] Aircrafts have become less noisy as a result of technical improvements, in part, due to international standards contained in the Chicago Convention on International Civil Aviation and in the EU directives mentioned above. These standards are taken into account by the authority when considering a request for a licence to use the airport. The Danish authorities do not allow aircrafts to land, if the operators do not have certificates demonstrating that they are in conformity with these standards.

200. High-speed ferries are regulated by noise rules under the Environmental Marine Protection Act[1263] and Statutory Order on the Environmental Permit of

1260. Concerning the municipal plans and the local plans, *see infra* paras 313–328.

1261. Concerning the approval system, *see supra* paras 62–63 and 65–66.

1262. Promulgation Order No. 1149 of 13 October 2017 on Aviation.

1263. Promulgation Order No. 1033 of 4 September 2017 on the Environmental Marine Protection Act, as amended several times.

High-speed Ferries.[1264] The Statutory Order states that a licence for new activities must be in accordance with the A-weighted values and the low-frequency regulations of the Statutory Order. The Environmental Agency is the competent authority.

§4. Evaluation of the Efficiency of the Legal Provisions

201. The concentration of residential activities and business in towns by means of spatial planning activities provides a good possibility to reduce the overall noise problem.[1265] Noise is, however, still a widespread source of nuisance and a health hazard in Denmark. In 2003, the 'National Strategy on Road Traffic Noise' highlighted the health effects of road traffic noise, and for the first time, there was a specific estimate of the economic consequences of the effects. At the same time, there was a renewed focus on the disturbance caused by the noise. The disturbance was quantified through a new investigation of the relationship between road traffic noise levels and house prices. In this way, it was possible to calculate the impact of road traffic noise on the society:

- 800–2,200 people hospitalised and 200–500 incidents of premature deaths each year;
- more than one in four dwellings in Denmark are exposed to road traffic noise above the noise limit for new dwellings (i.e., approximately 705,000 dwellings affected);
- 6.1% of the population is regularly disturbed by traffic noise inside their dwelling;
- a total cost to the society of DKK 8.7 billion each year.

In 2010, several research projects confirmed the negative impact of road traffic noise on health and well-being, and that the problem has not been reduced. The health effects are unchanged, and the number of exposed dwellings has not decreased. Thirty per cent of Danish homes are exposed to noise levels that exceed the threshold value of 58 dB (L_{DEN}), and noise problems are concentrated in cities. Approximately 10% of the noise-exposed dwellings in Denmark are located at the national roads. The rest are located at municipality roads. The main challenge in reducing road traffic noise is therefore related to the municipality roads, as 90% of the dwellings exposed to road traffic noise above the noise limits are located at municipality roads. The number of dwellings exposed to road traffic noise above the recommended limit (55 dB) has remained quite stable despite the increase in traffic. In 2003, 700,000 were exposed to a level of noise above the recommended limits for road traffic, and 60,000 were exposed to a level of noise above the recommended levels from airports or railways.[1266] The recent estimation, which is based on data from 2012 shows that 723,000 dwellings are exposed to noise that exceeds the recommended limits (58 dB L_{den}). Noise of 68 dB L_{den} or more heavily burdens

1264. Statutory Order No. 1735 of 21 December 2015 on Permits to High-Speed Ferries.
1265. Concerning the spatial planning, *see infra* Part III.
1266. OECD, *Environmental Performance Reviews. Denmark 2007*, at 178.

approximately 141,000 dwellings.[1267] A lack of public participation in the action planning was highlighted by the Centre for Strategy and Evaluation Services in its 2015 assessment of the Danish implementation of the END.[1268]

1267. Danish EPA, *The Danish National Road Noise Strategy*, https://eng.mst.dk/air-noise-waste/noise/traffic-noise/national-road-noise-strategy/ (visited on 15 Jul. 2019).

1268. Centre for Strategy & Evaluation, *Evaluation of Directive 2002/49/EC relating to the Assessment and Management of Environmental Noise*, at 9.

Chapter 7. Major Accidents, Hazards and Chemicals

§1. Major Accidents and Hazardous

202. There are currently two international instruments relating to major non-nuclear industrial hazards: the International Labour Organization (ILO) Convention Concerning the Prevention of Major Industrial Accidents signed in Geneva on 22 June 1993 and the UNECE Convention on the Transboundary Effects of Industrial Accidents signed on 17 March 1992 in Helsinki. A hazardous installation is defined as a fixed industrial plant/site at which hazardous substances are produced, processed, handled, stored, used or disposed of in such a form and quantity that there is a risk of an accident involving hazardous substances that could cause serious harm to human health or damage to the environment, including property. A hazardous substance is defined as an element, compound, mixture or preparation which, by virtue of its chemical, physical or (eco)toxicological properties, constitutes a hazard.

The ILO Convention requires the parties to provide the national policy and law on protecting of the employers, the public and the environment against major accidents in factories and industrial establishments. The aim is to prevent and mitigate the consequences of such accidents where they do occur. The standards, including the standard on BATs, apply to major hazard installations (excluding nuclear and military installations, and transport outside of an installation other than by pipeline). The ILO Convention sets out the systematic identification of major hazard installations, and rules on control and responsibilities of competent authorities and employers, as well as the workers' rights and responsibilities. The definition of employee is any individual working at, or on behalf of, a hazardous installation. This includes management and labour, as well as (sub)contractors. The employers are obliged to set up and maintain a documented system of major hazard control including emergency plans and safety procedures. The ILO Recommendations on the Prevention of Major Industrial Accidents from 1993 contain the guidelines for the international transfer of information to be organised by the ILO and the rapid compensation of victims of accidents. It also provides that ratifying States take the related ILO Code of Practice into account when formulating national policy, and that multinationals should ensure that they provide the same standards in all their establishments.

The UNECE Convention on the Transboundary Effects of Industrial Accidents and the Protocol on Civil Liability and Compensation for Damage Caused by the Transboundary Effects of Industrial Accidents on Transboundary Waters (signed in 2003) are based on the interests of the present and future generations' need for protection against the effects of industrial accidents. The Convention translates Principle 18 of the Rio Declaration (1992), on the obligation of the parties to '*immediately notify other States of any natural disasters or other emergencies that are likely to produce sudden harmful effects on the environment of those States*' into a more practical mandate. Based on the Convention, the parties must design accident notification systems. In Article 9 of the Convention it is stated that 'the people living in the areas capable of being affected by an industrial accident' have the right to information, the right to participate in the prevention of and response to industrial actions and access to justice.

There are some International guidelines to be followed. The OECD published its second edition of its guidelines in 2003 as a result of the Inter-Organisation Programme for the Sound Management of Chemicals (IOMC).[1269] These guidelines involve audits as a systematic examination of a hazardous installation to help verify conformity with regulations, standards, guidelines and/or internal policies. Audits can include examinations performed either by, or on behalf of, management of a hazardous installation (self- or internal audit), or an examination by an independent third party (external audit). The Global Reporting Initiative (GRI) was established as an international, multi-stakeholder initiative to develop, promote and disseminate frameworks for voluntary reporting of the economic, environmental and social performance of an organisation. The 'OECD Recommendations of the Council concerning Chemical Accident Prevention, Preparedness and Response' of 15 January 2004 recommends that Member Countries establish or strengthen national programs for the prevention of, preparedness for and response to accidents, e.g., by means of the 'Major Accident Reporting Systems' (the MARS Scheme).

The UNEP Division of Technology, Industry and Economics is leading an international initiative to promote chemical accident prevention and preparedness, focusing on a 'Flexible Framework for Addressing Chemical Accident Prevention and Preparedness (Guidance)'. It offers guidance for governments wanting to develop, review or strengthen their national chemical accident and prevention programs. Its activities focus on raising awareness, improving the transfer of knowledge and information, fostering technological cooperation and partnerships, and implementing international conventions and agreements.

The activities of the EUR-OPA Major Hazards Agreement of the Council of Europe offers a platform for cooperation in the field of technological hazards, particularly in respect of knowledge, prevention, crisis management, post-crisis analysis and rehabilitation.

203. The EU has ratified both the UNECE Convention and the ILO Convention. Article 196 TFEU – in the Title XXIII TFEU on 'Civil Protection' – established the constitutional basis for cooperation between the EU and its Member States in order to improve the effectiveness of systems for prevention and protection against natural or man-made disasters. The EU's actions must aim to support and complement Member States' action at national, regional and local levels. The European Parliament and the Council, acting in accordance with the ordinary legislative procedure are required to establish the measures necessary to help achieve these objectives.

In 1976, the chemical release after the accident at Seveso in Italy, where a catastrophic breakdown at a chemical plant released a huge cloud of toxic dioxin-laden

1269. OECD, *Guiding Principles for Chemical Accident Prevention, Preparedness and Response. Guidance for Industry (including Management and Labour), Public Authorities, Communities, and other Stakeholders*. The IOMC was established by UNEP, ILO, FAO, WHO, UNIDO, and OECD as a follow-up to the 1992 UN Conference on Environment and Development (the second Earth Summit) to strengthen cooperation and increase international coordination in the field of chemical safety.

gas to the atmosphere, prompted the EU to adopt the first Directive on Control of Major Accident Hazards in 1982. In 1996, the Directive on the Control of Major Accident Hazards (Seveso I Directive)[1270] was passed. The Seveso II Directive[1271] replaced it – the provisions are now laid down in the Seveso III Directive.[1272] The major rationale for the passing of the new Directive was the change in the classification system of chemicals under the REACH Directive[1273] and the CLP Regulation[1274] that introduce globally harmonised classification systems for chemicals.[1275] The Directive relates to the control of dangers connected with major accidents involving hazardous substances (e.g., chemicals), particularly where potentially dangerous industries are sited close to residential areas. It devotes much attention to the potential trans-frontier effects of serious accidents and to compliance with regulators, especially through systematic inspections. Its objectives include better exchange of information among Member States, authorities, operators, neighbours etc. The Directive does not apply to certain activities and installations, such as military establishments, landfills, hazard caused by ionising radiation and the transport of dangerous substances outside the establishment. It applies to some thousands of industrial establishments where dangerous substances are present in quantities exceeding the thresholds stated in the Directive. On the basis of criteria included in this Directive, the Commission should assess whether, notwithstanding their hazard classification, there are dangerous substances which do not present a major accident hazard and, where appropriate, submit a legislative proposal to exclude the dangerous substance concerned from the scope of it, cf. Article 4. Article 5 requires developers of new establishments to submit a notification to the competent authorities within a reasonable period of time prior to the start of the construction of the operation. Without prejudice to the operator's responsibilities, Member States must set up or appoint the competent authority or authorities responsible for carrying out the duties laid down in the Directive, cf. Article 6. The dangerous substances are classified in two schedules, cf. Annex I. The first schedule deals with 'named substances', such as chlorine, methanol and petroleum products. The second schedule relates to ten 'generic categories of substances', such as very toxic or flammable products. Thresholds established for named substances take precedence over the

1270. Council Directive 96/82/EEC on the Control of Major Accident Hazards involving Dangerous Substances.

1271. European Parliament and Council Directive 2003/105/EC amending Directive 96/82/EEC on the Control of Major Accident Hazardous involving Dangerous Substances. The scope of the Directive was extended by the Seveso II Directive to cover risks arising from storage and processing activities in mining, from pyrotechnics and explosive substances and from the storage of ammonium nitrate and ammonium nitrate-based fertilisers.

1272. European Parliament and Council Regulation No. 2012/18/EU on the Control of Major Accident Hazards involving Dangerous Substances (Seveso III Directive).

1273. European Parliament and Council Regulation No. 1907/2006/EC concerning the Registration, Evaluation, Authorisation and Restrictions on Chemicals (REACH) establishing a European Chemical Agency. Concerning REACH, *see infra* para. 214.

1274. European Parliament and Council Regulation No. 1272/2008/EC on Classification, Labelling and Packaging of Substances and Mixtures. Concerning the CLP Regulation, *see infra* paras 214 and 216.

1275. It resulted in the Seveso III Directive of 4 July 2012 that replaced the Seveso II Directive by 1 June 2015, the same date that the new classification system established by the CLP Regulation entered into force.

generic categories. The establishment's capacity for producing or storing the dangerous substance(s) is the basis for the national authorities' decision on whether the activities falls within the scope of the rules, and if so, whether it is qualified as a 'lower-tier' or an 'upper-tier' establishment. Both the lower- and the upper-tier establishments must notify the competent authority of the presence of dangerous substances and are obliged to have a major accident prevention policy in place, cf. Article 7. Any changes in the amount or type of dangerous substances must be notified to the competent national authority. Article 8 obligates the Member States to require the operators to draw up a document in writing setting out the major accident prevention policy (MAPP) and to ensure that it is properly implemented. The MAPP must be designed to ensure a high level of protection of human health and environment. It must be proportionate to the major accident hazards. It must include the operator's overall aims and principles of action, the role and responsibility of management, as well as the commitment towards continuously improving the control of major accident hazards activities and ensuring a high level of protection. The MAPP must be implemented by appropriate means, structures and by a safety management system in accordance with Annex III of the Directive. Member States must ensure that the competent authority, using the information received from the operators in accordance with Articles 7 and 10, or following a request for additional information from the competent authority, or through inspections pursuant to Article 20, identifies all lower-tier and upper-tier establishment to or groups of establishments where the risk or consequences of major accident hazards may be increased because of the geographical position and the proximity of such establishments, and their inventories of dangerous substances (domino effects), cf. Article 9. Member States must require the operator of the upper-tier establishment to produce a safety report, cf. Article 10. Article 11 states that the Member States must ensure that the operator updates the MAPP, the safety management system and the safety report and informs the competent authority of the details of those updates in advance in case of changes in the installations, establishments, storage facilities and processes of nature and quantity of dangerous substances, which could have significant repercussions on major accident hazards, or could result in a lower-tier establishment becoming an upper-tier establishment or vice versa. The Member States must also ensure that all upper-tier establishments draw up an emergency plan for the measures to be taken inside the establishment, cf. Article 12.

Article 13 of the Directive requires that hazardous activities are included in the spatial planning and/or other relevant policies. These requirements apply for both lower- and upper-tier establishments where hazardous substances are present. The mentioned requirements recognise that planning can be directed towards the need, in the long term, for appropriate distances between establishments covered by the Directive and residential areas, areas of public use and areas of particular natural sensitivity or interest. The accidents in Enschede, the Netherlands (2000), Toulouse, France (2001) and Ghislenghein, Belgium (2004) dramatically demonstrated the importance of spatial planning in mitigating the effects of major accidents. Member States must ensure that the information referred to in Annex V of the Directive is permanently available for the public, including electronically, cf. Article 14. Article 15 requires the Member States to ensure public participation in the decision-making in the following situations: (a) planning of new upper-tier establishments;

(b) modification to existing upper-tier establishments; and (c) developments around such upper-tier establishments. Member States must also ensure, as soon as possible following a major accident, that the operator must be required to supply information to the competent authority, cf. Article 16. The competent authority has to ensure that any urgent, medium-term and long-term measures which may provide necessary, are taken, cf. Article 17.

Under the Directive, the Member States are called upon to inform the Commission about major accidents, which have occurred within their territory. Such data are part of the environmental information accessible online in the EU's MARS Scheme.[1276] The Commission evaluates the information received from the Member States on hazardous accidents, and informs all the Member States and the relevant industry on the result of the details and lessons learnt to help prevent similar accidents in the future. The information is covered by the rules of the Aarhus Convention concerning access to environmental information.[1277] In Article 222 TFEU the 'solidarity clause' calls for the EU and its Member States to act jointly in a spirit of solidarity and assist a Member State in its territory in the event of a natural or man-made disaster. There are also new EU rules regulating offshore hazardous activities laid down in the new Directive on Safety of Offshore Oil and Gas Operations[1278] that supplement the Seveso rules.

204. The Environmental Protection Act applies to activities involving hazardous plants and processes, cf. section 2(2) of the Act.[1279] In pursuance of section 7, the Minister for the Environment may lay down some regulations concerning hazardous activities. The first Statutory Order was published in 1984.[1280] The current provisions are laid down in a Statutory Order on Control of the Risk of Major Accidents involving Hazardous Activities.[1281] It is hereinafter referred to as the Statutory Order.

Section 4, nos 2 and 3 and Annex I of the Statutory Order implement the thresholds and the distinction between the upper-tier plants/activities and the lower-tier plants/activities. The municipal plans and the local plans must include information

1276. In the EU, the Major Accident Hazards Bureau (MAHB) maintains the eMARS Database. The purpose of the eMARS is to facilitate exchange of lessons learned from accidents and near misses involving dangerous substances in order to improve chemical accident prevention and mitigation of potential consequences. It is available at the internet, *see* https://emars.jrc.ec.europa.eu/en/emars/content (visited on 15 Jul. 2019).

1277. Concerning the provisions on access to environmental information, *see supra* para. 31.

1278. European Parliament and Council Directive 2013/30/EU on Safety of Offshore Oil and Gas Operations.

1279. Promulgation Order No. 681 of 2 July 2019 on Environmental Protection.

1280. The first general administrative rules on such activities that implemented the Seveso I Directive were established by Statutory Order No. 204 of 1 May 1984 on Great Accident Risk in Connection with Industrial Activities. It was replaced by Statutory Order No. 545 of 16 September 1988 and Statutory Order No. 520 of 5 July 1990 on Security Assessment in Connection with Hazardous Activities. The Seveso II Directive was implemented by Statutory Order No. 1666 of 14 December 2006 on the Control of Risks from Major Accidents caused by Hazardous Substances, as amended by Statutory Order No. 1694 of 22 October 2010. Seveso III was implemented by Statutory Order No. 124 of 6 February 2014.

1281. Statutory Order No. 372 of 25 April 2016 on Control of the Risk of Major Accidents involving Hazardous Activities.

on the location of such hazardous activities.[1282] The general obligations of all operators of hazardous activities concerning notification and safety documents are stated in section 7 of the Statutory Order. section 7(2) states that both the lower and the upper-tier establishments are obliged at any times to demonstrate to the competent risk authority that they have taken all necessary measures provided for in this Order. They must implement the measures set out in the company's security report. The activities covered by the Statutory Order cannot be established or commenced without prior environmental approval from the authorities under Chapter 5 of the Environmental Protection Act, cf. section 8 of the Statutory Order.[1283] Applications for approval must include the information concerning the issues listed in the Annexes to the Statutory Order implementing the requirements laid down in the Seveso III Directive. The information relates to the parts of the establishment that are important from a safety point of view, the sources of hazard and the conditions under which major accidents could occur, together with a description of the preventive measures planned. The application must describe arrangements that are necessary for the safe operation of the plant and for dealing with any malfunctions that may arise. The application must also give information relating to possible major accident situations, i.e., emergency plans, including safety equipment, alarm systems and resources available for use inside the establishment for dealing with a major accident, and the names of the person and his or her deputies or the qualified body responsible for safety and authorised to set the emergency plans in motion and to alert the municipal council as the supervisory authority and the police. The operation licence must cover conditions on prevention of the special hazardous risks. The conditions connected to the approval have to specify the security obligations of the operator. Information about changes at the plants has to be sent to the approval authority, cf. sections 8–10 of the Statutory Order. Risk undertakings shall regularly and at least every five years review and, if necessary, update the safety document or the safety report. The obligations for the operators of upper-tier plants/activities to prepare a report on the assessment of the vulnerability of the plants in accordance with the guidelines in Appendix 6 of the Statutory Order is laid down in section 11. The obligation to inform the authorities about major accidents is described in section 12. The obligations of the different authorities, including their cooperation duties, are stated in section 13.

205. Nuclear energy has its own specific environmental problems such as safety, management and disposal of waste, but this is not a very important topic in Denmark. In this context, it should be remembered that there are no commercial nuclear installations in Denmark, and that it is the very clear energy policy not to accept such installations. Already in 1974, there was a public debate on the nuclear safety problems. In 1976, the Government drew up an energy strategy plan for the period of 1976–1995. Under this plan, new electricity supply capacity was supposed to be realised by means of five nuclear power plants.

1282. Concerning the spatial planning rules, *see infra* paras 312–321, *see* especially para. 313 on the content of the municipal plans.

1283. Concerning the environmental approval rules, *see supra* paras 63–65.

Nuclear safety measures are based on Act on Nuclear Installations.[1284] This Act contains rules for the eventuality that the Parliament decides to establish atomic plants in Denmark. The Act was in some respects suspended by the Danish Parliament.[1285] The rest of the rules contained in the 1962 Act were to be suspended by the coming into force of the Act on Nuclear Safety Measures and Environmental Issues relating to Nuclear Installations.[1286] The latter Act contains regulations on safety and environmental protection measures in atomic plants, etc., but it has not entered into force.

The Government departed from the above-mentioned 1976 strategy plan. It initially planned to settle the matter by means of the Nuclear Damages Compensation Act. However, it informed the Parliament that it did not wish an immediate decision to be reached. The adoption of Resolution No. B103 on 'Public Energy Planning without Nuclear Power Plants'– a decision adopted by the Parliament on 29 March 1985 – stopped the entry into force of the Act. Thus, most of the Danish atomic regulations are still to be found in the Act on Nuclear Installations.

206. Environmental problems in connection with radioactive contamination are regulated by the Act on the Use of Nuclear Substances.[1287] This Act lays down explicit criteria but authorises the government to issue rules regarding safety measures in conjunction with the importation, production, use, storage, transport and disposal of radioactive substances. Pursuant to this Act, the National Board of Health has laid down some regulations in the Statutory Order on Nuclear Safety Measures regarding Accidents in Nuclear Installations[1288] and the Statutory Order on Ionizing Radiation and Radiation Protection.[1289] Radioactive substances of any kind may generally not be produced, imported or held without permission from the authorities. Places where radioactive substances are produced, prepared and used must be clearly marked with warnings of radioactivity.

207. The Danish nuclear waste legislation has been debated as very unclear and clearly insufficient to handle nuclear waste from the decommissioning of the nuclear facilities at Risø National Laboratory at the Danish Technical University and from the hospitals. The Minister of Health is responsible for the administration of the Act on Nuclear Installations.[1290] On 9 July 2013, Denmark notified the EU about the implementation of the Directive establishing a Community Framework for the Responsibility and Safe Management of Spent Fuel and Radioactive Waste.[1291]

1284. Act No. 170 of 16 May 1962 on Nuclear Installations.
1285. It was s. 42 of Act No. 332 of 19 June 1974 Nuclear Damages Compensation that suspended some of the Act on Nuclear Installations.
1286. Act No. 244 of 12 May 1976 on Nuclear Safety Measures and Environmental Issues relating to Nuclear Installations.
1287. Act No. 94 of 31 March 1953 on the Use of Nuclear Substances, as amended by Act No. 99 of 10 February 2009 and by Act No. 23 of 15 January 2018.
1288. Statutory Order No. 278 of 27 June 1963 on Nuclear Safety Measures regarding Accidents in Nuclear Plants, as amended by Statutory Order No. 502 of 1 October 1974.
1289. Statutory Order No. 84 of 2 February 2018 on Ionizing Radiation and Radiation Protection.
1290. Act No. 170 of 16 May 1962 on Nuclear Installations, as amended.
1291. Council Directive 2011/170/Euratom establishing a Community Framework for the Responsibility and Safe Management of Spent Fuel and Radioactive Waste.

There are no clear Danish statutory rules implementing these rules and the citizens living in the areas planned for the deposit of the waste from the research institute Risø[1292] will not accept this. In a Circular letter the Minister of Health and Prevention ordered the nuclear regulatory authorities to submit a progress report on nuclear safety to the Minister every third year, who will transmit the report to the Danish Parliament. The Danish Health and Medicines Authority sent its first report on the implementation of the Directive in 2015.[1293] On that basis the Commission sent several questions to Denmark in a letter of 13 June 2016.[1294] Answers to the questions were sent to the Commission.[1295] On 7 July 2018, Denmark received an open letter from the Commission for not having implemented the Directive correctly.

§2. Chemicals

I. International Obligations on PIC, Chemical Safety Strategies, Etc.

208. The SDG targets 6.3 and 12.4 are focused on the negative environmental and human health impacts from harmful chemicals. It is the ambition to promote the sound management of chemicals (SMC) leading to reduced negative impacts. Chemical substances are defined as basic substances and compounds thereof as they appear naturally or are produced industrially. Some of the chemicals present problems due to their persistence and accumulation in the environment. This is particularly the case with the heavy metals. Other chemicals present problems because of their immediate toxicity. This is, for example, the situation in relation to pesticides. Pesticides, i.e., plant protection products (PPPs) and biocides, can affect human health via their contamination of groundwater, the soil, food and even the air. Chemical products are both products and solid, liquid and gaseous mixtures of two or more chemical substances. They are used in industrial and agricultural production as well as in private households. The main sectors using chemicals are the iron and metals industry followed by the chemical industry, and the repair and service sector. Chemical substances cross borders in the form of products and chemicals and as pollutants. Chemical safety is therefore both an issue relating to ensuring global trade and an issue relating to environmental regulation and reduction of the negative impacts of the substances.

1292. The Danish Parliament decided in 2003 to work out a plan for a deposit of the nuclear waste that is located at the research institute, but the six areas that were proposed for the location the deposit all ran into significant opposition from the people living in those areas.

1293. Danish Health and Medicines Authority, *Council Directive 2011/70/EUROTOM foe the Responsible and Safe Management of Spent Fuel and Radioactive Waste, First report from Denmark,* August 2015.

1294. Commission Letter of 13 June 2016, ENER/ARES (2016) 984284.

1295. The letter is available on the internet: https://www.sst.dk/-/media/Opgaver/Strålebeskyttelse/Tilsyn-og-rådgivning/Internationalt-samarbejde/Afrapportering-om-radioaktivt-materiale/Besvarelse-af-Kommissionens-spoergsmaal-til-Danmarks-nationale-politik-og-program.ashx?la=da&hash=84FD1C6647A2D6C8DD392893F20BF477444B5444 (visited on 19 Jul. 2019).

In 1992, the problems related to chemicals were discussed at the Rio Conference. Chapter 19 of the 'Agenda 21', adopted at the Conference, entitled 'Environmentally Sound Management of Toxic Chemicals, including Prevention of Illegal International Traffic in Toxic and Dangerous Products', recognised the lack of sufficient scientific information for the assessment of risks entailed by the use of a great number of chemicals, and a lack of resources to assess chemicals for which data are at hand. In 2002 at the Johannesburg Summit, the ambition was to achieve SMC throughout their life cycle by implementing the 'Globally Harmonised System' of classification and labelling of chemicals (GHS). The States were encouraged to implement the GHS without delay with a view to having the system fully operational. On 6 February 2006, at the International Conference on Chemicals Management (ICCM) in Dubai, United Arab Emirates, the Strategic Approach to International Chemicals Management (SAICM) was adopted as a voluntary multi-stakeholder, multi-sectoral policy framework to promote chemical safety and support nations in achieving the goal agreed at the Conference. The UNEP and WHO have published the official texts of the SAICM. It comprises:

- the 'Dubai Declaration on International Chemical Management' expressing high-level political commitment to SAICM;
- an 'Overall Policy Strategy' which sets out its scope, needs, objectives, financial considerations underlying principles and approaches, and implementation and review arrangement;
- a 'Global Plan of Action' that serves as a working tool and guidance document to support the implementation of SAICM and other relevant international instruments and initiatives.

The UN Development Programme and UNEP (UNDP-UNEP) Partnership Initiative for the Integration of Sound Management of Chemicals into National Development Planning Processes was established in 2006 to support the fulfilment of the goal of the SAICM. It aims to raise awareness of the need for action that contributes towards strengthening the linkage between sound chemicals management and the development agenda. It builds up capacity for improved integration of chemicals management into development agendas, and ultimately to mobilise sustainable financing for the 'SMC'. The commitment to minimise the adverse impact of chemicals on human health and environment by 2020 is part of the '2030 Agenda for Sustainable Development' and its SDGs and targets adopted on 25 September 2015. On 2 March 2019, the Secretariat of the SAICM released an interim report outlining progress in the implementation of the guidelines for achieving the 2020 goal on SMC. With 31 May 2019 as the deadline, the Secretariat invites stakeholders to provide comments to the report.

There are several international instruments that prevent the risks of damage to the environment and human health caused by trading, transport, storage and handling of chemicals. The Rotterdam Convention was concluded on 10 September 1998.[1296]

1296. UNEP/FAO Convention on Prior Informed Consent Procedure for Certain Hazardous Chemicals and Pesticides. It is also titled the PIC Convention. The EU and Denmark are parties to the Rotterdam Convention.

Under this Convention, chemicals that are banned or severely restricted, in order to protect human health or the environment, should not be shipped internationally unless the importing country consents to the shipping. It contains a procedure for the export of specially regulated chemicals and a procedure for the export of chemicals, which are prohibited or strictly regulated in the exporting country. It also contains requirements on the labelling and classification of the listed chemicals. The Convention allows the parties to take action that is more protective of human health and the environment than that required pursuant to the Convention, provided that such action is consistent with the provisions of the Convention and is in accordance with international law.

The UNECE Convention on Long-Range Transboundary Air Pollutants (LRTAP) from 1979 also regulates the discharges of chemicals by air.[1297] A protocol on POPs was signed under this Convention on 24 June 1998. It was named the Heavy Metals Protocol (or the UNECE Protocol on POPs Protocol). Article 3 describes the basic obligations of the contracting parties. These are, in essence:

- to eliminate the production and use of the substances listed in Annex I (the substances that are to be phased out);
- to restrict the substances listed in Annex II of the use set out in that Annex (substances whose use is regulated); and
- to reduce emissions of the substances listed in Annex III of a set level in relation to a reference year determined in accordance with that annex (substances whose emissions the signatory countries committed themselves to reduce).

Article 14(1)–(3) of the Protocol governs the procedure for amendments to Annexes I–III of that Protocol.

The Stockholm Convention was adopted on 22 May 2001[1298] as a follow-up on the Decision by the UNEP on the need for obligations on implementation plans. The Convention refers to the precautionary principle and aims to reduce and eliminate twelve persistent organic pollutants from international production and use, to clean up old stockpiles and contaminated zones, to take appropriate measures so that waste is handled, transported and stored in an environmentally sound manner, and to identify new components to be included in the international regime. Its objective is to protect human health and environment from POPs. The parties to the Convention recognise in particular that POPs:[1299]

> possess toxic properties, resist degradation, bioaccumulate and are transposed, through air, water and migratory species, across international boundaries and deposited far from their place of release, where they accumulate in terrestrial and aquatic ecosystems.

1297. CLRTAP and its protocols are described *supra* in para. 74.

1298. The UNEP Convention on Persistent Organic Pollutants – also known as the POPs Convention. It entered into force on 17 May 2004. The EU and Denmark are parties to the Convention. The Council approved the Convention by Decision 2006/507/EC.

1299. This reasoning is cited by the CJEU in its judgment C-246/07 *Commission v. Sweden*, para. 2.

The Convention lays down restrictions on the production, use, export and import of intentionally produced POPs. This Convention and the above-mentioned POPs Protocol are both establishing:

- prohibition or severe restriction on the production and use of intentionally produced POPs;
- provisions on the environmentally sound disposal of wastes containing POPs; and
- provisions on the reduction of emissions of unintentionally produced POPs.

Both the POPs Protocol and the Stockholm Convention establish strict international regimes for the initial lists of POPs, and they both contain provisions for including additional chemicals to these lists.[1300] The Convention was amended in 2009 to add seven new dangerous chemicals to the list. Article 3 of the Convention provides that the parties must adopt the necessary legal and administrative measures as regards the chemicals listed in the Annexes. Furthermore, the parties revised obligations for DDT, heptachlor, HCB and PCBs as well as certain emission limit values (ELVs) from waste incineration,[1301] sinter plants and electric arc furnaces for secondary steel production. They also adopted a decision to update guidance on BAT to control emissions of POPs. In 2015, new Annexes were decided at the COP. The parties can no longer produce PCBs, and they are obliged to stop using this chemical. Existing equipment that contains PCBs or is contaminated with PCBs may continue to be used until 2025. With regard to the elimination of the use of PCBs in equipment by 2025, the implementation is subject to review by the COP.

The UNEP Minamata Convention on Mercury was adopted on 10 October 2013 with the aim to protect human health and the environment from the adverse effects of mercury (Hg). The Convention has currently 102 members.[1302] It entered into force on 16 August 2017.[1303] In addition to the control on mercury mines, trade in mercury, mercury products and disposal of mercury waste the Convention includes provisions on controlling and reducing atmospheric emissions of mercury and mercury compounds. Mercury occurs naturally in the environment. The problems arise due to the use of it in products and processes – e.g., the burning of solid fuels both in the private use of fuels, in the transport sector and in the industry. The Convention addresses all aspects of the life cycle of mercury, including the use of it as chemicals. Manufacture import and export of products containing mercury is prohibited from 2020 with the modification that it is possible for the States to get a five years exemption.

1300. The POPs included in the Stockholm Convention are also all included in the Rotterdam Convention.

1301. Stationary combustion accounts for 51% of the HCB emission in Denmark, *see* DCE, *Annual Danish Informative Inventory Report to UNECE*, 2015, at 43.

1302. The EU and Denmark are parties to the Convention on Mercury. Before the Convention was ratified, the EU implemented it by several provisions, including provisions in the new NEC Directive (Directive 2016/2284/EU), cf. this *see* the Recital 4 in the preamble on the Directive.

1303. Mercury is a chemical that is also covered by the 'Heavy Metal Protocol' from 1998, *see supra* para. 74.

There are also international provisions on chemicals as hazardous waste regulated by the Basel Convention.[1304] The coordination among these three Conventions – Basel Convention, Rotterdam Convention and Stockholm Convention – has resulted in the adoption of recommendations on cooperation. Also the international regimes on protection of the marine environment – OSPAR and HELCOM – protect the environment against the negative impact of chemicals.[1305]

II. EU Legislation on Export and Import

209. The first EU Regulation concerning Export and Import of Certain Dangerous Chemicals was adopted in 1992.[1306] The EU signed the Rotterdam Convention in 1998, and implemented it by means of the Regulation Concerning Export and Import of Dangerous Chemicals[1307] implementing the PIC principle for certain hazardous chemicals and pesticides in international trade more stringently. In its judgment of 10 January 2006 in Case C-178/03 *Commission v. Parliament and Council*, the CJEU annulled the Rotterdam Regulation, as it was based solely on the environmental substantive basis of the Treaty. The Court ruled that both the environmental Article in the Treaty (now Article 192 TFEU) and the article on common commercial policy (now Article 207 TFEU) were the appropriate substantive basis.

The current Regulation concerning the Export and Import of Hazardous Chemicals[1308] is based on both articles of the Treaty, and it is stricter in its protection than the Rotterdam Convention. It covers not only the substances mentioned in the Convention's list. All substances subject to restrictions and bans within the EU are covered by the Regulation. In addition, the Regulation is harmonised with the REACH and the CLP Regulations described *infra*. Chemicals subject to the PIC procedure and listed in Annex II of the Regulation may not be exported to countries participating in the 'Prior Informed Consent Procedure' established by the Rotterdam Convention without the importing country's specific consent.

The Regulation on the Banning of Exports of Metallic Mercury and Certain Mercury Components and Mixtures and the Safe Storage of Metallic Mercury[1309] is another important Regulation that puts a general ban on exports of mercury from the EU.[1310] The ban applies from 15 March 2001 to exports of: metallic mercury

1304. Concerning the Basel Convention, *see supra* para. 140.

1305. Concerning the OSPAR and the Helsinki Conventions, *see supra* para. 129.

1306. Council Regulation No. 2455/92/EEC concerning the Import and Export of Certain Dangerous Chemicals.

1307. European Parliament and Council Regulation No. 304/2003/EC concerning the Import and Export of Certain Dangerous Chemicals.

1308. European Parliament and Council Regulation No. 649/2012/EU concerning Export and Import of Certain Hazardous Chemicals that replaced European Parliament and Council Regulation No. 689/2008/EC concerning Export and Import of Dangerous Chemicals.

1309. European Parliament and Council Regulation No. 1102/2008/EC on the Ban of Exports of Metallic Mercury Compounds and Mixtures and certain Mercury Components and Mixtures and the Safe Storage of Metallic Mercury.

1310. The Regulation on the Banning of Exports of Metallic Mercury and Certain Mercury Components and Mixtures and the Safe Storage of Metallic Mercury is a result of the international obligation described in UNEP's 'Community Strategy Concerning Mercury' and 'Mercury Programme'.

(Hg), cinnabar ore; mercury chloride (Hg_2CL_2), mercury oxide (HgO); and the mixture of metallic mercury with other substances with a mercury concentration of at least 95% of weight. Mercury produced by certain industrial activities will have to be stored under conditions that guarantee the safety of humans and the environment. The storage permit must include requirements for regular visual inspections of the containers and the installations of vapour detection equipment to detect any leak. Member States must submit to the Commission a copy of any permit issued for a faculty designated to store mercury, as well as information about the application and market effects of the Regulation in their territory. Metallic mercury from these sources is considered waste. The Regulation is without prejudice to the Regulation on Shipment of Waste.[1311]

III. REACH and Information on Risks

210. The 6EAP explained the need for a new system for risk assessment and risk management of chemicals produced, used and placed on the market and to improve some of the procedural mechanisms concerning the import and export of dangerous chemicals to bring it into line with the PIC Convention.[1312] On 13 February 2001, the European Commission adopted a White Paper setting out the 'Strategy for a Future Chemical Policy'.[1313] The objectives that needed to be balanced within the overall framework of sustainable development regarding chemicals were stated as: (a) protection of human health and environment; (b) maintenance and enhancement of the competitiveness of the EU chemical industry; (c) prevention of fragmentation of the Internal Market; (d) increased transparency; (e) integration with international efforts; (f) promotion of non-animal testing; and (g) conformity within the EU's international obligations under the WTO.

The general EU rules on dangerous substances were changed by the 2006 Package on Registration, Evaluation, Authorisation and Restriction of Chemicals (the REACH Package), which entered into force on 1 June 2007.[1314] The REACH Package includes:

- the REACH Regulation[1315] that applies to all substances unless they are explicitly exempted from its scope;

1311. The Basel Convention and Shipment of Waste Regulation aims to reduce the exports of hazardous waste, *see supra* paras 140–142.
1312. The 7EAP is also focused on the need for a reduction of the health and environmental risks connected to the chemicals.
1313. COM(2001) 88 final.
1314. The EU institutions and the Member States have fifteen years – depending of the content of the provisions – in which they have to apply the different parts of REACH as binding law.
1315. European Parliament and Council Regulation No. 1907/2006/EC concerning the Registration, Evaluation, Authorisation and Restrictions on Chemicals (REACH) establishing a European Chemical Agency.

– the REACH Directive on the amendment of the 1976 Directive on Classification, Packaging and Labelling of Dangerous Substances.[1316]

The REACH Regulation (hereinafter referred to as REACH) is part of the implementation of the Stockholm Convention as it contains provisions specifying how substances should be assessed with regard to their POPs characteristics. The European Chemical Agency (ECHA) was established by Title X of the REACH Regulation.[1317] The Agency manages the technological, scientific and administrative aspects of the REACH system at EU level, aiming at ensuring that the legislation can be properly implemented and has credibility with the stakeholders. REACH is directly applicable at national level and a total harmonisation instrument with its substantive basis in the Treaties rule on the Internal Market.[1318] The Member States (incl. Denmark) have a duty to take part in the risk assessment of the substances, ensure the good functioning of the Internal Market and to ensure that information is provided to consumers in accordance with the secondary legislation of the EU.

The overall aim of the Regulation is to ensure a high level of protection of human health and environment against risks from chemicals, as well as ensuring free circulation of the chemicals on the internal market, while enhancing competitiveness and innovation.[1319]

The REACH regulates chemical substances, mixtures and articles which contain hazardous chemical substances that can be (unintentionally) released. The definitions of substances, mixtures, articles, producers, etc. are laid down in Article 3. Products other than chemical substances and mixtures are called 'articles', cf. Article 3(3):

> An object which during production is given a special shape, surface or design, which determines its function to a greater degree than does its chemical composition.

Article 2(2) excludes waste as defined in the Waste Framework Directive from the definition of substance, mixture or article and thus from the field of application of REACH. REACH creates the distinction between 'non-phase-in substances' covering those chemicals not produced or marketed prior to the entry into force of REACH in June 2008, and 'phase-in substances' covering those chemicals listed in EINECS, or those that have been manufactured in the EU, but not placed on the EU

1316. European Parliament and Council Directive 121/2006/EC amending Council Directive 67/548/EEC on the Approximation of Laws, Regulations and Administrative Provisions relating to the Classification, Packaging and Labelling of Dangerous Substances in Order to Adapt to the European Parliament and Council Regulation No. 1907/2006/EC concerning the Registration, Evaluation, Authorisation and Restrictions on Chemicals (REACH) establishing a European Chemical Agency.

1317. ECHA is located in Helsinki, Finland.

1318. The legal basis for such provisions on the Internal Market is now Art. 114 TFEU.

1319. Recital 29 and Art. 1(3) of the REACH clearly state that the provisions are underpinned by the precautionary principle. Recital 1, the first part of Recital 3 and Art. 1(1) are high lightening the principle of a high level of environmental protection. The 'principle of substitution' where suitable economically and available technologies are available is also guiding the interpretation and application of the provisions, cf. Recital 12 and Art. 1(1) of REACH.

market, during the last fifteen years – also called 'no longer polymers' in the Directive on Classification, Packaging and Labelling of Dangerous Substances.[1320]

Most of the provisions in the REACH concern chemicals and manufactures and importers of articles which contain substances. Article 3(37) of the REACH defines an 'exposure scenario' of relevance for substances as:

> the set of conditions, including operational conditions and risk management measures, that describe how the substance is manufactured or used during its life cycle, and how the manufacturer or importer controls, or recommends downstream users to control, exposures of humans and the environment.

As indicated in this definition, some substances may be released already during use. Other substances may potentially be released during recycling or waste handling. The REACH creates a single system for both 'existing'[1321] and 'new' substances that adversely affect human health or the environment.[1322] Companies are 'article producers' with REACH obligations towards consumers and inspecting/enforcing authorities, if they produce articles within the European Economic Area, regardless of how the articles are produced and where they are placed in the market, cf. Article 3(4). An 'article importer' is any company located outside the EES that imports articles from companies that are located outside the EEA, cf. Article 3(10)–(11).

In Recital 117, the Regulation contains references to the Aarhus Convention and to the Aarhus Regulation concerning access to environmental information.[1323] However, Article 118 is stating that with regard to documents held by the ECHA it is the Regulation regarding Public Access to European Parliament, Council and Commission Documents[1324] that applies. There is in turn an exception to this presumption in emergency situations and other situations where urgent action is essential to protect human health, safety or the environment.[1325] Article 117 of the Regulation regulates the obligations of the Member States in terms of reporting to the Commission on the operation of the Regulation. Under Article 119, the competent national

1320. Council Directive 67/548/EEC on the Approximation of Laws, Regulations and Administrative Provisions relating to the Classification, Packaging and Labelling of Dangerous Substances.

1321. The single system that is in contrast to the former EU legislation was based on the distinction introduced by Council Regulation 793/93/EC on the Evaluation and Control of the Risk of Existing Substances. Existing chemicals covered by this former Regulation were those that were placed on the EEC market between 1 January 1971 and 18 September 1981. The 'new' chemical substances were substances that were not listed in the European Inventory of Existing Commercial Chemical Substances (EINECs), which was published in 1990. It contained over 100,000 chemicals that are used in the EU market. New chemical substances were listed in the European List of New Chemical Substances (ELINCS).

1322. New substances for the 'candidate list' are identified continuously under the REACH, and the list is updated twice a year.

1323. Concerning access to environmental information under the Aarhus Regulation, *see supra* para. 31.

1324. European Parliament and Council Regulation No. 1049/2001/EC regarding Access to the European Parliament, the Council and the Commission Documents.

1325. Concerning the assessment by the European Ombudsman of the Commission's practice in respect to this test, *see* COM(2011) 208 final, *Report from the Commission, Aarhus Convention Implementation Report*, at 18.

authorities in the Member States must inform the general public about the risks arising from substances, where this is considered necessary for the protection of human health and environment. Member States must ensure that all information held by the public authorities relating to imminent threats to human health or the environment is immediately distributed to any members of the public who are likely to be affected. The Regulation contains a free movement clause in Article 128(1). Article 128(2) allows the Member States to maintain or enact national rules on the protection of workers, human health or the environment insofar as these rules are outside the scope of the Regulation. Article 129 contains the safeguard clause, allowing the Member States to take action where there is an urgent risk to human health or the environment. Denmark has used the safeguard clause in several situations in order to introduce a classification system reflecting the neurotoxic potential as expressed through the risk phase R48/20 on danger of serious damage to health by prolonged exposure through inhalation.

211. Some of the chemicals that are used in cosmetics cause allergic reactions and other health problems. The cosmetics are products in the internal market. The manufactures must protect the users against such effects through scientific assessment, and the need to submit the assessment information to ECHA through a cosmetic products notification portal. These obligations are established by the Regulation on Cosmetic Products[1326] which has been in force since 11 July 2013. Testing cosmetics on animals is not allowed in the EU.

Article 1 of the Regulation states in that prior to placing cosmetic products on the market the producer/importer must submit, by electronic means, a list of information to the Commission. The Commission must, without delay, make the information available electronically to all competent authorities and to poison centres (or similar bodies), cf. Articles 5–6. The responsible producers of cosmetics have to follow the rules set out in the Regulation. Cosmetic products have been regulated in Denmark since 1961, but this legislation is now replaced by the Regulation that is directly applicable. The current national supplementary provisions on the administrative set-up are laid down in the Statutory Order on Cosmetic Products.[1327]

212. The international obligations with respect to POPs laid down in the Stockholm Convention and the UNECE Protocol on POPs have been implemented into EU law by means of the Regulation on Persistent Organic Pollutants of 29 April 2004,[1328] hereinafter named the POPs Regulation.[1329] The substantive basis in the Treaty is Article 192(1) TFEU given that the Regulation and the mentioned international measures agreed on predominantly pursue an environmental objective – the elimination of persistent organic pollutants.

1326. European Parliament and Council Regulation No. 1223/2009/EC on Cosmetic Products.
1327. Statutory order No. 803 of 21 June 2013 on Cosmetic Products. The Statutory Order has its legal basis in the Act on Chemical Substances and Products, *see infra* para. 213 concerning the mentioned Act.
1328. European Parliament and Council Regulation No. 850/2004/EC on Persistent Pollutants.
1329. Concerning the international rules, *see supra* para. 208. The POPs Regulation entered into force on 20 May 2004.

The POPs Regulation is a supplement to the EU rules described supra (the REACH Regulation, the CLP Regulation, etc.).[1330] It is directly applicable in Denmark and in all other Member States, including those which are not yet parties to the Stockholm Convention and/or the POPs Protocol.[1331] It contains provisions regarding the production, placing on the market and use of chemicals, the management of stockpiles and wastes, and measures to reduce the unintentional release of POPs. Article 3 prohibits the production, placing on the market and use of substances on the list which constitutes Annex I of that Regulation. It regulates the use of substances on the list constituting Annex II. The lists of the substances that are subject to the release reduction provisions constitute Annex III. The Member States are required to set up emission inventories for unintentionally produced POPs, national implementation plans and monitoring, and information exchange mechanisms. Article 14(1) of the Regulation provided that whenever a substance is listed in the Stockholm Convention or the POPs Protocol, the Commission is, where appropriate, to amend Annexes I-III accordingly, in accordance with the cooperation procedure referred to in Article 16(2) thereof. The Commission Regulation from 2014[1332] ensured amendments on minimum concentration limits for brominated diphenyl ethers and perfluorooctane sulfonic acid and its derivatives (PFOS)[1333] implementing international obligations under the Stockholm Convention. The Regulation added hexachlorobutadiene, polychlorinated naphthalene, short-chain chlorinated paraffins and endosulfan to the list of substances controlled in line with the Convention. The amendments came into force on 18 June 2015. The most recently amendment was passed in 2016.[1334] On 22 March 2018, the Commission presented a proposal for an amendment of the Regulation.[1335] These amendments are adding new chemicals to the list in accordance with the amended Stockholm Convention.

The Directive on the Disposal of Polychlorinated Biophenyls (PCBs) and Polychlorinated Terphenyls (PCTs)[1336] lays down rules on the controlled disposal of PCBs, the decontamination or disposal of equipment containing PCBs and/or the disposal of used PCBs in order to eliminate them. With regard to unintentionally produced POPs, there are several EU instruments that have an impact either directly or indirectly on the reduction of releases of these substances. The main release control measures on the control of the industrial emission of POPs are set out in the IED.[1337] The definition of BAT in the IED directly corresponds with one in the

1330. The Regulation has been amended several times.
1331. In 2017, Denmark joined the Persistent Organic Pollutant Review Committee (POPRC) under the Stockholm Convention that reviews chemicals proposed for listing under the Convention according to the POPs criteria.
1332. Commission Regulation No. 1342/2014/EU amending the POPs Regulation as regards Annexes IV and V.
1333. In the judgment C-246/07 *Commission v. Sweden*, the CJEU stated that a proposal to list PFOS in Annex A to the Stockholm Convention presented by the Swedish Government to the body set up under the Convention was against the exclusive competence of the Commission.
1334. Commission Regulation 2016/460/EU amending Annexes IV and V.
1335. COM(2018) 144 final.
1336. Council Directive 96/59/EC on the Disposal of Polychlorinated Biophenyls (PCBs) and Polychlorinated Terphenyls (PCTs).
1337. The IED replaced the IPPC Directive and sectorial directives, *see supra* para. 61.

Stockholm Convention. Where relevant, BAT-AELs are developed for emission of POPs. Product standards as imposed by the RoHS 2 Directive on the Restriction of the Use of certain Hazardous Substances in Electrical and Electronic Equipment[1338] will also reduce the quantity of POPs. The emission from PCBs in Denmark owes mainly to combustion of diesel road transport and not to products.[1339]

213. The Chemical Substances and Products Act[1340] is the main Danish legislation supplementing the directly applicable EU regulations and implementing the directives that are regulating the management of chemicals.[1341] The Act applies both to chemical substances and to components of chemical products and is subordinate to other rules, including the REACH Regulation and the CLP Regulation, cf. Article 288 TFEU and section 7 of the Act.[1342] The objective of the Act is to prevent damage to health and to the environment that may arise from production, safekeeping, use and disposal of chemical substances and products, cf. section 1(1) of the Act. The Act is based on the 'prevention principle' and the 'cleaner technology principle', cf. section 1(2). Based on the Act, when deciding action to be taken, a balance must be stuck between the damage which the substance or the product may cause to the environment and the technical and economic consequences, including the costs, of possible action both for society and for the individual, cf. section 2(2). This balancing test is not in harmony with the precautionary principle.[1343]

The Minister for the Environment has the power to publish the statutory orders necessary to transform and enforce international obligations and EU rules, cf. section 7a of the Act. The Minister may lay down rules on the risk labelling of products, cf. section 22a–22c of the Act. Under section 23, the Minister may issue regulations on the storage and safekeeping of hazardous substances and products. The Danish EPA and the municipal councils are in charge of supervising and controlling that the provisions of the Act are observed. The councils must assist in the supervision and control of the labelling and storage provisions by retailers, etc.[1344] The 'Danish Chemical Action Plan 2010-2013' was presented in March 2010. The Plan builds on the former 'Action Plan for 2006-2009', and it provided DKK 173 million to ensure a significant reinforcement of the commitment to the EU policy on chemicals. The Action Plan takes as its starting point the goal agreed at the 2002 WSSD and the obligations stated in the REACH. PPPs were not covered by the Action Plan as they were covered by the 'Green Growth Agreement', that was signed in July 2009 for the period of 2010–2013.[1345] On 23 October 2013, a new

1338. European Parliament and Council Directive 2011/65/EU on the Restriction of the Use of Certain Hazardous Substances in Electrical and Electronic Equipment, concerning this Directive *see supra* para. 150.
1339. DCE, *Annual Danish Informative Inventory Report to UNECE*, 2015, at 44.
1340. Promulgation Order No. 115 of 26 January 2017 on Chemical Substances and Products.
1341. The REACH and CLP Regulations are described *supra* in paras 210–212.
1342. Concerning the general legal hierarchy and the sources, *see supra* paras 56–58.
1343. The 'precautionary principle' is not mentioned in the Act. This is not in harmony with the EU chemical legislations. Concerning the basic principles of EU environmental law, *see supra* paras 26–29.
1344. Section 46 of the Chemical Substances and Products Act.
1345. Concerning the political agreement on 'Green Growth', *see supra* paras 110 and 160 and *infra* para. 261.

political agreement on 'Chemical Strategy 2014-2017' was signed with a focus on the Danish contribution to REACH and CLP through assessing and regulating substances. The current political strategy 'The Joint Chemical Initiatives 2018-2021' was agreed on 17 November 2017 by the former Government,[1346] the Social Democratic Party, the Danish People's Party, the Red-Green Alliance, the Alternative, the Social-Liberal Party and the Socialist People's Party. The Strategy is focusing on informed consumers, fair conditions for enterprises, less impact on health and the environment, and effective regulation and control of the most harmful chemicals. The practice regarding sanctions by the Chemical Inspection Service of the Danish EPA will be evaluated during the Agreement period with a view to possibly tightening sanctions against repeated infringements of the regulations. Import controls based on a risk assessment will be strengthened as part of the Agreement. DKK 4 million was earmarked to promote products covered by an eco-labelling scheme, and to create more awareness of the scheme. It is also part of the strategy to contribute to the work on an evaluation of the effectiveness of the Minamata Convention in respect to the management of mercury in waste, safe storage and reporting.

IV. Authorisation and Restriction of Use

214. The EU rules on authorisation of substances of very high concern (SVHC) are laid down in Title VII of the REACH. The candidate list of 'SVHCs' is listed in Annex XIV as subject to a prohibition process.[1347] The SVHC list includes substances, the use of which after their respective 'sunset dates' is prohibited unless the EU on application has granted specific exemption by a user.

Annex VII of the REACH replaces the Directive on the Approximation of Member States' Laws relating to Restrictions on the Marketing and Use of Dangerous Substances and Preparations,[1348] and thus introduced a new restricted process aiming at regulating the manufacture, placing on the market or use of certain substances on their own. Before the REACH entered into force, companies notified 'new substances' under the former Directive under the so-called Notification of New Substances (NONS). These notifications are considered as registrations under REACH. Registration is required under REACH before a substance is imported or produced in quantities exceeding one ton per year can be marketed. The same registration obligation exists for articles containing substances above the threshold established by the REACH, cf. Articles 5–7. Registration means that a manufacturer or importer of substances has provided a registration dossier (covering physicochemical, toxicological and eco toxicological information and information about the identity and name of the producer or importer) to the ECHA and that the ECHA

1346. The coalition government in power consisted of the Liberal Party, the Conservative Party, and the Liberal Alliance. Concerning the different Danish coalition government, *see supra* in para. 4.

1347. Concerning the candidate list, *see supra* para. 210.

1348. Council Directive 76/769/EEC on the Approximation of Member States' Laws relating to Restrictions on the Marketing and Use of Dangerous Substances and Preparations.

has not receive any indication that the documentation is incomplete.[1349] If a company fails to register a substance, it will no longer be allowed to manufacture or import that substance. Annexes IV and V to the REACH set out substances that are exempted from the registration, evaluation and downstream user provisions, as sufficient information is already available.

The process for addition to the candidate list is set out in Article 59 of the REACH and involves the preparation of a dossier in accordance with the criteria listed in Annex XV. The ECHA must identify the substances that have to be included in the 'Authorisation List'. The Commission Regulation[1350] contained the first designation of six substances to be included in the Candidate List. The latest date by which the applications on inclusion of substances in the candidate list from the Member States' Committee to the Commission[1351] must be submitted is eighteen months before the respective sunset dates.

To be identified as SVHC – substances that have very hazardous intrinsic properties – the substances have to be listed in the 'candidate list' in Annex XIV[1352] as substances that fulfil one or more criteria mentioned in Annex III, cf. Article 57. These criteria are:

- substances meeting the criteria for classification as carcinogenic, mutagenic or toxic to reproduction (CMR category 1 or 2);
- persistent, bio accumulative or toxic (PBT) or very persistent and very bio accumulative (vPvB) substances;
- substances for which there is evidence or equivalent levels of concern about their negative effects as they are potentially dangerous to health or the environment and are used dispersive.

There is no need for evidence of exposure and risk of a substance to identify it as an SVHC. However, a merely hypothetical risk does not permit precautionary action. The CJEU has emphasised the normative nature of the decision on tolerability of risks. There must be some scientific foundation for believing that adverse effects may occur, although the Court does not necessarily require findings.

If a company lodge an application for authorisation for the use of a listed substance, it has to attach a series of studies and detained documents, including a chemical safety report, an analysis of alternatives and a socio-economic analysis, cf.

1349. REACH establishes a duty for producers, importers and downstream users of substances to ensure that those substances will not adversely affect human health or the environment.

1350. Commission Regulation No. 143/2011/EU amending Annex XIV to the REACH Regulation.

1351. The Commission makes decisions on including new substances on the candidate list in Annex XIV, cf. Art. 58(1) of the REACH. The ECHA is required to make recommendations on further substances at least every second year, cf. Art. 58(3). Such a recommendation for the inclusion of substances in Annex XIV to REACH was published by ECHA on the following dates: 9 Jun. 2009, 17 Dec. 2010, 20 Dec. 2011, 17 Jan. 2013, 6 Feb. 2014, 1 Jun. 2015, 10 Nov. 2016, 5 Feb. 2018 and 19 Dec. 2018.

1352. The 'candidate list' has been established according to the procedure described in Art. 59. It is adopted by Commission Regulations and published on the website of the ECHA. The DEHP was included in Annex XIV by Commission Regulation No. 143/2011.

Article 7(2) and Article 33 of REACH.[1353] Article 7(2) requires any producer or importer of articles to send a notification to the ECHA, if all his articles supplied during a year in all contain more than 1 ton of a 'candidate list' substance. The conditions established by Article 7(2) are:

- the substance is included in the Candidate List for authorization;
- the substance is present in articles produced and/or imported above a concentration of 0.1/ weight/weight;[1354]
- the total amount of substances present in all articles produced and/or imported, which contain more than 0.1 weight/weight of the substance, exceeds 1 ton per actor per year.

In its judgment of 10 September in Case C-106/14 *Fédération des entreprises du commerce et de la distribution (FC) et al.* the CJEU stated how to ensure a correct interpretation of Article 7(2) and Article 33 TFEU.[1355]

Applicants for authorisation of SEACs under the REACH Regulation must demonstrate that the risks associated with the use of the substances concerned are adequately controlled or that the socio-economic benefits of their use outweigh the risks. Applicants must also analyse whether there are other alternative substances or technologies (the 'substitution principle'). If there are, they may prepare substitution plans: if not, they should provide information about research and development activities, if appropriate. The Commission may amend or withdraw any authorisation on review if suitable alternative substances become available.

1353. The aim of Art. 33 of the REACH is to ensure that sufficient information is communicated down the supply chain to allow the safe use of articles.

1354. In January 2013, the Commission started a process by letter no. 2012/2195 against Denmark for its failing to implement Arts 7(2) and 33 REACH on the maximum concentration 0.1% weight/weight correct. This legal question concerning the interpretation was explained by the Danish EPA to the Danish Parliament in a Note of 22 March 2013. It was the Danish understanding of the mentioned rules that it is not the whole bicycle as such, but the different elements of a bicycle that had to be assessed under the 0.1% weight/weight maximum level. Germany and Sweden follow the same interpretation of the rules as Denmark.

1355. It was the France notice on an interpretation of the concept of article within the definition of 'article' as well as the question concerning notification and communication obligations that the Conseil d'État wanted to have the CJEU's interpretation of. The last-mentioned question was related to the obligations in a situation in which a substance of very high concern (listed in the candidate list) is contained in different components of the same article. The Court explains that it must be remembered that the Regulation aims to ensure a high level of protection of human health and the environment, including the promotion of alternative methods for assessment of hazardous substances, as well as the free circulation of substances on the internal market while enhancing competitiveness and innovation. In its interpretation of Art. 7(2), the Court, e.g., concludes: 'the producer is required to notify the ECHA of the presence of substances of very high concern in the article that producer is making or assembling. If that article is subsequently used downstream by a second producer as input in the production of a complex product, that second producer is then not required also to notify the ECHA of the presence of the substance in question in that article … .'

The ECHA carries out evaluations of testing proposals made by industry and checks for the registration dossiers in compliance with the registration requirements.[1356] The ECHA is required to check 5% of the dossiers in each tonnage band, and in May 2012 it announced that it would improve the quality of dossiers. Under the cooperative approach, the Agency work with Member States to choose particular sections of dossiers relating to substance safety. Member States must evaluate certain substances to clarify whether their use poses a risk to human health or the environment (known as 'substance evaluation').[1357] The objective is, if necessary, to request further information from the registrants of the substances to verify any suspected concern. In the end, the evaluation of substances and articles may conclude that the risks are sufficiently under control with the measures already in place. Otherwise, it may lead to the proposal of risk management measures such as restrictions, identification of substances of high concern, harmonised classification or other actions outside the scope of the REACH. Any risk assessment should include consideration of:

- the life cycle of the product;
- potential hazards to health and the environment;
- physical form (solid, powder, liquid, gas, etc.);
- how the product is handled (manually, automatically);
- if there is contact with workers/consumers;
- if there is a risk of emission to the environment;
- what happens to the product after use (disposal).

Annex I of the REACH sets out the details of how to carry out a 'Chemical Safety Assessment' (CSA) and how to document it in a Chemical Safety Report (CSR). The CSR is the key source from which the registration provides information to all users of chemicals through the exposure scenarios. It also forms the basis for other REACH processes including substance evaluation authorisation and restriction. The report can also be described as the main end point for data assessment under REACH. Producers and importers are obliged to register substances in a database managed by the ECHA.

Article 31(1) and Annex II of the REACH describe what information should be included in the hazard communication under each of the sixteen headings of the safety data sheets (SDS). The sixteen-section format is internationally agreed. The SDSs are the products of risk assessment in that they describe how to reduce exposure in accordance with the known properties of the materials. The communication of risk to consumers is, by means of the SDSs, supplied in an official language of the Member States where the substance or the mixture is placed on the market as a mechanism for transmitting safety information. According to Article 31(7) of the REACH, registrants and downstream users are required to prepare a CSR and must

1356. Articles 40–43 of the REACH regulate the dossier evaluation. Annex XV established the rules on dossiers.

1357. Articles 44–48 of the REACH regulate such evaluations. The assessment is made in coordination between the ECHA and the competent authorities of Member States.

place the relevant exposure scenario(s) (ESs) into an Annex to the SDS. The original requirements of REACH for SDSs have been further adapted by an update to Annex II (revision of Annex II) to take into account the rules of the CLP Regulation.[1358]

The ECHA and the Member States must consider the adoption of marketing and use restrictions for the particularly dangerous substances.

The chemical diastyl phthalate (DEHP) was included in Annex XIV to the REACH in 2011.[1359] On 26 August 2014, the Kingdom of Denmark submitted four dossiers in accordance with Annex XV of the Regulation, proposing, first that DEHP and three other chemicals, the three of the phthalates (diisobutyl phthalate (DIBP), dibutyl phthalate (DBP) and benzyl butyl phthalate (BBP)) to be added to the 'candidate list' of substances. Denmark wanted to ensure that the combined concentration of these endocrine-disrupting substances does not exceed 0.1% in goods intended for indoor use or likely to come into direct contact with skin or mucous membranes. The Member State Committee did not reach unanimous agreement on the proposal, but it did unanimously approve that part of the proposal aimed at identifying DEHP as an endocrine-disrupting substance for which there was scientific evidence of probable serious effects on the environment. On 12 December 2014, the Executive Director of the ECHA adopted the decision in harmony with the Committee's approval with reference to Article 57(f).[1360]

V. Classification, Packaging and Labelling

215. To confront the danger and given the reality of the extensive global trade in chemicals and the need to develop national programmes to ensure their safe use, transport and disposal, it was recognised that an internationally harmonised approach to classification and labelling would provide the foundation for such programmes. The purpose of the classification is to consider the hazards arising from the normal handling and use of substances and preparations in the form they are placed on the market.

The UNECE developed the first generation of the GHS, and it has been updated biennially. The GHG classifies chemicals by types of hazard and proposes harmonised hazard communication elements, including labels and SDSs. It aims at ensuring that information about physical hazards and toxicity from chemicals is available

1358. The CLP Regulation harmonises the provisions and criteria for the classification and labelling of substances and mixtures within the EU, taking into account the UNs Globally Harmonized System of Classification and Labelling of Chemicals – referred to as 'the GHS'.

1359. Commission Regulation No. 143/2011 amending Annex XIV of the REACH Regulation.

1360. The Czech chemical company Deza did not accept that the decision of the ECHA was in harmony with the principle of conferral, as the decision was based on implied powers. It was of the opinion that the identification of the substance under Art. 57(f) was in conflict with the fact that DEHP was already identified previously by virtue under Art. 57. It was also part of the Czech argumentation that the decision of the ECHA was in conflict with the 'principle of legal certainty' and the 'principle of protection of legitimate expectations'. The conflict on the interpretation of Art. 57 was solved by the CJEU by a judgment of 23 January 2019 in the Case C-419/17P *Czech*. The Court rejected the argumentation of Czech as unfounded.

in order to enhance the protection of human health and environment during the handling, transport and use of these chemicals. The GHS also provides the basis for harmonisation of rules and regulations on chemicals at national, regional and global level, which is an important factor also for trade facilitation.

216. The old Directive on Classification, Packaging and Labelling of Dangerous Substances[1361] was based on the Treaty rule on the internal market. Additional rules concerning preparations were contained in Directive Concerning the Approximation of the Laws, Regulations and Administrative Provisions of the Member States relating to the Classification, Packaging and Labelling of Dangerous Preparation.[1362] Both Directives are repealed by the Regulation on the Classification, Labelling and Packaging of Substances and Mixtures (the CLP Regulation),[1363] which entered into force on 20 January 2009.

The CLP Regulation combines the GHS approach with the REACH with effect from 1 June 2015, the same date as the Seveso III Directive replaced the Seveso II Directive.[1364] Title XI of the REACH contains the new rules on the classification and labelling of substances. The rules basically declare the above-mentioned rules of the Council Dangerous Substances Directive[1365] as these rules were amended by the REACH Directive applicable. The new labelling system for pure chemical substances entered into force on 1 December 2010. As for mixtures, the labelling system entered into force on 1 June 2015.

217. Sections 19–23 of the Danish Chemical Substances and Products Act[1366] contain provisions relating to the classification, packing, labelling and storage of hazardous substances and products. The essential provision is section 19, in accordance with which every producer or importer must, before selling or importing a substance or product, acquire such information about the substances and consequences thereof so as to enable him or her to classify in accordance with the provisions of the Act and the EU rules. Denmark was involved in the preparation of the 'Guidance for Suppliers of Articles. The REACH Duties to inform about candidate list substances' (July 2013). The basis for this guidance was first developed in a project financed by the Nordic Council of Ministers.

The Minister for the Environment may under section 20 classify hazardous substances and products as: explosive, combustible, highly inflammable, readily inflammable, inflammable, poisonous, corrosive, harmful to health and locally irritating. The statutory orders mentioned below sets out more detailed classification

1361. Council Directive 67/548/EEC on Classification, Packaging and Labelling of Dangerous Substances.
1362. Council Directive 1999/45/EC concerning the Approximation of the Laws, Regulations and Administrative Provisions of the Member States relating to the Classification, Packaging and Labelling of Dangerous Preparations.
1363. European Parliament and Council Regulation No. 1272/2008/EC the Classification, Labelling and Packaging of Substances and Mixtures.
1364. Concerning the Seveso III Directive, *see supra* para. 202.
1365. It is referring to Council Directive 67/548/EC on Classification, Packaging and Labelling of Dangerous Substances as it was amended by the European Parliament and Council Directive 2006/121/EC.
1366. Promulgation Order No. 115 of 26 January 2017 on Chemical Substances and Products.

criteria for hazardous chemical substances and products. The Statutory Order on the Classification, Packaging, Labelling, Sale and Storage of Chemical Substances, and Preparation[1367] implement the above-mentioned relevant EU rules. The chief purposes of the rules are to ensure that the packaging is solid and strong, and that no possibility of confusion with harmless substances and products can arise. The rules on labelling require that the label contain the commercial name of the substance or product, the name of the hazardous substance, the name and address of the producer, and the hazardous class of the goods. A special danger sign must be included on the label. In addition, the labels must carry standardised risk symbols and safety instructions. The Statutory Order provides the regulations for evaluating the inherent properties of chemical substances or preparation in relation to hazard identification and assessment in line with the environmental requirements in the relevant EU requirements.

Chapter 6 of the Act contains rules that limit of the occurrence and use of chemical substances. Section 30 authorises the Minister for the Environment to make concrete decisions or draw up regulations to restrict or prohibit the sale, importation and use of chemical substances and to regulate their purity and concentration. The conditions for the use of these powers are laid down in section 30a–30e of the Act. Under section 31 of the Act, the minister may lay down rules concerning the composition and the purity of chemical products, including the extent to which chemical substances may occur in the product as impurities. Under section 32, the Minister may also demand that, for special purposes or in particular products, only chemical substances that are specially permitted for such purposes and of certain purity may be used. In specific sectors, it is therefore a 'positive list' system. As stated *supra* the regulations – including REACH and CLP – are binding in its entirety and directly applicable in Denmark, so the just-mentioned Danish rules have to be used only if they fully conform to the EU rules.[1368] Chapter 8 of the Chemical Substances and Products Act established the rules on internal control and the obligations on the responsible producer and importer to supply information concerning the substance or product, including financial and accounting data, etc. upon requests to the EPA. Additionally, producers and the importers must, when so ordered, carry out or have carried out, at their own expense, research into the impacts of the substances or products 'if there is reason to assume that a substance or product has effects that are hazardous to health or harmful to the environment', cf. section 40(1) of the Act. If an order is not complied with within the specified time, the EPA may have the examinations carried out at the expense of the responsible party, cf. section 40(2). This applies even to a substance that has already been duly notified, cf. section 41.

1367. Statutory Order No. 1075 of 24 November 2011 on the Classification, Packaging, Labelling, Sale and Storage of Chemical Substances, and Preparation, as amended by Statutory Order No. 1493 of 12 December 2013.

1368. Concerning the regulations as an integrated part of national legislation, *see supra* para. 58.

VI. Special Goals: PPPs and Active Substances

218. Pesticides are PPPs and biocides, used particularly in farming, forestry and horticulture and gardening as herbicides (weed killers), insecticides and fungicides. The group also includes microbiological products that consists of living microorganisms (bacteria or viruses), as well as plant growth regulators. The other main group is biocides (non-agricultural pesticides). The latter group is used to preserve wood against insects and fungi in buildings and on livestock and pets, and to exterminate rats and mice.

The 6EAP recognised that the impact of pesticides on humans and the environment, in particular from pesticides used in agriculture, had to be reduced. In its 'Towards a Thematic Strategy on the Sustainable Use of Pesticides',[1369] the Commission recognised the need for detailed, harmonised and up-to-date statistics on sales and the use of pesticides at EU level. The Strategy included five legislative proposals. Two of these legislative proposals were published on the same day as the Strategy – a proposal on a new Pesticide Framework Directive[1370] and a proposal on a Regulation concerning the Plant Protection Products (PPPs) on the Market.[1371] A third legislative proposal was published a few days later on a Directive establishing a Framework to Achieve a Sustainable Use of Pesticides,[1372] and in December 2006 the proposal on a Regulation concerning Statistics on the Distribution and Use of PPPs was published. In late 2008, the Parliament and the Council reached a compromise agreement on the 'Pesticide Package'.

Since 25 November 2009, the systematic production of EU statistics has been promoted by the Regulation on Statistics on Pesticides.[1373] The Member States are obliged to collect data on the annual placing on the market. At five years intervals, they must also send data on the use of substances containing PPPs. The preamble to the Regulation states that neither the Commission nor most Member States currently have sufficient knowledge or experience to propose new measures regarding biocides.

The EU has adopted a two-track approach for minimising the risks associated with pesticides: (a) a ban or severe limit regarding the placing on the market of the most hazardous and risky pesticides; and (b) ensuring 'best practice' is adopted regarding the use of the remaining, authorised pesticides. It provides for the risk assessment of the PPPs commonly known as pesticides.

219. The core legislation regulating the approval of pesticides on the EU market is the Regulation Concerning the Planting of Plant Protection Products on the Market (the PPPs Regulation). It contains the rules on approvals of the insecticides, herbicides and fungicides to be placed on the market. Like other regulations it is

1369. COM(2006) 372 final.
1370. COM(2006) 373 final.
1371. COM(2006) 388 final.
1372. COM(2006) 373 final.
1373. European Parliament and Council Regulation No. 1185/2009/EC concerning Statistics on Pesticides.

directly applicable at national level and takes a total harmonising approach regarding the legislation of Member States as it is based on the Treaty rules on agricultural issues, cf. Articles 42–43 TFEU, and on the Internal Market rules, cf. Article 114 TFEU.

The PPPs Regulation[1374] replaced the Directive Concerning the Placing of Plant Protection Products on the Market (the PPPs Directive)[1375] and the Directive on Prohibiting the Placing on the Market and Use of Plant Protecting Products Containing Certain Active Substances.[1376] The scope of the Regulation is confined to PPPs as well as active substances, which include microorganisms. The provisions also cover the so-called safeness, synergists and co-formulants, which are basically substances that have little or no effectiveness themselves but are added to PPPs to increase the effectiveness or safety of the relevant PPPs. Article 1 of the PPPs Regulation refers to the 'precautionary principle'. The approval cannot normally exceed a period of ten years, cf. Article 5 of the Regulation.[1377] However, for 'low-risk substances', the approval period can be fifteen years. The approval procedure for PPPs is set out in Articles 7–21 of the Regulation. The producer of the active substance has to demonstrate that it is safe and in conformity with the criteria laid down in Article 4. Approval of an active substance may be conditional, cf. Article 6. Under Article 4, the approval of PPPs for use on the market is subject to it being demonstrated that, under the envisaged conditions, their use will not result in, *inter alia*, harmful effects on human or animal health, directly or indirectly (e.g., through drinking water) or in groundwater and in unacceptable effects on the environment. In essence, the process involves an application sent to the authorities of the relevant Member State (known as 'the rapporteur Member State'). The rapporteur Member State must prepare a report that is made publicly available by the European Food Safety Authority (EFSA), which is also the authority that will come to a conclusion on the approval of the active substances. This conclusion is the basis for a review report and a draft regulation drawn up by the Commission and submitted to the Committee on the Food Chain and Animal Health, cf. Article 13(1) of the Regulation. The final approval is adopted on the basis of the review report and other relevant factors taking the 'precautionary principle' into account as the guiding principle, cf. Article 13(2). After the approval has been made, the active substance

1374. European Parliament and Council Regulation No. 1107/2009/EC concerning the Placing of Plant Products on the Market – also known as the 'Authorisation Regulation', the 'Pesticide Regulation', or the 'PPPs Regulation'. The Regulation came into force on 14 Jun. 2011.

1375. Council Directive 91/414/EEC Concerning the Placing of Plant Protection Products on the Market. The standard approved by the Food and Agriculture Organization (FAO) under the United Nation were followed by the Commission in its updating of the active substances, *see* the CJEU's Case C-459/06 *Vishim Srl v. the Commission.*

1376. Council Directive 79/117/EC on the Prohibiting the Placing on the Market and Use of Plant Protecting Products Containing Certain Active Substances.

1377. Existing authorisations for plant products that were granted before 14 Jun. 2011 (the day on which the Pesticide Regulation entered into force) are valid until they are amended or withdrawn.

is placed on the EU list, which can be found in the Annex to the Commission Implementing Regulation.[1378] Approvals may always be reviewed in the light of new scientific and technical knowledge indicating that the substance may compromise the objectives of the WFD, cf. Article 21. Articles 14–20 of the PPPs Regulation regulate the review process.

220. The Framework Directive on Sustainable Use of Pesticides[1379] is based on the environmental substantive basis of the Treaties (now Article 192 TFEU). It is complementary to other EU environmental rules, including the Wild Birds Directive,[1380] the Habitats Directive,[1381] the WFD,[1382] the Regulation on Maximum Residue Levels of Pesticides in or on Food and Feed of Plant and Animal Origin[1383] and the PPPs Regulation describe *supra*.

The maximum residual levels (MRLs) are set as indicators by the EU scientific authorities for each pesticide used on each crop. The measures used in accordance with the Pesticide Framework Directive are not permitted to prejudice voluntary measures in the context of the EAFRD.[1384]

The Pesticide Framework Directive provides for a range of actions to achieve a sustainable use of pesticides by reducing the risks and impacts of such substances on human health and the environment. The Member States were required to set up their first National Action Plans (NAPs) no later than 26 November 2012.[1385] These plans should contain quantitative objectives, targets, measures, timetables and indicators to reduce the risks and impacts of pesticide use on human health and environment, cf. Article 4. As a mandatory part of this planning, the Member States must introduce Integrated Pest Management (IPM), alternative approaches and techniques in order to reduce dependency on the use of pesticides. Member States shall ensure that all professional users, distributors and advisors have access to appropriate training by bodies designated by the competent authorities, cf. Article 5(1). There is an obligation for the Member States to take measures to inform the general public and to promote and facilitate information and awareness raising programmes and the availability of accurate and balanced information, cf. Article 7. As for the preparation of such programmes, it is appropriate to ensure public participations in accordance with the Directive on Public Participation.[1386] In their strategies, planning and reporting, etc. they must use the harmonised 'risk indicators' as referred to

1378. Commission Regulation No. 540/2011/EC implementing Regulation (EC) No. 1107/2009 of the European Parliament and Council as regards the List of Approved Active Substances.
1379. European Parliament and Council Directive 2009/128/EC on the Sustainable Use of Pesticides.
1380. Concerning the Wild Bird Directive, *see infra* para. 241.
1381. Concerning the Habitats Bird Directive, *see infra* para. 241.
1382. The Water Framework Directive is described *supra* in paras 103–104.
1383. European Parliament and Council Regulation No. 396/2005/EC on Maximum Residue Levels of Pesticides in or on Food and Feed of Plant and Animal Origin. Plants treated with authorised pesticides in line with the product label can be marketed and consumed as safe food with pesticide residues within the minimum residue levels.
1384. Concerning the Support under the Regulation No. 1305/2013/EU on Support for Rural Development by the European Agricultural Fund for Rural Development (EAFRD), *see supra* para. 258.
1385. These plans must be reviewed at least every five years.
1386. European Parliament and Council Directive 2003/35/EC on Public Participation, as amended. The Directive is described *supra* in para. 32.

in Annex IV, as this Annex was amended by Commission Directive on 15 May 2019.[1387] The indicator on hazard-based harmonised risk indicators is based on the quantitates of active substances on the market under the Regulation concerning Statistics on Pesticides.[1388] This Regulation stipulates that the Member States have to transmit annually to the Commission their statistical data on pesticides placed on the market each year (pesticide sales statistics).

The Member States must ensure that distributors of pesticides have sufficient staff in their employment holding the certificate referred to in the Directive, cf. Articles 5(2) and 6. The Member States must also ensure that pesticide application equipment in professional use is subject to inspection at regular intervals, cf. Article 8 of the Pesticide Framework Directive. The health and safety requirements relating to the inspection of pesticide application equipment are described in Annex II. Under Article 8(4), the inspection must verify that application equipment satisfies the relevant requirements. The standards referred to in Article 8(4) must be established in accordance with the procedure provided for in Article 6(3) of the Directive Laying Down a Procedure for the Provision of Information in the Field of Technical Standards and Regulations on Information Social Services,[1389] cf. Article 20 of the Framework Directive. Pursuant to Article 9, there is an obligation to prohibit aerial spraying, albeit with some exceptions, cf. Article 9. The Member States may include provisions on informing persons who could be exposed to spray drift, cf. Article 10. The protection of the aquatic environment and drinking water must be ensured by means of appropriate measures, cf. Article 11. Member States must have due regard for the necessary hygiene and public health requirements and biodiversity, and the results of relevant risk assessment by reduction of pesticide use or restriction in specific areas, cf. Article 12. They must adopt the necessary measures to ensure listed operations (e.g., storage, handling, packaging, tank mixtures and disposal) undertaken by professional users – and where applicable by distributors – ensure, that the pesticides do not endanger human health or the environment, cf. Article 13. It is also mandatory to take all necessary measures to promote low pesticide-input by use of integrated pest management, giving wherever possible priority to non-chemical methods, so that professional users switch to practices and products with the lowest risk to human health and environment among those available for the same pest problem (known as the 'substitution principle'), cf. Article 14. The Directive on Machinery[1390] states that machinery for pesticide application can only be placed on the market if it does not endanger the health or safety of persons or the environment.

1387. Commission Directive 2019/782/EU on Machinery, amending Directive 2009/128/EC. The Directive is based on the Internal Market as the substantive basis of the Treaties – the basis is now Art. 114 TFEU.

1388. European Parliament and Council Regulation No. 1185/2009/EC concerning Statistics on Pesticides.

1389. European Parliament and Council Directive 98/34/EC Laying Down a Procedure for the Provision of Information in the Field of Technical Standards and Regulations on Information Social Services.

1390. European Parliament and Council Directive 2006/42/EC on Machinery, as revised by Directive 2009/127/EC.

221. Denmark made its first Pesticides Strategy before it was mandatory under the Pesticide Framework Directive. The first Danish Strategy covered the period 1987 to 1996. The aim was to decrees the amount of pesticides used with 50% compared to the use in 1981–1986. The 'Bichel Committee' recommended a new strategy that was passed with effect from 1990. After an Action Plan covering the period of 2004 to 2009, the Green Growth Plan covered the period from 2010 to 2012, but neither of these action plans were effective. Moreover, the political agreements on APAE III and the 'Green Growth Agreement' were the basis for a Buffer Zones Act[1391] that established restrictions on the use of pesticides. A protected zone was established around lakes and watercourses under this Act.[1392] However, the pesticide load increased by 35% in the period 2007 to 2012. The Danish 'Protect Water, Nature and Human Health. Pesticide Strategy 2013-15' under the Pesticide Framework Directive was passed by a former centre-left coalition government.[1393] The overall goal of the strategy was to reduce the pesticide load by 40% by the end of 2015 compared with 2011. The most important instrument used to reduce the pesticide load was an amended pesticides tax. It is this Strategy that is part of the evaluation of the Danish policy published by the Commission in October 2017.[1394]

222. The Biocides Regulation[1395] aims to improve the free movement of biocidal products and at the same time to ensure a high level of protection of human health and the environment.[1396] The Regulation is based on the Internal Market as the substantive basis (Article 114 TFEU). The precautionary principle is mentioned in Recital 3 of the Regulation and the principle of a high level of protection is mentioned in its Recital 4 as guiding principles.

The Regulation makes a distinction between existing active substances, which were on the marked during the transposition period set by the former Biocidal Directive and other substances. Biocidal products can only be placed on the market when it receives an authorisation from the national authorities, and such an authorisation can only be obtained once the active substances contained in the product has been approved under the Regulation by the EU institutions. The Commission has passed many Regulations that ensure the harmonisation of the processes and criteria under this Biocidal Regulation.[1397] Product categories like medical products, cosmetic products, veterinary medical products and PPPs, which already fall under the scope of another approval scheme, are exempted from the Regulation. The

1391. Act No. 1411 of 4 December 2017 on Buffer Zones.

1392. Concerning the 'Green Growth Agreement', *see supra* para. 110.

1393. This former coalition government consisted of the Social Democrats, the Social-Liberal Party and the Socialist People's Party.

1394. Commission, *Member State National Action Plans and on Progress in the Implementation of Directive 2009/128/EC on Sustainable Use of Pesticides*, COM(2017) 587 final.

1395. European Parliament and Council Regulation No. 528/2012 concerning the Making Available on the Market and Use of Biocidal Products.

1396. The Regulation replaced European Parliament and Council Directive 98/8/EC on Biocidal Products.

1397. Among these regulations are Commission Implementing Regulation No. 354/2013/EU on Changes of Biocidal Products Authorised in Accordance with Regulation No. 528/8/2012/EU and Commission Regulation No. 414/2013/EU Specifying a Procedure for the Authorisation of Some Biocidal Products in Accordance with Regulation No. 528/12/EU.

authorisation of a biocidal product can be recognised in other Member States in accordance with the mutual recognition procedures to avoid duplication of the evaluation. The application for mutual recognition takes place in two phases. There are two procedures which are relevant: mutual recognition in sequences in situations either an existing authorisation and mutual recognition in parallel is situations where the initial application for national authorisation and the application for mutual recognition are submitted at the same time.

223. The Danish rules concerning approval of pesticides and biocides are laid down in Chapter 7 (sections 33–35) of the Chemical Substances and Products Act and the above-mentioned PPPs Regulation and Biocidal Product Regulation. The most important Danish rules implementing the Pesticide Framework Directive and supplementing the Regulations are laid down in the Statutory Order on Pesticides.[1398]

In Denmark, there are special national requirements for pesticides to ensure the protection of groundwater. The approval system is based on – and refers to – the PPPs Regulation, the Framework Directive on Sustainable Use of PPPs and the Biocides Regulation, cf. section 33(1) of the Act.[1399] The responsible person for import, sale or use must apply to the EPA for an approval on a special application form, cf. section 33 of the Act. Permission may be granted under conditions relating to the content, quality, sale, importation, packaging, advertising and marketing of the product. The EPA may decide that the legal provisions and conditions for the use and storage of the approved pesticide must be notified on the label.

The conditions for applications are laid down in Annex 1 of the Statutory Order on Pesticides. The obligations on labelling are laid down in section 17(1) and Annex 2 of the Statutory Order. The fees to be paid are stated in Annex 4 and Annex 5. As for the marketing of biocides containing active substances, each biocide must be approved according to EU standards and within the deadlines laid down by the Commission in accordance with the Biocidal Regulation. Mandatory standards on labelling are described in section 4 and Annex 3. Biocide products containing active substances for which a non-inclusion decision was taken shall be removed from the market within twelve months of the entering into force of such decision unless otherwise stipulated in that non-inclusion decision. This also refers to products marketed with a pesticide approval in accordance with former Danish legislation, even though this approval has not yet expired. Accepted tolerances in the products and analysis of biocides are stated in Annex 4 of the Statutory Order.

The Minister for the Environment may, in order to reduce the total load of pesticides, including the burden on health, the environment and nature, lay down rules on limitation or prohibition on the use of pesticides on specific areas, but not areas for agricultural purposes, cf. section 38 of the Act.

224. It is only holders of a special authorisation granted by the EPA and their assistants that are allowed to use very toxic pesticides. Obligatory training of all

1398. Statutory Order No. 815 of 18 June 2018 on PPPs.

1399. Concerning the Framework Directive on Sustainable Use of PPPs, *see supra* para. 219, and concerning the Biocides Directive, *see supra* para. 222.

commercial users of pesticides has been undertaken in Denmark. It is the Danish implementation of the provisions in the Pesticides Framework Directive laid down in Statutory Order on the Education of the Professional Users of Pesticides.[1400] It is with some exemptions prohibited to use aircrafts as a mean to bring out the pesticides on the fields.[1401]

225. Many ODS are GHGs that are not controlled under the UNFCCC. The Vienna Convention for the Protection of the Ozone Layer of 22 March 1985 and the Protocol Montreal on Substances that deplete the Ozone Layer are regulating such substances. The Protocol requires reduction of the use of ODS as well as reporting on trade in ODS. Since the Protocol entered into force, 95% of production and consumption of all ODS has been phased out.

The Convention on the Protection of the Ozone Layer (the Vienna Convention) was signed under the UNEP in 1985, and it entered into force in 1988. Under the Convention, the Montréal Protocol on Substances that Deplete the Ozone Layer (1987) identified certain chlorofluorocarbons (CFCs) and halogens. The Protocol has been signed by 196 States (including the EU), achieving universal participation. It aims to ensure the control by its parties of the production and consumption of specific chemicals, none of which occur naturally: CFCs, halons, fully halogenated CFCs (HCFCs), methyl bromide and similar chemicals. It limits and phases-out production and use of various compounds that destroy stratospheric ozone. It sets specific targets for reduction and a timetable for doing so. The Protocol represents a major political and diplomatic achievement in the international effort to protect stratospheric ozone. Since the Protocol entered into force, 95% of production and consumption of all ODS has been phased out. Still there are challenges to cope with. In 2006, scientists recorded nearly the largest ozone hole ever over Antarctica, and new data indicates that the recovery of the ozone layer in this area will not be reached before 2065.

The first EU Regulation on Substances that Deplete the Ozone Layer[1402] established more stringent requirements rules on the production, export, supply, use and handling of substances that deplete the ozone layer than the Protocol did.[1403] Since 1995, the use of CFCs has only been allowed in medical products and laboratory analyses. The rate of CFCs has been declining markedly since 1989, primarily due to implementation of the Montreal Protocol and the Regulation. The next version of EU law on ODS – directly applicable in Denmark – was Regulation on Substances that deplete the Ozone Layer (the 2000 ODS Regulation).[1404] It established stricter control provisions than the former version and stricter provisions than those of the

1400. Statutory Order No. 411 of 4 December 2017 on the Education of the Professional Users of Pesticides.
1401. Statutory Order No. 1755 of 14 December 2015 on the Use of Aircraft to bring out the Pesticides on the Field.
1402. Council Regulation No. 3093/94/EC on Substances that Deplete the Ozone Layer.
1403. The Montreal Protocol was signed by the Council Decision No. 88/540/EEC on Ratification of the Montreal Protocol. Denmark ratified the Protocol on 1 Jan. 1989.
1404. European Parliament and Council Regulation No. 2037/2000/EC on Substances that Deplete the Ozone Layer.

Protocol. The Regulation provided for a phased restriction on the production, importation, exportation, placing on the market and use of hazardous substances such as CFCs, other HCFCs, halons, carbon tetrachloride, 1,1,1-trichloroethane, methyl bromide, hydrobromofluorocarbons (HBFCs), HCFCs and bromochloromethane (CH_2BrCl) – and in certain cases, products or equipment containing these substances. There were also provisions on recovering, recycling, reclamation and destruction of such substances. By way of example can be mentioned, use of methyl bromide as a biocide was banned by September 2006. On 18 March 2010, it was banned for use as a PPP, quarantine and pre-shipment. The 2000 ODS Regulation was substantially amended several times. It is now replaced by the 2009 ODS Regulation[1405] that came into force on 20 November 2009. The 2009 ODS Regulation is a consequence both of new knowledge and technologies as well as the additional measures adopted by the parties to the Montreal Protocol at their meeting in September 2007 and in November 2008. In 2007, the parties adopted Decision XIX/6 providing for an accelerated phase-out schedule for HBFCs. Following that Decision, the production phase-out date should be brought forward from 2025 to 2020. The reselling of recycled HBFCs should also be prohibited, and recycled HBFCs should only be used in maintenance or servicing of refrigeration, air conditioning and heat pump equipment when recovered from such equipment and only by the undertaking, which carried out or mandated the recovery. The 2009 ODS Regulation implements such stricter conditions, it progressively generalise the ban of the use of those substances covered by the 2000 ODS Regulation, and it provides for control measures, which are stricter than those provided for in the 2000 ODS Regulation. The substances covered by the Regulations are also covered by the CLP Regulation,[1406] that provides for the labelling of substances classified as ODS and the labelling of mixtures containing such substances. It also makes references to the WEEE Directive and the obligations based on the Montreal Protocol only to accept technologies approved by the parties to be applied to the destruction of controlled substances.

226. Taxes on the pesticides, PVCs and industrial F-gases are used in Denmark as part of the policy on reduction of chemicals.[1407]

VII. Enforcement

227. The harmonisation of enforcement across the EU in Member States is a key issue under the EU chemical legislation, including the REACH Regulation and the CLP Regulation. The 'ECHA Forum for Exchange of Information on Enforcement'

1405. European Parliament and Council Regulation No. 1005/2009/EC on Substances that Deplete the Ozone Layer.
1406. European Parliament and Council Regulation No. 1272/2008/EC the Classification, Labelling and Packaging of Substances and Mixtures (CLP Regulation) – *see supra* in para. 216.
1407. Concerning the taxes, *see supra* para. 12.

has been established to ensure the coordination and a network of national enforcement authorities. It has adopted a set of minimum inspection criteria, which should be utilised primarily in the context of the Market Surveillance Regulation.[1408]

The Forum 'Strategies and Minimum Criteria for Enforcement of Chemical Regulations' was published on 6 December 2017 and includes criteria on how to enforce the four regulations: the POPs Regulation,[1409] the REACH Regulation,[1410] the CLP Regulation[1411] and the Biocidal Regulation.[1412] It provides a framework and general recommendations for developing national enforcement strategies within the Member States. Denmark and the other Member States may – as long as they respect the EU rules – develop their national enforcement strategies and establish their enforcement priorities in accordance with national circumstances. The Danish rules on enforcement are laid down in the Act on Chemical Substances and Products.[1413] It is the Chemical Inspection Service (in the EPA) that is responsible for monitoring compliance with the chemical regulations that includes both the EU regulations and approximately fifty Statutory Orders. It works together with other national authorities in the EU and the EEA. There is a special Nordic cooperation on these inspections titled the 'Nordic Inspection Group'. The Scientific Committee of the European Environmental Agency's stated in its 'Chemicals for a sustainable future' that EU legislation regarding chemicals typically addresses separate environmental media, individual substances and their specific use. It recommended that the regulatory approach should be changed into a more holistic one in which the overall environmental burden of chemicals on the human and ecosystem health as well as the importance of binding legal standards on products are in focus.[1414]

1408. European Parliament and Council Regulation No. 765/2008/EC on the Setting of the Requirements for Accreditation and Market Surveillance relating to the Marketing of Products.
1409. Concerning the POPs Regulation, *see supra* para. 212.
1410. Concerning the REACH Regulation, *see supra* para. 214.
1411. Concerning the CLP Regulation, *see supra* para. 216.
1412. Concerning the Biocidal Regulation, *see supra* in para. 222.
1413. Promulgation Order No. 115 of 26 January 2017 on Chemical Substances and Products.
1414. EEA, *Chemicals for sustainable future*. Report of the EEA Scientific Committee Seminar 2017, at 12.

Chapter 8. Sustainable Energy

§1. Policy and Legislation

228. International concern about the issue of secure energy access is growing. The UN, the OECD and its International Energy Agency (IEA), the Energy Charter, the Johannesburg Renewable Energy Coalition (JREC), the International Renewable Energy Agency (IRENE) and the G8/G20 have strengthened the importance of a rational use of energy including energy efficiency, as the most important contribution to reaching energy security and climate goals comes from the energy that we do not consume. The UN declared that 2012 was the 'International Year of Sustainable Energy for All', and the Rio+20 Summit in June 2012 was an important opportunity for action. Among the 2015 Sustainability Goals is the SDG 7 on energy that include four pillars: (1) ensure universal access to affordable, reliable and modern energy services, (2) work with countries to make energy systems and usage more efficient, (3) work to increase the global share of renewable energy, and (4) ensure sustainable cities and transport on the basis of integrated solutions that combine RESs and efficiency measures with other aspects or urban design, such as sustainable mobility, transport and waste management.

The IEA has long emphasised to its members and the world that energy production and consumptions, which is not compatible with international environmental requirements is not sustainable. The IEA has assessed the threats and opportunities facing the global energy system based on a rigorous quantitative analysis of energy and climate trends in its World Energy Outlooks. It is the estimated in the IEA's 'Sustainable Development Scenario' that the coal-fired power plants on a global basis account for one-third of energy-related CO_2 emission today and that it will represent more than a third of cumulative locked-in emissions to 2040. The World Energy Outlook analysis from November 2018 (WEO 2018) shows that over 70% of global energy investments will be government driven and that this means that the States and their international organisations needs to focus on more sustainable energy solutions. The WEO 2018 finds mixed signals on the pace and direction of change. Oil consumption is estimated to be growing in coming decades, due to rising petrochemicals, trucking and aviation demand and that the oil markets are entering a period of renewed uncertainty and volatility, including a possible supply gap in the early 2020s. Demand for natural gas is on the rise, and solar PV is charging ahead, but other low-carbon technologies and especially efficiency policies is lacking behind. In the power markets, renewables have become the technology of choice, making up almost two-thirds of global capacity to 2040, thanks to falling costs and supportive government policies. It is estimated in the WEO 2018 that the share of renewables in energy generation today is 25% and that this share of renewables will rise to over 40% by 2040. This expansion brings major environmental benefits, but it is also requiring a reform of the energy infrastructure and policy. The WEO 2018 is also highlighting the unique transformation that is ensured by the digital economy, making it possible to use electric vehicles, smart grids, smart buildings, etc. It finds that higher electrification would lead to a peak in oil demand by 2030, and that it will reduce the amount of harmful local air pollutant, but it will at the same time have an impact on the amount of carbon emissions if the share of renewables and low-carbon sources of power is not going further up in the energy generation plants. Coverage by renewable energy resources by a higher share of the total electricity consumption gives rise to technology hailing and regulatory problems. Achieving an energy system that do not emit carbon or harm the environment with other emissions requires strong political signals and the right framework to develop, integrate and deploy new technologies.

229. The EU 'Climate and Energy Package' (2008) aims to achieve in 2020 a 20% share in energy consumptions, originating from RES and a 20% reduction in primarily energy use – based on projected levels – through improved energy efficiency. It is based on an ambition to do, focusing on competitiveness (reasonable prices), sustainability (towards a low CO_2 fossil future) and energy security of supply.[1415] In Article 194 TFEU, it is stated that the Member States should achieve the goals in a 'spirit of solidarity'. In 2018 the EU passed a new package on the '2030 Framework for Climate and Energy' with the ambition to make it possible to fulfil the obligations under the Paris Agreement.[1416] The secondary legislation included in the Package that will come into effect from 2021 includes higher targets in the field of GHG emission reduction, the percentage of energy from renewable sources and the energy efficiency compared to the current legal acts. None of those objectives, which are indissociably linked, can be regarded as secondary to the other. The flexibility of the Member States is compatible with further market integration, increased competition, the attainment of climate and energy objectives and the gradual shift towards a sustainable low-carbon economy in national climate programmes, national plans for renewable energy and energy efficiency. Based on Article 192(2) TFEU, Member States retain their power to determine the conditions for exploiting their energy resources, the choice between different energy sources and the general structure of energy supply, cf. Article 192(2)b TFEU.

The 'Third Legislative Package' on a truly competitive energy market was presented in September 2007 and accepted by the European Council in October 2008. The package includes the Directive on the Single Electricity Market,[1417] the Directive on the Single Natural Gas Market,[1418] and the regulations on access to the network for cross-border exchanges. The package entered into force on 3 March 2011. Under this package, RES faced 'priority dispatch' meaning that, subject to security concerns, they should be dispatched ahead of other forms of generation irrespective of the marginal cost. In its conclusions of 23 and 24 October 2014 on the '2030 Climate and Energy Policy Framework', the Council stressed the importance of a more interconnected internal energy market and the need for sufficient support to integrate ever-increasing levels of variable RESs. On 25 February 2015, the Commission adopted its strategy for an Energy Union with the title 'A Framework Strategy for a Resilient Energy Union with a Forward-looking Climate Change Policy'.[1419]

1415. Concerning the Climate and Energy Package from 2008, *see supra* in para. 82.
1416. Concerning the 2030 Framework for Climate and Energy, *see supra* para. 83.
1417. European Parliament and Council Directive 2009/72/EC concerning Common Rules for the Internal Market in Electricity.
1418. European Parliament and Council Directive 2009/73/EC concerning Common Rules for the Internal Market in Natural Gas.
1419. COM(2015) 80 final.

On 23 February 2017, the Commission presented a package of proposals for a recast of the Directive on Common Rules for the Internal Market in Electricity, the Regulation on the Electricity Market, and the Regulation establishing a European Union Agency for the Cooperation of Energy Regulators.[1420] In December 2018, a political agreement on the 'Clean Energy for All European Package' was reached between the Council, the European Parliament and the Commission with the ambition to completing the Energy Union and combating climate change. The role and rights of consumers, transparency and predictability for investors is promoted by the new Package, *inter alia,* by obligations on systematic monitoring of key indicators for an affordable, safe, competitive, secure and sustainable energy system. These data are relevant for the coordination at national level of climate and energy initiatives and at EU level for the cooperation between Member States. The new Regulation on Governance of the Energy and Climate Action[1421] is passed with the aim to ensure transparency and a dynamic governance process. It includes an integrated monitoring and reporting system as well as obligations for the Member States to publish and update their integrated national climate and energy plans (NECPs) every ten years on the delivery of 2030 targets, cf. Article 3.[1422] The plans must consist of the issues listed in Article 3(2) and they must ensure the fulfilment of the objectives and targets that are stated in Article 4.[1423] A binding template is provided in the Annexes to the Regulation. The Member States had to submit their first draft plans by the end of 2018, cf. Article 9, and the final plans must be submitted by the end of 2019, cf. Article 3(1). The Commission has to assess the NECP, cf. Article 13[1424] By 30 June 2023, and subsequently by 1 January 2033 and every 10 years thereafter, each Member State must submit to the Commission a draft update of the latest notified integrated NECP or shall provide the Commission with reasons justifying why the plan do not require updating, cf. Article 14(1). By 15 March 2023 and every two years thereafter, each Member State must report to the Commission on the status of implementation of its NECP, cf. Article 17. The Regulation is also making it mandatory for the Member States to develop long-term strategies no later than 1 January 2020, and to ensure consistency between their NECPs and their strategies, cf. Article 15.

The 2009 *Directive on the Promotion of the Use of Energy from Renewable Energy* (RES Directive) is in force until 1 July 2021.[1425] By its nature, the Directive

1420. COM(2016) 864 final.

1421. European Parliament and Council Regulation No. 2018/1999/EU on the Governance of the Energy and Climate Action. The Governance that is an important part of EU's '2030 Framework for Climate and Energy' is mentioned *supra* in para. 83.

1422. The first integrated NECPs will cover the period 2021–2030, taking into account the long-term perspective.

1423. Article 4 is, e.g., stating the obligation for the Member States to include in their NECP the instruments that they will use to ensure that they are contributing to achieving the Unions targets on renewable energy in 2030 referred to in the new Directive on Renewable Energy, and the indicative national energy efficiency contribution to achieving the Union's energy efficiency targets.

1424. On 18 Jun. 2019, the Commission published its assessment of Member States' draft plans, and it called on Member States to step up ambition in their plans to implement the Paris Agreement.

1425. European Parliament and Council Directive 2009/28/EC on the Promotion of the Use of Energy from Renewable Energy. On 1 Jul. 2021, European Parliament and Council Directive 2018/2001/EU on the Promotion of the Use of Energy from Renewable Energy replace it.

balances a wide range of global, EU and national interests. It includes an integration of definitions and criteria across multiple sectors, countries and regulatory levels, and it is proactive in stating that there is a need to promote international standards and certification systems in relation to the production of sustainable biofuels. It sets a mandatory 20% target for the amount of RESs in the EU for the overall share of energy from such sources in the Union's gross final consumption of energy in 2020. Each Member State is subject to individual, quantitative commitments on the final energy demand from RES by 2020 that are based on the economic, social and environmental criteria set out in Annex I, Part A, so that across the EU, the target of 20% is achieved by 2020.[1426] A new RES Directive was passed in 2018[1427] and has a broader scope establishing a common framework for the promotion of energy from renewable sources. The share of renewable energy has to increase to at least 32% of the EU energy use by 2030.[1428] The Member States shall set national contributions to meet, collectively, the binding overall Union target in their integrated NECPs in accordance with Articles 3 to 5 and 9 to 14 of the Governance of the Regulation on the Energy Union and Climate Action, cf. Article 4(2) of the 2018 RES Directive.[1429] It also lays down rules on financial support for electricity from renewable sources in the heating and cooling sector and in the transport sector, on regional cooperation between Member States, and between Member States and third countries, on guarantees of origin, on administrative procedures and on information and training. It also establishes sustainability and greenhouse saving criteria for biofuels, bioliquids and biomass fuels, cf. Article 1. The Directive promotes energy from renewable non-fossil sources in the form of wind, solar, aero thermal energy, geothermal energy, hydrothermal energy and ocean energy, hydropower, biomass, landfill gas, sewage plants, biofuels and biogas. At least 10% of propellants in transport in every Member State must be RESs in 2020[1430] and 14% by 2030.[1431] Some special provisions on renewable energy in the transport sector are included in the 2018 Directive, cf. Articles 25 and 27–29. By 31 December 2021, Member States must take measures to ensure the availability of fuels from renewable sources for transport, including with regard to publicly accessible high-power recharging points and other refuelling infrastructure as provided for in their national policy framework in accordance with the Directive on Alternative Fuels Infrastructure.[1432] Both the 2009 Directive and the 2018 Directive afford the Member States a wide discretion with regard to the specific policies to be implemented and measures to be taken in accordance with their national circumstances. It

1426. By 2020, Denmark is required to increase its share of RES in the final energy consumption to a level of 30%.

1427. European Parliament and Council Directive 2018/201/EU on the Promotion of Energy Renewable Sources. This new 2018 RES Directive has its legal basis in Art. 194 TFEU.

1428. The binding Union target for 2030 under the 2018 RES Directive is 32%, cf. the Recitals 8, 10, and 11, and Art. 3(1) of the Directive.

1429. Article 3(1) of the 2018 RES Directive.

1430. Article 3 of the 2009 RES Directive.

1431. Article 25 of the 2018 RES Directive.

1432. European Parliament and Council Directive 2014/94/EU on the Deployment of Alternative Fuels Infrastructure. The Danish implementation of the Directive is made as a general delegation of the competence to the Minister of Transport, cf. Act No. 1537 of 19 December 2017 on Alternative Fuel Infrastructure.

includes a range of market-based and economic instruments such as green tradable certificates, feed-in tariffs in relation to renewable energy, taxes, and subsidies that Member States may use to meet the common target of 20% RESs of the total energy used in 2020.[1433] Under the 2018 RES Directive, it is possible to establish support schemes for energy as well as electricity from renewable sources as long as these schemes comply with Articles 107–108 TFEU, cf. Articles 4–6. One reason for the above-mentioned flexibility in the RES Directive is the limits to the EU institution's competences. The general principles on subsidiarity and proportionality as well as the shared competences between the EU and its Member States in the fields of environmental law and energy law must be respected by the EU. Another rationale behind the flexibility is that the initiatives to be taken are not only in the hands of the Member States, but also a matter of initiatives from business and other private actors. The Directive allows cheaper renewable energy that is produced and consumed in one Member State to contribute to the target of another Member State. As part of fulfilling their performance, the Member States may use 'statistical transfers' of a specified amount of RESs across national borders.[1434] Furthermore, they can use 'joint projects' for the production of electricity, heating or cooling from RES (which may involve private actors), they can use 'cross-border schemes', and they can use joint projects between them and third countries for the production of RES electricity (which may involve private operators').[1435] These cooperation mechanisms can also be viewed in the light of the EU institutions' limited capabilities. The objectives of the mechanisms are:

- to promote the use of a European regulatory perspective;
- to promote the integration of RESs into the Union Energy Market through trade, joint projects and joint support; and at the same time;
- ensure respect for the 'principle of sovereignty'.

The Directive accepts all types of joint projects between Member States in the production of electricity, heating or cooling from RESs. Cooperation may also include third countries.[1436] However, the Directive does not leave full autonomy to the Member States. The regulatory concept used is a concrete effort to reduce the barriers, which the jurisdiction of Member States, etc., may represent to ensure a sustainable development. It is mandatory to introduce a Guarantee of Origin System for the RESs.[1437] The guarantees must be applied across energy sectors: electricity, heating and cooling. They must ensure the involvement of informed citizens in the transformation from a brown to green economy. The European Energy Certification System (EECS) framework is designed to give users confidence in the

1433. Denmark only uses green certificates on a voluntary basis. The main measures used in Denmark are feed-in-tariffs, subsidies and taxes. The Danish use of economic instruments as subsidies to energy production is described *supra* paras 11–15.
1434. The conditions for the Union's reneweable development platform and statistic transfer between Member States are laid down in Art. 8 of the 2018 RES Directive.
1435. Articles 6–11 of the 2009 RES Directive and Arts 8–13 of the 2018 RES Directive.
1436. Article 11 of the 2018 RES Directive.
1437. Article 15 of the 2009 RES Directive and Art. 19 of the 2018 Directive.

quality and method of energy output.[1438] The idea of common concern in resource management, biodiversity and climate change has led to the use of sustainability criteria on biofuels in the RES Directive, the Directive on the Quality of Petrol and Diesel Fuels,[1439] and the Regulation on Performance Standards for Vehicles.[1440] The Directive on the Quality of Petrol and Diesel Fuels and the 2009 RES Directive were both amended in 2015 to reduce the risks arising from indirect land-use change.[1441] The 2018 RES Directive includes rules on sustainability and GHG emission saving criteria for biofuels, bioliquids and biomass fuels in Articles 29–34. The new Directive is, e.g., limiting the possibility to make food and feed crop-based biofuels, bioliquids and biomass fuels under the criteria of sustainability biofuels etc.

Global, regional, national and local decision-making systems and regulations include efforts to increase energy efficiency and reduce energy consumption as central planks in sustainable development. The Energy Efficiency Directive (EED)[1442] is another important part of the Energy Union Strategy. The EED puts forward legally binding measures to step up Member States' efforts to use energy more efficiently at all stages of the energy chain. The main purpose of the Directive is to ensure that the Union's 2020 headline targets on energy efficiency of 20% and its 2030 headline targets on energy efficiency of at least 32.5% are met and paves the way for further energy efficiency improvements beyond those dates.[1443] The Member States must achieve cumulative end-use energy savings at least equivalent to:[1444]

– New savings each year from 1 January 2014 to 31 December 2020 of 1.5% of the annual energy sales to final customers by volume, averaged over the most recent three-year period prior to 1 January 2013. Sales of energy, by volume, used in transport may be excluded, in whole or in part, from that calculation.

1438. It provides a mechanism for accounting renewable energy on the basis of certificate systems (RECS). The Danish 'Energinet.dk' is responsible for the operation of the EECS RECS system in Denmark. The EU obligations were implemented in Denmark by means of Statutory Order No. 1323 of 30 November 2010 concerning Guarantee of Origin of the RES. The Statutory Order was amended by Statutory Order No. 138 of 10 February 2012.

1439. Council Directive 98/70/EEC on the Quality of Petrol and Diesel Fuels, as amended by European Parliament and Council Directive 2009/30/EC and Directive 2015/1513/EU.

1440. European Parliament and Council Regulation No. 443/2009/EC on Performance Standards for Vehicles as amended by Regulation No. 333/2014/EU to define the modalities for reaching the 2020 target to reduce GHG emissions from new passenger cars.

1441. These two directives were amended by European Parliament and Council Directive 2015/1513/EU.

1442. European Parliament and Council Directive 2012/27/EU on Energy Efficiency. The design of the Directive is based on the Commission's proposal of 22 June 2011 on a set of measures for increased energy efficiency, cf. COM(2011) 370 final. The Energy Efficiency Directive repealed in 2012 two existing Directives: (a) the Directive on the Promotion of Cogeneration based on a Useful Heat Demand in the Single Energy Market (2004/8/EC – known also as the Cogeneration Directive) and (b) the Directive 2006/32/EC on Energy End-use Efficiency and Energy Services (known also as the Energy Service Directive).

1443. The higher targets are set by Art. 1(1) of the European Parliament and Council Directive 2018/2002/EU to Directive 2010/31/EU on the Energy Performance of Buildings, and Directive 2012/27/EU on Energy Efficiency. It is amending Art. 1(1) of the Energy Efficiency Directive.

1444. The minimum cumulative end-use energy savings are laid down in Art. 7 of the Directive 2018/2002/EU, that is replacing the ordinary formulation of this Article.

- New savings each year from 1 January 2021 to 31 December 2030 of 0.8% of the annual final energy consumption, averaged over the most recent three-year period prior to 1 January 2019. By way of derogation from that requirement, Cyprus and Malta must achieve new savings each year from 1 January 2021 to 31 December 2030 equivalent to 0.24% of the annual final energy consumption, averaged over the most recent three-year period prior to 1 January 2019.

The targets regarding energy efficiency implies a decreased utilisation of energy inputs, whilst preserving an equivalent pace of economy activity with five priority areas for action: buildings, energy technology/innovations, transport-related energy, energy-using equipment and energy consumers' behaviour. The main elements of the directive are: (a) each Member State will establish an energy efficiency obligation scheme, (b) the public sector will be required to renovate 3% of their building stock by floor area annually to cost optimal levels, (c) billing of energy consumption should be based on the actual consumption well reflecting data from the metering, (d) there should be initiatives for small- and medium-sized enterprises to undergo energy audit and disseminate best practice, and (e) improvement of the efficiency in the energy generation. The Member States are ensured flexibility in how they calculate the amount of their energy savings, whilst ensuring that the required cumulative end-use savings equivalent to new annual saving of at least 0.8% are reached.[1445] When implementing the provisions the Member States should pay particular attention to synergies between energy efficiency measures and the efficient use of natural resources in line with the principle of circular economy.[1446] One of the most important of the state obligations under this Directive is the National Energy Efficiency Action Plans (NEEAP) that the Member States have to use to demonstrate their fulfilment of their obligation to achieve the amount of savings required. Sales of energy used in transport could be excluded, and alternative ways to achieve equivalent energy savings would be permitted provided that equivalence is maintained. The Member States must require the large companies to have an energy audit management system. Recognising the significant energy-saving potential in enterprises of all categories and types, the EED obliges Member States to develop programmes to encourage small and medium-sized enterprises to improve their energy efficiency by implementing energy audits and the recommendations that stem from these audits. Based on the Directive, Member States should also ensure that national energy regulatory authorities take an integrated approach encompassing potential savings in the energy supply and end-use sector. It calls for a highlighting of concrete examples of how energy management systems could help their businesses. The EED requires Member States to adopt long-term renovation strategies and establish minimum requirements for the energy performance of newly constructed buildings and existing buildings undergoing major renovation. Almost 50% of the Union's final energy consumption is used for heating and cooling, of which 80% is used in buildings. Consequently, the renovation of buildings is an

1445. Recital 12 of the amending Directive 2018/2002/EU.
1446. Recital 28 of the amending Directive 2018/2002/EU.

effective instrument in the energy saving rules. The Directive on Energy Performance of Buildings (EPBD)[1447] also contained provisions on building renovation and long-term strategies for mobilising investment in the renovation of national building stocks. As for new buildings, Member States are required under the EPBD to ensure that before construction starts, the technical, environmental and economic feasibility of high-efficiency alternative systems is considered and taken into account. These systems include decentralised energy supply systems based on energy from RESs, cogeneration, district or block heating or cooling. When setting energy performance requirements for technical building systems, Member States must use, where available and appropriate, harmonised instruments. All new buildings after 31 December 2020 must respect very high-energy-saving standards and to a large extent be powered by RESs. The Directive includes obligations on 'nearly zero-energy buildings' in Article 9.[1448] Public authorities will have to lead the way by ensuring that after 31 December 2018, all new buildings they own or occupy are 'nearly zero-energy building'. With effect from 10 March 2020, the provisions on long-term renovation strategies laid down in the EED is moved to the EPBD, cf. Article 2a of the EPBD.[1449] The new rules expands the scope of the national long-term renovation strategies and make it mandatory for the Member States to establish a comprehensive strategy to achieve a high decarbonised building stock by 2050.[1450]

The Energy Labelling Framework Regulation[1451] is another secondary legislation addressing energy efficiency in the context of the 2030 energy efficiency targets. It provides for the labelling of those products and the provisions of standard product information regarding energy efficiency, the consumption of energy and of other resources by-products during use. It also provides for supplementary information concerning products, thereby enabling customers to choose more efficient products in order to reduce their energy consumption. The Eco-design Framework Directive[1452] aims to enable energy-related products to reach a suitable level of environmental performance during their life cycle. It also aims to facilitate the free movement of energy-related products within the EU. The Commission's adoption of regulations implementing measures laying down generic and specific eco-design requirements is based on this directive. Such requirements are laid down in the Commissions regulations implementing the Eco-design Framework Directive – i.e., the requirements for household dishwashers,[1453] household washing machines,[1454]

1447. European Parliament and Council Directive 2010/31/EU on the Energy Efficiency of Buildings.

1448. 'Nearly zero-energy buildings' are buildings that have very high-energy performance in accordance with the criteria set out in Annex I of the Directive.

1449. This amendment is made by the European Parliament and Council Directive 2018/844/EU to Directive 2010/31/EU on the Energy Performance of Buildings, and Directive 2012/27/EU on Energy Efficiency.

1450. *See* the Commission's Recommendation of 8 May 2019 (2019/786/EU) on Building Renovation concerning the content of the new provisions of the EPBD.

1451. European Parliament and Council Directive 2017/1369/EU setting a Framework for Energy Labelling.

1452. European Parliament and Council Directive 2009/125/EC on establishing a Framework for the setting of Eco-design Requirements for Energy-related Products.

1453. Commission Regulation No. 1016/2010/EU with Regard to Eco-design Requirements for Household Dishwashers.

and certain lighting products in the domestic and tertiary sectors.[1455] These rules are directly applicable and therefore binding on Danish manufacturers and importers who plan to market or put into service energy-related products.[1456]

The EU's Energy Taxation Directive[1457] is currently under discussion as the Commission wants to revise this Directive, but several Member States will not accept it. Based on Article 192 TFEU, it is only possible for the EU to make a new energy tax directive if all the Member States accept this.[1458] The Directive introduced a minimum tax level across the EU that has been controversial. In April 2011, the Commission published a proposal adding a CO_2 taxation chapter to the existing rules. The proposed energy tax structure involves a single minimum rate for CO_2 emissions in relation to sectors not subject to the EU ETS. It is the intention to introduce minimum tax rates for energy based on the energy content of fuel rather than on volume. Based on this change, transport and heating will be taxed with reference to the quantity of generated energy, thus rewarding more energy-efficient behaviour.

230. The geographical situation gives Denmark good conditions for import as well as export of energy sources. During the period from 1955 to the mid-1970s, Denmark was nearly 100% dependent on the import of oil. Historically, Denmark has been dependent on third countries in regard to coal.[1459] Denmark has been a net exporter of natural gas since 1984,[1460] and it is anticipated to be a net exporter of oil up to and including 2021, and a net exporter up to 2025 of sales gas.[1461] The Danish development of wind energy policy has a long history. It started on by establishing small onshore wind turbines in the late-1970s. In the mid-1970s, government commitment to the rapid introduction of nuclear power, enshrined in the first official energy plan from 1976, led to significant debate about the alternatives. Denmark is now involved in the North Sea Energy Cooperation (NSEC) on concrete concepts for joint offshore projects or cluster projects. [1462]

On 29 March 1985, a majority of the Danish Parliament adopted a decision on public energy planning not involving nuclear power in the Danish energy sources. By this point, Danish energy policy was getting ready for a greater focus on combined heat and power production (also known as cogeneration and as CHP) and on RESs, especially winds, in the electricity supplies system. In 1986/87, the Danish Energy Agency and the Steering Group for RES implemented programmes to

1454. Commission Regulation No. 1015/2010/EU with Regard to Eco-design Requirements for Household Washing Machines.

1455. Commission Regulation No. 245/2009/EU as amended by Commission Regulation 347/2010/EU as regards the Eco-design Requirements for Fluorescent Lamps, etc.

1456. Concerning the regulations as part of national legislation, *see supra* para. 58.

1457. European Parliament and Council Directive 2003/96/EC restructuring the Community Framework for the Taxation of Energy Products and Electricity.

1458. Concerning Art. 192(2) TFEU, *see supra* para. 57.

1459. The coal is imported from countries like China, India, the United States, Australian, Indonesia, Russia and South Africa, *see Denmark's Draft Integrated National Energy and Climate Plan*, December 2018, at 31.

1460. *Denmark's Draft Integrated National Energy and Climate Plan*, December 2018, at 31.

1461. Danish Energy Agency, *Oil and Gas Production in Denmark 2013 and Subsoil Use*, June 2014, at 16.

1462. *Denmark's Draft Integrated National Energy and Climate Plan*, December 2018, at 32.

encourage the use of decentralised CHP district heating distribution in decentralised municipality-owned networks for towns with between 500 and 40,000 inhabitants. These initiatives paved the way for CHP district heating systems using gas turbines, gas engines, municipally waste and biomass. The next energy plan published in 1990 ('Energy 2000')[1463] and the following plan published in 1996 ('Energy 21')[1464] conformed the shift in priorities. The first offshore wind farm in the world became operational in September 1991 at a site northwest of the Danish island of Lolland and in the Baltic Sea.[1465] Since then, a number of Danish offshore wind farms have been installed. The first feed-in tariffs system was introduced in 1993 as a fixed price for wind-generated electricity.[1466] The first EU Electricity Directive was implemented in Denmark on the basis of a political agreement adopted on 3 March 1999.[1467] By means of that reform, it was decided to maintain the fundamental rule obliging all electricity consumers to purchase from RESs in the 'RE Market'. This obligation appears in the 'Electricity Reform Agreement' (1999).[1468] Under a political agreement dated 20 February 2002, the former Liberal-Conservative Government (2001–2011) and several other political parties established the political basis for an amendment of the Electricity Supply Act with regard to the inclusion of payment for minimum capacity, the handling of electricity overflow, the takeover of non-performing windmills, electrical safety, etc. The agreement created new opportunities for offshore windmills and the framework

1463. 'Energy 2000' included the first moratorium on building new coal-fired power plants – permission would not be given to build conventional power without utilisation of the heat production. According to this strategy, several initiatives have to be taken, e.g., the establishment of 4000 MW of offshore wind power before 2030.
1464. 'Energy 21' was more focused on energy efficiency and renewable energy than the former strategies. Wind power was given an important role in 'Energy 21' with a target for RES-E at 10% in 2005 and 50% in 2030. The 2005 target was exceeded by a factor of two in 2003, with an installed wind power capacity of around 3000 MW.
1465. This wind farm consists of eleven 450 KW turbines. A second offshore wind park became operational in October 1995, at Tunø Knob between Jutland and the island of Samsø, with a capacity of 5 MW based on ten 500 kW turbines.
1466. Concerning the feed-in tariffs system, *see supra* para. 15.
1467. Act No. 375 of 2 June 1999 on Electricity Supply.
1468. Obligations for energy companies to promote RES-E were included in the Electricity Reform Agreement. The minimum price of a green certificate was specified as DKK 0.10 per kWh. The agreement allowed consumers to pay a fine instead. The fine was fixed at DKK 0.27 per kWh. The 'RE Market' was notified to the Commission and approved on 3 Oct. 2000. On 22 Mar. 2000, a follow-up agreement to the reform was adopted to ensure the implementation of initiatives promoting environmental friendly electricity, a green energy market (RE market with green certificates), energy saving and offshore wind. On 19 Jun. 2002, the Liberal-Conservative Government and several other political parties entered into an agreement postponing the planned 'RES market' in green certificates and replacing it with a premium-based feed-in tariff system. The RES Market was finally dropped by means of Act No. 1392 of 27 December 2008 on Promotion of Renewable Energy. The obligation to purchase an increasing share of RES-E as part of the energy supply system was supplemented with priority access for electricity from RES-E and environment-friendly electricity (including energy produced in CHP). This change resulted from a number of complications relating to the operational principles of the green certificate system, including high transaction costs in a small national market. It was decided to replace the 'RES market' with complicated transitional rules for RES-E. These rules are still part of the legislation on feed-in tariffs and energy taxes.

conditions of decentralised CHP plants.[1469] A Danish 'Action Programme for Energy Saving' was agreed by most of the political parties in May 2001 with the establishment of the Electricity Saving Trust Fund. It covered the trade, service and manufacturing sectors so that purchase agreements and other schemes to promote energy-efficient electricity's appliances were promoted with the activities of the Trust Fund. The action programme was also to promote electricity-heating conversion to district heating and natural gas and to promote the utilisation of efficient electrical appliances pursuant to the objectives of the Electricity Saving Trust Act.[1470] Based on the action programme, all network undertakings in natural gas and the district heating area were to carry out energy saving and advisory services. In order to ensure efficiency and coordination in overall energy-saving activity, the Danish Energy Agency had to carry out the general planning with a particular view to the implementation of calls for tender under the action programme. Among the more specific initiatives included in the agreement was promotion of energy-efficient products with references to the EU ambitions in the 6EAP on new mandatory ego-design and labelling of products. An 'Action Plan for Renewed Energy Conservation' was presented in 2005 as the key element in the long-term energy strategy up to 2025, including new initiatives for heat saving in buildings. The grid and distribution companies (electricity, gas and heat) are responsible for promoting energy conservation among their consumers. The initiatives must be non-commercial, and under normal conditions, no grants are awarded for investment. The policy and legislation promoting cogeneration of electricity and heating (CHP) is also an important source to energy efficiency. The '2004 Energy Agreement' between most of the political parties included a change in the feed-in tariff structure and market prices in favour of the central utilities and the consumer-owned power companies were commercialised. The political plan set two targets on wind, of which the most important is installing two offshore wind farms in the North Sea and in the Baltic Sea. The construction began in 2008.[1471] The political 'Energy Agreement 2008'[1472] and its subsequently implementation in the Act on Promotion of Renewable Energy[1473] established the actual conditions for renewable energy. With the 'Strategy for Reducing Energy Consumption' from April 2009 it was announced that changes in building had to include RES facilities in the building's 'energy framework audit' for buildings not already equipped with heating. The '2012 Energy Agreement' contained a wide range of initiatives based on the ambition to

1469. In 2002, the Horns Rev Offshore Wind Farm was constructed in the North Sea as part of this agreement. It consists of eighty turbines with a total capacity of 160 MW. From 2002 to 2003, Nysted Offshore Wind Farm was constructed, and it consists of seventy-two wind turbines with a total installed capacity of 165.6 MW. Nysted Offshore Wind Farm is situated approximately 2 km from a Natura 2000 site and 4 km from a seal sanctuary. This meant special considerations applied in connection with the construction work, including limitation of and control over navigation in the area.
1470. Act No. 1209 of 27 December 1996 on Electricity Saving Trust.
1471. Niels I. Meyer, *Learning from Wind Energy Policy in the EU: Lessons from Denmark, Sweden and Spain*, at 350, and Preben Maegaard, *Danish Renewable Energy Policy*.
1472. This energy agreement covered the period 2008–2011, and it improved the level of support. Fixed feed-in tariffs from the former energy agreements were supplemented by new feed-in tariffs. All the tariffs were defined for the new RES plants covering a period of many years.
1473. Now Promulgation Order No. 356 of 4 April 2019 on the Promotion of Renewable Energy.

bring Denmark closer to the target of 100% in the energy and transport sectors by 2050, and energy companies must increase efforts on energy efficiency by 100% from 2015 to 2020 compared to 2010–2012. The current '2018 Energy Agreement' was agreed in June 2018 between all the political parties in the Parliament.[1474] It is part of this agreement to establish three offshore wind farms of a total of 2,400 MW by 2030,[1475] to phase out coal in electricity production before the end of 2030 and to allocate funding that sets a course towards a 55% share of renewable energy by 2030.

231. Denmark, Norway and Sweden have a common electricity market (Nord Pool) related to the electricity supply. The Danish rules are laid down in the Act on Electricity Supply[1476] as a minimum implementing the Electricity Directive.[1477] With the 'Energy Agreement 2012', the Danish Parliament expects to reach an overall 100% renewable share in electricity consumption in 2030.[1478] The 'Energy Agreement 2018' underlines the objective of the Energy Supply Act to increase the utilisation of data and digital solutions, and the creation of a smart energy system. It is the overall objective of rolling out smart meters to all consumers by 2020.[1479]

The Energy Supply Act aims to ensure that the energy supply is organised and executed in the most appropriate manner for the whole country. The objectives are energy security, economy, environment and consumer protection. Within this objective, the actors must provide the consumers with access to cheap electricity and continue to give consumers influence on the management of the electricity sector's values, cf. section 1. The approach of this Act is based on the obligation to purchase electricity from prioritised plants to safeguard a basis for the continued utilisation of environment-friendly and RES production and to ensure that all consumers of electricity make an equal contribution to this. Operation of power generation plants with an electric power greater than 25 MW is subject to having a licence, cf. section 10 of the Act. This also applies to plants that are interconnected including the sites where one part is based on RES technology. Section 11 prescribes a duty to seek prior permission for the construction of and substantial changes to installations, although this requirement does not apply to small facilities. In the case of RES plants, this means those with a capacity of 10 MW or less, whereas the minimum level for conventional plants is 5 MW. Cogeneration of electricity and heat (CHP) is very often a mandatory term in the permits given to the power plants that are not based on wind. RES and environment-friendly energy production are ensured grid

1474. The Liberal Party, Liberal Alliance, the Conservative People's Party, the Social Democrats, the Danish People's Party, the Red-Green Alliance, the Alternative, the Social-Liberal Party and the Socialist People's Party.

1475. The three new offshore wind parks will each have a capacity of minimum 800 MW. The first is to be tendered in 2019 or 2020. The next two wind parks will be established in 2021 and 2023, *see Denmark's Draft Integrated National Energy and Climate Plan*, December 2018, at 23.

1476. Promulgation Order No. 52 of 17 January 2019 on Electricity Supply.

1477. Concerning the Danish energy policy, *see supra* para. 230.

1478. *Denmark's Draft Integrated National Energy and Climate Plan*, December 2018, at 22.

1479. *Denmark's Draft Integrated National Energy and Climate Plan*, December 2018, at 35.

connection. It is the transmission and distribution companies that set tariffs. Methods for price setting are published and approved by the Energy Regulatory Authority.

The objective of the Natural Gas Supply Act[1480] is to ensure that the Danish natural gas supply is organised and implemented in accordance with consideration for security of supply, national economy, environment, and consumer protection, cf. section 1. The Act must ensure consumer access to inexpensive natural gas. Pursuant to section 2(2) of the Act, the provisions also apply in relation to biogas, gas from biomass, and other types of gas to the extent that these gases can technically and safely be injected into and transported through the natural gas system. The construction and operation of upstream production pipelines are subject to approval by the Energy Agency. Access to the pipelines must be based on non-discriminatory conditions. All persons have access to the transmission and distribution networks upon payment, although access may be refused on the basis of lack of insufficient capacity. Access may also be refused if access to the system would prevent the operator undertaking from carrying out PSOs assigned to it or on the basis of serious economic and financial difficulties. The transmission and distribution undertakings must carry out maintenance of the network and must reconstruct and develop the network to the extent applicable and/or necessary. The transmission and distribution companies have the power to set tariff levels. Methods for price setting are published and approved by the Energy Regulatory Authority. With the direct use of biogas in the decentralised cogeneration plants, there is a significant need for the establishment of biogas transmission connections from both existing and future biogas installations to the cogeneration plants that currently use natural gas. It has been shown that the establishment of these connections is a task that the biogas producers have considerable difficulty in carrying out. The Danish rules are both based on national traditions and on the implementing the Natural Gas Market Directive. The current use of RESs for heating and cooling buildings is comprised partly of the individual use of RESs and partly by the use of RES in the district heating system. The aim of the Heat Supply Act[1481] is explicitly to promote the most socio-economic and environment-friendly use of energy for heating buildings and for the supply of hot water, and a reduction in the dependence on oil. The Act states explicitly that the most socio-economic use of energy sources has the highest priority. The owner of heat-producing plants cannot replace conventional energy sources (natural gas) with CO_2-free energy sources without a permit from the municipality. As for the district heating, it is the projection in the Danish draft NECP (December 2018) that at least 90% of the energy in the district heating will be based on other sources than fossil fuels in 2030. The '2012 Energy Agreement' that has impact on the development of the transformation into a green heating sector includes economic support of annually 13.4 million EUR to promote the use of more waste in the sector.[1482] The district heating sector supplies around 60% of domestic housing with

1480. Promulgation Order No. 1117 of 5 September 2018 on Nature Gas Supply.
1481. Promulgation Order No. 64 of 21 January 2019 on Heat Supply. In the 1950s, the district heating system based on fuel oil was developed in Denmark. After 1978, the district heating plants gradually changed from oil to coal and natural gas. It is now based also on biomass and solar energy.
1482. *Denmark's draft Integrated National Energy and Climate Plan*, 21 December 2018, at 23.

heat, corresponding to 45% of the total heat requirement. All new heat supply projects have to be in harmony with the spatial planning, and municipalities must include heating planning in their mandatory review of their spatial plans every fourth year.[1483] The legal basis for putting an obligation on the owners of buildings located in areas with collective heating systems to use the common heating system is no longer in force.[1484] Methods for price setting on the basis of the 'full-cost recovery principle' for the use of the heating supply system are published and approved by the Energy Regulatory Authority.[1485]

232. The Danish Act on the Promotion of Renewable Energy (RES Act)[1486] is concerned with the regulation of the conditions for the establishment of and economic support to wind turbines, solar energy, biogas and other RES. It contains provisions on the establishment of RES facilities on land and on the marine territory, including the EEZ.

The RES Act involves rules on: (1) support for the financing of preliminary investigations by the developers of local wind turbines and solar energy facilities; (2) an option for the future neighbours to the proposed wind turbines or solar energy facilities to purchase not less than 20% of the shares in the wind turbine projects or solar energy projects and by doing this become co-owners; (3) a right of the neighbours living close to new turbines and solar energy facilities to be compensated by the developer for the loss of value of their properties due to the negative environmental impacts of the turbines and solar energy facilities; and rules on a guarantee scheme for financing preliminary investment in EIA, and other needed investments that local wind turbine associations need to make; and (4) the establishment of a public fund that could ensure local procreative projects – such as parks and other facilities – decided by the municipality or the neighbours to reinforce local countryside and recreational values as part of the acceptance of wind farms and solar energy facilities. The reason behind these rules is that if people living near the wind turbines or solar energy facilities get compensation and have the rights of ownership in the energy production, the consequence of this will be an acceptance of the wind power.

The mandatory obligation for Member States to implement the sustainability criteria on biofuels established by the RES Directive have been transformed in Denmark by means of the Act on Sustainable Biofuels,[1487] and the Statutory Order on Sustainable Biofuels.[1488] According to these rules, companies that sell fuels for land transport must ensure that biofuels make up at least 5.75% of the company's total annual sales. From January 2020, they must blend in at least 0.9% of advanced biofuels. Where biofuels/bioliquids are to be taken into account for the fulfilment of the mandatory RES targets, the Danish authorities must require the economic operators to show that the subsidiarity criteria have been fulfilled. Providing evidence of

---

1483. The previous rules in the Heat Supply Act and the Planning Act were repealed by the Act No. 1712 of 27 December 2018 on Cancellation of the Right to Impose a new Connection Obligation, and Recognition of Profits for Heat Pumps, etc.
1484. Statutory Order No. 904 of 24 June 2016 on Connection to the Public Heating Network.
1485. Concerning the 'full-cost recovery principle', *see supra* para. 13.
1486. Promulgation Act No. 53 of 18 January 2019 on the Promotion of Renewable Energy.
1487. Act No. 62 of 17 January 2019 on Sustainable Biofuels.
1488. Statutory Order No. 1044 of 7 September 2017 on Sustainable Biofuels.

compliance with the land-related criteria can take many forms, including aerial photographs, satellite images, maps, land register entries/databases and site surveys. For the purpose of GHG saving by means of the use of biofuels/bioliquids, the calculation must be based on the rules laid down in the RES Directive, cf. Article 19(1).

Denmark will fulfil the cumulative end-use energy-saving obligations set out in Article 7[1489] of the Energy Efficiency Directive (EED) exclusively by an energy efficiency obligation scheme that was established already in 2006. Under this scheme, the network and distribution companies are subject to energy-saving commitments. The latest agreement on the saving obligations covers the period 2016–2020.[1490] Chapter 5 of the Act on Promotion of Energy Efficiency imposes obligations on efficiency control on all big enterprises as an implementation of some of the provisions laid down in the Directive on Energy Efficiency.[1491] The implementation of energy efficiency obligations also involved an amendment to the Heating Supply Act, the Energy Supply Act; the Act on Municipal Cooling Facilities; and the Act on Energy Performance of Buildings. Section 6(1) of the Building Act[1492] determines that the 2018 Building Regulations[1493] can require terms in the permit appropriate to discourage unnecessary energy consumption in buildings.[1494] Since 1995, it has been possible under the Building Regulations[1495] to choose three different ways to comply with building regulations when applying for a building permit. The rules were amended in 2005 to ensure the implementation of the first EPBD, and again in 2010 to ensure the implementation of the second version of EPBD.[1496] These national provisions have been amended several times since. However, they were not changed in 2014 to ensure the implementation of the current EPBD. The Danish rules laid down in the 2018 Building Regulations must be observed both in cases where there is processing of an application for a building permit, and in situations where the developer is only obliged to give a written notification to the municipality. The Building Regulations contain requirements on the maximum energy consumption based on the energy frame. The frame includes a building's overall need for energy supplied for heating, ventilation, cooling, hot water and possible lighting. Establishment of solar collector and other RES facilities will require a prior building permit under the Building Act. It is mandatory for the authority under the municipal building procedure to ensure that other legislation

1489. Article 7 of the EED, as formulated in Directive 2018/2002/EU set out the cumulative end-use savings for the period 2014–2020 and for the period 2021–2030, *see supra* in para. 229.
1490. *Denmark's draft Integrated National Energy and Climate Plan*, December 2018, at 26.
1491. Act No. 345 of 8 April 2014 on the Amendment of the Act on Promotion of Savings in Energy Consumption, the Act on Heat Supply, the Act on Municipal District Cooling, and various other acts, was the Act that implemented the EED with effect from 5 Jun. 2014.
1492. Promulgation Order No. 1178 of 23 September 2016 on Construction of Buildings (as amended several times).
1493. Statutory Order No. 1615 of 13 December 2017 on Building Regulation of 2018.
1494. The national requirements on the energy performance of buildings were first introduced in Denmark in 1977 as the 'Building Regulations of 1977'. The provisions were laid down in the Statutory Order of 15 January 1977.
1495. The provisions were laid down in Statutory Order No. 4002 of 13 February 1995.
1496. Concerning the EPBD, *see supra* para. 228.

is complied with. The '2012 Energy Agreement' specifies that the long-term marginal costs of reducing energy consumption in buildings should be seen in relation to the costs of expanding the renewable supply.[1497]

The Act on the Promotion of Energy and Water Savings in Buildings was also changed in 2005[1498] and in 2011[1499] to ensure energy efficiency. The Act includes in Chapter 3 rules on energy labelling of new buildings when built. Large buildings (over 1,000 m^2) and public building (over 250 m^2) have to be assessed every seven years and labelled following the EU labelling scheme.

§2. Evaluation of the Efficiency of the Policy and Legislation

233. The National Renewable Energy Action Plans to be made by the Member States for fulfilment of the binding targets are important parts of the 2009 RES Directive.[1500] Under the new Governance Regulation, Denmark is committed to file in its draft Integrated NECP in 2018, and the final version of this first final NECP in December 2019 to the Commission by 1 January 2020 pursuant to Article 15 of the Regulation. The Danish draft NECP of December 2018 explain that the energy savings to be achieved by renovation of buildings in the period 2021–2030 under the Energy Efficiency Directive will be calculated in 2019.

The assessment of the 'Danish National Renewable Energy Action Plan' that was made by the European Renewable Energy Council (EREC) in its 'Mapping Renewable Energy Pathways towards 2020' resulted in the characteristic of the Danish policy as a 'frozen policy scenario'.[1501] It was also the opinion of EREC that the financial initiatives were in general insufficient to encourage the investment needed to reach the 30% target.[1502]

On 18 June 2019, the Danish draft NECP of 21 December 2018 – that was titled a froze policy scenario – was evaluated by the Commission. [1503] The Commission stated that Denmark's indication of a 55% share of renewable energy in the gross final consumption of energy by 2030 is significantly above the 46% share in 2030 that results from the formula in Annex II of the Governance Regulation. However, the projections made by the Commission based on the existing policies and measures only indicate a share of 48%. The Danish ambitions on energy efficiency are assessed as very low. It is recommended that Denmark in its final plan provide more

1497. *Denmark's draft Integrated National Energy and Climate Plan*, 21 December 2018, at 27.
1498. Act No. 585 of 24 June 2005.
1499. The current version of this Act is now Promulgation Order No. 636 of 19 June 2012 on the Promotion of Energy and Water Savings in Buildings, as amended several times.
1500. Concerning the RES Directive and the Governance Regulation, *see supra* para. 228.
1501. The EU Roadmap was published in March 2011, at 40ff.
1502. Concerning the relation to the RES Directive, *see supra* para. 231.
1503. Commission Staff Working Document, *Assessment of the Draft National Energy and Climate Plan of Denmark*, SWD(2019) 275 final, and *Denmark. Summary of the Commissions assessment of the draft National Energy and Climate Plan 2021-2030*. Available at: https://ec.europa.eu/energy/en/topics/energy-strategy-and-energy-union/governance-energy-union/national-energy-climate-plans (visited on 30 Jun. 2019).

clarity on planned policies and measures, the transport sector included. It is also part of the assessment that Denmark needs to include a list of all energy subsidies, in particular including fossil fuels, as well as information on concrete actions undertaken and planned to phase out such energy sources.

Part II. Nature Conservation and Management

Chapter 1. Biodiversity and Nature Protection Rules and Strategies

234. Nature conservation and management is regulated at international, EU and national levels. The vertical harmonisation between the biodiversity initiatives at international and EU levels is very clear.

One of the international nature-protecting conventions is the 1971 United Nations Educational, Scientific and Cultural Organisation (UNESCO) Convention on Wetlands of International Importance: the Ramsar Convention. It is the first Convention in this area, and the only Convention that deals with a particular ecosystem. Currently, the Convention has 138 contracting parties. Denmark ratified it in 1977. The EU has not ratified the Convention, but the protection of the species is supported by the EU as part of the Natura 2000 network. The Convention is concerned with protecting 'the fundamental ecological functions of wetlands as regulators of water regimes and as habitats supporting a characteristic flora and fauna, especially waterfowl'. Joining the Convention signals a commitment by the party to ensuring the conservation and 'wise use' of the wetlands that the Convention has designated as 'Wetlands of International Importance'. 'Wise use' was defined at a conference in 1987 (the same year the Brundtland Report was published) as the 'use of a wetland so that it may yield the greatest continuous benefit to present generations whilst maintaining its potential to meet the needs and aspirations of future generations'. Each party to the Convention is committed to draw up a list of wetlands in its territory, designating at least one site that meets the Convention criteria for inclusion on the list of 'Wetlands of International Importance' and protecting the ecological character of the listed sites. The choice of designated areas is made on the basis of their international significance in terms of ecology,[1504] botany, zoology, limnology or hydrology. The parties must, as far as possible, include such protection in national environmental planning, and consult other parties about the implementation thereof, especially with regard to transboundary wetlands, shared water systems and shared species.[1505]

The Council of Europe's Convention on the Conservation of European Wildlife and Natural Habitats, named the Berne Convention, is another binding international instrument in the field of nature conservation. The Preamble of the Convention

---

1504. Concerning the designation of international protected sites, *see infra* paras 241–242.
1505. Concerning the global Red List, *see supra* para. 21 and *infra* para. 251.

merely expresses the need for greater 'unity' and cooperation among States. No international authority is established by the Convention: and the form of the action to be taken is left to each contracting party, though the Convention does institute a Standing Committee of the Parties and the Bureau of this Committee.[1506] The Convention covers most of the natural heritage of the European continent and extends to some African States. It protects habitats of wild flora and fauna. It lists endangered species in two appendices according to the degree of threat and requires the parties to take such measures as imposing closed seasons, prohibiting the removal of such species (as required), and prohibiting the use of indiscriminate means of capture. Exceptions can be permitted in certain circumstances. The parties are also required to take appropriate measures to conserve the habitats of the species listed in the appendices. There is special provision for migratory species. 'Migratory' can be described as a cyclical, and therefore predicable phenomenon, whereby certain animals perform periodic movements between two separate geographic areas, one area usually being where they breed. Because species do not observe national boundaries during their migration, a problem arises as to who owns the species and who takes care of protecting the biodiversity.

The UNEP Convention on Migratory Species (the Bonn Convention) is also a very important convention. It was adopted in 1979. Both the EU and Denmark are parties to the Convention, which Denmark ratified in 1982. The Convention aims to achieve the conservation of terrestrial and marine migratory birds throughout their migratory routes. In Article 1(2) of the Convention, it is stated that the EU, as a regional economic integration organisation, exercises the rights and fulfils its responsibilities which the Convention attributes to the EU Member States. The Convention takes into account ecosystems in assessing conservation status of migratory species and thus considers these species in their ecosystem context. The species are protected as they require special attention because of their importance from the environmental, ecological, genetic, scientific, recreational, cultural, educational, social and economic points of view. The parties have agreed to provide strict protection for endangered migratory species, to conclude multilateral agreements for the conservation and management of migratory species, and to undertake joint research. In Article 2 of the Convention, it is stated that the parties must take steps to promote national policies for the conservation of wild flora and fauna at, or adapt it to, a level which corresponds in particular to ecological, scientific and cultural requirements while taking economic and recreational requirements and the needs of sub-species, varieties or forms of local risks into account.

The Convention defines several important terms that are also used in other conventions and in the EU Natura 2000 legislation, including the following definitions:

1506. Denmark and the EU ratified the Convention in 1979. On behalf of the EU, a Council Decision of 21 December 1998 approved the revision of Appendices II and III to the Berne Convention, adding four species to Appendix II and twenty-two to Appendix III. That Decision stated that the Wild Birds Directive already covered two of those species and the Habitats Directive covered three.

- 'migratory species' means the entire population or any geographically separate part of the population of any species or lower talon of wild animals a significant proportion of whose members cyclically and predictably cross one or more national jurisdictional boundaries;
- 'conservation status of migratory species' means the sum of the influence acting on the migratory species that may affect its long-term distribution and abundance;
- 'favourable conservation status' is described as indications for circumstances in which the migratory species is maintaining itself on a long-term basis as a viable component of its ecosystems, etc.;
- 'engaged' means that the migratory species is in danger of extinction throughout all or part of the territory of a State;
- 'range' means all the areas of land or water that a migratory species inhabits, stays in temporarily, crosses or overlies at any time on its normal migratory route; and
- 'habitat' means any area in the range of a migratory species which contains suitable living conditions for that species.

Danish legislation is also using these terms. The UN CBD from 1992 is the broadest international instrument. It requests the parties to protect the biodiversity as such. Both the EU and Denmark are members of the Convention, which they both ratified in 1993.[1507] The CBD is a convention with a multi-species management approach (i.e., a holistic approach). With regard to alien species that threaten ecosystems, habitats or species, the Convention requests the parties to prevent the introduction, control and eradication of them. It calls on the parties to examine the issues of liability and redress, including restoration and compensation, for damage to biodiversity except where such liability is purely a domestic matter. There are three objectives behind the Convention: the conservation and sustainable use of biological diversity, and the equitable sharing of benefits arising from the utilisation of genetic resources. The parties to the CBD are obliged to ensure an equitable balancing of interests of developed and developing countries and between the present and future generations. As far as possible and as appropriate, each party to the Convention must: (a) establish a system of protected areas or areas where special measures need to be taken to conserve biological diversity; (b) develop, where necessary, guidelines for the selection, establishment and management of protected areas or areas where special measures need to be taken to conserve biological diversity; (c) regulate or manage biological resources important for the conservation of biological diversity whether within or outside protected areas, with a view to ensure their conservation and sustainable use; (d) promote the protection of ecosystems, natural habitats and the maintenance of variable populations of species in natural surroundings; and (e) promote environmentally sound and sustainable development in areas adjacent to protected areas with a view to further protection of these areas. Biodiversity is defined in the Convention as:

1507. The participation in the CBD regime was approved by Council Decision No. 93/626/EC.

> the variability among living organisms from all sources, including, inter alia, terrestrial, marine, and other aquatic ecosystems and the ecological complexes of which they are part: this includes diversity within species, between species and of ecosystems.

The ecosystem-based approach – that was introduced under the Convention[1508] – has triggered a change of structure and development of new legal instruments as well as institutional development and cooperation. It is a regulatory approach integrating a specific focus on ecological preconditions and environmental governance features, aiming to consider the multilevel dynamics of polycentric regulatory institutions and the many actors taking part in the governance, as well as satisfying human needs in a way that do not compromise the integrity, or health, of ecosystems.[1509] The application of this approach is the primary framework for action under the Convention. The twelve Malawi Principles on the operationalisation of the ecosystem approach – that are complementary and interlinked – were adopted under the CBD at the COP5 in 2000.[1510] The decision at the COP5 stresses the need for ecosystem management to be undertaken at the appropriate spatial and temporal scales. The CBD was supplemented by a programme adopted at the COP7 covering work on marine and coastal biodiversity, and on the creation of a global network of marine protected areas (NMPA). At the COP9 in Bonn the findings from the first phase of the 'Economics of Ecosystems and Biodiversity' (TEEB) initiative with the goal to draw up global intention on the economic benefits of biodiversity was presented in the form of an interim report.[1511] This initiative on a global study of the economic aspects of biodiversity was promoted by a joint proposal presented by Germany and the EU. The report provided evidence on the significant economic losses and human welfare impacts due to degradation of biodiversity. In 2010, phase two of the study was presented at the COP10 in Nagoya, Aichi Prefecture, Japan, with a focus on biodiversity in the forest. At this COP10, the 'Strategic Plan for Biodiversity 2011-2020 and the Aichi Biodiversity Targets' were adopted.[1512] The

1508. The ecosystem approach was introduced at the Second Meeting of the Conference of the Parties (COP) held in Jakarta, Indonesia (CBD COP 2), decision 8, UNEP/CBD/COP/2/19, at 12. Concerning this COP2, *see* Britta Bohman, *Transboundary Law for Social-Ecological Resilience? A Study on Eutrophication in the Baltic Sea Area,* Stockholm University, 2017, at 83 and 196.

1509. Britta Bohman, *Transboundary Law for Social-Ecological Resilience?*

1510. UNEP/Cbd/COP/5/23, Decision V/6 Ecosystem approach, in Convention on Biological Diversity (CBD) Cop (ed.), Decisions Adopted by the Conference of the parties to the Convention on Biological Diversity at its Fifth Meeting, Nairobi, 15–26 May 2000, at 103–110.

1511. The size and timing of payoffs from maintaining ecosystem services, the benefits, which humans derive from nature, are often subject to uncertainty, because interaction between ecosystems services, climate change and biodiversity is complex. However, ecosystem services are often overlooked, because they come at a limited or zero cost to producers even though the value of these services is in fact large. The goods and services provided by nature (e.g., forests) are often not valued property.

1512. The 'Global Biodiversity Outlook. Summary for Policy Makers' from 2012 underscores that several critical, global, regional and local thresholds are closed or have been exceeded, so there is still not a legal framework in place that effectively implements the Aichi Targets.

Strategic Plan is an overall framework on biodiversity, not only for the biodiversity-related conventions but also for the entire UN system. The 2020 Aichi Targets set forth the goal of restoring at least 15% of the degraded ecosystem by 2020. Target 11 of the Targets states:

> By 2020, at least 17 per cent of terrestrial and inland water areas, and 10 per cent of coastal and marine areas, especially areas of particular importance for biodiversity and ecosystem services, are conserved through effectively and equitably managed, ecologically representative and well connected systems of protected areas and other effective area-based conservation measures, and integrated into the wider landscapes and seascapes.

The COP10 also approved a list of invasive alien species under the Strategic Plan in which it stated:

> By 2020, invasive alien species and pathways are identified and prioritized, priority species are controlled or eradicated, and measures are in place to manage pathways to prevent their introduction and establishment.

The Nagoya Protocol on Access to Genetic Resources and the Fair and Equitable Sharing of Benefits Arising from the CBD were also established under COP10. It entered into force on 12 October 2014. Sixty parties, including the EU and Denmark, have ratified the Protocol.[1513]

Ocean management and transboundary cooperation on the protection of the nature in the oceans and the sea are other important international issues. Under the Constitution of the Sea – the UNCLOS, which sets out the legal framework for all activities in the oceans and seas – the coastal States have the jurisdiction to protect the environment in the territorial areas and the EEZ.[1514] The UNEP has recognised the existence of 227 Transboundary Areas (TBCAs) worldwide, but very few of these areas involve MPAs.[1515] The obligations under the above-mentioned CBD to establish spatially defined marine spaces, where human activities have to be limited in order to ensure the survival and/or recovery of sensible marine species, have been the most effective instruments.

The ecosystem approach and the protection against invasive alien species established under the CBD are also governing the EU management of habitats, water, sea areas, agriculture, forest and fishery.[1516] The Invasive Alien Species Regulation

---

1513. The Protocol was implemented by the Danish Act No. 1375 of 23 December 2014 on Benefit-sharing in the Utilisation of Genetic Resources.

1514. Concerning the international protection of the marine environment, *see supra* para. 129.

1515. Xiao Recio-Blanco, *Transnational Area-Based Ocean Management: Finding Avenues for Regulatory Harmonization,* William & Mary Policy Review, Fall2015, Vol. 7 Issue 1, at 95–141.

1516. Concerning the Water Framework Directive, *see supra* para. 103 and concerning the Wild Birds Directive and Habitats Directive, *see infra* para. 241. *See also supra* paras. 130–131 and *infra* para. 255 concerning the MSFD (2008/56/EC), the Directive on Maritime Spatial Planning (2014/89/EU), and the European Integrated Maritime Policy. EU's agriculture, forest, and fishery legislation that is described *infra* paras 258, 273 and 280 is also influenced by the ecosystem regulatory approach.

(IAS Regulation)[1517] – that entered into force on 1 January 2015 – seeks to address the problem related to invasive alien species in the EU in a comprehensive manner focusing on prevention, early detection and rapid eradication. A list of invasive aliens was established based on information from the Member States. The risk assessment and scientific evidence have to be ensured at national level. The Commission has the competence to adopt the list on invasive alien species in cooperation with the Member States. On 13 July 2016, the list was adopted.[1518] The Commission has also the competence to design the format for the national authorities' permission of activities involving alien species of concern in the EU, [1519] and it has the competence to update its list on invasive alien species in cooperation with the Member States.[1520] A new update of the list is under preparation in 2019.

The Habitats Directive and the Wild Birds Directive contain the relevant and very strong provisions, including an explicit obligation to prevent invasive alien species invasive alien species prevention obligation. In the Preamble of the last-mentioned Directive it is stated that care should be taken in consultation with the Commission to see that the introduction of any species of wild birds not naturally occurring in the European territory of the Member States do not cause harm to local flora and fauna. Until 1987, nature conservation in the EU was influenced by the general climate of opinion in most Member States that such issues were an exclusive national competence. The Treaty of the Internal Market changed it. The Wild Birds Directive[1521] was the first directive protecting the habitats of migratory species that provided for the conservation of all species of naturally occurring migratory species in the wild state before the clear legal basis for secondary environmental legislation was part of the Treaty.[1522] It was followed in 1992 by the Habitats Directive.[1523] One of the arguments used by the EU to justify the proposal for the Habitats Directive was that it would transpose the Bern Convention and the Bonn Convention into EU legislation and ensure vertical harmonisation. The vertical harmonisation is, for example, illustrated by the consistency in relation to the term that is used in the Directive. The definition of the 'conservation status of a natural habitat', 'conservation status of species', 'favourable conservation status' and 'favourable conservation status of a natural habitat' clearly relate to the definitions in the Bonn

1517. European Parliament and Council Regulation No. 1143/2014/EU on the Prevention and Management of the Introduction and Spread of Invasive Species.
1518. Commission Regulation No. 2016/1131/EU adopting a List of Invasive Alien Species of Union Concern pursuant to Regulation No. 1143/2014/EU.
1519. Commission Regulation No. 2016/145/EU adopting the Format of the Document serving as Evidence for the Permit Issued by the Competent Authorities of Member States Allowing Establishment to carry out certain Activities concerning Alien Species of Union Concern pursuant to Regulation No. 1143/2014/EU.
1520. The list of invasive alien species was updated by Commission Regulation No. 2017/1263/EU of 12 July 2017.
1521. Council Directive 79/409/EEC on the Conservation of Wild Birds, as amended. *See* now the codifying European Parliament and Council Directive 2009/147/EC on the Conservation of Wild Birds.
1522. Concerning the treaty provisions used now under the Lisbon Treaty, *see supra* para. 56.
1523. Council Directive 92/43/EEC on Natural Habitats and the Wild Flora and Fauna.

Convention, cf. Article 1(1) of the Habitats Directive.[1524] Annex IV of the Habitats Directive included strictly protected species listed in Annexes I and II of the Bern Convention. In 1998, the European Council agreed on the 'Community Biodiversity Strategy'[1525] with a focus on the importance of integrating biodiversity considerations into relevant sectorial policies. This strategy is implemented by action plans. In 2001, EU's policy paper entitled 'The Biodiversity Action Plan for Economic and Development Cooperation' was published. In this paper, EU refers to the international targets, and it underscores the importance of the ecosystem approach as the guiding approach for the conservation and sustainable use of the natural resources. The EU has the following 2050 vision for biodiversity:

> By 2050, European Union biodiversity and the ecosystem services it provides – its natural capital – are protected, valued and appropriately restored for biodiversity's intrinsic value and for their essential contribution to human wellbeing and economic property, and so that catastrophic changes caused by the loss of biodiversity are avoided.

In May 2011, the 'EU Biodiversity Strategy 2020'[1526] was presented by the Commission. It was adopted in 2012 to halt biodiversity losses in the EU, restore ecosystems where possible and step up efforts to avert global biodiversity losses. With its Communication 'Enhancing Europe's Natural Capital',[1527] the Commission follows the ideas behind the above-mentioned Aichi Targets developed under the CBD with a green infrastructure approach as an integrated part of the EU biodiversity strategy. The Commission points out that investing in natural capacity has potential to contribute towards numerous important policy objectives, including environmental risk management and adaptation to climate change. It promotes Member States to develop national strategies on green infrastructure and to enhance policy integration to support such infrastructure. On 20 December 2018, the EU and its Member States submitted the CDM Notification initial reviews on the aspects of the scope and content of the post-2020 global biodiversity framework in which they call for the adoption of an ambitious follow-up on the existing Strategic Plan that is covering the period 2011–2020.

Denmark has a biodiversity strategy, but it is not a strong part of the Danish nature protection policy. In 2004, the former liberal-conservative coalition government published the 'Action Plan for Biodiversity and Nature Conservation in Denmark 2004-2009', which included initiatives to halt the decline in biodiversity by 2010. It laid down the following priority areas:

1524. In the preamble to the Habitats Directive, it is stated that land-use planning should encourage the management of features of the landscape, which are of major importance for wild fauna and flora. The planning ensures an horizontal coordination of different interests in land use; concerning spatial planning, *see infra* Part III. The two nature protection directives are described more in detail in para. 241.

1525. Communication of 4 February 1998 on 'European Community Biodiversity Strategy', COM(1998) 42.

1526. COM(2011) 244 final.

1527. COM(2013) 249 final.

- *first priority*: existing natural areas, including small biotopes and semi-natural areas (section 3 areas under the Nature Protection Act) within Natura 2000 sites and national parks;
- *second priority*: other existing natural areas, including small biotopes and semi-natural areas (section 3 areas under the Nature Protection Act) outside Natura 2000 sites and national parks;
- *third priority*: new small biotopes and semi-natural areas within Natura 2000 sites and national parks; and
- *fourth priority*: new small biotopes and semi-natural areas outside Natura 2000 sites, etc., that are linked ecologically with other natural areas.

Since 2009, Denmark has had an NAP dealing with invasive alien species. The IAS Regulation and the Commissions Implementation Regulations are converted into Danish legislation by statutory rules.[1528] The former centre-left coalition government's strategy 'A Sustainable Denmark' from October 2014 established some goals on a diverse nature and protection of the animals and habitats.[1529]

1528. Statutory Order No. 1285 of 12 November 2018 on the Prevention and Management of Invasive Aliant Species on the EU List and on a National List concerning a Prohibition of Trading Invasive Aliant Species. The Order has its legal basis in ss 31a, 70, 73, 78, 89 and 90 of the Nature Protection Act. The national list is Annex 4 to the Statutory Order.

1529. The Coalition Government that was in power until 27 Jun. 2019 has not passed an action plan on sustainability and its policy has been focused primarily on a strong position in the international competition – especially for the agriculture and food industry. On 27 Jun. 2019, the Social Democrat Government took power with the ambition to ensure a higher level of environmental protection. Concerning the different coalition governments, *see supra* para. 4.

Chapter 2. Monuments, Archaeological Nature and Landscape

235. In 1972, the UNESCO Convention on the Protection of World Cultural and Natural Heritage (World Heritage Convention) was signed. It aims at the preservation of immovable cultural property, including natural sites, such as geological formations and the habitats of endangered species of animals and plants. The term 'natural heritage' is defined in Article 2. It covers natural features consisting of physical and biological formations, or groups of such formations that are of outstanding universal value from an aesthetic or scientific point of view. The term 'cultural heritage' is defined in Article 1, which covers: monuments, groups of buildings and sites. Each State that is a party to the Convention is obliged to identify, protect, conserve, present and transmit to future generations its cultural and natural heritage. Article 8 of the Convention established the World Heritage Committee. This Committee defines the criteria on the basis of which a property belonging to a country's cultural or natural heritage may be included in either of the lists mentioned in the Convention. Denmark ratified the Convention in 1979. In 1994, the Jelling Mounds, Runic Stones and Church were added to the World Heritage List. The year after, Roskilde Cathedral was included. In 2000, Kronborg Castle was added to the list and, most recently, Illulissat Ice fjord in Greenland was included in 2004.

The Council of Europe's 'Convention for the Protection of the Architectural Heritage in Europe' of 1985 (the Granada Convention), as revised in 1992 in Valletta, is closely related to the above-mentioned UNESCO Convention. It is ratified by Denmark but not ratified by the EU. The Convention aims to protect the 'architectural heritage', which covers:

- *monuments*: all buildings and structures of conspicuous historical, archaeological, artistic, scientific, social or technical interest, including their fixtures and fittings;
- *groups of buildings*: homogeneous groups of urban or rural buildings conspicuous for their historical, archaeological, artistic, scientific, social or technical interest, which are sufficiently coherent to form topographically definable units; and
- *sites*: the combined works of man and nature, being areas, which are partially built upon and sufficiently distinctive and homogeneous to be topographically definable and are of conspicuous historical, archaeological, scientific, social or technical interest.

The parties to the Convention are required to map the monuments, groups of buildings and sites that fall within the categories set out above. As a party to the Convention, Denmark is obliged to ensure implementation of the protection goals under its legislation, e.g., by providing financial support for the maintenance and restoration of the architectural heritage on its territory.

There is also cultural heritage at sea. Section 2 of Part XI of the UNCLOS, approved by the EU and its Member States in 1994, protects sites of archaeological and historical nature at sea. Article 149 states that all objects of such interests must be preserved or disposed of for the benefit of mankind as a whole, with particular regard being paid to the preferential rights of the State or country of origin, the State of cultural origin or the State of historical or archaeological origin. In October 2000, the Council of Europe's 'European Landscape Convention' was signed in Florence. The EU is not a party, but Denmark is. By taking into account values in relation to landscape, culture and nature, the Convention aims to preserve the life and the quality of life for all. It is the most holistic convention on the protection of land and culture related to land. The Preamble of the Landscape Convention states that it is related to the legal texts of other existing convention in the field of protection and management of the natural and cultural heritage, regional and spatial planning, local self-government and trans-frontier cooperation, in particular the Berne Convention, the Granada Convention, the Biodiversity Convention (CBD), the Aarhus Convention, the European Charter of Local Self-Government and the World Cultural and Natural Heritage Convention. In 2005, the Council of Europe adopted an action plan as part of the implementation of the Convention. The aim of this plan is to develop and support integrated policies in the field of landscape and spatial planning.

236. Protection of cultural heritage, natural heritage and architectural heritage has a long history in Denmark.[1530] The means used to protect ancient monuments and historical buildings are planning, conservation, and general protection lines (protected zones). The field of nature conservation and management activities is characterised by a strategy of ensuring the necessary coordination of environmental administration, first and foremost, through spatial planning rules and the rules relating to coordination and integration based in the Planning Act.[1531]

The most important areas of Danish legislation protecting buildings are the Act on Conservation of Buildings and the Culture in the Cities[1532] and the Museums Act.[1533] The Heritage Agency is responsible for administrating the rules on protection of the listed buildings, although churches and churchyards are protected by special rules in the Act on the Buildings of the Danish National Evangelical Lutheran Church.[1534] Approximately 2,000 church buildings, most of which are medieval, are protected under this Act. Based on section 2 of that Act, the Minister of Ecclesiastical Affairs has the competence to protect the churches.

Denmark is rich in ancient sites and monuments. They are found all over the country: burial mounds, rock carvings, runic stones, road tracks, castle mounds, castle ruins, military fortifications, etc. The majority of historic buildings, sites, parks, forests and monuments have suffered extensive damage from traffic, and industrial and agricultural activities. Agriculture has, for example, caused considerable damage to the cultural heritage, destroying about eighty of the originally grave mounds, but Denmark still has a large number of protected grave mounds.

237. There is no clear definition in the Danish legislation of the term 'landscape'. The term is traditionally used to describe the landscape as scenery or as the

1530. Concerning the Danish history, *see supra* paras 35–36.
1531. Concerning the spatial planning, *see infra* Part III, Chapter 2.
1532. Promulgation Order No. 219 of 6 March 2018 on Conservation of Buildings and the Culture in the Cities.
1533. Promulgation Order No. 358 of 8 April 2014 on Museums.
1534. Promulgation Order No. 1156 of 1 September 2016 on the Buildings of the Danish National Evangelical Lutheran Church.

word covering the open countryside. In Danish landscape protection, there is a particular focus on topics such as hilly landscapes, geology, historic environment, beaches and coast and natural elements. The conservation measures in Denmark have changed in character from the protection of individual buildings and areas to protection of the whole urban environment, local environments and nature/culture.

From the 1930s until the 1970s, many conservation orders focused on conservation of elements of the landscape, such as heaths and manor house landscapes. Since the 1970s, orders have more often aimed to protect the habitats of plants and animals or the public access to such areas. A 'Strategy on the Cultural Environment' was presented to the Parliament in November 1995 and debated in January 1996. Under this Strategy, priority was given to particular landscape elements such as fences, dikes, hedgerows, old road systems and villages. However, entire landscapes were also covered. The ambition was to make the cultural heritage a significant dimension of future environmental policy, to strengthen public participation and to ensure a balance between protection and utilisation. Currently, the Ministry of Environment and Food and the Ministry of Culture (the Heritage Agency of this Ministry) lay down the overall guidelines for safeguarding valuable cultural environments. These protection plans have to be respected in the municipal planning under the Planning Act, cf. section 11a(1) no. 15 of this Act.[1535] One or several municipalities may jointly set up a local Cultural Environmental Council, which advises the authorities with a view to supporting the cultural heritage and values relating to buildings and structures in the local physical planning, cf. section 23a of the Museums Act.[1536] Under the Planning Act, in their municipal spatial planning the municipalities must designate and protect the cultural environment as 'a geographically delimited area that reflects significant features of our society's historical development', cf. section 11a, item 15, of this Act.[1537] Since the 2007 structural reform,[1538] the municipalities have been required to provide more details on, and to otherwise supplement, information about heritage assets already identified in the former regional plans. The municipal plan is legally binding on the authorities that make decisions relating to roads, buildings, etc. This means that all public authorities must respect the protection of the 'cultural heritage' mentioned in the municipal plan. Cultural heritage also includes individual buildings, monuments and combinations of elements in a cultural environment as defined by the UNESCO Convention. However, municipal efforts must be directed at showing human endeavours in all periods, i.e., from prehistoric times to the present. Local plans are required to contain restrictions to safeguard the cultural heritage assets.[1539] Such local assets comprise ancient monuments, buildings and cultural environments, including churches and their surroundings, with binding effect on private owners and users. In the legal wording, a building is 'worthy of preservation' when it is included in the

1535. Promulgation Order No. 287 of 16 April 2018 on Planning, as amended by Act Nos 1712, 1714 and 1715 of 27 December 2018.
1536. Promulgation Order No. 358 of 8 April 2014 on Museums.
1537. Concerning the municipal plans, *see infra* para. 313.
1538. Concerning the 2007 reform, *see supra* para. 52.
1539. Concerning the content of local plans, *see infra* para. 321.

local plans in accordance with section 15(2), item 14, of the Museums Act. However, it is only the building's exterior that is protected by this designation. A building that is deemed worthy of preservation may not be demolished, except with special permission from the municipality. It is possible to seek financial compensation, including compensation for expropriations (takings) if it is not possible after such designation to use the building in the same way as before, cf. section 49 of the Act.[1540] Approximately 300,000 buildings have been deemed worthy of preservation.

Since 1990, the Ministry of Environment has developed a close cooperation with the municipalities on the so-called Municipal Atlases, the aim of which was to evaluate the preservation value of each individual municipality's buildings. The purpose is particularly to establish the foundations for the strengthening of conservation values through municipal planning and the designation of buildings, which should be listed in accordance with the Planning Act. At the same time, the objective is to stimulate public interest in, and understanding of, the qualities and uniqueness of buildings and urban environments. Today, assessment is based on the Survey of Architectural Values in the Environment (the SAVE methods). The nationwide register of about 400,000 buildings is available on the Internet.

238. The Act on Conservation of Buildings and the Culture in the Cities[1541] aims to preserve the Danish architectural heritage. It includes buildings of historical or environmental value, including buildings which illustrate housing, working and production conditions and other significant characteristics of social development. One of the other important targets laid down in this Act is also the obligation in relation to public participation, cf. section 1 of the Act.

The Heritage Agency (under the Ministry of Culture) has the competence to decide on conservation of buildings of special value if the buildings are more than 50 years old (until the amendment in 1997, the criterion was 100 years). Such buildings are listed by that Agency. Medieval buildings erected before the Reformation in 1536 must be listed under the Act without a special resolution, i.e., they are automatically listed, cf. section 4 of the Act.

Any citizen can file a proposal concerning the listing of a particular building with the Heritage Agency. The Agency then assesses whether the building in question meets the criteria for protection by the rules under the Act, cf. section 3 of the Act. Listing requires that the building be of special architectural or cultural heritage value. The Agency may deem buildings 'worth preserving' by reason of their eminent value or under other special circumstances, cf. section 3(2) of the Act. Before the Agency takes its decision, it has to notify in writing: (a) the owner and the occupant of the building; (b) the municipal council; (c) the local Museums Council and the Regional Specialist Cultural Environmental Council if such councils exist in the local areas; (d) the associations authorised under the Act; and (e) associations and similar organisations which have local connections, have an interest in preservation

1540. Concerning the provisions on expropriation and take over in the Planning Act, *see infra* para. 328.
1541. Promulgation Order No. 219 of 6 March 2018 on Conservation of Buildings and the Culture in the Cities.

issues and which have submitted a written request to the Agency regarding notification, cf. section 6 of the Act. Within a period of three months, any private person, association or authority may comment on the proposal, after which the Agency takes its decision. This decision may be appealed to the Minister for Culture, who makes the final decision. The Agency has also the competence to list buildings on its own initiative, e.g., after consideration of particular types of buildings. The Historic Buildings Council advises the Agency, the twelve members of whom are appointed by the Minister for Culture.

There are many listed buildings – listed as being of special architectural or historical importance. At present, there are approximately 9,000 listed buildings based on this Act. Of these approximately 1,000 are publicly owned while 8,000 are privately owned. The immediate surroundings of a building, e.g., a garden, courtyard or wall, may also be listed. The most recent listed buildings are from July 2011.

When a building is listed, it is an offence to demolish it or alter it in a way that affects its character or appearance. The listing protects the entire building. The owners or occupants of listed buildings must maintain them in good condition, including ensuring that the roof and windows are free of leaks, so that they do not fall into disrepair, cf. section 9 of the Act. The owners must obtain permission from the Agency for any construction or modification of protected buildings, beyond routine upkeep, cf. section 10. Permission is also required to mount an aerial or to place a sign on the façade. The State does not pay any compensation to owners of listed building although it does give tax exemptions for the higher maintenance expenses. It is also possible to obtain subsidies to cover some of the extra costs connected with the owners' building works in relation to preservation that is needed to protect the buildings, cf. Chapter 4 of the Act. A building may be delisted if there is no longer any point in listing it.

239. There are many museums in Denmark – from the large national collections to small, private one-person museums. The State owns 7 museums, and approximately 115 are approved to receive State subsidies. A State-subsided museum can be owned by one or several municipalities or by an association whose objective is to run the museum, or by an independent institution.

The purpose of the Museums Act[1542] is it to promote the activities and cooperation of museums with a view to safeguard the Danish cultural and natural heritage, and to promote access to and knowledge about this heritage and its interaction with the world. The provisions of the Act apply to museums owned by the State and those receiving subsidies from the State. At State level, the responsibility for administration of the Museum Act is the Ministry of Culture, with a special responsibility placed with the Heritage Agency.

If traces of ancient relics or monuments are found during construction work or agricultural and forestry activities, the work must be suspended to the extent that it affects the ancient relic or monument. In such situations, the Agency or the nearest cultural heritage museum owned or subsidised by the State must be informed immediately about the item of cultural heritage found at that place, and the work must be suspended insofar as it affects the object, cf. sections 27 and 29 of the Act. There is

1542. Promulgation Order No. 358 of 8 April 2014 on Museums.

also a notification obligation on any person who finds in watercourses, lakes, territorial water, on the continental shelf, or in the deep seabed an ancient relic or monument, including shipwrecks, cargo or parts of such wrecks, which must be assumed lost more than 100 years ago, cf. section 28 and 28a of the Act. Based on the Act, no changes may be made to the condition of ancient relics or monuments on the seabed if they are in territorial waters and on the continental shelf, but not beyond twenty-four nautical miles from the base lines from which the width of the outer territorial waters is measured. Nor may changes be made to the condition of wrecks of ships or cargo which must be assumed lost more than 100 years ago if they are in the mentioned area. The listed types are subject to protection only after the owner has received notification from the Agency. In special circumstances, the Agency may grant exemptions from the rules. The owners and users are obliged to make legal any unlawful situation.

The Act also regulates subsidies which safeguard the cultural and natural heritage in connection with the physical planning and preparation of construction work, agriculture and forestry activities, etc., including archaeological and natural-history investigation tasks that are also regulated by the Act, cf. Part 8 of the Act.

240. An important preservation measure for the landscape is the protection lines around the beaches, seashores, forests, lakes and monuments, regulated by several rules under the Nature Protection Act.[1543] The objectives of the Act are not only to safeguard nature and the environment so that the development of society will prosper regarding human conditions, but it also has the target to improve, restore and provide areas that are important to flora and fauna, as well as to interests essential to the landscape and the history of mankind, cf. section 1 of the Act which includes the concept of sustainability. Within a distance of 300 m from the beaches and seashores, a distance of 300 m from forests, and a distance of 150 m from lakes with a surface area of at least 3 ha, and 100 m from an ancient monument no one may locate buildings, sheds and caravans without approval from the authorities, cf. sections 15–18 of the Act. The prohibitions do not apply to measures that have been ordered or permitted in accordance with the Watercourses Act.[1544] Neither does it apply to reforestation and planting in existing gardens.

1543. Promulgation Order No. 240 of 13 March 2019 on Nature Protection.
1544. Concerning the Watercourses Act, *see supra* paras 109–110.

Chapter 3. Parks, Natura 2000 Sites and Network

§1. Designation and Protection

241. The EU wildlife protection policy is built on international agreements and made vertically binding on its Member States. It consists of Natura 2000 network of protected areas and the strict system of species protection. The first pillar consists of the EU-wide ecological network of protected sites: the Natura 2000 Network. The aim of the network is to ensure the long-term survival of Europe's most valuable and threatened species and habitats. The establishment of this network of protected areas also fulfils some of the obligations established by the Bern Convention,[1545] the Bonn Convention[1546] and the CBD.[1547] At present, the main sources of information available on Natura 2000 sites are to be found on public websites run by the Member States. The second pillar consists of the provisions on the obligations of the Member States to establish preventive and restorative measures that ensure a strict protection of listed species throughout the territory of each Member State.

The Wild Birds Directive[1548] ensures the conservation of all species of naturally occurring birds in the wild state living in the total EU Territory. It covers the protection, management and control of these species and lays down rules for their protection. Recital 4 of the Preamble states that the species of wild birds naturally occurring on the European territory of the Member States are mainly migratory species. Such species constitute a common heritage, and effective bird protection is typically a trans-frontier environmental problem entailing common responsibilities. The Directive covers also nests, eggs and birds' habitats, cf. Article 1(2).[1549] The areas of distribution for the special migratory species that are listed in Annex I of the Directive are the subjects of special conservation measures, cf. Article 4(1).[1550] Each Member State is obliged to identify and classify SPAs for such species, paying particular attention to the protection of wetlands of international importance. All regularly occurring migratory species have to be protected, cf. Article 4(2)–(4). The Member States must take the necessary measures for the ecological functionality in the geographical sea and land, where any migratory species have their breeding, resting and wintering areas and staging posts along their migrator routes, cf. Article 4(2).[1551] A breeding site is defined as the place, where the individuals of the species have their breeding territories or their eggs and young. The Member States must

1545. UNECE Convention of 19 September 1979 on the Conservation of European Wildlife and Natural Habitats.

1546. UNEP Convention of 1 November 1983 on the Conservation of Migratory Species of Wild Animals.

1547. UNEP Convention of 5 June 1992 on Biological Diversity.

1548. European Parliament and Council Directive 2009/147/EC on the Conservation of Wild Birds.

1549. The ban of deliberate destruction of or damage to nests and eggs in Art. 5 cannot be limited to the period of breeding, cf. C-252/85 *Commission v. France.*

1550. There are 194 species and sub-species that are listed in Annex I as particularly threatened. Member States must designate SPAs for their survival and all migratory bird species.

1551. Concerning this obligation, *see* the judgment of the CJEU in the Cases C-418/04 *the Commission v. Ireland*; C-191/05 *Commission v. Portugal*, and C-235/04 *Commission v. Spain.*

inform the Commission so that it may take appreciate initiatives with the goal of ensuring the needed protection of these areas as well as the areas covered by Annex I. The Member States must classify in particular the most suitable territories in number and size to avoid pollution or deterioration of such areas, cf. Article 4(4). The CJEU has emphasised that the selection of sites and the delimitation of boundaries in the context of this Directive should be carried out on the basis of exclusively scientific ornithological criteria.[1552] The main provisions include obligations on the maintenance of the favourable conservation status of all wild bird species across their distributional range with the encouragement of various activities to that end. Each Member State must take responsibility for the living conditions of the birds on the whole territory of the EU, including:

- restrictions on the sale and keeping of wild birds, cf. Article 6;[1553]
- specification of the conditions under which hunting, and falconry may be undertaken, cf. Articles 5–6;[1554]
- birds listed in Annex III and conditions under which permission may be given for otherwise prohibited activities, cf. Article 6 and Annex III to the Directive, as well as Article 9;
- requirements to ensure that the introduction of non-native birds do not threaten the biodiversity.

Interference in a designed SPA is not permitted for economic or recreational reasons.[1555] The SPAs are now also protected under Article 7 of the Habitats Directive,[1556] and they are part of the Natura 2000 network. The Habitats Directive aims to promote the maintenance of biodiversity in international nature areas, taking account of economic, social, cultural and regional requirements. The key element of the Directive as the designation of Special Areas of Conservation (SAC), cf. Article 1(1)(k):

> designated by the Member States through a statutory, administrative and/or contractual act where the necessary conservation measures are applied for the maintenance or restoration, at a favourable conservation status, of the natural habitats and/or the populations of the species for which the site is designated.

1552. C-355/90 *Commission v. Kingdom of Spain.*
1553. In Art. 6(1), it is stated that Member States shall prohibit, for all the bird species referred to in Art. 1, the sale, transport for sale, keeping for sale, and the offering for sale of live or dead birds and of any readily recognisable parts or derivatives of such birds. The ban on hunting in Art. 5 cannot be deviated for activities connected to normal farming, forestry, or fishing, cf. C-412/85 *Commission v. Germany*. In the same judgment, it is stated that the exception in Art. 6 governs only listed activities in Annex III that is exhaustive.
1554. Eighty-two bird species that are listed in Annex II can be hunted. The hunting periods are limited by the rules, and hunting is forbidden when birds are at their most vulnerable period during their return migration to nesting areas, reproduction, and the raising of their chicks.
1555. C-57/89 *Commission v. Germany.*
1556. European Parliament and Council Directive 92/43/EEC on the Conservation of Natura Habitats and of Wild Fauna and Flora.

It is mandatory for the Member States to work together with the Commission on the designation of SACs with a view to setting up a coherent EU-wide ecological network of such areas under the title Natura 2000, cf. Article 3(1). The Member States' proposals for areas to be protected must be based only on conservation-related arguments, and such proposals must include a distinction between priority habitats and species and other areas. The Court has stated that the site selection should be exclusively based on the ecological criteria listed in Annex III of the Directive.[1557] On the basis of national proposals, the Commission draws up a common list of Natura 2000 sites, cf. Article 4(2). If the Commission and the Member States cannot agree on the list, the Council takes the decision, acting on a proposal made by the Commission. The decision is binding, cf. Article 288 TFEU.[1558]

The Natura 2000 network includes the SPAs as well as the SACs, cf. Article 3(1) and Article 7 of the Habitats Directive. The SACs and SPAs are SIC. Such sites contribute significantly to the maintenance or restoration of the natural habitats for species of community interest at a favourable conservation status. As regards other areas than habitats belonging to the Natura 2000 network as SICs, the Habitats Directive invites Member States to encourage the management of features of the landscape, in particular with a view to improve the ecological coherence of the network, in the decisions they make on land-use planning and development policy, cf. Article 10 of the Directive.

In 2005 by its judgment in Case C-6/04 *Commission v. United Kingdom and Northern Ireland*, the CJEU made an important decision on the application of the Habitats Directive also on the EEZ of the Member States.[1559]

242. Denmark has only protected 11.1% of its total area, less than the OECD average of 16.4%, although one-third of Denmark's protected areas are in the international IUCN's categories I and II.[1560] In June 1998, Denmark submitted the first final list to the Commission concerning the SAC covered by the Habitats Directive. However, the Commission did not accept that this Statutory Order correctly implemented Denmark's EU obligations.[1561] In 2018, the protected sites only covered 8.3% of its total area. A total of 17.7% of the Danish marine area Natura 2000 sites.

The current Danish mechanisms used to protect and restore nature – including the Nature 2000 sites – are the rules in the National Parks Act,[1562] the Environmental Objectives Act,[1563] the Forest Act[1564] and the Nature Protection Act.[1565] Five

1557. C-67/99 *Commission v. Ireland*; C-71/99 *Commission v. Germany*; and C-220/99 *Commission v. France*.
1558. Concerning Art. 288 TFEU, *see supra* para. 54.
1559. *See also* the Commission's *Guidelines for the Establishment of the Natura 2000 Network in the Marine Environment. Application of the Habitats and Birds Directives*, 2007.
1560. OECD, *Environmental Performance Reviews. Denmark. 2007*, at 89. *See also infra* paras 250, 252 and 255.
1561. The first statutory order on international protected areas was published in 2003 as the Statutory Order No. 477 of 7 June 2003 on the Demarcation and Administration of International Protection Areas.
1562. Promulgation Order No. 120 of 26 January 2017 on National Parks.
1563. Promulgation Order No. 119 of 26 January 2017 on Environmental Objectives.
1564. Promulgation Order No. 315 of 28 March 2019 on Forests.
1565. Promulgation Order No. 240 of 13 March 2019 on Nature Protection.

national parks have been established under the National Parks Act by statutory orders in Denmark – involving: Mols Bjerge (Mols Mountains), Thy Klithede, the Waddenzee, Skjoldungernes Land and Kongernes Nordsjælland, as the most unique and valuable natural areas and landscapes in Denmark. The national parks include both land and sea, which are designed as Natura 2000 sites and areas not designed as such. They included forests and open countryside with cultivated fields, grazing and hedgerows as well as villages and urban communities. The OECD has concluded that it is not clear that the conservation role of the parks in relation to other protected areas has been clarified as a result of the project.[1566] The establishment of national parks is based on broad local support, and each park must have a decentralised management system. The management is based on voluntary agreements and existing legislation. The Act stipulates rules on the competence of the Minister for the Environment to put limitations on the municipalities. The national parks prepared by the minister must however not contradict the municipal plans or local plans.[1567] The national parks are open to everyone. The Environmental Objectives Act[1568] lays down the administrative and procedural requirements for planning and administration of Natura 2000 sites. In section 36(1), it is stated that the Minister for the Environment appoints international nature protection areas on land and at sea. It is a misunderstanding of the competences as it is the Commission that appoints SACs. The Danish Minister can only appoint SPA if it is accepted by the Commission. It is also a misunderstanding of the Danish competences when section 36(2) of the Act states that the Minister can make changes to already designated SCIs. Declassification of such areas is also regulated by the EU, and the CJEU has generated key rulings regarding the criteria to be interrelated. The Act obliges the EPA[1569] to prepare Natura 2000 plans for the areas not situated in forest, cf. section 37. The final Nature 2000 plans are decided by the Minister, cf. section 45. There are several steps in the planning regulated by the Act. The first step is the basic analysis that has to be performed for each Natura 2000 sites, cf. section 40. It includes the description of the status of the areas' natural habitats and species, as well as the threats to them. The Natura 2000 plans are developed in accordance with parameters covering the 'designation criteria', i.e., the natural habitats and species on which the sites are designated as protected.[1570] The plans must ensure the favourable conservation status for the threatened species and habitats in each area. This includes establishing and preparing action programmes, as well as making sure that the action programmes that have been adopted are implemented and completed in accordance with the obligations under the Wild Birds Directive and the Habitats Directive as well as the Ramsar Convention.[1571] The Natura 2000 action plans are

---

1566. OECD, *Environmental Performance Reviews. Denmark. 2007*, at 95.
1567. Concerning the spatial planning, *see infra* Part III, Chapter 2.
1568. Promulgation Order No. 119 of 26 January 2017 on Environmental Objectives.
1569. Statutory Order No. 95 of 28 January 2019 on the Delegation of Power to the Environmental Protection Agency.
1570. Statutory Order No. 945 of 27 June 2016 on the Classification and Goals for the Quality of Natura 2000 sites.
1571. UNESCO Convention of 2 February 1971 on Wetlands of International Importance especially as Waterfowl Habitat, as amended by the Protocol of 3 December 1982 and the Amendments of 28 May 1987.

prepared by the municipalities as the practical implementation of the State's, Natura 2000 plans, cf. sections 38 and 46a–46b.[1572] Chapter 4 of the Forest Act[1573] contains similar provisions in relation to the duty to prepare Natura 2000 forest plans for areas that must remain wooded in perpetuity, within the Natura 2000 sites. Preservation of areas designated as forest reserve land and protection of natural habitats for species are among the foremost objectives of this Act.[1574] The planning process, as well as the environmental objectives, and the Natura 2000 forest plans are published in the Statutory Orders on Natura 2000 Forest Planning.[1575] The municipalities do not have a competence in the planning of these forest areas. The Natura 2000 plans under the Environmental Objectives Act and the Forest Act are part of the spatial planning as legally binding state plans at the highest level in the plan hierarchy under the Planning Act, cf. section 11(4) of this Act.[1576]

The former liberal-conservative coalition government that was in power from 2015 to 27 June 2019[1577] and the Danish People's Party signed the political agreement on the 'Food and Agricultural Package' (December 2015) and the political agreement on the 'Nature Package' (May 2016). These agreements are focused more on the promotion of the agricultural business interests than on the protection of biodiversity.[1578] The last-mentioned agreement includes initiatives on the reduction of existing Natura 2000 sites and the simplification of the legislation making it 'digitalisation ready'. The agreement also mentions the biodiversity of state-owned forests, the farmer's role as resource manager, the agreements on the nature protection with the farmers (that will receive full financial compensation) and the possibility of using modern nature conservation.[1579] As a reaction to the 'Food and Agricultural Package', a 2016 pilot letter from the Commission to the Danish Government states that the Commission's services have decided on their own initiative to initiate an investigation of the Danish policy and follow-up legislation.[1580]

243. The Nature Protection Act[1581] gives the authorities the power to use conservation orders to establish parks and preserve on a case-by-case basis. The Act

1572. Detailed provisions of these plans are laid down in Statutory Order No. 944 of 27 June 2016 on the Municipal Natura 2000 Action Plans.
1573. Promulgation Order No. 315 of 28 March 2019 on Forest.
1574. Concerning the Danish Forest Act, *see infra* para. 276.
1575. Statutory Order No. 946 of 27 June 2016 on the Preparation of Natura 2000 Forest Sites and Statutory Order No. 1595 of 6 December 2018 on the Demarcation and Management of International Nature Conservation Areas and Protection of Certain Species.
1576. Concerning the spatial planning hierarchy, *see infra* para. 306, and concerning the content of the municipal plans and local plans, *infra* paras 313 and 321.
1577. The liberal coalition governments that were in power until 27 June 2019 has not passed an action plan on sustainability. Its policy was focused primarily on the strong position of the Danish agriculture and industry in the international competition.
1578. This political agreement is connected to the Agreement on the 'Food and Agricultural Package' of 22 December 2015 that was signed by the same political parties to support the economic interests in the agricultural and other food producing sectors.
1579. The Danish Government that was in power until 27 June 2019 presented a proposal to the Commission on the shredding 25,800 ha of Nature 2000 sites around the country.
1580. EU Pilot 8540/16/ENVI, *Implementation in Denmark of Directives 91/676/EEC, 2000/60/EC, 92/43/EEC, in relation to the recent adopted agriculture package.*
1581. Promulgation Order No. 240 of 13 March 2019 on Nature Protection.

aims to improve, restore and provide for areas important to flora and fauna as well as to the interests essential to the landscape and the history of mankind. The Act states that a balance has to be struck between the environmental goals (e.g., by restricting people's access to the natural areas) and the recreational goals (e.g., the need to improve the quality of life). Under this Act, it is possible to take concrete decisions in relation to conservation, but this competence is not very often used as it is characterised as expropriation with full compensation, cf. Chapter 6 of the Act. The Minister for the Environment, the municipal councils and the Danish Society for Nature Protection – as an NGO representing the 'public concerned' – have the right to present proposals on conservation. Such proposals are presented for the national conservation boards that have the competence to make the final decision on conservation, cf. section 33(3) of the Act. On land areas or bodies of fresh water, the thirteen nature conservation boards make the decision on such conservation orders, cf. section 33(1).[1582] A conservation order may have the purpose of preserving the present state of the area concerned (*status quo* conservation), achieving a specified state of nature (nature restoration) or ensuring public access to the area. No activities may be carried out legally or in fact if the activities are contrary to the goal of the proposal for a conservation order, cf. section 37(2). The orders normally consist of terms that are considered necessary to achieve the objectives of the Act, cf. section 38. A conservation order legally affects everyone, i.e., the public as well as the owner of the relevant properties, cf. section 37. Therefore, public participation in the decision-making process has to be arranged when the initiative is announced, cf. section 36.[1583] After the announcement of a proposal, meeting is arranged for all interested parties. The final conservation order must be published by means of an announcement. Under the Act, the relevant nature protection boards may grant exemptions from the existing conservation orders, cf. section 50.

244. The general preservation, maintenance and re-establishment of biotopes and habitats are very important parts of the general rules under the Nature Protection Act.[1584] Under section 3 of that Act, a number of habitat types are now protected by general rules, which prohibit altering the state of the habitats. By far the majority of the protected habitats are privately owned, and their preservation depends in many cases on the owner's continued operation of them. The protection depends on the size of the relevant lake, etc. Lakes over 100 km^2 in extent, designated watercourses which total 28,000 km or more in length, heaths, bogs, marshes, moors, salt marshes, swamps, coastal meadows, humid permanent grasslands and uncultivated dry grasslands are covered by this general protection. It is prohibited to alter the state of such section 3 water areas if they cover more than 2,500 m^2, either separately or jointly. The general protection of natural habitats based on section 3 of the Nature Protection Act will normally not be subject to compensation under the expropriation rules. The municipalities have the competence to derogate from these restrictions, cf. section 65(3).

1582. Concerning the organisation of the councils, *see supra* para. 46.
1583. Concerning the right to public participation, *see supra* para. 32.
1584. Promulgation Order No. 240 of 13 March 2019 on Nature Protection.

245. The Minister for the Environment has the competence to take a decision on expropriation if such a decision is necessary to protect vulnerable nature, cf. section 60(1) of the Nature Protection Act.[1585] The municipalities have the power to take over land by expropriation if it is of special importance to protect Natura 2000 sites, cf. section 60(3) of the Act. The distinction between compensation-free regulation and expropriation is not always clear.[1586]

246. In 2014, in a partnership with private companies, the Government established 'The Danish Foundation'. With an initial capital of DKK 875, this Foundation will contribute to the diversity of nature. Under Chapters VII and VIII of the current Nature Protection Act, extensive works are initiated to restore natural areas that have been fully or partly ruined, for example by dewatering, drainage or overgrowth. These rules aim to secure preservation, maintenance and re-establishment of biotopes and habitats. The Lower Skjern River, which is the largest river in Denmark, has been restored by a specific project on the basis of a specific decision taken by the Danish Parliament in 1987. The proposal on the restoration project was published in 1997. It included re-establishment of a meandering river, natural water levels and water level fluctuation in the river and its valley. The purpose was to improve living conditions for the flora and fauna, to ensure a high level of water quality in the river and in the downstream lagoon, and to improve possibilities of outdoor recreation.

247. Eco-friendly management of nature is also ensured by means of state-ownership. By way of example may be mentioned, natural areas under the jurisdiction of the Ministry of Environment and Food of Denmark amounted to 188,000 ha. It also owns approximately 5,000 ha of coastal meadows, freshwater meadows, bogs and dry grassland.

Some of the areas are located in Margrethe Kog, where efforts to transform a coastline affected by saltwater into humid marshland have succeeded in replacing a valuable biotope with another valuable and biologically attractive area. These areas are protected by a special Act, namely Act on Margrethe Kog.[1587] The Wadden Sea area is an example of an area partly owned by the Ministry of Environment and Food of Denmark. The Ministry of Ecclesiastical Affairs of Denmark owns approximately 17,000 ha, consisting of 400–500 holdings operated as farm utilities. The Ministry of Defence of Denmark is also the owner of land, and it has adopted its own environmental strategy on the protection and safeguarding of a rich diversity. The Danish Ministry of Transport owns a number of areas (approximately 10,500 ha) along the west coast of Jutland, which are managed by the Ministry of Environment and Food. The state-owned areas are managed by the Danish Nature Agency on the basis of detailed management plans. These plans give instructions in relation to efforts to maintain and improve the national elements and the biodiversity of the natural areas. A number of forests are included in these areas, and the

1585. Concerning s. 73 of the Danish Constitution, *see supra* para. 30.
1586. Concerning this distinction, *see infra* para. 250.
1587. Act No. 92 of 2 March 1983 on Margrethe Kog.

management of such forests is now based on a near-nature forestry approach (otherwise known as a 'close-to-nature' forestry approach). The Ministry of Ecclesiastical Affairs owns approximately 17,000 ha, consisting of 400–500 holdings operated as farm units. The Ministry contributes to designating areas and safeguarding of the biodiversity in its areas. The Ministry of Defence is also the owner of land. This Ministry has adopted its own environmental strategy on the protection and safeguarding of a rich diversity. The Ministry of Transport owns a number of areas (approximately 10,500 ha) along the west coast of Jutland, which are managed by the municipalities[1588] and the Danish Coastal Authority that is part of the Ministry of Environment and Food and its Nature Protection Agency.[1589]

248. The coastal areas constitute important natural habitat types, and such areas are therefore a very important part of the protected areas in Denmark.[1590] The Bern Convention, the Bonn Convention, the Ramsar Convention, the Biodiversity Convention, as well as the EU's Natura 2000 rules, apply to these coastal areas if there are migratory species living or visiting the areas.[1591]

Coastal protection works, land reclamation activities and the construction of harbours and industrial and tourist facilities have resulted in a loss of marine habitats along the west coast. Most of the summer houses used by tourists (approximately 97%) are also located in coastal areas. Agenda 21 – from the 1992 UN Conference on the Environment and Development held in Rio de Janeiro – recommended the development and implementation of ICZM in all States. Such a management is defined as a decision-making process with a view to sustainable use, development and protection of seaside terrestrial and coastal marine areas and their resources. There are also provisions on the protection of coastal zones in the Helsinki Convention on the Protection of the Marine Environment of the Baltic Sea Region (HELCOM) which both Denmark and the EU are parties to.[1592] There are also guidelines for the identification of coastal ecosystem influences related to this Convention. In the Commission 'Proposal for a Recommendation concerning the implementation of Integrated Coastal Zone Management (ICZM)',[1593] the need for a stronger Community strategy regarding coastal zone management based on an ecosystem approach and use of spatial planning instruments was stressed.[1594] The obligation to improve the sea/land interface is now part of the Directive on Maritime Spatial Planning.[1595]

1588. Act No. 720 of 8 June 2018 on New Provisions on the Competences and a Reduction of the Complexity in Coastal Protection. This Act ensured that the municipalities have the competences in most cases.
1589. Danish Government, *Action Plan for Biodiversity and Nature Conservation in Denmark 2004-2009*, at 3.
1590. Concerning the Danish coastal zoning, *see infra* para. 309.
1591. Concerning the international protection of biodiversity, *see supra* para. 234, and *supra* para. 241 on the Nature 2000 network that is often located in the coastal areas.
1592. HELCOM Recommendation 15/1 of 8 March 1994 on Protection of the Coastal Strip.
1593. Proposal for a Recommendation concerning the implementation of Integrated Coastal Zone Management (ICZM), *see* COM(2001) 533 final.
1594. Recommendation of the European Parliament and of the Council of 30 May 2002 concerning the Implementation of the ICZM in Europe. This Recommendation encourages the implementation

In 1994, the Danish Planning Act and the Nature Protection Act were amended to ensure stronger protection of the coast than previously, providing that henceforth only buildings and constructions with a special need to be located near the coast should be allowed in the 300 m wide zone along the coastline in all rural areas and summer cottage areas (such a zoning is named 'protection lines'). A special Coastal Conservation Commission was functioning in 1996–2000 with the purpose of reviewing and determining the dune conservation areas and the beach protection line. The exact trajectory of the extended 300 m zone was to be decided by this Commission. If an area was already used for building purposes, summer cottage houses, harbours, etc., the 300 m zone should not cover these areas. The binding rules on protection lines are laid down in statutory orders. These rules are still in force and the individual protection lines are mapped by the Ministry of Industry, Business and Financial Affairs.[1596] Also the general 'restriction on use lines' in the urban areas protects the coast, cf. section 15 of the Nature Protection Act. In addition, this Act protects all semi-natural land areas larger than 2,500 m^2. Under the Planning Act, the building protection zone is maintained at 100 m in the urban and summer cottage areas. New constructions for leisure and tourism are only permitted if they are linked to the 'tourism-political considerations' and only in connection with urban areas or existing large tourist facilities. Changes to the existing state within the zone are prohibited when it comes to buildings, planting, fencing, etc. The municipalities act as the responsible authorities.

249. Protection of dunes is ensured by the Nature Protection Act and Statutory Order on the Conservation of Dunes.[1597] The dune protection lines exist along the West Coast of Jutland. The Statutory Order contains some prohibitions concerning construction, cultivation, hedge cutting and gravel pit exploitation. Fencing, grazing and other activities are also banned. No activities which are contrary to the protection may legally or in practice be carried out. The authorities may extend the protected areas. The decline in the size of area covered by dunes over the last 100 years due to planting and exploitation for recreational purposes (built-up areas) is estimated at 35%. The four general threats to the Danish dunes are:

- the invasion of non-native species, especially mountain pine and lodgepole pine trees;
- a lack of natural dynamic processes (over-stabilisation of dunes);
- ammonium deposition/eutrophication;
- site-specific threats concerning drainage, pressure from tourism, and barriers to habitat management due to land ownership.

Restoration projects are carried out, funded by the Danish State with the contribution of the EU LIFE+ financial instrument. The authorities may order measures

---

by the Member States of a coastal zone management strategy in the context of existing conventions with neighbouring countries, including non-Member States, in the same regional sea. Concerning ICZM, *see infra* para. 302.

1595. Concerning the MSPD, *see supra* para. 130.

1596. The Green Map on Denmark ('Grønt danmarkskort') is shown at the internet.

1597. Statutory Order No. 1061 of 21 August 2018 on the Conservation of Dunes.

at the expense of the owner as the landowners are generally responsible for the protection of the coasts. The State and the municipalities only pay for coastal protection in the case of particularly exposed stretches. Priority is accorded to the preservation of a number of coastal stretches in a natural state rather than to protect all locations where coastal disintegration and mitigation are taking place, and attempts are made to employ more nature-friendly coastal protection methods, e.g., sand feeding, instead of hefty sand breakwaters.

§2. Compensation

250. In the event of the use of conservation measures, compensation is paid according to the principles of expropriation under sections 39, 45 and 60 of the Nature Protection Act that follows the criteria established under the Constitution.[1598] The following criteria have been stated in case law with reference to section 73 of the Constitution as criteria that speak against the characterisation of the restrictions as expropriation: (a) if the aim of the restrictions is to take care of general public interests; (b) if the restrictions on the use of the property are general, i.e., a regulation covering all or a certain category of properties; (c) if the restrictions are not intensive/burdensome for the property owner; (d) if the restrictions are only related to possible future changes in the use of the properties or changes in the buildings. As regards compensation, the rules on conservation decisions differ from those for general restrictions. In order to avoid treating citizens differently, depending on to which rules reference is made, the authorities have chosen to regulate primarily through general restrictions on land use, e.g., by means of the protection of habitats in accordance with section 3 of the Nature Protection Act or by means of municipality plans/local plans based under the Planning Act. However, sections 47–49 of the Planning Act ensure that the owners have some protection based on the expropriation principles if the local plans affect the current business use of the property.[1599] The use of conservation measures is generally restricted to cases where the compensation-free rules of the legislation governing utilisation of the areas do not suffice for conservation purposes. If the conservation boards[1600] decide to protect a property, the owner may apply for compensation from the State or the municipality for the depreciation caused by this deprivation of the right of free disposal. If a decision to protect, first and foremost, aims to serve the interests of the municipalities, the regional conservation boards or the Environmental Protection and Food Appeals Board may decide that the municipal council must pay all or part of the compensation to the owner.

1598. Concerning the criteria on expropriation established by s. 73 of the Danish Constitution and case law, *see supra* para. 30.

1599. Concerning the take-over obligation, *see infra* para. 328.

1600. Concerning the organisation of the councils, *see supra* para. 46.

Chapter 4. Wildlife Protection and Trading

251. There are several important conventions and EU legislations protecting wildlife, including the rules on the wildlife trafficking. On an international level, such trafficking has become one of the world's most profitable organised crimes, and the problem is growing. The 2030 Agenda for Sustainable Development states in target 15.7 that there is a need for ambitious policies to end poaching and trafficking of protected species of flora and fauna, and to address both demand and supply of illegal wildlife products. The Convention on International Trade in Endangered Species and Wild Fauna and Flora (the Washington Convention – CITES) was decided under the IUCN already in 1973. CITES entered into force in 1975. Currently, there are 183 parties although not all the parties have accepted later amendments to the Convention. Denmark ratified the Convention in 1977. The EU became a party to the Convention on 8 July 2015.[1601]

Wildlife administration is part of the Danish Nature Agency's field of work. A red list has been drawn up by the Agency identifying species at risk of extinction as part of the Red List Categories of the IUCN that was launched in 1994. The categories have been developed by the IUCN for classifying species at high risk of global extinction. This system replaced other systems based on more subjectively threatened species categories. Based on the established IUCN criteria, the global Red List of threatened birds has been published regularly since 1974. The 1997 Red List covers both plant and animal species: in total 3,142 species, of which 343 have disappeared (i.e., 'extinct' species), 1,608 are threatened ('critically endangered' or 'vulnerable') and 1,191 are 'rare'. A Danish Red List for birds was developed in 2003. The status on the red-listed birds that was published in January 2009, covering 1,256 species of insects, fungi and vascular plants, showed that one in three of the species for which sufficient data is available is categorised, to a greater or lesser extent, as threatened or no longer found in Denmark. The assessment of Danish species on the basis of the IUCN categories aims to provide a basis to evaluate development trends of biodiversity in Denmark and to fulfil the obligations laid down in the Biodiversity Convention. Today, a number of species from the Danish Red List are experiencing an improvement in population size in Danish nature, often due to highly target-specific efforts. Examples of such species include the otter, the green tree frog and several species of orchids. The white-tailed eagle, black stork and eagle owl have all returned to Denmark in recent years. Bans or limitations on hunting have also helped a number of species, such as the mute swan, the cormorant and the common seal.[1602]

1601. The Council ratified the Convention by its Decision No. 2915/451/EU. The Convention was changed by the 'Gaborone Amendment' that made it possible for regional economic integration organisations – such as the EU – to become party to the Convention. The amendment of the Convention entered into force in November 2013.

1602. In a case assessed by the Aarhus Compliance Committee, the Appeals Board has stated that it was not competent to carry out an evaluation of the municipality of Hillerød for an extensive culling of juvenile rooks protected under the Wild Birds Directive. At the time of the decision taken by the municipality to cull the rooks, there was no prohibition against such an activity in the legislation in force. The municipality was acting in its capacity as landowner. Thus, at that time, provided certain conditions were met, landowners were allowed to cull such birds on their land

The CITES Convention aims to protect listed animals and plants against overexploitation through a common legislation and control of the international trade of such species – whether they are treated as live or dead specimens, parts or derivatives.[1603] To achieve this, it regulates international trade in certain species of wild fauna and flora that are, or may be, threatened by trade. The Convention is based on a system of permits and certificates that must be presented before specimens of protected species are allowed to leave or enter a country, and that can only be issued if certain conditions are present. It accords various degrees of protection to over 35,000 species. Species can be listed in one of the three Appendixes:

(1) Annex I includes species that are threatened with extinction and that are – or may be – affected by international trade. In general, all international commercial trade in such species is banned. Some trade may be allowed under exceptional circumstances.
(2) Annex II includes species that are not necessarily threatened with extinction. They may become threatened if the trade is not closely controlled. Some species are listed because they look like species on the list.
(3) Annex III includes species subject to legislation within a particular Member Country and for which the cooperation of other parties is needed to control international trade.

The parties are all required to implement the provisions of the Convention. The European Community has implemented the Convention since 1984. To ensure a harmonised implementation in its Member States, the CITES provisions have been implemented by the CITES Regulation (also named 'the Basic Regulation').[1604] It goes beyond the Convention in many respects. The provisions are covering trade between Member States, and they include non-CITES listed species, imposing stricter import restrictions on some species and empowering the EU to suspend imports of species from particular exporting countries.[1605] In February 2016, the Commission presented the 'EU Action Plan Against Wildlife Trafficking'.[1606] The current CITES Regulation has been amended several times to add new species to the list of protection transforming the amendments made to the CITES Convention into national legislation.[1607] The Regulation provides the general legal framework as binding provisions at national level as it lays down the provisions for all the Member States' international trade as well as their import, export and re-export of

without a licence or any kind of prior authorisation, and the State authorities could not stop the killing of the protected birds. Concerning the Danish Hunting and Wildlife Management Act, *see infra* para. 254.

1603. Article II of the CITES.

1604. Regulation No. 338/97/EC on the Protection of Species of Wild Fauna and Flora by Regulating Trade therein. Concerning regulations as directly applicable in the Member States, *see supra* para. 58.

1605. Commission, *Analysis and Evidence in support of the EU Action Plan against Wildlife Trafficking*, staff working document of 26 February 2016 SWD(2016) 38 final, at 36.

1606. COM(2016) 87 final. The strategy was adopted by the Council on 21 Jun. 2016.

1607. The provisions of the CITES Regulation have been amended by the Commission Regulation No. 1497/2003 of 18 August 2003.

specimens of species listed in the four Annexes to the Regulation. Rules on the documents required as well as the procedures to be followed for such trade, import, export or re-export are also laid down in the Regulation. There are four Annexes (A, B, C and D) to the Regulation of which the first three largely correspond to Annexes I, II and III of the Convention. Annex D (the monitoring list) includes species that might be eligible for listing in one of the other Annexes and for which the import level is therefore monitored. It also establishes a number of bodies at EU level, i.e., the Committee on Trade in Wild Fauna and Flora, the Scientific Review Group, and the Enforcement Group, all of which consist of representatives of the Member States and are convened and chaired by the Commission. The Commission Regulation on the Implementation of the CITES Regulation (the Implementing Regulation) is laying down detailed rules concerning the implementation of the CITES Regulation.[1608] The Permit Regulation[1609] regulates the design of permits, certifications and other documents provided for in the CITES Regulation. Permits and certifications issued by one Member State on the basis of these EU rules are valid throughout the whole territory of the EU. The application of the CITES Regulation in Denmark is based on administrative rules.[1610] The Danish EPA and the Agricultural Agency have the power to make decisions on wildlife trafficking that involves Danish citizens or the Danish territory on behalf of the EU. Illegal trade of parrots between 2009 and 2011 was prosecuted by the Danish Prosecution Service and the illegal trafficking was sanctioned by Danish courts by a financial penalty amounting to EUR 87,000, confiscation of 11 eggs, 31 parrots and a trade profit amounting to EUR 28,500.[1611]

252. The International Whaling Commission (IWC) established in 1946 protects some types of whales with a focus on the twelve large whale species that were the target for commercial fishing in the 1940s. Whales are also protected by the CBD, the CITES, the Bonn Convention, the Bern Convention and the Habitats Directive.[1612] The EU is not a member of the IWC as it cannot accede to the Convention, which reserves membership to States only.

Denmark is a party to the IWC, and the national authorities responsible for the Danish Realm are in a special situation in this regard. Greenland and the Faroe Islands, that are both part of the Danish Realm, have a policy accepting the hunting of whales, and Denmark represents them in the IWC.[1613] The Habitats Directive prohibits the hunting of whales in the territories of EU Member States, and at an IWC meeting in 2008/2009, the Commission represented the EU's position based

1608. Commission Regulation No. 865/2006/EC laying down Detailed Rules concerning the Implementation of Council Regulation No. 338/97/EC on the Protection of Species of Wild Fauna and Flora by regulating Trade therein, as amended by the Commission Regulation No. 2019/220 of 6 February 2019.

1609. Commission Regulation No. 792/97/EC on the Implementation of the CITES Regulation.

1610. Statutory Order No. 266 of 21 March 2019 on the Protection of Wildlife in Situations of Trafficking.

1611. Commission, *Analysis and Evidence in support of the EU Action Plan against Wildlife Trafficking*, Staff working document, SWD(2016) 38 final, at 62.

1612. Concerning the international protection of biodiversity, *see supra* para. 234, and concerning the Habitats Directive, *see* para. 241.

1613. Concerning the Danish Realm and its relation to the EU, *see supra* paras 1 and 4.

on a mandate from the Council.[1614] Denmark did not support the EU stance and invoked Declaration No. 25 TEU on 'Representation of the interests of the Overseas Countries and Territories referred to in Article 227(3) and 5(a) and (b) of the Treaty Establishing the European Community' in support of the whaling activities on its territories. Denmark's reliance on this Declaration at the IWC has prevented the EU from presenting a united stance on the prohibition of hunting of the whales. At the seventy-first IWC meeting, Denmark clarified its position in relation to the EU policy. At the meeting, the representative for Denmark stated that while Denmark as an EU Member State is bound by the EU common position, because Denmark has overseas territories that are not part of the EU it may, in specific cases where the interests of Greenland and the Faroe Islands diverge from those of the EU, need to deviate from the common EU position. At the meeting, it was also stated that when Denmark made an intervention, it would be to pursue the interests of its overseas territories, in particular the whaling rights of Greenland. However, Declaration No. 25 is not included in the Lisbon Treaty, and other EU Member States are arguing that it is not possible for Denmark to act against the binding obligations established by the Habitats Directives.[1615]

The North Atlantic Marine Mammal Convention Organisation (NAMMCO) protects some of the other whales, and since the EU has ratified this Convention, the Habitats Directive on the prohibition of whaling binds Denmark. Transposition by Denmark of the norms is to be made within the context of the principles of loyalty and sincere cooperation.[1616]

253. The Nature 2000 protection established by EU legislation is among the strongest protection of wildlife. Once a site has been classified as an SPA under the Wild Birds Directive and/or an SAC under the Habitats Directive – and is listed as a Natura 2000 site (SCI) in the legislation and on the webpage – the national authorities in the Member States have obligations to protect the species covered by the specific classification in that Natura 2000 site against any significant negative effect, cf. Article 6(2) of the Habitats Directive.

The Member States must establish the necessary conservation measures involving, if need be, appropriate management plans specially designed for the sites or integrated into other development plans, and appropriate statutory, administrative or contractual measures which correspond to the ecological requirements of the natural habitat types presented on the sites, cf. Article 6(1). The Member States must oblige the competent national authorities to take all necessary initiatives to protect Natura 2000 sites. Article 6(3) of the Directive establishes a mandatory procedure to be followed by the national authorities – e.g., the Danish authorities – on a preliminary examination of all new plans and projects, which are likely to have significant effect on a Nature 2000 site (either individually or in combination with

1614. The Proposal of 2 June 2008 on Council Decision No. 9818/08 establishing the Position to be Adopted on behalf of the European Community with regard to the Proposal for amendments to the Schedule of the International Convention on the Regulation of Whaling.

1615. Concerning the principles and rules binding the Member States, *see supra* paras 55–58.

1616. The 'principle of sincere cooperation' is laid down in Art. 4(3) TEU. This principle and the 'principle of loyalty' are important in CJEU case law.

other plans or projects). In *the Waddenzee Case* (C-127/02) and several other judgments, the CJEU has stated that a proposal for a project or a plan is to be subject to AA ensured by the responsible national permitting authority if it cannot be excluded on the basis of objective scientific information that the proposed project/plan will have significant effects on the relevant species at the Nature 2000 site in view of the site's conservation objectives, either individually or in combination with other plans or projects. The steps to be made are the following:

- screening for AA;
- AA;
- assessment of alternative solutions;
- assessment where no alternative solutions remain and adverse impacts cannot be ruled out, i.e., the imperative reasons of overriding public interest test and compensatory measures.

The aim of such an AA is to avoid damage that can harm the integrity of the European 2000 network and its features. An AA also involves assessment of the cumulative effects. In the light of the conclusion of the assessment of the implications for the Nature 2000 site – and subject to the provisions of Article 6(4) – the national authorities are only permitted to agree to the proposed plan or project if they have ascertained that it will not adversely affect the integrity of the site concerned and, if appropriate, after having obtained the opinion of the general public, cf. Article 6(3). If, in spite of negative assessment of the implications for the protected species at the relevant Natura 2000 site and in the absence of alternative solutions, a proposed plan or project must nevertheless be carried out for imperative reasons of overriding public interest, including those interests of a social or economic nature, in such situations, the national authority must take all compensatory measures necessary to ensure that the overall coherence of the Natura 2000 network is protected. The Commission must be informed about the compensation works that have been decided, cf. Article 6(4).[1617] Where the site concerned hosts a priority natural habitat type and/or a priority species (Annex IV species), the only considerations which may be raised under Article 6(4) as the reasoning for permitting the project/plan are those relating to human health or public safety, to the beneficial consequences of primarily importance to the environment or, further to an opinion from the Commission, to other imperative reasons of overriding public interest. The provision on the strict protection of the special species listed in Annex IV is found in Article 12 of the Directive and explained in a Guidance on Strict Species Protection published by the Commission in 2007. It is settled case law of the CJEU that the Member States must ensure the protection of such species by effective measures.[1618] The

1617. The Danish Western High Court accepted by a judgment of 27 June 2013 the legality of the Danish Act No. 647 of 15 June 2010 (as amended by Act No. 159 of 1 March 2011) on the Test Centre Østerild established for the testing of new 250 m wind turbines close to Natura 2000 sites. On 9 Jun. 2012, the European Commission accepted the Test Centre Østerild project.

1618. C-98/03 *Commission v. Germany* and C-383/09 *Commission v. France*. The obligations are described by Henrik Schoukens, *Saving the Common Hamster with the EU Habitats Directive: A Mandatory Recovery Effort, A Remediation of Parts Non-Compliance or An Exercise in Futility?*, in The Nordic Environmental Law Journal, 2017, Vol 1, at 59–97, and Jan Darpö and Yaffa

national derogations from this protection can only be authorised if the species have reached favourable conservation status and the derogations are in line with one of the grounds for the derogations laid down in Article 16(1). This EU protection of the species is also an implementation of the obligations under the Bern Convention of species listed in Annex I and II of that Convention. The Danish provisions on the mandatory AA under the Article 6(3)–(4) of the Habitats Directive as well as the other obligations for the national authorities described in this Directive and the Wild Bird Directive are laid down in the Statutory Order on the Protection of International Protected areas (the Habitats Statutory Order).[1619] The Statutory order has its legal basis in several acts, including the Environmental Objectives Act,[1620] the Forest Act,[1621] the Nature Protection Act[1622] and the Hunting and Wildlife Management Act.[1623]

254. The purpose of the Hunting and Wildlife Management Act is to ensure a protection against overhunting of diverse and numerous game populations and to provide the basis for sustainable administration of such populations. Since 1944, all hunters have been required to provide information about the game they have shot, specifying both the species and the county. Changes in the number of game shot provide a picture of the size of the population. The information is gathered in connection with the annual renewal of game licences. Ducks and seabirds are monitored from the air. All hunters must have a game licence, cf. section 44 of the Act. Before the first acquisition of a licence, the applicant must demonstrate that he or she has the necessary knowledge about common wildlife and about the regulations on hunting and wildlife conservation, and that he or she has the practical proficiency in using a firearm, cf. sections 44 and 45 of the Act. The applicants must pay a fee for the game licence. The Act is based on the principle that only species (mammals and birds) for which hunting seasons have been laid down by means of statutory orders may be hunted, thus generally protecting all other mammals and birds. Chapter 5 of the Act regulates the manner of hunting and which firearms, etc. may be used. Hunting periods and the preservation of wildlife are regulated in Chapter 6. A prohibition against the deliberate destruction of birds' nests is also laid down in the Act. The owner of a property is the holder of the right to hunt on his or her land. Nobody else has the right to use firearms on the property unless the holder of the right has granted him permission, cf. sections 1 and 5 of the Act. An amendment of the Act[1624] included the legal basis for the establishment of advisory services for

Epstein, *Thrown to the Wolves – Sweden Once Again Flouts EU Standards on Species Protection and Access to Justice*, in The Nordic Environmental Law Journal, 2015, Vol 1, at 7–20.

1619. Statutory Order No. 1595 of 6 December 2018 on the Demarcation and Management of International Nature Conservation Areas and Protection of Certain Species.

1620. Promulgation Order No. 119 of 26 January 2017 on Environmental Objectives.

1621. Promulgation Order No. 315 of 28 March 2019 on Forests.

1622. Promulgation Order No. 240 of 13 March 2019 on Nature Protection.

1623. Promulgation Order No. 265 of 21 March 2019 on Hunting and Wildlife Management.

1624. Act No. 514 of 12 June 2009 on the amendments of the Nature protection Act, the Hunting and Wildlife Management Act and other acts (Protection of certain Animal Species, etc.).

the protection of Annex IV species,[1625] as well as additional measures for the protection of vulnerable species, including management plans. Indigenous species cannot be hunted unless the authorities give a special permission for the species and the conditions. Currently forty-five species can be hunted.

255. The World Commission on Protected Areas (WCPA) under the IUCN has the marine environment as its priority area. Protected areas for wildlife on the sea have been established at regional level, e.g., under the Helsinki Convention,[1626] the OSPAR Convention[1627] and the NMPA. As a protection of the ecosystems, the Habitats Directive and the Wild Bird Directive apply to internal waters, the territorial sea, the EEZ and the continental shelf.

The CJEU has stated that the Natura 2000 rules also apply to waters under the Member States' jurisdictions and in waters where they exercise sovereign rights, *see* Case C-6/04 *Commission v. UK and Northern Ireland*. This judgment was made before the new clear statute in Article 11 of the CFP Regulation made it mandatory for the Member States to follow a clearly described procedure taking measures for the control of fishing activities in Nature 2000 areas.[1628] In this judgment, the CJEU established that the granting of fishing licences within an SPA is a 'plan' or 'project' within Article 6(3) of the Habitats Directive. The issuing of annual cockle fishing licences must be based on an assessment following the criteria in that Article.[1629] Another important judgment stating that these directives apply to the Member States' EEZs is the Case C-127/02 *Waddenzee*. The Member States of the EU are required to protect and preserve the marine environment, prevent its deterioration or, where practicable, restore marine ecosystems in areas where they have been adversely affected, cf. Article 1(2)(a) of MSFD.[1630] This Directive provides the opportunity to complete current efforts to identify and designate MPAs under the Habitats Directive (i.e., SACs), the Wild Birds Directive (SPAs), the HELCOM Baltic Sea Action Plan (BSAP) and the OSPAR NMPAs. The Habitats Directive, the Wild Birds Directive, the MSFD and the Framework Directive for Maritime Spatial Planning (FMSP Directive)[1631] are all means used to implement these obligations.

1625. Annex IV species are protected by the Habitats Directive.

1626. HELCOM Baltic Sea Action Plan (BSAP) approved by the Council in 1994. Under Art. 13 of the Convention, the HELCOM Recommendation 15/5 has established a system of coastal marine Baltic Sea Protected Areas (BSPA). The NMPA can be defined as areas of seawaters that are given special protection through legal provisions because of their significance for series for a number of reasons.

1627. It is laid down in its Annex V on the Protection and Conservation of the Ecosystems and Biological Diversity of the Maritime Area and the corresponding Appendix 3. The OSPAR Ministerial Meeting in September 2010 adopted the 'North-East Atlantic Environmental Strategy for 2010-2020', which has as its overarching objective the implementation of an ecosystem approach.

1628. European Parliament and Council Regulation No. 1380/2013 on the Common Fisheries Policy (CFP Regulation). Concerning this Regulation, *see infra* para. 280.

1629. Concerning fishing activities, *see infra* paras 279–285.

1630. European Parliament and Council Directive 2008/56/EU establishing a Framework for the Community Action in the Field of Marine Environmental Policy. Concerning this Directive, *see supra* para. 130.

1631. European Parliament and Council Directive 2014/89/EU establishing a Framework for Maritime Spatial Planning. Concerning this Directive, *see supra* para. 131. The structure, functioning and

256. Almost 23% of the Danish Baltic Sea waters have been included in the SCIs sites. After an assessment by the Commission, a new binding legislation that included additional marine habitats was published in 2010.[1632] In 2011, eight marine habitats were expended or introduced as new protected sites by means of an amending statutory order.[1633]

A preliminary assessment for the National Monitoring and Assessment Programme for the Aquatic and Terrestrial Environment (NOVANA) system of thirteen habitats and seventy-nine species found that three habitats and twenty-two species were in an unfavourable condition and thirteen species had disappeared. Some 22% of Denmark's mammals, 13% of birds, 16% of freshwater fish, 14% of amphibians and 10% of plants are threatened according to the IUCN categories.[1634]

---

progress of marine ecosystems have to be fully considered, marine species and habitats must be protected, and the human-induced decline of biodiversity must be prevented. Marine regions or subregions are used as the units to which the objectives of MSFD apply.

1632. Statutory Order No. 63 of 11 January 2010 on the amendment of the Statutory Order on the Design and Administration of International Protected Sites and the protection of certain Species.

1633. Statutory Order No. 1079 of 25 November 2011 on the amendment of the Statutory Order on the Design and Administration of International Protected Sites and the protection of certain Species.

1634. OECD, *Environmental Performance Reviews. Denmark 2007*, at 99ff. The Statutory Order No. 1048 of 28 August 2013 on Special Restriction of Fisheries in Natura 2000 Sites aims to reduce the negative impact of fisheries on the Nature 2000 sites.

Chapter 5. Agricultural Resources

257. Farmers produce food and bioenergy, and they are participating in the management of the landscape. Farming can have positive as well as negative impacts on the environment and the living conditions. The production is heavily dependent on natural resources, such as soil, water and climate. Overexploitation of land use, water consumption and pollution, as well as erosion and degradation of the soil, are some of the negative impacts.[1635] Pesticides, including POPs, are among the most significant sources of pollution. Biodiversity, landscape degradation and decline, fire and GHG emissions are other important negative impacts. Among the positive aspects are the farmers' production of food and biomass (as resources for renewable energy), and their contribution towards improving resilience of the nature, and to CO_2 storage (sinks) facilities. In the agricultural landscape, decisions on landscape structures and functions play a fundamental role with the farmers as the key actors.

The competences relating to agriculture is shared between the EU and its Member States, cf. Article 4(2)(d) TFEU. The agricultural policies of the EU are traditionally production- and income-oriented in a market context characterised by individual choices, whereas environmental protection, nature conservation, zoning and spatial planning, etc. are concerned with wider common goals on the protection of the soil, water and habitats as well as the challenges related to climate change. The types of means used to reduce the negative consequences are: (a) statutory management requirements putting restrictions on land use and production; (b) conservation orders and other case-by-case decided restrictions; (c) subsidy schemes and other economic instruments; (d) voluntary agreements; and (e) education/training and information services.

258. The substantive basis for secondary law on agricultural issues is Articles 38 and 43 TFEU in the 'Agricultural Chapter'. The CAP is defined by the Union, cf. Article 38 TFEU. The CAP was originally established in the 1960s on the basis of high guaranteed prices. However, environmental problems emerged in connection with the growth of agriculture, and set-aside requirements were introduced in 1988 as a measure to reduce the large and costly production surplus under the guaranteed price system and to deliver some environmental benefits. Three major reforms of the CAP have taken place (in 1992, 1999 and 2003/2004)[1636] before the last reform was passed in 2013 as the '2013 CAP Reform'. The next CAP beyond

1635. On a global basis, agriculture accounts for approximately 40% of land use and 85% of water consumption.

1636. At the end of 2003, the Rural District Programme was renewed along two lines: growth and development *versus* nature and environment. Agri-environmental schemes became compulsory for the Member States. It included a number of schemes: (a) an extension of the particularly sensitive agricultural areas; (b) protection of the aquatic environment and nature by agreement between the authorities and farmers; (c) extensive buffer zones either as spray-free margin strips or as spray-and-fertiliser-free strips; (d) organic farming; (e) testing different concepts of grazing associations and nature plans; and (f) forest schemes.

2020 is under preparation.[1637] The draft regulations on the CAP beyond 2020 present new rules that is focused more on a result-driven policy. The Member States have to prepare CAP Strategic Plans in accordance with minimum requirements established in the future 'CAP Strategy Regulation'. The new rules also establish networks that have to facilitate the successful implementation of the CAP Strategic Plans. All the regulations established by the current as well as the future CAP are directly applicable at national level and therefore part of Danish legislation.[1638]

The 2003–2004 reform introduced 'cross-compliance' obligations and 'Good Agricultural and Environmental Conditions' (GAEC). It included rules on land use, as well as a special payment for the production of crops on non-set-aside land dedicated to energy crops. In September 2006, the Commission adopted twenty-eight agri-environmental indicators to assess the interaction between the CAP and the environment.[1639] The '2013 CAP Reform' was adopted on 16 December 2013 by the Council of EU Agriculture Ministers.[1640] The budget is fixed for the period 2014–2020. In line with 'Europa 2020', the overall CAP objectives are: [1641]

- viable food production;
- sustainable management of natural resources and climate change;
- balancing territorial development;
- fostering the competitiveness of agriculture.

It is the ambition behind the '2013 CAP Reform' to enhance the overall environmental performance of the CAP through the greening of direct payments[1642] by means of certain agricultural practices that are beneficial for the climate and the environment and that all farmers will have to follow, which goes beyond the mandatory cross-compliance requirements. The Regulation on Support for Rural Development by the European Agricultural Fund for Rural Development (EAFRD)[1643] seeks to establish a coherent and sustainable framework for rural development by mandatory requirements on direct payments only to 'active farmers' in the meaning of Article 9 of the Regulation on Direct Payments to Farmers[1644] and on the basis of 'SWOT' analyses. In its preamble, the EAFRD states its relation to the EU's

1637. The Commission proposal on the Multiannual Financial Framework (MFF) 2017–2021 (titled MFF Regulation), COM(2018) 322 final, as well as the Commission's proposal on the 'CAP Strategy Plan Regulation' of 1 June 2018, COM(2018) 392 final.
1638. Concerning the regulations as part of national law, *see supra* para. 58.
1639. COM(2006) 508 final.
1640. The '2013 CAP Reform' covers the period 2014–2020.
1641. Support for this programme is co-funded by the EU under the European Parliament and Council Regulation No. 1305/2013/EU on Support for Rural Development by the European Agricultural Fund for Rural Development (EAFRD) and the national Exchequer.
1642. Direct payments are provided by the European Agricultural Guarantee Fund (Pillar 1) of the CAP. The primary aim of this subsidy scheme is to provide income support for farmers. The subsidies should also contribute to achieving other objectives related to land use. There is a national budget ceiling for each Member State.
1643. The European Parliament and Council Regulation No. 1305/2013/EU on Support for Rural Development by the European Agricultural Fund for Rural Development (EAFRD).
1644. European Parliament and Council Regulation No. 1307/2013/EU establishing Rules for Direct Payments to Farmers under Support Schemes within the Framework of the Common Agricultural Policy.

overall policy – as described in 'Europa 2020' – and the need for a sustainable development of rural areas with focus on a limited number of core priorities.[1645] Among these priorities are restoring, preserving and enhancing ecosystems that are related to agriculture and forestry, the promotion of resource efficiency and the shift towards a low-carbon economy in the agriculture, food and forest sectors. Member States have to programme these measures to ensure: (a) that they help to achieve one or more EU priorities for rural development and (b) to meet the needs of rural areas. They have the competence to define national or regional supplementary minimum requirements on the basis of the framework established by the CAP, taking into account the specific characteristics of the areas concerned, including soil and climate conditions and existing farming systems, land use, crop rotation, farming practice and farm structures. It introduced rural development measures to be used to motivate the framers to take specifically sensitive agricultural areas out of production ('set-aside' of land).[1646] The '2013 CAP Reform' replaced the single payment scheme ('SPS Scheme')[1647] with the basic payment scheme ('BPS Scheme')[1648] for farmers with the simplification of the regulation as the guiding principle. The economic support is subject to the cross-compliance obligations.[1649] It is accepted that the Member States applying BPS can continue to use this scheme until 2020, and Denmark is among the Member States that decided to use this possibility.[1650] Since 2015, every farmer who claims a direct payment and has more

1645. The annual ceiling (the maximum amount that can be paid) for the expenditure financed by the EAGF has to take into account the maximum amounts laid down for that fund under the multi-annual framework provided for in Council Regulation No. 1311/2013/EU.
1646. European Parliament and Council Regulation No. 1310/2013/EU laying down Transitional Provisions on Support for Rural Development.
1647. The 'SPS Sheme' is an income support scheme for farmers decoupled from production. It was introduced by the '2003 CAP Reform'. The objectives of this support scheme is to provide basic income support to farmers and to deliver basic goods to European society. The supports were to the farmers based on historical data (at regional or individual farmers level). The supports were for managing their land to minimum standards for crop production, animal welfare and the environment (cross-compliance standards).
1648. The basic income support scheme for farmers is based on payment entitlements. Eligibility for the BPS Scheme or, as the case may be, the Single Area Payment Scheme, is a precondition for the farmers to receive other direct payment such as green direct payment, the redistributive payment, the payment for areas with natural or other specific constraint and the payment for young farmers. In order to achieve direct payments, farmers have to activate their payment entitlements together with eligible agricultural land. The support is independent of agricultural production and income, cf. the definition in European Court of Auditors, *Basic Payment Scheme for farmers – operationally on track, but limited impact on simplification, targeting and the convergence of aid levels*, 2018, at 6–7. The aim of the BPS is the same as the aim of the SPS: to provide a basic income support to farmers without distorting production decisions.
1649. In addition to the Basic Payment, each farm (holding) will receive a payment per hectare for respecting certain agricultural practices beneficial for the climate and the environment. Member States have to use 30% of the national envelope in order to pay for this. The relevant measures that are required are: maintaining 5% permanent grassland; crop diversification involving at least three crops (none accounting for more than 70% of the land and the two main crops together not exceeding 95%) and maintaining an ecological focus area of at least 5% for farms with more than 15 ha (exemption for farms comprising more than 75% grassland).
1650. The Danish authorities have decided to earmark 2.7–2.8% of the direct payments for voluntary coupled support targeting beef and veal, and they have allocated 0.3% of the envelope for areas

than 15 ha of arable land is obliged to have 5% of his arable land covered by ecological focus areas, which improve biodiversity, maintain attractive landscapes and brings benefits for the environment. All payment entitlements activated in 2019 in a Member State or in a region should have a uniform unit value. The CAP Horizontal Regulation[1651] provides farm advisory services helping farmers to assess the performance of their agricultural holding and to identify the necessary improvements, GAEC, agricultural practices beneficial to the climate and the environment set out in the Regulation establishing Rules for Direct Payments to Farmers. Evidence collected through Article 10 of the CMEF serves for measuring the performance of the CAP.[1652] Under the CAP Horizontal Regulation, the Member States have to set up and operate an integrated administration and control system (titled the 'integrated system') for certain payments under the EAFRD and the Regulation on Direct Payment for Farms. The sample of farmers to be checked under the cross-compliance requirements shall be selected by the Member States using a risk analysis for 'on the spot' (OTS) checks of areas related to aid schemes, greening payment, rural development and animal aid schemes to whom the relevant requirements and standards apply.[1653] Where the requirements of GAEC under the direct payment provisions are not complied with at any time in a given calendar year, and the non-compliance in question is the result of an act or omission directly attributable to the farmer who submitted the aid application in the calendar year concerned, the total amount of direct payments granted or to be granted must be reduced.

259. On 28 February 2014, Denmark and the Commission made their Partnership Agreement on the implementation of the 2013 reform in Denmark. The implementation of the programmes is jointly funded with the EU.

In the period 2014–2020, more than EUR 7 billion are invested under the CAP in the Danish farming sector and rural areas.[1654] Denmark has used its flexibility to adopt both direct payments and the RDP to the specific national needs by the transfer of EUR 287 million from its original direct payment envelope to its rural development funds.[1655] The Danish Agricultural Aid Act[1656] and the Statutory Order on

---

with natural constraints (for up to 100 ha for farms on small islands), *see* The European Commission's info from 2016, available at https://ec.europa.eu/info/publications/cap-your-country_en (visited on 15 May 2019).

1651. European Parliament and Council Regulation No. 1306/2013/EU on the Financing, Management and Monitoring of the CAP.

1652. In the preamble of the CAP Horizontal Regulation it is stated that the main elements of the 'integrated system' are: (a) the provisions concerning a computerised database with the identification system for agricultural parcels, aid applications or payment claims and the identification and recording of payment entitlements; whilst taking into account (b) the evolution of the policy, in particular, by the introduction of payment for agricultural practices beneficial for the climate change and the environment and the ecological benefits of landscape features.

1653. Commission Implementation Regulation No. 809/2014/EU.

1654. European Commission's info from 2016, available at https://ec.europa.eu/info/publications/cap-your-country_en (visited on 15 May 2019).

1655. About 5% in 2015, 6% in 2017, and 7% thereafter, *see* https://ec.europa.eu/info/publications/cap-your-country_en (visited on 15 May 2019).

1656. Promulgation Order No. 231 of 22 March 2018 on the Administration of the EU's Regulations under the CAP on Agricultural Aid.

Cross-compliance[1657] lay down the criteria for receiving economic support under the above-mentioned EU programmes. The provisions contain all the key requirements that have to be respected in national legislation concerning the use of fertiliser and PPPs.[1658] There is also a Statutory Order on the Granting of Support to Organic Production[1659] and a Statutory Order on the Granting of Environmental Support to the Owners and Tenant of Agricultural Holdings.[1660] The Danish Agriculture Agency under the Ministry of Environment and Food is the managing authority with respect to the national administration of EU funds.[1661] The Danish Agricultural Advisory Service supports the producers and their organisations by means of professional advice. Many farmers hire agricultural crop consultants, who are employed by local agricultural organisations for help in devising the required plans for manure use and for filing reports about the use of manure and fertilisers. Municipalities have also the option of cooperating with these consultants to give advice to farmers about more efficient production methods, to certify adequate storage capacity for manure and for other tasks. Producer organisations, which are truly owned and controlled by the farmers themselves, have the potential to empower farmers and facilitate delivery of services that respond to their needs.

260. Organic production and labelling of organic products are covered by the Regulation on Organic Production and Labelling of Organic Products.[1662] With effect from 1 January 2021, these rules will be replaced by the rules laid down in a new Regulation.[1663] Both Regulations are directly applicable at national level.[1664]

Pursuant to Article 1 of the 2007 Regulation in force, it applies to the following products originating from agricultural activities (including aquaculture) where such products are placed on the market or are intended to be placed on the market: (a) live or unprocessed agricultural products; (b) processed agricultural products for use as food; (c) feed; and (d) vegetative propagative material and seed for cultivation. Organic means coming from or related to organic production, cf. Article 2(c). Organic production is an overall system of farming management and food production that combines BEPs, a high level of biodiversity, the preservation of natural resources, the application of high animal welfare standards and a production method

1657. Statutory Order No. 1036 of 26 July 2018 on cross-compliance.
1658. Concerning the restrictions on use of pesticides, *see supra* paras 218–224.
1659. Statutory Order No. 94 of 28 January 2010 on the Granting of Support to Organic Production. The provisions were, e.g., amended after the 'Partnership Agreement' was signed, *see* Statutory Order No. 1301 of 9 December 2014, and by Statutory Order No. 86 of 28 January 2015. The latest amendments to the provisions are laid down in Statutory Order No. 93 of 28 January 2016.
1660. Statutory Order No. 95 of 28 January 2010 on the Granting of Environmental Support to the Owners and Tenant of Agricultural Holdings. These provisions were also amended after the 'Partnership Agreement' was signed. *See, e.g.,* Statutory Order No. 1300 of 9 December 2014 and by Statutory Order No. 86 of 28 January 2015. The latest amendments were established by Statutory Order No. 92 of 28 January 2016.
1661. Statutory Order No. 1273 of 27 November 2017 on the Competences of Agriculture Agency.
1662. European Parliament and Council Regulation No. 834/2007/EC on Organic Production and Labelling of Organic Products.
1663. European Parliament and Council Regulation No. 2018/848/EU on Organic Production and Labelling of Organic Products. In 2014, the Commission presented the proposal for this new Regulation as part of the new CAP reform, cf. COM(2014) 180 final.
1664. Concerning the regulations as part of national legislation, *see supra* para. 58.

in line with the preference of certain consumers for products produced using natural substances and processes. Organic farming differentiates itself from conventional farming by the targets that it sets itself to meet in terms of greater respect for the environment, nature and livestock welfare. GMOs and products produced from or by GMOs are prohibited in organic production.[1665] The objectives of the Regulation is to establish a sustainable management system for agriculture that: (i) respects nature's systems and cycles and sustains and enhances the health of soil, water, plants and animals and the balance between them; (ii) contributes to a high level of biological diversity; (iii) makes responsible use of energy and the natural resources, such as water, soil, organic matter and air; and (iv) respects high animal welfare standards and in particular meets animals' species-specific behavioural needs. It also aims to ensure a high quality of produced products. Furthermore, it aims to produce a wide variety of foods and other agricultural products that respond to consumers' demand for goods produced by the use of processes that do not harm the environment, human health, or animal health and welfare, cf. Article 3. Organic production must be based on the appropriate design and management of biological processes. The use of chemicals is only accepted in cases where the appropriate management practices either do not exist or where such practices would have unacceptable environmental impacts, cf. Article 4. There are special principles applicable to farming stipulated in Article 5, special principles in relation to organic food stipulated in Article 6, and special principles on organic feed stipulated in Article 7. The general rules on production are laid down in Articles 9 and 10. The general farm production rules are laid down in Articles 11–17. The Danish supplementary rules to the Regulation are contained in the Act on Organic Production[1666] and the Statutory Order on Organic Agricultural Production.[1667]

261. Several political agreements have been made since the 1980s to reduce the emission of compounds of nitrogen (N) and phosphorus from agricultural activities causing eutrophication[1668] by the enrichment of water nutrients. This policy has, however, been changed by the political agreements made in 2015–2016.

The first Danish political agri-environmental action plan with the objective of reducing the emissions of nitrogen (N) into surface waters was the 'NPO Action Plan', which was finally agreed upon as a Parliamentary Decision in May 1985. The Environmental Support Act for this action plan was not passed until January 1987. In March 1987, the Ministry of Environment presented a 'Marginal Land Strategy' with the goal of protecting the open land by means of conservation of non-cultivated or extensively cultivated areas and of protecting environmentally sensitive areas. The first Danish APAE I was agreed upon in 1987. The main task of this Plan was to reduce discharges of nutrient salts into the waters surrounding Denmark by 50% and to reduce phosphorus (P) emissions by 80% before 1993. The initiatives led to a reduction in the impact of urban wastewater on the recipients.

1665. Concerning GMOs, *see infra* paras 297–301.
1666. Promulgation Order No. 21 of 4 January 2017 on Organic Farming.
1667. Statutory Order No. 1316 of 19 November 2018 on Organic Agricultural Production.
1668. The 'eutrophication' is causing an accelerated growth of algae and higher forms of plant life to produce an undesirable disturbance to the balance of organisms present in the water and to the quality of the water concerned.

However, it did not reach the desired quality targets, as P concentration is still high. This was partly due to accumulation in the sediment of P that had been discharged in the past. In 1991, the Ministry of Agriculture presented an 'Action Plan for a Sustainable Development within the Agriculture' to the Danish Parliament. In February 1998, the political parties in the Danish Parliament agreed on the APAE II. On the basis of this agreement, important rules on the control of container use as storage vessels for livestock manure, including measures to prevent water pollution by run-off and seepage into the groundwater and surface water of liquids containing livestock manures, etc. were passed by the Danish Parliament. Measures were directed towards the individual farmer and included the establishment of slurry tanks with a nine-month storage capacity and obligations to grow winter crops on 65% of the surface area. In January 1999, an 'Action Plan on Development in Organic Farming' was passed with the target of 170,000 ha increase in such farms before 2003. In 2002, an 'Action Plan for Reducing Ammonia Volatilisation' related to the agricultural activities was published with the ambition of ensuring a total reduction of about 9,500 tonnes of nitrogen per year. In October 2003, the Government published the 'Pesticide Plan 2004–2009' for reducing pesticide consumption. The Plan was based on targets for the establishment of spray-free buffer zones along identified watercourses and lakes, as well as initiatives to protect Danish groundwater. A 'Manure Action Plan' was implemented in 2004 by tightened distance requirements from 20 March 2004 to protect neighbour areas by introducing zones where new farming facilities are not allowed. The political agreement on the 'APAE III covering the ten-year period 2005–2015 was concluded in April 2004. It was closely related to the Danish implementation of the WFD and the Habitats Directive. Organic farming was one of several elements in the APAE III. It had the objective of reducing excess P by 50%. The means to ensure this reduction was a crop-free buffer zone of 10 m along rivers and lakes before 2009 (covering close to a 30,000 ha agricultural area) and a further 20,000 ha agricultural area before 2015. The buffer zones were to be established by voluntary transfer of set-aside land along lakes and rivers. The leaching of nitrogen from agricultural activities was to be reduced by a minimum of 13% by 2015, as compared with 2003. The rules on late crops and the rules on the use of nitrogen in livestock manure were tightened. The 'Green Growth Agreement' from June 2009[1669] included initiatives on promotion of a market-based organic sector, promotion of the localisation of biogas plants as part of municipal spatial planning: reduction in the harmful effects of pesticides (e.g., by creation of the framework for cultivation in accordance with guidelines for integrated pest management); reduction in the NH_3 burden; reduction in the loss of nutrients in connection with feeding; digestion of feed; the use of livestock manure; stimulation of the cultivation of perennial energy crops; and the financing of the green growth in the agricultural sector under the EU RDP. After many political initiatives reducing the negative impact from agricultural activities, the former Liberal-Conservative Government made a political agreement with the Liberal Alliance and the Danish People's Party on the abolishment of the Act on Buffer Zones with effect from January 2016 as well as the removal of the general standards on fertiliser use.

1669. The 'Green Growth Agreement' was agreed between the Liberal-Conservative Coalition Government, the Social-Liberal Party and the Danish People's Party.

The political agreement of 22 December 2015 between the same parties on the 'Food and Agricultural Package' accepted a higher emission from agricultural activities.[1670] It is the ambition behind this agreement to establish a target regulation of agriculture with effect from August 2019. The new legislation that is under development as a follow-up on this agreement will be based on four main principles:[1671]

(1) The accepted leaching of nitrogen from the fields to the coastal water is deafferented geographically in order to meet the nitrogen target set in the water basin plans. In the calculation of the leaching access, the average retention from the zone to the coast water body is taken into account.
(2) Each agricultural farm receives a leaching permit to leaching its nitrogen to the aquatic environment. The maximum leaching from the root zone per hectare (kg N per hectare) will be stated in the permit. The maximum nitrogen leaching will be equally designed in a catchment area.
(3) Flexibility in the farmers use of instruments (e.g., catch crops, buffer strips, reduced nitrogen application, etc.) is accepted.
(4) The reduction of the production caused by the new regulatory approach will be combined with a compensation to the farmers.

The challenge related to the reduction of the protection of water was highlighted by the EU Commission in its pilot letter on the implementation problems connected to the just-mentioned political agreement.[1672]

262. The just-mentioned political agreement on the 'Food and Agricultural Package' from 22 December 2015 was followed by an amendment of this Act that came into force in August 2017.[1673] The very large farms and some other agricultural activities are not permitted to be established or commenced without prior operating licence in accordance with the Act on Environmental Approval for Livestock Holdings.[1674] The Act coordinates several aspects of nature protection, environmental protection, EIA obligations, zoning and planning, cf. section 1(1). Section 1(2) states that the Act specifically aim at:

1670. Statutory Order was Statutory Order No. 280 of 16 March 2016 on Agricultural Use of Fertilisers during the 2015/2016 Planning Period, Statutory Order No. 1055 of 1 July 2016 on Agricultural Use of Fertilisers during the 2016/2017 Planning Period, Statutory Order No. 963 of 12 July 2017 on Agricultural Use of Fertilisers during the 2017/2018 Planning Period, Statutory Order No. 1008 of 2 July 2018 on Agricultural Use of Fertilisers during the 2018/2019 Planning Period and Statutory Order No. 762 of 29 July on Agricultural Use of Fertilisers during the 2019/2020 Planning Period.
1671. Danish Ministry of Environment and Food, *Overview of the Danish Regulation of Nutrients in Agriculture & Danish Nitrates Action Programme*, June 2017, at 6–7.
1672. EU Pilot 854040/16/ENVI, *Implementation of Directives 91/676/EC, 2000/60/EC, 92/43/EEC, in relation to the recently adopted agriculture package*, May 2016.
1673. Act No. 204 of 28 February 2017 on New Regulation of Livestock Holdings, etc., and General rules on Spreading of Manure, etc.
1674. Concerning the environmental approval system, *see supra* paras 64–69.

1) preventing and limiting of the pollution of air, water, soil and subsoil and limiting nuisance caused by odour, light, noise, dirt and flies from livestock farms, including from the production, storage and use of livestock manure, etc.; 2) limiting the use and waste of mineral resources and other resources; 3) promoting the use of the best available techniques (BAT), including cleaner technology; 4) promoting recycling and limiting problems associated with waste disposal; 5) protecting nature and its populations of wild flora, wildlife and habitats; 6) creating and retaining valuable built-up areas, cultural and urban environments, as well as landscapes; 7) ensuring that exposed coastal areas continue to represent an important nature and landscape resource; and 8) involving the general public in cases in accordance with the law.

Livestock farming with an NH_3 emission of more than 3,500 kg NH_3-N per year must not be established without prior approval from the municipal council, cf. section 16a(1) of the Act. Based on section 16a(2), it is also mandatory to apply for a prior approval if the livestock farm has:

- more than 750 dots for lakes;
- more than 2,000 dots for fattening pigs (over 30 kg); or
- more than 40,000 dots for poultry (chicken, turkeys, guinea fowl, ducks, geese, quails, pheasants, partridges, or ratites that are kept captive for breeding, production of meat or eggs for consumption or supply of wild species for release).

Based on the amended Act the permit thresholds are now linked to the production area of the installation. Some of the livestock installations are only covered by national law, others – the biggest livestock installations[1675] – are covered by the IED as it has been implemented into Danish legislation. The IED requirements must be respected by the pig and poultry installations above the thresholds and installations having an NH_3 emission above 3,500 NH_3-N per year, cf. section 16a.[1676] The same is the case for the intensive rearing of poultry or pigs with more than 40,000 places for poultry, more than 2,000 places for production pigs (over 30 kg), or more than 750 places for sows, cf. section 16a(2).[1677] Applications for the establishment, expansion or modification of livestock farms must be submitted to the municipal council via the digital self-service system 'Husdyrgodkendelse.dk'. The half-automatised decision-making system consists of GIS maps on sensitive areas, etc., algorithms and calculation systems. The authorities assessment of the applications

1675. The livestock installation having an ammonia emission above 3,500 kg NH3N per year. Concerning the new rules, *see* Jussi Kaupilla and Helle Tegner Anker, *The Role of Permits in Regulating Livestock Installations and Manure Spreading: Experiences from Denmark and Finland*, European Energy and Environmental Law Review, 27(3), June 2018, at 97–98.

1676. *See supra* para. 61 concerning the IE Directive, and *infra* para. 265 concerning the Environmental Approval for Livestock Holdings Act. In 2003, the Danish Minister for Environment asked the competent authorities to make sure that EIAs relating to pig farms focused especially on Natura 2000 sites, as implemented in Denmark by means of statutory rules. Concerning Natura 2000 sites, *see supra* paras 234 and 241–242.

1677. These thresholds are the same as those established by s. 6.6. of the Annex I to the IE Directive.

must include the following issues: (a) the use of BAT; (b) protection of soil, groundwater, surface water as well as nature with its population of wild flora, fauna and their habitats; (c) limitation of any nuisance caused to neighbours (odour, noise, fly and light nuisance, waste production, etc.); and (d) landscape interests. In order for an application to be successful, it must be shown that the applicant has taken the necessary measures to prevent and limit pollution by using BAT and that the farm can generally be operated at the location without affecting the surroundings in any way that is incompatible with the environmental rules on protection of the surroundings. The environmental approval system is only covering the installation in which the animals are located. The screening and impact assessment under the IEA Directive[1678] and the screening and AA under Article 6 of the Habitats Directive are in the Danish digitalised legislation transformed into general provisions allowing categories of projects under some thresholds stated to be executed without being subject to an individual AA.[1679] Based on a recent judgment from the CJEU, it is, however, problematic to use such prior standards and thresholds based on an AA as alternatives to individual assessments under Article 6 of the Habitats Directive.[1680] The just-mentioned exemptions from these individual assessment described by EU legislation are part of the Danish digitalisation strategy.

263. The land spreading of manure and other organic fertilisers are subject to the general regulation in the Act on Agricultural Use of Fertiliser and Plant Bags[1681] and the Act on Regulation of Livestock Installations, etc., and General Rules on Speeding of Manure, etc.[1682]

Pursuant to these acts, the Minister for the Environment has also laid down rules on the use of manure and other organic fertilisers in agriculture with a view to protect groundwater, lakes and watercourses against pollution. The statutory orders established general critical deposition values combined with maps on sensitivities of the groundwater and habitats being affected significantly[1683] as alternatives to the individual assessment under the EIA and Article 6 of the Habitats Directive's provisions. The assessment under the IEA rules and the assessment under Habitats Directive are part of these general provisions and the supplementary statutory rules.[1684] The Danish thresholds that are included in the assessment are laid down in the statutory orders on the yearly nitrogen forecast,[1685] the Statutory Order on the

1678. Concerning the EIA Directive, *see supra* para. 32.
1679. Statutory Order No. 1467 of 6 December 2018 on the Approval of Livestock Installations.
1680. Joint Cases C-293/17 and C-294/17 *Coöperatie Mobilisation for the Environment UA*.
1681. Promulgation Order No. 996 of 25 June 2018 on Agricultural Use of Fertiliser and Plant Bags.
1682. Now Promulgation Order No. 1020 of 6 July 2018 on Regulation of Livestock Installations, etc., and General Rules on Speeding of Manure, etc.
1683. These maps have constitutive effects.
1684. Statutory Order No. 718 of 8 July 2019 on the Approval of Livestock Holdings.
1685. Statutory Order No. 214 of 16 March 2018 on the Nitrogen Forecast for the Planning Period 2017/2018, and Statutory Order No. 248 of 19 March 2019 on the Nitrogen Forecast for the Planning Period 2018/2019. The rules are part of the implementation of the Nitrates Directive.

Approval of Livestock Holdings,[1686] and the Statutory Order on Commercial Animal Husbandry, Livestock Manure, Silage, etc.[1687] Based on CJEU case law, it is, however, problematic to use such prior standards and thresholds based on an AA as the alternative to individual assessments under the Article 6 of the Habitats Directive.[1688] The CJEU has stated that the Annex IV species have to be respected by extensive farming.[1689]

264. The Statutory Order on Commercial Animal Husbandry, Livestock Manure, Silage, etc.,[1690] established very detailed and complicated conditions on manure and silage utilisation as fertiliser. Liquid manure and silage effluent must not be applied to areas without vegetation, areas which are frozen, or which are covered in snow.

As a general rule, no manure must be spread on fields in the period from the harvest until 1 February, unless the manure is applied to areas with growing vegetation or areas with crops growing the following winter. Manure must not be spread in a way or on such areas that risk direct contamination of lakes, watercourses, including artificial draining facilities or in the case of heavy rain. If it is applied on a field without vegetation, it must be ploughed within twelve hours after application. It must never be used in forests. Pursuant to the Act on the Use of Fertilisers by Agriculture and on Nutrient-reducing Measures,[1691] the requirements on green cover on fields in the autumn are laid down in the Statutory Order on the Requirement for establishment of Targeted Catch Crops during the Plan Period 2018/2019[1692] that only covers one year. It applies to areas with crops that are included in the after-crop land area located as ID15 areas by a GIS map with legally binding effects.[1693] However, the notice do not apply to companies, having a later crop area which is less than 10 ha, or land authorised for organic farming or undergoing reorganisation with a view to obtaining authorisation for organic farming on 1 February 2018. As a consequence of the political agreement on the 'Food and Agricultural Package' (December 2015), these administrative rules replace the statutory rules that established the 'harmony rules'.[1694] In May 2016, the Commission found that the amendment was not in harmony with the EU obligations[1695] as the aim of the former

1686. Statutory Order No. 1467 of 6 December 2018 on the Approval of Livestock Holdings.
1687. Statutory Order No. 116 of 23 January 2019 on Commercial Animal Husbandry, Livestock Manure, Silage, etc.
1688. Joint Cases C-293/17 and C-294/17 *Coöperatie Mobilisation for the Environment UA.*
1689. Concerning these obligations, *see* the European Commission, *Farming for Nature 2000. Guidance on how to support Nature 2000 farming systems to achieve conservation objectives, based on Member States' good practice experiences*, 2014, and Henrik Schoukens, *Saving the Common Hamster from Extinction with the EU Habitats Directive: A Mandatory Recovery Effort, A Remediation of Past Non-Compliance or An Exercise in Futility*? The Nordic Environmental Law Journal, 2017, Vol 1, at 59–97.
1690. Statutory Order No. 116 of 23 January 2019 on Commercial Animal Husbandry, Livestock Manure, Silage, etc.
1691. Promulgation Order No. 338 of 2 April 2019 on the Use of Fertilisers by Agriculture and on Nutrient-reducing Measures Act.
1692. Statutory Order No. 1037 of 27 July 2018 on the Requirement for Establishment of Targeted Catch Crops during the Plan Period 2018/2019.
1693. The GIS map on the ID15 areas is included in the Statutory Order No. 1038 of 27 July 2018.
1694. Concerning the Danish 'harmony rules', *see* Danish Ministry of Environment and Food, *Overview of the Danish Regulation of Nutrients in Agriculture & Danish Nitrates Action Programme*,

fertilisation norms was to ensure that crops were not overly fertilised relative to their needs, and that the nitrogen content of manure was used appropriately. Agricultural enterprises that are involved in plant breeding, livestock breeding, forestry or a combination of these may register with the 'Danish Registry of Fertiliser Accounts' and then purchase commercial fertiliser without paying the nitrogen tax.[1696] An enterprise has to be registered if it is a livestock holding with more than 10 livestock units, stocking density is more than 1.0 livestock unit per ha, or the enterprise receives more than 25 tonnes of manure or other organic fertiliser in the plan period. A plan period extends from 1 August to 31 July in the following year. Once the enterprise has been entered in the register, it is covered by the rules regarding fertiliser use, including the obligations to draw up fertiliser plans and fertiliser status accounts containing key figures on the use of nitrogen (commercial fertiliser and livestock manure). The consumption must not exceed the fixed quota established for the individual enterprise. The quota is calculated on the basis of the size, crop, previous cropping and nitrogen standard of the crop in the climate area concerned, and the soil texture of the fields of the enterprise. In addition, guiding norms for the use of P and potassium are given to each enterprise. The Danish Agricultural Agency is responsible for checking the use of fertiliser products in organic production. Each year, the holdings must submit fertiliser budgets to the Agency to account for the quota, fertiliser consumption and the use of manure. Regulation and control are solely carried out at holding level.

265. The Statutory Order on the Prohibition of Straw Burning[1697] has established strong restrictions on the farmers' permit to burn the straw from grain and seed crops in the field. Only a few seed grass crops are exempted. However, the burning of small amounts of waste straw, etc. is permitted, and it is possible to obtain a dispensation.

266. The whole of Denmark has been designated as an NSA under the Nitrate Directive.[1698] In 2002,[1699] 2005[1700] and again in 2008,[1701] the Commission decided to allow Denmark a derogation in relation to the Directive until 31 July 2012. These derogations allows, by means of a case-by-case decision under certain conditions, an amount of livestock manure to be applied to the land on cattle farms each year, including by animals themselves, to up to 230 kg N/ha. On 23 October 2012, the Commission accepted the Danish request for a new extension of the derogation until

---

June 2017, at 8–9. Now the historical Statutory Order No. 845 of 12 July 2011, as amended by Statutory Order No. 928 of 16 July 2010 on the agricultural use of fertiliser and on plant cover. These former norms reflected the economically optimal nitrogen needs for the crop in harmony with the former Danish Nitrates Action Programme.

1695. The Commission's EU Pilot 8540/16/ENVI *Implementation in Denmark of Directives 91/676/EEC, 2000/60/EC, 92/43/EEC, in relation to the recently adopted agriculture package.*
1696. Concerning the use of taxes in Denmark, *see supra* para. 12.
1697. Statutory Order No. 1459 of 7 December 2015 on the Prohibition of Straw Burning.
1698. Concerning the Nitrate Directive, *see supra* para. 106.
1699. It was made by the Commission Decision No. 2002/915/EC.
1700. It was made by the Commission Decision No. 2005/294/EC.
1701. It was made by the Commission Decision No. 2008/664/EC.

31 July 2016,[1702] and a new extension of the derogation until 31 December 2018 was accepted on 29 March 2017 on strict conditions. The very short time limits of this last extension is a consequence of the challenges that the Commission find is related to the political agreement on the 'Food and Agricultural Package'.[1703] The cattle farms are required to cultivate at least of the 80% grassland. No later than three weeks after ploughing grassland, new crops must be established. The Ministry of Environment and Food of Denmark should also increase the frequency of control and monitoring of the cattle farms that make use of the exception.

267. The Watercourses Act[1704] states that cultivation, soil treatment, planting, modification of the ground layout, the erection of fencing and the construction of buildings must not be carried out in a rural area within a 2 m border along natural or watercourses and lakes or those targeted as high priority in the municipal plan.[1705] There are rules in the Environmental Protection Act, the Nature Protection Act and the Water Supply Act that protect the drinking water against pollution caused by the agricultural activities.

Section 11a of the Water Supply Act states that the Minister for the Environment shall issue regulations that designate the following groundwater areas with constitutive effect:

1) areas with drinking water interests,
2) areas with special drinking water interests,
3) recovery catches for general water supplies outside the areas mentioned in paragraph 2;
4) Sub-areas within the areas referred to in paragraphs 2 and 3 which are particularly sensitive to one or more types of pollution (sensitive recovery areas), indicating the type or types of pollution that are considered to be sensitive; transfer,
5) Sub-areas within the sensitive recovery areas, cf. No. 4, based on an assessment of land use, pollution threats and the natural protection of water resources, where a special effort to protect water resources is needed to safeguard drinking water interests (focus areas), and
6) borehole protection areas for wells that recover groundwater for general water supplies.

The strict protection of drinking water dates back to an amendment of several environmental acts in 1998.[1706] It was an amendment to the Environmental Protection Act, the Water Supply Act and the Nature Protection Act that introduced rules

---

1702. The conditions to be respected are explained in the Commission's letter of 23 Oct. 2013, C(2012) 7182.

1703. The challenges are described in the pilot letter EU Pilot 8540/16/ENVi.

1704. Promulgation Order No. 127 of 26 January 2017 on Watercourses as amended by Act No. 72 of 8 June 2018.

1705. Concerning the Watercourses Act, *see supra* para. 109.

1706. The amendment was made by Act No. 479 of 1 July 1998 on the Amendment of the Environmental protection Act, the Water Supply Act and the Planning Act (Protection of the Drinking Water Resources and the water Supply). The design of this amending Act was based on the 'Drinking Water Report' of December 1997.

on compensation for farmers in cases where they make an agreement with the authorities and in situations where the authorities give them an administrative order on reduction of pesticide and fertiliser consumption.[1707] The rules make it clear that the drinking water plans must include: (a) designation of vulnerable abstraction areas that are sensitive to nitrates and pesticides; (b) target areas for which efforts to protect water resources are required in order to safeguard drinking water resources; and (c) the setting of priorities for target areas. For each target area, the municipal councils prepare an action plan with detailed information about the need for protection and guidelines for the activities as well as time schedules for the authorities' actions to protect these areas. If the farmer pollutes the groundwater as part of normal legal activities, the owner of a water supply plant may ask the public authority to make an agreement with the farmer – and the land farmer can order full compensation for reduction of the polluting activities. In cases where it is not possible to issue an agreement, the municipal councils are also empowered to give an administrative order with a legal basis in section 24 of the Environmental protection Act – and by doing so restrict the right of use, including restriction of cultivation in nitrate-sensitive and pesticide-sensitive abstraction areas. Agreements as well as orders may only be used in cases where existing farming results in loads on the water resources which require intervention to safeguard drinking water interests. In some cases, the right to use the land can be restricted to such an extent that a takeover in whole or partial of the property may be appropriate. Based on the Nature Protection Act, expropriation of land is possible in the event that one or several landowners prevent a project that is widely accepted by other landowners. For the purpose of preventing or controlling the entry of nitrates into protected groundwater as a result of agricultural use of land, the municipal council has the power to designate 'NSAs' on a case-by-case basis, cf. section 26a of the Environmental Protection Act. Provided the municipal councils pay full compensation to the farmer, they have the competence to make an agreement with the owner regarding the future practice in that area.[1708] The valuation authorities decide on the extent of the financial compensation, including the question of a takeover in whole or partial. The owners of the water supply plants make the payments to the owners of agricultural land in the area in return for the latter accepting restrictions on the manner in which they farm the land. The same applies if the authorities issue the polluter with an order concerning future farming activities.

268. Compost containing organic matter and plant nutrients can be used as soil improvers and fertiliser. The levels of xenophobic chemicals in sludge have, however, raised concerns about the current use of sludge and other organic waste products as fertilisers on arable land. The Statutory Order on the Application of Waste Products in Agriculture (including forestry),[1709] therefore, defines certain cut-off values for the maximum concentration of organic contaminants and heavy metals in

1707. Concerning the protection against pollution for the activities of the farmers, *see supra* para. 116.
1708. Concerning expropriation, *see supra* paras 30, 145, and 150.
1709. Statutory Order No. 1001 of 27 June 2018 on the Application of Waste Products in Agriculture.

sludge to be distributed on agricultural land; *see* the general regulation in the Statutory Order on the Utilisation of Ash from Gasification and Incineration of Biomass and Biomass Waste in Agriculture.[1710]

269. The Chemical Substances and Products Act[1711] and the Statutory Order on Pesticides[1712] established the rules on the use of plant protection.[1713] The farmers are only allowed to use approved chemical products for plant protection. Importers of PPPs must apply for governmental approval of the relevant substances and products in accordance with the EU pesticides rules.[1714]

The current Statutory Order on the Designation of Drinking Water Resources[1715] sets binding restrictions on the use of pesticides on the mapped areas with binding effects of the maps. The municipalities have to adopt an action plan for the protection of the drinking water against pesticides in accordance with the national maps, cf. section 11(1), no. 5 of the Water Supply Act. The action plans must be based on vulnerability to a pesticide contamination that has been identified through the finding of PPPs in groundwater.

270. The Danish Land Allocation Act[1716] regulates the sale of a plot of land that has been separated from the property, the application procedure and the issuance of a permit, etc.

The Agricultural Holdings Act[1717] is regulating the ownership. Until 1967, it did not allow individual holdings (except the very smallest) to be closed down. It was drastically changed in 1967 by an Act[1718] enabling the merger of farms if the size after amalgamation did not exceed 75 ha. The aims of the Act in force are:

1) Ensure proper and multi-faceted use of agricultural properties, taking into account agricultural production, nature, environment and landscape values;
2) Ensure the sustainable development of agricultural industries and improve the competitiveness of these industries;
3) Respect settlement and development in rural areas and
4) Preserve the self-service as the predominantly holding and operating form in agriculture and ensure the necessary production base for the agricultural industries.

1710. Statutory Order No. 818 of 21 July 2008 on the Utilisation of Ash from Gasification and Incineration of Biomass and Biomass Waste in Agriculture.
1711. Promulgation Order No. 115 of 26 January 2017 on Chemical Substances and Product.
1712. Statutory Order No. 815 of 18 June 2018 on Pesticides.
1713. Concerning the restrictions on use of pesticides, *see supra* para. 223.
1714. Concerning the restrictions on import and export, *see supra* paras 218–224. Concerning the taxation of inputs from fertilisers and pesticides, *see supra* para. 12.
1715. Statutory Order No. 209 of 12 March 2018 on the Designation of Drinking Water Resources. The Statutory Order has its basis in Act No. 45 of 23 January 2018 on Designation of Area to Protect Ground Water Resources against Pollution that is cost by Pesticides.
1716. Promulgation Order No. 31 of 4 January 2017 on Land Allocation and Public Purchase and Sale of Real Estate for Agricultural Purposes, etc.
1717. Promulgation Order No. 27 of 4 January 2017 on Agricultural Holdings.
1718. The ownership provisions laid down in the Agricultural Holding Act were changed by Act No. 114 of 1967.

An agricultural holding is understood to mean an entity used for agricultural purposes, as for the land is set out in the Act on the Operation of Agricultural Properties,[1719] and which is operated by the same natural or legal person. The agricultural entity can consist of one or more agricultural properties, areas without agricultural duty and rented areas, cf. section 2(3). The properties listed as agricultural properties in the Geodata Agency's Land Register are covered by the scope of the Act, cf. section 2(1).[1720] Such properties are subject to agricultural obligations under the Act, cf. section 2(2). At the owner's request, a property may, at, be listed as an agricultural property in the Land Register if the property is 2 ha or more and used for agriculture, forestry, horticulture, including flower nursery, orchard, nursery, or similar agricultural business, and is provided with a residential building, cf. section 4. The current version of the Act lays down the goal of sustainable and differentiated cultivation of agricultural properties with respect to agricultural production, the nature, the environment and the landscape.[1721] The lands of an agricultural holding must be utilised in a proper agricultural way. At least once in each election period, the municipal councils must cooperate with the Ministry of Environment and Food of Denmark on the preparation and publishing of an analysis of the agricultural activities to ensure that the agricultural interests are included in the municipal plans, and local plans.[1722] As almost all the agricultural land is privately owned, questions of compensation for interference on behalf of nature protection play an important role.[1723]

271. The Environmental Performance Index (EPI) constructed by Yale University for the OECD Countries in 2008 and 2014 ranks countries according to criteria such as environmental health and ecosystem vitality.[1724] In 2008, Denmark was number 25 out of 149 countries in this ranking. In 2014, it was number 13 out of 178 countries. The agricultural index was part of the ecosystem vitality, and it was composed in terms of: (a) management of water irrigation; (b) livestock concentration; (c) pesticide monitoring; (d) vegetative cover in agricultural landscapes; (e) biomass burning in agriculture; (f) agricultural subsidies; (g) nitrogen loads in the bodies of water; (h) biological health and productivity of agricultural soils; (i) wildlife in agricultural lands; (j) agricultural crop diversity; (k) area of eco-verified production; (l) conservation areas on private lands; and (m) net GHG emissions from agricultural activities. The ranking of Denmark has to be understood in the context of the intensiveness of most agricultural production in Denmark.[1725] The large farms

1719. Promulgation Order No. 958 of 10 July 2017 on the Operation of Agricultural Properties.

1720. The Geodata Agency shall change the Land Register's listing of properties as agricultural properties in conformity with the changes that are resulting from the law's rules on listing and lifting of agricultural duty.

1721. The environmental protection goal was introduced in Denmark by the Agricultural Holdings Act in 1986.

1722. There are restrictions on the localisation of the livestock farms with reference to the municipal spatial planning system and zoning. *See infra* Part III, especially para. 332, concerning obligation for the developer of non-agricultural installations, etc., to have a rural permit.

1723. Concerning the agricultural sector, *see supra* paras 245 and 250.

1724. Concerning the EPI, *see supra* para. 21.

1725. Concerning the Danish agricultural sector, *see supra* para. 9.

are characterised by two trends, intensification and specialisation, which have a pronounced and often negative effect on the environment. The dominant role of nitrogen and agriculture in the Danish landscape has become a great potential danger to the environment.[1726]

1726. Concerning the environmental challenges, *see supra* paras 20 and 23.

Chapter 6. Forests

272. Forests cover roughly 30% of the Earth's land area. According to FAO estimates, some 13 million ha of forests is lost every year. Forests have a number of environmental benefits: biodiversity and landscape conservation; their impact on global and regional climates; protection of groundwater against pollution; and the protection against filter dust, salt, etc., from the air. Of all ecosystems, tropical forests contain the greatest diversity in terms of species, genetic material and ecological processes. Furthermore, such areas are cultivated more extensively than farmland, using considerably less fertiliser and pesticides. Globally, however, forest areas continue to decrease. The forest area has remained stable or has slightly increased in most OECD countries.[1727] The indicators used by the OECD refer to the intensity of use of forest resources (timber).

There is no comprehensive legally binding instrument at global level related to forest. The Bern Convention on the Conservation of European Wildlife and Natural Habitats – as implemented into EU law by the nature directives – is protecting some of the forest species. At the Rio Conference in 1992, the forests were given an increasingly important role in the context of sustainable development and environmental conservation. This resulted in the UNFCCC, the Biodiversity Convention (CBD), the Convention on Combat Desertification (UNCCD), and the agreement on the 'Forest Principle' concerning a global consensus on the management, conservation and sustainable development of all types of forests and Chapter 11 in Agenda 21 which outlines possible ways for combating deforestation at a global level.[1728] Deforestation involves the conversion of forest to another land cover type. There is no common definition of 'forest'. The current, global definition of 'forest' included in a set of Food and Agricultural Organization's (FAO) and UNECE's documents is:[1729]

> Land with tree crown cover (or equivalent stocking level) of more than 10 percent and area of more than 0.5 hectares (ha). The trees should be able to reach a minimum height of 5 meters (m) at maturity in situ. May consist either of closed forest formations where trees of various storeys and undergrowth cover a high proportion of the ground; or open forest formations with a continuous vegetation cover in which tree crown cover exceeds 10 percent. Young natural stands and all plantations established for forestry purposes which have yet to reach a crown density of 10 percent or tree height of 5 meters are included under forest, as are areas normally forming part of the forest area which are temporarily unstacked as a result of human intervention or natural causes, but which are expected to revert to forest.

1727. OECD, *Environment at a Glance 2013. OECD Indic*ators, at 44.

1728. It was the same conference that resulted in the Biodiversity Convention (CBD) and the Convention to Combat Desertification and the Framework Convention on Climate Change (UNFCCC).

1729. *See* http://www.fao.org/docrep/005/y4171e/y4171e10.htm. FAO defined the term 'forest' between 1990 and 2000 in the Forest Resource Assessment.

Both at global and regional levels there are initiatives on the protection of forests. The UN International Arrangements on Forests (IAF) that EU is taking part in have the same overall aim as the pan-European 'Ministerial Conferences on the Protection of Forests in Europe' (MCPFE).[1730] The EU and its Member States have all signed the resolutions under MCPFE. In the first part of the 1990s, the Pan-European policy has been focused on issues related to ecological sustainability and environmental protection, but in 1998 it shifted towards socio-economic aspects. In 2003, the parties to the Vienna Declaration set an overall forest policy that aims to achieve a balance between the economic, ecological, social and cultural roles of forests in the context of sustainable development.

In respect to forests, the COP5 (2000) – held under the CBD – has adopted the 'Ecosystem Approach' as a codex for the management of land, water and living resources in a sustainable and equitable way. The 'UN Forum on Forests' (UNFF) was established in 2000 by the United Nations Economic and Social Council (ECOSOC) with the main objective to promote the management, conservation and sustainable development of all types of forests and to strengthen long-term political commitment to this end. Its activities should be based on the Rio Declaration, the Forest Principles, Chapter 11 of Agenda 21 and the outcome of the Intergovernmental Panel on Forests (IPF) and Intergovernmental Forum on Forests (IFF) Processes – the IPF/IFF Processes – and other forest-related agreements. It should foster a common understanding of sustainable forest management by 'Non-Legal Binding Instruments on Forests'. The ambition is to facilitate implementation of forest-related agreements and fostering a common understanding of sustainable forest management by 'Non-Legal Binding Instruments on Forests'. In 2002, an 'Expanded Programme of Work on Forest Biodiversity' was adopted at the COP6. The 'Intergovernmental Panel on Forests' and the 'Intergovernmental Forum on Forests' have since worked on new initiatives on Actions towards Sustainable Forest Management. The World Summit on Sustainable Development (WSSD) held in Johannesburg in 2002 addressed and emphasised the role of sustainable forest management. In October 2008, the COP9 adopted a decision on 'Forest Diversity'. The Rio+20 Conference on Sustainable Development (2012) declaration called for holistic and integrated approaches to sustainable development and for the promotion of integrated and sustainable management of natural resources and ecosystems. The importance of forests is also addressed by several of the UN sustainability goals from 2015, including goal no. 15 that addresses the need for sustainable management of trees and forests. A forest ecosystem is a dynamic complex of plants, animals and microorganism communities, and their environment that interact as a functional unit that reflects the dominance of ecosystem conditions and processes by trees. Humans, with their cultural, economic and environmental needs, are an integrated part of many forest ecosystems.[1731] Both the arising climate changes, global population growth, multiple exploitations of forest, and the growing demands

1730. Forty-three European countries are involved in this process relating to the development of a common understanding regarding the protection and sustainable management of forests in Europe by means of resolutions, guidelines and criteria (the 'Pan-European Process').

1731. European Environmental Agency, *European forest ecosystems. State and trends*, EEA Report no. 5/2016, at 12.

on the utilisation of the land for other purposes as well as on the exploitation of the forests are all challenges to forest biodiversity that have to be covered by environmental law. The key functions of the forest ecosystem are defined by the European Environment Agency in its report on the state and trends in the European forest ecosystem as:[1732]

> energy capture from the sun through photosynthesis and its conversion to organic substances, which leads to processes such as the production of biomass, the cycling of water and nutrients, and decomposition.

The International Tropical Timber Agreement and the International Cooperative Programme on assessment and monitoring of air pollution effects on forests, the 'ICP Forests', are also important in the protection of forest at international level.[1733] At pan-European level, the MCPFE means that forty European countries are involved in a process relating to development of a common understanding regarding the protection and sustainable management of forests in Europe by means of resolutions, guidelines and criteria (the 'Pan-European Process'). The EU and its Member States have all signed the resolutions made by the MCPFE. At the Ministerial Conference on the Protection of Forest in Europa held in Oslo, Norway, on 14–16 June 2011, these parties signed the '2020 Forests Objectives'. These objectives are as follows[1734]

To ensure and demonstrate that all forests in the EU are managed according to sustainable forest management principles and that the EU's contribution to promote sustainable forest management and reduce deforestation at global level is strengthened, thus:

- contributing to balancing various forest functions, meeting demands and delivering vital ecosystem services;
- providing a basis for forestry and the whole forest-based value chain to be competitive and viable contributors to the bio-based economy.

The condition of forests can also be seriously affected by natural factors such as extreme weather conditions, attacks from parasites and diseases or human influences such as climate change, fires and air pollution (degradation). When forests remain forests but lose their ability to provide ecosystem services or suffer from major changes in species composition due to overexploitation, exotic species invasion, pollution, fires, etc., it results in degradation.

Several means are used under the UNFCCC, which focuses on the importance of forests.[1735] According to the use of CDM under the Kyoto Protocol[1736] 'forest' is defined by the Marrakesh Accord (COP7) as an area of more than 0.5–1.0 ha with

1732. European Environmental Agency, *European forest ecosystems. State and trends*, EEA Report No. 5/2016, at 12.
1733. The ICP Forest was launched in 1985 under the CLRTAP in response to wide public and political concern over extensive forest damage caused by air pollution. The CLRTAP is described *supra* in para. 74.
1734. COM(2013) 659 final, at 6.
1735. Concerning the international climate rules, *see supra* para. 80.

a minimum tree crown cover of 10–30%, with the term 'tree' defined as a plant with the capacity of growing to more than 2–5 m height. Over the last decade, increasing attention has been paid to the role of the world's forests in the carbon cycle (as sinks), and as the raw material (biomass) for the production of biofuels.[1737] Deforestation accounts for some 20% of the global CO_2 emissions.[1738] The possibility of compensating developing countries for the reduced emission ensured by stopping the deforestation and degradation (REDD) was proposed at COP11 (2005) by some developing countries. Negotiations under the UNFCCC have been focussed on the important role of avoiding deforestation in mitigating climate change, especially since the adoption of the Bali Road Map at COP13 (2007). The Durban Decision (COP17) included the possibility of REDD+ (reduction of emissions from deforestation and forest degradation, promotion of forest conservation, sustainable management of forests, and enforcement of forest carbon stocks) to be part of a new post-2020 climate agreement. There is no distinction in the definition laid down in the climate rules between 'natural forest' and 'plantation forests'. These definitions have been criticised for allowing continued unsustainable exploitation of forest resources as the conversion of natural forest to plantation is not classified as 'deforestation'.[1739] Accounting of Removal Units (RMUs) in the form of emissions and removals of emissions from afforestation, reforestation, deforestation, forest management, cropland management and grazing land management activities (LULUCF activities) can be chosen by a party 'as verifiable changes in carbon stocks' in the commitment period 2013–2020.[1740] It can also be applied under the Paris Agreement.

273. Forests are the dominant natural habitats across most of Europe. In the EU, forests cover over 40% of the land. Some 60% of forests are owned by several million of private owners. Their individual share of the areas covered by forests is small and often fragmented. Nearly 25% is protected as Natura 2000 sites.[1741] Traditionally, the most important function of forests has been – and still is in many parts of the World – used as a renewable source of timber and other products. The EU is one of the largest producers, traders and consumers of forest products in the world. EU policies relevant for forests have shifted from focusing on agriculture and trade issues towards other issues – especially with a focus on the importance of the forest ecosystems.

There is no special reference in the TFEU on forest policy. The policy is part of both environmental and agricultural policies. The EU does not have a mandate for

---

1736. The definition was important for developing countries as the Kyoto Protocol limited carbon sequestration under the CDM to afforestation and reforestation. Concerning these instruments, *see supra* para. 80.

1737. Concerning the sustainability criteria used to reduce the negative consequences of the production of biofuels, *see supra* para. 229.

1738. Commission, *Addressing the challenges of deforestation and forest degradation to tackle climate change and biodiversity loss*, COM(2008) 645 final, at 5.

1739. The most important direct cause of forest destruction is typically the change in land use (deforestation).

1740. Articles 3(3) and (4) of the Kyoto Protocol.

1741. COM(2013) 659 final, at 2.

a common forest policy. In principle, forest policy is thus still a national matter. However, EU environmental legislation is also covering forests. The substantive basis for such secondary instruments is Article 192 (environmental policy) or Article 194 (energy policy). The EU protection of the biodiversity in the forest areas is to be found in the Biodiversity Strategy, the Habitats Directive and the Wild Birds Directive[1742] The protection under the ELD of Natura 2000 sites ensures enforcement of the protection.[1743] The marketing of forest reproductive materials is regulated by a directive[1744] that has its substantive basis in the agriculture treaty rule (now Article 43 TFEU). The protection of the forest against harmful organisms has also its basis in this treaty rule, and the CAP is used as the main source of funds in the forest sector. On 15 December 1998, the European Council adopted the first EU 'Forestry Strategy' on the basis of a proposal of 20 May 1998 from the Commission.[1745] It established some principles relating to responsibility for forest policy, implementation of international commitments and the integration and support of forest programmes developed by the Member States through the CAP, the RDP and other programmes. The 6EAP identifies the need to base the draw up, implementation and evaluation of environmental policies on a knowledge-based approach and, in particular, the need to monitor the multiple roles of forests. In 2003, the Commission presented an 'Action Plan on Forest Law Enforcement, Governance and Trade' (Action Plan on FLEGT) with a focus on governance reforms and capacity-building. It identifies the setting up of a licensing scheme as a measure to ensure that only legally produced timber is used. The Forest Action Plan 2007–2011 and the co-financing of forest measures under the Rural Development Regulation were important instruments for the realisation of the strategy.[1746] In 2010, the Commission adopted a Green Paper on 'Forest Protection and Information – Preparing Forests for Climate Change',[1747] which sets out options for a EU approach to protection of forests and to inform about forest resources and the importance in the climate policy. The EU's Biodiversity Strategy[1748] involves a forest management plan in line with sustainable forest management. Based on the Commission's proposal 'Supporting forests and the forest sector: a new approach for a new EU Forest Strategy',[1749] the Council adopted a new Forest Strategy on 19 May 2014. This new framework is based on the ambition to ensure that the multifunctional potential of EU forests is managed in a sustainable and balanced way, enabling the forests' vital ecosystem services to function correctly. With reference to the Ministerial Conference on the Protection of Forest in Europa held in Oslo, Norway, on 14–16 June 2011 – that resulted in the '2020 forest objectives' – the EU Strategy is stating that these objectives have been developed together with Member States and stakeholders to address the three dimensions of sustainable development in an integrated way, providing a holistic approach to forest management and policy.

1742. Concerning the Habitats and the Wild Birds Directives, *see, e.g., supra* para. 241.
1743. Concerning the Environmental liability Directive, *see infra* para. 336.
1744. Council Directive 1999/105/EC on the Marketing of Forest Material.
1745. COM(98) 649 final.
1746. COM(2006) 302 final.
1747. COM(2010) 66 final.
1748. 'EU Biodiversity Strategy to 2020', COM(2011) 244 final.
1749. COM(2013) 659 final.

The FLEGT Action Plan from 2003 resulted in directly applicable legislation at national level consisting of two pieces of legislation.[1750] One of these instruments was the FLEGT Regulation[1751] allowing for control of timber to EU from countries entering into bilateral FLEGT Voluntary Partnership Agreements (VPA) with the EU.[1752] In 2008, the Commission laid down more detailed rules on acceptance and verification by means of the Regulation on detailed measures for the implementation of the FLEGT licence scheme for import of timber into the EU.[1753] This implementation strategy is based on Voluntary Partnership Agreements (VPAs) with countries and regional organisations that place legally binding obligations on the parties. The EU has been negotiating the FLEGT VPAs with timber-producing partner countries. The partnership agreements create a legally binding obligation for the parties to implement a licensing scheme and to regulate trade in timber and timber product, identified in those FLEGT VPAs. The EU FLEGT Facility provides technical assistance to governments and other stakeholder groups in timber-exporting countries as a supporting measure in the negotiation of VPAs. This is a bilateral treaty between EU and a timber-exporting country. The agreement is combined with a Timber Legality Assurance System set up in the exporting country and a 'FLEGT licence' ensured by the exporting country. The timber exported under a 'FLEGT licence' is treated as legal. The other directly applicable legislation under the FLEGT Action Plan is the EU Illegal Timber Regulation[1754] that prohibits the placing on the EU market of illegally harvested timber and products from such timber. This Regulation has its substantive basis in the environmental rule of the Treaty (now Article 192 TFEU). It lays down the obligations of operators who place timber and timber products on the market. It requires EU traders who place timber products on the EU market for the first time to exercise 'due diligence' established by Article 6 and monitoring obligations and organisations, cf. Articles 8–9. The core of the 'due diligence' notion is that operators undertake a risk assessment exercise so as to minimise the risk of placing illegally harvested timber, or timber products containing illegally harvested timber, on the EU market. It defines timber and timber products in Article 2(a) as the timber and timber products sets out in the Annex. Once on the market, the timber and timber products may be sold on and/or transformed before they reach the final consumer. To facilitate the traceability of timber products, economic operators in this part of the supply chain (referred to as traders in the regulation) have an obligation to keep records of their suppliers and customers.

1750. Concerning the problems related to the system, *see* Karin Buhmann and Iben Nathan, *Plentiful Forest, Happy People? The EU's FLEGT approach and its impact on human Rights and Private forestry sustainability schemes*, in the Nordic Environmental Law Journal, 2012, Vol. 2, at 53–82.

1751. Council Regulation No. 2173/2005/EC on the Establishment of a FLEGT Licensing Scheme for Imports of Timber into the European Community.

1752. Its substantive basis is the common commercial policy, now Art. 107 TFEU.

1753. Commission Regulation No. 1024/2008/EC laying down detailed Measures for the Implementation of the Council Regulation No. 2173/2005/EC on the Establishment of a FLEGT Licensing Scheme for Imports of Timber into the European Community.

1754. European Parliament and Council Regulation No. 995/2010/EC laying down Obligations of Operators who place Timber and Timber Products on the Market.

The Forest Forum Regulation[1755] was established to implement forest monitoring and protecting activities from 2003 to 2006 in the following areas: (a) atmospheric pollution; (b) fires; and (c) biodiversity, climate change, carbon sequestration and soils. A follow-up measure was the LIFE+ Regulation[1756] covering the period 2007–2013. The monitoring programme is now part of the UNFCCC monitoring activities and the International monitoring activities under the CLRTAP. The protection of forest is also an important part of the EU's climate policy and law. In 2010, the Commission presented the 'Green Paper on Forest Protection and Information in the EU: Preparing Forest for Climate Change'.[1757] The Effort Sharing Decision (EDS) and the EU ETS Directive include provisions for the use of LULUCF in the EU reduction commitment. With the new LULUCF Regulation in the 2030 Climate and Energy Framework,[1758] the Member States have to ensure that GHG emissions from LULUCF are offset by at least an equivalent removal of CO_2 from the atmosphere in the period 2021–2030. This is known as the 'no debit' rule. The scope of the LULUCF is extended as from 2021 to cover all land uses (until 2021, only forests are included). Up to a certain limit, credits obtained under the LULUCF Regulation can be used to reach the target for the non-ETS sector in accordance with the Effort Sharing Regulation. As a Member State, Denmark has the obligation under this Regulation to reduce its GHGs by 39% in relation to its 2005 levels. From 2021 to 2030, Denmark must meet its commitments under the Paris Agreement, cf. Article 4(3) in Annex I of the Regulation.[1759] The limit on the use of credits obtained under the Regulation for Denmark is 14.6 million credits.[1760]

274. Unlike other Scandinavian countries, Denmark is not a country in which forestry plays an important economic role. Around 2,000 people are employed in the primary forest sector, while secondary wood production employs around 14,000 people and is a major export business.[1761]

Approximately 13% of Denmark is forested. The total forest area in Denmark has more than doubled during the last 100 years.[1762] Based on OECD's indicators, the annual change of forest resources in Denmark is 27% and the intensity of use is going down.[1763] It is the ambition to have about 25% of the total land area forested

1755. European Parliament and Council Regulation No. 2152/2003/EC concerning Monitoring of Forests and Environmental Interactions in the Community.
1756. European Parliament and Council Regulation No. 614/2007/EC concerning the Financial Instruments for the Environment (LIFE+).
1757. COM(2010) 66 final.
1758. European Parliament and Council Regulation No. 2018/841/EU on the Inclusion of GHG Emissions and Removals from Land Use, Land-Use Change and Forestry (LULUCF).
1759. European Parliament and Council Regulation No. 2018/842/EU on the Binding Annual Greenhouse Gas Emission Reductions.
1760. *Denmark's Draft Integrated National Energy and Climate Plan*, December 2018, at 15.
1761. The Danish Forest & Nature Agency, *The Danish National Forest Programme in an International Perspective*, at 8.
1762. Communication from the Commission to the Council and the European Parliament *Reporting on the Implementation of the EU Forest Strategy*, COM(2005) 84 final, at 9.
1763. OECD. *Environment at a Glance 2013. OECD indicators*, at 44.

by the end of the twenty-first century.[1764] The former liberal-conservative coalition government[1765] that was in power until 27 June 2019 had an afforestation plan to double the forest area in Denmark over the next 80–100 years. This objective entails that 20–25% of Denmark will be covered by forest landscapes by 2090. Seventy-two per cent of the forest area is privately owned (approximately 2,652,000 ha), while the remaining 28% is publicly owned, mainly as state forests. The Danish Nature Agency is the largest forest producer and the manager of an area of 186,000 ha. Approximately two-thirds (108,000 ha) is afforested, which amount to a quarter of Denmark's forests. The rest of the State forest areas consist of lakes, bogs, meadows, sand dunes and moorland. As part of the implementation of the agreement relating to 'APAE II', DKK 120 million were to be used for 25,000 ha of afforestation.

275. The protection of forests is a very old policy and law in Denmark.[1766] In 1994, the Danish Ministry of Environment adopted the 'National Strategy for Sustainable Forest Management'. The short-term objective of the strategy was to ensure the existence of at least 5,000 ha of virgin forest by the year 2000, of which 1,500 ha were privately owned. In addition, traditional forestry management was to be ensured on at least 4,000 ha (coppice forest, grazing forest and selective felling). In the long term, the aim was to ensure the existence by the year 2040 of at least 40,000 ha of virgin forest. It was also the ambition to facilitate forest management using traditional forestry practice to designate areas left to become overgrown naturally and thereby help to enhance natural forest areas.

As a follow-up, in 1994 the Government presented a position paper on an overall forestry policy to the Danish Parliament. This encompassed the following central points. The aim of the environmental forest policy was to double the Danish forest area in the following seventy to eighty years and thus reduce timber imports. Realisation of this goal would necessitate afforestation of approximately 5,000 ha annually, which was considerably more than the approximately 2,500 ha that were planted annually in the 1990s. In addition, some forest areas were to be converted to natural forest and virgin forest, and environmentally sound forms of forestry would be practiced in other areas. This was to be achieved via multiple-use forestry, which means that the productivity of the forest had to be increased while at the same time protecting the environment, the living conditions of animals and plants and the open air.[1767] In 2001, a broad political consensus was reached on a set of operational guidelines for sustainable forest management at management unit level, based on the Pan-European Guidelines. One of the central elements of the near-to-nature forest management practices in the mentioned guidelines was to utilise the natural processes, such as natural regeneration, to the maximum extent. This principle of management was part of the 'Danish National Forest Strategy' of June 2002, the implementation of the 'EU Forestry Strategy' and the Pan-European measures, seen

1764. *Denmark's Sixth National Communication and First Biennial Report to the UNFCCC*, at 65 and 178.

1765. Concerning the different coalition governments that has been in power in Denmark, *see supra* the notes in para. 4.

1766. Concerning the historical background, *see supra* paras 35–38.

1767. Concerning the amendment of the legislation, *see infra* para. 276.

as a long-term exercise where the conversion of specific areas only takes place, for instance, at the optimal rotation age or when stands are to be logged anyway, i.e., due to instability, health, etc. In the Danish Forest Strategy, it is stated that it is the ambition to ensure that the Danish forests can: (a) deliver high-quality wood products to society; (b) offer good opportunities for outdoor recreation, particularly near urban areas; (c) conserve biological diversity; (d) create economic possibilities and render the rural areas attractive with regard to nature, and contribute to maintaining residence in the rural areas; (e) strengthen landscape functions with regard to biological diversity and landscape amenities; and (f) have environmental protection functions, for instance, the protection of groundwater, the production of renewable mineral resources, and acting as CO_2 sinks. As more specific target goals, the mentioned Danish strategy states that 10% of the total forests will have biodiversity conservation as the primarily management objective before 2040. It is the ambition to increase the forest areas so that forest landscapes cover 20–25% of Denmark after one tree-generation (80–100 years). This 2002 strategy that is now sixteen years old has not been replaced by a new strategy.

276. The Danish Forest Act[1768] regulates the conservation, protection and the utilisation of forests. The Act ensures that areas protected as forest reserves remain forests. When it was amended in May 1996, emphasis was placed on the intangible and ecological values of forest as a consequence of national and international strategies.[1769] By use of building lines, section 17 of the Nature Protection Act prescribes that the location of buildings, sheds and caravans without permission is not allowed within 300 m of publicly owned forests of any size and private forests of more than 20 ha.

In 2009, an amendment of the Forest Act was aimed at facilitating owners' management of their forests according to the near-nature principles. Based on the Act, the overall aim is now to ensure a sustainable and multiple-use management of the forest and to manage them in line with the overall management of the countryside. Instead of clear-cut systems, forest owners are to a greater degree applying near-to-nature forest management regimes. Such management involves advisory services and information about good and multiple use of forest management. The Danish Nature Agency is responsible for the implementation of the policies. Upon the administration of the Act, importance must be attached to ensuring that forests are managed in order to increase and improve wood production and to protect landscape and amenity, nature conservation, cultural heritage and environmental protection interests, as well as recreational activity interests, cf. section 1(3) of the Act. Forests owned by the State, the municipalities, religious institutions or foundations and large private forests are open to the public, cf. section 23 of the Act. The publicly owned forests create the framework for recreational activities. Forest visits are among the most popular activities in that approximately 91% of the adult population visits a forest at least once a year. Every year, the publicly owned forests receive 25 million visits. The visitors are free to go wherever they wish, day or night.

1768. Promulgation Order No. 122 of 26 January 2017 on Forests.
1769. Concerning the Danish forest policy, *see supra* para. 275.

The areas that are formally registered as forest reserves may not be used for purposes other than forestry, unless the owner obtains an exemption from the Danish Nature Agency, cf. Chapter 3 of the Act. The criteria for 'forest reservation' are laid down in Chapter 2 of the Act. Preservation of areas designated as forest reserve land, as well as the protection of natural habitats and habitats for species are among the foremost objectives of the Act. Forest reserves must be kept covered with trees that form, or which will come to form, a closed high forest within a reasonable period of time, cf. section 8 of the Act. Livestock is prohibited, and lakes, watercourses, bogs, meadows, salt marshes and swamps, heath and dry grasslands situated in protected forest areas must not be cultivated, drained, planted or changed in any other way irrespective of their size. During the development of high forest, the health, production and stability of the forest must be ensured through adequate cultivation means such as thinning and adjustment of the combination of tree species and the dispersion of diameter class. Old trees and dead wood in adequate quantities may be left for natural degradation and as habitats for animals and plants. Sections 9, 10 and 11 of the Act accept several modifications to protection of forest reserve land. Based on section 6, the Agency may also allow the forest reservation duty to be cancelled for an area. A municipal council can also send the application for a cancellation to the Agency if the municipal plan for the relevant area includes the forest in a project for a new road. The permissions and declarations must be recorded in the Land Register. The registrations are binding on all owners of and holders of liens on the real estate. Sections 14–28 of the Act contain provisions on the duty of the Minister for the Environment to prepare 'Natura 2000 forest plans' for the wooded reserved areas, i.e., areas that must be wooded in perpetuity, within Natura 2000 sites. It is mandatory to make a prior habitat assessment as described in the Habitats Directive.[1770] Implementation of the strict liability rules established by the ELD to protect the Natura 2000 sites in the forest is ensured by section 59a–59i of the Act.[1771] The principle of compensation is flexible so that the landowners are able to adjust their production structure when it is needed. In pursuance of the Environmental Protection Act, the Minister for the Environment has laid down provisions on the use of sludge in forests.[1772]

277. The Nature Protection Act promotes the enlargement of the forest areas. The Forest Act also introduced subsidy schemes to promote the planting, for example, of native deciduous trees.

Based on section 29 of the Forest Act, the Minister for the Environment may provide State subsidies for: the enhancement of good and multiple-use forestry in the existing forests; the permanent preservation of forest areas as untouched forest; the afforestation of agricultural land, the tending of these new stands and compensation for loss of income provided that the areas are made subject to a forest reservation

1770. Concerning the mandatory habitat assessment, *see supra* para. 241.
1771. Concerning the Danish implementation of the Liability Directive, *see infra* paras 337–341.
1772. Statutory Order No. 1001 of 27 June 2018 on the Application of Sludge, Sewage and Compost, etc., for Agricultural Purposes.

duty; the development of products from the forest and timber industry; consulting services in the forestry industry; and information, advisory and investigation activities.

278. Forest management, crop management and grazing land management activities are chosen to be included in the Danish accounting of RMU and LULUCF in the commitment period under the Kyoto Protocol and the EU ETS.[1773] Afforestation is therefore a useful climate policy instrument.

After the submission of its Fourth National Communication under the UNFCCC, Denmark has chosen Article 3(3) and (4) of the Kyoto Protocol for forest management. Therefore, projections for forestry now include CO_2 removals in forests existing as of 1 January 1990 in addition to removals in new forest areas under Article 3(3) of the Protocol.[1774] Afforestation on 18,000 ha of privately owned farmland, corresponding to the forest binding of 323,000 tonnes CO_2 was subsidised from 1990 to 2007.[1775] However, the afforestation efforts are running behind schedule. This is mainly due to the high cost levels associated with afforestation activities in both publicly owned as well as privately owned forests, and competition with other land uses, mostly agriculture, which eventually constrain afforestation efforts.[1776] In March 2009, the contribution from managed forestry was estimated at 2.8 Mt CO_2 on average for the ten-year period 1997–2006. This estimate was much higher than the specified maximum of credits as RMUs for Denmark at 0.183 Mt CO_2. However, according to the estimates from August 2009, the forests were expected to be a source in 2008–2012 with an average annual net emission of 0.490 Mt CO_2. This estimate was much higher than the annually maximum of debits at 0.183 Mt CO_2 (183 Gg) between 2008 and 2012.[1777] In the Sixth report to the UNFCCC, the CO_2 removals from forest management averaged 4107.2 Gg for the period 2008–2011, much higher than the specified maximum of credit as the removal units for Denmark at 183 Gg.[1778] The projection in Denmark's 'Seventh National Communication on Climate Change' to the UNFCCC, afforestation will be a net sink of approximately 720 kt CO_2 eqv per year until 2020, and deforestation would be a source of 84 kt CO_2 eqv per year until 2020.[1779]

1773. Concerning RMU and LULUCF as instruments used in the climate regime, *see supra* para. 272.
1774. Concerning the Danish use of RMU and LULUCF, *see infra* para. 278.
1775. *Denmark's Fifth National Communication on Climate Change,* at 180.
1776. The Danish Forest & Nature Agency, *The Danish National Forest Programme in an International Perspective*, at 30, and *Denmark's Sixth National Communication and First Biennial Report to the UNFCCC*, at 179.
1777. *Denmark's Fifth National Communication,* at 183–184.
1778. *Denmark's Sixth National Communication and First Biennial Report*, at 180.
1779. *Denmark's Seventh National Communication and Third Biennial Report,* at 255.

Chapter 7. Fish Resources

279. The regimes for the conservation of marine living resources address the sustainable use of targeted stocks, incidental catch of other species, depletion of biodiversity and degradation of marine ecosystems. The effect of industrial fishing and pollution at the sea on biodiversity are some of the rationalities for the restrictions agreed on regarding human activities causing harm to fish resources.

The UN Geneva Convention on Fishing and Conservation of Living Resources of the High Seas (1958) recognised the special interests of coastal states. It states that all States have the right to engage in fishing on the high seas, subject to: (a) their treaty obligations; (b) the interests and rights of coastal states; and (c) the provisions contained in the Convention. All States must also adopt, or cooperate with other States in adopting, such measures for their respective nationals as may be necessary for the 'conservation of living resources on the high seas'. This refers to the expression of the just-mentioned means of the aggregate of measures rendering possible the optimum sustainable yield from those resources so as to ensure a maximum supply of food and other marine products. A conservation programme should be formulated with a view to securing, in the first place, the supply of food for human consumption; *see* Article 2 of the Convention. The Convention entered into force on 20 March 1966, and it was regarded as codifying existing international law. Marine living resources are subject to the exclusive rights of States in their internal waters, territorial seas (out to 12 nautical miles) and a 200 nautical mile EEZ under the UNCLOS.[1780] Under Articles 55–75, this Convention established a regime to deal with the overexploitation of fish stocks in 1982. The objective of the EEZs was to ensure coastal States' exclusive authority and to promote cooperation in the conservation, management and development of living resources. Article 62(4) states that nationals of other States fishing under the EEZ must comply with the conservation measures and other terms and conditions established in the laws and regulations of the coastal State. Articles 63 and 64, respectively, deal with straddling and highly 'migratory' fish stocks. 'Straddling fish' have migratory paths that take them into two or more jurisdictions during their travel. Some marine mammals are listed as highly migratory and thus protected by Articles 64 and 65. On the high seas, the living resources are in principle free for use and exploitation by vessels of all nations. Article 117 lays down the duty of States to take, or to cooperate with other States in taking, the measures for their nationals that may be necessary to conserve the living resources of high seas.

In 1999, the FAO established an International Plan of Action for the Management of Fishing Capacity. An agreement on straddling and migratory fish was an important issue under the second Earth Summit in Rio de Janeiro in 1992, but it was not signed, partly because of a dispute between Canada and the EU. Only Agenda 21, Chapter 17 on the 'Protection of the Oceans', addresses the issue. The 1993 FAO Compliance Agreement to 'Promote Compliance with International Conservation and Management Measures by Fishing Vessels on the High Seas' and the 1995 UN Straddling Stocks Agreement on Conservation and Management of Straddling

1780. Concerning UNCLOS, *see supra* para. 129.

Fish Stocks and High Migratory Fish Stocks[1781] were signed with a view to preserve the marine environment as well as to protect marine living resources. They address threats to the long-term sustainability of fisheries and the contribution of fisheries to food supply, including overexploitation of important fish stocks, modification of ecosystems, etc. The UN Straddling Stocks Agreement is built on three pillars. It sets out principles on which conservation and management should be based and established, and it states that management must be based on the precautionary approach and the best available scientific information.[1782] The second pillar ensures that the conservation and management measures are adhered to and complied with, and that those who fish for the stocks do not undermine them. Coastal States as well as States fishing on the high seas must, in giving effect to their duty to cooperate in accordance with the Convention, take measures to prevent or eliminate overfishing and excess fishing capacity and ensure that levels of fishing efforts do not exceed those commensurating with the sustainable use of fishery resources. For this purpose, the primarily responsibility of the flag State is reaffirmed, and the framework for action by States other than the flag States is set out with safeguards against abuse (flag State jurisdiction). The third pillar contains provisions for the peaceful settlement of disputes.[1783]

High seas fishing are only partially regulated, and this is done partly by the FAO Agreement to Promote Compliance with International Conservation and Management Measures by Fishing Vessels on the High Seas (1993),[1784] and partly by regional agreements. The marine areas associated with the individual species are divided into zones based on designations under the auspices of the International Council for the Exploration of the Seas (ICES).

The Rio Conference in 1992 focused on biodiversity, including the fish stocks and their ecosystems, resulting in the Convention on Biodiversity (CBD). Fishery targets for 2020 are now laid down under the CBD in the Decision by the COP on the 'Biological Diversity on the Strategic Plan for Biodiversity' (2011).

Examples of regional conventions are the Convention on Fishing and Conservation of the Living Resources in the Baltic Sea and the Belts of 1982, the Convention for the Conservation of Salmon in the North Atlantic Ocean of 1982 with the EU, Denmark, the Faroe Islands, and Greenland as the parties, [1785] and the Convention on Future Multilateral Cooperation in the Northwest Atlantic Fisheries (NAFO) of 1978 with the EU, Canada, Cuba, Denmark, France, Iceland, Japan, Norway, the Republic of Korea, Russia, Ukraine and the United States of America as the parties. The NAFO was signed in 1978. The northern shrimp fisheries in the high seas of the Atlantic (the Flemish Cap) are, for example, subject to the management of NAFO. The Atlanto-Scandian herring stock in the Northeast Atlantic is controlled

1781. As 'migratory' fish do not observe international ocean boundaries during their travels, the UN Agreement for the Conservation and Management of Straddling Fish Stocks and highly Migratory Fish Stocks (1995) covers the questions of who owns the fish in areas beyond the national jurisdiction.
1782. Concerning the 'precautionary principle', *see supra* para. 28.
1783. The EU is a party to all the above-mentioned agreements.
1784. Concerning the international instruments, *see infra* para. 279.
1785. The North Atlantic Salmon Conservation Organisation – NASCO – is the intergovernmental organisation established in 1983 under the Convention.

by means of an agreement between the EU, Norway, Iceland, the Faroe Islands and the Russian Federation. The Northeast Atlantic Fisheries Commission (NEAFC) decides the annual transferable fishing quota (TAQ). Fishing of the oceanic redfish stock in the high sea of the Irminger Sea is covered by a regional agreement involving Russia, the Faroe Islands, Greenland and the EU and controlled by the NEAFC.

280. Fishing has substantial and severe impacts on EU's coastal and marine environments. The powers in relation to fisheries are in principle shared between the EU and its Member States, cf. Article 4(2)(c) TFEU. However, exclusive competence applies to the conservation of marine biological resources under the CFP, cf. Article 3(1)(d) TFEU.[1786] Before the Lisbon Treaty, fisheries policy was an area of exclusive EU competence, and Member States were not allowed to impose their own national rules on those activities. Article 38 TFEU explicitly mentions the CFP and the extension of the Internal Market to cover this policy. Article 38(1) TFEU states that references to the CAP are to be understood to include fisheries. CFP and the CAP have joint objectives and the same substantive basis, i.e., Articles 38 and 43 establish one of the legal bases for both policies.[1787]

The history of the CAP and the CFP is different. In 1983, the Community system for the conservation of fishery resources was established by the Regulation on the Conservation and Management of Fishery.[1788] The Council Regulation on Fisheries and Aquaculture[1789] established a system for management of exploitation of living aquatic resources so as to promote sustainable development. Fishing in Community waters was managed on the basis of an annual EU law fixing the total allowable catches (TAC) per fish stock and dividing the quotas among the individual Member States. The regulation was based on biological advice on fisheries and prognoses for the development of fish stocks. In July 1999, the EU recommended that the fisheries and marine ecosystems should be integrated in a CFP of the Community in coordination with nature protection policies.[1790] At the World Summit on Sustainable Development in 2002, the EU signed up to achieve the Active Maximum Sustainable Yield by 2015 and the new 2020 fisheries target adopted by the parties to the Biodiversity Convention at the COP10.[1791] The first EU 'Biodiversity Action Plan for Fisheries'[1792] was followed by a new Biodiversity Action Plan in 2006,[1793] which aims primarily to clarify responsibilities concerning implementation of the existing law and promotion of the 'actions on the wider countryside and marine environment' with an ecosystem approach as the guiding principle. The Council adopted biodiversity targets in March 2010, and the Commission described the targets in May 2011 as part of the new biodiversity strategy: 'Our life insurance, our

1786. Concerning the exclusive competences of the EU, *see supra* para. 56.
1787. Concerning the importance of the legal bases, *see supra* para. 57.
1788. Council Regulation No. 170/83/EEC establishing a Community System for the Conservation and Management of Fish Resources.
1789. Council Regulation No. 3760/92/EEC establishing a Community System for Fisheries and Aquaculture.
1790. COM(99) 363 final.
1791. Concerning CBD, *see supra* para. 234.
1792. COM(2001) 162 final.
1793. COM(2006) 216 final.

natural capital: An EU Biodiversity Strategy to 2020'.[1794] The next CFP was established in 2000–2002 by the CFP Framework Regulation (also referred to as the 'basic' conservation Regulation)[1795] and the Regulation on the Common Organisation of the Markets in Fishery and Aquaculture Products.[1796] The CFP Framework Regulation describes the scope of the CFP as encompassing 'conservation, management and exploitation of living aquatic resources, aquaculture, and the processing and marketing of fishery and aquaculture products'. In April 2009, a Green Paper analysed the shortcomings of the current CFP[1797] and the Communication on 'Reform of the Common Fishery Policy'[1798] states the need for a better future for fish and fisheries, as well as the marine environment. The Communication of 13 July 2011 entitled 'Reform of the Common Fisheries Policy' sets out the potential challenges, objectives and orientations for the current CFP. The Regulation on the European Maritime and Fishing Fund[1799]– the 'EMFF' – that is covering the period 2014–2020 provide a new well-defined framework for the implementation of the policy together with the Regulation on the 2013 CFP Regulation.[1800] The Preamble of the EMFF Regulation states that the scope of the funding should include support for the CFP for the conservation of marine biological resources, for management of fisheries and fleets exploiting those resources, for fresh water biological resources and aquaculture. The 2013 CFP Regulation (hereinafter the CFP Regulation) repealed the above-mentioned 2002 CFP Regulation as the directly applicable law in all Member States from 1 January 2014. The fundamental objective of the Regulation is the exploitation of living aquatic resources on the basis of measures designed to protect and conserve such resources, provide for their sustainable exploitation and minimising the impact of fishing activities on marine ecosystems, cf. Article 2. It shall ensure that fishing and aquaculture activities are environmentally sustainable in the long term and managed in a way that is consistent with the objectives of achieving economic, social and employment benefits, and of contributing to the availability of food supplies, cf. Article 2(1). Article 2(3) of the CFP Regulation is stating that it shall implement the ecosystem-based approach to fisheries management. This means the structure, functioning and progress of marine ecosystems must be fully considered, marine species and habitats must be protected, and human-induced decline of biodiversity must be prevented. The CFP shall implement the ecosystem-based approach known from the MSFD to fisheries management so as to ensure that the negative impacts of fishing activities on the marine ecosystems are minimised and shall endeavour to ensure that aquaculture and fisheries activities avoid the degradation of the marine environment, cf. Article 2(3) of

1794. COM(2011) 244 final.
1795. European Parliament and Council Regulation No. 2371/2002/EC on the Conservation and Sustainable Exploitation of Fisheries Resources.
1796. European Parliament and Council Regulation No. 104/2000/EC on the Common Organisation of the Markets in Fishery and Aquaculture Products.
1797. COM(2009) 163 final.
1798. COM(2011) 417 final.
1799. European Parliament and Council Regulation No. 508/2014/EC on the European Maritime and Fisheries Fund. This fund is one of the ESI funds mentioned *supra* in para. 15.
1800. European Parliament and Council Regulation No. 1380/2013/EC on the Community Fisheries Policy EU.

the CFP Regulation. Article 3(22) makes it possible for Member States having a direct management interest in the fishery to be affected to propose conservation measures to request the Commission to adopt the relevant spatial conservation measures by means of delegated acts. The Member States have, however, to do it by consensus. Denmark has on this basis stopped a Swedish initiative in 2018. Measures for the conservation of marine biological resources are established in Part III of the CFP Regulation. They may include:

- multi-annual plans that contain conservation measures to restore and maintain fish stocks above levels capable of producing maximum sustainable yield in accordance with Article 2(2), cf. Articles 9–10;
- targets for the sustainable exploitation of stocks;
- measures for the purpose of adopting the number of fishing vessels to available fishing opportunities;
- incentives, including those of an economic nature, to promote fishing methods that contribute to more selective fishing, to avoidance and reduction, as far as possible, of unwanted catches and to promote fishing with low impact on the marine ecosystem and fishing resources;
- measures on the fixing and allocation of fishing opportunities;
- measures to achieve the objectives of Article 15 on loading obligation;
- minimum conservation reference sizes;
- pilot projects on alternative types of fishing management techniques and on gears that increase selectivity or that minimise the negative impact of fishing activities on the marine environment;
- conservation measures to be adopted by the Member States pursuant to Article 11;
- technical measures.

Decisions that are made at EU level about TAC and fishing quotas are based on scientific advice. The ICES is in many of these areas – including the Baltic Sea and the North Sea – the relevant Council. Advices received from ICES will have an impact on the management of the fishing activities as the Commission can follow such advices as the basis for stronger protection of certain stocks in the areas where ICES have competences. By way of example of relevance for Denmark may be mentioned, on 27 June 2019 the ICES published its evaluation of the implementation of the Baltic Sea Multiannual Plan,[1801] stating that the ecosystem is undergoing a fundamental change and that it is not in equilibrium state. It has major consequences for fisheries and eco-management in this region. The Commission can also request ICES to provide new precautionary maximum sustainable yield (MSY) ranges for selected stocks. Each year, the Council[1802] fixes quotas in regulations for

1801. ICES Special Request Advice, *Baltic Sea Ecoregion*, published 27 June 2019. The Baltic Sea Multiannual Plan for cod, herring and sprat in this region was established by the Commission Regulation No. 2016/1139/EU.

1802. *See, e.g.*, Council Regulation No. 2018/2025/EU Fixing for 2019 and 2020 the Fishing Opportunities for Union fishing Vessels for certain deep-sea Fish Stocks.

EU Member States on the basis of scientifically determined TACs, and of the interests of fishermen and consumers. The fisheries are managed by multi-annual plans and governed by the ecosystem approach and the precautionary principle. It entails a transformation to a policy where fishing opportunities allocated to Member States shall ensure relative stability of fishing activities of each Member State for each fish stock or fishery. Article 10 of the CFP Regulation is stating that the Commission shall prepare multi-annual plans for the regional marine areas. Where necessary, the EU adopts measures to protect vulnerable marine habitats such as deep-sea corals, and reduce unintended catches of seabirds, seals and dolphins. Under Article 11 of the Regulation, Member States are empowered to adopt conservation measures not affecting fishing vessels of other Member States that are applicable to waters under their sovereignty or jurisdiction and that are necessary for the purpose of complying with their obligations under Article 13(4) of the MSFD, [1803] Article 4 of the Wild Birds Directive and Article 6 of the Habitats Directive. Article 11 provides more clarity for Member States and specify the procedural steps to follow in their control of fishing activities.[1804] These rules implement the judgment of the CJEU in Case C-127/02 *Waddenzee* concerning fishing licence related to the protected site.[1805] The criteria on 'GES' adopted by the Commission on 17 May 2017[1806] under the MSFD is focused on several fish-related criteria, including the levels of pressure of the fishery activity, reproductive capacity of the stock, the productivity of key species, etc. However, the measures used have to be compatible with the objectives set out in Article 2 of the CFP Regulation, they have to meet the objectives of the relevant EU legislation that they intend to implement, and they have to be at least as stringent as such measures. The Member States shall inform the Commission about their allocation method. A control regime is established under the IUU Regulation[1807] and by the Regulation on Establishing a Community Control System for Ensuring Compliance with the Rules of the Common Fisheries Policy.[1808] The IUU Regulation is implementing the UN Provisions of the UNCLOS relating to the Conservation and Management of Straddling Fish Stocks and Highly Migratory Fish Stocks (the 1995 UN Fish Stocks Agreement)[1809] and the FAO Agreement to Promote Compliance with International Conservation and Management Measures by Fishing Vessels on

1803. *See* concerning the MSFD that aims to achieve 'GES' in the marine environment by 2021, *see supra* para. 130.
1804. This is explained by the ClientEarth in *Article 11 of the EU Common Fisheries Policy*, July 2014.
1805. The judgment established that the granting of fishing licences within a special, protected area is a 'plan' or 'project' within Art. 6(3) of the Habitats Directive. The Member States must enforce the legislation by applying the rules established by the Environmental Liability Directive in situations where fishing activities damage the Natura 2000 sites. Concerning this, *see infra* para. 336.
1806. Commission Decision No. 2017/848/EU laying down Criteria and Methodological Standards on Good Ecological Environmental Status of Marine Waters and Specifications and Standardised Methods for Monitoring and Assessment.
1807. European Parliament Regulation No. 1005/2008/EC on Establishing a Community System to Prevent, Deter and Eliminate Illegal, Unreported and Unregulated Fishing.
1808. European Parliament Regulation No. 1224/2009/EC on Establishing a Community Control System for Ensuring Compliance with the Rules of the Common Fisheries Policy.
1809. On 19 Dec. 2003, Denmark, the EU, and the other Member States of the EU became parties to the 1995 UN Fish Stocks Agreement. All the Member States signed a declaration recalling that as members they have transferred competence to the EU in respect of certain matters governed by the Agreement, which were specified in an Annex to the Agreement.

the High Seas (1993 FAO Compliance Agreement)[1810] by use of minimum requirements to be applied by flag states to the registration and authorisation of vessels for fishing on the high seas – using a certification system. The main objective of the FAO Agreement is to prevent vessels from undermining the effectiveness of conservation and management measures by merely re-flagging fishing vessels that have been caught poaching the international fishing agreements. As the world's largest market, the EU enhances its action against IUU fishing with trade consequences for third countries. Access to EU ports is now only authorised for fishing vessels flying the flag of a third country, which are able to provide accurate information about the legality of their catches and have this information validated by their flag State. A certificate is required under the regulation as a precondition for the import of fishery products into the EU. That certificate should contain information demonstrating the legality of the products concerned. It should be validated by the flag State of the fishing vessels, which caught the fish concerned, in line with its duty under international law to ensure that fishing vessels flying its flag comply with international rules on conservation and management of fisheries resources. Under this scheme, the conditions, procedures, etc. according to which checking, inspection and verification activities of third countries' vessels are made and carried out by the Member States. The above-mentioned international agreements on fisheries predominantly set out the principle that all States have a duty to adopt appropriate measures to ensure sustainable management of marine resources and to cooperate with each other.

The Regulation Concerning the Use of Non-indigenous Species and Locally Absent Species in Aquaculture[1811] established the framework governing aquaculture practices in relation to such species implementing the international obligations that are accepted by the Member States.[1812] The Member States must monitor and inspect such activities. Any movements of non-indigenous species have to be controlled by a permit system. Also, the Regulation concerning the Making Available on the Market and Use of Biocidal Products[1813] provides for rules concerning the authorisation for the use of certain alien species for particular purposes. In Annex I, the MSFD specifies the protection against non-indigenous species introduced by human activities. The Preamble to the Directive states that these international obligations must be taken fully into account by the Member States when they implement the Directive.

281. Fish has been caught in Denmark from the very earliest times, and right from the start, the implements used were fundamentally the same as those used today: nets, traps and hooks. The development of the railway system at the end of the nineteenth century and the installation of motors in boats at around 1900 led to a tremendous increase in offshore fishing. Fresh fish could then be transported over

1810. Denmark and the other Member States are parties to the 1993 FAO Compliance Agreement through the EU – concerning the agreements *see supra* para. 279.

1811. European Parliament and Council Regulation No. 708/2007/EC concerning the Use of Non-indigenous Species and Locally Absent Species in Aquaculture.

1812. Concerning the international protection of biodiversity, *see supra* para. 234.

1813. European Parliament and Council Regulation No. 528/2012/EU concerning the Making Available on the Market and Use of Biocidal Products.

great distances. The boats were able to go further out to sea, and larger, more efficient equipment, for instance, the Danish seine, came into use. Fishing was hereafter a real business, and the numbers employed in it grew rapidly. In 1913, there were about 12,000 full-time fishermen. Those who engaged in it had other work as smallholders, day labourers, etc. The fishing was done in fresh water or close to the coast, though freshwater fishing had never been particularly significant. The first known full-time fishermen can be dated back to the seventeenth century, in the Limfjord area and elsewhere. The fish was normally salted or dried; fresh fish was the preserve of the coastal population. Since 1900, enormous improvements have been made to ships, equipment, engines and electronic equipment; the 12,000 fishermen in 1913 caught approximately 66,000 tonnes, while the 4,500 in 2000 caught 1.5 million tonnes.[1814] The total catch by Danish fishermen from salt-water fishing has fallen in terms of quantities during the period 2003–2013 from 1.0 million tonnes to 670,000 tonnes in 2013.[1815] The total catch by Danish fishermen from salt-water fishing amounted to 672,000 tonnes in 2016. [1816]

The seas around Denmark are characterised by intensive fishing. Industrial fishing began in the North Sea at the end of the 1940s with herring fishing. Later, species such as sand eel, Norway pout and sprat were added to these. The ratio of species was altered, and by 1998, sand eel accounted for 60%. Sand eel is the most common kind of fish in the Danish fishing industry; in terms of cash value, however, cod surpasses it. The fishing grounds are the North Sea, the Skagerrak, the Kattegat, the Sound, the Belt Sea, the Baltic, the Limfjord and the fjords of Ringkøbing and Nissum. Most of the catches come from the North Sea and the Skagerrak. The most important species of fish caught for immediate human consumption are cod, plaice and herring; examples of other species are hake, dover sole and turbot. Fishing for Norway lobster, deep-water prawn and common mussels is also of importance. If all fish landed are listed in order of value, the order runs as follows: cod, sand eel, plaice, herring and Norway lobster. Eel also used to be important, but after a serious diminution of stocks in the 1970s, it has been of less significance.

Since 1985, there has been a fisheries partnership agreement between the EU and Greenland/Denmark.[1817] Greenland is associated to the EU as one of the overseas countries and territories (OCTs) covered by TFEU Articles 198–204 and Protocol No. 34. A special status and commercial agreement linked to withdrawal were agreed by the EU, Denmark and Greenland in protocols to the amended treaty. The current agreement is covering the period from 1 January 2013 to 31 December 2018. In June 2014, a joint declaration was signed by Greenland, Denmark and the EU on the continuation and further strengthening of their relations and cooperation in the following areas: (1) sustainable managing of fish stocks and the marine environment as well as providing fishing opportunities for the vessels of EU Member

1814. Concerning the economy of Danish fishing activities, *see supra* para. 9.

1815. *Statistical Yearbook 2014*, at 405. Concerning the Danish fishing activities, *see also infra* para. 281.

1816. *Statistical Yearbook 2017,* in the section titled 'Business sectors'. Concerning the economy, *see supra* para. 9.

1817. Concerning the partnership agreement, *see infra* para. 280.

States; (2) education and training, tourism and culture; (3) natural resources, including mineral resources; (4) energy, climate, environment and biodiversity; (5) Arctic issues; (6) the social sector, mobility of workforce, social protection systems, food safety and food security; and (7) research and innovation in areas such as energy, climate change, disaster resilience, natural resources, including mineral resources, and sustainable use of living resources. It was published as the Council Decision on relations between the European Union on the one hand, and Greenland and the Kingdom of Denmark on the other.[1818]

The Faroe Islands accepted to become part of an agreement among the EU's coastal States on the management of the fish stocks of mackerel for 2014, including mutual access to each other's fishing grounds. This agreement was the basis for solving a conflict between the EU and the Faroes. In 2014, the Kingdom of Denmark, in respect of the Faroe Islands, notified the WTO Secretariat of a request for consultation with the EU regarding the former dispute on the prohibition of import of herring catch by the Faroe Islands into the Member States (including Denmark). The prohibition on import was the reaction from the EU on the Faroe Islands' catch of mackerel beyond the quota accepted in the EU. In 2017, the Commission published a long-term management plan for the fisheries in the North Sea as a follow-up on the compromise that was made between the EU and Denmark/Faroe Islands.[1819]

282. The Act on Fisheries[1820] is the framework law regulating all aspects of fisheries. The Act includes provisions aiming at preservation of species, e.g., TAC quotas, minimum size limits and fishing prohibitions. It covers both fishing in salt water and fresh water. The goals of sustainable fishing practices are stated in section 1 of the Act. The Danish fisheries are under the administrative jurisdiction of the EU institutions[1821] and the Ministry of Environment and Food of Denmark. Thus, the national law primarily consists of the above-mentioned EU regulations and administers the EU quotas and other joint preservation measures and regulates local fish stocks such as mussels and fishing close to the coast. The conservation measures necessary to achieve the aims of the EU regulation must be formulated in the light of the available scientific information and may include, per species or group of species: the establishment of zones where fishing is prohibited or restricted to certain periods, types of vessel, fishing gear or end-uses; the setting of administration and control of the fishing activities; and the restriction of fishing activities, in particular through catch limits. For each fish species, minimum sizes, fishing seasons and quotas are stipulated.

283. Commercial fishing is only allowed if the persons or firms are registered at the Ministry of Environment and Food of Denmark, cf. sections 11–12. The rules on the qualifications of fishermen and enterprises for commercial fishing are laid

1818. Council Decision No. 2014/137/EU.

1819. Commission Regulation No. 2017/1180/EU amending Regulation No. 2017/117 establishing Fisheries Conservation Measures for the Protection of the Marine Environment in the North Sea.

1820. Promulgation Order No. 261 of 21 Mach 2019 on Fisheries.

1821. Concerning EU legislation on fisheries, *see supra* para. 280.

down in sections 14–25 of the Act. Anyone can practice angling under the conditions set by the Ministry, cf. sections 26–27. Sections 28 and 29 of the Act also regulate fishing in fresh water. The owner of a property is the holder of the right to fish in waters that are closer to his or her property than to other properties. Nobody else has the right to fish in private waters unless they have the permission of the holder of the right. Chapters 5 and 6 of the Act regulate how to fish, what equipment to use, which periods of fishing and how to preserve the fish. A licence can have expiry date, if the authorities decide it, cf. section 36(2). The catch quota management trials include a provision, which require the multi-species fishery activities to stop fishing as soon as the quota for any of the species is reached. The Danish implementation of the obligations under the EU rules on IUU fisheries was ensured in 2012 by an Act amending the Fisheries Act[1822] that was related to the establishment of an advisory council, fisheries in certain water basins, EU point system for illegal fishing activities, etc. The rules in this Act are mainly penalised by means of sanctioned especially through economic sanctions such as confiscation. Confiscation of offenders' unlawful financial profit or the tools used to gain the profit is turned out to be an important measure. Confiscation may be defined as a compulsory surrender of property, whether it in the form of money, objects (e.g., fishing tools) or rights, in consequence of a breach of the rules. Section 132(1) of the Act includes a special provision that a catch may be confiscated. In fisheries cases, very large confiscation claims are often imposed on offenders, including foreign offenders. The follow-up on the Regulation on the EMFF with administrative competences was ensured by the Act on a Maritime and Fishing Fund.[1823] The power established in this Act to establish administrative on state aids in accordance with the Regulation has resulted in several statutory orders.[1824]

284. By an amendment in 2002 of the Act on Fisheries in 2002,[1825] a Catch-Share Programme was introduced for the Danish herring fishery on an experimental basis. It entered into force in 2003 under the name of Individual Transferable Quota (ITQs), whereby ITQs were allocated according to vessels records for the previous three years (grant fathering). Recent entrants can obtain quota loans for a period of time. A vessel owner can transfer the quota utilisation to another fishing vessel in his or her possession, and if there is more than one new owner, the quota utilisation can be split among them and transferred proportionately to other vessels. The political reasoning behind the experiment was the ambitions of modernising of the fishing fleet. The programme was extended to other fish stocks and made permanent in 2007.[1826]

1822. The Fisheries Act was amended by Act No. 388 of 2 May 2012 Advisory Committee, Fishing of Salmon in certain Water Systems, EU Point System for serious Violations, Seizure of Fishing Gear, etc., and Criminal Regulation of Certain Extra-territorial Violations.
1823. Act No. 1361 of 16 December 2014 on a Maritime and Fishing Fund.
1824. This competence has been used as the basis for Statutory Order No. 472 of 26 April 2019 on Subsidies to Storage of Fishing Products, Statutory Order No. 873 of 27 June 2019 on Subsidies to Investment in Aquaculture and Statutory Order No. 252 of 20 March 2019 on Subsidies to Municipality Projects on Water Restoration.
1825. Act No. 369 of 6 June 2002 on the amendments to the Fisheries Act.
1826. It was made by Act No. 317 of 31 March 2007 on the amendments to the Fisheries Act.

The normal categories of fishing seasons in Denmark are thirteen months calculated, from 1 January, cf. section 36a of the Act. More detailed rules are laid down in the Statutory Order on Catch Share.[1827] Fishing in the Kattegat is regulated both with the TAC and the number of fishing days. There are three seasonally closed areas to protect cod in the Baltic Sea (1 May–31 October in Bornholm Deep, Gdansk Deep and Gotland Deep). A near-total ban in the Øresund Sea on towed dishing gear has been in place since 1932, and it was made stricter in 2009. Since 2009, the EU has operated a scheme with real-time closures in the North Sea and Skagerrak in areas with presence of juvenile cod, haddock, whiting and saithe.[1828]

All Danish commercial marine fisheries are managed by the ITQ/TVQ system[1829] with the Danish oyster fisheries, as the last to come under the system.[1830] Fishermen holding quotas can form 'quota pools' privately to manage the responsibility to ensure that aggregate member landings do not exceed the total quota share. Some national rules for the conservation of fish resources are laid down to regulate, *inter alia*, Danish quotas, fishing periods per species and the use of large and small fishing ships. The statutory rules on the conditions for commercial fishing are established by the Minister for Food, Fisheries, and Equal Opportunities and Nordic Cooperation in different rules on fish stocks, cf. for example, Statutory Order on the Fishing of Eel in Fresh Water and Sea Water.[1831] These rules also focus on the difference between EU zones and other fishing zones. The Danish catches have dropped from 1.5 million tonnes to less than half that volume over the past decade mainly due to a dramatic drop in the catches of sand eel in the North Sea and decreases in other food fish catches.[1832]

285. In the harbour, the control authorities calculate the catch per species by means of a special sorting system, and on the basis of these calculations, the authorities will draw up a report stating the percentage of illegal catch. If the control is carried out at sea, such calculation is impossible, and the inspectors will simply estimate the contents of the cargo. Sensor monitoring of fishing vessels can be established on a voluntary basis with a full video monitoring system. Six vessels have accepted to have four video cameras and other electronic surveillance equipment installed so that catches and discards can be monitored very precisely. The Ministry of Environment and Food of Denmark has established a complete database to facilitate sustainable fishery certification and to supply retailers with all relevant data and documentation for the Danish fisheries certification of sustainability. The Catch Quota Management (CQM) is a results-based management system that

1827. Statutory Order No. 1446 of 1 December 2016 on Catch Share.
1828. European Parliament, Directorate-General for Internal Policies, Policy Department. Structural and Cohesion Policies B, *Fisheries in Denmark*, at 26.
1829. TVQ is the abbreviation for the 'Transferable Vessel Quota' shares.
1830. Statutory Order No. 1471 of 11 December 2018 on the Commercial Fishing of Mussels and Oyster.
1831. Statutory Order No. 1551 of 11 December 2015 on the Fishing of Eel in Fresh Water and Sea Water.
1832. The Danish fishing fleet in 2013 was composed of 2,742 vessels; *see* European Parliament, Directorate-General for Internal Policies, Policy Department. Structural and Cohesion Policies B, *Fisheries in Denmark*, at 10.

started in Denmark as a scientific project from September 2008 to September 2009 gathering extensive data from the above-mentioned six vessels. In 2010, a new trial with CQM and full documentation was carried out, in which the Danish Ministry puts the operational aspects into a management and control context. A Council Regulation regarding Fishing Opportunities for certain Fish Stocks[1833] established the provision for the use of CQM in the EU Member States for certain fish stocks. In Denmark, fishing vessels must be registered, and the owner needs a licence from the Danish Agency of Fisheries under the Ministry of the Environment and Food. The licence requirements are prescribed in the annual statutory orders. From the mid-1980s, the government attempted to reduce the fishery capacity and overfishing through vessel decommissioning, policies limiting vessel entry, and vessel investments and regulations limiting fish mortality, e.g., by restricting the number of days at sea. In the period 1987–1991, there was a reduction of the Danish fleet of 17,233 gross tonnes and 70,499 kilowatts. The reduction was compensated by subsidies granted under Act on Subsidies and State Guarantees on Borrowed Money to the Fisheries.[1834] Since the adoption of this Act in 1987, licences are given only to applicants who have received closing-down assistance in a period of five years after their vessels were struck off the Ships' Register. New licences are only granted to applicants that have been active in commercial fishing for at least two years and who have withdrawn an old fishing vessel from the fleet. The licence is normally given only for a fishing vessel of the same capacity as the withdrawn vessel. From 1989 to 2006, 1,272 vessels were removed at a total public cost of DKK 1.4 billion. The number of vessels holding ITQs has been substantially reduced since 2003 by means of the transfer of quotas. As intended by the ITQ reform, some of the Danish vessels holding ITQs are brand new and have replaced vessels that were more than twenty-five years old.[1835]

286. Around 30% of Danish marine fish species are currently red listed.[1836] Fishing and navigation may disturb the ecological balance of coastal areas. The disruption can be minimised by the proper use of fishing resources and by only slight interference with the avifauna. As long ago as 1951, a statutory order[1837] prohibited navigation and fishing in the waters around the Rømø Dam. There are also other statutory orders protecting different sensitive areas.

The mandatory protection of Natura 2000 sites as described in the Habitats Directive is also relevant for fishing activities.[1838] The obligations to ensure EIA and the protection of species under the Habitats Directives are implemented in the Act as

1833. Council Regulation No. 219/2010/EC amended Regulation No. 53/2010 as regard Fishing Opportunities for Certain Fish Stocks and following the Bilateral Fishing Agreements of 2010 with Norway and Fareos Islands.

1834. Act No. 875 of 23 December 1987 on Subsidies and State Guarantees on Borrowed Money to the Fisheries.

1835. *Nordic experience of fisheries management seen in relation to the reform of the EU Common Fisheries Policy*, TemaNord 2009:579.

1836. Concerning the international protection of such species, *see supra* para. 255.

1837. Statutory Order No. 44 of 12 February 1951 on Denmark's Ratification on 24 May 1934 of the International Convention on the Establishment of Certain Uniform Rules on Immunity for State Ships with Additional Protocols as concluded in Brussels on 10 April 1926.

1838. Concerning EU fishery legislation, *see supra* para. 280.

section 10a–10j. The Danish Statutory Order on the Coordination of the Environmental Assessment and Digital Self-service on Plan, Programmes and Projects [1839] and the Statutory Order on Habitat Protection[1840] implement the protection of the habitats and the wild birds in respect to activities covered by the Act on the Continental Shelf and the Subsoil Act. The Statutory Order on Special Fishing Conditions in Natura 2000 Sites[1841] as a Protection is an implementation that is based on the Fisheries Act. The rules on environmental liability were established by an amendment to the Fisheries Act in 2008, cf. section 10a–10j, in Chapter 3a of the Act.[1842]

In accordance with the Watercourse Act, the municipal council may decide that fishing or sailing is not permitted to take place in certain watercourses, or that fishing, or sailing may only take place under specified conditions.[1843]

287. The MSFD has implemented the Marine Strategy Framework,[1844] and the Directive on Maritime Spatial Planning was implemented in 2016 by the Act on Maritime Spatial Planning.[1845] The ministries are currently working on the first strategic maritime planning. No draft has been presented for the public yet.

288. The freshwater fish farms have been regulated since 1989 by means of a feed quota, i.e., the maximum permissible feed utilisation during the course of a year. A fish farm is subject to the operational licence system laid down in accordance with Chapter 5 of the Environmental Protection Act[1846] and Statutory Order on the Approval of Fresh Water Fish Farms.[1847]

The licensing authority has the power to decide more stringent terms as part of the licence. The rules also require that fish farms have a sedimentation basin such that the sludge settles in it rather than being discharged into the watercourses. There are rules on discharge levels for certain specified substances, on internal control of the inlet and outlet, and on operating records, as well as the coordination of administrative decision-making. Where a fish farm do not function properly from the point of view of environmental protection, e.g., where it do not comply with or consider requirements laid down pursuant to this Act, the municipal council may require that the necessary improvement or renewal of the plant be carried out. Where pollution cannot be remedied, the council may issue a prohibition on future operation of the fish farm, and possibly order its removal, *see* section 41 of the Act.

1839. Statutory Order No. 121 of 4 February 2019 on the Coordination of the Environmental Assessment and Digital Self-service on Plan, Programmes and Projects, it has its legal basis in the SEA and EIA Act.
1840. Statutory Order No. 1595 of 6 December 2018 on the Demarcation and Management of International Nature Conservation Areas and Protection of Certain Species.
1841. Statutory Order No. 1048 of 28 August 2014 on Special Fishing Conditions in Natura 2000 Sites.
1842. Concerning environmental liability, *see infra* para. 337.
1843. *See supra* paras 109–110 concerning the Danish legislation on watercourses. The water quality in freshwater area has to respect the water basin management plans, *see supra* para. 108.
1844. Act No. 522 of 26 May 2010 on Marine Strategy Framework.
1845. Concerning Act No. 615 of 8 June 2016 on Maritime Strategic Planning, *see supra* para. 133.
1846. Concerning the environmental approval system, *see supra* paras 62–66.
1847. Statutory Order No. 1317 of 20 November 2018 on Environmental Approval of Listed Activities.

Denmark was among the European pioneers in systematic pond farming of trout 100 years ago. In 1914, Denmark had approximately 140 trout farms, primarily producing for export. In Denmark, there are now approximately 220 farms, of which five are organic.

289. Marine aquaculture has existed in Denmark for many years. The offshore aquaculture farms are covered as listed activities by the Environmental Protection Act's Chapter 5, the Statutory Order on Approval of Listed Activities[1848] and Statutory Order on Salt-water Based Fish Farms.[1849] The owners of the farms that did not have a licence were obliged to apply for an operating licence under this Act no later than 15 March 2014. Currently, there are still farms that do not have a licence. Of more than twenty marine farms that exist in Denmark, one is converted to organic production. Stocks must have lived under ecological conditions for a year before they can be sold as organic.

Marine fish farms located close to the coast must respect the Planning Act and the Nature Protection Acts rules on coast protection.[1850] If the farm is located more than – or partly more than – 1 nautical mile from the coast, it is regulated by the water plans to be established under the Water Basins Planning Act and the Act on Marine Strategic Management.[1851] The location must not be in conflict with the international protection of Nature 2000 areas,[1852] and it must be assessed under the EIA rules before a licence is granted.[1853] The nitrogen emission from this sector was 62,400 tonnes to the sea area in 2016.

1848. Statutory Order No. 1567 of 7 December 2016 on the Approval of Fresh Water Fish Farms.

1849. Statutory Order No. 640 of 17 September 1990 Salt-water Based Fish Farms. The approval of the fish farms is also regulated by the general Statutory Order No. 1317 of 20 November 2018 on Environmental Approval of Listed Activities, *see supra* para. 63 concerning the Danish approval system, and *supra* para. 133 concerning the maritime spatial planning obligations.

1850. Concerning the spatial planning, *see infra* Part III, Chapter 2.

1851. Concerning the Danish river basin legislation, *see supra* para. 108, and concerning the Danish implementation of MSFD, *see* para. 132.

1852. Concerning the Nature 2000 sites as protected by the Wild Birds Directive and the Habitats Directive, *see supra* para. 241.

1853. Concerning the EIA rules, *see supra* para. 32.

Chapter 8. Subsoil, Minerals and Hydrocarbons, Etc.

290. The Mining Waste Directive[1854] is one of the directives that establish minimum environmental requirements as a protection of the subsoil. It covers the management of waste resulting from prospecting, extraction, treatment and storage of mineral resources and from quarrying. The Offshore Security Directive is another important directive protecting the marine environment from the environmental consequences of extraction. A number of subsoil activities decisively influence the habitats.

The Mining Waste Directive provides for measures, procedures and guidance that the Member States had to transpose to national law by 1 May 2008 to prevent or minimise the adverse effects on the environment and risk to health resulting from the management of waste from the extractive industries.[1855] It requires the Member States to establish national law that makes it mandatory for the operator to have an extractive waste management plan included in the application for an approval of extractive activities or included in the EIA, cf. Article 5. Such management plans shall be reviewed every five years and/or amended, if substantial changes have taken place in the extractive activities. The Member States have to report to the Commission on any high-risk facilities of which some also falls under the Seveso III Directive[1856] and/or IED.[1857] The holders of authorisation are the liable 'operators' within the meaning of the ELD. As a circular economy action, the Commission published a draft to a guiding document in 2019 on best practices in the waste management plans.[1858]

Under the Directive on Prospection, Extraction and Production of Hydrocarbons,[1859] the Member States shall ensure that no extractive activity start without an authorisation under the minimum conditions laid down in the directive. In this context, the national licensing authority is required to consider the technical and financial risks, and where appropriate, the previous record of responsibility. Since 1991, minimum requirements on the improvement of the protection onshore and offshore of workers' health and security have been established in the Mineral-Extracting

1854. European Parliament and Council Directive 2006/21/EC on the Management of Waste from Extraction Industries. The Directive aims to prevent or reduce as far as possible any adverse effects on the environment. The Directive is mentioned *supra* in para. 147.

1855. The Commission opened legal proceedings against Denmark, France, UK and Bulgaria related to non-conformity.

1856. European Parliament and Council Directive 2012/18/EU on the Control of Major Accident Hazards involving Dangerous Substances.

1857. Such facilities are known as 'Category A Facilities'. Denmark has reported to the Commission that there do not exist any Category A facilities in Denmark, cf. Commission, *Report on the Implementation of Directive 2006/21/EC on the Management of Waste from Extractive Industries and amending Directive 2004/35/EC*, COM(2016) 533 final, at 4.

1858. Eco Efficiency Consulting and Engineering Ltd, *Development of a guidance document on best practices in the Extractive Management Plans. Circular Economy Action* of 22 January 2019. The report is made in collaboration with WEFalck, Pöyry Finland Oy, Botond Kertész & CRS Ingeneria.

1859. European Parliament and Council Directive 94/22/EEC on the Conditions for granting and using Authorisations for the Prospection, Exploration and Production of Hydrocarbons.

Industries Drilling Directive.[1860] This Directive did not protect the marine environment, and it did not reflect the best regulatory practices for major accident prevention. The Seveso III Directive is not covering the offshore activities, so until 2013 there was no EU legislation ensuring a protection of the marine environment against the risks connected to major hazardous activities.[1861] A review of offshore oil and gas operations was launched by the Commission in its communication 'Facing the challenge of the safety of offshore oil and gas activities'.[1862] In 2011, the Commission presented the draft on a 'Regulation on Safety of Offshore Oil and Gas Prospection, Exploration and Production Activities'[1863] in the light of the Deepwater Horizon accident experience in the Gulf of Mexico. The proposal is the background for the Safety of Offshore Oil and Gas Operation Directive[1864] that came into force on 18 July 2013. It aims to ensure the protection of the marine environment and in particular to achieve or maintain GES by 2020 at the latest, an objective set out in the Marine Strategic Framework Directive.[1865] The provisions of this Directive apply not only to future offshore oil and gas installations and operations but is – subject to transitional arrangements – also covering existing installations. The general principles of risk management established by Article 3 of the Directive are based on the 'polluter pays principle'. Offshore hydrocarbon operations and installations are only accepted in areas appointed by the licence, cf. Article 4(4) and Article 6. Member States shall ensure that decisions on granting or transferring licences to carry out offshore oil and gas operations take into account the capacity of an applicant for such a licence to meet the requirements for operations within the framework of the licence as required by relevant provisions of EU law, especially this Directive, cf. Article 4. In particular, when assessing the technical and financial capability of the applicant for a licence, due account under Article 4(2) shall be taken of:

- the risk, the hazardous and any other relevant information related to the licensed area concerned, including, where appropriate, the cost of degradation of the marine environment referred to in Article 8(1) letter c) of the MSFD;
- the particular stage of offshore oil and gas operations;
- the applicants' capabilities, including any financial security, to cover liabilities potentially deriving from the operations in question, including liability for potential economic damages where such liability is provided for by national law; and

1860. Council Directive 92/91/EEC concerning the minimum Requirements for Improving the Safety and Health Protection of Workers in the Mineral-Extraction Industries through Drilling.

1861. The Seveso Directive is not covering offshore activities, *see supra* para. 203.

1862. COM(2010) 560 final.

1863. COM(2011) 688 final. Concerning the background, *see also* JRC Science and Policy Report, *Safety of offshore oil and gas operations: Lessons from past accident analysis. Ensuring EU hydrocarbon supply through better control of major hazards*, 2012.

1864. European Parliament and Council Directive 2013/30/EU on Safety of Oil and Gas Operation. Art. 192(1) TFEU is the substantive basis for this Directive. The deadline for the Member States to transpose measures in the Offshore Safety Directive in national legislation was 19 Jul. 2015.

1865. This relation to the MSFD is stated in the Preamble of the Offshore Safety Directive. Concerning the MSFD, *see supra* para. 130.

- the available information relating to the safety and environmental performance of the applicant, including in relation to major accidents, as may be appropriate to the operations for which the licence was required.

Article 5 of the Directive is demanding the Member States to ensure that the public is given early and effective opportunities to participate in the decision-making relating to operations that can have significant effects on the environment.[1866] The holders of authorisation are the liable 'operators' within the meaning of the ELD.[1867] The operators must ensure verification of their capacity by independent verification as a necessary assurance system, cf. Article 17. Member States shall ensure that the operator is financially liable for the prevention and remediation of environmental damage caused by offshore oil and gas operations carried out by, or on behalf of the operator, cf. Article 7. The operators must prepare and submit different documents listed in the Directive, including emergency response plans, taking into account the risk assessment undertaken as part of the major hazardous reporting, cf. Articles 11 and 14. These plans must include an analysis of oil spill response effectiveness, and the plans have to be updated over time when appropriate. Member States must also ensure that the operators of a well prepare the notification to be submitted to the competent authority, cf. Articles 11(1) and 15. Member States must require operators and owners to prepare a document setting out their corporate major accident prevention policy. The operators have to make their policies in accordance with the criteria laid down in Articles 19 and 28–30. It is mandatory for all Member States to adopt the common accident-reporting format to be used by the responsible operators in their reporting on major hazards (RoMH). The operators must use these standardised documents when they report on major hazards and immediate risk, cf. Articles 12–13. Member States must also ensure that the overseas operators that are domiciled in their jurisdiction are reporting any major hazards, cf. Article 20. As of 19 July 2016, the national provisions on offshore safety etc. must be binding on owners and operators of planned production installations as well as operators planning or executing well operations. All Member States have to cooperate with offshore neighbours in emergency response planning and emergency preparedness and response, and they have to establish mechanisms for reporting of safety concerns, cf. Articles 22–23, Article 27 and Articles 31–32.

There are three Danish acts regulating the extraction of materials and hydrocarbons in the subsoil: the Mineral Resources Act,[1868] the Subsoil Act[1869] and the

1866. Concerning such obligations established in accordance with the Aarhus Convention, *supra* para. 32.

1867. The Offshore Safety Directive is also amending the Environmental Liability Directive so that the extraction activities are covered by the liability rules listed in Annex III of the Environmental Liability Directive. Environmental damage to the seawaters within the entire continental shelf and EEZ of the Member States is covered by the Environmental Liability Directive after this amendment. Concerning the Environmental Liability Directive, *see infra* para. 336.

1868. Promulgation Order No. 124 of 26 January 2017 Mineral Resources, as amended by Act No. 427 of 18 May 2016 and Act No. 720 of 8 June 2018. *See infra* paras 291–292 concerning extraction on land.

1869. Promulgation Order No. 1190 of 21 September 2018 on the Utilisation of the Danish Subsoil.

Safety of Offshore Oil and Gas Operation Act.[1870] The Danish State has the right to exploit the seabed within the EZZ and the continental shelf limits.[1871] Section 2 of the Act on the Continental Boundaries[1872] states that natural resources are owned by the State and may only be explored and exploited with the permission of the Minister for Climate, Energy, and Utilities.

291. The total area in Denmark that is designated for the extraction of sand gravel and pebbles currently amounts to approximately 930 km^3. When all the main natural resources are included, 93 million tonnes of materials were extracted in Denmark, which is equivalent to 16.4 tonnes per inhabitant.[1873] Around 75% of the mineral resources extracted in Denmark are extracted on land (this part amounts to approximately 5 km^2 per year), while the remaining part is extracted from the seabed. It is estimated that at the present level of activity, the area of seabed directly affected by marine aggregate extraction will be 1–3 km^3 annually.

The Mineral Resources Act[1874] regulates the exploitation of lignite, flint stone, gneiss, granite, gravel, lime, kaolin, bog iron ore, chalk, coal, clay, mould, sand, sandstone, peat, stone, diatomaceous earth, travertine, marl, CH_4 extracted from deposits from quaternary layers, bog lime, ochre ore and shells on land. The Danish Nature Agency is the overall responsible authority in the administration of this Act, while the regional councils are responsible for the mapping of areas for future supply activities and the spatial planning for the exploitation of mineral resources.[1875] It is the five regional councils that are responsible for the mineral resources mapping, the mapping of existing ram materials in the sub-soil and the 'case-by-case' administration of permits under the Act. Non-commercial removal of a limited quantity of stones and boulders, and preliminary investigations regarding mineral resources in a specific area limited to 200 m^3 do not need a permit, but the activities must still to be notified to the council. The council has four weeks to decide whether a permit is necessary, or whether it is acceptable to carry out the extraction without a permit, or if there is a need to set certain conditions for the extraction.

The administration has to be based on prioritising and weighing the environmental interests as part of the weighing of the following interests listed in section 3 of the Act: (a) the quantity and quality of mineral resources and the sound exploitation

1870. Promulgation Order No. 125 of 6 February 2018 on Safety of Offshore Oil and Gas Operation.
1871. *See* the Convention concerning the Continental Shelf of 1958 (ratified by Denmark in 1963) and the UNCLOS (ratified by Denmark in 2004). Concerning the UNCLOS, *see supra* para. 129. The Danish rules are laid down in Promulgation Order No. 1189 of 21 September 2018 on the Continental Shelf and certain Pipeline Plant in the Territorial Sea.
1872. Promulgation Order No. 1189 of 21 September 2018 on the Continental Boundaries.
1873. *Statistical Yearbook 2017*, at 408.
1874. Promulgation Order No. 124 of 26 January 2017 on Mineral Resources, as amended by Act No. 427 of 18 May 2016 concerning the Changes needed to ensure Harmony with the Act on Strategic Environmental Assessment of Plans and Programmes and the Environmental Impact Assessment of projects (EIA) and Act No. 720 of 8 June 2018 concerning new Rules on the Competence in Cases related to Coastal Protection.
1875. Concerning the Mineral Resources Act, *see infra* para. 292 and concerning the national planning *infra* para. 307.

of raw material resources, as well as commercial considerations; and (b) environmental protection and water supply interests, protection of archaeological and geological interests, nature protection, including conservation of landscape values and scientific interests, expedient urban development, infrastructure constructions, agricultural and forestry interests, prevention of sand drift, coastal protection, fishery interests, inconveniences for marine and air traffic and changes in current and seabed conditions. Section 1 of the Act states that the main goals are:

- to ensure that exploitation of mineral resources deposits on land and on the seabed takes place as an element of sustainable development after a comprehensive weighing of interests and an overall evaluation of the factors mentioned in section 3 of the Mineral Resources Act;
- that extraction and after-treatment of mineral resources are planned in such a way that the after-treated area may be integrated in another use;
- to ensure the sources for supply of mineral resources also in the future;
- that mineral resources are used in accordance with their quality; and
- that waste products are used instead of natural mineral resources to the greatest possible extent.

292. The five regional councils are obliged to take the landscape and the environmental consequences of extraction on land into consideration in their mapping of the plan for extraction and supply of mineral resources, cf. section 5a of the Mineral Resources Act.[1876]

This planning process must include public participation, cf. section 6a. The planning activities at land are part of the spatial planning activities, and they have to be coordinated with the municipal planning activities under the Planning Act. An SEA must be included in the decision-making on new spatial plans.[1877] Under section 11(4) no. 7 of the Planning Act, municipal plans must not contradict the extraction planning made by the regional councils. The municipal plan shall be accompanied by a report describing the premises on which the plan is based, including the provisions established by the mineral resources plan that are relevant to the planning of land use within the geographical area covered by the municipal plan, cf. section 11e(1) no. 10 of the Planning Act. Pursuant to section 7 of the Mineral Resources Act, a permit from the regional councils are required for the commercial extraction of mineral resources and for the establishment of installations at the extraction site on land for such activity. Permits for extraction on beaches and other coastal stretches with no continuous land vegetation are granted by the Danish Nature Agency, cf. section 7(4) of the Mineral Resources Act and section 16b of the Coastal Protection Act.[1878] Permits for extraction on beaches and other coastal stretches with no continuous land vegetation shall be granted only with the consent of the Danish Coast Authority. Permits for raw material extraction activities, which can be assumed to have a significant impact on the environment, may be granted only on

1876. Promulgation Order No. 124 of 26 January 2017 on Mineral Resources, as amended by Act No. 427 of 18 May 2016 and Act No. 720 of 8 June 2018.
1877. Concerning SEA of plans and programmes, *see supra* para. 32.
1878. Promulgation Order No. 57 of 21 January 2019 on Coastal Protection.

the basis of an EIA, during which the general public, public authorities and NGOs have had the opportunity to express their opinions.[1879]

293. In relation to the extraction of marine aggregates – such as gravel and sand pumping, and the extraction of stones – the rules providing for protection are laid down in the Mineral Resources Act. Until January 1997, it was possible to extract marine aggregates (stone, gravel and other natural deposits) on the seabed without being subject to regulation. Many reefs were reduced in size and scope until the amended Mineral Resources Act[1880] came into force.

Under the Raw Material Act, all extraction of marine aggregates must now be undertaken in the designated areas, where the commercial and environmental interests have been weighed against each other. A permit from the Danish Nature Agency is required, cf. section 20 of the Act. The Agency makes a call for tender on extractions followed by a licensing process. The rules on the competition conditions laid down in this Act were changed in 2015.[1881] The aim of the changing rules was to ensure a stronger procedure in the competition on the marine mineral resources. Under section 23 of the Act, permits for mineral resources extraction activities that can be assumed to have a significant impact on the environment, may be granted only on the basis of an EIA, during which the general public, public authorities and NGOs have had the opportunity to express their opinions.[1882]

294. The Subsoil Act[1883] applies to all construction places on the continental shelf that have not been subject to private commercial utilisation prior to 23 February 1923. The aim of the Act is to ensure appropriate exploitation of mineral resources and use of the subsoil. The mineral resources covered by the Act include hydrocarbons, sulphur, rock salt, bromine, helium, other genuine gases, geothermal heat, store of natural gas and storage of CO_2 (known as CCS). All producing oil and gas fields in Denmark are located in the North Sea. The production has a major impact on Denmark's energy supply as well as its economy. The first oil discovery in the North Sea was made in 1966 by the privately owned firm, A.P. Møller and their partners in the Danish Subsoil Consortium (DUC). The Dan field was the first field to produce oil. It has accounted for nearly 28% of the total Danish oil production since 1972. In 1982, A.P. Møller was granted exclusive rights to explore in the entire Danish area. Since holding the first licensing round in 1984, the State has participated in all licences awarded for the extraction of hydrocarbons extraction. Six licensing rounds have been held during the period 1984–2006. The Danish North

1879. Concerning the EIA provisions, *see supra* para. 32.
1880. It was amended by Act No. 484 of 12 June 1996 on the Amendment of the Mineral Resources Act and the Act on the Continental Shelf.
1881. It was changed by Act No. 178 of 24 February 2015 on the amendments to the Auction Scheme and other Rules on the Extraction of Mineral Resources at Sea as a result of the Government's competitive Policy drafting and Evaluation of the Mineral Resources Act, amendments resulting from the transfer of the Coastal Protection Act to the Ministry of Environment and clarification of the implementation of the Marine Strategy Framework Directive, etc. The Act on Coastal Protection Act and the Marine Strategic Management Act were also amended by this Act.
1882. The detailed rules are laid down in ss 11–12 of the Statutory Order No. 1680 of 17 December 2018 on Mineral Resources Extraction on the Seabed on the Continental Shelf.
1883. Promulgation Order No. 1190 of 21 September 2018 on the Utilisation of the Danish Subsoil.

Sea Fund is acting on behalf of the Danish State in licence issues. The objective of the Fund is to help secure a financial return as high as possible for the State in relation to oil and gas activities. The Fund also participates in technical, financial, legal and commercial discussions with the operator and other co-licensees to determine which exploration and production activities are to be initiated.

The Minister for Climate, Energy and Utilities has the competence to grant the rights to exploitation on the Danish seabed and subsoil, cf. section 2 of the Act. The power is delegated to the Energy Agency. There are four types of licences for offshore oil and gas operations: (1) licence for preliminary investigations for up to three years; (2) exploration licence; (3) production licence; and (4) exploration and production licence.[1884] Permission can be granted as an exclusive right to explore hydrocarbons, etc. in the continental shelf. In 1997, an 'open-door' procedure was introduced for unlicensed areas in all Danish onshore and offshore areas, with the exception of the western part of the North Sea. This 'open-door' procedure is now one out of four possible procedures, cf. section 12 of the Act. The other three procedures are: (1) general tender round, which is the main rule; (2) mini round based on an unsolicited application; and (3) neighbour-block procedure, which can be used when special geological or procedural conditions are present. The 'open-door' procedure is not used in the North Sea. It is only used in areas where the situation in which oil and gas have not been discovered before. Oil companies can continually apply for licences in the 'open-door' area within an annual application period from 2 January to 30 September. If the Agency receives more than one application for the same area, the 'first-come, first-served' policy applies in accordance with the licence conditions. The implementation of the Directive on Prospection, Extraction and Production of Hydrocarbons[1885] is first and foremost based on an interest in the protection of health and safety for the employees. The Danish implementation of the provisions of the Safety of Offshore Oil and Gas Operation Directive[1886] promote a high level for health and safety the employees. The Directive was implemented in 2014.[1887] The Danish Act stipulates that an approval for the extraction of hydrocarbons must be granted before the development of an installation can be initiated. Such approvals are granted pursuant to section 27 of that Act and must ensure that health and safety aspects are factored into the general design phase.[1888] This amendment includes the provisions on the obligations for the operator to use an independent verification, the obligations on risk management and reduction of risks as well as rules on final removal of an oil and gas installation. The Danish independent authority is responsible for assessing and accepting reports on major hazards,

1884. Stevens & Bolton LLP, *Civil liability, financial security and compensation claims for offshore oil and gas activities in the European Economic Area. Final Report*, at 35.

1885. European Parliament and Council Directive 94/22/EEC on the Conditions for Granting and Using Authorisations for the Prospection, Exploration and Production of Hydrocarbons.

1886. Promulgation Order No. 125 of 6 February 2012 on Offshore Security.

1887. Act No. 1499 of 23 December 2014 on an amendment to the Act on Offshore Safety, the Marine Environmental Protection Act and the Act on Environmental Damage.

1888. By the amendment of the Act – by Act No. 287 of 15 April 2009 – it was clarified that the construction of new installations, extensions to or the commissioning and modification of existing offshore installations must contribute to higher safety standards. The implementation of European Parliament and Council Directive 2005/36/EC EU on the Recognition of Professional Qualification formed part of the amendment.

assessing design notification and assessing notification of well operations and the other duties stated in Article 8 of the Directive is the Ministry of Industry, Business and Financial Affairs. Denmark is ordered to ensure at all times the independence and objectivity of this competent authority from the Ministry of Energy, Climate and Utilities that deals with the economic development of offshore natural resources. The rules in the Offshore Safety Directive on the protection of the marine environment by the rules on public risk management planning and the environmental liability are laid down in the Marine Environmental Protect Act and the Act on Environmental Damage.[1889]

In 2015, an Act[1890] amended the Subsoil Act to transpose some of the Safety of the provisions laid down in the Offshore Oil and Gas Operation Directive into Danish legislation. It included a new Chapter 7a on technical requirements, the definition of the responsible operator, insurance and other sorts of financial security instruments as well as the scope of the licences. Section 10 stipulates that oil and gas production must be carried out in a manner that prevents any waste of hydrocarbons. To meet this requirement, the operator must submit a development plan to the Agency for approval before starting to develop a discovery. The development plan must include a production plan and a description of the installations. Each licence includes terms specifying the exploration that the licensee must carry out, including time limits for the individual seismic surveys and exploration wells. The decisions concerning exploitation must be based on an EIA, cf. section 28a of the Act. More detailed provisions are laid down in Statutory Order on the Environmental Impact Assessment of Projects for the Supply of Hydrocarbons, the Protection of Natura 2000 Sites and the Establishment of Pipelines in the Danish Territorial Seawater and Continental Shelf.[1891]

Licences to exploration of hydrocarbons and the recovery of such materials are generally granted for a six-year term, cf. section 13(1) of the Act. In some cases, the work programme of the licence may stipulate that the licensee is obliged to carry out specific work, such as the drilling of an exploration well, or otherwise to relinquish the licence by a certain date before the six-year licence term expires. It is possible for the Agency to renew the six-year licence by up to two years, provided that the licensee, upon carrying out the original work programme, is prepared to undertake additional exploration commitments. In exceptional cases, the exploration term may be extended beyond ten years, i.e., if it is considered appropriate to give the licensee sufficient time to clarify the production potential of a marginal discovery. *See* section 13(2) of the Act concerning the possibility of granting a licence for a period of thirty years. All contemplated licence transfers, extensions and the associated conditions must be submitted to the Agency for approval.

1889. Concerning the Marine Protection Act, *see supra* para. 131, and concerning the Environmental Damage Act, *infra* para. 341.
1890. Act No. 535 of 29 April 2015 amending the Act on Continental Shelf and certain Pipeline Plant in the Territorial Sea to ensure the implementation of the Safety of Offshore Oil and Gas Operation Directive.
1891. Statutory Order No. 434 of 2 May 2017 on the Environmental Impact Assessment of Projects for the Supply of Hydrocarbons, the Protection of Natura 2000 Sites and the Establishment of Pipelines in the Danish Territorial Seawater and Continental Shelf.

295. Geothermal heat is an RES used for the district heating supply together with other forms of energy sources. The hot water is found in porous and permeable sandstone layers, and it is pumped up to the surface via wells. Geothermal heat production is possible because the temperature in the subsoil layers typically increases by 25°–30°C for every 1,000 m of depth. The utilisation of the heat in the subsoil is part of the State-ownership, and applications are invited by means of a call for tenders.

The Subsoil Act[1892] regulates the geothermal heat by means of a licence system, cf. section 18 with a reference to section 5 of the Act. The tender system related to specific areas and criteria, cf. section 18b. The assessment of applications includes an EIA[1893] and Natura 2000 protection.[1894] Applications can be submitted twice a year for permission for exploration and extraction of geothermal energy for district heating supply. Application deadlines are 1 February and 1 September. The permits are granted for six years, cf. section 18c. During that period, a work programme must be implemented, which is agreed between the applicant and the Danish Energy Agency. If the investigations lead to a decision on the establishment of a geothermal plant, the permit can be extended up to thirty years for the purpose of recovering geothermal energy.

296. The Danish geology is very suitable for CO_2 storage (CCS) and combined with biomass it is expected that the energy production could be carbon negative. The subsoil storage of CO_2 must take place at locations with suitable geological conditions. In Denmark, this will typically be a porous and permeable sandstone layer at depths of more than 1,000 m approximately. Another possibility would be to inject the CO_2 into the fields of the North Sea.

In the report 'Power to the People' from 2009 by the Danish Energy Association, it was estimated that CCS could help to remove 7.5 million tonnes of CO_2 by 2025 and just under 17 million tonnes of CO_2 by 2050. The CCS Directive[1895] was implemented into Danish law in the form of an amended Danish Subsoil Act as a new section 5(3) on the competences of the Minister for Climate, Energy and Utilities to decide on new administrative rules, and section 23e–23v[1896] on the allocation of exploration and storage licences in connection with the deployment of CCS. So far, the CCS technology has not been a part of the Danish public energy policy. In September 2009, Vattenfall postponed their plans to build a full-scale CO_2 plant for coal power in North Jutland. The project was hampered by strong local protests due to a fear of leakage of CO_2.

1892. Promulgation Order No. 1190 of 21 September 2018 on the Utilisation of the Danish Subsoil.
1893. Concerning the EIA provisions, *see supra* para. 32.
1894. Concerning the protection of habitats, *see supra* para. 241.
1895. European Parliament and Council Directive 2009/31/EC on the Geological Storage of Carbon Dioxide.
1896. The CCS Directive was implemented into Danish legislation by Act No. 541 of 30 May 2011 amending the Subsoil Act (implementation of the CCS Directive, Exploration and Extraction of Geothermal Energy, Injunctions for Third-party Access to Installations for the Extraction, Treatment and Transport of Oil and Gas, etc.).

Chapter 9. GMOs

297. Uncertainty about the consequences of production, import and exports, and use of GMOs, especially the living modified organism (LMO), the need for control over their release and public concern about the consequences of release into the environment has resulted in guidelines and rules on biosafety agreed on at international level. Sustainable development of biotechnology involved in various grown crop produces (GM crops for cultivation) is one of the important issues. Veterinary vaccines containing one or more GMOs are commercially available on the international market for veterinary purposes. GM papaya is an example of production based on engineering cultivated in many places, e.g., in the US, China, Brazil, Indonesia, Mexico, Australia and Vietnam. A number of such GM papayas are resistant to the papaya ring spot virus, which is one of the major limiting factors for commercial production of papaya. Authorisation of such GMOs is highly controversial in the EU, as a number of Member States – including Denmark – have raised concerns, for example, in relation to a GM type of potato, and some Member States have invoked safeguard clauses against GMOs that have already been authorised.

GMOs are any organism – with the exception of human beings – in which the genetic material (DNA) has been altered in a way that do not occur naturally by mating and/or natural combination.[1897] There is a difference between LMOs and GMOs. The former category only includes GMOs that are capable of growing (and typically refers to agricultural crops), whereas the category of GMOs includes both such organisms and organisms which are not capable of growing. The objective is to contribute to ensuring an adequate level of protection, specifically focusing on transboundary movements of LMOs. Biosafety means a system of biological, chemical and physical conditions and measures, which prevent the accidental release of GMOs and their products into the environment and/or the transfer of genetic information by them. The international discussion on biosafety is related to the precautionary principle stated in Principle 15 of the Rio Declarations:

> Where there are threats of serious or irreversible damage, lack of full scientific certainty of the danger of a technology should not be used as a reason for postponing cost-effective measures to prevent environmental degradation.

Furthermore, Agenda 21 from the Rio Conference (1992) states that only when adequate and transparent safety and border-control procedures are in place the global community will, at large, be able to derive maximum benefit from, and be in a much better position to accept, the potential benefits and risks of biotechnology. The CBD[1898] recognises that genetic resources are under the jurisdiction and sovereignty of national governments, cf. Article 15(1). The parties to the Convention may consequently regulate access to their plant genetic resources. However, Article

1897. This definition is stated in Art. 2(2) of the European Parliament and Council Directive 2001/18/EC on the Deliberate Release into the Environment of Genetically Modified Organisms, as amended by Directive 2015/42/EU as regards the Possibility for the Member States to Restrict and Prohibit the Cultivation of Genetically Modified Organisms.

1898. Concerning the CBD, *see supra* para. 234.

15(2) places a caveat requiring resource-providing States not to impose restrictions that hinder access to genetic resources and thereby restrain conservation and the sustainable use of biodiversity. According to Article 15(3) and (7), the benefits arising from the utilisation of genetic resources as well as subsequent applications and commercialisation must be shared in a fair and equitable way with the development country providing such resources as the developing country is the country of origin. It requires benefit-sharing to financially enable developing countries and increase incentives for countries sustainably to protect their resources. Any utilisation of genetic resources generating benefits is a ground for benefit-sharing. Article 19 of the CBD includes provision to create a protocol setting out the safe transfer, handling and use of any LMO resulting from biotechnology where required. It is the background for the agreement on the Cartagena Protocol on Biosafety (from 29 January 2000). The Protocol aims to protect the local biological diversity from possible adverse impacts arising from the transboundary movement of GMOs intended for release into the environment, e.g., commercial planting of crops or trial planting in the fields for scientific research. The Protocol came into force in September 2003 with an explicit reference to Principle 15 of the Rio Declaration in Article 1. It makes it clear in Articles 10(6) and 11(8) that products from new technologies must be based on the precautionary approach and must allow developing countries to balance public health against economic benefits. The parties to the Protocol are required to take measures for the safe handling, packaging and transport of LMOs that are subject to transboundary movement. It features a set of procedures, including the PIC obligations for LMOs that are to be intentionally introduced into the environment and a more simplified PIC procedure for LMOs that are intended to be used directly as food or feed or for processing. The Protocol makes it possible for countries to ban imports of LMOs with reference to the precautionary principle.[1899] Article 23 of the Protocol sets out minimum requirements for public awareness, consultation and participation in decisions relating to LMOs. There are also intentions on bringing new rules into the Aarhus Convention (on access to information, public participation and access to justice) facilitating stronger biosafety.[1900] Textually, the amendment to the Aarhus Convention (which has not yet entered into force),[1901] that was agreed in 2005 under the second Meeting of the parties to the CBD, would represent a new wording of Article 6(11) and amend it with 'a new Article 6*bis*'.[1902] The 'Nagoya Protocol on Access to Genetic Resources and the Fair and Equitable Sharing of Benefits' was adopted in October 2010 in Nagova, Aichi

1899. Concerning the PIC procedure, *see supra* para. 28.

1900. The rights to access to environmental information and the rights to participation are described *supra* in paras 31–32.

1901. The amendment was agreed in May 2005, with the EU and its Member States joining in the consensus. The EU ratified the amendment to the Convention in 2008. However, further five ratifications are required from the parties, who were parties to the Convention at the time the amendment was adopted in order for the amendment to enter into force.

1902. This new Art. 6*bis* requires parties to provide for early and effective information and public participation prior to making decisions on whether to permit the deliberate realise of GMOs into the environment and placing on the market of GMOs. The new text of the Convention also states that the requirements should be complementary and mutually supportive of the provisions of their

Prefecture, Japan. It adds to the Convention that the regimes for access and benefit-sharing must 'contribute to the conservation of biological diversity and the sustainable use of its components', cf. Article 1 of the Protocol. The definition of the term 'utilisation of genetic resources' is established by the Protocol as 'research and development on the genetic and/or biochemical composition of genetic resources, including through the application of biotechnology as defined in Article 2 of the Convention'.

298. The Resolution on International Undertaking on Plant Genetic was adopted by the FAO Conference in 1983 as a non-legally binding agreement. A legally binding instrument was adopted by the FAO Conference as the Treaty on Plant Genetic Resources for Food and Agriculture (ITPGRFA) on 3 November 2001. This Treaty lays down specific conditions for access to a number of crop plants and their wild relatives. The rules were negotiated under the FAO's Commission on Genetic Resources with a focus on plant genetic resources as being essential to sustainable agriculture and food security. It covers 'any genetic material of plant origin of actual or potential value for food and agriculture'. It aims at guaranteeing food security through the conservation, exchange and sustainable use of the world's plant genetic resources, as well as for fair and equitable benefit-sharing arising from the use thereof – in harmony with the CBD.[1903] Each contracting party to the Treaty shall promote an integrated approach to the exploration, conservation and sustainable use of plant genetic resources for food and agriculture. The focus at the seventh session of the governing body of the ITPGRFA was on the implementation of the '2030 Agenda for Sustainable Development'.

The European Community and its Member States signed the Treaty on 6 June 2002.[1904] It was highlighted by the Commission in its proposal for the Council decision concerning the conclusion of the Treaty that the provisions of the Treaty ensure the preservation of agricultural biodiversity in harmony with the CBD.[1905] On 9 October 2017, the Council adopted conclusions, setting out the EU's position for the seventh session. It called on the governing body of the ITPGRFA to enhance the function of the existing multilateral system, expanding its scope and improve its function.

There are major differences in biotechnology regulation between various countries and in particular between the EU and the USA. Since the 1990s, the EU has followed the precautionary approach both with respect to food safety and protection of the environment. In 2003, the USA challenged EU legislation on GMOs with reference to the WTO Agreement on the Application of Sanitary and Phytosanitary Measures (the 'SPS Agreement'). In the *EC Biotec Case*, the USA argued that the

---

national biosafety framework, and consistent with the objective of the Cartagena Protocol on Biosafety. The competences for the parties to provide for exceptions, confidential information and the transparency of decision-making are stated in Annex I bis under the title 'Modalities referred to in Article 6*bis*'.

1903. Article 1(1) of the Treaty on Plant Genetic Resources for Food and Agriculture.

1904. There are 127 contracting parties to the Treaty on Plant Genetic Resources for Food and Agriculture (ITPGRFA), including the EU and its Member States. The Treaty came into force on 29 Jun. 2004.

1905. COM(2003) 602 final.

measures were affecting the approval and marketing of biotech products in an 'arbitrary and unjustifiable' manner and in conflict with the 'SPS Agreement'. The Panel Report from September 2006 found that EU had violated the 'SPS Agreement', but it also dismissed many of the claims made by the USA.[1906]

299. At EU level, the GMO rules are guided by the precautionary principle stated in the Treaty, cf. Article 191(1) TFEU. The GMO rules are based on the TFEU's substantive basis for regulation of the Internal Market (now Article 114), the agricultural issues, public health issues or environmental protection.

EU has implemented the Cartagena Protocol by the directly applicable Regulation on Transboundary Movements of GMOs,[1907] and the Regulation on Genetically Modified Food and Feed[1908] transposes the Cartagena Protocol into EU law. These Regulations are based on the internal market provisions.[1909] The first-mentioned Regulation governs unintended transboundary movements of GMOs as well as exports of GMOs to third countries. It establishes the procedures for the transboundary movement of GMOs with mandatory obligations to respect the PIC principle, information on the Biosafety Clearing House set up by the Cartagena Protocol,[1910] and requirements on identification and accompanying documentation. The last-mentioned Regulation on Genetically Modified Food and Feed puts in place a centralised, uniform and transparent procedure for all applications for placing on the market whether they concern the GMO itself or the food and feed products derived from this. It makes a distinction between: (a) exports of GMOs, where the PIC obligations must be respected; and (b) unintentional transboundary movement, where the Regulation establishes a general duty for the Member States to take appropriate measures to prevent such movements, cf. Article 14(1). If an unintended movement occurs, there is an obligation to ensure information to the public and consult the affected or potentially affected states. The Regulation applies without prejudice to the Directive on the Deliberate Release of GMOs (the GMO Directive).[1911] With respect to the rules on confidentiality, the rules of the directly applicable Regulation, the rules of the Cartagena Protocol and the rules of the Directive are comparable. By deliberate release is meant any intentional introduction into the environment of the modified organisms for which no specific containment measures

---

1906. *See* WT/DS291/R, WT/DS292/, WT/DS293.

1907. European Parliament and Council Regulation No. 1946/2003/EC on the Transboundary Movements of Genetically Modified Organisms.

1908. European Parliament and Council Regulation No. 1830/2003/EC concerning Traceability and Labelling of Genetically Modified Organisms and the Traceability of Food and Feed Products Produced from Genetically Modified Organisms. The Regulation is based on three Treaty rules: the agricultural substantive basis (now Art. 38 TFEU); the Internal Market (now Art. 114 TFEU); and the rule on public health (now Art. 168 TFEU).

1909. The legal basis is Art. 114 TFEU.

1910. The Biosafety Clearing House is a mechanism to facilitate exchange of LMO and assist the parties to better comply with their obligations under the Protocol.

1911. European Parliament and Council 2001/18/EC on the Deliberate Release of Genetically Modified Organisms. The GMO Directive is also based on the Internal Market. It includes a reference to this principle in Arts 1 and 4. The latter Article is stating that Member States must ensure that all appropriate measures are taken to avoid adverse effects on human health and environment that might arise from the deliberate release or their placing on the market of GMOs.

are used to limit their contact with people and the environment. The Directive was amended in 2015 as regards the possibility for the Member States to restrict or prohibit the cultivation of GMOs in their territory.[1912] The just-mentioned amendment has also impact on the decision-making regulated by the Regulation on Genetically Modified Food and Feed that is quite similar to – and relies on the detailed risk assessment requirements of – the GMO Directive. Together those two secondary legal instruments establish a comprehensive legal framework for the authorisation of GMOs, which is fully applicable to be used for cultivation purposes throughout the Union as seeds or other plant propagating materials ('GMOs for cultivation'). The amended Directive ensures the Member States more influence on the use of GMOs on their territory.[1913] Companies applying for an authorisation for placing GMOs on the market must file an application with the competent national authorities in the EU Member State where they first want to market the GMO. The application must be accompanied by documentation in accordance with Annex III and an environmental risk assessment in accordance with Annex II of the Directive. Some guidance notes on the risk assessment procedure are connected to Annex II.[1914] Article 4(1) of the Directive established the basic standard for granting the authorisation for a release. The decision on the application for an authorisation is taken on a case-by-case basis taking into account all the information and risk assessments provided by the applicant. Authorisation under the Regulation may only be granted if the applicant shows that the food or feed do not have adverse effects on human health, animal health or the environment.[1915] It is also assessed if the authorisation could mislead the consumers, or if it differs from the food or feed it intends to replace to such an extent that this is nutritionally a disadvantage. EFSA, the Commission and the Member States are involved in the decision-making process. During the authorisation procedure, Article 26b(1) ensures the Member States the right to demand that the geographical scope of the written consent or authorisation is adjusted to the effect that all or part of their territory is to be excluded from the use of the GMOs in the cultivation of land. Based on the new Article 26b(3), the Member States are able to ban GMO crops based on an approval list of grounds that

---

1912. European Parliament and Council Directive 2015/412/EU is amending the Deliberate Release into the Environment of Genetically Modified Organisms Directive as regards the possibility for the Member States to restrict or prohibit the cultivation of GMOs in their territory.
1913. The amendment is a result of four years of discussion that started on 13 Jul. 2010 by the Commission proposal on a co-existence regulation that grants Member States more flexibility, cf. COM(2010) 375 final. This proposal on a revision aimed to provide a legal basis for the Member States to decide on GMO cultivation on other grounds than those based on scientific assessment of environmental and health risks accepting also ethical and moral criteria. The Council did not accept this proposal and stopped the decision-making on the revision until 2012. On 12 Jun. 2014, a compromise text was accepted by the Council. On 13 Jan. 2015, the European Parliament adopted the draft on an amendment to the Directive with reference to a compromise reached between the Council and the Parliament in December 2014.
1914. Commission Guidance Document for the Risk Assessment of Genetically Modified Plants and Derived Food and Feed, 6–7 March 2003.
1915. Article 4(2) concerning food and Art. 16(2) concerning feed.

include town and country planning, land use, socio-economic impacts, co-existence, agricultural policy objectives and public policy.[1916] The current authorisation process consists of seven steps:[1917]

(1) The applicant that develops a new GMO must scientifically assess and document the human and animal health implications and environmental safety of the relevant GMO.
(2) The developer must apply for authorisation in the Member State where it wants to commercially realise the GMO.
(3) The national authority then files the documentation with the EFSA.
(4) The EFSA prepares an opinion based on a scientific risk assessment conducted by independent experts, and submits this report to the Commission and all the Member States.
(5) The demand from a Member State on a geographical restriction of the authorisation is submitted to the Commission.[1918] The restrictions or prohibitions adopted should refer to the cultivation, and not to the free circulation and import of genetically modified seeds and plant propagating materials.
(6) The Commission submits a recommendation, either to grant or refuse the authorisation, to the Standing Committee on the Food Chain and Animal Health.[1919]
(7) The Standing Committee, which is composed of Member States representatives, may accept or reject the applications by means of a qualified majority on the basis of EFSA's advice the Commission can decide on an authorisation if there is no qualified majority reached in the Standing Committee.

A new point 1a is inserted in Article 26a making it mandatory for the Member States from 3 April 2017 to take appropriate measures in border areas of their territory with the aim of avoiding possible cross-border contamination into neighbouring Member States in which the cultivation of those GMOs is prohibited unless such measures are unnecessary in the light of particular geographical conditions. The environmental policy objectives used for justification of a ban must relate to other environmental impacts than the risks to health and environment assessed during the

1916. Council of the European Union, *EU Countries get more latitude on the cultivation of GMO*, 10 December 2014.

1917. In 2010, for the first time in twelve years, the EU authorised the cultivation of a GM crop, namely BASF's Amflora potato (GM potato EH92.527-1). The application was submitted by the developer BASF (BASF is the World's largest chemical company) to the Swedish authorities. Despite this authorisation, several Member States have banned cultivation of the potato with reference to the safety clause in Art. 23 of the Directive. Following a request from the Commission, the Panel on Genetically Modified Organisms and the Panel on Biological Hazards were asked to deliver a statement the assessment of the scientific elements supporting the prohibition notified by Austria in June 2010 on the placing on the market of the potato. In 2012, the EFSA's GMO Panel concluded that to date no grounds exist that would lead to reconsideration of its opinion on the type of potato.

1918. This demand has to be sent at the latest forty-five days from the date of circulation of the assessment report under Art. 14(2) of the Directive, or from receiving the opinion of the EFSA under Arts 6(6) and 18(6) of the Regulation.

1919. The Commission normally follows the opinion of the EFSA. Art. 26 b(2) of the amended Directive is stating the time scheme and procedure to be followed by the Commission.

scientific risk assessment carried out by the EFSA. No later than 3 April 2019, the Commission must report to the European Parliament and the Council regarding the use made by the Member States on the new rules established by the amended GMO Directive, including the effectiveness of the provisions enabling the Member States to restrict or prohibit the cultivation of GMOs in all or part of their territory and the smooth functioning of the internal market.

Placing recombined pharmaceuticals that contain or consists of GMOs on the market is regulated by the Regulation on the Procedures for the Authorisation and Supervision of Medicinal Products for Human and Veterinary Use[1920] which protect human health, the health of animals and the environment.

300. The Directive on the Contained Use of Genetically Modified Microorganisms (the GMM Directive)[1921] is based on the environmental substantive basis of the Treaties, and consequently lays down the minimum standards. The Member States are permitted to take more stringent measures.[1922] The GMM Directive regulates activities involving GMMs such as genetically modified viruses or bacteria and cell cultures of higher organisms under conditions of containment.[1923]

The Directive prescribes a consent procedure when premises are used for the contained use of GMMs in situations relating to risk classification. Measures concerning the evaluation and the 'best use of biotechnology' with regard to the environment are stated in the Directive to be the guiding principle. Member States are required to take all measures necessary in order to avoid the contained use having negative consequences. Article 5 provides that the user must apply the general principles, and the appropriate containment and other protective measures set out in the Directive so as to keep workplace and environmental exposure to any genetically modified microorganisms (GMM) to the lowest reasonable practical level, and that a high level of safety is ensured. The Directive requires a minimum of containment and protection measures of a general nature. The prevention of accidents must be ensured by control measures and equipment that are checked and maintained adequately. When contained uses is to be carried out in premises for the first time, the operator is required before commencing any use to submit to the competent authorities a notification containing at least the information listed in Annex V, Part A, B, or C as appropriate, cf. Article 6. The Directive lays down a system of four risk classifications (containment categories) ranging from high risks (Class 4), moderate risks (Class 3), low risks (Class 2) and no or negligible risks (Class 1), cf. Article 7. The attribution of a particular activity to one of the risk categories must be based on a risk assessment to be performed by the operator, using the criteria laid down in Annex III. Class 3 or a higher class of contained use may not proceed

1920. European Parliament and Council Regulation No. 726/2004/EC on the Procedures for the Authorisation and Supervision of Medicinal Products for Human and Veterinary Use. The Regulation is based on two Treaty rules: the legal basis for secondary legislation on the internal market (now Art. 114 TFEU) and the legal basis for secondary legislation covering public health issues (now Art. 168 TFEU).

1921. European Parliament and Council Directive 2009/41/EC on the Contained Use of Genetically Modified Organisms.

1922. Articles 192 and 193 TFEU and concerning the use of these articles, *see supra* paras 57–58.

1923. Activities in a closed environment in which the population and the environment is limited.

without prior consent of the competent authority, which must communicate its decision in writing. Before a contained use commences, the Member States must ensure that the operator sets up an emergency plan in order to react effectively in the event of an accident. There is also an obligation to ensure that any persons at risk of being affected by an accident are informed of all aspects relating to their safety.

301. Danish legislation on GMOs is older than EU legislation. It dates back to 1986,[1924] inspired by the Recommendation on registration of some biotechnological projects,[1925] and it was replaced in 1991 by the Act on Environment and Genetic Engineering,[1926] which implemented the GMM Directive. The supplementary Danish provisions to the Transboundary Regulation on Transboundary Movements of GMOs,[1927] that transposes the Cartagena Protocol, that establishes the procedures for the transboundary movement of GMOs, are laid down in a Statutory Order[1928] under this Act. The enforcement of the provisions laid down in the Regulation concerning Traceability and Labelling of Genetically Modified Organisms and the Traceability of Food and Feed Products Produced from Genetically Modified Organisms is ensured by a Statutory Order[1929] that has its legal basis in the Danish Act on Food.[1930]

The goal of the Act on Environment and Genetic Engineering[1931] is to contribute to safeguarding nature and the environment, thus ensuring sustainable development with respect to human conditions of life and for the protection of flora and fauna with regard to the utilisation of recombinant techniques on GMOs, cf. section 1(1) of the Act. The practical administration of the provisions laid down in the Act is delegated to the EPA. The Act prohibits any import, transport, release, trade and marketing which is not in harmony with the statutory rules, cf. section 6. As this provision includes provisions on transport, it is broader than the directives. It is a framework legislation leaving a wide discretion for the Minister for the Environment in laying down the detailed provisions. The implementation has to be EU conform. Decisions on experimental release are made by the Agency on the basis of Part B of the GMO Directive.[1932] The authorities in the other Member States are allowed to comment on the projected release. The Act requires that all kinds of research involving, or resulting in, recombinant GMOs or cells, must be done in

1924. Act No. 288 of 4 June 1986 on the Environment and Genetic Engineering.
1925. Council Recommendation No. 82/472/EEC of 30 June 1982 on Registration of some Biotechnological Projects.
1926. Act. No. 356 of 6 June 1991 on Environment and Genetic Engineering.
1927. European Parliament and Council Regulation No. 1946/2003/EC on the Transboundary Movements of Genetically Modified Organisms.
1928. Statutory Order No. 34 of 19 January 2012 on Transboundary Movements of GMOs.
1929. Statutory Order No. 641 of 13 May 2015 on Penalties for Violation of Certain Regulations on Genetically Modified Food.
1930. Promulgation Order No. 999 of 2 July 2018 on Food.
1931. Promulgation Act No. 9 of 4 January 2917 on Environment and Genetic Engineering. The present version of the Act is based on the implementation also of the 2015 amendments to the GMO Directive. It was amended by Act No. 646 of 8 June 2016 on the procedure to be respected in situations in which Denmark wants to use the new competences laid down in the 2015 amendments to the GMO Directive.
1932. Concerning the GMO Directive, *see supra* para. 299.

laboratories that are classified in accordance to a new system, under strict safety and health rules, cf. section 7 of the Act and Statutory Order on the Approval of Production Using Genetically Modified Micro-organisms.[1933] Section 8 of the Act states that a production process using or resulting in recombinant GMOs or cells must be approved by the Agency before production can take place in Denmark. The most important statutory orders are the Statutory Order on Conditions related to Protection of the Environment, Nature and Health to be Respected in the Approval of GMOs,[1934] Statutory Order on Transport and Notification of the Transport of GMOs Authorised to Marketing in a Third Country,[1935] and Statutory Order on the Deliberate Release into the Environment of Genetically Modified Organisms.[1936] Products made by use of genetic technology may not be deliberately released, e.g., exposed in the open land as part of a research project or for the purpose of achieving a desired effect on the environment, without an approval from the Agency, cf. section 9(1) no. 1 of the Act.[1937] It is also mandatory to have an authorisation to 'deliberate release for the marketing of genetically modified organisms which constitute or form part of products', cf. section 9(1) no. 1 of the Act. The Agency must involve the Commission, the competent authorities in all the Member States, stakeholders, the general public and NGOs in the processing and handling of the application, cf. section 9a(1). Denmark has established a web-based system both for the regular public consultation and for the application process that is based on the digitalised self-service system. The Agency must involve the Commission, the competent authorities in all the Member States, stakeholders, the general public and NGOs in the processing and handling of the application, cf. section 9a(1). In section 2a and section 9a(2) it is stated that the Minister for the Environment in connection with an application for a license for the cultivation of a genetically modified crop must submit a recommendation on whether or not to request an exclusion from the Danish geographical area to a Committee set up by the Danish Parliament.[1938] If the Committee does not agree with the Minister's recommendation, the Committee must inform the Minister about this and the reasons for its assessment. Section 4(1) ensure that the Minister has the authority to lay down rules on temporary restriction and prohibition of cultivation of a genetically modified crop or of a group of genetically modified crops defined by crop or property if there are serious reasons for this. In this connection, the Minister must lay down rules on the temporary prohibition of sowing or planting of these genetically modified crops. The relevant GMO can be placed in the market and cultivated anywhere within the EU after the approval

---

1933. Statutory Order No. 225 of 19 March 2009 on the Approval of Production Using Genetically Modified Micro-organisms.
1934. Statutory Order No. 1387 of 25 November 2015 on Conditions related to Protection of the Environment, Nature and Health to be Respected in the Approval of GMOs. The Order has its legal basis in Act on Environment and Genetic Engineering.
1935. Statutory order No. 226 of 19 March 2009 Transport and Notification of the Transport of GMOs Authorised to Marketing in a Third Country.
1936. Statutory Order No. 37 of 19 January 2012 on the Deliberate Release into the Environment of Genetically Modified Organisms.
1937. In relation to the words 'placing on the marketing' the definition is laid down in s. 9(7) as 'making available to third parties'.
1938. These rules are based on the flexibility that the Member States were ensured by the 2015 amendments to the GMO Directive.

given by the competent authorities in a Member State. The approval must be renewed after ten years. Denmark has ensured a strong inspection by specialist inspectors of all activities in the country notified under the GMO Directive.[1939]

The Act on GMO Farming[1940] regulates the commercial production, sale and transport of GMO crops. It is the competence of the Minister for Food, Fisheries, and Equal Opportunities and Nordic Cooperation to publish statutory rules[1941] and administer those rules on a case-by-case basis. The Act establishes the legal framework for the regulation of co-existence between GMO farming and organic farming. Sections 9–12 of the Act establish a compensation system to farmers if the use of GMOs causes damage to their conventional farming activities.

1939. Commission, *Report on Experience of Member States with Directive 2009/41/EC of the European Parliament and of the Council of 6 May 2009 on the Contained Use of Genetically Modified Micro-organisms (recast) for the period 2006-2009*, COM(2012) 398 final, at 6–7.

1940. Promulgation Act No. 28 of 4 January 2017 on GMO Farming.

1941. The most important is Statutory Order No. 1559 of 11 December 2015 on Cultivation, etc. of Genetically Modified Crops.

Part III. Zoning and Land-Use Planning

Chapter 1. Introduction

302. Spatial planning can be defined as planning that seeks to protect nature and the environment while respecting the living conditions of people, plants and animals. The spatial planning system involves conflicting interests, which are balanced against each other. The level of cooperation between the nature conservation and spatial planning sectors regarding the planning of global or regional ecological networks is one of the important issues. Spatial planning is also important as a means to exercise due care in approving new developments that may be at enhanced risk of natural hazards such as storm events, flooding or erosion. In respect of open space, the goal of strategic land-use planning is to maintain the functionality of the natural environment and multi-functionality of the cultural landscape, to improve protection against hazardous situations, to preserve endangered areas from the encroachment of urban development, to reduce uneconomic use of space, all of which imply consequences for the impact of economic growth.

The protection of and restrictions on new development in coastal areas by spatial planning – considering future flood risks associated with climate change – is also an important part of the adaptation to climate change. It is critical to ensure that the spatial planning framework provides adequate protection for the natural environment from the impact of climate change, by preventing forms of development that would further compromise natural systems and by encouraging development or interventions that will enhance the resilience of the natural environment to adapt to potential climate change impacts. Therefore, those responsible for planning decisions should seek to protect and restore biological diversity, prioritise action that enhances climate change resilience by restoring natural systems, and where possible avoid actions that undermine natural processes. Land-use planning also functions as a preventive measure to reduce the hazardous effects of industrial accidents in accordance with Article 6 and Annex IV to the UNECE Convention on the Transboundary Effects of Industrial Accidents by 'public safety zone'.[1942]

In its EAPs, the EU focuses on spatial planning as an important means to avoid unnecessary increases in the need for mobility and to ensure a balance between modernisation of public services and environmental protection. However, EU legislation only ensures certain pieces of legislation as well as guidelines in relation to spatial planning. The reason for the lack of general, more explicit EU legislation in

1942. Concerning the spatial planning as an instrument in the protection against major accidents under the UNECE, *see supra* para. 202.

relation to physical planning is Article 192(2) TFEU, which states that EU initiatives on town and country planning must be decided by the Council acting unanimously.[1943] There are clear provisions in the Maritime Spatial Planning Directive (MSPD) – as its name indicates – on mandatory spatial planning.[1944] The ICZM system that was adopted in 2002 by the Council and Parliament is also relevant as a means to protect sensitive areas.[1945] The ICZM system ensures a shared responsibility for the biodiversity and other important environmental media involving all the parties concerned: maritime communities, local residents and businesses, users of recreational facilities, holidaymakers, fishing communities and environmental NGOs. Each Member State has to develop a national management strategy in consultation with all types of coastal stakeholders. The MSPD is connected to the ICZM, and it ensures a higher priority to the ecosystem approach in the decision-making situation on activities in the coastal area. Coastal communities depend on their natural environment for a variety of ecosystems services.[1946] Important EU rules on protection of the internationally protected Natura 2000 sites are laid down in the Habitats Directive, and the Wild Birds Directive ensures protection of sensitive areas against damage.[1947] Provisions relating to the protection of urban and suburban areas against projects and plans with great environmental consequences are also laid down in the EIA Directive and the SEA Directive.[1948] The legislation included in the CAP is an important means to ensure sustainable development in the rural area.[1949] There are also obligations for the Member States to set up provisions on spatial planning. Article 13 of the Directive contains obligations to ensure that major accidents are prevented, and consequences of accidents are taken into consideration in the spatial plans.[1950]

303. All infrastructure facilities – such as roads, railways and aerodromes – in Denmark are decided by an act. The Parliament decides in special situation in which new facilities are very controversial to ensure the legal basis for the facilities by a special act. It was for example the case when the Parliament passed the Act on the Establishment of Ørsted Test Centre[1951] that made it possible to erect seven test wind turbines of up to 250 m total height. It was also the case when the Parliament passed the Act on the Design and Construction of a Wild Pig Fence along the Danish-German Land Border.[1952] The last-mentioned Act made it possible for the EPA to give the Nature Protection Agency a licence to establish almost 70 km long

1943. Concerning the legislative procedure used in the EU, *see supra* para. 57.
1944. Concerning the MSPD, *see supra* para. 130.
1945. Concerning this communication, *see supra* para. 248.
1946. All coastal States have access to the EMSA Clean SEA Net mentioned in *supra* para. 133.
1947. The NATURA 2000 provisions are described *supra* in para. 241.
1948. Concerning these procedural rules, *see supra* para. 32.
1949. Concerning CAP, *see supra* para. 258.
1950. Concerning the Seveso III Directive, *see supra* para. 203.
1951. Act No. 647 of 15 June 2010 on the Establishment of the Østerild Test Centre. The Østerild Test Centre Act was amended by Act No. 159 of 1 March 2011. By its judgment of 27 June 2013, the High Court West accepted that the decision-making processes on this Act were in harmony with the EIA Directive.
1952. Act No. 694 of 8 June 2018 on the Design and Construction of a Wild Pig Fence along the Danish-German Land Border.

wild boar fence consisting of a strong steel-mat fence along the Danish-German border as a protection of Danish pigs against the spread of African swine fever. The Act is very problematic as it makes it possible to establish the fence in habitats sites, and it is also problematic under the Bern Convention and the Schengen Agreement.[1953] The work was started up in the German city Padborg in spring 2019, and it is expected to last until December 2019.

In Denmark, large development projects, such as the construction of bridges and roads, are approved in accordance with special legislative acts on the new project passed by the Parliament. Naturally, such special acts are not covered by the rules of the Planning Act. Interactions with neighbouring countries on spatial planning are rather limited partly because of the territorial isolation of Denmark.[1954] There is some cooperation with Germany on terrestrial sites crossing the border between South Denmark and Germany. Denmark, Germany and the Netherlands also cooperate under the aegis of the Trilateral Cooperation on the Protection of the Wadden Sea.[1955] There is also some cooperation with Sweden on the development of the Oresund Region.

304. Planning activities are regulated in Denmark under the Planning Act,[1956] which mainly lays down the powers of the authorities, the procedural rules and the aims and the contents of planning. The spatial planning activities regulate the use of property. Land-use planning ensures a general binding framework for case-based decision-making, usually established at different levels, including the local and regional levels, determine the character and intensity of land use and activities which may often have a major impact on environmental conditions.

The purpose of the Act, as laid down in section 1, is to ensure that the overall planning synthesises the interests of society. The planning activities must contribute to protect the country's nature and environment, so that sustainable development of society with respect to people's living conditions and the conservation of wildlife and vegetation are secured. Based on section 1(1):

> The Act aims to ensure a coherent planning that unites the social interests in land use, helps to safeguard the country's nature and environment and creates a good framework for growth and development throughout the country, so that

1953. The Act on the Design and Construction of a Wild Pig Fence has its background in a political agreement between the former liberal-conservative coalition Government and the Danish People's Party. They agreed to spend DKK 123.9 million on the efforts to protect against African swine fever, of which DKK 30 million will be provided by industry as co-financing.
1954. Concerning the geographical isolation, *see supra* para. 3.
1955. Concerning the protection of the Wattenzee under the Act on National Parks, *see supra* para. 242.
1956. Promulgation Order No. 287 of 16 April 2018 on Planning, as amended by Act No. 1714 of 27 December 2018 (concerning the spatial planning in areas with a high level of odour, dust and other sorts of air pollution, the right to use summerhouses on the island Læsø in the winter period, expropriation to ensure the fulfilment of local planning and maritime spatial planning for transport infrastructure), by Act No. 1715 of 27 December 2018 (on strategic planning for villages), and by Act No. 1712 of 27 December 2018 (concerning cancellation of the right to impose a new connection obligation, recognition of profits for heat pumps, etc.).

social development can take place on a sustainable basis with respect for human life conditions, conservation of animal and plant life and increased economic prosperity.

The Act especially aims towards, cf. section 1(2):

1) To ensure appropriate development in the whole country and in the individual administrative regions and municipalities, where the development must be based on overall planning and economic considerations; 2) the establishment and the preservation of valuable buildings, settlements, the urban environment and landscapes; 3) creating a good framework for business development and growth; 4) ensuring that the open coasts continue to comprise an important natural and landscape resource; 5) biodiversity is supported, and that pollution of air, water and soil and noise pollution is prevented; 6) involving the public in the planning process as much as possible; and 7) that the versatility of the housing composition is promoted through the possibility of planning for rental properties in the cities.

The restrictions established by the content of the spatial plans are only relevant for future changes in the actual activities and use of the properties, and the spatial plans are typically passed without economic compensation, as the State do not expropriate and take over the title of the land. It only restricts the future use of the land in various ways.

305. An important focus of the spatial planning activities is the development of possible binding frameworks for land use. The spatial planning is carried out at three levels: national planning by directives on issues of special national interests, municipal planning and local planning. The planning is focused on good business and growth conditions, as well as on the protection of the environment and nature.

Denmark is divided into five types of settlements at national level: (1) Greater Copenhagen and the Oresund Region; (2) the remaining part of Zealand; (3) Eastern Jutland; (4) town regions; and (5) small-town regions. The Ministry of Industry, Business and Financial Affairs has an active role in ensuring overall national spatial planning considerations in the municipal planning. The Danish Business Authority[1957] ensures that spatial planning is designed to ensure that a distinct difference is kept between rural, urban and summer cottage areas and that the special national planning interests are respected. The regulatory approach has been changed from an Act that, first and foremost, ensured a long-term approach on a high level of environmental protection to an Act promoting business development and growth.[1958] In

1957. It is an agency under the Ministry of Industry, Business and Financial Affairs.

1958. City planning has been developed in Denmark since 1922. The first real spatial planning measure relating to the development of cities was passed in 1949. Zoning activities were established in 1969, and the spatial planning system, composed of three regulatory levels, was established in the 1970s. The planning and zoning activities both formed part of a modernisation strategy in a Planning Act in 1991. The attention to the broader duty of care of governmental planning authorities

2015, this was done by replacing the Minister for the Environment with the Minister for Business as the political responsible minister in the former government.[1959] On 9 June 2016 a political agreement on 'A Denmark in Better Balance – Better Framework for Municipalities, Citizens and Companies throughout the Country' was made between the former coalition government, the Danish People's Party and the Social Democrats, and it was followed up by several amending acts.[1960] The Danish Business Authority is obliged to monitor trends and make use of: (a) the competence laid down in section 3 of the Act on Planning Act;[1961] (b) the competences relating to objections laid down in section 29 of the Act regarding municipal spatial planning and local planning; and/or (c) the right to complain laid down in section 59 of the Act to appeal to the Spatial Planning Appeals Board. It is a supervisory obligation for the Minister for Business to veto proposals on a municipal spatial plan and on local plan on behalf of all governmental ministers if such proposals are in conflict with national interests, cf. section 29. This competence includes only the situations in which the municipal and local draft plans are in conflict with one of the following four categories of national interests: (1) the ambitions on growth and business development; (2) binding protection of the nature and environment; (3) culture and landscape conservation; and (4) interests in national and regional facilities.[1962] A veto is binding on the municipality that receives it.

One of the above-mentioned purposes of the Planning Act is that the authorities must ensure that the inhabitants of the municipality can participate in decision-making on the content of the spatial plans, cf. section 1(2) no. 6, and the procedure described in Chapter 6 of the Act.

There are provisions in the Planning Act requiring proposals for plans at national, municipal and local levels to be presented at an early stage; the authorities must ensure that the plans are debated involving public participation; and it must be possible for citizens to make objections to the proposed plans. The citizens' objections are, however, not binding on the administrative authorities. If an authority with relevant authority – neighbour municipality, a regional council or a state authority with competence to take care of special state interests – casts a veto,[1963] the planning authority cannot itself make the final decision. If the planning authority and the authority vetoing the plan cannot find a solution, the Minister for Business takes

---

in making new land use plans to prevent forms of development that are associated with special risks has had a high priority in the Danish spatial planning, but the importance of these instruments is not as strong as it was earlier.

1959. It is now the Minister for Industry, Business and Financial Affairs.

1960. Act No. 668 of 8 June 2017 on the Modernisation of the Planning Act, Better Framework for the Municipalities, the Citizens and Business in the whole Country, Act No. 1714 of 27 December 2018 concerning Spatial Planning in Areas with a high level of Odour, Dust and other Forms of Air Pollution, the right to Use the Summer houses on the Island Læsø the whole Year, Expropriation as part of the Realisation of Local Plans and Maritime Spatial Planning for Transport Infrastructure, and Act No. 1715 of 27 December 2018 on Strategic Spatial Planning for the Development in the Villages.

1961. Concerning national spatial planning, *see infra* para. 307.

1962. Act No. 688 of 8 June 2017 ensured the Municipalities more Flexibility by a Change in the Veto Rules limiting the Competence of the Minister to Veto the Municipality Planning when significant National or Regional Interest were concerned.

1963. Concerning the veto rules, *see infra* paras 318 and 325.

over the competence to make the final decision on the plan. Thus, it is not a question of a complaint or of ex officio interference, but of a change of competence on account of disagreements between the authorities involved. The Minister also has the power to interfere ex officio. The Act is therefore part of the Danish implementation of the obligations in relation to public participation established by the second pillar of the Aarhus Convention.[1964] The Agenda 21 obligations are part of the activities regulated by the Planning Act. Before the end of the first half of the local election period, the municipal councils must publish a 'Local Agenda 21 Strategy' on their contribution to a sustainable development. The strategies must include political objectives for contributions to reduce negative effects on the environment; ensuring public participation; and ensuring horizontal coordination of decisions made in different sectors. It is mandatory to make digitalised planning documents and all other data of relevance for the use of each real estate available on the Internet for visitors using the interactive GIS software.[1965] Info on the areas that are already nature protected, and the areas that are planned to be included in the protected areas is included in another map titled 'The Digitalised Maps',[1966] that is coordinated with other maps in Plandata.dk.[1967]

SEA procedures that involve public participation have – based on the SEA Directive and implemented into Danish law by the 'SEA and EIA Act'[1968] – to be applied to all planning reports.

1964. The procedural rules are described *supra* in paras 31–32.

1965. Section 54b of the Planning Act, Statutory Order No. 735 of 13 June 2017 on the Registration of New Information on the Use and Possible Use of Real Estates based on Spatial Plans and Dispensation from the Rural Zoning, and Statutory Order No. 1191 of 24 September 2018 on the Digitalised Planregister Plandata.dk. The homepage is at https://planinfo.erhvervsstyrelsen.dk/plandatadk (in Danish – visited on 27 Aug. 2019). Included in the information are the proposal on new local plans, all the spatial plans, the decisions on zoning and data from the housing and building register (BBR).

1966. The Ministry of Industry, Business and Financial Affairs' Digitalised Green Maps is part of the general Plandata.dk.

1967. The Ministry of Business' Plandata.dk is available at http://kort.plandata.dk/spatialmap (in Danish – visited on 27 Aug. 2019).

1968. Promulgation Order No. 1225 of 25 October 2018 on Strategic Environmental Assessment of Plans and Programmes and the Environmental Assessment of Projects (the SEA and EIA Act). The SEA procedures include an evaluation of the possible impact on protected habitats, the impact on the coherence of any ecological network that might be affected by the spatial plan and other environmental, economic and social consequences of the implementation of the specific planning project, *see supra* para. 32.

Chapter 2. Spatial Planning

§1. National Spatial Planning and Flood Risk Management Plans

306. After each election of the Parliament, the Minister for Business is obliged to submit a national report on behalf of the Government. The report and, in particular, its analysis guide the spatial planning context in Greater Copenhagen, the municipal spatial development planning in other parts of Denmark as well as special issues of national interest that have to be respected in the municipal planning, cf. section 2(2) and (3) of the Planning Act.[1969]

The Minister for Industry, Business and Financial Affairs is also obliged to publish an overview of the national interests in terms of municipal planning every fourth years, cf. section 2a of the Act. This overview must include information about the interests and considerations arising from new legislation, action plans, national planning decisions and agreements between authorities. It is possible for the Minister to publish this overview in a digital form.

307. The Minister for Industry, Business and Financial Affairs has the power to lay down binding rules on the content and quality of the spatial planning and the competence to issue binding concrete national directives, cf. section 3.

To ensure the protection of national planning interests, including the quality of planning, the Minister can as part of the national planning process decide those specific conditions which form the basis of the interpretation of the provisions of the Act by municipal and local planning, cf. section 3(1) of the Act. The Minister has also the competence to publish national planning directives relating to issues of national spatial planning interests. Such directives are published as statutory orders. Before the Minister submits a national planning report or a report on the national planning interests, a proposal must be published and sent to the affected regional and municipal councils with a time limit of at least eight weeks for the submission of comments on the proposal, cf. section 22a. Digital publication of the draft national spatial plan directives is possible. The Minister has, e.g., used this competence to make a directive on the establishment of a harvesting station at Søndervig, Ringkøbing-Skjern Municipality.[1970]

The Minister may confer the legal status of a municipal plan on rules established in accordance with section 3(1) of the Act. In special cases, the Minister may also determine that development projects envisaged in a rule established in accordance with section 3(2) may be initiated without a municipal or local plan and without a permit in accordance with section 35(1) on zoning. In special situations, the Minister also has the power to decide to order the municipal councils to make use of their provisions of the Act, including their competence to produce a municipal plan or local plan with a specified content, cf. section 3(4). In situation where the legally mandated tasks of other authorities are affected, or where it is of major importance for the State, the Minister can decide to take over the authority granted to the

1969. Promulgation Act No. 287 of 16 April 2018 on Planning, *see infra* paras 307 and 310.

1970. Statutory Order No. 275 of 12 April 2018 on the Establishment of a Harvesting Station at Søndervig, Ringkøbing-Skjern Municipality.

municipal councils in accordance with the Act, cf. section 3(5). Finally, the National Parks Act allows the Minister to create parks that have to be respected as state plans in the planning hierarchy.[1971] It is also possible for the Minister to order the municipal councils to provide information for use in the national planning work, cf. section 5. For the purposes of formulating comprehensive national spatial planning, public authorities, concession holders and similar establishments must provide information as to the preparation or implementation of investigations, planning and major construction undertakings, which might be of significance to the planning.

308. The Planning Act[1972] and the Act on Assessment and Management of Floods Risks[1973] are the two acts implementing the Floods Directive[1974] into Danish law. A Statutory Order,[1975] guidelines published by the Nature Protection Agency in June 2014 and the maps on the risk areas established by the Coastal Authority establish the framework for the municipal risk management planning. There are ten areas in twenty-two municipalities that are involved in the flooding risk management. The provisions that have to be followed by the municipalities in their risk management planning are laid down in Chapter 3 of the Act on Assessment and Management of Flooding Risks and sections 6–9 of the Statutory Order on the Assessment and Management of Flood Risks.[1976]

§2. Coastal Zoning and Planning for Retail Trade

309. Planning for coastal areas is a very important issue. Chapter 2a of the Planning Act includes rules on areas near the coast, which have to be kept as free as possible of development and installations that do not need to be located near the coast. The protection was made less strong already in 2014,[1977] and again as part of the reform of the Planning Act in 2017–2018.

The main rule is that within a 3 km wide designated zone, land may only be re-designated as an urban zone if there is a specific planning-related or functional jurisdiction for location near the coast, cf. section 5a.[1978] Section 5b(1) states that it

1971. Promulgation Order No. 120 of 26 January 2017 on National Parks. Concerning this Act, *see supra* para. 241.
1972. An amendment to the Planning Act made it very clear that activities related to adaptation to climate change are accepted as a legal criterion in spatial planning. The amendment was made by Act No. 579 of 18 of June 2012 on Local Planning Risk Management.
1973. Act No. 1505 of 27 December 2009 on the Assessment and Management of Floods Risks.
1974. European Parliament and Council Directive 2007/60/EC on the Assessment and Management of Floods Risks.
1975. Statutory Order No. 894 of 21 June 2016 on the Assessment and Management of Floods Risks.
1976. The Danish implementation is described by Martin Jebens, Carlo Sorensen and Thorsten Piontkowitz, *Danish Risk Management Plans of the EU Floods Directive*, available at https://orbit.dtu.dk/ws/files/127609958/e3sconf_flood2016_23005.pdf (visited on 29 Jun. 2019).
1977. Section 5 concerning the possibility to establish special pilot projects that accepted developments in the coastal areas. It was introduced by Act No. 1529 of 27 December 2014 amending the Planning Act and the Nature Protection Act.
1978. Concerning the coastal areas that are important areas for the international protected species, *see also supra* para. 248. The coastal zone, which comprises the rural zones and summer cottage areas located in coastal areas, is shown in a map appended to the Planning Act.

is only possible to include new areas in the planning of development in rural areas at – or near to – the coast if there are special planning reasoning or a functional reasoning for establishing new facilities, building etc. in the coastal area. Harbour facilities used for transport and other very important infrastructural installations (e.g., wind turbines) can be established on land that requires the reclamation of territorial water areas and areas which are under special coastal protection (e.g., as Nature 2000 sites) in very specific situations. Establishment of all other facilities is only permitted if there are special reasons for accepting it. Holiday and leisure facilities must be located in accordance with coherent considerations arising from tourism policy and only in connection with existing urban communities or large holiday facilities. Existing coastal cottage areas must be maintained as such for holiday and leisure purposes unless there are special planning reasons or functional reasons for changing the area to urban areas, cf. section 5(1). Special rules on the possibility for the municipalities to obtain a permit from the Minister for Industry Business and Financial Affairs to plan for development of new costal cottage areas are laid down in section 5b(4) and (5). A number of conditions have been laid down for such a change, including the inclusion of existing cottage grounds that have not been utilised. It is a precondition not more than 6,000 new cottage grounds are established. The competence for the Minister to make such a national planning directive on the change of the areas to urban areas is the above-mentioned section 3.[1979] The aim of this new provision that was established in 2017 is to ensure more local flexibility in such coastal areas.[1980] Section 4a of the Act establishes another competence for the Minister to approve between 0 and 15 areas for innovative, sustainable tourism projects in the coastal zone if the areas have a significant potential for growth and development in coastal and nature tourism. Such a decision is made by the Minister on the basis of applications submitted by the municipalities after the Minister has invited them to do so. The applying municipalities must prove that there are already existing tourism activities in the area where they want to have new tourism facilities and that the application is in accordance with the coherent considerations in the municipal council for tourism and planning strategy.

310. The rules laid down in Chapter 2d of the Planning Act on retail trade that aim to ensure maintenance of shop variety in small- and medium-sized towns, as well as in individual areas in large towns, were eased by the reform of the Planning Act in 2017.[1981] The eased rules were the result of the political agreement of 9 June 2016 on ‘A Denmark in Better Balance – Better Framework for Municipalities, Citizens and Companies throughout the Country’ that was concluded to ensure a liberalisation of the retail rules in order to increase both competition and productivity.

1979. *See supra* para. 307. Such a change was ensured by Statutory Order No. 1017 of 3 July 2018 on the Transfer of Coastal Cottage Areas to Urban Areas in Fanø, Stevns, Vordingborg and Aarhus.
1980. The Planning Act was changed by Act No. 668 of 8 June 2017 as a follow-up on the political agreement of 9 June 2016 on ‘A Denmark in Better Balance – Better Framework for Municipalities, Citizens and Companies throughout the Country’.
1981. Act No. 668 of 8 June 2017 Act on amendment of the Planning Act, the Nature Protection Act and the Act on Access to Environmental Information (Modernisation of the Planning Act, Better Framework for Municipalities, Citizens and Businesses throughout the Country).

The rules require that municipal councils introduce specific statements concerning the location of large shopping centres in the municipal plans. Section 5l of the Act states that the municipal spatial planning for retail must:

1) Promote a varied store offering in small and medium-sized cities as well as in the individual neighbourhoods of the larger cities.
2) ensure that areas for retail purposes are laid out where there is good accessibility for all modes of transport, and so the transport distances associated with purchasing are limited, and
3) Create a good framework for well-functioning markets with an efficient store structure.

The plans have to ensure that new shopping facility locations are located in places with good accessibility for all types of traffic, including pedestrians, cyclists and public transport. Section 5m and 5n stipulates that new shopping areas must be located in the central part of towns or districts where there is a sufficient customer base, i.e., to make room for shops that cannot be placed in the city centre. In municipalities where no town has more than 20,000 citizens, the municipality has the competence to establish shopping areas in the central part of the district. There are no limits for non-grocery stores in the Act. For grocery shops, the maximum store size is 5,000 m^2 in city centres and district centres, cf. section 5q(1). It is possible to add 200 m^2 for staff facilities, cf. section 5q(2). The municipalities have the competence to make decisions on the maximum size in their municipal plans if the city has more than 20,000 citizens, cf. section 5p.

§3. Planning in Greater Copenhagen

311. There are special planning rules for the capital, Copenhagen, and the areas around the capital.[1982] These areas constitute a single urban region with coherent housing and labour market areas and common regional recreational and green spaces transcending the municipal boundaries. Chapter 2c of the Planning Act mandates the Minister for Industry, Business and Financial Affairs and the municipalities in Greater Copenhagen to take responsibility for the development in the Greater Copenhagen.

The Minister must be, in dialogue with the municipalities, responsible for the administrative regions and lay down the overall planning principles for the spatial development of Greater Copenhagen in concrete national planning directives, as well as a directive on the retail in this area, cf. sections 3 and 5j(2). The latest directives were passed in 2018 and 2019.[1983] Planning in this area has to be in harmony with the decision made by the Minister, and it has to be based on an assessment of development in the region as a whole and must maintain the main principles of the

1982. Included in the area are all the municipalities in the Region Capital, except Bornholm and Greve, Køge, Roskilde, Solrød and Stevns Municipalities, cf. s. 5h of the Planning Act.

1983. Statutory Order No. 1488 of 11 December 2018 on the Retail in the Capital Area and Statutory Order No. 312 of 28 March 2019 on the Spatial Planning in the Capital Area (The Finger Plan 2019).

overall 'finger city' structure, cf. section 5i and 5j. The 'finger city' structure, with the fingers as urban corridors extending radically from central Copenhagen along railway lines is the fundamental basis for urban development. The Greater Copenhagen Area is divided into four zones with different provisions for municipal planning: (1) the core urban region, where urban development and regeneration will take place within existing urban zones and consider opportunities to strengthen public transportation are encouraged; (2) the peripheral urban region (the finger city adopted in 1947) where urban development and new urban functions are located with consideration for the existing and decided infrastructure and the strengthening of public transportation; (3) the green wedges between the urban 'fingers' and across them; and (4) the rest of Greater Copenhagen, where urban development is local and takes place in connection with the municipal centres or as the completion of other urban communities.

§4. Strategic Planning for Villages

312. On 1 January 2019, a new Chapter 2b on strategic planning for villages was included in the Planning Act.[1984] The new provisions were passed with the aim of promoting growth, employment and settlement throughout the whole country. The new section 5a and 5b means that the municipalities are obliged to carry out strategic planning as part of their municipal planning in which they decide how all villages and challenged rural areas can become an attractive place for settlement. The municipalities have to cooperate with each other on this strategic planning.

§5. Municipal Plans

313. In 2003, an amendment of the Planning Act[1985] made it possible to change harbour areas and industrial areas, which were no longer used for business activities, into areas with a mixed of urban functions such as residential areas and business areas. This urban regeneration is an important aspect of the municipalities' urban policy. It has to be decided as part of the municipal planning process.[1986]

Each municipality must have a municipal plan covering a period of twelve years, cf. section 11(1) of the Act. The municipal plans must contain the objectives for development and land use in urban areas and in the countryside, and guidelines for the utilisation of rural zones and for the distribution of construction in urban and rural zone building respectively. Each municipal council must produce a municipal plan containing general guideline for matters of vital importance for the promotion

1984. It was made by two acts: Act No. 1714 and Act No. 1715 of 27 December 2018 on amendment of the Planning Act and the Maritime Spatial Planning Act.

1985. Act No. 440 of 10 June 2003 Amendment of the Planning Act (Changes of the Cities).

1986. The 2007 structural reform had the consequence that the former regional planning was incorporated in the new municipal plans by 2009, *see supra* paras 48 and 52.

of suitable urban and building development, etc., cf. section 11(2). Municipal planning can be developed into an important tool for cooperation and dialogue with citizens, neighbouring municipalities, regional councils and the State regarding the development of the municipality. These other authorities have the option to object to the planning of a municipality.[1987] If the plan is passed, it is binding on all authorities. They must respect the final municipal plan, and the municipal council must work to achieve implementation of the requirements laid down in its own municipal plans, *inter alia*, through the exercise of the powers conferred on the council by law, cf. section 12.

Municipal planning implements common national interests, as it establishes the main requirements and guidelines for land use and infrastructure in each county. It serves as part of the decision-making basis for local planning activities in the municipalities.

314. The municipal plan must contain: (a) a general structure with the overall objectives for development and land use in the municipality; (b) a framework for the content of the local plans; and (c) guidelines for the rural areas. These plans are not binding on citizens.

The municipal plans must not be contrary to the draft to or the final version of national plans or to instructions given by the Minister in accordance with section 3, cf. section 11(4) nos 1 and 2. Under section 11(4), it is also mandatory for the municipal council to respect a higher hierarchy for the following provisions and plans:

- provisions on protection of drinking water laid down in accordance with the Water Supply Act;[1988]
- Nature 2000 plans and municipal action plans on protection of Nature 2000 sites that are established under the Environmental Objectives Act,[1989] as well as the Nature 2000 plans established under the Forest Act;[1990]
- municipal flood risk management plans;[1991]
- regional councils' raw material extraction plans under the Mineral Resources Act;[1992] and
- maritime spatial plans established under the Act on Maritime Spatial Planning.[1993]

The mandatory themes to be covered by municipal planning are stated in section 11a of the Planning Act in twenty-eight points. Among these issues are:

1987. Concerning the veto competences, *see supra* para. 305 and *infra* para. 319.
1988. The provisions on protection of the drinking water and water supply areas are described *supra* in para. 115.
1989. The provisions on Nature 2000 plans in the Environmental Objectives Act are described *supra* in para. 242.
1990. The Forest Act is described *supra* in para. 276.
1991. These plans are established to ensure the implementation of the Floods Directive, *see supra* para. 107.
1992. The raw material planning is described *supra* in para. 292.
1993. Concerning the maritime spatial plans, *see supra* in para. 133.

- the designation of summer house districts and other areas for recreational purposes;
- the different areas for different use in the urban zone – including the location of areas for housing, areas for business, location of major centres, major traffic facilities and other technical installations, and major public institutions;
- the location of establishments, etc. for which special requirements must be met with regard to their location for the purpose of preventing pollution and major hazardous accidents;
- the size and location of areas reserved for agricultural purposes, including a designation and protection of especially valuable agricultural areas;
- the utilisation of land for the exploitation of stone, gravel and other natural resources in the ground;
- the protection of nature preservation interests, including the designation and protection of nature reserves especially worthy of preservation – including Nature 2000 sites;
- protection against flooding risks; and
- the implementation of directives or decisions made by the Minister for the Environment in accordance with sections 3 and 5j of the Act.

The municipal structure plan may contain guidelines concerning other matters of importance for land use and building development in the municipality, cf. section 11a. It is mandatory to include a map on the protection of Nature 2000 sites, connections to the 2000 Natura Network and other nature protection areas, cf. section 11a(2). The municipal council must follow the content of its own municipal structural plan both in its local planning and its decision-making. Apart from household and small wind turbines, such turbines may only be erected in areas designated by reservations and guidelines in the municipal plan. In its planning, the municipal council must ensure that it gives consideration to neighbouring residences, nature, the landscape, cultural-historical values, agricultural interests and the possibility of exploiting renewable energy resources.

315. In their municipal planning municipalities must establish the framework for the content of local planning in the individual parts of the municipality with regard to a list of purposes, cf. section 11b of the Planning Act.

The list contains of the following sixteen purposes: (1) the distribution of buildings according to nature and purpose of use; (2) areas with mixed city functions; (3) building conditions (including frameworks for the preservation of settlements or urban environments); (4) urban regeneration and conversion of urban areas; (5) urban transformation areas where the use of buildings and undeveloped land for business, port or similar activities must be changed for residential, institutional, center, recreational or commercial purposes compatible with residential use; (6) the supply of public and private services; (7) areas for retail purposes (including maximum gross occupancy areas for the individual stores); (8) institutions and technical facilities (including heat supply conditions); (9) areas for recreational purposes; (10) traffic infrastructure; (11) transfer of land to urban area or cottage areas; (12) the order of development and changed use of land for urban purposes, the urban redevelopment areas and cottage areas mentioned in point 5; (13) the use of water bodies and the design of water bodies in an urban conversion area within or in connection with a port's covering works; (14) the establishment of mitigation measures to protect against flooding or erosion in the planning of urban development, location of special technical facilities, altered land use, etc. in the designated areas that may be exposed to floods or erosion; (15) ensuring that commercial areas along the highway are prioritised for transport and logistics companies and other heavy-transport companies; and (16) the location of 'consequence areas' around business areas reserved for production companies and transformation areas within 'consequence areas'.

Based on section 11e it is mandatory for the municipal councils to include an explanation of the preconditions that have been decisive for the design of the municipal plan. It is also mandatory to explain the connection with other municipalities' municipal planning to ensure a coordination of the mitigation measures used to prevent flooding or erosion, etc., in the designated areas that may be exposed to floods or erosion, cf. section 11e(1) no. 14.

It is mandatory for the municipalities to include the strategic planning for villages and the new provisions on retail when they make the next revision of their municipal plan, cf. sections 11f.

316. Before the end of the first half of the election period of the municipal councils, the municipal council must publish a strategy for municipal planning and, in addition, it may publish such a strategy whenever the council considers it necessary or appropriate, cf. section 23a of the Planning Act.

The strategy must contain information about planning that has been carried out since the latest revision of the municipal plan, the municipal council's assessment and strategy for development and the council's decisions: in order to revise the municipal plan as a whole; or to revise it for special topics or areas and to adopt parts of the municipal plans for a new period of four years. The municipal council must make a draft public and set a time limit of eight weeks for submission of ideas, proposals on amendments, etc. and for comments on the published strategy, cf. section 23a(5). After the expiry of the time limit, the municipal council must take a position on the submitted comments, and it may adopt amendments in connection with this position. When a public announcement has been made, the municipal council may prepare a draft municipal plan, cf. section 23b. The council may also produce proposals to amend the municipal plans that have not been decided on in the strategy. Before such proposals are prepared, the council must solicit ideas, proposals, etc. in preparation of the planning work. It must conduct an information campaign to encourage public debate on objectives and details of the planning, cf. section 23d. Any municipal council or who demands to have his or her minority opinion on the plan proposal entered in the minutes has the same possibility in such situations as mentioned above, cf. section 24(2). When the proposal for a municipal plan supplement has been published, there is a period of public consultation. After the expiry of a time limit of eight weeks, the municipal council must take a position on the submitted comments, and it may adopt amendments in connection with this position, cf. sections 24(3) and 27.

317. Simultaneously with publication, the proposed plan and other materials must be notified to the Ministry of Industry, Business and Financial Affairs, to the official representation of other states, to the regional councils, to the neighbouring municipalities, to the local cultural environmental council where relevant and to the relevant national park fund created pursuant to the National Parks Act, sections 25 and 26. Neighbouring municipal councils can protest against another municipal's planning proposal if the proposal is of considerable importance for the development of the objecting municipality, cf. section 29b(1) of the Act.

318. A proposed plan may not be adopted in final form if the Minister for Business or another Minister, the regional councils or neighbour municipalities, in accordance with the stipulations in section 29, 29a or 29b of the Planning Act have notified the municipal council in writing about it objections to the proposal before the expiry of the time limit stated in the plan, cf. section 28. If the municipal council cannot arrive at an agreement with the objecting authority, the dispute may be brought before the Minister for Business.

If the final plan is substantially affected by the amendments, then it may not be adopted before the appropriate authorities or persons – who are not necessarily the same as those bringing about the amendments as a result of their objections – have been given the opportunity to comment on the plan. It is also mandatory to send the amended plan to the Minister for Business, cf. section 27(2) of the Act.

§6. Local Planning

319. The municipalities may adopt local plans at any time if the proposed local plan complies with the relevant municipal planning framework for the relevant local plans.

The local plans establish binding rules for the citizens on how properties in specific geographical areas may be developed and used. They differ considerably in content and extent. Some local plans regulate land use or parcelling-out and development in new urban areas; others regulate the use of specific properties, while others regulate a single theme (e.g., relating to the facades of the buildings in the relevant area). Proposals for local plans and the final local plans are the only planning instruments that have a direct and binding effect on the citizens/property owners and users in relation to future changes of the land use or changes in the buildings, cf. sections 17(1) and 18 of the Planning Act. Property owners may not act in breach of a draft to or a final local plan by changing the use of their property or by erecting new buildings in a manner that conflict with the content of the precise conditions laid down in the local plan. The local plan does not require the property owner to change the current use of the property.

320. Many major development projects require a local plan to be decided as the basis for the decision-making by the authorities on permits. The municipal council must prepare a proposal for a local plan if a developer presents a project that is in accordance with the municipal plan but which lacks the local plan that will make the project possible, cf. section 13(2) of the Act. Local plans must also be produced before the subdivision of larger areas or before major building and investment works, including demolition of buildings, are carried out.

Permits under the Building Act[1994] or under the Act on Parcelling Out of Real Estates[1995] cannot be given until the local plan has been finally adopted or approved. The municipal council may grant exemptions from the provisions of a local plan, provided such exemptions do not contradict the purpose of the plan or if the exceptions are limited in time, cf. section 19(1) of the Planning Act. More extensive exemptions may require a new local plan. The purpose of the local plan must be stated in the plan. The local plan must not contain provisions contrary to a municipal structure plan, and it must be accompanied by an account of how it fits into the municipal structure plan and to the other planning for the area, cf. section 13(1). Under section 13(1), it is mandatory for the municipal council to respect a higher hierarchy for the following provisions and plans:

- provisions on protection of drinking water laid down in accordance with the Water Supply Act;[1996]
- Nature 2000 plans and municipal action plans on protection of Nature 2000 sites that are established under the Environmental Objectives Act[1997] as well as the Nature 2000 plans established under the Forest Act;[1998]
- municipal flood risk management plans;
- regional councils' mineral resources extraction plans under the Mineral Resources Act;[1999]
- maritime spatial plans established under the Act on Maritime Spatial Planning.[2000]

321. A local plan may regulate numerous issues related to land use that often involve many conflicting interests. Based on section 15 of the Planning Act, the local plan may contain provisions on twenty-eight listed issues. Among these issues are:

- transfer of areas comprised by the plan into urban zones or summer house districts;
- the use of the area, including provisions to the effect that specified areas must be reserved for specified purposes;
- the size and delimitation of properties;
- roads, paths and other matters of importance to traffic, including rights of access to traffic areas with a view to separation of the various kinds of traffic;
- the location of tracks, pipes and transmission lines, including power supply lines;

1994. Promulgation Order No. 1178 of 23 September 2016 on Construction of Buildings.
1995. Promulgation Order No. 769 of 7 June 2018 on the Parcelling Out of Real Estates.
1996. The provisions on protection of water supply areas are described *supra* in para. 115.
1997. The provisions on Nature 2000 plans in the Environmental Objectives Act are described *supra* in para. 242.
1998. The provisions in the Forest Act are described *supra* in para. 276.
1999. Mineral resources extraction planning is described *supra* in para. 292.
2000. Concerning the maritime spatial plans, *see supra* para. 133.

- the location of buildings on the sites, including the ground level at which a building must be constructed;
- the extent and external appearance of buildings, including provisions for the regulation of the density of dwellings;
- the use of the individual buildings;
- the layout, use and maintenance of the open areas, including provisions on regulation of the ground, fences, conservation of plants and other matters pertaining to plants, and the lighting of roads and other traffic areas;
- the preservation of landscape features in connection with the development of an area allocated for urban purposes or a summer house district;
- the provision of or connection to communal facilities situated within or outside the area comprised by the plan as a condition for using new buildings;
- provision of screening facilities such as a green belt, a baffle, a wall or similar construction as a condition for bringing use new buildings into use or changed use of an area without buildings;
- the establishment of landowners' associations for new single-family house areas, industrial areas or areas for leisure-time dwellings, including landowners' compulsory membership, and concerning the right and duty of the association to be in charge of the establishment, operation and maintenance of communal areas and communal facilities;
- the preservation of existing buildings, so that buildings may only be demolished, converted or in other ways altered subject to the permission of the municipal council; keeping an area free from new buildings if buildings may entail a risk of collapsing, flooding or other damage which may involve danger to the users' life, health or property;
- the cessation of the validity of expressly mentioned negative easements if the continued validity of the easement will be contrary to the purpose of the local plan; and
- the prohibition of major building works in existing buildings, so that such works can only be carried out subject to the permission of the municipal council or if they are required by a public authority in accordance with the law.

The local plans can be very detailed. In order to ensure the implementation of decisions under section 3 of the Act, the Minister for Business may order the municipal council to produce a local plan of a special project. The Minister also has the power to produce a national directive with the same legal effects as a local plan, cf. section 3(3) of the Act.[2001] The local plan must also state whether its implementation is dependent on permits or examinations granted by authorities other than the municipal council. The local plan must be accompanied by a report describing how the local plan relates to the municipal plan and other planning in the area. The report prepared in connection with local plan proposals for development projects in coastal areas must give information about the effects on the visual environment, and justification must be presented for the structures intended to be taller than 8.5 m. In addition, the report must describe other possible conditions that are important in safeguarding the interests relating to nature and open-air recreation. The report must

2001. Concerning national spatial planning, *see supra* para. 307.

also state whether realisation of the local plan depends on permits or exemptions from other authorities than the municipal council, cf. section 16 of the Act.

322. Determination of noise-sensitive areas is also part of local planning. Such plans provide for the creation of foreclosure measures, as noisy businesses need to be protected against claims from neighbours, cf. section 15a the Planning Act.[2002] It is only possible to include areas that are affected by air pollution, odours, dust, etc., from production companies and transport facilities, etc., in the areas for residential purposes, and recreational use if the local plan contains provisions that limit the risk for neighbouring complaints, cf. section 15b.

The report accompanying a local plan proposal associated with entering into a development agreement must contain information on how the content and design of the provisions of the local plan proposal are related to the protection of the interest of the operators in the polluting companies against any risk for neighbouring complaints, cf. section 16(8).

323. The municipal council may prohibit activities that legally or in practice may be prevented by a local plan before the plan is passed, cf. section 14. The prohibition may be imposed for a period of up to one year. The municipal council must ensure a notification of the prohibition to the Land Registry as regards the property in question. However, registration is not necessary for the ban to be valid.

324. After adoption of a proposal for a local plan, the municipal council must publish the final proposal together with a brief description of its content and the legal effect of it. The council may publish alternative proposals. Any member of the council with a dissenting opinion, in relation to a proposal on the local plan, can demand the council to ensure that this opinion is included in the minutes of the municipal council. The council must simultaneously publish the dissenting opinion of the member concerned and a brief statement by that member stating his or her grounds, cf. section 24(2) of the Act.

Simultaneously with publication of the proposal, the municipal council must give notice in writing to: the owners of properties covered by the plan and the tenants and users of these properties; the owners of properties outside the area of the plan and the tenants and users of these properties to the extent to which in the opinion of the municipal council the plan is of material importance to them; locally based associations and similar associations which have asked the municipal council in writing to be informed of proposals for local plans, cf. section 26.

325. Objections to and proposed amendments to a proposal for a local plan must be sent to the municipal council within a time limit fixed by the municipal council. The hearing period must not be less than eight weeks from the date of publication,

2002. Local planning has to take into account the terms in the permits that the polluting plans have received as well as Guidelines No. 3/2003 on Noise in the Areas Transformed from Business Areas into Residential Areas ensure flexibility in relation to noise levels, *see supra* paras 192 and 312.

cf. section 23(5) of the Planning Act. If an objection against a plan from the residents in the area is made in time, the local plan proposal can be adopted no earlier than four weeks after the expiry of the opposition period, cf. section 27(1). It is possible for the municipalities to make changes to the proposal before the final decision on the content of the local plan. If the changes involve significant consequences for anyone other than those who have objected, the plan may not be adopted without such persons being given the opportunity to express their views on the plan, cf. section 27(2).

326. According to section 28(1), the Minister for Business and other ministers are guaranteed influence on local planning through a right of veto. It is mandatory for the Minister for Business to use this competence if the proposal on the local plan conflicts with the national interests[2003] or with provisions on coastal protection, cf. section 29(1)–(2). If a state authority, on the basis of the special interests, which it protects, objects to a proposal for a local plan in due time, the local municipal council cannot make a final plan until the municipal council and the authority concerned have agreed on the content of the plan. If such agreement is not arrived at, the dispute may be brought before the Minister, cf. section 28(3). The Minister may decide that the municipal council cannot finally adopt a local plan. In such a case, the plan can only have legal effect in accordance with the Act if the Minister approves the plan.

327. Immediately after the final adoption or approval of a local plan, the municipal council must ensure publication of an announcement of the final plan in accordance with rules laid down by the Minister. The announcement shall among other things state whether the plan is different from the proposal previously published, cf. section 24 of the Act. The municipal council shall further send a copy of the published announcement to the authorities, persons and institutions mentioned in sections 25–26 of the Act.

When a proposal for a local plan has been published, properties comprised by the proposal cannot be built on or used in other ways if this entails a risk of prejudicing the content of the final plan, cf. section 17 of the Act. When the public announcement of a final local plan has taken place, there may neither legally nor in practice be established a new project or any change of the use of the location unless an exemption has been granted in accordance with the rules in sections 18 and 19 of the Act.

328. The municipal council may expropriate real estate that is privately owned or private rights to real estate when the expropriation is materially important for ensuring the implementation of urban development in compliance with the municipal plan or in realising a local plan. Expropriation cancels all rights to the property unless specifically provided for otherwise, cf. section 47 of the Act. The owner has the right to full economic compensation for the expropriation.[2004]

2003. Concerning the competence of the Minister for Business, *see supra* para. 306.

2004. Concerning the right to compensation and expropriation, *see supra* paras 30, 245 and 250.

An owner of real estate that is used for agriculture, market gardening, plant nursery or fruit orchards may, if the property is in whole or in part transferred from a rural area to an urban area or summer cottage area, within four years after the transfer, demand that the municipality assumes ownership of the property or the part of it. The ownership has to be transferred for an amount to be decided by the valuation authorities pursuant to sections 47 and 50, cf. section 47a of the Planning Act.[2005] When a local plan has allocated a property or part of a property for a public purpose, the owner may demand that the municipality shall take over the property – or the relevant part thereof – against payment of compensation, cf. section 48(2) of the Act. When a local plan provides that a building may not be demolished without the permission of the municipal council, and such permission is refused, the owner may demand that the municipality take over the property against payment of compensation, cf. section 49 of the Act. The valuation authorities, pursuant to the Public Roads Act,[2006] determine the amount of economic compensation for expropriation and whether claims are justified in accordance with the above-mentioned sections, cf. section 50 of the Planning Act. It is the duty of the owner of real estate to remove any buildings and activities that constitute an infringement of the Planning Act. If the infringement consists or an unlawful use of the property, that use has to stop without compensation, cf. section 63 of the Act.

2005. Compensation to the private owner is based on the same rules that apply to expropriation of property.

2006. Promulgation Order No. 1520 of 27 December 2014 on Public Roads, as amended several times.

Chapter 3. Urban, Rural and Summer Cottage Zoning

329. Pursuant to Chapter 7 of the Planning Act, Denmark is divided into urban zones, summer cottage areas and rural zones. Based on section 34(2) of the Act, urban zones are areas allocated as building zones for urban development by an urban development plan or town planning by law and areas transferred to urban zones by a local plan. The municipal plan lays down the guidelines for the utilisation of rural zones and for the distribution of construction in urban and rural zone building respectively.

The municipal council may decide to transfer areas from an urban zone or summer cottage area to a rural zone in accordance with the municipal plan. The municipal may also, after it has received an application from the owner concerned, transfer land from an urban zone or summer cottage area to a rural zone if the transfer is unobjectionable based on planning considerations, cf. section 45 of the Act.

Decisions on permits in relation to the transfer of areas from urban zone or summer cottage areas to rural zone must not be taken by the authorities until the owners of the affected lots have had the opportunity to submit comments. The municipal council must set a time limit of at least eight weeks, for the consultation of the neighbours, cf. section 45(3) of the Act.

The municipality must pay compensation to the owners for expenses and economic losses that they incur in situations where their estates are transformed to a rural zone by means of a local plan in the interest of common interest.[2007]

330. Summer cottage areas are allocated for summer cottage development by law and areas transferred to summer cottage districts by a local plan. Approximately 15% of the coastal zone is presently built up or reserved for summer cottage districts or other holiday and leisure facilities. Property in a summer cottage area cannot be used for any other purpose than dwelling unless this has been otherwise established in a local plan or in one of the older by-laws plans that remain in force. The zone boundaries, however, are regulated by the planning.

Unless otherwise established in the local plans no more than one dwelling may be built or fitted up on an independent property in such areas without a permit from the municipal council, cf. section 39 of the Planning Act. Except for short-term holiday use, a dwelling in the summer cottage area may not be used for overnight purposes from 1 November to 1 March, unless the dwelling was used for permanent residence when the area was designed as a summer cottage area and the right to use it as a permanent residence did not lapse later because of non-use within three years, cf. sections 40 and 56 of the Act.

A person who receives a pension or has taken voluntary early retirement, a person under the unemployment benefit system or a person receiving anticipated (i.e., disability) pension in accordance with the Social Pensions Act, who owns a dwelling in a summer cottage area has a personal right to use it permanently when he or

2007. Section 46 of the Act, and concerning expropriation, *see supra* paras 30, 245 and 250.

she has owned the property for eight years. The change in the use by the mentioned persons of the dwelling to permanent residence do not require a permit, cf. section 41 of the Planning Act. It is not possible for people that is not a Danish citizen to buy a summer house without a special dispensation.[2008]

331. Rural zones are the remaining areas, cf. section 34(4) of the Planning Act. The rural zones include the countryside and many villages. The main purpose of the provisions on rural zones is to prevent sprawl in the countryside and to protect valuable landscape and biodiversity. On application by an owner, the municipal council may transfer an area from an urban zone or a summer cottage district to a rural zone if the area is next to a rural zone and the transfer is not contrary to the municipal and local spatial planning.

332. In rural zones, the owner is not allowed to make a parcelling-out or a division of land without permission from the municipal council unless the area parcelled-out is added to an existing farm, cf. section 35(1) of the Planning Act. The above-mentioned rules on parcelling-out are supplemented by rules laid down in the Act on Parcelling Out of Real Estates[2009] and Statutory Order on the Control of the Administration of Parcelling-out.[2010]

A rural permit from the municipality is generally required for the construction of buildings or a change in the use of existing buildings in the rural areas, unless the buildings are necessary for the cultivation of the property concerned as farm or forestry land or for the carrying on of fishery, cf. sections 35 and 36(1) of the Planning Act. In section 36(1) of the Act it states that a permit in accordance with section 35 is not required if the activities are included in the twenty-eight issues listed in this subsection, including: parcelling-out in accordance with the provisions of the Agricultural Property Act[2011] for joint operation with an existing agricultural property or the rules on parcelling-out of a forest property in accordance with section 6(1) nos 5 and 6 of the Agricultural Property Act. It is also relevant if the construction is commercially necessary for the relevant estate's operation as an agricultural or forestry property or for the practice of fishery or it is necessary to make it possible to explore mineral resources in the subsoil. For manure storage installations, a permit must be granted for a location desired in relation to field operations, unless important considerations related to the landscape, nature, the environment and to neighbours militate decisively against location.

2008. Denmark has a special situation under EU legislation based on a Protocol that is connected to the Lisbon Treaty. This special restriction for non-Danes to buy summer house was a compromise that Denmark made with the European Community in 1992 to ensure a Danish yes to changes in the treaty. The Danish rules are laid down in Act No. 265 of 21 March 2014 on the Acquisition of Real Estate. There is also a special Act No. 949 of 3 July 2013 on Summer Cottage and Camping regulating the ownership and rental of summer houses.
2009. Promulgation Order No. 769 of 7 June 2018 on Parcelling Out of Real Estates.
2010. Statutory Order No. 1447 of 29 November 2018 on the Control of the Administration of Parcelling-out.
2011. Promulgation Order No. 27 of 4 January 2017 on Agricultural Property.

333. A permit for parcelling-out, construction or change in the use of land that is subject to local planning obligations under section 13(2) of the Act may not be granted until the required plan has been made public, cf. section 35(2). For coastal areas, permits may only be granted if the matter for which the permit was applied is not in conflict with national planning interests in the area.

Part IV. Liability Questions

Chapter 1. Environmental Versus Civil Liability

334. It is important to make a division between environmental liability and civil liability for environmental damage. Civil liability covers traditional damage, personal injury and property damage, including economic loss, whereas environmental liability covers the ecological damage and contaminated sites. Liability for environmental damages can be defined as the instrument that make the operator that causes environmental damage or a risk for such a damage pay for the preventive and remedying of the damage.[2012] For liability to be an appropriate response, three criteria must be fulfilled: (1) there must be one or more identifiable responsible operators; (2) the damage must be concrete and quantified; and (3) there must be a causal relationship between the activities of the operator and the damage/risk of damage.

One of the first conventions on civil liability for environmental damage was the Paris Convention on third-party liability in the field of nuclear energy accidents in 1960. Other important instruments are the UNECE Convention on the Transboundary Effects of Industrial Accidents (1992), the Liability Protocol under the UNEP Basel Convention on the Control of Transboundary Movements of Hazardous Waste and Their Disposal (1999). This Protocol shall apply to damage due to incidents during a transboundary movement of hazardous waste and their disposal. The operator who notifies a transport in accordance with Article 6 of the Basel Convention shall be liable – based on strict liability – for damage until the disposal has taken possession of the waste. Thereafter, the disposer shall be liable, cf. Article 4 of the Protocol. If two or more persons are liable according to Article 4, the claimant shall have right to seek full compensation for the damage from any or all of the persons liable, cf. Article 4(6). The objective is to provide for a comprehensive regime of civil liability and for adequate and prompt compensation for damage resulting from transboundary movement of hazardous waste. The protocol is not in force. Denmark has signed it in 2000, but not ratified it. EU has not signed it. Another liability regime is established under the Cartagena Protocol on Biosafety (connected to the CBD). The Protocol is an international agreement which aims to ensure the safe handling, transport and use of LMOs resulting from modern biotechnology that may have adverse effects on biological diversity, also taking into account risks to human health (2000).[2013] The Protocol came into force in 2003. Both Denmark and the EU have ratified the Protocol.

2012. Concerning the 'polluter pays principle', *see supra* para. 28.
2013. Concerning the regulation of LMOs, *see supra* para. 297.

The conventions on civil liability for environmental damage are first and foremost conventions relating to the protection of the maritime environment. All sea are more or less interconnected, and the jurisdictions (and sovereignty) of states do not cover High Sea Areas, so it is clearly relevant to ensure common responsibility for protection of such areas. The International Convention Relating to Intervention on the High Seas in Cases of Oil Pollution Causalities was passed in 1969 in direct response to various coastal oil spill catastrophes during the 1960s, especially the Torrey Canyon Disaster in 1967. The 1969 International Convention on Civil Liability for Oil Pollution Damage (CLC) based on strict liability of accidental oil spills at sea was signed in Brussels during the IMO International Legal Conference on Maritime Pollution Damage. A new updated CLC was signed in 1992. This strict liability scheme is combined with the compulsory insurance under the International Convention on the Establishment of an International Fund (the IOPC Fund Convention).[2014] The Fund Convention applies only to damage occurring within the territory of a contracting party, including the territorial seas. The aim is to provide 'full and adequate' compensation to any person suffering from pollution damage, as defined by reference to the CLC or costs for measures to prevent or minimise such damage. The International Convention on Limitation of Liability for Maritime Claims 1976 (the 'LLMC 76') as amended by the 1996 Protocol is also relevant in this respect. The Bunker Convention was adopted on 23 March 2001 and entered into force on 21 November 2008. It aims to ensure that adequate, prompt and effective compensation is available to persons who suffer damage caused by spills of oil, when carried as fuel in ships' bunkers. The Convention on Liability and Compensation for Damage in Connection with the Carriage of Hazardous and Noxious Substances by Sea (the HNS Convention)[2015] is based on the concept established by the CLC and Fund Conventions. The HNS Convention establishes a comprehensive regime covering pollution damage from hazardous and noxious substances carried by ships, as well as the risks of fire and explosion caused by such substances. The damage includes loss of life, person injury and loss of or damage to property.

The EU is not a party to the above-mentioned IMO conventions, as the IMO only accepts sovereign states as parties to its conventions. The EU has authorised its Member States, in the interest of the EU, to ratify the conventions. Denmark has ratified all of them. The EU has also supported the fulfilment of the conventions by passing its own legislation. Under the Directive on the Insurance of Ship-owners for Maritime Claims,[2016] owners of seagoing ships flying the flag of a Member State's shipping registry and other seagoing ships entering a port of a non-Member State of 300 gross tonnage and above are required to maintain insurance or other financial securities to cover the vast majority of third-party maritime claims up to the limits

2014. The Fund Convention entered into force on 22 Aug. 1978.
2015. The HNS Convention was originally adopted in 1996. A new Convention was accepted in 2010.
2016. European Parliament and Council Directive 2009/20/EC on the Insurance of Shipowners for Maritime Claims.

of liability established by the above-mentioned 'LLMC 76'. These rules on insurance were implemented into Danish legislation by an act[2017] that amended several acts on marine security.

335. The 1993 UNECE Convention on Civil Liability for Damage Resulting from Activities Dangerous to the Environment – the Lugano Convention – introduced a European regime on environmental liability based on strict liability. However, the Convention has an insufficient number of parties and is therefore not in force.

Neither Denmark nor the EU has ratified it. The Convention was, however, an important inspiration for the EU legislative process resulting in the ELD.[2018] Denmark, Germany and the UK opposed the use of the Lugano Convention as the basis for an EU regime, partly because it differs from their own established regimes. The objectives of the Convention are: (a) to provide for adequate compensation in relation to transboundary damage; (b) to deal with grave and imminent threats of damage from dangerous activities by means of strict liability; (c) to facilitate the burden of proof for victims of pollution; and (d) to provide for strict, joint and several liability for the operator in the field under the 'polluter pays principle'. 'Operator' means the person who exercises the control over a dangerous activity. The strict liability in principle covers all types of damage caused by dangerous activities, organisms and certain waste installations or sites as well as permanent deposits of waste. The geographical scope of the Convention is determined by a provision that the incident causing damage must take place within the territory of a State party, irrespective of where the damage is suffered. Such activities in the field of dangerous substances, biotechnology and waste are further defined in the Convention using a very wide definition of dangerous activities. The Convention covers traditional damage as well as ecological damage.

336. The principle of establishing a concept of environmental liability as part of the enforcement instruments was already mentioned in the former Directive on Shipments of Hazardous Waste.[2019]

A first initiative on the environmental liability regime was a draft directive presented in 1989 to combat damage caused by waste. A second step was the Green Paper[2020] presented in 1993. The same year, some European countries signed the Lugano Convention.[2021] The primarily objective for a Community action was to improve the implementation of the 'precautionary principle' as well as the 'prevention principle' and the 'polluter pays principle', by stimulating prevention of environmental damage and by making the polluter pay for restoration of environmental

2017. The implementation into Danish law of the LLMC 76 was ensured by Act No. 251 of 30 March 2011 amending the Maritime Act, the Maritime Safety Act and the Seamen's Law (Duty of Insurance for Maritime law, Implementation of the Convention on Working Conditions in the Fisheries Sector, etc.).
2018. Concerning the Environmental Liability Directive, *see infra* para. 336.
2019. Council Directive 84/631/EEC on Shipments of Hazardous Waste. This Directive is now replaced by the Regulation 1013/2006 on Shipments of Waste.
2020. COM(93) 47 final.
2021. The Lugano Convention is mentioned *supra* in para. 335.

damage. The aim was also to create a horizontal instrument that improved the implementation and enforcement of EU environmental legislation. The secondary objective was to take away potential competition distortions in the internal market resulting from diverging national regimes. The next step made by the Commission in the process of the establishment of a general strict environmental liability regime as part of the EU environmental legislation was to publish the White Paper on 9 February 2000.[2022] With reference to this initiative and on the basis of the environmental principles codified in the Treaty, the 6EAP stated:

> Thus, one of the important tasks for the Community is to ensure those who cause injury to human health or cause damage to the environment are held responsible for their actions and that such injury and damage is prevented wherever possible.

The Commission presented its proposal on the ELD in January 2002, and in June 2003, the Council agreed in principle on a financial liability regime for environmental damage caused by companies. The Directive was finally adopted in April 2004 as an alternative to the ratification of the Lugano Convention.[2023]

The objectives of the ELD's environmental liability regime are to: (a) implement the 'polluter pays principle', the 'prevention principle' and the 'precautionary principle' enshrined in Article 191(2) TFEU;[2024] (b) strengthen the implementation of EU environmental legislation through prevention of damage to the environment (biodiversity, water and land) and where environmental damage has occurred, through remediation of damaged natural resources and services to their baseline condition at the time the damage occurred; (c) ensure that money raised through liability is used for effective restoration of the environment; and (d) reduce distortions in the Internal Market. The definition of the 'environmental damage' that is the objective of the ELD is stated in Article 2(1), and it ensures a close connection to the quality standards established in other EU directives. Environmental damage means:

(a) damage to protected species and natural habitats is any damage that has significant adverse effects on reaching or maintaining the favourable conservation status of habitats or species protected by the Habitats Directive or the Wild Birds Directive.[2025] The significance of such effects is to be assessed with reference to the baseline condition, taking account of the criteria set out in Annex I of the ELD;
(b) water damage is any damage that significantly adversely affects:

2022. COM(2000) 66 final.
2023. European Parliament and Council Directive 2004/35/EC on Environmental Liability with Regard to the Prevention and Remedying of Environmental Damage. The Directive was amended by the Directive 2006/21/EC on the Management of Waste from Extractive Industries, through the Directive 2009/31/EC on Storage of Carbon Dioxide, and through the Directive 2013/30/EU on Safety of Offshore Oil and Gas Operations.
2024. Concerning these principles as part of EU environmental law, *see* Suzanne Kingston, Veerle Heyvaert and Aleksandra Covoski, *European Environmental Law*, 2017, at 91–103.
2025. Concerning the Habitats Directive and the Wild Birds Directive, *see supra* paras 234 and 241.

(i) the ecological, chemical and/or quantitative status and/or ecological potential as defined in Directive 2000/60/EC with the exception of adverse effects where Article 4(7) of the Directive applies, or
(ii) the environmental status of the marine waters concerned, as defined in Directive 2008/56/EC, in so far as particular aspects of the environmental status of the marine environment are not already addressed through Directive 2000/60/EC; [2026]

(c) land damage is any land contamination that creates a significant risk of human health being adversely affected as a result of the direct or indirect introduction, in, on or under land, of substances, preparations, organisms or micro-organisms.

The ELD holds the operators, whose activities have caused environmental damage or an imminent threat of such damage, financially liable for remedying the environment. Imminent threat of damage means a sufficient likelihood that the environmental damage will occur in the near future as defined in Article 2(9). The definition of 'operator' in Article 2(6) is:

> any natural or legal, private or public person who operates or controls the occupational activity, or, where this is provided for in national legislation, to whom decisive economic power over the technical functioning of such an activity has been delegated, including the holder of a permit or authorisation for such an activity or the person registering or notifying such an activity.

It is the same definition of the 'operator' that is used in several other directives, including the Industrial Emission Directive.

Members States are obliged to transform the ELD into national law by means of binding rules requiring the operators to take any necessary preventive initiative and to ensure that those operators responsible for the damage/risk of damage are preventing and remedying the environment. The operators have to be demanded by national legislation to take care of the risks of environmental damage and to pay the costs of their own prevention of the damage as well as the remediating activities. They also have to pay compensation to the authorities that have used their supervisory power. To this effect, the ELD provides for two distinct but complementary liability regimes in Article 3(1):

– *Strict liability* for environmental damage caused by any of the occupational activities listed in Annex III, cf. Article 3(1)(a). The activities listed in Annex III of the EDL are activities that are regulated by EU environmental directives and regulations. Amongst the relevant activities are activities covered by the IED, the Waste Framework Directive, other waste directives, the Waste Shipment Regulative, the REACH Regulation, the GMO Directives, the Directive on Geological Storage of Carbon Dioxide and the Offshore Safety Directive.

2026. These two water directives are described *supra* in paras 103, 178, and 290.

- *Negligence liability* for damage to protected species and national habitats caused by any occupational activities other than those listed in Annex III and to any imminent threat of such damage occurring by reason of any of those activities, cf. Article 3(1)(b). The relevant occupational activities are activities carried out in the course of an economic activity, a business or an undertaking, irrespective of its private or public, profit or non-profit character.

The ELD envisages different remedial measures depending on the type of environmental damage. Annex II sets out a common framework in order to ensure the remedying of environmental damage. When it comes to damage to protected species and natural habitats as well as water damage, the competent authorities have an element of discretion in deciding which measures the responsible operator has to take, given the remedial options available to restore the damaged natural resources either in situ or elsewhere. However, the remedial measures must sufficiently make up for the environmental damage. When deciding between options, the authorities have to consider various factors, such as the effect of each option on public health and safety, the benefits for the overall environment, the costs and implementation time, the likelihood of success, the possibility of future and collateral damage, the distance to the damaged site, and social, economic and cultural concerns, as well as other relevant factors specific to the locality. The operator must bear the costs for the prevention and remedial actions taken pursuant to the ELD, and the financial security has to be assured by means of a security over property or other appropriate guarantees from the operator that has caused the damage or the imminent threat of damage, cf. Article 8(1) and (2). However, Article 8(2) accepts that during implementation of the EDL, the Member States may decide to have some exemptions from this codification of the 'polluter pays principle'. If the full costs of the prevention/remediation would be greater than the recoverable sum or if the operator cannot be found, the national authorities are allowed to decide not to seek to recover the full cost. Furthermore, under Article 8(3) the operator do not have to bear the cost when he or she can prove that the environmental damage or imminent threat of such damage: (a) was caused by a third party and occurred despite the fact that appropriate safety measures were in place; or (b) the damage resulted from compliance with a compulsory order or instruction emanating from a public authority. National exceptions from the 'polluter pays principle' are also possible pursuant to Article 8(4) that grants the Member States the choice to provide a 'permit defence' and/or a 'state-of-the-art defence'. Denmark has implemented both the 'permit defence' and the 'state-of-the-art defence' into the existing environmental acts as part of the rules on environmental liability.[2027] Article 4(2)–(4) avoids duplication with international liability legislation that is effective in the EU.[2028] The rules also avoid overlaps with the civil liability regimes that exist in Member States. The latter means that so-called traditional damage, i.e., personal injury and damage to goods and property, is dealt with under national civil liability legislation, cf. Recital 14 to the ELD. Member States may supplement the requirements of the ELD with

2027. Concerning the Danish implementation, *see infra* para. 340.
2028. Concerning the international conventions, *see supra* para. 334.

their own national liability rules, cf. Article 16(1). The Directive is without prejudice to any provisions of national regulations concerning cost allocation in cases of multiple-party-causation, in particular in relation to the apportionment of liability between the producer and the user of the product, cf. Article 9. Denmark has opted for proportionate liability.[2029]

337. The Danish law of liability and compensation for environmental damage resulting from activities dangerous to the environment is very complicated. The implementation of the ELD was achieved by means of a combination of the Environmental Damage Act[2030] and the Act on the Implementation of the ELD.[2031] These Acts entered into force on 1 July 2008 – more than one year after the ELD deadline for the implementation. Denmark opposed EU involvement in liability issues and its implementation of the rules is clearly based on a minimalist approach.

The special chapters on environmental liability that were included in the existing environmental acts establish rules on the identification of the responsible operators, the obligations on such operators to inform the supervisory authorities of any environmental damage and their obligations to avoid any environmental damage. These chapters can be found in:

- Chapter 9a (section 73a–73i) of the Environmental Protection Act;[2032]
- Chapter 11a (section 68–68h) of the Water Supply Act;[2033]
- Chapter 11a (section 60–60j) of the Watercourse Act;[2034]
- Chapter 4a (section 38a–38j) of the Contaminated Soil Act;[2035]
- Chapter 5a (section 54a–54i) of the Environmental Approval of Livestock Holdings Act;[2036]
- Chapter 11a (section 77a–77h) of the Nature Protection Act;[2037]
- Chapter 8a (section 53a–53k) of the Hunting and Wildlife Management Act;[2038]
- Chapter 3a (section 10a–10j) of the Fisheries Act;[2039]
- Chapter 7a (section 33a–33j) of the Mineral Resources Act;[2040]
- Chapter 8a (section 59a–59i) of the Forest Act;[2041]

2029. Concerning the Danish exceptions, *see infra* para. 338.
2030. Act No. 466 of 17 June 2008 on Supervision, Prevention and Remediation of Environmental Damage. It is now the Promulgation Order No. 277 of 27 March 2017 on Supervision, Prevention and Remediation of Environmental Damage. Concerning the Danish implementation by the Environmental Damage Act, *see infra* para. 341.
2031. Act No. 507 of 17 June 2008 on the Amendment of Several Environmental Acts as the Implementation of the Environmental Liability Directive.
2032. Promulgation Order No. 681 of 2 July 2019 on Environmental Protection.
2033. Promulgation Order No. 118 of 22 February 2018 on Water Supply.
2034. Promulgation Order No. 127 of 26 January 2017 on Water Courses.
2035. Promulgation Order No. 282 of 27 March 2017 on Contaminated Soil.
2036. Promulgation Order No. 520 of 1 May 2019 on Environmental Approval of Livestock Holdings.
2037. Promulgation Order No. 240 of 13 March 2019 on Nature Protection.
2038. Promulgation Order No. 265 of 21 March 2019 on Hunting and Wildlife Management.
2039. Promulgation Order No. 261 of 21 March 2019 on Fishery.
2040. Promulgation Order No. 124 of 26 January 2017 on Mineral Resources.
2041. Promulgation Order No. 315 of 28 March 2019 on Forest.

- Chapter 3a (section 25a–25i) of the Environment and Genetic Engineering Act;[2042]
- Chapter 14a (section 47a–47k) of the Environment Marine Protection Act.[2043]

There are – in harmony with the liability concepts established by the ELD – two sets of liability rules that are used in cases of environmental liability in these chapters. The supervisory authorities – in most cases the municipal councils, according to the relevant environmental acts – are responsible for the correct handling of the complicated legal rules by sorting out the environmental damage from other adverse effects. With respect to soil contamination, the competent authorities are the regional councils. The Danish EPA is the supervisory authority in cases concerning some IE activities, maritime pollution and in GMO cases. The starting point in the Danish implementation of the ELD is the 'official principle' putting the obligations to clarify the situation first and foremost on the supervisory authorities. This implementation of the ELD is not in harmony with the goals and rules of the Directive, as it does not make the operators the primarily responsible actors. According to the Ministry of Environment and Food's guidelines on how to use the environmental liability rules, there will be very few cases based on these rules per year – in the order of five to fifteen – where an adverse effect on the environment or nature involves environmental liability. Until now – eleven years after the provisions came into force in Denmark – only one case has been handled under the environmental liability rules.[2044] The vast majority of cases where an adverse effect on the environment or nature is identified are therefore handled in accordance with the traditional Danish approach to restoration and liability for pollution as described *supra*. The supervisory authorities are obliged to investigate whether the pre-existing Danish laws regulating the effects of occupational activities on the environment apply in a particular instance of damage to the environment or whether the case is covered by the special rules implementing the ELD. The use of the special rules on environmental liability are only relevant, if it is possible to find the responsible operator, and if it is possible to clarify how the adverse effect was caused, including whether it was caused by occupational activities.[2045] To assist the authorities in the very difficult adjudication of the few cases covered by the rules on environmental liability, the Ministry of Environment and Food published 'Guideline on the Definition of the Environmental Damage in the Act on Environmental Objectives'.[2046] The Act on the Implementation of the ELD has, as already mentioned above, modified several environmental acts by putting new chapters into the existing rules but

2042. Promulgation Order No. 9 of 4 January 2017 the Environment and Genetic Engineering.

2043. The rules were amended by Act No. 1499 of 23 December 2014 as an implementation of the rules in the Directive 2013/30/EU on Safety of Offshore Oil and Gas Operation regarding the operator's responsibility for major industrial incidents at the marine area, *see supra* para. 290. It is now Promulgation Order No. 1033 of 4 September 2017 on Environmental Marine Protection.

2044. On 12 December 2018, the Danish EPA agreed with Holbæk Municipality's assessment that an environmental damage to the aquatic environment was the result of fertiliser spills in the Tuse Å system in September 2018.

2045. Concerning damage caused to Nature 2000 sites by negligence, *see infra* para. 339.

2046. Guidelines No. 4/2008 on the Definition of the Environmental Damage in the Environmental Objectives Act.

without changing the existing powers of the supervisory authorities. There are rules in the new chapters on the competences of the supervisory authorities to take decisions on whether there *is not* an environmental damage, or any liable operators covered by the special environmental liability rules. Municipal councils (or in cases of soil pollution the regional council) do not have the power to take a decision stating that the damage is covered by the environmental liability rules. They must respect the competence of the Ministry of Environment and Food of Denmark to take such decisions. The local and the regional councils must halt their decision-making process and send the case to the EPA asking for a formal decision on the categorisation of damage as covered by the environmental liability rules in the special chapter of the relevant acts.[2047] The municipal councils or regional councils must present a draft decision to the Agency, which must then make a statement on the case.[2048] This Statutory Order sets out a consultation scheme for whether there is any environmental damage and who is responsible for that damage. The statement of the EPA is binding on the local and regional councils. The persons, authorities and NGOs with standing may complain about all decisions made according to these rules, including the statement made by the Agency on 'environmental damage' and on the identification of the responsible operator. The Guidelines explain that the supervisory authorities are only obliged to take a specific decision not to use the environmental liability rules, if the supervisory authority is requested to take such a decision by a company, person, authority or organisation that is entitled to complain against a final decision made under the environmental damage chapter of the relevant act. The environmental liability rules do not entail supervisory authorities to undertake more investigative or enquiring supervision than the obligations they have in normal cases.

338. Denmark uses both the exceptions accepted by Article 8(4) of the ELD – and not only as an exception from the financial responsibility. In the Danish implementation, it is an exception from all the obligations that the operator has under the ELD. The strict liability caused by agricultural activities is shared between the users (the farmers) and the manufacturers or importers in cases of certain products under Chapter 9a of the Environmental Protection Act, Chapter 5a of the Livestock Approval Act and Chapter 4a of the Contaminated Soil Act. If the adverse effects are a result of the application of pesticides, biocides, GMOs or the use of waste (e.g., the spreading of sewage sludge) or fertiliser for agricultural purposes and the farmer has followed the user guide given by the importer or producer of such materials, some special rules on the responsibility of the importer or producer established in the mentioned acts will put the strict responsibility on the importer or the producer and not on the operator of the agricultural facilities. This primarily liability for the operator (i.e., the producer or the importer) of the hazardous products means that when using the products correctly, the farmer will not be liable for any environmental damage resulting from the use of the products.

2047. *See* the list of the relevant chapters and acts, *supra* in para. 337.

2048. Statutory Order No. 1460 of 7 December 2015 on the Mandatory Hearing concerning Environmental Damage.

Section 73b(4) of the Environmental Protection Act establishes strict liability for the manufacturer and importer of products (e.g., pesticides and GMO) that cause an environmental damage. Environmental liability is only relevant, if the damage causes significant human health problems or damage to Natura 2000 sites or to the water. The liability entails that the manufacturer/importer is just as liable for environmental damage, which may be regarded as development damage, i.e., damage that has occurred as a result of emissions or activities (including use of product), that were not considered able to cause pollution according to the technical and scientific knowledge at the time when the emission or activity took place. Concerning this, cf. Article 8(4)b of the EDL. It accepts exceptions granted from the obligations of the operators to pay the costs of remedial actions based on the 'state of art defence'.[2049] In the Danish implementation, this exception is misunderstood. It is regarded as an exception from the general obligations of the operators to take any precaution into account as the strict liable individuals. The possibility of using exception from strict liability for 'development damage' is applied in the Danish rules regardless of whether the effects from the use of the product are in accordance with the conditions laid down in the licences.[2050]

According to the liability rules, strict liability is also modified if the environmental damage stems from activities accepted by statutory rules that the operator is obliged to follow. Finally, if the damage is the result of an expressly permitted effect, i.e., an expressly permitted emission or event, and the operator has showed no irresponsible behaviour, he or she will not be liable. It is the operator that has to prove the existence of such situations.[2051]

339. The negligence rules are used in cases where a non-Annex III occupational activity causes environmental damage to Natura 2000 sites as covered by the environmental liability chapters in the relevant environmental acts. The relevant acts are: the Nature Protection Act, the Forestry Act, the Hunting and Wildlife Management Act, the Tøndermarsken Act, the Mineral Resources Act, the Water Supply Act, the Watercourse Act and the Fisheries Act.[2052]

Negligence will be found where the polluter has not exercised the caution required of an individual or an enterprise in the conduct of that exact type of owner's use.[2053] In this connection, the standards that were in force at the time of the act (or failure to act) apply. Therefore, previous environmental legislation may be relevant when taking decisions on justifiability. In general, it is a condition for liability that there must be a causal relationship between the event, what gives rise to liability and the damage and that the damage is foreseeable. In the case of liability based on negligence, the delimitation between foreseen ability and negligence is particularly complicated. The negligence may consist in either action or a failure to act when the law (including a failure to obtain a licence prescribed by law) requires

2049. The provisions laid down in Art. 8(4) are mentioned *supra* in para. 336.

2050. Ministry of Environment's Guidelines No. 4/2008 on the Definition of Environmental Damage in the Act on Environmental Damages.

2051. Concerning the 'permit defense' permitted by Art. 8(4) of the EDL, *supra* para. 336.

2052. Concerning the definition of Annex III's occupational activities in the ELD, *see supra* para. 336 and concerning the relevant chapters and acts, *see supra* para. 337.

2053. Concerning negligence, *see infra* para. 344.

action. The obligation of the property owner to inspect installations, deposits, etc., that are likely to cause environmental damage depends on the likelihood of the occurrence of such damage. The harmfulness of the substances, etc. in question, the sensitivity of the Natura 2000 sites and the property owner's knowledge of technical and other conditions are likely to cause the pollution are also important. Therefore, in order for the action/inaction to be considered negligent, the actual damage must be a consequence of risky activities. In cases where there is environmental damage caused to Natura 2000 sites and where the negligence rules are the relevant basis for the supervisory authority's reaction, the EPA must assess whether the damage has been caused by negligence or not. Only in situations where there is insufficient basis to take a decision on whether the exception from the 'environmental liability' rules is applicable, the supervisory authority will, according to the rules, be able to order those responsible for the occupational activity to provide information and undertake any type of investigation, preventive measure and remedial action. If it is impossible to hold anyone liable, it is no longer relevant to consider whether the adverse effect on nature or the environment constitutes environmental damage, unless this environmental damage could affect another Member State. In such cases (i.e., where there is an adverse effect on nature or the environment that could affect another Member States, but where it is not known which particular occupational activity has caused the adverse effect), the EPA itself must clarify whether it can be determined that the effect is a consequence of negligence.

340. Strict liability applies in cases where the environmental damage is caused by 'Annex III occupational activities' under the ELD. Such activities include:

- agricultural or industrial IE activities regulated under the Environmental Approval for Livestock Holdings Act or under the Environmental Protection Act;
- handling of waste from extraction industries in accordance with the Mineral Resources Act;[2054]
- water extraction in accordance with the Water Supply Act;
- damming of water in accordance with the Watercourse Act;
- damage caused by offshore extraction of oil and gas, ships or aircraft that are dumping waste covered by the Marine Environment Act; and
- activities covered by the Environment and Genetic Engineering Act.

The Danish authorities have included activities not mentioned in Annex III in the scope of strict liability by means of the rules laid down in the Contaminated Soil Act in the concept of strict liability. They have also chosen to use the proportionate liability rules in the implementation of Article 9 of the ELD concerning the cost allocation between multiple parties.

2054. Promulgation Order No. 124 of 26 January 2017 on Mineral Resources, as amended by Act No. 427 of 18 May 2016 and Act No. 720 of 8 June 2018 as the provisions were changed to ensure the implementation of the European Parliament and Council Directive 2006/21/EC on the Management of Waste from Extractive Industries.

341. The Environmental Damage Act[2055] is only relevant in situations where the EPA states that the damage to the environment is within the scope of the ELD as implemented by the chapters in all the different environmental acts.[2056]

The objectives of the Environmental Damage Act are to ensure that the responsible polluter prevents any environmental damage or guarantee the covering of the costs of environmental damage covered by the above-mentioned environmental acts, and to guarantee payment of the costs of restoring the damaged environment, etc. The Act only applies to environmental damage or to an imminent threat caused by diffuse pollution where it is possible to establish a causal link between the damage and the individual polluter. Sections 4, 7(2) and 8(2) of the Environmental Damage Act obliges the supervisory authority to assess whether there is a situation covered by exceptions from the rules on environmental liability – and in situations covered by such an exception to stop the use of the environmental liability rules.[2057] Sections 4 and 7(2) of the Act transform the general exceptions laid down in Article 4 of the ELD into Danish law. Therefore, the Act does not cover environmental damage, or the imminent threat of such damage caused by an act in an armed conflict or a natural phenomenon of exceptional, inevitable and irresistible character. Furthermore, the Act does not apply to activities that are subject to the international marine conventions ratified by Denmark (the Convention on Civil Liability for Oil Pollution, the Fund Convention, the Bunker Convention and the HNS Convention), or nuclear risks, etc.[2058] The 'occupational activities' that are covered by the strict liability concepts are defined in section 5(2) of the Act using the same definition as the one established in Article 3(10) and Annex III to the ELD. The Act uses the definitions of 'environmental damage' as it is defined in the ELD. The responsible individual actors are defined in section 12 as 'the addressee to the decision of the administrative authority'. This Danish focus on the addressee of the administrative orders is not a correct implementation of the ELD as the Directive is based on the concept of the responsible 'operator'.[2059] The addressee is obliged to cover the costs of the supervisory authority in accordance with the rules in the Statutory Order on the Costs Covering in Connection with Administration and Supervision in Accordance with the Environmental Damage Act.[2060] Pursuant to Chapter 2 of the Act, the responsible operator is required to have an insurance cover or other adequate guarantees for the cover of the cost of the Ministry of Environment and Food of Denmark. The 'baseline condition' for natural resources is defined in conformity with Article 2(14) of the ELD in section 16 of the Act as the conditions of the natural resources and their exploitation opportunities were at the time when the

---

2055. Promulgation Order No. 277 of 27 March 2017 on Supervision, Prevention and Remediation of Environmental Damage.

2056. Concerning the Danish environmental acts that have chapters on environmental liability, *see supra* para. 337.

2057. Concerning the exceptions in the Danish legislation, *see supra* para. 338.

2058. Concerning Art. 4 of the ELD, *see supra* para. 336.

2059. It is not always clear for the authorities who is the responsible operators based on the criteria established by the ELD, and if the authorities choose to send their orders to other actors than the 'operators', the addresses for the orders are then based on the Danish rules.

2060. Statutory Order No. 1337 of 25 November 2015 on the Costs Covering in Connection with Administration and Supervision in Accordance with the Environmental Damage Act.

damage occurred. Preventive measures are defined in section 13 in identical terms to those used in Article 2(10) of the ELD. The definitions of 'remedial measures', 'natural resource' and 'services' laid down in sections 14, 16 and 17 relating to internationally protected species and habitats (Natura 2000 sites) also follow the definitions in the ELD. The definition of remedial measures in relation to soil pollution is focused on removal of the pollution and rehabilitation or equivalent alternatives on the same basis as the ordinary Danish rules in the Contaminated Soil Act.[2061]

Damage caused by activities that are the consequences of necessary water management activities made on the basis of water management planning is not covered by the Environmental Damage Act, cf. sections 8(2) and 17 of that Act.[2062] In such cases, the rules laid down in the original text of the relevant environmental acts on the competences of the supervision authorities must be followed.[2063] It follows from section 3 that the Act do not apply to environmental damage if more than thirty years have passed since the emission, event, or incident that led to the environmental damage. This limitation period comes from Article 17 of the ELD. The limitation period in section 48 of five years during which the supervisory authority may initiate recovery procedures is an implementation of Article 10 of the ELD.

2061. Concerning contaminated soil, *see supra* paras 170–187.
2062. Concerning the environmental Damage Act, *see supra* para. 242.
2063. Concerning the list on relevant chapters and acts, *see supra* para. 337.

Chapter 2. Civil Liability

342. The Product Liability Directive[2064] was the first EU directive on strict civil liability. It is a minimum harmonisation directive, and it deals with strict liability for defective products that have been put into circulation. It states that the producers are liable for damage caused by defective products. Article 3(1) of the Directive defines 'producer' as being the manufacturer of a finished product, the producer of any raw material or the manufacturer of a component part or any person who by putting a name, trademark or other distinguishing feature on the product presents himself as its producer. The injured person must prove the damage, the defect in the product and the causal relationship between the damage and the defect. The word 'damage' means damage caused by death or by personal injury, as well as damage to an item of property intended for private use or consumption other than the defective product, with a lower threshold of EUR 500.

The Danish Product Liability Act[2065] imposes strict liability on producers for any injury to a third party caused by a defect in their product and implements of the Directive. The Act provides that liability to pay damages becomes statute-barred after three years from the date on which the injured party became aware or ought to have become aware of: (a) the damage; (b) the defect; and (c) the name and residence of the producer in question. The three-year limitation rule is supplemented by a rule that the liability for damages expires after ten years from the date on which the producer puts the product into circulation.

343. The Danish Act on Strict Liability for Pollution Cost by Heavily Polluting Activities[2066] is private tort law. It is based on a very traditional liability concept.[2067] The Act came into force in July 1994. It is based on the recommendation in the Report of the Committee constituted by the Minister of Justice on 'Liability for Heavily Polluting Activities.[2068] The Act has only been used in very few cases.

The Act stipulates that the liability for environmental damages caused by particularly polluting enterprises will be adjudicated on an objective basis (i.e., without putting the blame on the enterprise), as it introduces a regime of strict liability in respect to damage caused by activities on real estate. Strict liability will only apply in relation to the industrial or public activities included in the list attached to the Act. The strict liability do not apply to all the polluting activities of such enterprises, rather only to the types of activities that have caused the enterprise to be included in the list in 1995.[2069] Liability is triggered if there is an impact on the environment (air, water, soil) coming from an establishment and causing death, bodily injury or damage to property. Pure economic loss is recoverable under the

2064. Council Directive 85/374/EEC on the Approximation of the Laws, Regulations and Administrative Provisions of the Member States concerning Liability for Defect Products.
2065. Promulgation Order No. 261 of 20 March 2007 on Product Liability.
2066. Promulgation Order No. 994 of 9 September 2014 on Strict Liability for Pollution Costs by Heavily Polluting Activities.
2067. This Act is *not* related to the Environmental Liability Directive.
2068. Committee Report No. 1237/1992 on Liability for Heavily Polluting Activities.
2069. For example, in relation to agricultural holdings only matters relating to the manure tank can justify strict liability.

Act. It remains the case that a balancing exercise will be necessary: weighing the cost of restoration against the ecological gains achieved by the restoration. The Act may help owners of property to restore their land: it does not deal with the situation where there are no proprietary interests in the harmed natural resources unless it is the environmental authorities that restore the land and ask for compensation. Based on the Act, the polluter responsible may have to pay compensation for restoration of the environment made by the authorities; however, the cost of restoration should not be considered to be out of proportion merely because it exceeds the economic value of the damaged natural resources. The injured party must prove that the damage was caused by someone's act, so all the other aspects in relation to proving causation, etc. is still on the plaintiff. Under the Act, the period of limitation is thirty years from the time when the action was performed and five years from such time as the injured party became aware of the pollution. There are very few court cases based on this Act.[2070] The Supreme Court made a principal judgment in 2017 that is very difficult to understand.[2071]

There is a specific set of liability rules in relation to claims for damages caused by atomic installations considered in Act on Liability for Nuclear Damage.[2072] Section 7 of this Act imposes strict liability on the owners of nuclear plants for damage caused by nuclear accidents. However, this liability regime is of little relevance since there are no nuclear power plants in Denmark, only nuclear research at the Danish Technology University. The rules are in accordance with the Paris Convention on third party liability and supplementary conventions. The Act also covers laboratories, where there are only small quantities of nuclear material and also any practices dealing with the extraction of nuclear fuel and treatment of non-irradiated natural uranium, cf. section 1 of the Act.

344. Negligence is the most important legal basis in Denmark as the courts use this unwritten law in most of the cases concerning economic loss caused by pollution. Demonstrating liability in environmental cases on the basis of the negligence rules involves certain difficulties.[2073]

The injured person has the burden of proving that the damage has caused the harm due to wrongful behaviour. Another difficulty is to establish the causal link between the damage and the particular activity. The distance between the affected area and the activity is one determining factor. The time lag between the interference and the materialisation of damage is another challenge for the injured party

2070. The Supreme Court did not use the Act on Strict Liability for Pollution Cost by Heavily Polluting Activities in a judgment published in the Danish Law Reports 2002, at 780.

2071. The West High Court used the Act in a judgment of 7 May 2015 (V.L. B-0140-14), which the Supreme Court uphold in 2017, *see* Danish Weekly Law Reports 2017, at 2510. The case concerns the fact that the content of heavy metal cadmium in the sludge deposited at a water utility's waste water purification plant exceeded the limit value for the application of sludge on agricultural land. The case concerned the question of whether a district heating plant that was one of the responsible polluters should bear all the additional costs of disposal of the sludge to a waste incineration plant in Germany. The answer of the Supreme Court was 'yes'. The Court stated that the district heating plant should compensate the loss of the water utility.

2072. Promulgation Order No. 993 of 9 September 2014 on Compensation for Nuclear Damage. Statutory Order No. 467 of 16 September 1974 brought the Act into force.

2073. Concerning the demonstration of negligence, *see supra* para. 339.

who must prove liability. An additional problem relating to establishing liability arises when the effects from various polluters cumulate, making it almost impossible to link cause and effect, since the private law principle do not accept joint and several liability. If the person has suffered the damage or a person, for whom the person who suffered damage is responsible, has by his or her own fault contributed to the damage, the compensation may be reduced or disallowed having regard to all the circumstances. Compensation of loss or damage caused by impairment of the environment is limited to the costs of measures of reinstatement or preventive measures actually undertaken or to be undertaken.

Under the Environmental Protection Act, special rules were already drawn up in the 1970s to cover the risk of pollution caused by leaking oil tanks. The courts' case law on liability for oil tanks has, however, not accepted the statutory rules as clear enough to make a change from traditional negligence thinking. In its judgment of 18 June 1991,[2074] the Danish Supreme Court ruled that an innocent property owner, who had never been the user of the tank, could not in accordance with the Environmental Protection Act be ordered to pay the cost of removing the polluted soil caused by the tank unless otherwise stipulated by clear legal rules. On 3 February 1998, in another judgment the Supreme Court ruled that a property owner who had been the user of the tank could not be ordered to pay either, provided he or she had not acted against the normal standard of good behaviour (known as the 'culpa rules').[2075] In the just-mentioned cases and in other cases, the Danish Supreme Court has stated that the duty to pay restoration costs depends on whether or not any clear legislation specifies strict liability for harm to the environment (the principle of legality). This is the case even though environmental statutes frequently attempt to counteract environmental risks. Such judgments have produced regulatory irrationality. In practice, the court judgments had as a consequence that no Danish environmental authorities wanted to use their power to demand the polluter to clean up polluted soil until the Act on Contaminated Soil came into force.[2076] Neither have they wanted to restore the polluted environment themselves on the basis of these rules as it is very doubtful whether the polluter has any duty to pay the restoration costs. The current rules on soil pollution laid down in the Soil Contamination Act were passed to solve the problems in relation to the public expenditure in such cases.[2077] Actions for compensation under the 'culpa rules' are subject to a limitation period of typically three years from the date on which the claimant knew or ought to have known of the damage. In cases of personal injury or death caused by environmental pollution, the limitation period is thirty years under the Statute of Limitations Act.[2078]

Compensation claims can also be based on the so-called law of nuisance.[2079] This is the unwritten court-made legislation handling the conflicting interests between neighbours by means of a so-called tolerance of nuisance targets. The owners' right

2074. This judgment is published in the Danish Weekly Law Reports 1991, at 674.
2075. This judgment is published in the Danish Weekly Law Reports 1998, at 549.
2076. Concerning the Contaminated Soil Act, *see supra* para. 183.
2077. Concerning the Contaminated Soil Act, *see supra* paras 170–187.
2078. Promulgation Order No. 1238 of 9 September 2015 on Statute of Limitations.
2079. Concerning the unwritten law of nuisance, *see supra* para. 34.

to enjoy their properties is restricted by their neighbours' right to enjoy their surroundings. Thus, an owner is not allowed to exercise or abuse his or her right of ownership to such an extent that the activities/change of the use of the property interfere seriously (above the 'tolerance limits') with the comfort and convenience or quality of life of his or her neighbours. Based on this, no neighbour is allowed to initiate activities that may result in unreasonable or unnecessary damage or nuisance on a neighbouring property. The source of complaints might not amount to nuisance if the activity is deemed to be typical in the relevant local area. A breach of the tolerance limit (nuisance) has several consequences. Notably, it gives the neighbour a right to compensation (damages) on the basis of strict liability, and it may lead to an injunction. The right to compensation do not depend on the activity being unlawful: even activities that have been formally approved or accepted by a local plan can be assessed as an activity that goes beyond the tolerance limit.

When deciding whether something is unreasonable or unnecessary, importance should be attached to what is technically or economically feasible. The courts have on this basis generally rejected nuisance law against wind turbines on the grounds that the interference does not exceed what is to be expected as a result of general societal development. If the general requirements of a minimum distance to neighbours, noise standards, etc. specifically established for wind turbines are followed by the owner of the turbines, this will be enough to protect him or her against the compensation claim.[2080] Compensation to the neighbours of the wind turbines was therefore rejected in this judgment.

2080. This judgment of the Danish Supreme Court is published in the Danish Weekly Law Reports 2009, at 2680.

Chapter 3. Criminal Liability

345. Environmental crimes are acts that breach environmental legislation and cause significant harm or risk to the environment. Some crimes under environmental law have a cross-border character. On 4 November 1998, the Council of Europe (UNECE) adopted the Convention on the Protection of the Environment through criminal law. The convention that is not in force obliges the parties to introduce special provisions on enforcement by criminal actions. The sanctions available must include imprisonment and pecuniary sanctions and may as an option include reinstatement of the environment. EU did not take part in the Convention as it only accepts national states as parties.[2081] On 4 November 1998, Denmark signed the Convention, but Denmark has not ratified it. As an alternative to this Convention, Denmark presented a proposal for a third-pillar framework decision to be adopted by the Council of the EU. However, the Commission did not agree that this was the right solution and instead decided to present a proposal for a new directive in 2001.

In January 2003, on the initiative of Denmark, the Council adopted the Framework Decision on the Protection of the Environment through Criminal Law.[2082] The CJEU annulled this Decision for infringing the Treaty,[2083] holding that on account of both their aim and content, several articles of the Decision had as their main purpose the protection of the environment and could have been properly adopted on the basis of the environmental provisions of the Treaty (now Article 192 TFEU). As a follow-up to that judgment, preparation of a special directive on criminal enforcement was started in 2007. It resulted in the Directive on the Protection of the Environment through Criminal Law.[2084] The objective of this Directive is to ensure more effective protection of the environment by the enforcement of existing EU environmental rules in criminal cases. The key responsibility for ensuring effective implementation and enforcement of EU legislation lies with the national authorities and very often at local level. The obligation for the Member States to adopt measures only relates to the provisions of the legislation listed in Annex A to the Directive, which oblige Member States, when implementing that legislation, to provide for prohibitive measures. It is mandatory to provide for criminal penalties in national legislation in respect of serious infringements of provisions of EU environmental law. If it is necessary for the achievement of the objectives, the EU institutions can, on the basis of CJEU case law, oblige Member States to provide for criminal sanctions, even where EU law do not expressly provide for such sanctions. Provisions on penalties are also included in EU secondary legislation on different subjects. By way of example may be mentioned Article 34 of the Offshore Safety Directive[2085] stating that the Member States must lay down rules on penalties applicable to infringements of national provisions adopted pursuant to this Directive. They must take all measures necessary to ensure that the provisions are transformed into

2081. Articles 13(1) and 14 of the Convention.
2082. Council Framework Decision No. 2003/80/JHA on the Protection of the Environment through Criminal Law.
2083. C-176/03 *Commission v. Council.*
2084. European Parliament and Council Directive 2008/99/EC on the Protection of the Environment through Criminal Law.
2085. Concerning the Offshore Safety Directive, *see supra* para. 290.

national law.[2086] The penalties that the Member States use as sanctions must be effective, proportionate and dissuasive. They must notify the Commission without delay of any subsequent amendment affecting them.

346. Each of the Danish environmental acts has sections on penalties for breaches of its rules and indications on the level of sanctions. Enterprises and other legal persons may incur criminal liability under these special environmental rules as well as under the Criminal Code.[2087] The latter includes special rules in its section 196 on the sanctions for the most serious types of environmental crime and establishes the legal basis for considerably stricter penalties for this type of crime. The procedural remedies contained in the Administration of Justice Act[2088] apply in actions brought by the public prosecutor.

The Danish municipalities that are the supervisory authorities in most cases are important actors in enforcement of the legislation in Denmark.[2089] The decision to start a case against a company or an institution is made by the supervisory authorities that contact the police and ask them to bring the case to the courts. The courts decide on the level of sanctions. In the last part of their content, the environmental acts include provisions on criminal sanctions. Unless a heavier penalty is due pursuant to the Criminal Code, the penalty for the criminal environmental activities is only a fine. Imprisonment of up to four years is possible under the Criminal Code Act if a breach is committed repeatedly or for gross negligence, or results in extreme damage to the environment. The fines set so far for environmental crimes have not been very high. Up to now, there have been no cases where the person responsible for the criminal activities has been imprisoned for a breach of the environmental legislation. In the event of very serious violations of the Environmental Protection Act, the courts may dismiss an operator from the right to operate a company subject to approval under this Act. The actual or intentional financial gain – or savings – that the responsible person(s) have planned to get from the illegal action is also relevant for the use of sanction. There are also provisions laying down that profit resulting from criminal activity may be confiscated in accordance with the rules laid down in the environmental acts with reference to the Criminal Code. Confiscation is possible even if the breach did not result in damage to the environment or a risk of such damage. If profits cannot be confiscated, the process of setting fines or the inclusion of additional fines will take this into consideration. The limitation period in relation to criminal liability is stated in the specific rules on criminal sanctions and is normally five years. If the State or a local authority commits a breach, it will also be treated by the just-mentioned rules. Therefore, a fine may be imposed on the State or the local authority in question.

2086. The Member States had to notify those national provisions to the Commission by 19 July 2015.
2087. Promulgation Order No. 1156 of 20 September 2018 on the Criminal Code, as amended.
2088. Promulgation Order No. 1284 of 14 November 2018 on Administration of Justice, as amended.
2089. Concerning the public actors taking part in the sanctioning, *see infra* para. 346.

Part V. Access to Justice

Chapter 1. General

347. The UNECE Convention on Access to Information, Public Participation and Access to Justice in Environmental Matters (the Aarhus Convention) marks a definitive step forward in the field of environmental democracy and human protection as it seeks to protect the right of every person of present and future generations to live in an environment adequate to his or her health and well-being. To do so, it sets minimum standards empowering members of the public and the 'public concerned' to hold public authorities to account by providing tools to the following three pillars: (a) access to environmental information; (b) participation in decision-making; and (c) access to justice in matters relating to the environment.[2090] Both the EU[2091] and Denmark[2092] are parties to this Convention.

The access to justice is called the 'third pillar' of the Convention. Article 9(1) states that each party to the Convention shall, within the framework of its national legislation, ensure access to justice for any individuals with a direct, personal and legitimate interest as well as for the 'public concerned' to a review procedure before a court of law or another independent and impartial body established by law. The Convention determines which issues are covered by the right to have the validity of the decision resolved. Any person that has not received the requested environmental information – as such a right is established by Article 4 – has a legal right to a review of this decision.[2093] Under Article 9(2), the parties also have to ensure that the 'public concerned'[2094] and any person with a direct, personal and legitimate interest have access to a review procedure to challenge the substantive and procedural legality of acts and omissions relating to operating licences for specific activities for which public participation is required under Article 6 of the Convention. The same is the case in connection with other relevant provisions of this Convention,

2090. Concerning the Aarhus Convention as an important 'mixed agreement' on procedural rights. The rights to environmental information and public participations are described *supra* in paras 31–32.

2091. On 17 February 2005 Council ratified the Convention on behalf of the European Community with a reservation for the obligations resulting from Art. 9(3).

2092. On 29 September 2000, Denmark ratified the Convention with reservations for the Faroe Islands and Greenland.

2093. The rights to environmental information is described *supra* in para. 31.

2094. The term 'public concerned' means: the public affected or likely to be affected, or having an interest in, the environmental decision-making. For the purposes of this definition, NGOs promoting environmental protection and meeting any requirements under national law are deemed to have an interest, cf. Art. 2(5). This term is not used in Danish legislation, *see supra* in para. 32.

including the rules on public participation in plans and programmes, cf. Article 9(2) *in fine*. Furthermore, the rules on access to justice also cover situations where there are significant problems with enforcement of EU or national environmental legislation, cf. Article 9(3). Pursuant to this subsection of Article 9, in cases where Article 9(1) or Article 9(2) does not apply the parties to the Convention have to ensure that the members of the 'public concerned' have access to an administrative or judicial procedure. Under Article 9(4), it is mandatory for the parties to ensure timely, adequate and effective remedies, including relief as appropriate. The process shall be fair and not prohibitively expensive.

In some cases presented by the NGOs to the ACCC, the Committee has found that neither the TFEU, as interpreted by the CJEU, nor the Aarhus Regulation grants sufficient administrative or judicial redress as required by the Convention in cases concerning the policy and decisions of the EU institutions.[2095] The ACCC recommended that the CJEU should modify its case law on standing before the EU Courts, or in the alternative, that the EU should amend the Aarhus Regulation, or should adopt new legislation.[2096]

The access to justice obligations have been implemented into EU legislation with consequences for the European Parliament, the Council, the Commission and other bodies at EU level by Article 10 of the Aarhus Regulation. The Article states that NGOs which meet the criteria set out in Article 11 are entitled to make a request for an 'internal review procedure' whereby those who meet the criteria can request an EU institution or body to reconsider an 'administrative act' under EU environmental law. Proceedings before the CJEU in cases where the EU institution or body fails to act in accordance with Article 10(1)–(2) are also granted to the NGOs by Article 12 of the Regulation. The general substantive basis for individuals' access to the CJEU against the EU institutions is found in Article 263(4) TFEU.[2097] It allows natural and legal persons to challenge decisions of the EU institutions addressed to them and decisions which take the form of regulations provided they are of direct and individual concern to them.[2098] Under Article 41(1) of the Charter, everyone has the right to have his or her affairs handled impartially, fairly and within a reasonable time by the institutions and bodies of the EU. But, this right has to be read in the light of Article 263(4) TFEU – it cannot go beyond, cf. Article 52 of the Charter.

348. The implementation by the CJEU of the access to justice obligations as these obligations must be respected by the Member States is in harmony with

2095. *See* the Aarhus Convention Compliance Committee's assessment of 17 March 2017 in Case ACCC/C/2008/32.

2096. At the meeting of the parties under the Convention in September 2017, no agreement was reached between the ACCC and the EU on the findings, and the adoption of a decision was postponed until the meeting in 2021. On 11 Jun. 2018, a draft Council decision was published with a request to the Commission asking it to submit a study on the Union's option for addressing the findings of the ACCC and, if appropriate, in view of the outcome of the study, a proposal for a Regulation amending the Aarhus Regulation.

2097. Natural and legal persons (NGOs, companies and citizens) are 'non-privileged applicants' under the Treaty.

2098. The access to justice is based on the 'individual concern' criteria – the classic rules of 'standing'.

Article 9 of the Convention. It is well-established case law that the detailed procedural rules governing actions for safeguarding an individual's right under EU law must not be less favourable than those governing similar domestic actions (principle of equivalence) and must not make impossible or excessively difficult in practice to exercise rights conferred by EU law (the 'principle of effectiveness'). The Danish administrative appeal bodies as well as the courts have an obligation to follow this case law.

Article 9 of the Aarhus Convention has been implemented into EU law through Article 6 of the Access to the Environmental Information Directive, Article 11 of the EIA Directive and Article 25 of the IED for the review of legality of certain acts and omissions at national level. In 2003, the Commission presented a proposal for a Directive on Access to Justice,[2099] establishing an obligation for the Member States to guarantee that the 'public concerned' might initiate administrative or judicial proceedings. Qualified entities in a Member State were also planned to have recourse to such proceedings in another Member State, but the proposal was not accepted by the Council. The proposal was withdrawn in 2014 owing to resistance at Member State level. The interpretation by the Danish authorities (and the national authorities in other Member States) of Article 9 of the Convention's criteria on 'sufficient interest' and 'impairment of a right', etc., has to be in harmony with the EIA Directive, the IED and case law of the CJEU[2100] that is focusing on the fulfilment of the goals of the Aarhus Convention, which is to give the 'public concerned' a wide access to justice.[2101] Moreover, the CJEU has stated that the procedural rights serve the purpose of ensuring the effective implementation of EU environmental law at national level.[2102] Case law makes it clear that the right to a review covers both the substantive and the procedural legality of the contested decision in its entirety.[2103] In the CJEU's interpretation of Article 9(2) of the Convention with consequences for the national authorities' interpretation of the concept of access to justice, the Court has stated that the NGOs must have access to a review procedure by national courts or other impartial bodies established by national law to challenge the decision by which a national authority has given a ruling on a request for development consent.[2104] The Member States should allow environmental NGOs to have access to justice, given that they are deemed under EU secondary legislation to have 'sufficient interest' or 'rights which may be impaired', depending on which one of the two admissibility criteria for the court action is used in the national procedural

2099. COM(2003) 624 final.

2100. Concerning the CJEU case law on access to justice, *see, e.g.,* Jan Darpö, *Article 9.2 of the Aarhus Convention and EU Law. Some Remarks on CJEU's Case Law on Access to Justice in Environmental Decision-Making*, in Journal for European Environmental & Planning Law, Vol. 11 (2014) Brill & Nijhoff, at 367–391, the Commission's Communication of 28 April 2017, *Notice on Access to Justice in Environmental Matters*, C(2017) 2616 final, and Jan Darpö, *On the Bright Side (of the EU's Janus Face). The EU Commission's Notice on Access to Justice in Environmental Matters*, Journal for European Environmental & Planning Law, 2017, at 373–398.

2101. In C-263/09 *Djurgården,* the Swedish environmental code that required the organisations to have at least 2,000 members was found to be in breach of Art. 11 of the EIA Directive.

2102. C-72/95 *Kraaijeveld.*

2103. C-137/14 *Commission v. Germany.*

2104. C-263/08 *Djurgården* (paras 37–39) and C-115/09 *Trianel* (para. 59).

law.[2105] In its judgment on the *Slovak Brown Bear*,[2106] the CJEU found – with reference to the 'principle of equivalence' and the 'principle of effectiveness' – that the Member States have a Union law obligation to interpret, to the greatest extent possible, the procedural rules of environmental law in accordance with the objectives of Article 9(3)[2107] and the objective of effective judicial protection of the rights conferred by EU law. The NGOs must be able to challenge before a national court an administrative decision liable to be contrary to EU environmental law.[2108] It is their role under environmental law to challenge the procedural or substantive legality of decisions, acts or omissions which have an environmental impact. The CJEU has also derived access to justice under the rules on public participation in the draw up of action plans for improving ambient air quality under the Air Quality Directive.[2109] In two of its other judgments, the CJEU has stressed the need for correct transposition of air and drinking water directives in order to ensure that the persons concerned can ascertain the full extent of their rights to a healthy environment at national level.[2110] In one of its preliminary rulings, the CJEU found that the German legislation, by setting up an additional requirement, interfered with adequate access to justice.[2111]

2105. C-115/09 *Trianel.*

2106. C-240/09 *Slovak Brown Bear.*

2107. Article 9(3) is not a provision that is directly applicable at national level as the criteria on sufficient interest and impairment of rights are subject to the adoption of national legal criteria.

2108. It is for the referring court to interpret, to the fullest extent possible, the procedural rules relating to the conditions to be met in order to bring administrative or judicial proceedings in accordance with the objectives of Art. 9(3) of the Convention.

2109. C-237 *Janecek.*

2110. C-361/88 *Commission v. Germany* and C-59/89 *Commission v. Germany.*

2111. With reference to the national rules on standing, the German court has not accepted the case presented by the local chapter of Friends of the Earth on the annulation of a permit to build and operate a coal-fired plant in an area close to a Natura 2000 site.

Chapter 2. Administrative Appeals

§1. Goals, Time Limits and Substantive Limitation

349. In Denmark, in most environmental cases, the first instance is the municipalities[2112] – although in some cases it is an agency under the Ministry of Environment and Food of Denmark or the thirteen nature conservation boards[2113] – that have the authority to make the decision. Administrative appeals (also named recourse) of such decisions to the appeals boards are a very important means to ensure control in relation to decision-making covering nature protection, planning, polluting activities, etc.[2114] Any complaint leads to insecurity and can interfere with the legal position of the party to whom the decision is addressed.

The appeal authorities' possibility of influencing the municipality's municipal and local plans as an instance of recourse is limited. If procedural errors are made during the preparation of a plan, this constitutes a point of law, which can be considered by the appeal authorities, but they will presumably be disinclined to let ascertained errors have any influence on the validity of that spatial plan. A broad delimitation of the circle of complainants is consequentially of no great importance in such matters. However, it may ensure that the central authority has the opportunity to point out to the municipalities that the procedural rules must be observed, and that the provisions of the local plan must be in accordance with the law.

350. There are three preconditions that the complainant has to respect to get the appeals board to accept the case for a review: (1) the person's right to complain has to be proved; (2) the time limits for bringing the case to the appeals boards must be respected; and (3) the complaint has to be uploaded at the electronic webpage for appeals as it is mandatory to file the document electronically.[2115]

The environmental acts include the time limits to be observed, cf., *inter alia,* section 62(1) of the Planning Act and section 101(1) of the Environmental Protection Act. The time limit for lodging a complaint is four weeks from the day the decision was notified. The Environment and Food Appeals Board can declare a case dismissed if it is not received electronically. The appeals board may also decide not to dismiss a complaint that is not filed with digital self-service if there are special conditions that make the complainant not likely to be able to use digital self-service.[2116] In cases accepted for review, the appeals board must follow the administrative rules principle under the assessment procedure, including the 'right

2112. Concerning the role of the municipalities, *see supra* para. 48.

2113. Concerning the competences in cases on conservation, *see supra* para. 46.

2114. The term 'administrative appeals' is used to describe the situation where an administrative decision can be brought before another administrative authority which – when some procedural prerequisites have been satisfied – is under an obligation to reconsider the decision.

2115. Act No. 86 of 28 January 2014 on the Mandatory Digital Self-service when Filing a Complaint and Compulsory Forwarding of a Complaint on a Local Plan to the Nature and Environmental Appeals Board, etc. This Act made the use of the portal for electronic appeals mandatory. It came into effect on 1 Feb. 2014.

2116. Such a competence is ensured by s. 21(2) of the Act on the Environment and Food Appeals Board.

of contradiction' by consulting the complainant and the addressee during the procedure if new information emerges on which the directly involved parties could have interest in making some comments.

351. The main rule is that the appeals boards have the competence to investigate both the formal decision-making process that has been applied at first instance and the content of the decision. However, in order to achieve a reduction of the cases that the appeals boards have to review, several acts limit the recourse to legal questions or leave it to the appeals boards themselves to assess the extent of the examination to be carried out – including the competence to decide that it will be limited to the objections submitted by the complainant.

Appeals against the spatial planning – and several other issues – can be made only on legal issues and not on the discretionary part of planning decisions. Questions of legality, including compliance with the traditional principles of administrative law and compatibility with the plans also fall within the term 'legal issues'. River basin management plans and Nature 2000 plans may be appealed to the Environment and Food Appeals Board regarding the procedural provision of such plans.[2117] The appeals boards may also have the competence to limit their review of a decision to the matters complained of.[2118] The re-examination may have the result that the decision is upheld, amended completely or partially, or annulled without a new decision being taken in its place. In case of a breach of the procedural rules, misinterpretation of the statutory rules or decisions not respecting the administrative principles,[2119] the appellate authority may declare the decision invalid and/or refer it back to the first instance. However, an invalid decision may also be substituted by a new decision, e.g., by correction of procedural errors. The appeals boards have no powers regarding sanctions.

352. Whether an administrative appeal has the (injunctive) effect of suspending the appealed decision until the appeal body has taken its decision depends on the specific provisions laid down in the environmental acts in question. If no such provisions exist, the general rule is that an appeal of a licence (approval) do not have an injunctive effect although specific circumstances may lead to another result. It is normally laid down in the rules that an appeal relation to bans, prohibitions, etc., has an injunctive effect, e.g., section 95 of the Environmental Protection Act and section 87 of the Nature Protection Act. Based on certain statutory rules, the appeals board decides whether an appeal has the effect that the decision is without legal effect until the decision has been assessed by that body. If the complaint has an injunctive effect, the party affected must await the decision of the recourse instance.

353. In some cases, by means of ouster clauses in the relevant environmental act or statutory order, the Parliament has left the final administrative decision-making

2117. Section 36 of the Water Basin Management Planning Act and s. 56, No. 2, of the Environmental Objectives Act.
2118. Section 11 of the Environment and Food Appeals Board Act.
2119. The general public law principles are described *supra* para. 30.

to the local authorities. In such cases, it is possible to have decisions made by the municipalities evaluated by another body.

The State Supervisory Authority (Ankestyrelsen) under the Ministry of Social Affairs and the Interior has the competence to evaluate the legality of municipality actions.[2120] All legal and natural persons may ask for a supervisory check of whether a municipality has complied with the legislative requirements. Such a procedure can only be initiated where there is no other administrative appeal possibility. The Authority is not obliged to carry out an assessment – it determines itself whether a complaint should lead to further investigations. It may review the legality of the decisions and omissions, and it may issue its guiding opinion on the matter. If relevant, it can bring the case to the courts, and it may annul or suspend clearly illegal decisions.

§2. Types of Recourse Bodies

354. The appeals boards responsible for the assessment of the handling of administrative appeals in the areas of environmental law are established by legal acts as (in principle) independent from the ministries in the handling of the individual complaint – including the Ministry of Industry, Business and Financial Affairs and the Ministry of Environment and Food of Denmark. This means that, first and foremost, the functional independence of the members of the recourse body must be guaranteed, and also that some of the basic principles of judicature must subjected to the body's procedure. When establishing such recourse systems, the legislator must consider what type of body is best suited to handle the task at hand. If the lawmaker wishes to inspire confidence in the administrative recourse system, it is natural to create a system similar to that of the law courts, which in a 'law and order context' are thought to command greater confidence than administrative bodies.

On 1 February 2017, the complaint system was reorganised by the two acts on the Environment and Food Appeals Board[2121] and the Spatial Planning Appeals Board[2122] that replaced the former Environment and Nature Appeals Board. In these acts, the focus are now primarily on ensuring a quick and effective treatment of the complaints in the Complaints House, where officials are primarily those who carry out the work on handling complaints – and who also make the decisions. The use of independent chairmen has been limited to the appointment of two professors of law who perform the task as a secondary activity. In exceptional situations, the two boards of appeal are composed with experts, judges and/or politicians – depending on the type of conflict and legal area.

355. Appeals in cases concerning the acts that are administrated under the Ministry of Environment and Food of Denmark of Denmark can be brought before the

2120. The Ministry of Social Affairs and the Interior is responsible for the governance of municipalities and regions.
2121. Act No. 1715 of 27 December 2016 on the Environment and Food Appeals Board.
2122. Act No. 1658 of 20 December 2016 on the Spatial Planning Appeals Board.

Environmental Protection and Food Appeals Board. It is the only appeal instance in the administrative environmental decision-making system. Its competence covers decisions made up of sixty-four environmental acts, acts on agriculture, fisheries and food issues. Its competences are regulated both by these sixty-four acts and by a special act on the composition of the Board in different cases.

The Environment and Food Appeals Board consist of: a chairman appointed by the Minister for Business (who has to involve the Minister for the Environment in a hearing before the appointment); two members appointed by the two High Courts among the members of the courts; sixteen expert members who are appointed by the Minister for Business and Growth; four representatives of the general public appointed by the Danish Parliament (who are appointed among the members of the political parties), cf. section 2 of the Act on the Environment and Food Appeals Board. The Chairman of the Board and his deputies must have passed a law degree. The composition of the Board may differ from one case to another depending on which environmental or food legislative act the contested decision is based on. The Board is divided into nine subsections, which are constituted by the members just mentioned, and supplemented by two expert members depending on which of the sixty-four legal acts the cases are related to: (a) industrial relations; (b) soil contamination; (c) groundwater and water supply conditions; (d) agricultural issues; (e) marine conditions; (f) freshwater conditions; (g) food; (h) veterinary issues; or (i) representatives of the general public, cf. section 3. The members are appointed for a period of up to four years at a time. The chairman may decide on behalf of the board in all cases that do not contain questions of major or principal importance, and in cases whose decision is solely due to a legal assessment, cf. section 8. However, it is in most cases the staff and not the chairman that makes the decisions. In the very few cases in which the claims are handled by the Board with experts, judges and/or representatives of the political parties, the decision has to be discussed at a meeting, unless the chairman finds it inconsequential that the decision is taken by the board on a written basis. If a complaint contains several objections, the Environment and Food Appeals Board may limit its review to the essentials, cf. section 11. It is possible for this Appeals Board to limit the re-examination if it wants to as long as the issues related to the cases do not conflicts with the fulfilment of EU legislation and international obligations. To obtain the needed documentation on the factual situation it is possible for the Appeals Board to decide – if it is deemed necessary – to make its own investigation at a property. The police must provide the Board with assistance in exercising this power, cf. section 16 of the Act.

356. In cases concerning spatial planning under the Planning Act and the Maritime Spatial Planning Act, administrative appeals can be brought before the Spatial Planning Appeals Board Act.[2123] This Appeals Board is also part of the Ministry of Industry, Business and Financial Affairs, and the members are appointed without the involvement of the Minister for the Environment.

All its members must have knowledge of and insight into spatial planning. They are appointed by the Minister for Business for a period of four years. The Board consists of a chairman and one or more substitutes for him, one member appointed

2123. Act No. 1658 of 20 December 2016 on the Spatial Planning Appeals Board.

by the presidents of the Higher Courts among the members of the courts, one member with knowledge of and experience in concrete spatial planning, two members with knowledge of and insight into growth and business development, one member with knowledge of and insight into cultural and landscape conditions, one member with knowledge of and insight into the natural and environmental conditions and four representatives of the general public appointed by the Danish Parliament (who are appointed among the members of the political parties). The Chairman of the Board and his deputies must have passed a law degree. The members are appointed for a period of up to four years at a time. The chairman may decide on behalf of the Board in all cases that do not contain questions of major or principal importance, and in cases whose decisions are solely due to legal assessment, cf. section 4(1). The Appeals Board must consist of all members, and the Appeals Board must make decisions by ordinary majority of votes at a meeting, or by written processing in cases that cannot be decided by the chairman or a deputy for him alone. In case of a tie, the chairman's vote in the individual case is decisive, cf. section 4(2).

The Act on the Spatial Planning Appeals Board states that the Board itself may allow a third party and a public authority, having a legal interest in the outcome of a case, to take part in the processing of the case as a support to the complainant or a support to the accused authority, cf. section 5.

357. Administrative appeals in cases concerning energy-related issues, including environmental administration (e.g., EIAs and SEAs) of energy production facilities in the marine area, can be brought before the Energy Appeals Board. This Appeals Board is also part of the Ministry of Industry, Business and Financial Affairs. It consists of a chairperson as well as a number of experts in all aspects of energy-related issues with comprehensive knowledge of energy matters. The Appeals Board is composed of three, five or seven members depending on the nature of the case. Its remit covers all cases in which the Energy Agency is the first instance. It can assess decisions made under the Carbon Dioxide Allowances Act, the Continental Shelf Act, the Electricity Act, the Heating Act, the Promotion of Renewable Energy Act and the Subsoil Act.

§3. RIGHTS OF COMPLAINT (ACCESS TO JUSTICE)

358. Since the 1980s, the environmental acts have provided that certain environmental organisations (NGOs) have the right of complaint within the appeal systems. The Act on the Implementation of the Aarhus Convention changed these rules in the description of the public concerned.[2124] *Typically,* an appeal against a decision or an omission can be appealed by:

2124. Act. No. 447 of 31 May 2000 on the Implementation of the Aarhus Convention. Concerning the Aarhus Convention and its focus on access to justice, *see supra* para. 31.

- Local environmental organisations whose main objective is to protect nature and the environment, provided they have notified the relevant authority (municipality) in advance about their interest in the type of cases that they wish to be informed of, and they have documented the relevance of their objectives by their statutes.[2125]
- Local environmental organisations whose main objective is to safeguard essential recreational interests, provided they have notified the relevant authority (municipality) in advance about their interest in the type of cases that they wish to be informed of, and they have documented the relevance of their objectives by by-laws.
- National environmental organisations whose main objective is to protect natural resources and the environment, and/or whose objectives are to safeguard essential recreational interests.[2126] An organisation can, of course, look after both a collective and a common interest. When the Danish Angling Society makes a complaint against the discharge of wastewater into the watercourses, the organisation invokes both the anglers' economic interest in the fish stocks paid by them and the common interest in preserving the Danish fish stock.
- Certain specified business and interest organisations covering specific interests have the right to appeal within their specific sphere of interest.[2127]

359. Any individual with a direct, personal and legitimate interest (individual significant interest) in the outcome of a case has the right of complaint in the appeal

2125. By way of example it may be mentioned, s. 100(1)–(2) of the Environmental Protection Act ensures that local environmental associations working primarily to protect the environment have the right to appeal the decisions taken by municipalities or by the Ministry of Environment and Food to the Environment and Food Appeals Board. It is a precondition that such associations have informed the municipal council of the types of decisions of which they wish to be notified, cf. s. 76(1). It is also a precondition that the local organisation is not part of a national organisation with rights of appeal.

2126. By way of example it may be mentioned, claims under s. 100(3) can be filed to the Environmental Appeals Board by some nationwide associations and organisations. If they, according to their statutes, have the protection of nature and environment as the main purpose, they can appeal decisions according to some the provisions. Under s. 100(4), nationwide associations and organisations that, according to their statutes, are expected to handle significant recreational interests may appeal against the same of the decisions when the decision affects such interests, and the complaint aims to protect nature and the environment. Claims to the Spatial Planning Appeals Board can also be made by national associations and organisations if their main object is either to protect nature and the environment or to safeguard essential user interests within an area. Their right to complain is depending on the following conditions: (a) they have by their own statutes or regulations documentation for the relevant objectives; and (b) they represent at least 100 members, cf. s. 59(2) of the Planning Act.

2127. Under s. 99 of the Environmental Protection Act, the Danish Fisheries Association can appeal against the decisions of the municipal council and the minister regarding issues of pollution of streams, lakes or the sea; the Freshwater Fisheries Association of Denmark can appeal against the decisions of the municipal council and the minister as regards issues relating to water pollution and lakes; the Labour Council's Business Council may appeal against the decisions of the municipal council and the minister when significant employment interests are affected; and the Consumer Council may appeal against the decisions of the municipal council and the minister to the extent that the decisions are essential and fundamental.

systems. If there is no legislative basis for delimitation in an act, there is a presumption that everybody who has an individual and material interest in the decision has the right of complaint. Guidance to decision-making concerning delimitation of the persons with a right of complaint may be obtained from the judicial delimitation of who has access to justice in the court system.[2128]

The party to whom the decision is addressed clearly belongs to the category of persons enjoying a right of complaint. There are also other persons who in one way or another will be affected by a decision, even when the decision is not addressed to them and cannot properly be said to concern their rights. Their right of appeal as complainants depends partly on whether the act under which the decision is made is to be understood in the sense to protect the group of persons to which they belong. Of relevance is also whether their interest in contesting a decision balances private and public interest in the decision having immediate legal force.

In the preparatory works of the Environmental Protection Act, the decisive criterion of whether associations, etc., should be considered to have a right of complaint on the basis of having an 'individual and significant interest' is whether the association in question can be said to represent a group of persons whose individual, material interests are directly affected by the decision. Thus, for example a house owners' association must be able to appeal a decision to grant permission to establish a dumping site near the members' properties if the site could conceivably cause inconvenience to the members. If the association do not represent such a group, or if the group of persons represented by the association has no direct connection with the said matter, it will have no right of complaint. Section 59 in the Planning Act follows the same concept, and it includes the funds with the goal of taking care of national parks in the groups with access to justice. A person with a right of complaint may of course permit somebody else to lodge a complaint on his behalf, e.g., a lawyer or an association (trade association, agricultural society, nature conservation society or NOAH – Friends of the Earth Denmark). It must be clearly established that such an authorisation exists.

360. A right of complaint for public authorities is very common in environmental legislation. The approach to such an initiative by the authorities is different from one act to the other act. Therefore, only some examples will be mentioned here.

Based on the Nature Protection Act, all authorities have the right of complaint, cf. Section 86(1). Right of complaint is ensured by the Minister for Environment and anyone else with a legal interest in the outcome of the case, including the National Park Fund created pursuant to the National Parks Act, cf. section 59(1) of the mentioned Act.

The regional council and the municipal council are allowed to complain over each other's decision under the Contaminated Soil Act. The regional and the municipal councils also have the competence to appeal the decision of the Minister for Environment, cf. section 82(2). The municipal council may complain the decision of the Minister for the Environment under the Environmental Protection Act,

2128. Concerning standing for NGOs, *see infra* para. 371.

cf. section 98(2) of this Act. The Minister for Industry, Business and Financial Affairs has right to complain about the decisions of the municipalities under the Planning Act, cf. section 59(1).

§4. Fees and Appeals Boards

361. An appeal to the Environmental Protection and Food Appeals Board as well as an appeal to the Spatial Planning Appeals Board require payment of a fee amounting to DKK 900 for private persons and DKK 1,800 for business and NGOs (at the 2016 level), which is reimbursed if the appeal is successful in wholly or in part.

Until 2004, applicants to the appeals boards were not charged for starting a procedure. It was changed in 2004, where everyone that made an appeal to the former Nature Protection Appeals Board had to pay DKK 400. The regime for appeals to the former Nature and Environmental Appeals Board was changed by several acts.[2129] The fee is now decided by the Act on the Environment and Food Appeals Board[2130] and the Act on the Spatial Planning Appeals Board.[2131] The fees are returned to the applicant if: (a) as a result of the appeal, the decision at issue is amended or repealed; (b) the complaint is wholly or partly upheld by the Appeals Board; or (c) if the complaint is rejected by the appeals board for some procedural reasons. Insofar as the appeals boards have not received payment for handling an appeal, the boards set a time limit for payment of the amount required. If the fee is not paid within this time limit, the appeal is denied.

The claimant has to pay DKK 4,000 as the fee on appeals to the Energy Appeals Board in cases concerning compensation for CO_2 taxes.[2132]

362. In April 2012, the ACCC made a decision concerning compliance by Denmark in respect of access to justice in accordance with Article 9(4) of the Aarhus Convention.[2133]

The Committee holds that the requirement for fair procedures under Article 9(4) means that the process, including the final ruling of the decision-making body, must

2129. It was changed by Act No. 1608 of 22 December 2010 on the Nature and Environment Appeals Board Accordingly, on 1 Jan. 2011, a fee amounting to DKK 500 was changed on private persons and a fee amounting to DKK 3,000 was charged on others, such as enterprises, NGOs and authorities. Act No. 580 of 18 June 2012 changed this level into DKK 500 for everyone, *see infra* para. 362 concerning the critic of the former discrimination by the Aarhus Convention Compliance Committee.

2130. Act No. 1715 of 27 December 2016 on the Environment and Food Appeals Board and Statutory Order No. 132 of 30 January 2017 on Fees for Bringing Complaints to the Environment and Food Appeals Board.

2131. Act No. 1658 of 20 December 2016 on the Spatial Planning Appeals Board and Statutory order No. 108 of 28 January 2017 on Fees for Bringing Complaints to the Spatial Planning Appeals Board.

2132. Section 8 of the Statutory Order No. 664 of 19 June 2006 on the decision-making by the Energy Appeals Board.

2133. The Aarhus Convention Compliance Committee's Case ACCC/C/2011/57.

be impartial and free from prejudice, favouritism or self-interest. The Danish distinction between individuals that have to pay DKK 500 and NGOs that have to pay DKK 3,000 as a fee, when they appeal to the Nature and Environmental Appeals Board is not in itself necessarily unfair. However, the Committee considers that the relationship between the average individual net income and the NGOs financial capacity to have access to justice is not clear. Moreover, the financial capacity of any particular NGO to meet the costs of access to justice may depend on a number of factors, including the amount of the NGO's membership fee, the number of members, and the amount of resources allocated for access to justice activities in comparison to other activities among other factors. It is also stressed that the Convention explicitly recognises the importance of the role that the NGOs can play in environmental protection. When assessing if the Danish fee regime is 'prohibitively expensive', apart from the amount of the fee as such, the Committee considers the following aspects of the system as a whole to be particularly relevant: (a) the contribution made by appeals by NGOs to improve environmental protection and the effective implementation of the Danish Livestock Act; (b) the expected result of the introduction of the new fee on the number of appeals by NGOs to the Appeals Board; and (c) the fees for access to justice in environmental matters as compared to fees for access to justice in other matters in Denmark.

The Compliance Committee stated in its decision that it is evident based on the statistics that the NGO efforts resulted in the repeal of a large number of illegal decisions, a halt on many potentially environmental harmful activities, and the imposition of measures for limiting other harmful effects on the environment. The statistics alone provided sufficient evidence of the contribution made by appeal by NGOs to improve environmental protection and the effective implementation of the Danish Act on the Environmental Approval for Livestock Holdings. The Committee finds that the fee system was indented to, and was likely to, result in a decrease of the number of appeals filed against environmental decisions by the NGOs. It was the conclusion of the Committees' assessment that the fee amounting to DKK 3,000 that the NGOs had to pay was a breach of the requirements in Article 9(4) of the Convention, that the access to justice procedures must not be prohibitively expensive.[2134]

2134. After this decision, the fee to be paid was changed by law, *see supra* para. 361.

Chapter 3. Juridical Remedies

§1. The Court System

363. The Danish law courts have a constitutional basis which allows them a special status in the administration of law and justice. It is a system of general courts that deals both with civil cases, including cases on public law issues, and criminal cases.[2135] There are no constitutional courts.

The courts are established to ensure that the government and all the administrative authorities respect the law, cf. section 63 of the Constitution. Consequently, the natural function of the law courts has been to interpret the 'rule of law'. It is a consequence of the division of power between the administrative authorities and the courts. The courts must also ensure that the legislation enacted by the Danish Parliament is in accordance with the Danish Constitution, EU law and international laws that Denmark has undertaken to observe. It is possible to bring cases concerning the content of legal acts passed by the Danish Parliament on the basis of the Danish Constitution – typically as cases on expropriation made by environmental legislation without full compensation. In this respect, the position of the courts is, however, to be very careful in the constitutional review. Issues concerning the correct implementation of international conventions and EU directives are other examples of cases concerning the Danish Parliaments act that can be handled by the courts. In the more than 170 years under the Danish Constitution, it has only happened once that the Supreme Court has set aside a piece of legislation adopted by the Danish Parliament.[2136] EU environmental law is binding, but such sources are not important in the environmental cases handled by the courts.[2137] The courts have primarily been instituted to afford legal protection to citizens with the purpose, *inter alia*, of ensuring that the statutory rules as well as the binding legal principles are observed by the administration.[2138]

2135. Criminal cases are those cases concerning unlawful activities that are investigated by the police and presented by the police in the courts.

2136. The judgment is published in the *Weekly Judicial Review* 1999 at 841. The Supreme Court stated that the legislative power had exceeded the limits laid down in Section 3 of the Constitution for the distribution of powers between the legislative, executive and judicial authorities. Concerning this judgment as only example, *see* Marlene Wind, *Do Scandinavians Care about International Law?* iCourts Working Paper Series No. 74, https://papers.ssrn.com/sol3/papers.cfm?abstract_id=2833215 (visited on 5 Nov. 2019) – Nordic Journal of International Law (forthcoming).

2137. In the judgment published in the Weekly Law Review 2017, at 824, the Supreme Court ruled of the CJEU Case 441/14 *Ajos*. Based on Danish legal tradition, it was not possible for the Danish courts 'in applying the interpretive methods recognized by Danish courts' to respect the CJEU's preliminary ruling. In its interpretation of the Employment Directive, the CJEU had in its preliminary ruling included the fundamental human rights (including the principle of non-discrimination). The Danish Supreme Court assumed that as the CJEU had not in its preliminary ruling in the *Ajos* case referred to the provisions in the Treaty that are listed in the Danish Accession Act, the Danish Supreme Court 'would be acting outside the scope of its powers as judicial authority' if it was to disregard the provisions of the Danish Act. Concerning this Danish judgement, *see* Ole Terkelsen, *The Ajos Case and the Danish Approach to International Law*, in European Public Law, Vol. 24, Issue 2, 2018, Kluwer Law Online, at 183–193.

2138. Concerning the administrative law principles, *see supra* para. 30.

364. There are three stages in the juridical system: the lowest Courts of First Instance (twenty-four district courts), the two High Courts, and the Supreme Court, cf. sections 59(1), 63(2) and 78(4) of the Danish Constitution.[2139] None of the courts is formally specialised in administrative cases – or in environmental law cases.

It is possible to bring an action directly to the courts without exhausting the administrative appeal procedure. All decisions taken by the appeals boards can be challenged before the district courts. The length of a procedure at first instance is generally about one year. The judgment made by the city court may be appealed to one of the two higher courts – the Eastern High Court (which handles cases from Jutland) or the Western High Court (which handles cases from the rest of the country). The provisions on their competences and procedural rules are laid down in the Administration of Justice Act.[2140] The rules on where to bring a case against are laid down in Chapter 22 of the Administration of Justice Act. If it is a case brought against the authorities, the provisions on where to bring it are laid down in sections 239 and 240. A court may have jurisdiction in a civil case on grounds of residence, but jurisdiction can also be based on other facts, such as the venue of tort. Actions seeking punishment, compensation or redress for environmental damage or pollution may be brought either in the district where the tort was committed or in the defendant's place of residence. Real estate cases may be brought before the court in the district where the real estate is situated. The parties to a case may also agree to bring the case before a court other than the one that would normally be competent under the law. The referral to court normally has no injunctive effect, but statutory rules in the relevant environmental act may ensure injunctive effect, and the courts may decide that the assessment that is made suspends the enforcement of the decision taken by the administrative authority.

365. The Administration of Justice Act establishes the main principles, the institutes and the procedural rules governing the civil and criminal procedure with the overall objective of ensuring enforcement of the substantive legal rules.

The procedure is founded on the principles of due process, under which the court must be objective and impartial, and the decisions must be uniform in cases that are similar to one another. In general, court hearings are public, and proceedings are oral. Civil cases may be dealt with in writing where the defendant fails to appear in a case under appeal or in other exceptional circumstances. Due process of law (including cases on the public law issues) entitles a party to a civil lawsuit to receive notice of the alleged breach of the law and a hearing in which the party may defend its action. The plaintiff's non-appearance in court will, in normal circumstances, result in a rejection of the case. Should the defendant not appear at the court hearing, the court normally passes judgment in favour of the plaintiff. The parties to the case have a right to attend all court meetings, to study files, to engage in the 'right of contradiction' and to examine witnesses. In general, court proceedings and documentation are open to the public and the proceedings are oral. Civil procedure is based on the principle of negotiation, including in cases concerning appeals of

---

2139. Concerning the Danish courts, *see supra* para. 6.

2140. Promulgation Order No. 1284 of 14 November 2018 on the Administration of Justice Act, as amended.

administrative decisions. The most important consequence of this principle is that it is the parties who furnish the material, such as claims, allegations and evidence, and the court is not authorised to take up issues beyond the framework established by the parties. There are some exceptions to this principle. An exception of practical importance is the fact that the law courts are obliged to guide parties who appear without legal counsel. All courts act freely in relation to matters of formality. Furthermore, the courts may propose an objection to the parties with a view to the clear-up ambiguities and incompleteness. The principle of negotiation is not applicable in criminal cases where it is up to the court to reach, as far as possible, a proper judgment on the merits of the case.

366. The rules of the Administration of Justice Act contain the principle that courts must have first-hand evidence. Parties, witnesses and expert witnesses must testify directly before the court hearing the case. The assessment of evidence is based upon the basic rule of freedom to consider evidence. Expert witnesses may be heard at the request of the parties or at the initiative of the court. The court frequently chooses them from master lists of various organisations and institutions. Third parties may also testify as witnesses.

A claim submitted to the courts must be well founded, actual and sufficiently clear. In this respect, it is important to stress that all parties in civil cases may present evidence and arguments, limited by rules of relevance. A party to a case may demand that the other party produce the documents in court, but under sections 298–299 of the Act, the court considers whether the documents must be produced. In this connection, the court may decide that the evidence can be adduced in a different manner. Under section 300, it is always presupposed that the party requesting that the opposing party produce documents may state the facts that are to be proven (i.e., a more specific fact in dispute). This disputed fact must be relevant for the case, it must be probable that the documents in question are relevant, and it must be probable that the opposing party has the documents in question. If the opposing party refuses to produce the documents and is under a duty of secrecy, he or she may in certain circumstances be exempted from production.

The most important example of rights asserted with respect to environmental issues under private law (liability or nuisance claim) is the private right to compensation for breach of the obligation not to harm neighbouring houses. Private law restrictions are also stipulated in the form of easements that are attached to properties, opposable to third parties and transferred together with the transfer of title to the properties in question. Such easements are, however, seldom used as the basis for protection of nature.

Most cases related to the lack of compliance with the environmental acts (based on public law) are submitted to the courts by the relevant authority. A citizen's possibility as the opposing party to the administrative authorities of presenting his or her case depends on the information that can be procured – either under the rules on disclosure under the Act or under the rules on access to documents laid down in the

Administrative Procedures Act.[2141] The law courts are restricted by the 'negotiation' maxim. This means that to a large extent the assessment of the administrative decision by the court depends on who appears as having a right of action and how this person or organisation acts. The courts may review both the interpretation of the legal substantive standards – including the interpretation of EU law – the procedural rules and to some extent the discretionary powers used by the administrative authorities. Within the environmental field, the rules are often so vague and imprecise that it is difficult for the law courts to re-examine a decision. The courts of law must have some precise written rules or some ordinary principles of law to base their decisions on. In very few cases, the courts decide to initiate a preliminary ruling procedure at the CJEU. The administrative authorities enjoy a wide measure of discretion as generally the courts cannot review discretionary decisions taken by the authorities. The courts restrict themselves to examining the accuracy of the findings of the facts and the interpretation of the statutory rules as well as the respect for the administrative principles[2142] – verifying, in particular, that the decisions made by the relevant authorities are not vitiated by a manifest error or a misuse of powers, and that the authorities did not clearly exceed the bounds of their discretion. Irrespective of whether the substantive rules are precise or imprecise and irrespective of differences in the legal positions of those involved they also ensure that the administration is respecting the procedural rules. The courts may annul administrative decisions if they are not in harmony with the general public law principle or if the interpretation of the wording of the statutes is not correct. The judgment itself, including the facts and grounds (which in court hearings are always public), may be reported in the press. A prohibition against public reporting may be issued but may only refer to part of the proceedings.

§2. Juridical or Administrative Appeal

367. It is the general starting point in Danish law that complaints about administrative decisions are dealt with by administrative appeals bodies. Not many environmental matters in Danish law are brought before the ordinary courts; within the environmental protection field, it is not traditional to have the substantive questions tried by a court.

Bringing cases to the appeals boards is easy, fast and cheap compared with a review of a decision by the courts. In most cases, it will also be necessary to have the assistance of a lawyer in court cases. The knowledge level in respect of environmental issues is higher in the administrative appeal systems compared to the knowledge in the courts. Moreover, the appeals boards are bound by the 'official' maxim (i.e., the principle that the content and form of proceedings depend on the activity of the judge and not on the parties) to assist the private persons in resolving the matter. In contrast to this, the courts are bound by the 'negotiation' maxim, according to which the main burden of procuring material for the proceeding rests

2141. Concerning the special provisions on the use of the Administrative Procedures Act in environmental cases, *see supra* para. 31.

2142. Concerning these principles, *see supra* para. 30.

on the parties, so that the function of the judge is mostly supplementary. This fact, too, renders the administrative recourse procedure more attractive than that of the courts of law. It is not possible for the appeals boards to ask the CJEU for a preliminary ruling on the interpretation of EU secondary legislation[2143]– so in this respect, it is the courts that are in the strongest position. The enforcement of the legislation is also an issue that can only be handled by the courts.

368. Danish law does not require that the administrative recourse process should be employed before bringing the matter to the courts of law unless otherwise expressly prescribed by law. By instituting special expert instances of appeal, particularly boards of appeal such as the ones that exist under the environmental law, the incentive for citizens to bring the matter before the courts is reduced. In this connection, it should be borne in mind that the re-examination carried out by the Danish courts cannot be or become as intensive as that of the administrative appeals boards.

§3. Access to Justice

369. There are no statutory rules on the identification of the individuals and environmental organisation having access to justice in the environmental acts brought to the courts in civil cases. The question on standing is regulated by unwritten principles and not in the Administration of Justice Act[2144] or in the many environmental acts. In general, citizens and enterprises with an individual, significant interest in the outcome of the procedure will have standing.

There is no *actio popularis* in Denmark. It is up to the courts to decide who has access to the review procedure before a court. A party to a civil case is defined as a person, association, etc., by whom or against whom a claim is made regarding the issue of the case. This definition, therefore, includes both plaintiff and defendant. Based on the traditional Danish approach to standing, this means that, the person in question must be protected by the rules according to which the matter has been settled, and that the person in question must have been affected by the decision in a manner that is significant as compared with other citizens.

370. The legislator is of the opinion that the implementation of the Aarhus Convention into Danish legislation has to be made by the courts on a case-by-case

---

2143. The Environment and Food Appeals Board stated that it did not have the competence to bring the legal question to the CJEU. In was stated in its decision of 13 March 2019, journal number NMK-10-00904 concerning the interpretation of the Habitats Directive in a case on the approval of a marine aquaculture farm. The reasoning of the board was based on CJEU's Case 222/13 *The Danish Telecommunication Complaints Board.* The CJEU stated in this case: 'Those guaranties and impartiality require rules, particularly as regards the composition of the body and the appointment, length of service and the grounds for abstention, rejection and dismissal of its members, in order to dismiss any reasonable doubt in the minds of individuals as to the imperviousness of the body to external factors and its neutrality with respect to the interest before it … .'

2144. Promulgation Order No. 1284 of 14 November 2018 on the Administration of Justice Act, as amended.

assessment, and that the access to justice at the appeals boards is the most important part of the Danish fulfilment of this Convention. It is also presumed that the point of departure is a certain correspondence between the category having a right of complaint and the category having access to justice.

When, for example, the Nature Protection Act assigns a right to lodge complaints to the Danish Society of Nature Conservation, the society in question might also have a right of action. The Society has some common objectives that the Act has accepted in the administrative appeal system, and it must also be possible to safeguard these objectives by bringing an action before a court. If a person or an association of persons has such a connection with or interest in a decision that a right of complaint is presumed to exist, it could not be presumed as the main rule that there would not also be a right to take the matter further and obtain a definitive, enforceable decision before the courts. Conversely, it would be impractical if the person withstanding did not have the possibility, before bringing an action, or trying to achieve redress through a recourse examination. The use of the administrative appeal system would typically be quicker and cheaper for both the individual and the society compared with bringing the case to the courts. Only special circumstances or conditions merit a different determination of the concept of interest in the two relations.

371. Danish court practice on access to justice for environmental organisations (NGOs) in matters related to nature protection, pollution and other environmental matters is scarce and not well established. The starting point is that delimitation of the right of action is the same as the delimitation for the right of complaint.[2145]

If an association invokes the interests of a group of private persons, the courts must require that the association can be said to represent the interests of the persons in question. Based on judicial practice, a fixed structure with board and membership fees will often be a prerequisite for the association's appearance as a party (unless an express authorisation exists). In Danish judicial practice, it has been presumed that the Danish Anglers' Association may act as an agent for its local committees in civil actions for damages against polluters. The local committees may be compensated for the loss suffered as a result of destruction of the fish stocks. The amount is intended to cover the cost of supplying new fry. On the other hand, the courts have not been prepared to accept claims for damages arising out of financial loss due to smaller yields in a period of time during which pollution occurred. It is presumed to be a case of non-economic damage if the association's members are not able to practice a recreational interest for a period of time. In 1994, in a case against the Ministry of Transport, the Eastern High Court held that Greenpeace Denmark had a right of action in a case on the EIA procedure.[2146] This decision came despite the lack of legal basis in the statutory rules, and despite Greenpeace not being entitled to invoke its members' economic interests as being affected by the decision of the Ministry. In its judgment, the Court found that Greenpeace had an actual and concrete dispute relating to the Ministry's duty to conform to a specific EIA in connection with a bridge project based on a specific new development act.

2145. Concerning the right of complaint, *see supra* paras 358–359.

2146. This judgment is published in the Danish Weekly Law Reports 1994, at 780.

The Court stated that Greenpeace had obtained legal recognition of its functions through a right of appeal in two general environmental acts (the Environmental Protection Act and the Act on Environmental Marine Protection). The acceptance of the right of action was also based on the structure of the organisation. In another case related to EIA, the Supreme Court accepted the Danish Bicycle Association.[2147] It must likewise be presumed that when, for example, the Danish Anglers Society pursuant to the Fisheries Act is entitled to lodge complaints with the administrative authorities, this association might also have the right to complaint to the courts in cases under this Act in order to safeguard the special common interest in the fish stock. However, the Act says nothing about this. In the judgment of case *Danish Anglers Association and the Anglers Association v. the Ministry of Environment,* the NGOs were granted legal standing by the Western High Court.[2148] The NGOs wished to overturn the Danish Nature Agency's decision on the introduction of beavers in the Danish nature. The court found that the Associations had a concrete, significant and individual interest in the outcome of the case. As they had put fish out in the surface water where the beavers were supposed to live and get their food, their access to justice was accepted. They had protected economic interests in the case. A case was lodged in August 2011 to the court system by a number of neighbours to the Test Centre, Østerild established by a special act.[2149] The Western High Court accepted access to justice for the 'Organisation for a Better Environment' in relation to the claim regarding the validity of the Act.[2150]

Acceptance by the courts of a legal interest on the part of associations with a programme on environmental protection etc. can – based on the mentioned judgments – be considered to be dependent on:

- *The structure of the association.* Only associations with a fixed structure are accepted as a party to a case.
- *The association's objective and possible recognition by law.* The association may only be a party to the case if the objective of the association is protected by law and is relevant to the case in question. If an act – e.g., the Environmental Protection Act – expressly recognises the association as being entitled to look after the interests in question, the association is obviously entitled to present a claim before the courts of law.
- *The association having a concrete interest in the matter.* An association is considered a party if it has suffered financial loss or if its rights have been infringed in a way that is comparable to an infringement of an individual's legal position.

372. As mentioned above, the Danish public environmental and planning law do not contain rules on standing for environmental organisations in civil cases. Nor does the Act on Strict Liability for Pollution Cost by Heavily Polluting Activities contain such provisions, although the subject was discussed during the preparation

2147. This judgment is published in the Danish Weekly Law Reports 2000, at 1103.
2148. This judgment is published in the Danish Weekly Law Reports 2001, at 1594.
2149. Act No. 647 of 15 June 2010 on the Establishment of Østerild Test Centre.
2150. This judgment is published in the Danish Weekly Law Reports 2012, at 1160.

of this Act.[2151] It was stressed that the advantage of including a right of action for environmental organisations was that this would be both in compliance with the general or individual deterrence views which form the basis of environmental legislation and, at the same time, in compliance with the developments in the other EU Member States (e.g., with regard to trade, called for inclusion of such rules). The majority of the members of the committee, however, did not consider that there were grounds for including a rule on standing for the organisations. It was argued that such a right of action in the court system would constitute a serious breach of one of the fundamental principles of Danish tort law. Moreover, the majority supported their conclusion by the fact that the rules on the public authorities' right to interfere, with a consequent right to claim a refund of the expenses by the wrongdoer, combined with the introduction of strict liability for damage would adequately prevent damage to the environment. If it was necessary to introduce stricter rules for preventive reasons it should – according to a majority of the committee – be done by way of extending criminal liability in relation to concrete areas of the law, e.g., by means of higher penalties for breaches of relevant provisions of environmental legislation. The Danish Parliament followed the committee's recommendation.

373. On 29 April 2008, the ACCC stated in a decision[2152] that Denmark did not fulfil its obligations under the Convention as no one was able to challenge the extensive culling of rooks by the Danish municipality of Hillerød in several locations that it owned. The rooks are listed in Annex II of the Wild Birds Directive with the effect that they cannot be hunted in Denmark unless four criteria set out in the Directive are met. One of the rook colonies was situated on a water purification plant, another at a garage and others close to a town dwelling. The municipality intended to cull 1,500 juvenile rooks to reduce a problem caused by the breeding behaviour in the rook colonies. In cooperation with the State Forest District of the Danish Nature Agency, under the Ministry of Environment, and the municipality, a number of persons related to the municipality were allowed to cull the juvenile rooks during the period from 1 May to 15 June 2006. The communicant claimed that the municipality's decision, taken in its capacity as landowner, breached the Wild Birds Directive.[2153] The communicant had tried to bring the case before the Nature and Environmental Protection Appeals Board, but had been informed by the Board that it did not have jurisdiction with regard to the implementation of EU directives. In its reply, the Appeals Board informed the communicant that his request had been forwarded to the Danish Nature Agency for possible action. The communicator never received a reply from the Agency. The Danish rules were amended with the effect that landowners were no longer allowed to cull rooks on their land or elsewhere without a licence granted by the Agency. However, the changes in the statutory rules did not ensure access to justice as the rules on administrative appeal were not amended. The Compliance Committee concluded that it was not convinced that the lack of opportunity for the communicant to initiate a criminal procedure in itself

2151. Report No. 1237/1992 on Strict Liability for Pollution Cost by Heavily Polluting Activities.
2152. Aarhus Convention Compliance Committee case ECE.PP/2008/5/Add.4.
2153. The Wild Birds Directive is described *supra* in paras 234 and 241.

amounted to non-compliance by Denmark. It noted the limited case law with regard to standing for NGOs in these situations outside the criminal procedure. As far as standing for such organisations is concerned, it stressed the importance of applying the approach reflected in the decision by the Western High Court in 2001 on acceptance of the standing for two NGOs as a minimum level of standing for access to justice in cases relating to the protection of wildlife.[2154]

§4. Group Claims

374. The rules on 'access to justice for group claims' are stated in Chapter 23a (section 254a–254 k) of the Administration of Justice Act.[2155] Under this Act, a 'group action' means a suit brought by someone without specific authority to sue on behalf of the members of the group. The group members are not parties to the action and do not need to be active. Nevertheless, a judgment in the case applies for and against all of the group members. Such a group action can be relevant in environmental law cases. However, group actions are only permitted if the action cannot be more effectively or equally well processed in another manner (e.g., in the form of a test case) and if certain other special conditions for a group action exist. Stringent requirements are imposed concerning the suitability of the representative and counsel of the group to conduct the group action. However, the members of the group are able to leave the group during the litigation and in such circumstances would thereby not be bound by the judgment. The members of the group must be informed in a suitable manner of the procedure, their rights to leave the group and also receive an advice on important decisions and other procedural steps in the action. The members also have the right to intervene and thereby become a party to the group action, and they have the right to appeal against the judgment. The court has to be active in directing the action, both as regards formal and substantive issues. A settlement made by the representative of the group is subject to court approval in order to bind members of the group. The court is empowered to award joint damages for distribution among the members of the group by means of a special post-trial distribution procedure, in which the court and defendant need not participate. Customary Danish principles concerning liability for litigation costs also apply to group actions. Under certain circumstances, members of the group are not liable for litigation costs.

§5. The Costs, Legal Aid and 'Timely Procedure'

375. The Administration of Justice Act contains provisions on legal aid, including access to free legal aid, also for environmental organisations, cf. sections 327 and 328 of the Act. The basic conditions for obtaining such legal aid from the Ministry of Justice consist of economic criteria and the need to show reasonable grounds for initiating a process before the courts.

2154. This judgment is described *supra* in para. 372.
2155. The rules on group claims came into force on 1 Jan. 2008.

The economic criteria for single citizens and married applicants (meaning people living together) are stated in the Statutory Order on Free Legal Aid.[2156] For NGOs, the economic criteria are based on practice with focus on the organisation as such and the people who have a direct interest in the activities of the organisation. There are problems regarding the obligations under Article 9(4) of the Aarhus Convention to ensure a timely and cheap procedure. Often, it takes several years for the courts to resolve environmental cases brought, and the costs of litigation are typically very high. In some of the notes connected to legal acts that preclude access to administrative appeal it is stated that the courts should pay particular attention to the obligations arising from the Convention in relation to the cost of litigation just as a means for the Parliament not to have new problems with the Compliance Committee.

2156. Statutory Order No. 1372 of 28 November 2018 on Free Legal Aid.

Selected Bibliography

AirClim, ClientEarth and European Environmental Bureau. *Clearing the Air. A critical Guide to the New National Emission Ceilings*, Directive, 2017.

Andersen, Michael Skou. *The Decline and Revival of Environmentally-Related Taxation in Europe*. In Akihisa Mori et al. (eds), 'The Green Fiscal Mechanism and Reform for Low Carbon Development'. Routledge, 2018.

Basse, Ellen Margrethe. *The Existing Regulatory Conditions for 'Energy Smart Water Utilities': Promotion of Sustainable Energy Transition.* In L. Squintani and H.H.B. Vedder with M. Reese and B. Vanheusden (eds.), 'Sustainable Energy United in Diversity. Challenges and Approaches in Energy Transition in the EU', European Environmental Law Forum (EELF) Book Series, Vol. 1, 2014, at 111–136.

BertelsmanStiftung, *Sustainable Governance Indicators. 2014 Denmark Report*, edited by Finn Laursen, Torben M. Andersen and Detlef Jahn.

BertelsmanStiftung, *Sustainable Governance Indicators. 2017 Denmark Report*, edited by Finn Laursen, Torben M. Andersen and Detlef Jahn.

Birnie, Patricia & Alan Boyle. *International Law and the Environment*. 3rd edn. Oxford, 2009.

Bohman, Britta. *Transboundary Law for Social-Ecological Resilience? A Study on Eutrophication in the Baltic Sea Area*, Stockholm University, 2017.

Borja, Angel, Mike Elliott, Jacob Carstensen, Anna-Stiina Heiskanen and Wouter van de Bund. *Marine Management – Towards an Integrated Implementation of the European Marine Strategy Framework and the Water Framework Directives*, Elsevier, 2010 Oct 20.

Christensen, Thomas Budde & Tyge Kjær. *Planning for Sustainable Transport: The Case of Copenhagen*. In Werner Gronau, Karl Reiter & Robert Press (eds), 'Transport and Health Issues'. Mannheim 2011, at 122–134.

ClientEarth. *Article 11 of the EU Common Fisheries Policy*. July 2014 (available at the Internet).

Darpö, Jan and Yaffa Epstein. *Thrown in the Wolves – Sweden Once Again Flouts EU Standards on Species Protection and Access to Justice*, in the Nordic Environmental Law Journal, 2015, Vol. 1, at 7–20.

Darpö, Jan. *Article 9.2 of the Aarhus Convention and EU Law. Some Remarks on CJEU's Case Law on Access to Justice in Environmental Decision-Making*, in Journal for European Environmental & Planning Law, 2014, at 367–391.

Selected Bibliography

Darpö, Jan. *On the Bright Side (of the EU's Janus Face). The EU Commission's Notice on Access to Justice in Environmental Matters*, in Journal for European Environmental & Planning Law, 2017, at 373–398.

Ebbeson, Jonas (ed.). *Access to Justice in Environmental Matters in the EU*. Kluwer International Law, 2002.

Ebbeson, Jonas. *A Modest Contribution to Environmental Democracy and Justice in Transboundary Contexts: The Combined Impact of the Espoo Convention and Aarhus Convention*, in Review of European Community & International Environmental Law (RECIEL), Vol. 20, No. 3, 2011, at 248–257.

Ebbeson, Jonas. *Protection of the Marine Environment of the Baltic Sea Area – The Impact of the Stockholm Declaration*. In M.H. Nordquist, L.N. Moor & S. Mahmoudi (eds), 'The Stockholm Declaration and Law of the Marine Environment'. Martinus Nijhoff Publishers, 2003, at 155–164.

Ebbeson, Jonas. *Public Participation and Privatisation in Environmental Matters: An Assessment of the Aarhus Convention*, in Erasmus Law Review, Vol. 4, No. 2, 2011, at 71–89.

Ebbeson, Jonas. *The Notion of Public Participation in International Environmental Law*. In Jutta Brunée & Ellen Hey (eds), 'Yearbook of International Law', Vol. 8 (1997), at 51–97.

Frid, Rachel. *The Relations Between the EC and International Organizations. Legal Theory and Practice*. Kluwer International Law, 1995.

Glasbergen, Pieter. *Co-operative Environmental Governance. Public-Private Agreements as a Policy Strategy*. Dordrech, Boston, London, 1998.

Golub, Jonathan (ed.). *New Instruments for Environmental Policy in the Europe*. Routledge, 1998.

Hallo, Ralph E. (ed.). *Access to Environmental Information in Europe. The Implementation and Implications of Directive 90/313/EEC*. Kluwer Law International, 1996.

Hermind, Benét and Ulla Eikard. *Denmark*. In Ralph E. Hallo (ed.), 'Access to Environmental Information in Europe'. Kluwer Law International, 1996, at 59–70.

Jans, Jan H. & Hans H.B. Vedder. *European Environmental Law*. Europa Law Publishing, 2012.

Kauppita, Jussi and Helle Tegner Anker. *The Role of Permits in Regulating Livestock Installations and Manure Spreading: Experience from Denmark and Finland*, in European Energy and Environmental Law Review, Vol. 27, No. 3, 2018, at 88–100.

Kingston, Suzanne, Veerle Heyvaert and Aleksandra Cavoski. *European Environmental Law.* Cambridge University Press, 2017.

Kiss, Alexandre & Dinah Shelton. *Manual of European Environmental Law*. 2nd edn. Cambridge, 1997.

Koeman, N.S.J. *Environmental Law in Europe.* Kluwer Law International, 1999.

Krämer, Ludwig. *EU Environmental Law*. 8th edn. Sweet & Maxwell, Thomson Reuters, 2016.

Koopmann, Hans-Martin. *Voluntary Action of Business and Industry. A Legal Analysis of Voluntary Agreements and Self-Regulation*. University of Rotterdam, 2000.

Langlet, David. *Scale, Space and Delimitation in Legal Governance – Perspectives from the Baltic Sea*, Marine Policy, Elsevier, Vol. 98, 2018, at 278–285.

Larsson, Marie-Louise. *The Law of Environmental Damage. Liability and Reparation.* Stockholm University, 1997.

Long, Ronan Joseph. *The Marine Strategy Framework Directive: A New European Approach to the Regulation of the Marine Environment, Marine Natural Resources and Marine Ecological Services*, in Journal of Energy and Natural Resources Law, Vol. 29, No. 1, 2011, at 1–44.

Pettersson, Maria and Patrik Söderholm. *Industrial Pollution Control and Efficient Licensing Processes: The Case of Swedish Regulatory Design*, ISSN 2071-1050, in Sustainability, Vol. 6, Issue 8, 2014, at 5401–5422, www.mdpi.com/journal/sustainability.

Recio-Blanco, Xiao. *Transnational Area-Based Ocean Management: Finding Avenues for Regulatory Harmonization*, William & Mary Policy Review, Vol. 7, Issue 1, 2015, at 95-141.

Revesc, Richard L, Philippe Sands and Richard B. Steward, *Environmental Law, the Economy and Sustainable Development.* Cambridge University Press, 2010.

Sands, Philippe, Jacqueline Peel, Adriana Fabra and Ruth MacKenzie. *Principles of International Environmental Law.* Cambridge, 2018.

Schoukens, Henrik. *Saving the Common Hamster with the EU Habitats Directive: A Mandatory Recovery Effort. A Remediation of Past Non-Compliance or An Exercise in Futility?*, in the Nordic Environmental Law Journal, 2017, Vol. 1, at 59–97.

Seerden, René & Kurt Deketelaere (eds). *Legal Aspects of Soil Pollution and Decontamination in the EU Member States and the United States.* Intersentia, 2000.

Seerden, René & Mikael Heldeweg (eds). *Comparative Environmental Law in Europe, An Introduction to Public Environmental Law in the EU Member States.* Tilburg, 1996.

Shapovalova, Darian. *The Effectiveness of the Regulatory Regime for Black Carbon Mitigation in the Arctic*, in Arctic Review on Law and Politics, Vol. 7, Issue 2, 2016, at 136–151.

Terkelsen, Ole. *The Ajos Case and the Danish Approach to International law*, in European Public Law, Vol. 24, Issue 2, 2018, Kluwer Online, at 183–193.

De Waard, Boudewijn (ed.). *Negotiated Decision – Making.* Den Haag, 2000.

Weiss, Edith Brown. *The Evolution of International Environmental Law*, in Japanese Y.B. International Law, Vol. 54, 2011, at 1-27.

Wetterstein, Peter (ed.). *Harm to the Environment – The Right to Compensation and the Assessment of Damages.* Oxford, 1997.

Wind, Marlene. *Do Scandinavians Care about International Law?,* in Nordic Journal of International Law, (forthcoming), https://papers.ssrn.com/sol3/papers.cfm?abstract_id=2833215 (visited 5 November 2019).

List of documents from public authorities and institutions

Danish Commission on Climate Change Policy. *Green Energy – The Road to a Danish Energy System without Fossil Fuels.* September 2010.

Selected Bibliography

Danish Economic Councils. *Economy and Environment 2009. English Summary.* Copenhagen, 2009.
Danish Economic Councils. *Economy and Environment 2010.* Copenhagen, 2010.
Danish Economic Councils. *Economy and Environment 2011*. Copenhagen, 2011.
Danish Economic Councils. *Economy and Environment 2012*. Copenhagen, 2012.
Danish Economic Councils. *Economy and Environment 2013*. Copenhagen, 2013.
Danish Economic Councils. *Economy and Environment 2014*. Copenhagen, 2014.
Danish Economic Councils. *The Public Service Obligation Tariffs in Denmark*, Notes published on the Internet. Copenhagen, 2014.
Danish Economic Councils. *Economy and Environment 2015*. Copenhagen, 2015.
Danish Economic Councils. *Economy and Environment 2017*. Copenhagen, 2017.
Danish Energy Agency. *Green Taxes for Trade and Industry Description and Evaluation*. Copenhagen, June 2000.
Danish Energy Agency. *The Green Certificate Market in Denmark. Status of Implementation*. Copenhagen, 2001.
Danish Energy Agency. *A Visionary Danish Energy Policy 2025*. Copenhagen, January 2007.
Danish Energy Agency. *Wind Turbines in Denmark*. Copenhagen, 2009.
Danish Energy Agency, Danish Energy Federation and Danish Business Agency. *Energy Industry Analyses*. Copenhagen, May 2011.
Danish Energy Agency. *Energy Statistics 2010*. Copenhagen, November 2011.
Danish Energy Agency. *Oil and Gas Production in Denmark 2013 and Subsoil Use*. June 2014.
Danish Energy Agency. *Denmark's Energy and Climate Outlook 2018. Baseline Scenario Projection Towards 2030. With Existing Measures (Frozen Policy).* April 2018.
Danish Forest and Nature Agency. *Strategy for Natural Forests and other Forest Types of High Conservation Value in Denmark*. Copenhagen, 1994.
Danish Forest and Nature Agency. *The Danish National Forest Programme in an International Perspective*. Copenhagen, 2008.
Danish Government. *A Shared Future – Balanced Development – Denmark's National Strategy for Sustainable Development*. Copenhagen, 2002.
Danish Government. *Making Markets Work for Environmental Policies. Achieving Cost-Effective Solutions.* Copenhagen, 2003.
Danish Government. *The World Summit in Johannesburg and Denmark's National Strategy for Sustainable Development*. Copenhagen, 2003.
Danish Government. *Action Plan for Biodiversity and Nature Conservation in Denmark 2004–2009.* Copenhagen, 2004.
Danish Government. *Danish Strategy for Adaptation to a Changing Climate*. Copenhagen, 2008.
Danish Government. *Denmark's Fifth National Communication on Climate Change. Under the United Nations Framework Convention on Climate Change and the Kyoto Protocol*. Copenhagen, 2009.
Danish Government. *An Integrated Marine Strategy*. Copenhagen, July 2010.
Danish Government. *Our Future Energy*. Copenhagen, November 2011.
Danish Government. *Energy Strategy – From Coal, Oil and Gas to Green Energy.* Copenhagen, February 2011.

Danish Government. *Denmark at Work. Plan for Growth in the Blue Denmark.* Copenhagen, December 2012.

Danish Government. *Climate Policy Plan. Towards a Low Carbon Society*. Copenhagen, August 2013.

Danish Government. *The Government Presents a Comprehensive Danish Export Strategy*, Copenhagen, May 2014.

Danish Government. *A Sustainable Denmark*. October 2014.

Danish Government. *Denmark Without Waste II – A Draft on Strategy for Waste Prevention*, Copenhagen, February 2015.

Danish Government. *The National Reform Programme. Denmark 2015*. Copenhagen, March 2015.

Danish Government. *A Stronger and More Secure Digital Society. The Common Public Digitalisation Strategy 2016-20.* 2017.

Danish Government. *Simple Rules. Less Bureaucracy – Digital Actuality*. Copenhagen, 2017.

Danish Government. *The National Convergence Programme. Denmark 2018.* Copenhagen, April 2018.

Danish Government. *Denmark's Draft Integrated National Energy and Climate Plan.* Copenhagen, December 2018.

Danish Ministry of Agriculture. *The Agricultural Holdings Act with Specific Attention to Structural Aspects*. Copenhagen, 1990.

Danish Ministry of Climate, Energy and Building, *Denmark's Sixth National Communication and First Biennial Report, Under the United Nationals Framework Convention and Climate Change*. Copenhagen, December 2013.

Danish Ministry of Climate, Energy and Building, *Denmark's Seventh National Communication and Third Biennial Report, Under the United Nationals Framework Convention and Climate Change*. Copenhagen, December 2018.

Danish Ministry of Defence. *Environment and Nature Strategy of the Ministry of Defence 2012-2015*. Copenhagen, 2016.

Danish Ministry of Economic Affairs and Business. *The Danish Maritime Cluster – An Agenda for Growth*, Copenhagen, 2008.

Danish Ministry of Economic Affairs and the Interior. *Economic Survey – August 2014*. Copenhagen, 26 August 2014.

Danish Ministry of Environment and Energy. *Ends and Means in Environmental Policy*. Copenhagen, 1990.

Danish Ministry of Environment and Energy. The Environmental Protection Agency (ed.). *Scientific Symposium on the North Sea Quality Status Report*. Copenhagen, 1993.

Danish Ministry of Environment and Energy. *Strategy for Sustainable Forest Management.* Copenhagen, 1994.

Danish Ministry of Environment and Energy. *Natur– og Miljøpolitisk Redegørelse. 1995* (Communication Regarding the Policy of Nature and Environmental Protection). Copenhagen, 1995.

Danish Ministry of Environment and Energy. *The Environmental Protection Agency: 'Lovgivning og praksis – forurenet jord' (Law and Practice – Polluted Soil).* The Soil Pollution Committee's Report No. 1/1995, Copenhagen.

Selected Bibliography

Danish Ministry of Environment and Energy. *Biological Diversity in Denmark. Status and Strategy*. Copenhagen, 1996.

Danish Ministry of Environment and Energy. *Energy 21. The Danish Government's Action Plan for Energy*. Copenhagen, 1996.

Danish Ministry of Environment and Energy. *Energy 21. The Governmental Energy Action Plan 1996*. Copenhagen, 1996.

Danish Ministry of Environment and Energy. *The Environmental Protection Agency: 'Betænkning om forurenet jord' (The Report on Polluted Soil)*. The Soil Pollution Committee's Report No. 2/1996, Copenhagen, 1996.

Danish Ministry of Environment and Energy. *The Environmental Protection Agency: 'Agreement Relating to Action Plan for the Aquatic Environment'*. Copenhagen, February 1998.

Danish Ministry of Environment and Energy. *The Environmental Quality Status in Denmark in 1997*. Copenhagen, 1998.

Danish Ministry of Environment. *Denmark Without Waste. Recycle More – Incinerate Less*. Copenhagen, November 2013.

Danish Ministry of Environment. *Layman's Report: Odense Pilot River Basin. Pilot Project for River Basin Management Planning. Water Framework Directive Article 13*. Copenhagen, 2007.

Danish Ministry of Environment. *The Environmental Protection Agency. Recycling in Denmark. Policy, Legislation and Activity*. Copenhagen, 1990.

Danish Ministry of Environment. *Report on Denmark's Implementation of the HELCOM Baltic Sea Action Plan, BSAP*. Copenhagen, 18 May 2010 (Case No. BLS-465-00129).

Danish Ministry of Environment. *Denmark Without Waste II. A Draft on a Plan on a More Resource Efficient Denmark*. Copenhagen February 2015.

Danish Ministry of Taxation. *How Is Income Taxed?* Copenhagen, 2008.

Danish Ministry of Transport. *The Danish Government's Action Plan for Reduction of the CO_2– Emissions of the Transport Sector*. Copenhagen, 1996.

DANVA. *Water in Figures. DANVA's Statistics and Benchmarking 2017*. Skanderborg, 2017.

DCE (Danish Centre for Environment and Energy, Aarhus University) *Vandmiljø og Natur 2010 (Water Environment and Nature 2010)*. Aarhus University, Aarhus, 2011.

DCE. *Projection of SO_2, NO_x, NH_3 and Particle Emission 2010-2030*. Report No. 7, Aarhus University, Aarhus, 2011.

DCE. *Projection of SO_2, NO_x, NMVOC, NH_3 and Particle Emission 2012-2035*. Report No. 81, Aarhus University, Aarhus, 2013.

DCE. *Annual Danish Informative Inventory Report to UNECE, Emission Inventories from the Base Year of the Protocols to Year 2013*. Report No. 145, Aarhus University, Aarhus, 2015.

DCE. *Annual Danish Informative Inventory Report to UNECE. Emission Inventories from the Base Year of the Protocol to Year 2016*. Report No. 267, Aarhus University, Aarhus, 2018.

European Commission. *Report from the Commission. Aarhus Convention Implementation Report*. COM(2011) 208 final, Brussels, 14 April 2011.

European Commission. *Taxation Trends in the European Union. Data for the EU Member States, Iceland and Norway*. Brussels, 2011.

European Commission. *A Clean Air Programme for Europe.* COM(2013) 918 final, Brussels, 18 December 2013.

European Commission. *Development of Guidance on Extended Producer Responsibility (EPR).* Brussels, 2014.

European Commission. *Fact Sheet: 2014-2020 Rural Development Programme for Denmark*. Brussels, 12 December 2014.

European Commission. *Implementation in Denmark of Directives 91/676/EC, 2000/60/EC, 92/43/EEC in Relation to the Recently Adopted Package,* letter 8540/16/ENVI, Brussels, May 2016.

European Commission. *The EU Environmental Implementation Review. Country Report – Denmark*, SWD(2017) 39 final – Staff working document, Brussels, 2017.

European Commission. *Assessment of the Draft Integrated National Energy and Climate Plan of Denmark, SWD(2019) 275 final*. Brussels, 2019.

European Commission. *Denmark.* Summary of the Commission's *Assessment of the Draft Integrated National Energy and Climate Plan 2021-2030*, Brussels, 2019.

European Environment Agency (EEA). *The European Environment – State and Outlook 2010* (SOER 2010). Copenhagen, 2011.

European Parliament. Directorate-General for Internal Policies. Policy Department. Structural and Cohesion Policies B. *Fisheries in Denmark*. Copenhagen 2013.

European Environmental Agency (EEA). *Air Quality in Europe 2013 Report*, EEA Report No. 9/2013, Copenhagen, 2013.

European Environment Agency (EEA). *The European Environment – State and Outlook 2015. Synthesis Report*. Copenhagen, 2015.

European Environment Agency (EEA). *Application of EU Emission Trading Directive. Analysis of National Responses under Article 21 of the EU ETS Directive in 2014*, Technical Report No. 3/2015, Copenhagen, 2015.

European Environmental Agency (EEA). *NEC Directive Status Report 2014. Reporting by Member States under Directive 2001/81/EC of the European Parliament and of the Council of 23 October 2001 on National Emission Ceiling for Certain Atmospheric Pollutants*. EEA Report No. 7/2015, Copenhagen, 2015.

European Environmental Agency (EEA). *Reporting and Exchanging Air Quality Information Using e-Reporting*. Technical Report No. 3/2015, Copenhagen, 2015.

European Environmental Agency (EEA). *European Forest Ecosystems. State and Trends*. Report No. 5, Copenhagen, 2016.

European Environmental Agency (EEA). *National Emission Ceiling Directive.* Copenhagen, 2016.

European Environmental Agency (EEA). *Air Quality in Europe – 2017 Report.* Report No. 13/2017, Copenhagen, 2017.

European Environmental Agency (EEA). *European Bathing Water Quality in 2017.* Copenhagen, 2017.

European Environmental Agency (EEA). *Chemicals in the European Waters. Knowledge Development*. Report No. 18/2018, Copenhagen, 2018.

European Environmental Agency (EEA). *NEC Directive Reporting Status 2018.* Copenhagen, 2018.

Selected Bibliography

Hey, Christian. *EU Environmental Policies: A Short History of the Policy Strategies*, EU Environmental Handbook, Secretary General of German Advisory Council on the Environment, https://pdfs.semanticscholar.org/445e/f8210932ca2b848b8d8b0d46072b592d97ae.pdf (published on the Internet without information on the year of publication).

Local Government Denmark. *The Danish Local Government System.* Copenhagen, 2009.

McCormick, John. *Environmental Policy in the European Union.* Hampshire, 2001.

NERI. *The Danish Air Quality Monitoring Programme. Annual Summary for 2005.* NERI Technical Report No. 584, University of Aaarhus, Aarhus, 2005.

Nordic Council, *Plans and Budget 2019. Summary.* Publication No. 2019:712, Copenhagen, 2019

Norden. *Environmental Action Plan 2009-2012.* Copenhagen, 2008.

Nordiska Ministerrådet. *Planer och Budget 2011.* Copenhagen, 2012.

OECD. *Tax Policy Reforms in Denmark.* Danvers, 2004.

OECD. *Applying Strategic Environmental Assessment. Good Practice Guidelines for Development Cooperation.* Paris, 2006.

OECD. *Environmental Performance Reviews. Denmark. 2007.* Danvers, 2008.

OECD. *Extended Producer Responsibility: A Guidance Manual for Governments*, 2011.

OECD. *Environment at a Glance 2013. OECD Indicators.* Paris, 2013.

Statistics Denmark. *Statistical Yearbook 1998.* Copenhagen, 1999.

Statistics Denmark. *Statistical Yearbook 2011.* Copenhagen, 2011.

Statistics Denmark. *Statistical Yearbook 2014.* Copenhagen, 2014.

Statistics Denmark. *Statistical Yearbook 2017.* Copenhagen, 2017.

Stevens & Bolton LLP. *Civil Liability, Financial Security and Compensation Claims for Offshore Oil and Gas Activities in the European Economic Area. Final Report.* European Commission – DG Energy, 14 August 2014.

Wilhjelm Committee. *Danish Nature – Status, Trends and Recommendations for Future Biodiversity Policies.* Ministry of Environment, Copenhagen, 2001.

World Heath Organization Regional Office for Europe and Joint Research Center (JCR). *Burden of Disease from Environmental Noise. Quantification of Healthy Life Years Lost in Europe*, Copenhagen, 2011.

Index

The numbers here refer to paragraph numbers.

Index

Index

Index

www.ingramcontent.com/pod-product-compliance
Lightning Source LLC
LaVergne TN
LVHW021003300926
849160LV00007B/237